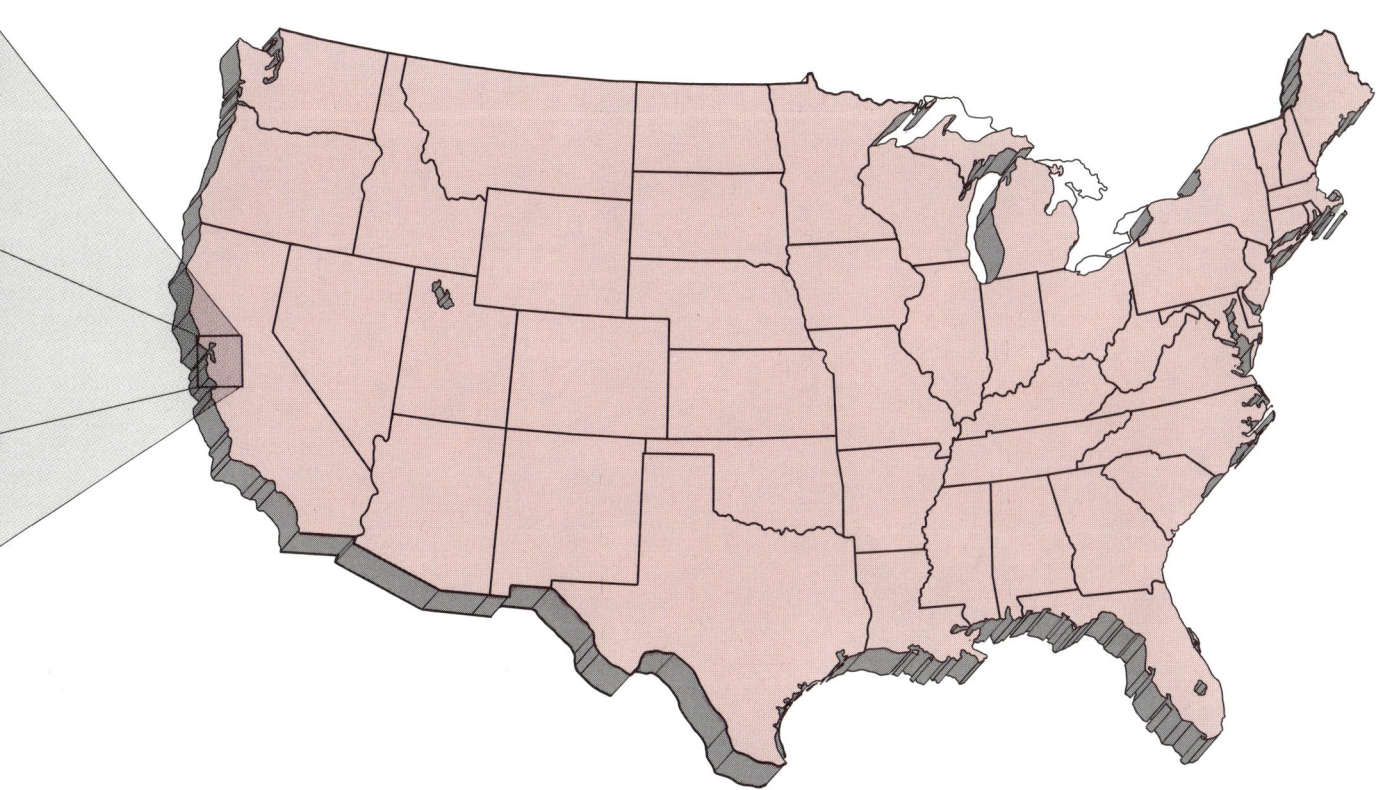

    The front cover picture, an image generated via satellite, shows part of central California, including the San Francisco-Oakland-San Jose metropolitan area. The brightest red color indicates vegetation, whether natural or cultivated. Urbanized areas - streets, rooftops, docks, etc. - show up as a blue-gray shade. Areas without healthy vegetation, such as bare soil or rock, exhibit lighter shades. Water bodies are dark blue to black.

    On the left is the equivalent area represented in the form of a map adapted from a U.S. Geological Survey sheet originally at a scale of 1:500,000. The image and the map are both versions of reality, each providing different data and having different uses.

HUMAN GEOGRAPHY
Culture, Interaction, and Economy

HUMAN GEOGRAPHY
Culture, Interaction, and Economy

Keith D. Harries
University of Maryland Baltimore County

Robert E. Norris
Oklahoma State University

Merrill Publishing Company
A Bell & Howell Company
Columbus   Toronto   London   Sydney

Cover Photo: Courtesy of NASA

Published by Merrill Publishing Company
A Bell & Howell Company
Columbus, Ohio 43216

This book was set in Frutiger.

Administrative Editor: Kathy Nee
Production Coordinator: Molly Kyle
Cover Designer: Cathy Watterson
Text Designer: Cynthia Brunk

Copyright © 1986 by Merrill Publishing Company. All rights reserved. No part of this book may be reproduced in any form, electronic or mechanical, including photocopy, recording, or any information storage and retrieval system, without permission in writing from the publisher. "Merrill Publishing Company" and "Merrill" are registered trademarks of Merrill Publishing Company.

Library of Congress Catalog Card Number: 86-60389
International Standard Book Number: 0-675-20141-1
Printed in the United States of America
 2 3 4 5 6 7 8 9—91 90 89 88 87

PREFACE

This book is closely related to an earlier general geography text, *Geography: An Introductory Perspective,* that appeared in 1982. Our intention has been to build on that foundation to produce a text specifically for human and cultural geography courses. To do so, we have developed the human geography content of the earlier title, substantially revising and rewriting some chapters and adding several new ones to add greater depth and balance. The coverage of cultural geography, particularly, has been strengthened. In addition, a chapter on "Geography at Work"—applied geography—has been added in recognition of the growing importance of this subfield of the discipline.

In the difficult process of attempting to write a book that would be all things to all students and all instructors, these reviewers were extremely helpful: D. Brooks Green and Paul L. Butt, University of Central Arkansas; Richard E. Zeller, Florida State University; James M. Bingham, Western Kentucky University; Michael Garrett, Bemidji State University; Sam Robinson, Elgin Community College; Christopher J. Smith, SUNY at Albany; Michael Libbee, Central Michigan University; Kathleen E. Braden, Seattle Pacific University; Richard V. Smith, Miami University; and Roger P. Miller, University of Minnesota. In practice, however, it is impossible to accommodate all preferences, and the shortcomings of the final product are the result of our own deliberate and often difficult choices.

An early draft was typed by the effervescent Charlene Fries with her usual dazzling speed and accuracy. Colleagues and others made numerous helpful suggestions over the years. We are indebted to Dr. Stephen W. Tweedie of Oklahoma State University for bringing to our attention Desmond Morris's work on the geography of gestures. Suzanne Spears, medical illustrator and calligrapher extraordinaire, suggested the frivolous additional toponym types.

At Merrill, Pam Cooper gave the idea initial encouragement. Kathy Nee took over the project and provided nothing but constructive encouragement; we are particularly grateful for her patience and persistence.

The book contains some cartography from the earlier text, but much is new. The new and revised graphics were prepared at the Cartographic Service of the University of Maryland, Baltimore County, under the capable supervision of its former director, Scott Edmonds, now president of Maryland Cartographics, Inc. Other cartographers involved in the project at UMBC were Scott Morris and Kevin Lear. We appreciate their good work and their efforts to meet their deadline.

PREFACE

In the preface to the previous book, we encouraged readers to communicate with us if they found errors or omissions. Once again, we invite readers' comments. Each will be acknowledged and used to improve future editions. We can be contacted at the Department of Geography at either the University of Maryland—Baltimore County, Catonsville, MD 21228 or Oklahoma State University, Stillwater, OK 74078

Keith D. Harries Robert E. Norris
Columbia, Maryland Stillwater, Oklahoma

CONTENTS

1 Fundamentals of Geography — 1

WHY LEARN GEOGRAPHY? 1

WHAT THIS BOOK IS ABOUT 2

THE HISTORY OF GEOGRAPHY 2
   The Greeks | The Middle Ages | The Age of Discovery | The Age of Exploration | Environmental Determinism

CONCEPTS IN GEOGRAPHY 9
   The Human and Physical Worlds: Interaction | Maps and Mapping | Map Scales | Thematic Maps | Regions | Cultural Processes and the Landscape | Geometry of Space—Location, Distance, and Distribution | Geographical Change | Application: Geography as a Useful Science

REGIONAL VERSUS TOPICAL GEOGRAPHY 20

CONCLUSION 20   KEY WORDS 20   REFERENCES 21

2 World Population — 23

THE DEVELOPMENT OF HUMANS AND THE HUMAN RACES 23
   Human Development | Migration | Race

POPULATION GEOGRAPHY 28
   The Demographic Transition | Population Pyramids | U.S. Population Geography | World Population Density, Distribution, and Wealth

POPULATION AND FOOD 41

CONCLUSION 44   KEY WORDS 45   REFERENCES 45

CONTENTS

3 The Elements of Cultural Geography — 50

THE CONCEPT OF CULTURE 50

CULTURAL PROCESSES 50

ARTIFACTS 51

SOCIOFACTS 52
    Geojurisprudence | Regional Social Philosophy | Spatial Rights | Geographic Variation in Statutes

MENTIFACTS 57

CONCLUSION 59   KEY WORDS 59   REFERENCES 59

4 Geography of Language — 63

THE NATURE AND USE OF LANGUAGE 63

WORLD LANGUAGE PATTERNS 66
    Indo-European Languages | Other Language Families

HISTORICAL GEOGRAPHY OF THE ENGLISH LANGUAGE 70

MULTILINGUALISM 71
    The Soviet Union | India

BILINGUALISM 75

PLACE NAMES 77

CONCLUSION 81   KEY WORDS 81   REFERENCES 81

5 Geography and Religion — 85

WHAT IS RELIGION? 85

TRADITIONAL RELIGION 86
    Animism | Zoroastrianism: Example of a Predecessor

THE MAJOR RELIGIONS 89
    Judaism | Christianity | Islam | Hinduism | Buddhism

RELIGION AND SPATIAL PROCESSES 99
    Landscape Influences | Sociopolitical Influences

CONCLUSION 100   KEY WORDS 102   REFERENCES 102

6 Material Culture — 105

ARCHITECTURE 105
    Ancient Architecture | Medieval Architecture | Colonial Architecture

BORDERS, WALLS, AND FENCES 115
    Ancient Borders | Modern Borders | Walled Cities | Walls and Fences

MONUMENTS, BURIAL SITES, AND SHRINES 124
Ancient Structures | Modern Monuments | Cemeteries | Shrines

OTHER ITEMS OF MATERIAL CULTURE 128

CONCLUSION 128   KEY WORDS 128   REFERENCES 129

7 Selected Topics in the Cultural Geography of the United States 131

DIVERSITY AND PATTERN IN RACE AND ETHNICITY 131
Current Patterns | The Rural Frontier | The Urban Frontier

RELIGION 140

THE URBAN SCENE 143

PASTIMES 146

CULTURE REGIONS 147

CONCLUSION 150   KEY WORDS 152   REFERENCES 152

8 Social Processes 155

SOCIAL SPACE 155

AGGREGATION AND BEHAVIOR 156

BASIC CONCEPTS IN HUMAN SPATIAL INTERACTION 158
Perception | Density, Crowding, and Personal Space

INTERACTION THROUGH MOVEMENT 165
The Journey to Work | The Journey to Shop | Social Trips | Social Characteristics and Interaction | Migration Processes and Patterns

INTERACTION THROUGH COMMUNICATION 173

CONCLUSION 176   KEY WORDS 176   REFERENCES 176

9 The Geography of Social Problems 181

HEALTH AND DISEASE 182
Mapping Disease and the Search for Causes | Patterns of Health Care

CRIME AND JUSTICE 192
Regional Variation | Urban, Suburban, and Rural Crime | Crime Factors

CONCLUSION 199   KEY WORDS 200   REFERENCES 200

10 Economic Geography: Primary Production 203

PRINCIPLES OF PRIMARY PRODUCTION 204
The Physical Environment | Economic Factors | Cultural Factors | Political Factors

CONTENTS

GEOGRAPHY OF AGRICULTURE 205
Subsistence Herding | Subsistence Farming | Commercial Herding | Commercial Farming

EXTRACTIVE INDUSTRIES 221
The Fuels | Metals Production | Nonmetallic Mineral Production

GEOGRAPHY OF FORESTRY 226

GEOGRAPHY OF FISHING 229

CONCLUSION 230   KEY WORDS 231   REFERENCES 231

11 Economic Geography: Secondary and Tertiary Economic Activity   235

MANUFACTURING 235

PRINCIPLES OF INDUSTRIAL LOCATION 236

ORIGIN OF MANUFACTURING 238
Industrial Revolution

LIGHT INDUSTRY 239

HEAVY INDUSTRY 241
Location of Heavy Industry

HIGH TECHNOLOGY INDUSTRY 245
Machine Tools | Chemicals | Computers | Transportation Equipment

TERTIARY ECONOMIC ACTIVITY 251

PRINCIPLES OF RETAIL LOCATION 251

RETAILING 252
Grocery Stores

CONCLUSION 255   KEY WORDS 256   REFERENCES 256

12 Rural Settlement Patterns   259

PRINCIPLES OF SETTLEMENT AND LAND USE 260
Farmstead Location | Patterns of Settlement | Physical Factors and Settlement Patterns

ANCIENT SETTLEMENT PATTERNS 263
Land Reform | Roman Influence on Rural Settlement

RURAL SETTLEMENT IN THE MIDDLE AGES 266

MODERN RURAL SETTLEMENT 269
Europe | Asia | Africa | Latin America | North America

RANGE AND TOWNSHIP 271

RURAL SETTLEMENT IN THE UNITED STATES 273

CONCLUSION 275   KEY WORDS 275   REFERENCES 275

13 Urbanization and Urban Places — 279

HISTORICAL GEOGRAPHY OF URBANIZATION 281
  Recent Urban Population Trends

THEORETICAL CONCEPTS 287
  Locational Competition | Accessibility, Interaction, and Land Value | Hierarchy

REGULARITIES IN URBAN STRUCTURE 292

PLANNING THE URBAN ENVIRONMENT 295

CONCLUSION 296   KEY WORDS 296   REFERENCES 296

14 The Quality of Urban Life — 299

THE SOCIOECONOMIC ENVIRONMENT 300

THE PHYSICAL ENVIRONMENT 304

A QUALITY OF LIFE STUDY OF U.S. METROPOLITAN AREAS 308

CONCLUSION 311   KEY WORDS 315   REFERENCES 315

15 The Bounded Earth — 319

PERSONAL SPACE 320

PERSONAL PROPERTY 321

LOCAL GOVERNMENTS 323
  Special Districts | Townships | Counties

CITY BOUNDARIES 328

STATE BOUNDARIES 329

INTERNATIONAL BOUNDARIES 335

OCEAN BOUNDARIES 336

MULTINATIONAL BOUNDARIES 339

CONCLUSION 341   KEY WORDS 341   REFERENCES 341

16 Politics and Location — 345

NATIONALISM AND NATION-STATES 345
  Historical Development of the State Idea | Colonialism | Decolonization | Assimilation or Separation | Nation-States

IMPACT OF LOCATION 351
  Relations with Other States | Buffer States | Landlocked States | Corridors and Proruptions

INTERACTION AND ECONOMICS 355
  Migrants and Refugees | Haves and Have-Nots | Industrialization, Modernization, and Development

ECONOMICS AND POLITICS 361
  Life Cycles of States | The Cost of Arms

CONCLUSION 362   KEY WORDS 364   REFERENCES 365

17 Geography at Work — 376

APPLIED GEOGRAPHY 367

SUBJECT MATTER OF APPLIED GEOGRAPHY 368
  Approaches and Methods | Case Studies

CONCLUSION 374
  Elements of the Geographic Perspective

KEY WORDS 376   REFERENCES 376

GLOSSARY 378

APPENDIX A Climatic Classification 389

APPENDIX B The United States Population Data Sheet of the Population Reference Bureau, Inc. 393

APPENDIX C 1985 World Population Data Sheet 397

1
Fundamentals of Geography

WHY LEARN ABOUT GEOGRAPHY?
WHAT THIS BOOK IS ABOUT
THE HISTORY OF GEOGRAPHY
CONCEPTS IN GEOGRAPHY
REGIONAL VERSUS TOPICAL GEOGRAPHY

The island of Capri in the Tyrrhenian Sea off the west coast of Italy near Salerno. (Photo courtesy of the Italian Government Travel Office.)

WHY LEARN ABOUT GEOGRAPHY?

Ignorance of geography has become an embarrassment to the American people. In the mid-1980s, a newspaper reported that, in a test ranking the achievement of students in eight industrial countries, Americans "wore the dunce cap" in math, science, and geography. One-fifth of the sixth graders in a Dallas school could not find the United States on a world map. Although not last in geography, American students trailed those from Sweden, England, and Canada—countries where geographic education has traditionally been strong. Geography is a vital component of a liberal arts education—education about the world we live in—to help us understand what makes civilization tick.

Liberal arts education, including geography, tends to have been overlooked in the quest for technical excellence. The energy reserves of the Soviet Union or the consequences of bilingualism in Canada seem insignificant when we are struggling to learn electrical engineering, accounting, or medicine. Yet geography, like history, sociology, economics, and other social science and humanities disciplines, helps us understand how our civilization got where it is today. Such studies do not help us solve a problem in an engineering class, but they help us know why there is a science of engineering and why engineering deals with the problems that it does.

Geography helps us put affairs into perspective at the local, regional, national, and international levels. Geography is implicit in many decisions regarding local government, marketing, military strategy, and personal choices about where to live. At a broader level, geography has traditionally brought together perspectives from the physical and social sciences to solve problems.

CHAPTER 1 FUNDAMENTALS OF GEOGRAPHY

Geography is to place as history is to time. Just as historians are primarily concerned with interpreting events in the temporal dimension, so geographers are concerned with *where* things happen. Naturally, neither viewpoint is exclusive; historians must concern themselves with where things happen and geographers must take time into account. In practice, geography and history complement each other, just as many other disciplines are closely and beneficially interrelated.

Despite the relevance of geography to understanding contemporary issues, emphasis on geography has faded in U.S. schools. An editorial in the *National Geographic Magazine* explains how this came about (Grosvenor, 1984). In 1904, the Society decided to popularize geography, which was separating at that time from geology. William Morris Davis, a Harvard professor noted for his work in physical geography, objected to this popularization, wanting to keep geography scholarly and academic. Toward this end, he helped found the Association of American Geographers, which is still the principal organization of academic geographers in America. The split between popular and academic geography weakened the discipline as the National Geographic Society went in one direction and academic geographers in another. There has lately been a reconciliation between the two societies. The Association of American Geographers is now committed to strengthening geographic education and popularizing research findings, while the National Geographic Society has launched a new journal, *National Geographic Research,* as part of an expanded program of support for geographic research.

WHAT THIS BOOK IS ABOUT

Geography is divided into two broad areas: physical and human. Physical geography is concerned primarily with the relationship between humans and the physical environment. Physical geographers look, for example, at the relationship between climate and human behavior *(bioclimatology)*. They also look at the relationship between rock types and the shape of the surface of the earth and what that means for human use of the earth *(geomorphology)*. Some reconstruct ancient conditions *(paleoenvironments)* to see how climate and vegetation has changed over hundreds of thousands of years, thus providing clues about current conditions and changes.

This book, however, concerns human geography. While human geography must take into account the physical environment (agricultural patterns can only be understood in the context of climates, for instance), its main concern is to interpret human behaviors and the patterns they produce on the land. Human geographers usually categorize information in a way that relates logically to major human phenomena. Population is a fundamental topic since we are concerned with patterns that relate to people. We then consider cultural geography, the study of ways of life of peoples, out of which stems more detailed consideration of three components of culture: language, religion, and material objects or artifacts. To illustrate the influence of cultural processes in a familiar context, Chapter 7 deals with selected aspects of the cultural geography of the United States. Then a series of four chapters deals with social and economic patterns. Next, forms of human settlement become the focus of attention as we consider rural and urban communities and discuss the quality of life in urban areas. Two chapters are then devoted to the political aspects of geography. The concluding chapter, "Geography at Work," shows how to apply geography in real problem-solving situations.

Figure 1–1 illustrates the relationship between geography and other disciplines, which are grouped under the humanities and the physical, biological, social, and mathematical sciences. Geography appears with the social sciences, because it is primarily concerned with human occupancy of the earth and its methods are predominantly scientific rather than humanistic. Various subfields of geography are shown along the lower part of the chart, under the disciplines to which they most strongly relate. This book is concerned with the 'human geography' category, which has its strongest ties to the several social sciences listed, and to history from the humanities column. Human geographers also use mathematical sciences extensively in their research, although we will not deal with mathematical applications. Each chapter has an outline at the beginning, and a list of key words at the end. The key words appear in the Glossary at the end of the book, and several Appendixes provide supplementary data on a variety of topics. Like most geography texts, this book emphasizes maps. Geography instructors sometimes spend a whole class session discussing the processes that underlie the patterns you see on a single map. This is consistent with the emphasis in geography on the "where" of things.

THE HISTORY OF GEOGRAPHY

Geography dates back to humans' first descriptions of places. People have always talked about environ-

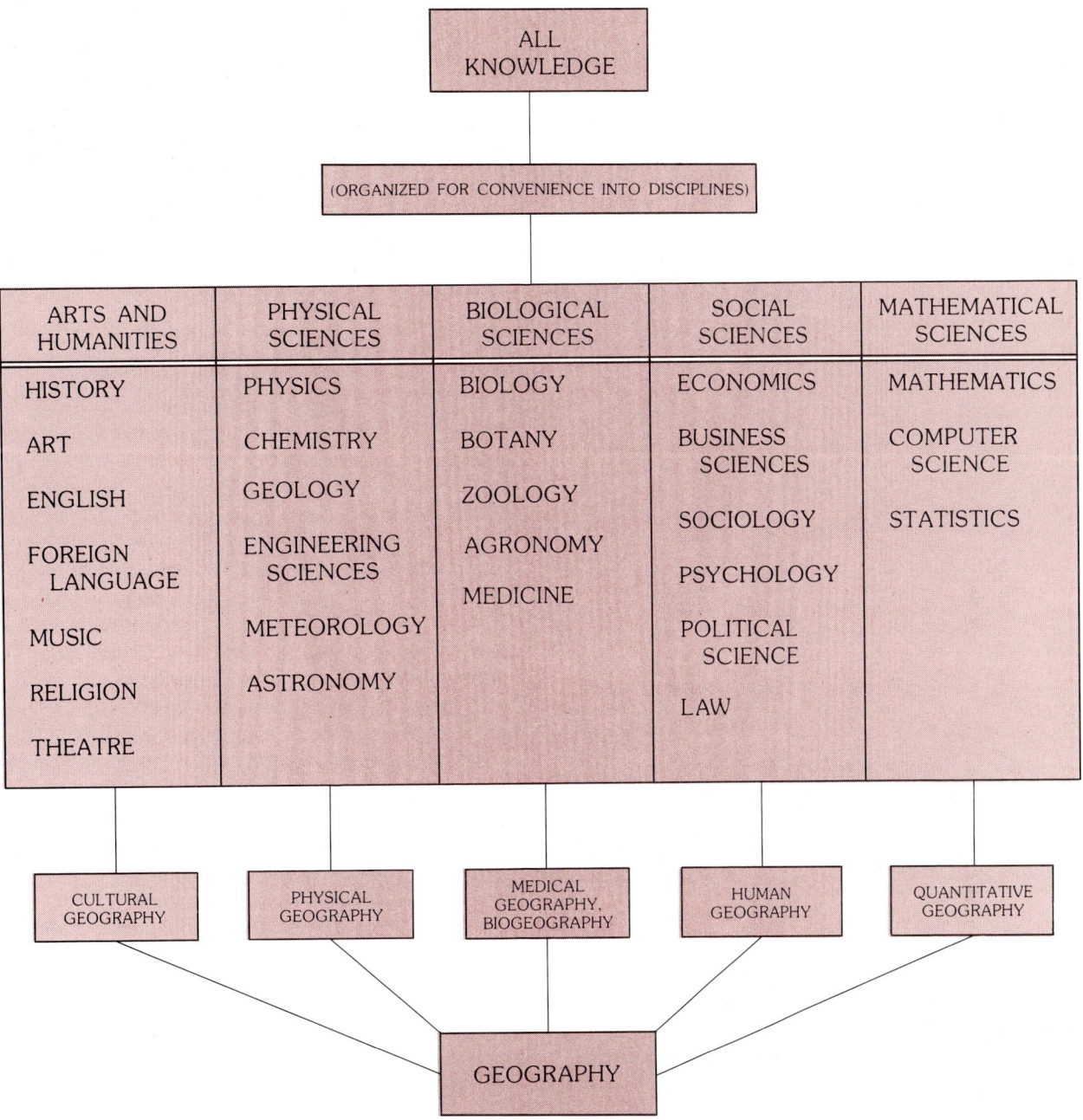

FIGURE 1-1 Relationship between geography and other disciplines.

mental conditions where they live, and sometimes they set out in search of better circumstances. They explored new places that might provide greater safety or a better food or water supply or places where commodities such as flint or salt might be found. Besides searching for useful items, humans have also demonstrated a natural curiosity about what lies beyond the horizon. Thus, the history of the human race is laced with tales of travel, migration, and expeditions into the unknown. Those who journeyed reported their findings to those who stayed home, and their descriptions of what lay beyond the next hill were the beginnings of geography.

People who lived thousands of years ago made many observations about the world around them. The Egyptians, for example, determined the number of days in a year, how to measure land area, and how to orient buildings with reference to compass points. The Phoenicians, known for their travels and explorations into previously unknown regions, developed navigational skills and reported place-to-place differences in climate and landforms. Although threads of geographical knowledge came from every civilization in every part of the world, the ancient Greeks were the first to record the information in a thorough and organized way. Geography, therefore, truly began with the writings of the ancient Greek scholars.

The Greeks

The first geographer may have been the Greek poet Homer, who lived during the ninth century B.C. His adventure poem, the *Odyssey,* included a geographical description of various places in the Mediterranean region. About 500 years after Homer, Hecataeus wrote *Descriptions of the Earth,* the first book known to have been written for the purpose of describing the earth. Of course, the world according to Hecataeus was again essentially the Mediterranean area (Figure 1–2).

By the fifth century B.C., Greek writers began to go beyond mere description by attempting to explain earth processes. Plato, during the fourth century B.C., was the first to say the earth was round rather than flat. At about the same time, Eudoxus postulated that climatic zones (klima) circle the round surface of the earth. During the third century B.C., Aristotle noted that the shadow of the earth on the moon was circular, and that average temperatures decrease with increasing distance from the equator. At about the same time, Alexander the Great extended the Greeks' geographic knowledge by making measurements during his expeditions of conquest. As a student of Aristotle, Alexander had learned to observe and record distances and locations, so his reports back to Greece included a wealth of geographical information.

The last of the great Greek scholars known for their works in geography were Eratosthenes (273–192 B.C.) and Strabo (64 B.C.–A.D. 20). Eratosthenes is often called the father of geography because he coined the term *geography,* from *geo* ("the earth") and *graphos* ("to write" or "describe"). He was the first person to measure accurately the circumference of the earth using sun angles and mathematics (see Figure 1–3). He also wrote about Eudoxus's climatic zones, and went on to describe the earth as having two frigid polar regions, two temperate areas, and a torrid belt near the equator. Eratosthenes made a map of the known world (Figure 1–4) that included Europe, Asia (India), and Africa (Libya).

Strabo, on the other hand, presented little that was new; rather, he is famous because of his 17-volume *Geography,* a compilation of all the Greek geographical knowledge prior to his time. In fact, most of the information we have about the Greeks before Strabo is based on his writings. Some scholars have called Strabo's work the single most important writing handed down from antiquity.

The ancient Greeks provided geographers with a name and a framework within which to work. Obviously, many of their theories and concepts were wrong; on the other hand, many were amazingly accurate. Of great importance was their setting the stage for the study of the earth as the home of humans. Unfortunately, the inquiry the ancient Greeks began into how and why things in the natural world work as they do did not continue in an orderly progression through time.

During the Roman era, geographical writings consisted primarily of local land surveys and encyclopedias of local environments. The Romans' contribution to geography was more in what they did than in what they wrote. Through the forced spread, or diffusion, of their language, education, religion, and countless other cultural factors, the Romans changed the human geography of a large part of the known world. They also were leaders in matters of law and order, and one practice with lasting impact on ge-

FIGURE 1–2 The world according to Hecataeus. This map, drawn by the Greek scholar Hecataeus during the fourth century B.C., depicts the world known to the Greeks at that time. Notice that Africa and Asia are included in one land mass and Europe in another, and that everything outside was thought to be ocean.

THE HISTORY OF GEOGRAPHY

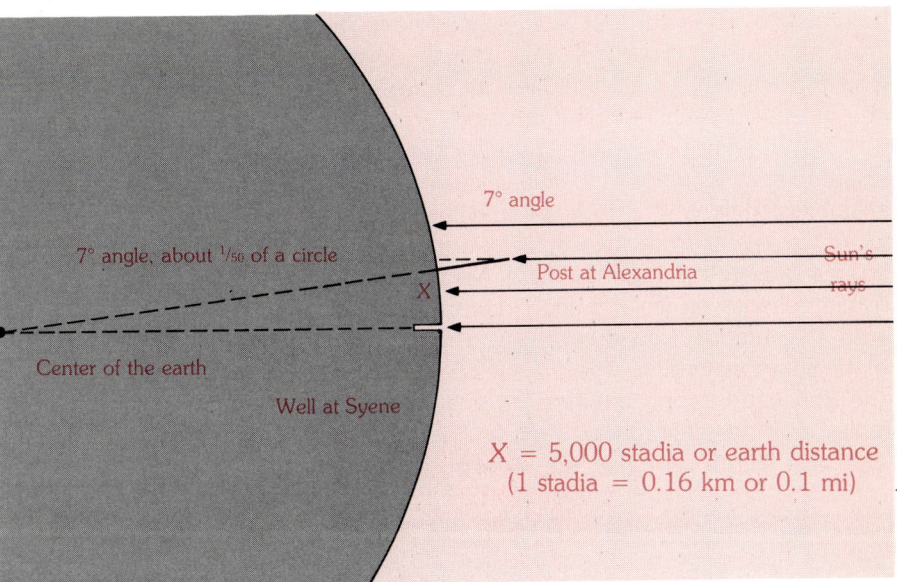

FIGURE 1–3 Eratosthenes's calculation of the circumference of the earth. On June 21, the vertical rays from the sun penetrated to the bottom of a well at Syene, whereas in Alexandria, the rays formed a shadow at a 7° angle to a vertical post. Distance X was calculated at 5,000 stadia, based on an estimate that a camel caravan traveled the distance between these two cities in 50 days (100 stadia per day). Distance X also represents an arc distance of 1/50 the earth's circumference. (Adapted from Tarbuck and Lutgens, *Earth Science*, 4th ed. [Merrill Publishing Co., 1985], p. 412.)

ography was their use of precise demarcations of political units. The Roman era was followed by the Middle Ages, a period noted for its lack of impact on intellectual writings.

The Middle Ages

The time between the fifth and fifteenth centuries A.D. is known as the Middle Ages. During the thousand years from the fall of the Roman Empire until the age of global exploration, the Christian religion became a binding force in human affairs. Scholars were killed and books burned in a misguided religious fervor. Many people were shackled by serfdom or bound to their local areas by superstition and fear. Geography, as well as other social sciences, was therefore retarded on both theoretical and descriptive levels. The end of the period was marked by the Reformation in religion and the Renaissance in schol-

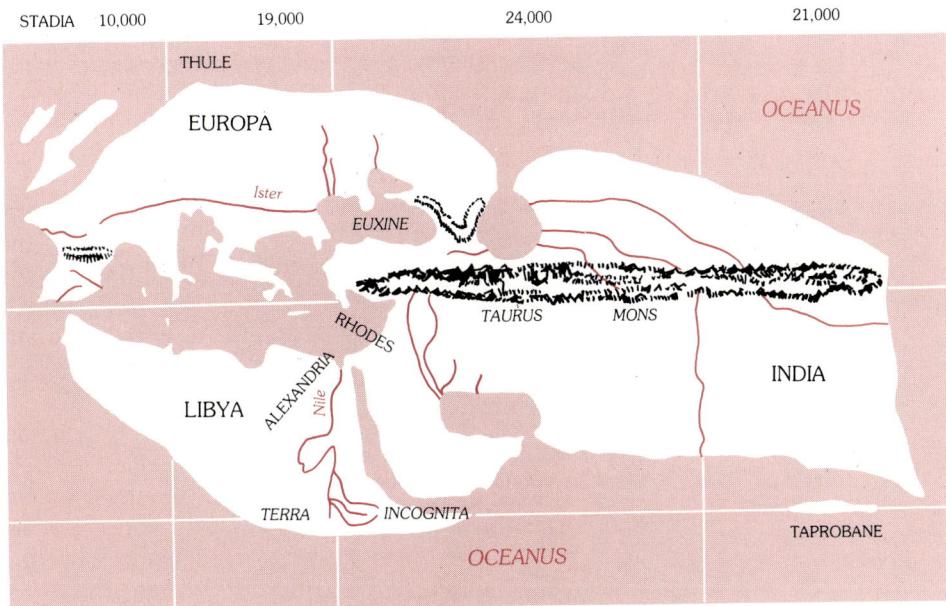

FIGURE 1–4 The world according to Eratosthenes, who lived during the second century B.C. Notice how much more information had been obtained since the Hecataeus map in Figure 1–2.

arship. Another factor that aided scholarly endeavors near the close of the Middle Ages was the invention of the printing press, the machine that gave scholars the means for exchanging information.

Travel did not cease during the Middle Ages, but many records were lost and little is known about the major expeditions. We do know that the Vikings explored areas far from their homeland from the fifth to the eleventh centuries. These Norsemen established colonies on Iceland and Greenland, and traveled to Labrador, Newfoundland, and perhaps even as far south as Virginia. The crusades from Europe to the Holy Land during the eleventh and twelfth centuries took people into new regions. During the seventh and eighth centuries, the Moslems moved outward from their home base in Arabia. The Chinese sent explorers to India during the seventh century, and as far west as Europe by the thirteenth century. Perhaps the most famous traveler of the period was Marco Polo. Like Strabo, Marco Polo is noted for faithfully describing in writing the people and places he saw. He journeyed for 24 years (1271–1295), from Venice to Peking overland, and back to Venice by boat (Figure 1–5), a truly incredible journey for the time. His account of his experiences has fascinated readers for centuries.

The Age of Discovery

The Age of Discovery began early in the fifteenth century, somewhat overlapping the Middle Ages.

ATHENS TODAY

Athens, once the seat of the great Greek civilization, is now one of the noisiest, most overcrowded, most polluted cities in the world. With nearly four million people, Athens is growing at the rate of about 150,000 per year. Most of the migrants come in search of jobs, leaving many outlying towns and villages nearly empty. About 40 percent of the population of Greece now live in Athens, and at the current growth rate, over half the national population will be in the city in about 15 years.

A recent Greek govenment study reported that Athens is the noisiest city in Europe, and probably in the world. The noise comes from overcrowding, industry, and automobiles. Cars are everywhere. Despite the fact that gasoline costs well over $3 per gallon, Greeks purchase more than 100,000 new automobiles a year. They need cars because the public transportation system is poor.

The automobile also carries much of the blame for pollution in Athens. Smog is thick most of the time, and there are few parks with oxygen-producing green plants to ease the suffocating conditions. Smog not only hinders breathing and irritates the eyes, it also causes decay of the marble of the ancient ruins through the attack of sulfur dioxide. Overcrowding strains the inadequate sanitation and sewage facilities, adding to the pollution problem.

THE HISTORY OF GEOGRAPHY

Prince Henry established a school of navigation in 1416 at Cape Saint Vincent on the southwest coast of Portugal. Cape Saint Vincent was the embarkation point for numerous Portuguese sea expeditions led by captains trained at one of the world's first geographic research centers. Prince Henry's goal was to find a sea route to the Orient by sailing around Africa, and many other discoveries were made in the process. His seamen were trained to make locational notations on charts and to describe in writing the places they visited. Geographical knowledge was thus extended and recorded with each cruise.

By the end of the fifteenth century, Columbus had sailed to America three times, Vasco da Gama had sailed to India, and John Cabot had "rediscovered" Nova Scotia. Numerous lesser-known captains had sailed, explored, and recorded their findings.

By 1550, some 60 years after Columbus's first voyage of exploration, the outlines of all the continents except Australia and Antarctica had been recorded on maps (Figure 1–6). That brief period was the true golden age of discovery. In addition, information from the many interior expeditions helped fill in the maps. During the sixteenth century, the Age of Discovery became the Age of Exploration. Magellan sailed around the world, and Balboa, Cortez, Pizarro, de Soto, Coronado, and a host of other captains, pirates, and seekers of fortune explored the Western Hemisphere.

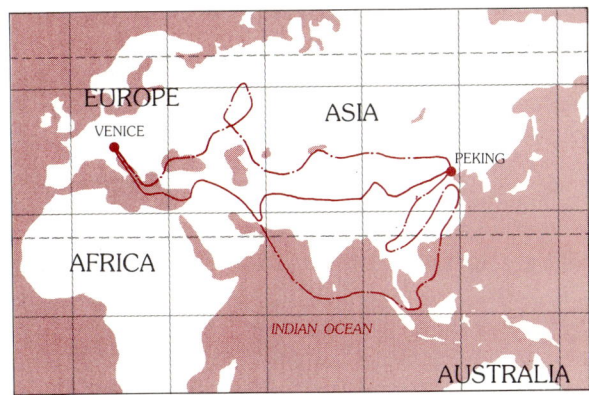

FIGURE 1–5 Marco Polo's two trips to China. We know the routes Marco Polo traveled from his discussion of the places he visited. (It is approximately 5,100 miles [8,200 km] from Venice to Peking.)

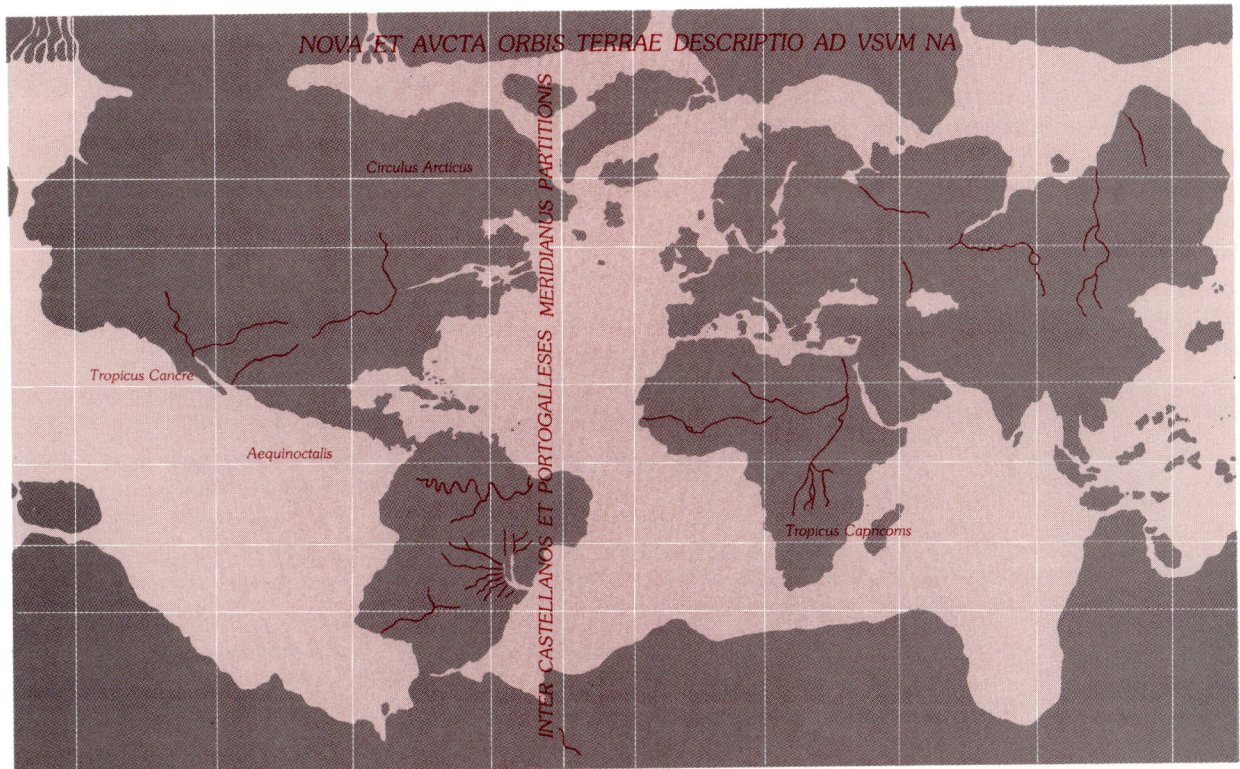

FIGURE 1–6 Mercator's world map of 1569, the most accurate to that date. It was used as a navigational chart because a straight line drawn on it was equal to an arc on the globe.

CHAPTER 1 FUNDAMENTALS OF GEOGRAPHY

The Age of Exploration

The Age of Exploration usually is dated from about 1550 to 1850, although significant expeditions occurred after that time. During this period, a flood of information about the world came rolling back to scholars in Europe. At the same time, the scholars themselves were making many scientific discoveries. The period is noted for the attempts to combine the "knowledge of the classics with knowledge of the land." Bernhard Varen (known as Varenius) was one person who successfully united the two kinds of information. His *General Geography,* published first in 1650, influenced geographic thought for at least 100 years. The explorers brought back to the scholars more than locational data and information about the natural world. They also described the people who lived in the newly "discovered" lands. Thus, human geography began to appear as part of the discipline.

The Age of Exploration ended with the work of two other German geographers, Alexander von Humboldt and Karl Ritter, both of whom died in 1859. Their work has influenced geography ever since. Many people refer to them as the founders of modern geography; more specifically, Humboldt is considered the creator of modern physical geography and Ritter, the originator of cultural geography. Although the two were contemporaries, they differed in their approach to the subject. Von Humboldt was a traveler and writer who carefully described what he saw, then attempted to explain it through the formulation of hypotheses. Ritter, on the other hand, did not travel as much, and is noted more for his lectures than his writing. As a teacher, he contributed to the concepts of the interconnection of humans and their earth home. Ritter described the earth as an organic entity, hypothesizing an organic unity between humans and nature. This viewpoint was promulgated by his immediate successors and brought geography into an era of disrepute, as we will see.

Environmental Determinism

Geography first became recognized as an academic discipline in 1874, when it appeared in German universities as a field of advanced study. The emphasis was on von Humboldt's and Ritter's philosophical approach to the new discipline. Basic speculations centered on the influence of the natural environment on culture and human social progress.

During the latter part of the nineteenth century, the application of extreme generalizations to the relationship between humans and their environments became the focus of geography in Germany. This method was epitomized by Friedrich Ratzel's work. Ratzel, known as the father of political geography, also started what is called *anthropogeography,* which viewed geography only in terms of human experience. He took Ritter's idea of an organic world and applied it to cultures. Ratzel suggested, by analogy, that groups of individuals, especially states, were in a struggle with one another for space. Only those states with adequate space would be able to survive. This concept, based on Charles Darwin's ideas of biological entities struggling for survival, is called *Social Darwinism.*

Ratzel's disciples extended the analogy of cultures as biological entities into the philosophy of *environmental determinism.* Adherents of this philosophy believed in a cause-and-effect relationship between humans and their environment. They stated that the physical environment *caused* humans to be the way they were, both in physical makeup and in their cultural activities. Free will was considered unimportant, because humans were subject to the same natural laws as plants and animals.

The ideas of environmental determinism took root in the United States through the teachings of Ellen C. Semple at the University of Chicago. Trained in Germany by Ratzel, Semple explained in her book, *American Geography and Its Geographic Conditions,* how the environment shaped history. From 1903 to 1932, she influenced many geographers who became convinced that the environment determines human activity and taught this concept to others.

Ellsworth Huntington, a prominent U.S. geographer who taught for many years at Yale University, discussed how areas of the world that show progress in economic activity—and civilization in general—correspond closely to areas of "high climatic energy." He claimed that an invigorating climate *resulted* in human progress. The ideas of the environmental determinists held sway in geography until 1940, when Huntington died (Figure 1–7).

During the first half of the twentieth century, geography was retarded by the influence of environmental determinism, and by the split between popular and academic geography. The misuse of geography by the Nazis in Germany, and the lack of theoretical advances by American geographers, only added to the woes of the discipline.

Since about 1950, however, dramatic changes have transformed geography in America and most other countries. The most important change was the acceptance by geographers of *probability theory,* which states that the natural world contains *uncertainty.* In adopting probability theory, geographers in effect rejected environmental determinism. Concepts

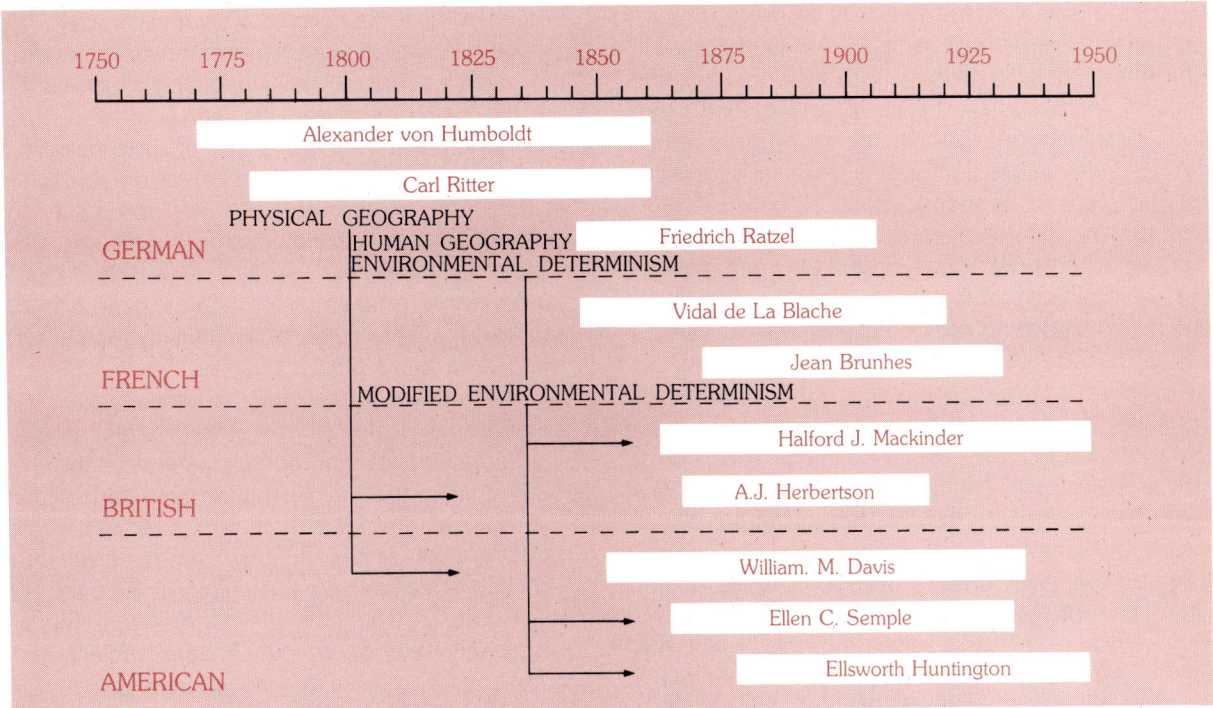

FIGURE 1-7 Life spans of ten prominent geographers from four countries.

and methods from the science of statistics (which is based on probability theory) were applied to geography and other social sciences. Computers came into use in universities, permitting rapid processing of large amounts of geographic information. Led by innovators such as Harold H. McCarty at the University of Iowa and William L. Garrison at the University of Washington, the 'young Turks' of geography used the new concepts, methods, and technology to create what has been called a *quantitative revolution.* This meant a new emphasis on the analysis of statistical information and the expression of geographic concepts with mathematical statements. The years between 1950 and 1970 were a period of extraordinary transformation in geography.

Because of continuing technological innovation, the modern era continues to develop even more precise measurements. Since the Soviet *Sputnik* satellite in 1957, satellites have sent an avalanche of new information back to earth. Satellite imagery matched with computer technology continues to increase spectacularly our knowledge of the earth. Geographers are employed in the new field of *remote sensing* as interpreters of satellite images. Geography has moved from the ancient travelers' general descriptions of the earth to the exact descriptions provided by satellite images.

CONCEPTS IN GEOGRAPHY

The Human and Physical Worlds: Interaction

The concept underlying all geographic studies is that the earth is the home of the human race, and that much human behavior is conditioned, though not determined, by the earth environment. Climate, topography (the shape of the earth's surface), the geographic arrangement of people and resources in areas, and numerous other factors illustrate the role of the physical environment as the backdrop to human behaviors. Though traditionally separated for convenience, physical and human geography are closely related. The elements of physical geography include the earth's atmosphere, land and water, and soils and vegetation. These are such important elements that each has its own subdiscipline; for example, meteorologists and climatologists study the atmosphere, geomorphologists study the land, pedologists specialize in soils, and plant geographers concentrate on vegetation. Physical geography is the integrating discipline concerned with all these physical elements.

Human geography includes all the activities of humans. It is sometimes called *cultural* or *social ge-*

ography, although these terms usually refer to subcategories of human geography. As we noted, culture refers to such things as race, language, and religion. Social aspects include processes and problems associated with humans living in groups (society). Besides culture and society, human geography includes study of economic, political, and urban affairs, for example (see Figure 1–1).

Two aspects of the relationship between humans and their physical environment demand comment. One is the mediating effect the environment has on human behavior. For example, humans respond to the weather by wearing different types of clothing. Our sport and leisure activities are tempered by environmental conditions, as are vital economic realms, such as agriculture. The other aspect of the relationship is the human impact on the environment. We modify the landscape, the atmosphere, the vegetation, and the earth's waters. Although some modifications do not seem to harm the environment, many literally destroy it. Geographers are concerned with both aspects of the relationship between humans and the evironment.

Maps and Mapping

Maps are vital tools for the geographer. Because any geographic distribution can be mapped, maps are available on an extraordinary variety of topics. Maps may vary from simple, hand-drawn line sketches showing the general location of roads, to the highly complex and colorful renditions of data from satellites, produced entirely by computers. Geographers use maps not only to store and illustrate information, but also to suggest explanations of phenomena under study. Comparing different maps can suggest what conditions control various distributions. At the simplest level, for example, a comparison of population distribution maps and topographic maps may show that people have avoided the steepest or most flood-prone lands, and comparisons of crop and climate maps may show that certain crops are limited to specific climatic types.

Map Scales

The appearance of geographical, or *spatial,* distributions on a map varies depending on the map's level of resolution. This corresponds to our visual perceptions of the real world; for example, the landscape looks much different when we fly over it at 30,000 feet (about 9,000 meters) than it does when we walk or drive across it. Materials such as wood or human hair are virtually unrecognizable if we look at them under an electron microscope. Similarly, map information can vary depending on how closely it portrays the earth's surface. This relationship between areas on the earth's surface and areas on the map is known as *map scale.*

A large-scale map is used to portray a *small* area of the earth in great detail. A map that shows only one city block, for example, would be large-scale. A small-scale map shows a *large* area without detail. World maps are always small-scale, because it is impossible to show detail of anything as large as the world on a single piece of paper.

Map scale is usually indicated on maps as a bar scale (graphic scale) or representative fraction (ratio). The bar scale shows graphically what distance on the map equals a mile, or kilometer, or some other unit. The representative fraction (RF) states how many units of distance on the earth's surface are represented by one unit on the map. An RF of 1:2,000 means that one unit on the map (inch, centimeter, foot, millimeter, or any unit) equals 2,000 of the same units on the earth's surface. A map on which about 2.5 inches equals a mile (or 4.1 cm = 1 km), is the equivalent of an RF of 1:24,000. When the denominator, or number on the right of the RF, is very large (say 75,000,000), we are dealing with a very small-scale map, sometimes called *global scale,* because a map at this scale usually shows the world. A relatively small number, say 600, indicates a large-scale map, or what we can call *local scale.* The easiest way to remember this relationship, perhaps, is to think of the RF as a fraction; 1/75,000,000th is very small, whereas 1/600th is (relatively) large. The ultimate large-scale map would have an RF of 1:1. It would be the same size as the earth itself, and is obviously impossible!

Small areas of the earth portrayed with large-scale maps can be shown with relatively little error. When large areas are shown on small-scale maps, however, error is inevitable, because it is impossible to represent the round earth on a flat piece of paper. Cartographers (map scientists) have devised many ways to minimize this problem with various *map projections.* All have advantages and disadvantages, depending on which parts of the world need to be represented most accurately.

Thematic Maps

Thematic maps usually present only one category of information. Thematic maps might show population distribution or the occurrence pattern of a disease. Various types of thematic maps can be made from

CONCEPTS IN GEOGRAPHY

the same information. Each of the maps in Figures 1–8, 1–9, 1–10, and 1–11 (statistical, dot, choropleth, and isoline maps) was constructed from the data shown on the first map.

The Statistical Map To map crime in an urban area, one might choose a single crime category, such as murders. The resulting *statistical map* (Figure 1–8) would contain quantities (number of murders) per unit area (such as a city block) for some given time period. The statistical map portrays the spatial distribution of the occurrences of murder. We cannot, however, determine much about the pattern, density, or dispersion of murder by observing the statistical map. To portray the data more effectively, the numbers can be changed to dots or symbols.

The Dot Map To achieve a more effective visual impression, the statistical map can be converted to a *dot map*. The dot map is easy to make, and contains the same information as the statistical map, yet gives the spatial distribution in a much different form. On the dot map, quantities are portrayed by dots rather than by numbers, with each dot representing a certain unit of magnitude. For example, if one dot represents 10 crimes, then a city block with 50 crimes would contain five dots (Figure 1–9). The dots are placed randomly within each block and represent the *relative* location of the crimes. The resulting spatial distributions can be analyzed in terms of their patterns, densities, and dispersions. In practice, police departments usually use pins on large wall maps to represent crimes, with one pin per crime. This is convenient, as they can add pins daily and remove them at the end of a time period, say a month, so the map can be started again. The pin map is still a kind of dot map, however.

The Choropleth Map The *choropleth map* is another way to increase the visual impact of the spatial arrangement of geographic facts. The word *choropleth* comes from the Greek words *choros* ("place") and *pleth* ("fullness"). Each place (area) on a choropleth map is shaded completely (fully) because each value is related to area. The original data, such as the crime statistics in Figure 1–8, are divided into intervals, then each interval is assigned a shade to depict magnitude clearly (Figure 1–10). Each shade on the resulting map thus represents a range of quantities instead of exact amounts. Information contained in

3	5	7	6	5	2
4	8	8	8	6	5
5	10	9	6	4	2
4	6	7	5	5	2
4	5	5	4	3	1
3	3	4	4	1	1

FIGURE 1–8 Schematic representation of a statistical map. The first step in making most statistical maps is to plot the numerical values for what is to be represented. Plotting is done by small unit areas, as shown here. (From Harold H. McCarty/James B. Lindberg, A PREFACE TO ECONOMIC GEOGRAPHY, © 1966. P. 31. Adapted by permission of Prentice-Hall, Inc., Englewood Cliffs, N.J.)

FIGURE 1–9 Schematic representation of a dot map. On dot maps, a dot represents each occurrence. For example, in an area where 7 is the numerical value, 7 dots are placed at random. The lines that separate the areas are removed after all dots are placed. (From Harold H. McCarty/James B. Lindberg, A PREFACE TO ECONOMIC GEOGRAPHY, © 1966. P. 33. Adapted by permission of Prentice-Hall, Inc., Englewood Cliffs, N.J.)

CHAPTER 1 FUNDAMENTALS OF GEOGRAPHY

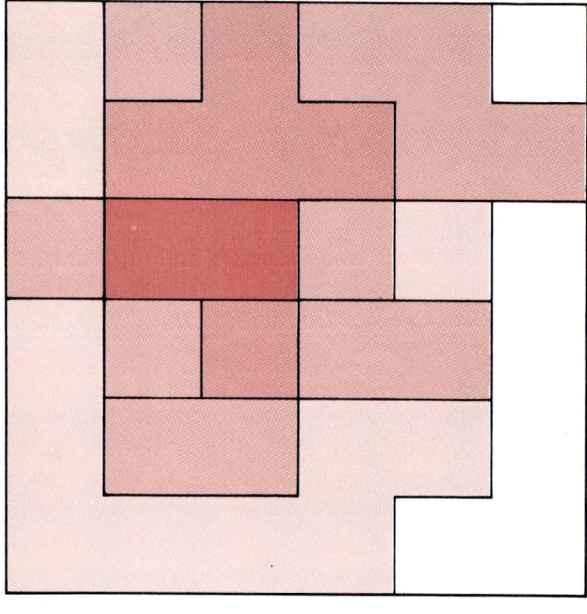

☐ 1–2 ☐ 3–4 ☐ 5–6 ☐ 7–8 ■ 5–10

FIGURE 1–10 Schematic representation of a choropleth map. Choropleth maps use shades of colors instead of dots to represent categories (intervals) of numerical values. (From Harold H. McCarty/James B. Lindberg, A PREFACE TO ECONOMIC GEOGRAPHY, © 1966. P. 34. Adapted by permission of Prentice-Hall, Inc., Englewood Cliffs, N.J.)

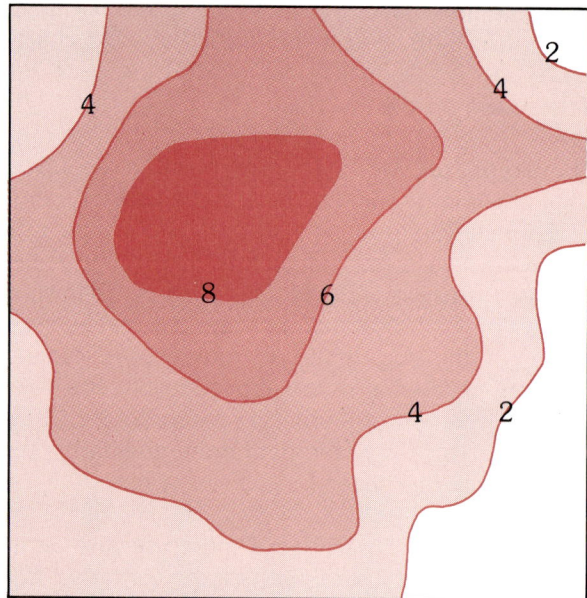

FIGURE 1–11 Schematic representation of an isoline map. Isoline maps are created by interpolating values between actual numerical values. The lines connect locations with equal values. (From Harold H. McCarty/James B. Lindberg, A PREFACE TO ECONOMIC GEOGRAPHY, © 1966. P. 35. Adapted by permission of Prentice-Hall, Inc., Englewood Cliffs, N.J.)

the original data is sacrificed for a more effective visual display.

A common use for choropleth maps is to portray information about political units such as counties, states, and nations. Areas of high and low color value can be distinguished from each other quickly and easily.

The Isoline Map In choropleth mapping, political boundaries define the statistical areas of the map. These boundaries are removed or ignored for *isoline maps* (Figure 1–11). Isolines (from the Greek *isos,* which means "equal") are lines that connect points of the same value. For example, all points 50 feet (15 m) above sea level might be connected by a line, called a contour line. This kind of map, with contours at specified intervals (say 5 ft or 1.5 m), is called a *contour map* or *topographic map* (Greek *topo,* meaning "place") because it tells us about the shape of the land. Many isolines have the prefix "iso" in their name, so it is easy to recognize what kind of lines they are. Examples include isobars (showing barometric pressure), isotherms (showing tempera-

ture), isohyets (showing precipitation), isobaths (showing depths of water bodies), and isochrones (showing time). The spaces between adjoining lines on isoline maps can be shaded to enhance the visual effect, as in Figure 1–11. The shaded zones can be thought of as *regions,* because they contain an element that is more or less homogeneously distributed throughout that area. TV weather forecast maps are good examples of this practice.

Correct interpretation of isoline maps is important in geography, and the clue to successful interpretation is understanding what an isoline represents. As an example, consider an isoline map of elevations. Each isoline (contour) represents a certain distance above sea level. "Walking" along a contour, then, would mean that you were always at the same level, never moving up- or downhill. Where contour lines are close together, the elevation changes rapidly; where they are widely spaced, the elevation change is gradual. With practice, one can visualize the hills and valleys of the actual landscape by looking at a topographic map.

Regions

Regional analysis has always been an important part of geography. Geographers analyze regions not only

CONCEPTS IN GEOGRAPHY

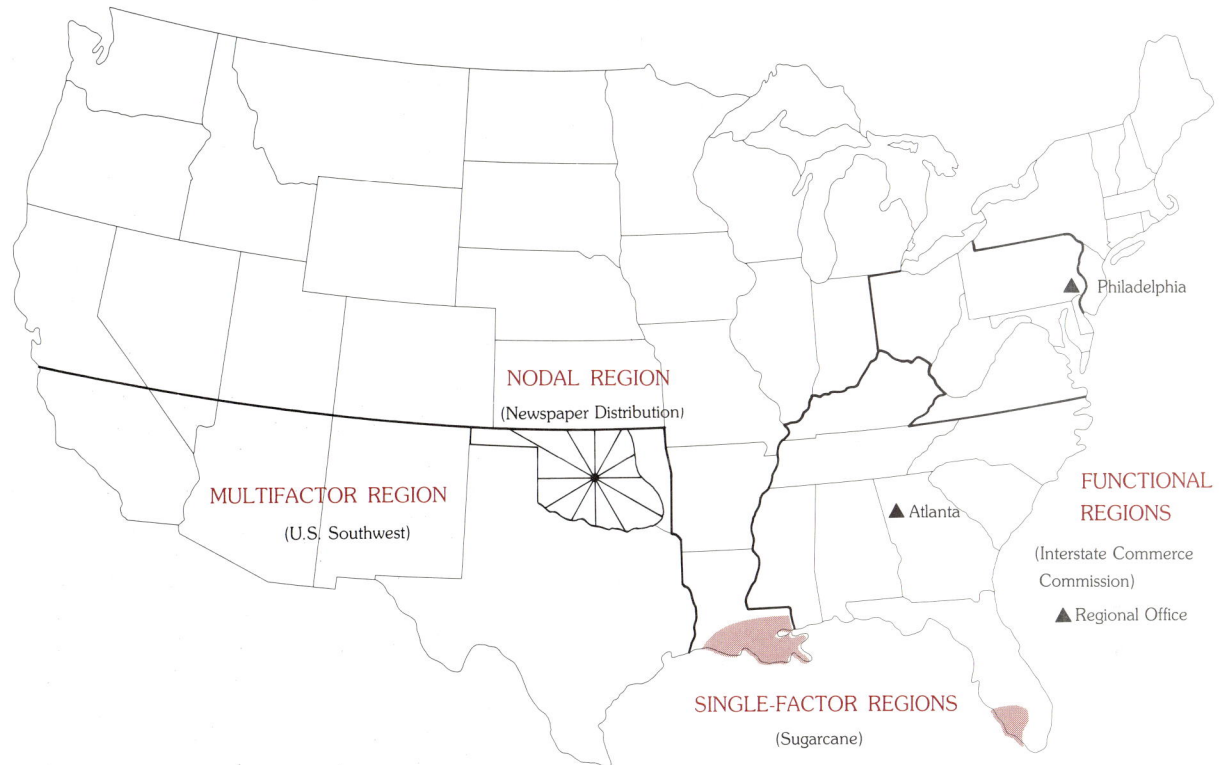

FIGURE 1–12 Four types of regions: (1) *functional* regions, designated by political boundaries; (2) *multifactor* regions, such as the U.S. Southwest; (3) *nodal* regions, such as the distribution area of the *Oklahoma Observer* newspaper; and (4) *single-factor* regions, such as the sugarcane areas of Louisiana and Florida.

to discover what they are like and why, but also to compare one region to another. Regions are areas of the earth's surface, sometimes outlined quite vaguely or arbitrarily, and sometimes defined on the basis of precise boundaries. A region may be a very large area, such as the Moslem world, stretching from India across the Arabian and Saharan Deserts to the west coast of Africa. Or a region may be small, such as the sugarcane growing area of southern Louisiana (Figure 1–12). The underlying concept of a region is the existence of some characteristic found throughout.

The characteristic used to establish a region may not be visible on the landscape, but it can be mapped. For example, a *nodal region* can be identified through the movement of something from one point (a *node*) to many other points. The distribution area of a newspaper is an example of a nodal region—the publishers' offices are the node, and the delivery points outline the region. We can observe the newspaper delivery trucks, but we cannot actually see the outline of the delivery region. Using information provided by the newspaper, however, we can show the region on a map (Figure 1–12). Nodal regions usually are established on the basis of a *single factor,* such as newspapers, migrants to a city, school attendance, or any of a multitude of things that move to or from a node and outlying points. The nodal region and *market area* concepts are closely related.

There are other types of single-factor regions in addition to nodal regions. For instance, the Moslem world and Louisiana's sugarcane area are single-factor regions based on a type of religion and a type of agriculture, respectively. The Rocky Mountain region exhibits mountainous landforms throughout, and is a single factor region. The Gobi Desert in Asia is a region based on the single factor of low amounts of rainfall. A region can thus be outlined by a human factor, which may be cultural, social, or economic, or it can be described by a physical factor such as landform or climate.

It is sometimes convenient to use more than one factor to outline a region. *Multifactor regions* are areas such as the U.S. Southwest, where a wide range of more or less homogeneous characteristics

13

CHAPTER 1 FUNDAMENTALS OF GEOGRAPHY

exists (Figure 1–12). For example, the Southwest may be identified on the basis of significant cultural traits (Hispanic population and Spanish language, large Indian population, Catholic religion), economic factors (oil and gas, cattle ranching), and physical factors (Sunbelt climate). The problem with the multifactor region concept is that geographers and other social scientists often do not agree on where the boundary of a given region should be drawn. (See the section on "Culture Regions" in Chapter 7.)

Boundaries of *functional regions* (Figure 1–12) are determined quite precisely. As the name implies, functional regions are established to perform a function. The function is usually an administrative one, such as those performed by federal agencies. Almost all large companies have sales regions or "territories," and distribution regions. Functional regions tend to be similar to nodal regions, because each area generally has a major city that serves as an administrative center for the region. The borders of these functional regions usually correspond to existing political boundaries; in fact, all political divisions can be considered functional regions.

Cultural Processes and the Landscape

Interpretation of landscapes has a long tradition in geography. Geographers continue to analyze patterns and forms produced by human activity. The concept underlying this work is that local environments, both human and physical, shape the patterns and forms observed in various cultures. The rectilinear patterns seen over much of the American landscape, for example, have their roots in surveying and planning techniques dating back to the Romans, who preferred straight highways over those that conform to the contours of the landscape. Large round fields seen today in America result from the use of center-pivot irrigation systems—irrigation technology has produced a distinctive pattern on the land.

Building materials and architectural styles are often explicable in terms of local resources and traditions. In a region rich in lumber, for example, homes and other structures tend to be built of wood. An abundance of clay may contribute to a cityscape of brick. Limestone and granite have been popular materials for major public edifices such as cathedrals, libraries, and universities. In less-developed countries that lack the machinery to excavate clay for brick or the energy to fire the necessary kilns, materials such as mud and straw have been used to manufacture building materials. Similarly, clothing materials tend to be of local origin when trade and wealth are not developed. In a technologically-oriented society such as the U.S., on the other hand, clothing materials are commonly synthetic, and few people think in terms of making clothing from locally available substances.

Building styles say a great deal about the needs, preferences, and resources of the people who built them. Family size, structure, and lifestyle are often reflected quite clearly in the homes of a particular time period. The tenements of nineteenth century industrial cities reflected low incomes and general ignorance of the principles of public health. Modern condominiums express preferences for smaller families and the avoidance of yard work in favor of various leisure pursuits. New emphasis on the use of insulating materials in construction reflects increasing energy costs and general awareness that fossil fuels are nonrenewable. Subtle changes are occurring in the orientation and design of homes in efforts to conserve energy (fewer and smaller windows, for example), and these make a lasting imprint on the landscape, providing monuments to technological and economic change. (Chapter 6 discusses this topic in greater detail.)

Geometry of Space—Location, Distance, and Distribution

Location   There are various ways to deal with locational information, depending on the degree of accuracy required. One approach is to give a place a *nominal location.* The answer to the question "Where do you live?" might be "The United States of America." This is not a very precise response, but it does give an idea of which part of the earth you are located in. The answer can be more exact with only names of places. The sequence might be: (1) The U.S. South; (2) the state of Maryland; (3) the city of Columbia; and (4) Thunder Hill Road. Thus, by giving only nominal responses, you have increased the degree of accuracy to make known a fairly precise location (Figure 1–13a).

Another type of nonmathematical locative system is called *relative location.* Before a relative location can be given, a nominal location must be known. For example, if someone does not know where Columbia is, you can refer to places that are known, such as Washington, D.C. and Baltimore. Thus the location of one place is given *relative* to the location of some other place (Figure 1–13b).

Relative locations are important in geography for reasons other than merely describing where something is located. For example, the relative location of the Middle East with respect to the location of Europe, Asia, and Africa is of interest to political geographers. Economic geographers are concerned with

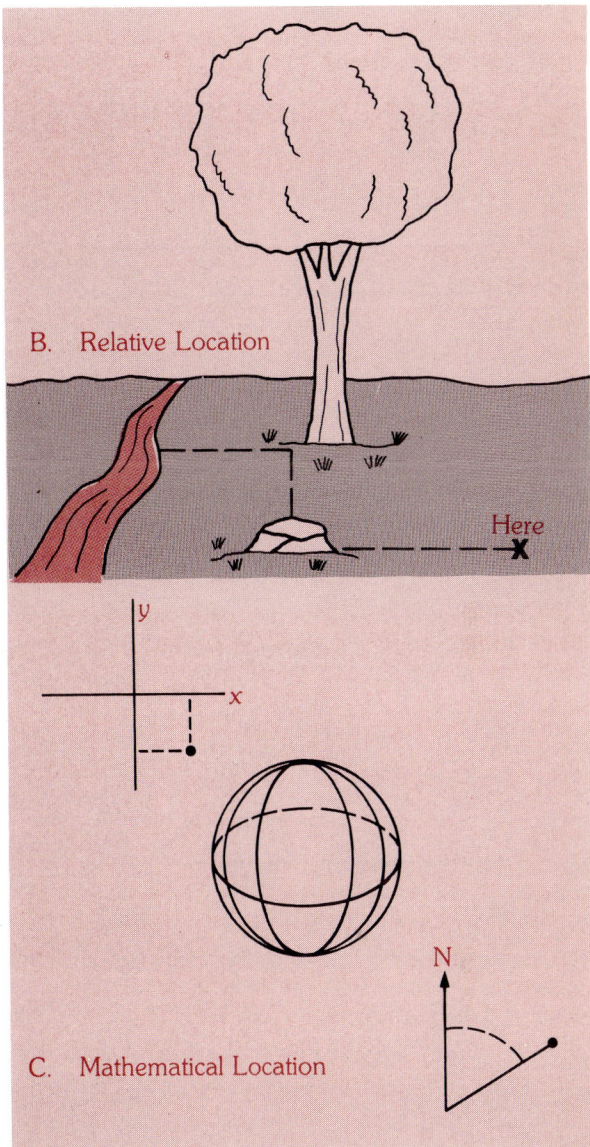

FIGURE 1–13 Three common locative systems.

the location of iron ore relative to the location of coal. Relative locations suggest relationships, and relationships lead to explanation.

The most precise description of location is given by the *mathematical location* system, of which there are two types: latitude and longitude and polar coordinates (Figures 1–13c and 1–14). The better known of these systems is the *latitude and longitude scheme*, based on the Cartesian coordinate system. This system for precise location of individual points was designed in the seventeenth century by the French mathematician René Descartes. Descartes's system starts with two perpendicular lines; for convenience, we designate the lines (axes) as *X* and *Y* (Figure 1–14a). Additional lines parallel to the axes form a grid. Locations are made on the grid by moving so many units away from the *X*-axis and so many units away from the *Y*-axis. The axes correspond to the equator and prime meridian, respectively (Figure 1–14b and c).

Latitude and longitude are expressed in degrees because they are formed through angular measurements at the center of the earth. Latitude measures distances north and south of the equator, and longitude measures east and west of the prime meridian. The grid lines are created by rotating the angles. Each grid line, therefore, is a particular angular distance from the original axis. Latitude lines are parallel to one another and are also called *parallels*. Longitude lines form wedges that come together at the poles. The location of any point on the earth's surface is given as two angles, interpreted as distances from the two axes. For example, 47°36′ N (latitude), 122°20′ W (longitude) is the location of Seattle, Washington. Although scientifically precise, this location information may not be as meaningful as the relative designation of, say, 150 mi (241 km) north of Portland, Oregon, depending on what kind of information one needs.

The other type of mathematical locative method is a direction and distance measure known as the *polar coordinate system*. This system is used in surveying and navigation, and we mention it here because it can be used to record the location of sampling points in geographic field exercises. We take a

CHAPTER 1 FUNDAMENTALS OF GEOGRAPHY

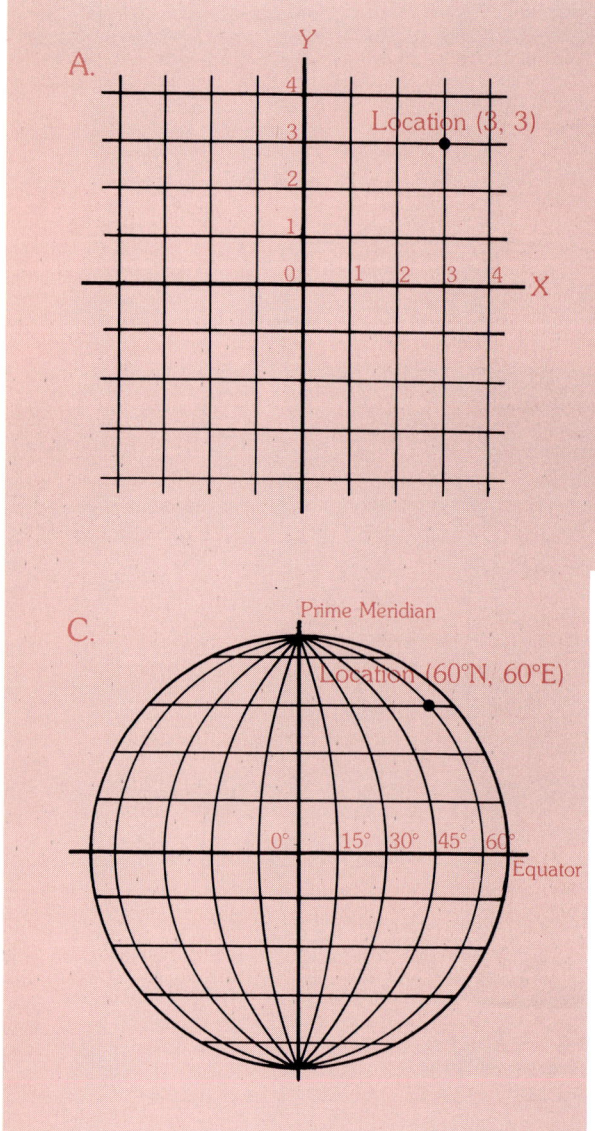

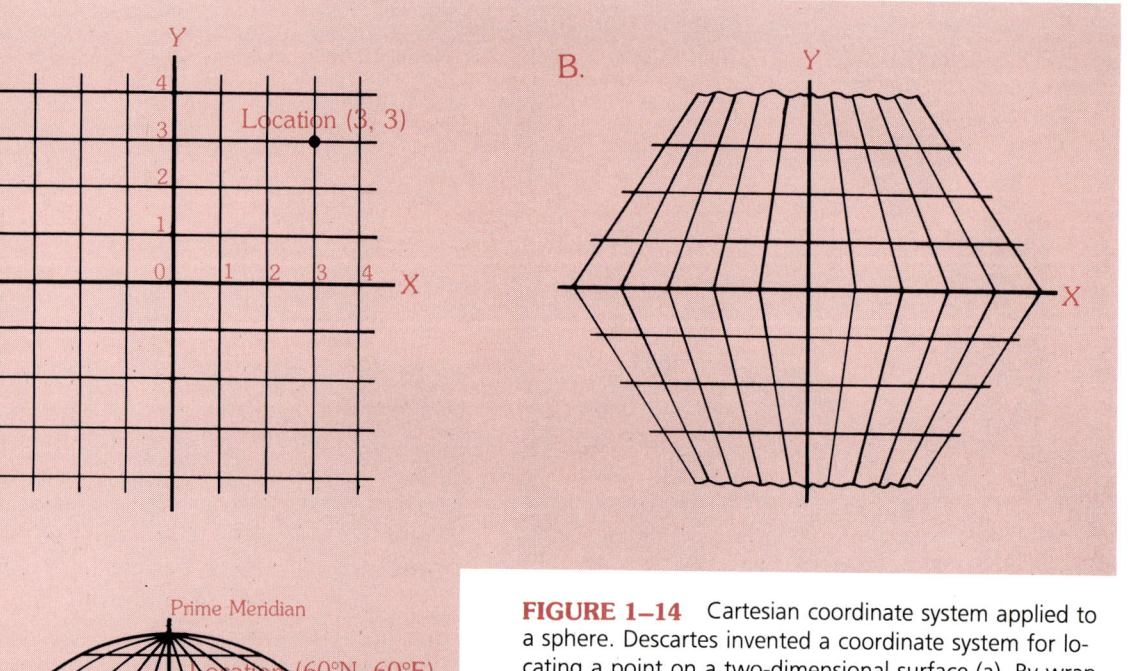

FIGURE 1–14 Cartesian coordinate system applied to a sphere. Descartes invented a coordinate system for locating a point on a two-dimensional surface (a). By wrapping the flat surface around a sphere and pulling the ends together at top and bottom, one can apply the two-dimensional surface to a three-dimensional surface (b). The latitude and longitude system is an adaptation of the Cartesian coordinate system (c).

known location such as a bench mark (a marked point of known elevation) as the origin and record other locations according to their direction and distance along straight lines from the origin. Locations based on direction and distance are a combination of relative and mathematical systems; however, any point on the globe can be designated. For example, if the North Pole is considered the origin and the prime meridian a base line, then any place can be found as an angle from the base line and the distance from the North Pole.

Distance Distance is simply the space between two points. Measured with a standard unit such as the mile or kilometer, the result is called *absolute distance* and is what most people probably think of when they deal with distance. But many other forms of distance pertain to geography. These are *relative distances*, since they are measured with respect to other factors.

In economic terms, distance is relative to the cost of movement from one place to another. There is a cost involved in any movement, whether in monetary terms or in expenditure of energy. Movement includes the travel of people, goods, or ideas. This *economic distance* can be much different than absolute distance. For example, the cost of shipping something by water usually is about one tenth the cost of shipping it overland (Figure 1–15), so the least-cost route between two places may be much longer than the least-absolute-distance route (Figure 1–16). Another example of economic distance is in the construction of new routes. The question is whether it is more expensive to minimize the cost of construction or to minimize eventual user costs. The cost of constructing a stretch of highway in mountainous terrain can be 50 times or more the cost of construction on flat land. A situation such as that shown in Figure 1–16 would require careful consideration: should the new highway be built through the expensive mountain route, thus saving eventual user costs, or should

FIGURE 1–15 Land and water transportation systems: (a) railroad yard and adjacent highway in Salt Lake City, Utah; (b) ships moving up the St. Lawrence Seaway near Quebec City.

it go the greater absolute distance and save the tremendous cost of construction? Perhaps a compromise between the extremes would be best.

The factors of *time* and *direction* also affect distance. The expression "time is money" can apply if time is the critical expense factor for the situations in Figure 1–16; the least-absolute-distance routes may be the least-cost routes. Maps that indicate travel times from a single point, such as the central business district of a city, may distort absolute distances according to ease of movement, because travel time is not equal in all directions. Direction of movement must also be considered a distance factor, since movement from point A to point B may not be as easy as movement from B to A ($A \rightarrow B \neq B \rightarrow A$). A common example in urban areas is the one-way street pattern (Figure 1–17a). Another example is that of two points located at different elevations (Figure 1–17b); the absolute distance between the points may be the same in either direction, but the ease of movement is not the same, and distance is important only when movement is necessary.

Another relative distance factor may be termed *psychological distance*. Perceptions of distance vary—what may seem like a long trip to some individuals may seem short to others. Even the same route going and coming can seem different to one traveler, depending on road conditions, anticipation of what waits at the end of the trip, the beauty or safety of various routes, and so on. Thus, we must consider time and direction in calculating psychological distance.

Distance can also be thought of in terms of the obstacles encountered along the path of movement. These obstacles create *friction* to movement. If the friction increases, movement is more difficult either in terms of cost, time, direction, or behavioral factors. The absolute distances between places are distorted by the friction factors. For example, shoppers may go to a suburban mall farther from their homes

CHAPTER 1 FUNDAMENTALS OF GEOGRAPHY

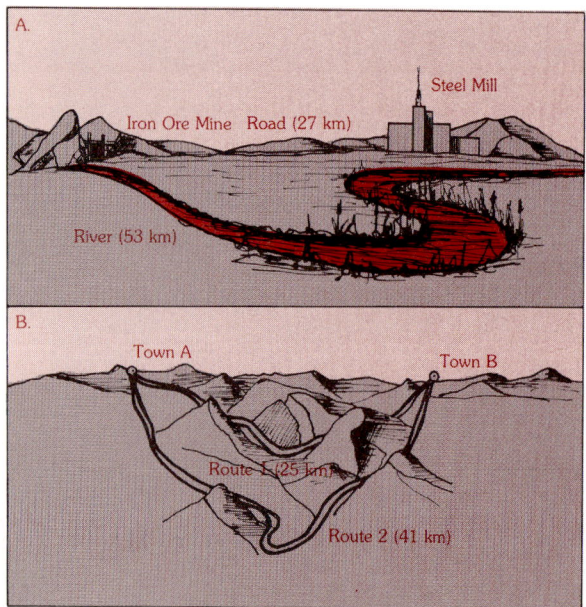

FIGURE 1–16 Examples of economic distance. The shortest actual distance may be more expensive than a longer route, as in (b).

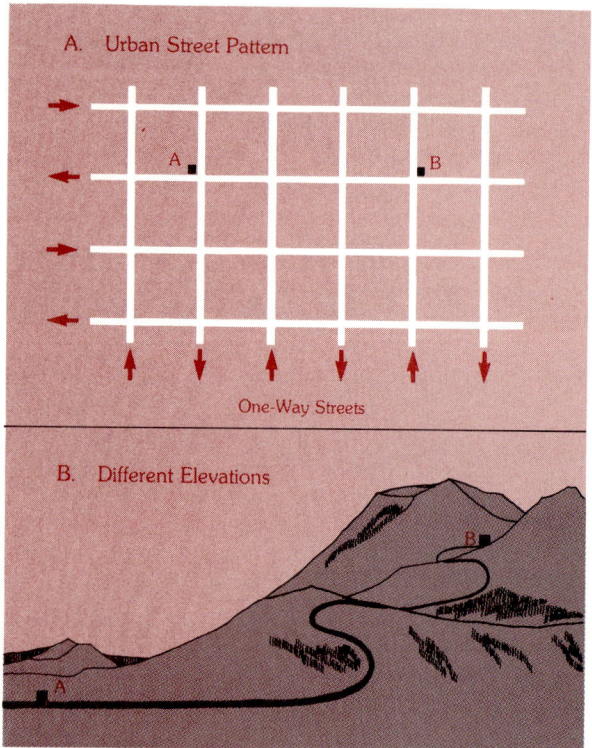

FIGURE 1–17 Examples showing that the friction of distance is not the same from A to B as it is from B to A.

rather than to nearer downtown stores to avoid the friction of traffic congestion.

Distribution A main concern of geography is how things are distributed on the face of the earth. This interest in *spatial distribution* is one feature that distinguishes geography from other sciences. Spatial distributions are important to geographers because they are the basis of all maps, and because they implicitly pose the question "Why?" The central question in geography, then, is why things are distributed as they are.

The elements common to all spatial distributions are *pattern, density,* and *dispersion*. These three elements relate to the locations of the objects under study but are otherwise independent of one another. Consider the location of towns. Let us call the objects (towns) *geographic facts,* because they exist and have specified locations. We can then define *pattern* as the geometric arrangement of the individual geographic facts (Figure 1–18a). The geometric arrangement of towns can be described with terms such as *linear* (found along a river or road), *centralized* (arranged around the largest place), *uniform* (distributed evenly over the landscape), or *random* (scattered haphazardly). A spatial distribution pattern can help describe that distribution, but, more importantly, it can be compared to the pattern of another distribution. Comparisons provide useful explanations of the processes underlying the distributions. For example, the clustering of cases of cancer in homes near a chemical dump may suggest the role of the chemicals as causative agents in the cancers.

Density is the number of geographic facts per unit area (Figure 1–18b). Density makes sense only with regard to the size of an area. It is also an important measure for comparative purposes. A comparison of the number of towns in counties of varying sizes requires the use of a ratio, such as towns per square mile or kilometer. (For a more detailed discussion of density of a particular type—*population density*—see the section "Density, Crowding, and Personal Space" in Chapter 8.)

The third element of all spatial distributions, *dispersion*, is the degree to which the objects (geographic facts) are spread apart from one another (Figure 1–18c). As with density, dispersion makes sense only with regard to a designated area. For example, the distribution of towns in two counties of equal size can have indentical patterns and densities but can be spread out differently. They can be *agglomerated* (located close together) or *dispersed*

CONCEPTS IN GEOGRAPHY

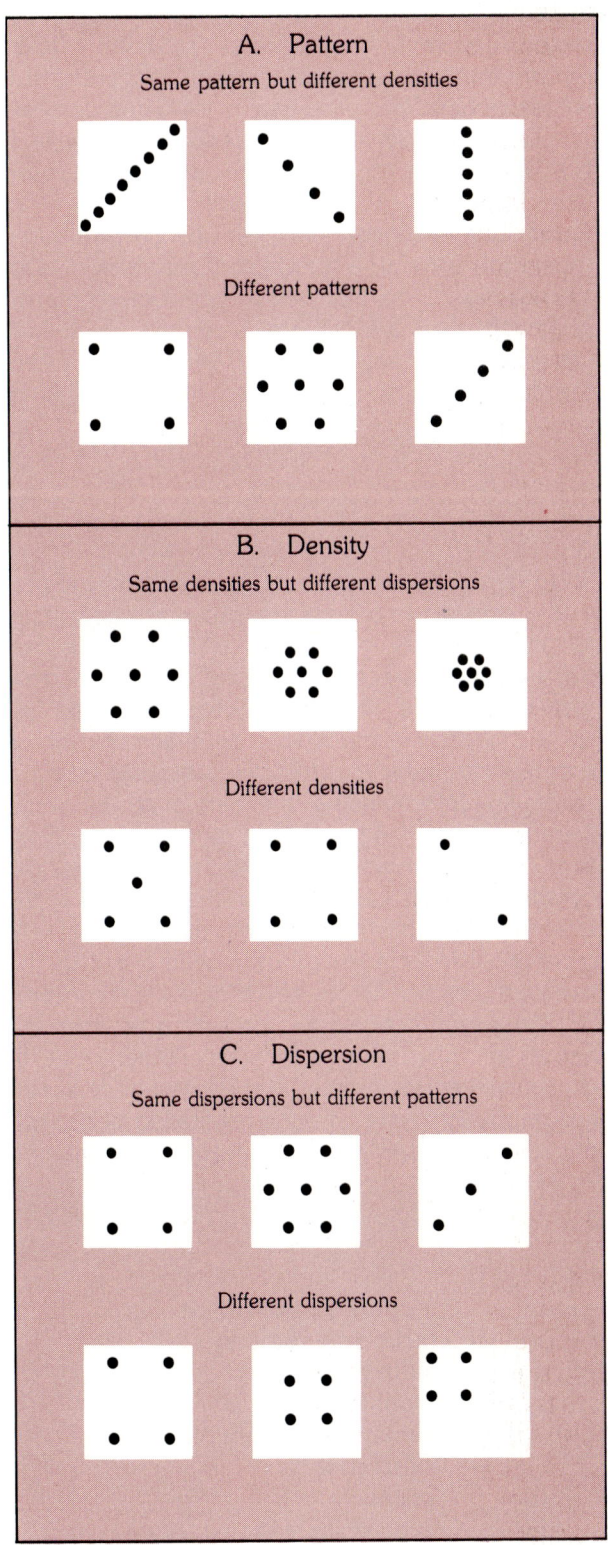

FIGURE 1–18 Comparisons of the three elements of spatial distribution—pattern, density, and dispersion.

(spread throughout the area). Two or more spatial distributions can be compared by comparing their dispersions.

Geographical Change

The concept of change is by no means unique to geography, yet an understanding of change in the context of geography can contribute to our understanding of processes and patterns on the land. We are confronted with change in both the human and physical environments, and these changes interact with each other. Long-term increases in precipitation, for example, may result in more frequent flooding and curtailment of development in floodplains. A devastating earthquake may elicit changes in building codes. Human attitudes toward the environment may change in the direction of greater respect for nature, resulting in the survival of endangered species, the setting aside of aesthetically valuable lands for recreational purposes, and improved air and water quality. A decline in respect for the natural environment would result in deterioration of environmental quality. A dramatic example of change is apparent today along the southern margins of the Sahara Desert, where *desertification* is extending the area of the desert and contributing to famine conditions among the peoples of the region. Here, change in the physical environment has traumatically affected the human population.

Diffusion Processes Although geography is preoccupied with areas and places, the relationship between geography and time can be important indeed. Changes often occur because new ideas spread from person to person, ultimately resulting in modification of life style. The attraction of small cars, with their low gasoline consumption, spread rapidly in the 1970s when gas prices were rising quickly. Other changes, both trivial and significant, have spread more or less rapidly, including hybrid corn, the use of herbicides and pesticides, kindergarten, microcomputers, Christianity, the English language, and AIDS. Geographic change is not always positive. Diseases spread over time, and may cause heavy mortalities if the host areas are not ready to deal with them. Wars bring changes, usually unwelcome, in both time and space. Geographers describe the spread of phenomena as *diffusion*. Research on diffusion processes shows that certain regularities can be seen when ideas, or diseases, or other phenom-

19

ena spread across the landscape, as we will see in Chapter 8.

Application: Geography as a Useful Science

Like other scientific fields, modern geography has both "pure" and "applied" aspects. Pure geography is concerned with the formulation of concepts, principles, and laws to allow better understanding of human geographic behavior. This type of geography tends to rely heavily on the use of mathematical and statistical "models," generalizations about processes or sets of interrelationships. Applied geography, on the other hand, is the use of geographic principles, methods, and perspectives in problem-solving situations. Numerous problems—market research, urban planning, industrial location, recreational planning, military strategy, disease control, emergency medical facility siting, school siting—demand an understanding of geographic patterns. Chapter 17 will explore the nature and scope of applied geography in greater detail.

REGIONAL VERSUS TOPICAL GEOGRAPHY

Geographers generally approach problems from either a *regional* or a *topical* perspective. The regional approach begins with a region, such as New England. Then we make descriptive observations about the physical and human elements that compose the region. The topical or *systematic* approach, on the other hand, begins with a topic such as population distribution, then analyzes various aspects of the topic, such as density, age structure, and family size. A topical study is concerned with all places the topic is found, rather than with all things in a particular region. Frequently, the nature of the problem determines whether a regional or topical approach (or some combination of the two) is more appropriate.

This book uses the topical approach to geography. This is not to suggest that topical analysis is "best"; its use here merely reflects our belief that an introduction to geography can be covered more thoroughly through a topical approach than in a region-by-region manner. Most introductory human geography texts are organized topically, unless they are courses in "world regional geography," where the emphasis is on regions and their interrelationships.

CONCLUSION

This chapter outlines the history of geography to provide a perspective on the role into which geography has evolved today. Interest in the subject of geography has existed since humans first began to explore their earth home. The Greeks were among the first to record their contributions to geography. Some progress was made in the Middle Ages, but dramatic strides in understanding the nature of the world were made in the Ages of Discovery and Exploration. In the nineteenth and early twentieth centuries, geography suffered a setback from the influence of the environmental determinists, only to reemerge as a progressive social science in the second half of the twentieth century. Seven key geographical concepts provide a study framework: interaction between the human and physical worlds, maps and mapping, regions, cultural processes, the geometry of space, geographical change, and the application of geography to problem-solving.

KEY WORDS

absolute distance
agglomerated distribution
applied geography
choropleth map
contour map
density
diffusion
dispersed distribution
distance
dot map
economic distance
environmental determinism
equator

friction of movement
functional regions
global scale
graphic scale
human geography
interaction
isolines
large-scale map
latitude
local scale
longitude
map scale
mathematical location

REFERENCES

multifactor region
nodal region
nominal location
pattern
physical geography
polar coordinate system
prime meridian
psychological distance
quantitative revolution
region
relative distance

relative location
representative fraction
remote sensing
single-factor region
small-scale map
spatial distribution
statistical map
systematic geography
thematic map
topical geography

REFERENCES

BAKER, J. N. *A History of Geographical Discovery and Exploration.* Boston: Houghton Mifflin, 1931.

BROEK, JAN O. M. *Geography: Its Scope and Purpose.* Columbus, OH: Charles E. Merrill, 1965.

GROSVENOR, GILBERT M. "Geography Has Been Losing Ground in Our Schools," *National Geographic Magazine,* 166 (1984).

JAMES, PRESTON E. *All Possible Worlds: A History of Geographical Ideas.* Indianapolis, IN: Bobbs-Merrill, 1972.

JAMES, PRESTON E., and JONES, CLARENCE F., eds. *American Geography: Inventory and Prospect.* Syracuse, NY: Syracuse University Press, 1954.

KOLARS, JOHN F., and NYSTUEN, JOHN D. *Geography: The Study of Location, Culture, and Environment.* New York: McGraw-Hill, 1974.

McCARTY, HAROLD H., and LINDBERG, JAMES B. *A Preface to Economic Geography.* Englewood Cliffs, NJ: Prentice-Hall, 1966.

MEYER, ALFRED H., and STRIETELMEIR, JOHN H. *Geography in World Society: A Conceptual Approach.* Philadelphia: J. B. Lippincott, 1963.

MURPHEY, RHOADS. *The Scope of Geography,* 2nd ed. Chicago: Rand McNally, 1973.

PLATT, ROBERT S. "Determinism in Geography." *Annals,* Association of American Geographers, 38 (1948): 126–31.

ROBINSON, ARTHUR H., SALE, R. D., and MORRISON, J. *Elements of Cartography,* 4th ed. New York: John Wiley, 1978.

TARBUCK, EDWARD J., and LUTGENS, FREDERICK K. *Earth Science,* 2nd ed. Columbus, OH: Charles E. Merrill, 1979.

THOMAS, WILLIAM L. JR., ed. *Man's Role in Changing the Face of the Earth.* Chicago: University of Chicago Press, 1956.

THOMSON, J. OLIVER. *History of Ancient Geography.* Cambridge: Cambridge University Press, 1948.

WEIGERT, HANS W., and STEFANSSON, VILHJALMUR, eds. *Compass of the World.* New York: Macmillan, 1945.

2
World Population

THE DEVELOPMENT OF HUMANS AND THE HUMAN RACES
POPULATION GEOGRAPHY
U.S. POPULATION GEOGRAPHY
WORLD POPULATION DENSITY, DISTRIBUTION, AND WEALTH
POPULATION AND FOOD

Victoria, Hong Kong, located on a strip of land reclaimed from the sea. (Wolfgang Kaehler Photography)

THE DEVELOPMENT OF HUMANS AND THE HUMAN RACES

Human Development

The family of humans, a group of creatures called *hominids,* probably emerged in Africa about 5 million years ago. Humans are referred to as *Homo sapiens,* from the Latin meaning "man, the wise."

Though apes and humans have common ancestry, it is not true that humans are "descended from apes." The family tree branched, with humans developing on one side and apes and their relatives on the other. What distinguishes the hominids from the apes is bipedal (two-legged) posture. Other creatures, such as the kangaroo, can stand on two legs, but humans have taken advantage of the availability of arms for advanced toolmaking, a uniquely human trait.

As humans evolved, toolmaking became increasingly sophisticated, beginning with stone scrapers, advancing to stone blades, and eventually achieving the great efficiency of the bow and arrow. Over the next 2 million years, the human brain size gradually increased. Compared to gorillas, with about 500 cm^3 (about 31 in^3) of brain, *Australopithecus,* the first of the hominids, reached 600 cm^3. *Homo erectus,* by about 600,000 years ago, had reached 900 cm^3, which compares to today's 1,450 cm^3. This brain size was reached some 100,000 years ago (McEvedy and Jones, 1978, p. 13).

Exactly how the human species of today developed from *Homo erectus* is not clear. Evidence from Greece dated to 500,000 years ago is thought to link *Homo erectus* and *Homo sapiens.* Skeletons found there lack clear characteristics of either *erectus* or *sapiens.* The earliest *sapiens,* perhaps 200–300,000 years ago, were Neanderthal people, so called because of fossil discoveries in the Neander valley in Germany. Evidence is sketchy, and there is still considerable disagreement, but one suggestion is that a branch of the Neanderthals migrated to Southwest Asia some 100,000 years ago, following initial evolution in Europe. Compared to us, the Neanderthals were heavy-boned people with massive, out-thrust faces accommodating large teeth, and with the backs of their heads protruding markedly. Some quarter-million years ago, it's likely that Africa had the highest population density. Open woodlands were favored habitats, as they supported herds that could be hunted. Humans and grazing animals were inseparable, and deserts, forests (both cold and warm), and tundra regions contained no people, as they either had no grazing herds or, as in the case of the tundra, were too cold.

Climatic change a couple of hundred thousand years ago gave rise to massive ice accumulations known as the Riss and Würm glaciations. So much water was "locked up" in the form of ice that world sea level may have dropped as much as 150 m (500 ft) and large areas of continental shelves were exposed, offering new hunting and gathering opportunities. People who had migrated poleward retreated to lower latitudes, as Europe became too cold for human occupancy. The Riss glaciation lasted until about 125,000 BP (Before the Present), and was followed by a warmer period, the Riss-Würm interglacial. After the onset of the Würm, people were more successful in adapting to cooler northerly environments, using technological advances such as fire, clothing, and shelter. Northerly groups of people developed lighter skin color, to allow the skin to synthesize vitamin D by sunlight. Darker skins at higher latitudes blocked scarce sunlight (short winter days, cloudy climate) and prevented formation of vitamin D, leading in turn to a bone-weakening disease called rickets, if milk or fish (the only other sources of D) were not available. At lower latitudes, sunlight was so abundant that dark skin didn't matter, but in the north, biological selection favored lighter skins, as darker-skinned peoples became victims of rickets.

The Würm glaciation ended about 10,000 years BP. In the later part of the Würm, *Cro-Magnon* people emerged, evolving from Neanderthals. No Neanderthal fossils more recent than 40,000 BP have been found. Evolution from Neanderthal to Cro-Magnon probably did not occur in all Neanderthal groups. European Neanderthals, for example, seem to have died out. In other regions, however, Neanderthals evolved into Cro-Magnons, who were lighter-boned and flatter-faced. The skull, instead of being rather elongated, became more rounded. Why did skull shape change? The massive teeth and jaws of the Neanderthals may have been an adaptation to the use of teeth for chewing hides to soften them for making clothing, and for other "gripping" chores. When tools improved, the need for large teeth and jaws disappeared. Another theory is that, as language became more sophisticated, the upper throat (pharynx) enlarged to accommodate the demand for a greater variety of sounds. The enlargement of the pharynx is thought to have contributed to the arching of the skull and its corresponding shortening (Campbell, 1982). Cro-Magnon people probably migrated to Europe some 20–30,000 years BP, after evolution partially in Southwest Asia ("Modern Man: Mid-East Origins", 1979). Evolutionary change had finished by about 30,000 BP, yielding modern humans—people like us.

How many of our ancestors were on earth at any given time? *Australopithecus* (debatably a human ancestor owing to evidence that the type coexisted with hominids more clearly related to man) probably did not leave Africa, and its population has been estimated at between 70,000 and a million. *Homo erectus* ranged much farther, from Europe to Indonesia, and a total population at any given time of 1.7 million has been suggested—about the same as the 1980 population of the Miami, Florida, metropolitan area! Migration across Beringia (the land now submerged under the Bering Strait) into the Americas occurred about 45–10,000 BP. Then, accompanied by a warming trend around 12,000 BP, came an increase in the size of the human population. By 12,000 BP, the total had grown to more than twice what it had been around 100,000 BP—about 4 million (McEvedy and Jones, 1978). Gradually, as improvements occurred in food production, and, in the last couple of hundred years, in public health, the rate of population increase accelerated. As the population grew, it also diffused, or spread, through the process of *migration*. (See Chapter 8 for further discussion of diffusion.)

Migration

Migration takes many forms. In this discussion, we refer to the long-term relocation of large groups of people, over substantial distances. *Long-term, large,* and *substantial* are purposely left undefined, as they are intended only to provide a general idea of the types of human movement under consideration.

Prehistoric Migrations By about 300,000 BP, *Homo* had spread over most of Africa and into southern, western, and central Europe, Southern

THE DEVELOPMENT OF HUMANS AND THE HUMAN RACES

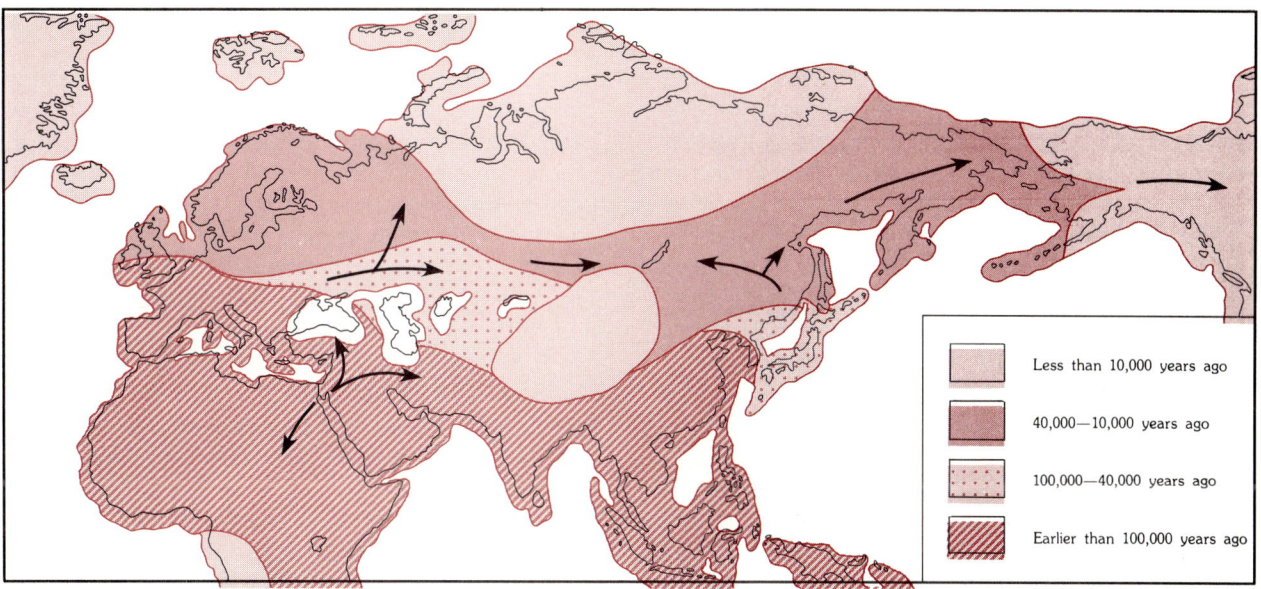

FIGURE 2–1 Colonization of the world by *Homo sapiens*. Until about 10,000 years ago, glaciation confined humans to southern Europe and Asia. Technological advances allowed migration farther north. (From *The Mystery of Migration*, edited by Robin Baker, copyright © 1980 by the Viking Press.)

Asia, Central China, and Indonesia. Australia was reached about 32,000 BP, and the Americas about 10–45,000 BP, via Beringia (Figure 2–1). There were two major phases of migration into North America:

- 40–19,000 BP: Hunter/gatherers from northeastern Siberia entered North America and spread rapidly south to Central America, which was reached about 20,000 BP. Southern South American was colonized around 12,000 years ago.
- 8–10,000 BP: Northwestern Pacific people, ancestors of the Eskimos and Aleuts, spread around the southern part of Beringia, reaching southwest Alaska and the Aleutian Islands about 8–10,000 years ago. They then migrated along the Arctic coast, reaching the eastern Canadian Arctic about 5,000 BP and northern Greenland about 4,000 BP (Baker, 1981).

Patterns of early human occupancy were severely restricted by climatic conditions. Regions of initial habitation were at relatively low latitudes in Africa, southern Europe, and Asia. Major migrations to the north became possible only as the climate moderated from the bitter cold of the ice age, and the technologies of fire use and clothing developed. Even today, the northern fringes of North America, Europe, and Asia are very sparsely populated. The Southern Hemisphere is essentially devoid of people south of about 50°S latitude, where the only major land mass is the frigidly inhospitable continent of Antarctica. Though modern humans have access to vast energy supplies and sophisticated techniques for making clothing and shelter, the coldest lands of the earth are avoided much as they have been throughout the existence of *Homo sapiens*.

Ancient Migrations Though many migrations throughout history have been forced by conquest or slavery, such movements of people have nevertheless had the effect of changing the population geography of regions. The Romans, for example, imported slaves from Africa, Gaul, Britain, and the River Rhine region. As many as 600,000 of the people of Rome may have been "foreign" slaves. Invasions of Britain by the Angles, Saxons, Jutes, and Vikings not only changed the population geography of Britain, but also contributed the basis of the English language, *Aenglisc*, the language of the Angles (see Chapter 4). Invasions from central Asia into neighboring areas also redistributed population to some extent. Vandals, Goths, and Huns invaded the Roman Empire, for example, and the Mongols invaded China and Asia Minor (Turkey). A combination of voluntary migrations and migrations forced by famine, disease, or military invasion kept populations in a more or less constant state of increase, decrease, and mixing (Jones, 1981).

Modern Migrations Beginning about the seventeenth century, European expansion led to major international migrations to two kinds of environments. First, the warm coastlands of the Americas, ranging from Virginia to Brazil, were accessible by sea and permitted the production of exotic crops such as sugar, cotton, and tobacco. These tropical crops demanded labor, which was not adequately available locally. Europeans could not be recruited in sufficient numbers, so African slaves were soon imported. Altogether, about 12 million Africans were transported to the New World. Following the abolition of slavery, Asian Indians and Chinese became the new supply of cheap labor, particularly to Malaysia, Indonesia, Sri Lanka, Fiji, Hawaii, South and East Africa, Mauritius, and California. As a result of this contract labor system, many laborers stayed in their adopted countries following the expiration of their contracts, giving rise to significant local populations.

The second kind of environment that stimulated massive migrations was that of middle-latitude grasslands and deciduous woodlands. This environment was attractive to Europeans, as they could adapt to it with relatively little difficulty. Between 1820 and 1930, about 60 million Europeans migrated to the Americas, South Africa, Australia, and New Zealand. This was the most massive migration of people in history (Jones, 1981). More recently, we have seen the migration of Vietnamese, Cubans, Mexicans, Haitians, Filipinos, and others to the U.S. in large numbers, for a variety of reason. (See Chapter 8 for further discussion of migration processes and patterns.) Migrations since the eighteenth century are summarized in Figure 2–2.

Race

Among the concurrent evolutionary changes was the emergence of several racial groups, identified on the basis of certain physical characteristics. Why did such groups develop? The most important process has been *natural selection,* the survival of those better adapted to their environments, and the consequent perpetuation and amplification of the adaptive traits. The other major process in racial development is *genetic drift,* the accidental change in the genetic structure of a population. Geographic isolation plays a significant role in both selection and drift—in more isolated populations, the processes can continue undisturbed and therefore have their maximum effect (Howells, 1975).

The distribution of racial groups does not conform neatly to patterns that would be expected on the basis of adaptive processes alone. Dark skin, for example, is due to concentration of the substance *melanin,* which acts as a protective screen against sunlight. It is reasonable, then, to suggest that people living in low-latitude areas, where the sunlight is most intense, would develop dark skin pigmentation as a defense mechanism. But why, then, would forest dwellers in more or less dense shade in tropical rain forests have dark skin? The explanation may lie in migration processes that also explain other anomalies: these people may have developed their dark skin elsewhere, perhaps in the warm steppes or savannas, and then moved at a later time to the forest.

Other adaptive traits of racial groups include the paleness of northern Europeans, a high-latitude people living in a generally cloudy climate and therefore

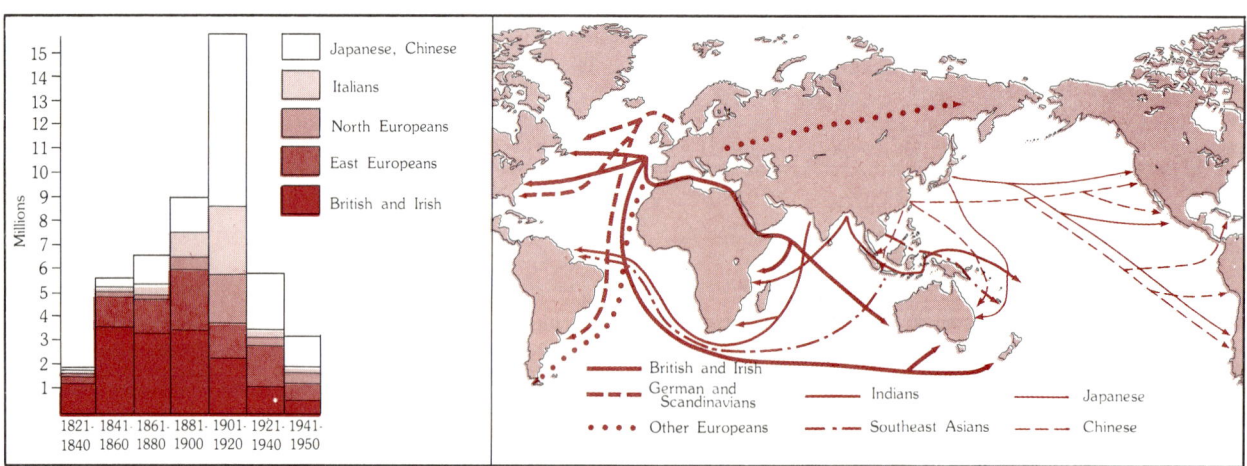

FIGURE 2–2 World migrations since the eighteenth century. From *The Mystery of Migration,* edited by Robin Baker, copyright © 1980 by the Viking Press.)

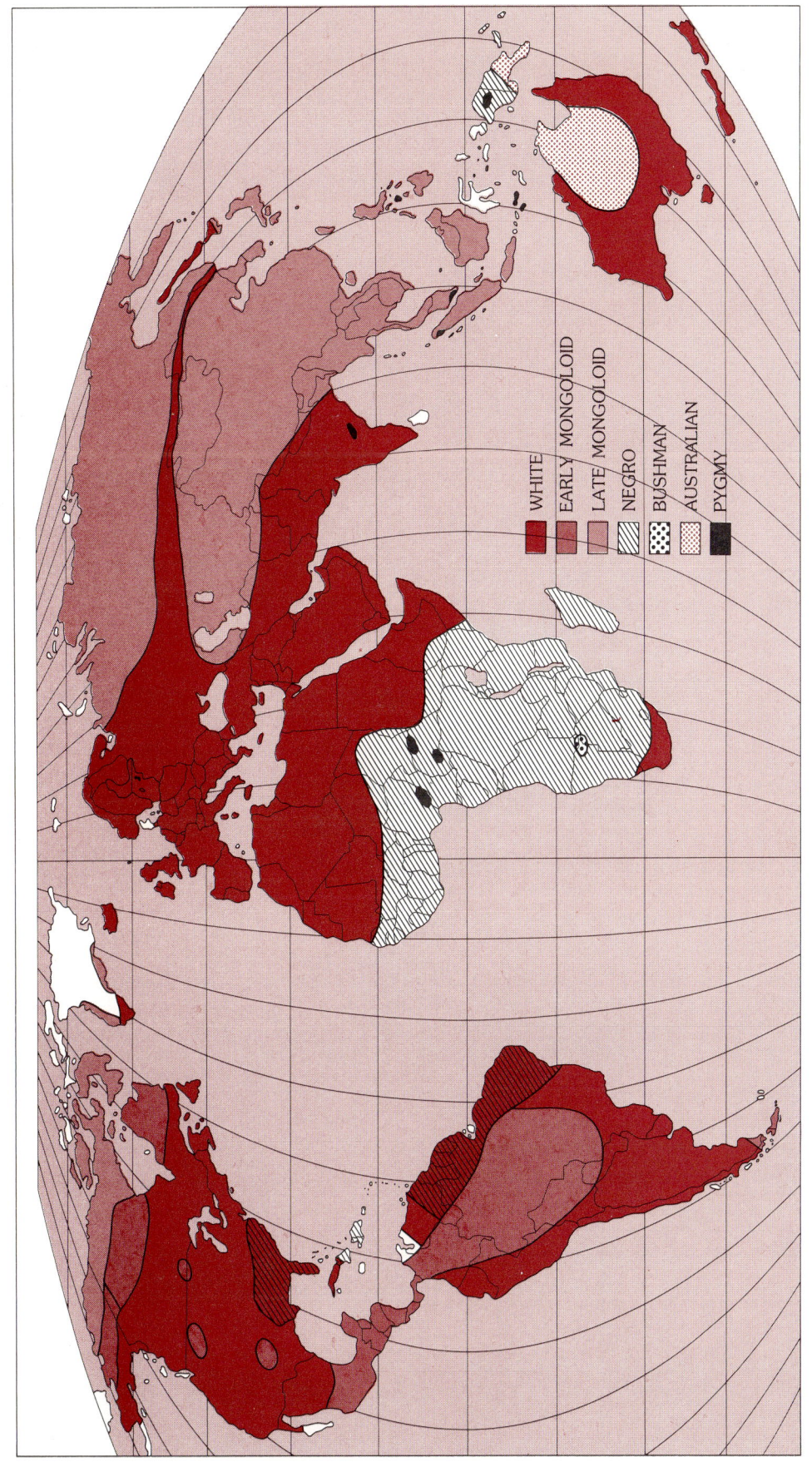

FIGURE 2-3 World distribution of seven major racial groups. (From "The Distribution of Man" by William H. Howells, copyright © 1960 by Scientific American, Inc. All rights reserved.)

without need for protective skin color. Oriental people, particularly in cold eastern Asia, are well adapted to their frigid winter. Eyes have double lids (giving the distinctive almond appearance), and facial features, well padded with fat, generally provide good protection against the cold. Another observable aspect of adaptation is body bulk. Compact specimens, with large volume in relation to surface area, are better able to resist cold than lanky types with a smaller volume-to-area ratio. Indeed, tall, slender types tend to be found in hotter climates, and more compact people in frigid areas (Howells, 1975).

The classification of people into racial groups is difficult because racial distinctions became blurred as people's mobility increased. One simple classification divides peoples into *mongoloid* (East Asia, the Americas), *caucasoid* (Europe, the Americas, Australia, South Asia, much of the Arab world), and *negroid* (most of sub-Saharan Africa and parts of the Americas). Because this three-part classification is considered too generalized, however, most modern classifications contain up to a dozen categories to describe the complexity. Figure 2–3 shows a seven-part classification. Whites, or caucasoids, are retained as a single group, but mongoloids are divided into "Early" (more recent) and "Late" (older) groups. This classification also distinguishes among dark-skinned negroid peoples, who are found in Australia and the island chain to the north of it, as well as in Africa and in those parts of the Americas to which blacks were taken as slaves (or to which they have subsequently migrated). The Bushmen in Southwest Africa, who are actually rather light skinned compared to most other African negroids, provide an interesting anomaly because the Bushmen live in an environment of intense sunlight.

Race is at the root of as much tension and potential and actual conflict as any other problem in the world today. What are the facts? What do racial differences really mean? In a document issued by UNESCO in 1964, more than 20 distinguished international scholars lent their names to a lengthy statement dealing with the biological aspect of race. Parts, including those with geographic implications, have been excerpted in the box on page 29. In Chapter 7, we will look at the issue of race from a cultural rather than a biological perspective and discuss the relationship between the concepts of race and ethnicity.

Race and Migration Figure 2–3 generalizes the geography of races; in reality, increases in mobility in recent centuries have given rise to some degree of racial mixing, with the result that millions of people do not fit a simple scheme of racial identification. However, we should not exaggerate the effects of migration and genetic mixing. Americans look at the racial diversity around them, and perhaps tend to assume, erroneously, that such racial blending is going on everywhere in the world. While the U.S. has absorbed many immigrants of diverse racial backgrounds, the source areas of those migrants are likely to remain essentially the same genetically. It is unlikely that the world is headed toward a blending of all peoples into one race. Repeated massive migrations, such as those from Europe to the Americas, are unlikely in the future, and the contribution of racial mixing in the U.S. to racial change on a global scale is minimal (Brues, 1977).

POPULATION GEOGRAPHY

As we have said, the world's human population increased from perhaps 1.7 million 100,000 years ago to about 4 million 10,000 years ago. In the last 10,000 years, population has increased over a thousandfold, to about 5 billion, and much of that change has actually occurred in the last few hundred years (Figure 2–4). Barring a nuclear catastrophe, we can be confident that, by the year 2000, the world population will be around 6 billion, or about the equivalent of 1,500 Detroits.

The rate of increase is staggering. Every 30 seconds, about 117 live babies are born and some 46 people die, for a net increase of 71 new inhabitants. This means over 200,000 new mouths to feed each day, or nearly 75 million a year (Haupt and Kane, 1980). When population growth rates are mapped, we see a division between the more developed countries (MDCs), with generally low rates, and the less

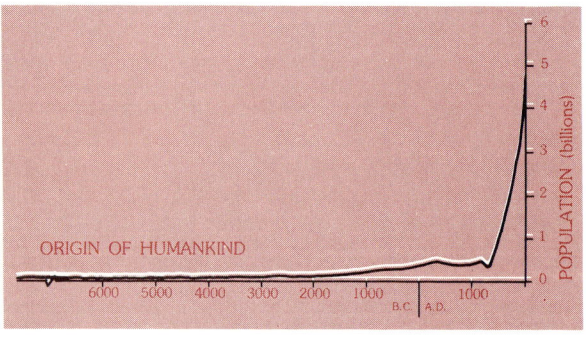

FIGURE 2–4 Growth of the world's population. (Adapted from Chester Zimolzak and Charles A. Stansfield, Jr., *The Human Landscape: Geography and Culture,* 2nd ed. [Charles E. Merrill, 1983], p. 35.)

developed countries (LDCs), with high rates (Figure 2–5). The brunt of the burden of population increase, then, is borne by those nations least prepared for it (Figure 2–6). Similar patterns of regional difference emerge when one considers patterns of fertility rates and death rates (Figures 2–7 and 2–8). The highest fertility rates are found in LDCs, particularly in Africa, where some nations have rates exceeding 6.0, several times the rates of some European nations (Figure 2–7). Death rates (Figure 2–8) also tend

BIOLOGY, GEOGRAPHY, AND RACE

- All people living today belong to a single species, *Homo sapiens,* and are derived from a common stock. There are differences of opinion regarding how and when different human groups diverged from this common stock.
- Biological differences among human beings are due to *differences in hereditary constitution* and to the *influence of the environment* on this genetic potential. In most cases, those differences are due to the interaction of these two sets of factors.
- There is great genetic diversity within all human populations. Pure races—in the sense of genetically homogeneous populations—do not exist in the human species.
- Nearly all classifications recognize at least three major stocks. Since the pattern of geographic variation of the characteristics used in racial classification is a complex one, and since this pattern does not present any major discontinuity, these classifications . . . cannot claim to classify humankind into clear-cut categories; moreover, on account of the complexities of human history, it is difficult to determine the place of certain groups within these racial classifications, in particular that of certain intermediate populations.
- It is not possible from the biological point of view to speak in any way whatsoever of a general inferiority or superiority of this or that race.
- The human species, which is now spread over the whole world, has a past rich in migrations, in territorial expansions and contractions . . . . For long millenia, human progress in any field seems to have been increasingly, if not exclusively, based on culture and the transmission of cultural achievements and not on the transmission of genetic endowment.
- As entities defined by distinctive traits, human races are at any time in a process of emergence and dissolution.
- It has never been proved that interbreeding has biological disadvantages for humankind as a whole. Therefore, no biological justification exists for prohibiting intermarriage between persons of different races, or for advising against it on racial grounds.
- As a rule, the major stocks extend over vast territories encompassing many diverse populations that differ in language, economy, culture, etc. There is no national, religious, geographic, linguistic, or cultural group which constitutes a race *ipso facto* (by virtue of the fact itself); the concept of race is purely biological.
- Most racial classifications of humankind do not include mental traits or attributes as a taxonomic criterion [a criterion for classification]. The peoples of the world today appear to possess equal biological potential for attaining any civilizational level. Differences in the achievement of different peoples must be attributed solely to their cultural history. Neither in the field of hereditary potential concerning overall intelligence and the capacity for cultural development, nor in that of physical traits, is there any justification for the concept of "inferior" or "superior" races.

Source: After UNESCO. *Proposals on the Biological Aspects of Race.* August, 1964. Reprinted in *Biological Anthropology: Readings from Scientific American,* San Francisco: W. H. Freeman & Co., pp. 220–22.

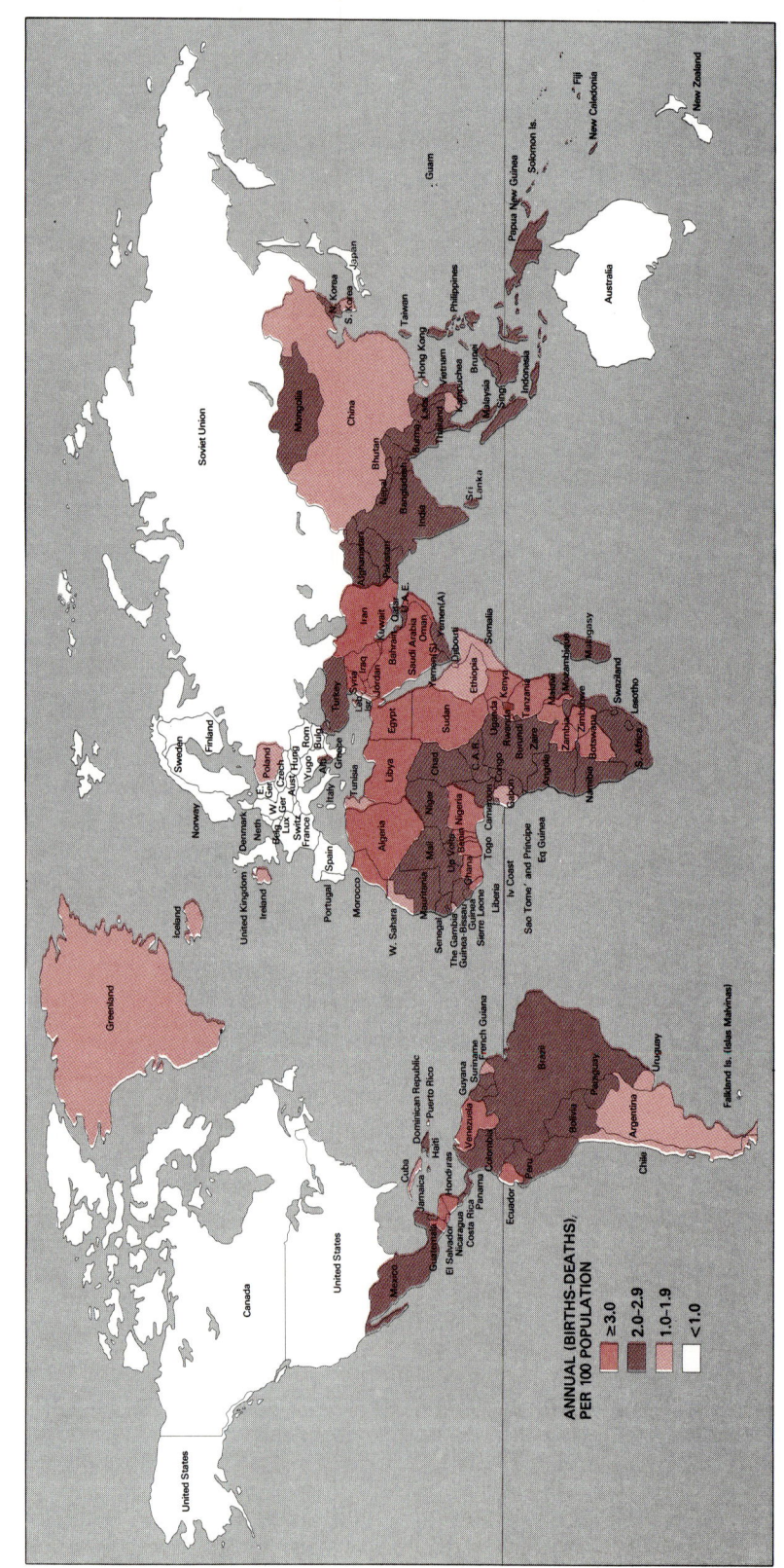

FIGURE 2-5 World natural population increase. (From Population Reference Bureau.)

FIGURE 2–6 The Deccan, an interior plateau of India, where dry conditions combine with wind erosion and occasional water erosion to create a difficult agricultural environment. (Photo courtesy of Gordon Oosterman, the National Council for Geographic Education, and the Great Plains National Instructional Television Library.)

to be highest in the LDCs of Africa and southern Asia, where rates exceeding 20 per 1,000 are not uncommon, compared to 9 in the United States (Table 2–1).

The Demographic Transition

Typically, nations go through a four-stage change process over time known as the *demographic transition* (Figure 2–9). In *Stage 1* (no growth), both birth rates (BR) and death rates (DR) are high, resulting in little or no population increase. Death rates may fluctuate considerably in Stage 1 in response to periods of famine or disease epidemics. Presently, there are no clear examples of nations at Stage 1, as death rates, even in LDCs, are relatively low compared to birth rates. In 1985, for example, the death rate for all LDCs was 11, but their birth rate was 31, leading to a population doubling time of 34 years, compared to 100 years for the U.S. (see Appendix B). Stage 1, then, is an historical relic—a remnant of the period when public health and nutritional standards were low and death rates were correspondingly high, more closely matching birth rates.

At *Stage 2* (rapid growth), the birth rate remains high, but the death rate decreases because of public health advances. This situation is typical of many LDCs today where growth rates are high. As shown in Figure 2–5, more than a dozen countries have annual rates of natural population increase of 3 percent or more, meaning that the population doubles in 23 years or less. Among the nations representative of Stage 2 are Ghana (BR 47, DR 15), Bolivia (BR 42, DR 16), and Saudi Arabia (BR 42, DR 12).

In *Stage 3* (slow growth), the death rate is relatively low, but the birth rate is declining, giving slower growth. China (BR 19, DR 8) and Indonesia (BR 34, DR 12), with population doubling times of 65 and 32 years, respectively, and birth rate declines exceeding 20 percent between 1950 and 1975, may be classified as Stage 3 nations (see Mauldin, 1980). The United States (BR 16, DR 9) also is in this category.

Finally, in *Stage 4* (stagnation), birth and death rates are both low, giving a very low rate of increase. The most extreme examples are found in Europe, where Sweden and the United Kingdom have doubling times exceeding 1,000 years. In both nations, birth and death rates are low—11 and 11 in Sweden and 13 and 12 in the United Kingdom. In all, at least 24 nations anticipate either zero population growth (ZPG) or an actual decline in numbers.

Excessive rates of population growth in LDCs lead to chronic problems—malnutrition, unemployment, disease—but zero population growth has economic and social consequences, too. The cost of supporting expanding populations of elderly and shortages of workers are causes of concern. Responses include encouragement of childbirth by introducing or increasing government grants based on family size (France), attempts to suppress abortion (Hungary), and encouragement of immigration (Sweden).

The process of demographic transition is by no means inevitable for any particular nation. It is merely a convenient way of describing, in a generalized way, a series of stages that today's MDCs have been ob-

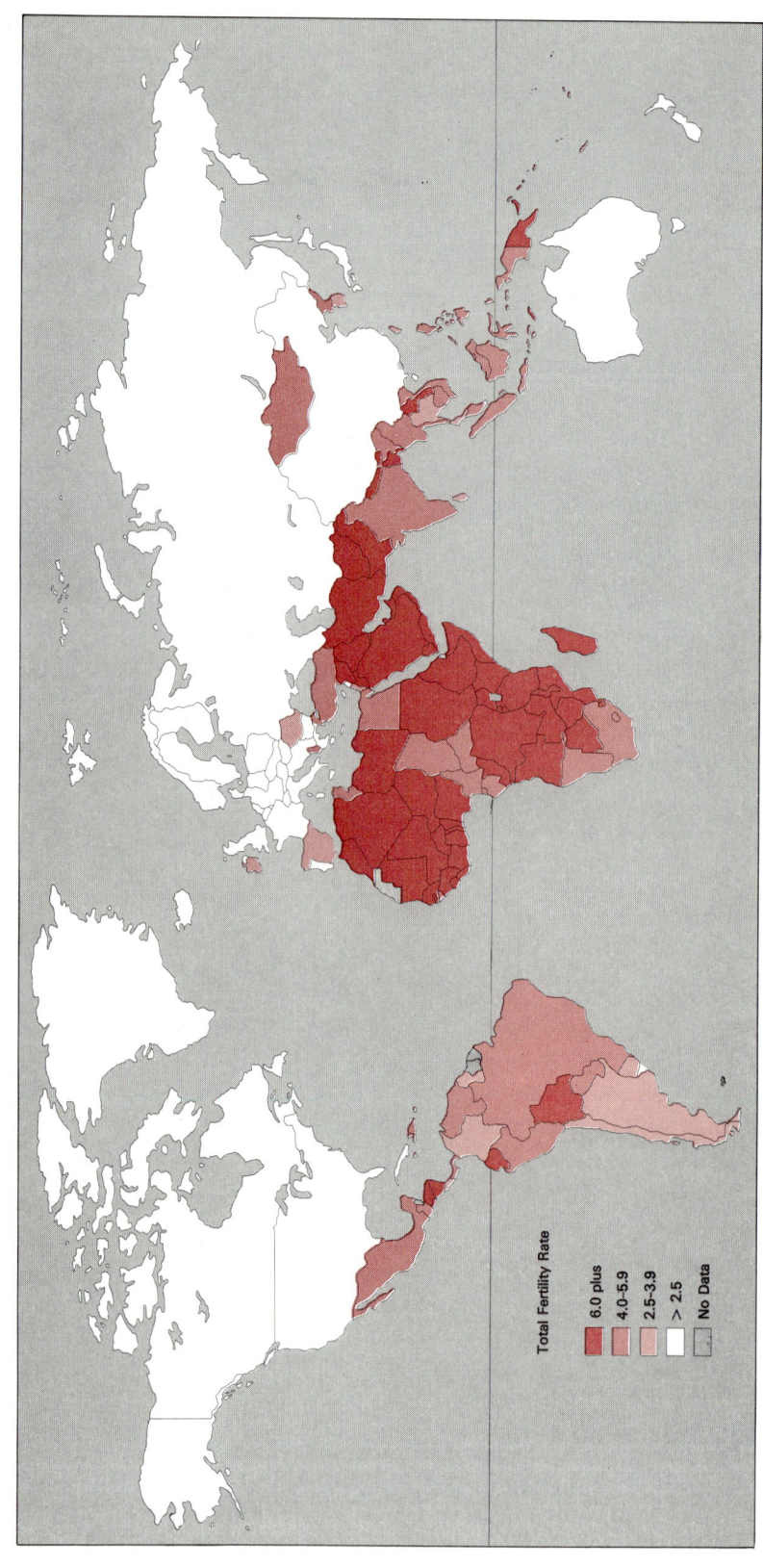

FIGURE 2–7 World fertility rates. (From Population Reference Bureau, 1981. Reproduced by permission.)

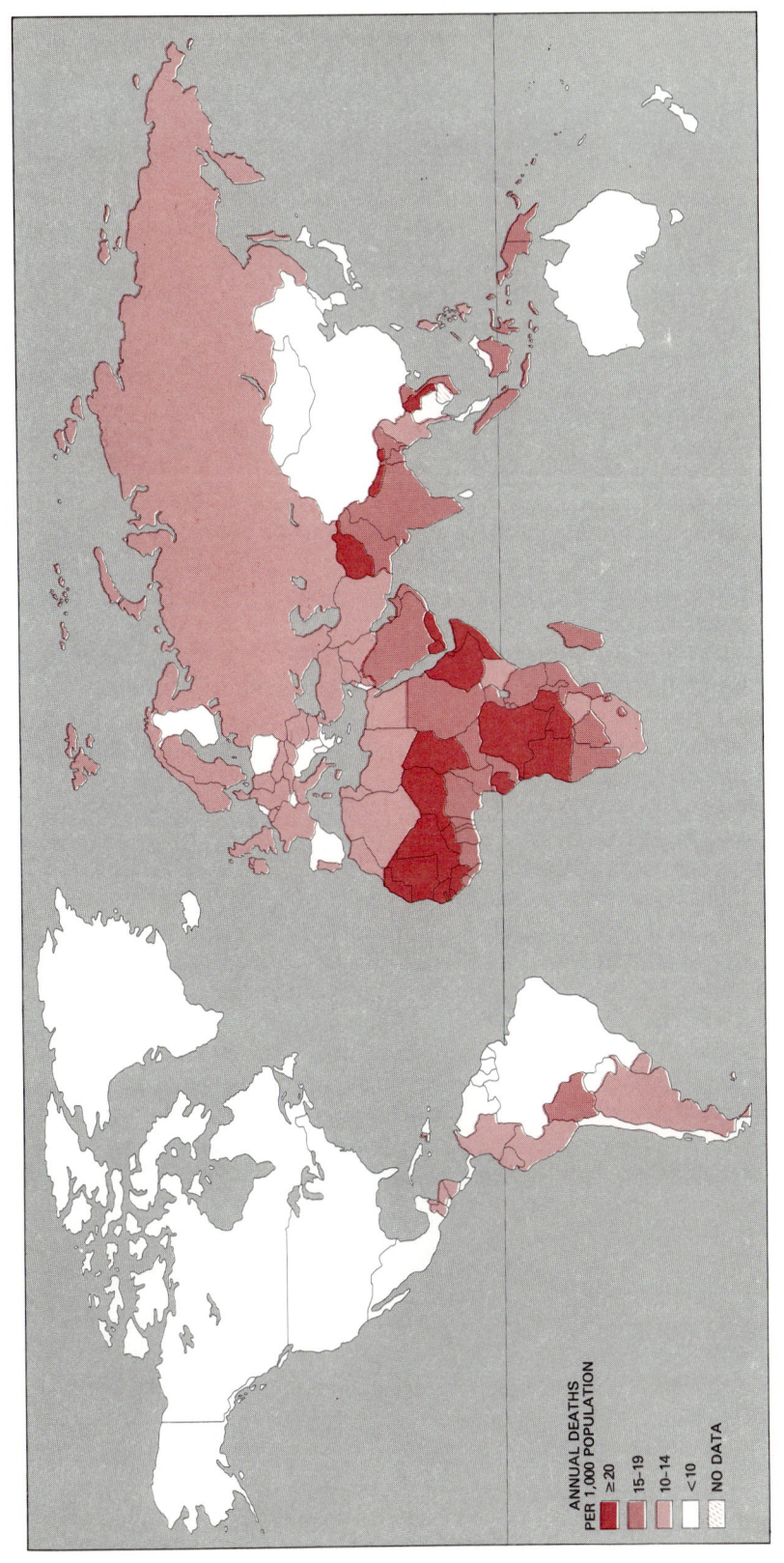

FIGURE 2–8 World death rates. (From Population Reference Bureau, 1981. Reproduced by permission.)

CHAPTER 2 WORLD POPULATION

TABLE 2–1 Comparative demographic data, 1985

Area**	Population (Millions)	Birth Rate*	Death Rate*	Natural Annual Increase (%)	Years to Double Population	Infant Mortality Rate	Life Expectancy at Birth
World	4,845	27	11	1.7	41	81	62
MDCs	1,174	15	9	0.6	118	18	73
LDCs	3,671	31	11	2.0	34	90	58
Africa	551	45	16	2.9	24	110	50
Asia (not Soviet Union)	2,829	28	10	1.8	39	87	60
Soviet Union	278	20	10	1.0	71	32	69
Latin America	406	31	8	2.3	30	62	65
Europe	492	13	10	0.3	240	15	73
Oceania	24	21	8	1.2	56	39	71
United States	239	16	9	0.7	100	11	75

*For definitions of rates, see box on page 36.
**For more detail on specific nations, see Appendix B. For detail on the United States, see Appendix C.
Source: Abstracted from Appendix B.

served to follow. It is possible, however, that explosive rates of population growth will be maintained in many LDCs, and that population may, in reality, be limited by starvation and disease. Thus far in the 1980s, for example, hundreds of thousands of Ethiopians died as a result of famine caused by drought. Such events raise the specter of the dire predictions of the famous British economist Thomas Robert Malthus (1766–1834). Malthus pointed out, in *An Essay of the Principle of Population as it Affects the Future Improvement of Society*, that population tends to increase *geometrically* (1, 2, 4, 8, 16, 32, . . .), whereas food supply increases *arithmetically* (1, 2, 3, 4, 5, 6, . . .). Therefore, noted Malthus, population will tend to outstrip food supply, causing famine, war, and disease.

Yet Malthus opposed birth control because he feared the practice would result in severe limitations on family size, which in turn would lead to society's economic stagnation. Population should be limited, he thought, through the practice of "moral restraint." This suggestion was ineffectual, and the birth rate in Britain remained high until publication of birth control information was legalized in 1877. Since that time, adoption of birth control techniques has become widespread, particularly in MDCs.

Population Pyramids

The demographic transition is a useful concept to help us understand how the rate of natural increase of a population relates to trends in birth rates and death rates. Another graphic device that enables comparisons of population characteristics between nations is the *population pyramid*. Population pyramids, which may or may not be pyramid-shaped (Figure 2–10), indicate the proportions of the population in specific age categories, by sex. The pyramid can also tell us something about rate of population in-

FIGURE 2–9 Four-stage demographic transition model.

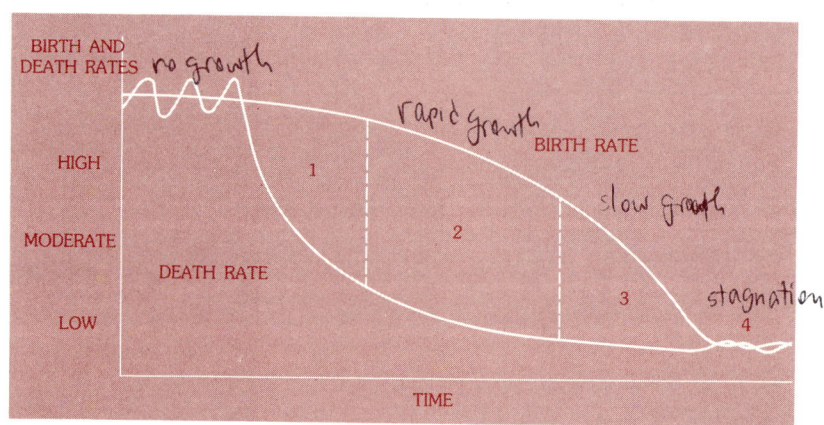

POPULATION GEOGRAPHY

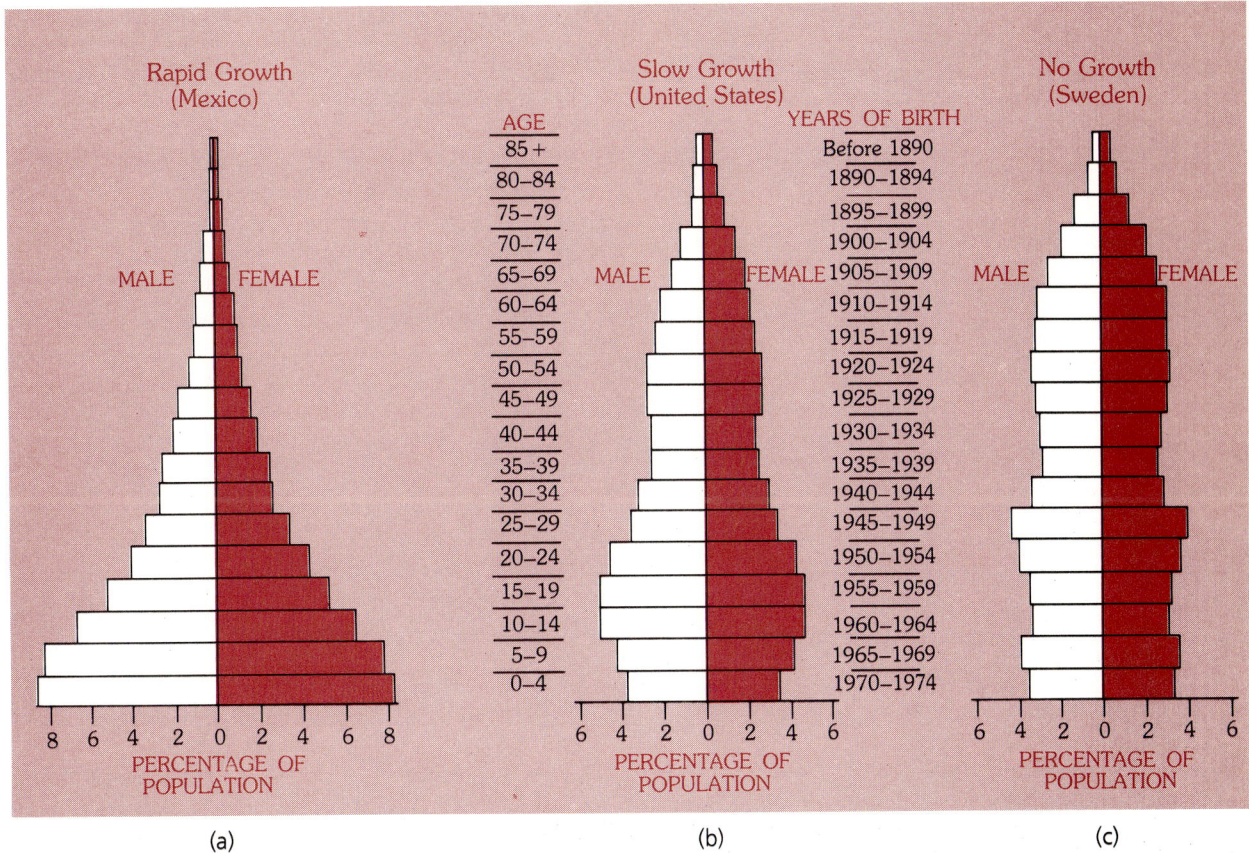

FIGURE 2–10 Population pyramids showing age/sex structure of rapid-growth, slow-growth, and no-growth nations. (From *Social Education* and Population Reference Bureau. Reproduced by permission.)

crease, just on the basis of its shape. Three pyramids, or profiles representative of three types of age/sex composition, are shown in Figure 2–10. The *rapid growth* model (Figure 2–10a), using Mexico as an example, shows the high proportion of young people. One can see that virtually every younger age group (*cohort*) is bigger than the next older group. This indicates that Mexico's population is increasing rapidly, with a doubling time of 22 years.

Figure 2–10b represents the profile of the U.S. population, illustrating *slow growth*. The shape of the profile provides information on the impact of historical events on the population's age/sex composition. The depression of the 1930s, during which the birth rate dipped dramatically and there was net emigration, shows in profile as the "pinched" middle. The baby boom following World War II is illustrated by the bulge near the base, and the more recent decline in the birth rate is expressed by the narrow base.

The third profile (Figure 2–10c) illustrates a country of *no growth*—Sweden. This profile is rather straight-sided, indicating approximately similar proportions of population in each age cohort. Birth and death rates have been low over a long period, and the population is aging. The median age (than which half the population is older and half younger) in Sweden is about 35, compared to 17 in Mexico and 29 in the United States. The *dependency ratio* in Sweden is increasing, and about 4 million workers currently support about 1.6 million retired persons.

The importance of understanding the age/sex composition of populations cannot be overemphasized, as this information, along with other data, holds the key to understanding future fertility trends and the demands likely to be placed on the world's nations, regions, and cities. The demand for schools is strongest among 5- to 25-year-olds. The need for health services is greatest among the youngest and oldest. The need for employment is strongest among those between about 20 and 60 years of age. Information like this can help us anticipate future demands for resources. (See Appendix B for more information on world population.)

35

CHAPTER 2 WORLD POPULATION

POPULATION TERMINOLOGY

- *Age/Sex structure* Proportion of males and females in specific age categories. Knowledge of age-sex structure helps in understanding population trends.
- *Birth rate* Number of births per 1,000 population in a given year.
- *Cohort* A group of people sharing a common demographic experience. For example, the birth cohort of 1968 would be the people born in that year; other examples are marriage cohorts and school class cohorts.
- *Death rate* Number of deaths per 1,000 population in a given year.
- *Demographic transition* Process of historical change from high birth and death rates to low birth and death rates. (See Figure 2–9.)
- *Dependency ratio* Ratio of the dependent part of the population to the productive part. The dependent part is usually considered to be those persons under 15 and over 65.
- *Fertility* Reproductive performance, whether for a person, a couple, a group, or a population. The Total Fertility Rate is the average number of children born to a woman. For the U.S., this rate was 1.8 in 1980.
- *Mortality* Deaths as a component of population change.
- *Natural increase/decrease* Surplus/deficit of births over deaths in a population in a given period.
- *Population density* Population per unit of area. The distinction is often made between *arithmetic* density (population per area) and *physiological* density (population per productive area).
- *Population pyramid* Chart showing the age/sex structure of the population. The chart may not be pyramid-shaped. (See Figure 2–10.)
- *Zero population growth* Static or equilibrium population, occurring when births plus immigration (persons coming into the country) equals deaths plus emigration (persons leaving the country).

Source: Based on definitions in Arthur Haupt and Thomas T. Kane, *Population* Handbook (Washington, DC: Population Reference Book, 1980).

U.S. POPULATION GEOGRAPHY

The geography of people in a particular nation can give us valuable clues about patterns of regional development and demands for various resources. We may also be able to anticipate tensions and conflicts between different population groups as immigrant clusters expand and shift. Information about the changing size of particular age and sex cohorts is critical if we are to understand present and future trends in productivity and social organization.

What can we learn from a study of the population geography of the United States? When we look at U.S. population density (Figure 2–11), we see high density zones in the northeast and on the Pacific Coast. Densities are low in the mountain, desert, and Great Plains regions. This distribution is explained by a combination of conditions and processes. First, the *natural environment* discourages settlement in some regions, where terrain is rough, or climate is extreme. This explains the relative emptiness of the Rocky Mountains (terrain, climate), and of the southwestern desert and the Great Plains (climate). Even within these sparsely inhabited areas, we find clusters of settlement where terrain is more hospitable or irrigation may be available, as in the Ogden-Salt Lake City-Provo area of Utah and the Imperial Valley in California.

Comparable environmental controls are at work in Canada, where the majority of the population clusters in the southern part of that vast territory. The extremely severe winters in northern Canada and the Canadian Rockies make those regions less attractive. The west coast of Canada also exhibits a significant population cluster centered on Vancouver. Winters there are extremely mild because of the warming influence of the ocean, and the area is sometimes jokingly called the "Canadian Riviera," comparing it to the mild south coast of France.

A second major influence on population distribution in the U.S. and Canada has been the location of *ports-of-entry* of foreign immigrants. New arrivals

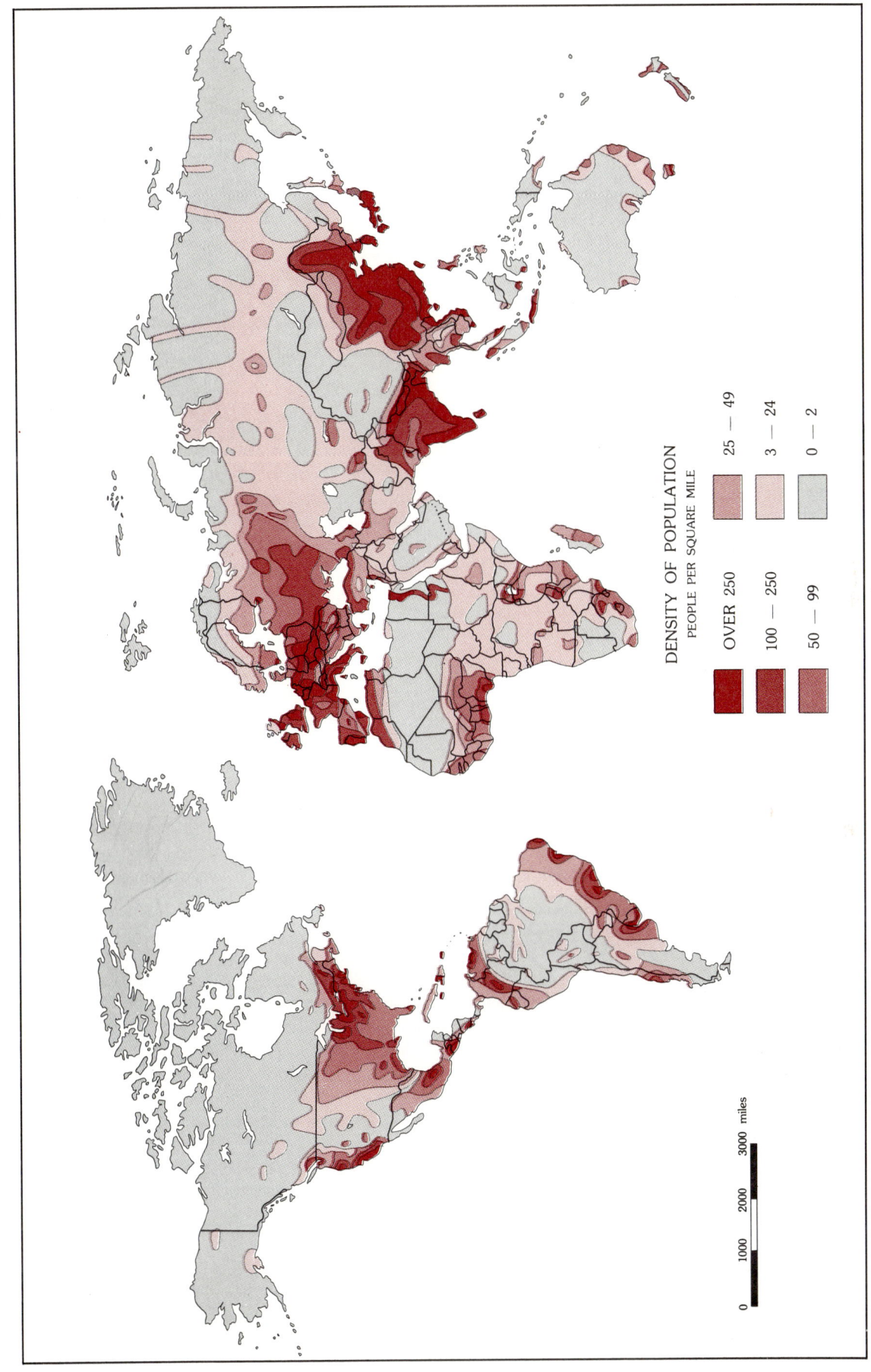

FIGURE 2–11 World population density. (From Chester Zimolzak and Charles S. Stansfield, Jr., *The Human Landscape: Geography and Culture*, 2nd ed. [Charles E. Merrill, 1983], p. 30.)

tended to make their homes in the cities or regions where they first arrived. Increased mobility in recent decades has made this factor less important. In general, poor immigrants, such as recent arrivals from Cuba, Haiti, and southeast Asia, lack the resources to move beyond their arrival point. Middle-class immigrants are able to be more selective in their choice of destinations. Historically, however, the mold has been set by the masses of immigrants who formed the nuclei of today's great population concentrations. These regions attract more new arrivals because they tend to offer more employment opportunities, and they contain ethnic clusters capable of offering comfort and security to new arrivals.

A third major influence on U.S. population distribution has been the migration from farms to cities. In 1930, the farm population was over 30 million, or about a quarter of the U.S. population. By 1980, the total farm population had shrunk to under 8 million, or about 3 percent. The urban or city population has grown as farm population has diminished. (We will see more details of trends in urbanization in Chapter 13.)

Population geography is dynamic. The population map, like a cloudy sky, is never the same from one moment to the next. People are born, die, move, leave the country, or enter it. Two additional major controls over the population geography of an area, then, are, *population increase or decrease* and *internal migration*.

What did the 1980 Census tell us about the characteristics and trends of U.S. population?

Census Findings In the early 1980s, it was estimated that the U.S. population exceeded 232 million, making it the fourth-ranking nation in terms of population size, exceeded only by China, India, and the Soviet Union (see Appendix B, World Population Data Sheet). The 1980 Census of Population revealed what Calvin Beale, a researcher at the U.S. Department of Agriculture, has called "the six demographic surprises of the 1970s" (Population Reference Bureau, 1982):

- *Fewer Births* Early in the 1970s, it was predicted that births in the decade would exceed 40 million. In fact, there were only 33 million, about a quarter less than the most popular forecast. The low total was attributed to delayed marriage and childbearing, as well as increased abortion.
- *Fewer Deaths* Some 21 million deaths had been expected in the 1970s but the actual total was nearer 19 million. Life expectancy increased much more than had been expected (3.4 years compared to a projected 6 months).
- *Smaller Households* Between 1970 and 1980, average household size declined from 3.14 to 2.76 persons, smaller than the lowest Census Bureau projection. Small nonfamily and one-parent households increased faster than had been predicted.
- *Greater Shift to South and West* The west region, including the mountain states, grew twice as fast as expected (8.3 million compared to a projected 4 million). Growth in the South was 62 percent more than predicted—12.5 million compared to a predicted 7.8 million (see Figure 2–12).
- *Nonmetropolitan Growth* The rate of nonmetropolitan growth was nearly 16 percent, three times what had been expected.
- *Illegal and Refugee Immigration* Both types of immigration contributed a larger-than-expected share to U.S. population growth. Illegal and refugee immigration have become perplexing problems. As a nation of immigrants, it is morally inconsistent for the U.S. to close the door to new arrivals. The impact of illegal immigrants on specific areas such as Southern California, West Texas, and South Florida has been dramatic. Local school systems and other social services have been severely stressed. The complexity of the problem was symbolized by a cartoon depicting a tired, confused Liberty (Figure 2–13).

Geographic Implications of Current Trends Mobility will be reduced in the 1980s from the "normal" level of 20 percent of households moving each year to about 16 percent. Fewer people will be available in the prime moving ages, 22–25. Expensive housing and the possible continuation of high interest rates also will tend to suppress migration. Population gains in the South and West will continue, particularly in the Mountain states, owing to their massive energy reserves. The strength of this migration stream will depend to some extent on changes in energy technology, which relates in turn to the world price of oil. Programs for the extraction of oil from oil shale suffered a setback when world oil prices declined in the early 1980s, for example. Thus we see a relationship among resources, technology, and population dynamics. Ultimately, water will be the critical resource limiting population growth in the West. Although energy-related migration will be significant, most overall growth will be seen in suburbs and resort/retirement places. The birth rate

U.S. POPULATION GEOGRAPHY

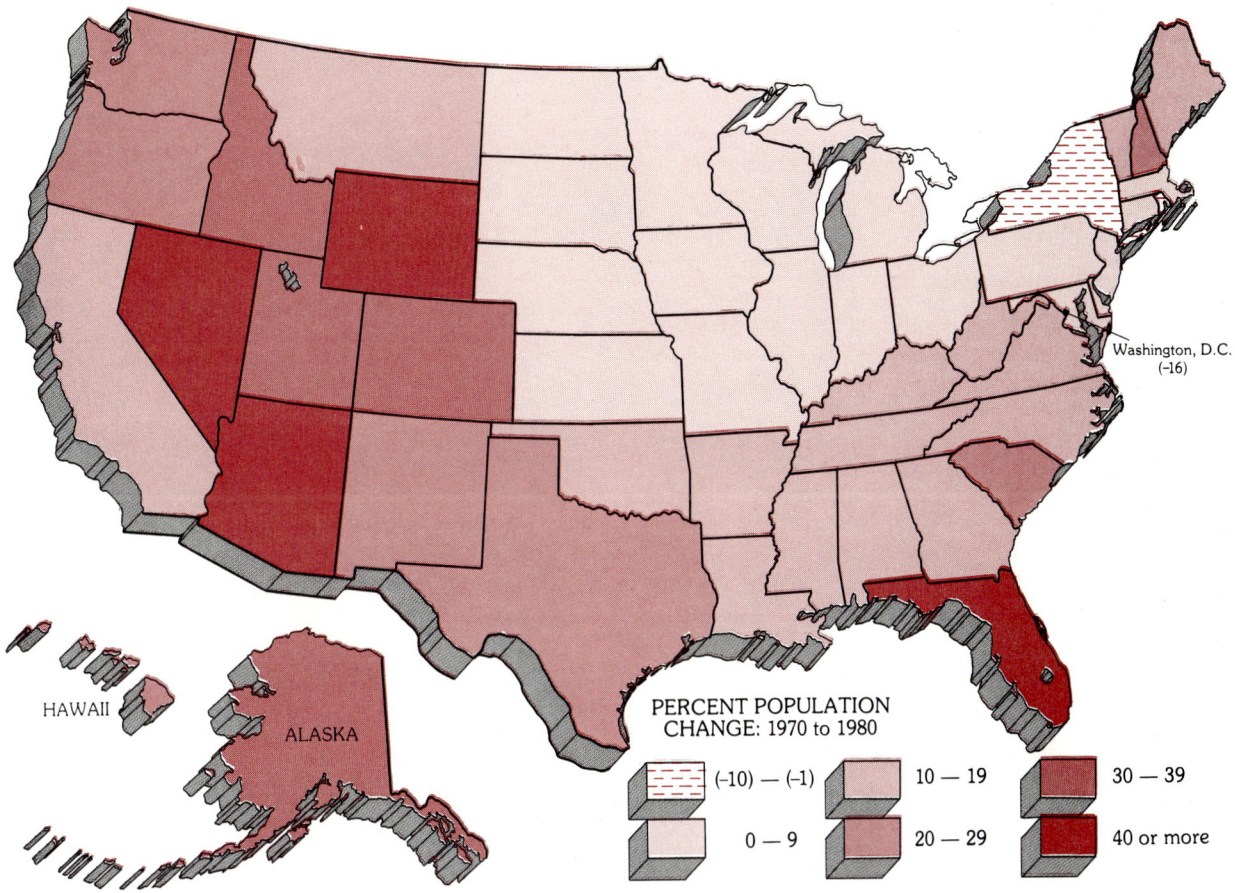

FIGURE 2–12 Percent of population changes of states from 1970 to 1980. U.S. population grew 11.4 percent in the decade.

FIGURE 2–13 An exhausted Liberty figure, her torch burned out, grapples with the intricacies of immigration reform proposals. (Reprinted with permission of the *Albuquerque Journal*.)

CHAPTER 2 WORLD POPULATION

probably will be highest in the West because of a combination of economic growth and the location in the West of the largest proportion of potential childbearers. Migration to nonmetropolitan areas will continue, perhaps at a lower rate if unemployment remains at the relatively high levels of the early-to-mid-1980s.

The number of households will increase in the 1980s much faster than the rate of population increase. This increases the demand for housing units. With smaller families and high housing costs, it is reasonable to expect a continuation in the trend toward small housing units in multi-unit structures. The detached ranch-style home will be a less prominent feature of suburban growth. These trends have implications for the rate of loss of agricultural land (higher densities mean less per capita land consumption).

Continued decline in death rates will make the elderly an increasingly important group. Some states have attracted large numbers of retirees. In Florida in 1980, 17.3 percent of the people were 65 and older. (See Appendix C, U.S. Population Data Sheet.) Nevada, Arizona, Florida, Hawaii, Arkansas, and New Mexico are experiencing rapid increases in the number of elderly attracted by climatic and recreational amenities.

The three major types of immigration—*legal, illegal,* and *refugees*—will continue to make a major contribution to U.S. population growth. The best estimate is that the net inflow (taking into account those who leave the U.S.) will be on the order of three-quarters of a million to a million a year. Port and border areas will be most strongly influenced by the substantial flow of immigrants. (See Figure 8–14 and the related discussion in Chapter 8.) Many immigrants to these border areas are Hispanics, who are often Catholics, and more likely to adhere to their church's proscription against birth control or abortion. These religious adherences have implications for population growth rates in regions receiving Hispanic immigrants. Another factor in the immigration picture is that Mexico's young adult population—the prime migration-prone age group—will double by the year 2000, increasing the probability of immigration from Mexico. An "unknown" in this situation is the condition of the Mexican economy. If it remains depressed, as it was in the early 1980s, Mexicans will have more incentive to leave (Population Reference Bureau, 1982).

You can by now appreciate the complexity of population dynamics. Multiple factors, including regional attractions, or lack of them, determine the size, age, and sex structure of the population. Perhaps the single most important fact about population is its *dynamic* nature. The only certainty is change.

WORLD POPULATION DENSITY, DISTRIBUTION, AND WEALTH

The most striking characteristic of the map of world population density in Figure 2–11 is the unevenness between and within nations. Indeed, the distribution of population is so uneven that about three billion people live on only 10 percent of the earth's land surface (Figure 2–14). The regions of greatest concentration—East Asia, South Asia, Europe, and northeastern North America—show up clearly on the map. Do these high-density areas have any particular characteristics in common? Reference to the map of world climates in Appendix A, Figure A–1, shows that the major population clusters are located in moderate climate regions, those classified as "C" (humid warm) and "A" (humid tropics). The desert zones ("B"), cold humid regions ("D"), and the polar zones ("E") are, with some important exceptions, relatively empty areas.

There is no question that *Homo sapiens* has, quite naturally, tended to dwell and thrive in the more hospitable regions of the earth—those that are not excessively hot or cold or excessively wet or dry. We must remember, however, that the population map of today is a product of thousands of years of evolution, adaption, migration, famine, and disease. Differences in population density patterns within and between similar natural environments may reflect the influence and predominance of social factors over environmental conditions. Generally, however, cultural and environmental factors are interrelated.

As we have said, high population densities in northeastern North America reflect the historical accident that the northeastern seaboard was the closest point of contact with Europe. It was also a region with a rather hospitable climate, similar to that which many immigrants had known in their European homelands. It is understandable, then, that this region became a major population nucleus. Had the initial surges of population to North America come from East Asia instead of Europe, then Seattle or Portland or San Francisco or Los Angeles might have become the premier city of the continent instead of New York.

The most extensive region of high density on earth is East Asia. China has about one billion people, or somewhat less than a quarter of the world's population. China's highest densities are associated with cities and with the plains and valleys of great

40

FIGURE 2–14 Irrigation canal in China. (Photo by Jerome Wyckoff.)

Chinese rivers such as the Huang He and Chang Jiang* (formerly Huang Ho and Yangtze Kiang). These river basins are productive agricultural areas.

The European population cluster, with more than half a billion people, also has major concentrations along rivers and coastal zones. These concentrations are often around major cities such as Paris on the Seine and London on the Thames. In Europe, however, the attraction of river basins is not linked to agriculture, as it is in East or South Asia, but to industry. The industrial revolution in Europe led to a substantial population redistribution during the last 300 years, from a dispersed rural population to a highly urbanized population that depends on nonagricultural employment. Great coalfields, such as the Ruhr in Germany, served as magnets at which industries developed and cities grew. The recent dependence on petroleum products has meant a new orientation toward port cities where petroleum products are refined or used as raw materials for other products.

Although there are other nodes of population outside the areas we have discussed (for example, the Nile Valley, Nigeria, Java, and California), the four major concentrations together account for such a significant proportion of the world's population (around 70 percent) that other regions seem sparsely peopled or empty by comparison.

World population and wealth distributions are sometimes viewed as a contrast between the Northern and Southern Hemispheres (Figure 2–15); however, this is an oversimplification. China, with its 1982 census showing a population exceeding one billion, is in the Northern Hemisphere, so the North-South split is more credible if we define the boundary as approximately 30–35° North latitude.

POPULATION AND FOOD

The pressure of population on available resources in many regions, not just in the more densely inhabited zones, is such a cause for continuing concern that it is appropriate to conclude this chapter with a discussion of the issue of food supply for the earth's billions. The world food supply, like population, is unevenly distributed. Food availability, taken for granted in MDCs, is a source of continuing crisis in LDCs. Food shortages do not have to reach famine levels for serious problems to arise. In many regions, hunger—defined as a constant insufficiency of essential nutrients—causes serious ongoing difficulties in the form of infant mortality, impaired development, and disease.

Knight and Wilcox (1976) have concisely summarized the nutritional problem in a chart where the axes of each graph represent percent *starch*, percent *animal* sources (milk, meat, eggs, animal fats), and percent *other* sources, all measured in calories (Figure 2–16). Data for African and Asian nations (Figure 2–16a and b) are seen to cluster toward the top end of the graphs, meaning that people in these nations consume high percentages of starch and low percentages of animal sources. In Latin America (Figure 2–16c), some nations are more dependent on animal products. The difference between the majority of developed nations (Figure 2–16d) and other countries is striking. The largest cluster is seen to be relatively less dependent on starches. For the United States,

*New Pinyin alphabet spellings

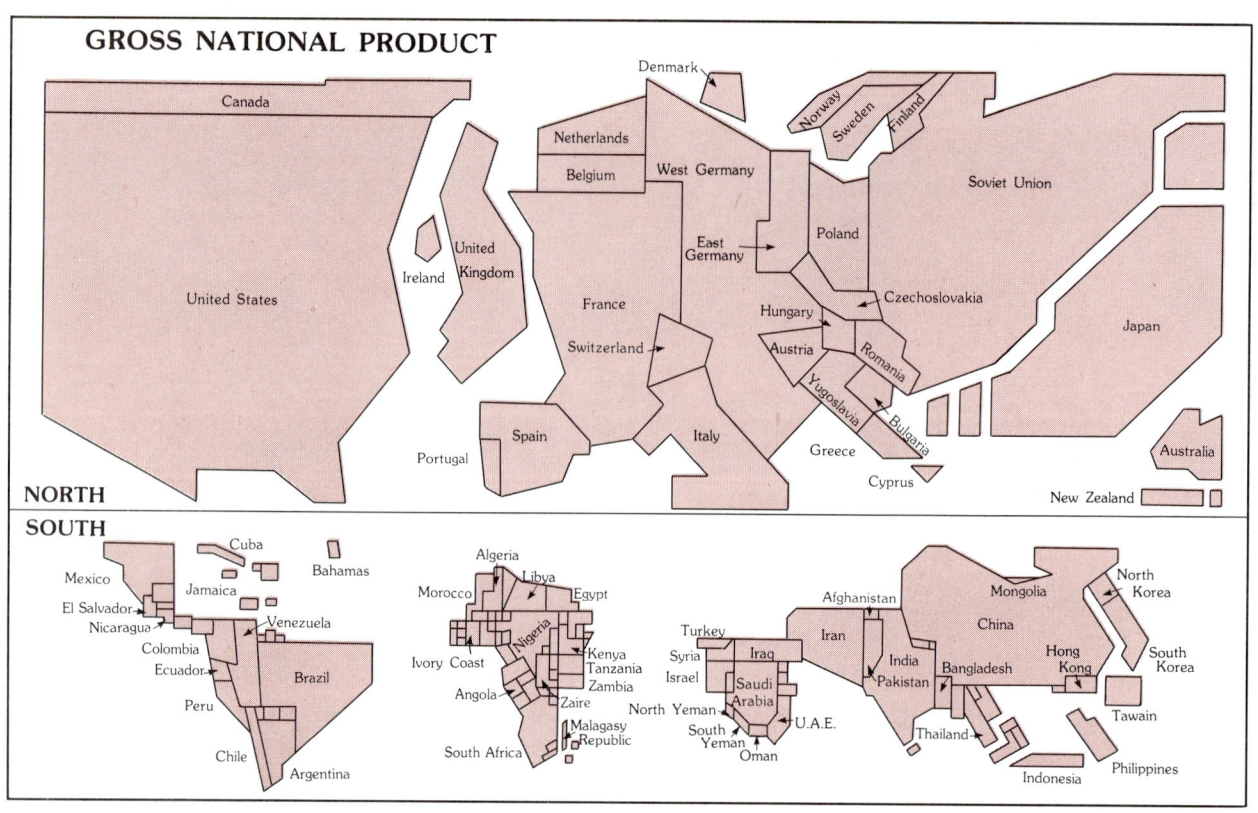
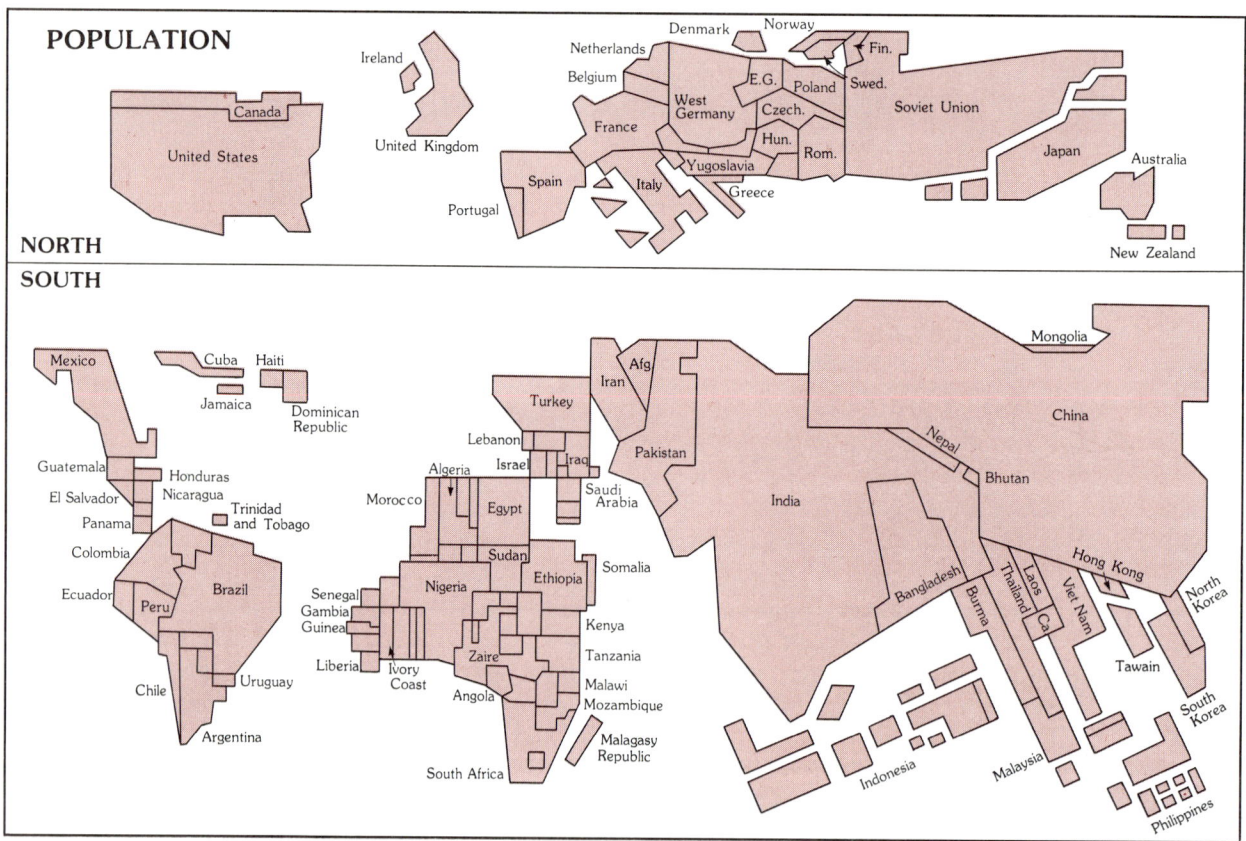

FIGURE 2–15 The world turned upside down. This *cartogram*, in which the areas of nations are proportional to either Gross National Product (upper set) or population (lower set), illustrates the popular concept that the division between wealthy nations with slow population growth and poor nations with rapid growth is a division between the northern and southern hemispheres. The latitudes of nations on the cartogram shows that this concept is an oversimplification. (Copyright 1981 by Newsweek, Inc. All rights reserved. Reprinted by permission.)

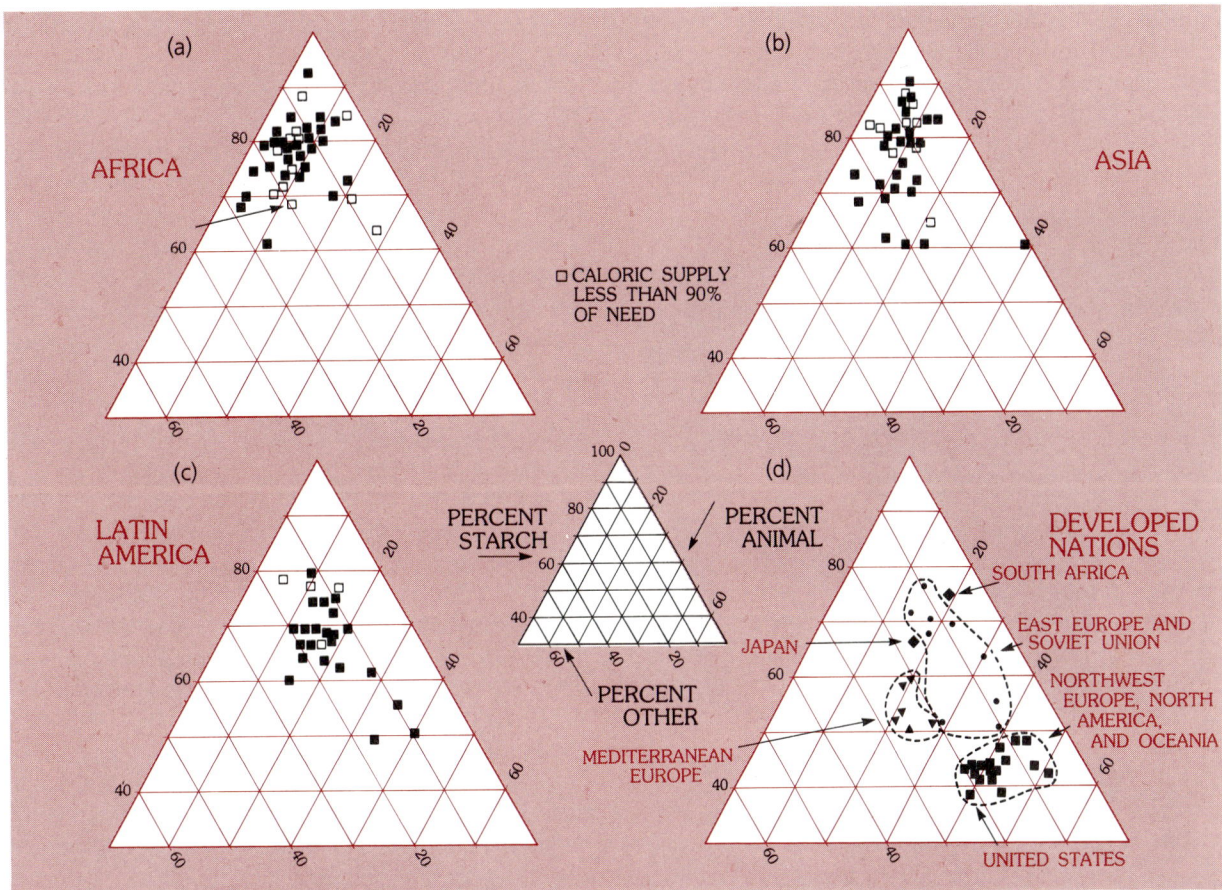

FIGURE 2–16 Dietary composition of national caloric intake. (From C. Knight and R. Wilcox, *Triumph or Triage? The World Food Problem in Geographical Perspective* [Washington, D.C.: Association of American Geographers, Resource Papers for College Geography No. 75–3, 1976]. Reprinted by permission.)

the diet is about 38 percent starches, 40 percent animal sources, and 22 percent other sources.

The preference of MDCs for animal products is extraordinarily inefficient. For example, when corn is grown and fed to a hog, most of the energy of the corn (some 90%) is lost in fueling the hog's metabolism, and relatively little is used for growth. Thus, it is generally more efficient (in the sense of increasing total food supply) for humans to eat plant materials directly rather than converting them into animal products. An exception occurs when the only available crop is grass; human stomachs, which are in most respects quite versatile, are not adept at digesting grass, so grazing livestock in such situations makes sense (Knight and Wilcox, 1976).

Rice is one of the world's most important food crops, and the staple food of the southern Chinese. In Hong Kong, the amount of land devoted to rice production (Figure 2–17) declined drastically from 23,353 acres (94.5 km^2) in 1954 to 2,780 acres (11.3 km^2) in 1976. The trend toward production of more valuable crops such as vegetables and flowers has made it necessary for Hong Kong to import most of the rice it needs. With competent management, however, the oceans show some potential for increased food production. In Japan, for example, laver seaweed that grows on ropes is dried and pressed into sheets called "black paper" that are then used as food (Figure 2–18). The use of seaweed as food is not uncommon; the Welsh make seaweed into a substance called "laver bread."

Unfortunately, the pressure to produce food, brought on by growing population or crises such as drought or insect infestations, can result in long-term damage to the environment, which further reduces a population's ability to meet its own needs. For example, in the Sahel region of Africa, a combination of drought, overgrazing, and excessive cultivation of grain crops has resulted in destruction of the soil resource, and in the southward advance of the Sahara,

CHAPTER 2 WORLD POPULATION

a process called *desertification*. Starvation in Ethiopia in the mid-1980s is related to desertification. It has been estimated that about 630 million people worldwide live in drylands, and some 50 to 78 million are in areas subject to desertification (Hare, Kates, and Warren, 1977).

In Bangladesh, population pressure has caused changes in how people utilize their water resources. They have moved into flood-prone areas and have cut forests and failed to maintain river embankments, actions that encourage erosion and increase flooding problems. Furthermore, there has been a breakdown in the traditional system of digging ponds, which capture runoff, and using the fill to create high ground for flood-protected homesites. The breakdown of this system has reduced the availability of water for food production in the dry season, and brought greater vulnerability to floods (Dutt and Ahmed, 1974).

Food is the product of a complex interweaving of food preferences, traditional practices, technological changes, environmental opportunities, and needs. In some regions, increasing population has created such rapidly escalating needs that the only immediate answer is emergency assistance from nations with food surpluses, or the resources to buy such surpluses. The Ethiopian crisis, however, showed that warning signs of impending disaster are not necessarily heeded by countries in a position to assist, and victim countries themselves may hinder relief efforts for political reasons. The seriousness of the situation is illustrated by Table 2–2.

FIGURE 2–17 A rice paddy in Hong Kong. (Photo courtesy of Barbara Weightman, the National Council for Geographic Education, and the Great Plains National Instructional Television Library.)

FIGURE 2–18 Cultivating seaweed in Ago Bay, Honshu, Japan. (Photo courtesy of Robert E. Cramer, the National Council for Geographic Education, and the Great Plains National Instructional Television Library.)

CONCLUSION

Geography is concerned with the human occupancy of the earth—hence, the theme of population geog-

TABLE 2-2 Annual rate of increase in food production compared to population growth.

Region	Food Production 1961–1970	Food Production 1971–1975	Population 1961–1970	Population 1971–1975	Increase in Food Production per Capita 1961–1970	Increase in Food Production per Capita 1971–1975
	(percent per year)					
Developed Regions						
North America	2.4	1.9	1.3	0.9	1.1	1.1
Western Europe	2.3	1.9	0.8	0.6	1.5	1.3
Oceania	3.4	1.3	1.9	1.7	1.5	0.7
Eastern Europe and USSR	3.2	2.1	1.0	0.9	2.2	1.1
Total	2.7	2.0	1.1	0.9	1.6	1.2
Developing Regions						
Africa	2.9	0.5	2.5	2.7	0.4	−2.1
Latin America	3.0	2.7	2.8	2.7	0.3	−0.1
Far East	2.7	2.8	2.5	2.5	0.2	0.3
Near East	3.3	3.7	2.7	2.8	0.7	0.9
Asian centrally planned economies	2.8	2.4	1.7	1.7	1.1	0.7
Total	2.9	2.5	2.3	2.3	0.6	0.2

Source: Food and Agricultural Organization, *Billions More to Feed* (Rome: FAO, 1976), p. 8.

raphy underlies much of this book. The human species evolved over a very long time, and until relatively recently, increased slowly in numbers. During the course of the evolutionary process, certain adaptive physical traits developed which we now categorize into *races*. In recent centuries, population numbers have increased dramatically as standards of health and nutrition have improved, thus reducing death rates. Meanwhile, birth rates have tended to remain high, yielding fast increases in population, particularly in LDCs, where the technology of birth control has been adopted slowly, if at all. Populations are increasing so rapidly in some areas that the demand for food causes food producers to adopt pastoral and cropping practices that damage soils and other aspects of the natural environment, ultimately reducing the capacity of that environment for food production. Social organization, which is often interrelated with agricultural practices, may break down, leading to additional stresses in the country involved.

KEY WORDS

Australopithecus
BP—Before the Present
caucasoid
Cro-Magnon
demographic transition
desertification
genetic drift
hominid
Homo erectus
Homo sapiens
migration
mongoloid
natural selection
Neanderthal
negroid
population pyramid
race
Sahel

REFERENCES

BAKER, ROBIN. *The Mystery of Migration*. New York: Viking Press, 1981.

BORGSTROM, GEORG. *The Food and People Dilemma*. Belmont, CA: Duxbury Press, 1973.

BRUES, ALICE M. *People and Races*. New York: Macmillan, 1977.

CAMPBELL, BERNARD G. *Humankind Emerging*, 3rd ed. Boston: Little, Brown, 1982.

CLARKE, JOHN I. *Population Georgraphy.* Oxford: Pergamon Press, 1965.

DUTT, ASHOK K., and AHMED, NAWAJESH. "Population Pressures in Bangladesh." *Focus* 25, Nos. 3 and 4 (November–December, 1974).

HARE, F. KENNETH, KATES, ROBERT W., and WARREN, ANDREW. "The Making of Deserts: Climate, Ecology, and Society." *Economic Geography* 53 (1977): 332–46.

HAUB, CARL. *The United States Population Data Sheet.* Washington, DC: Population Reference Bureau, 1982.

HAUB, CARL, and HEISLER, DOUGLAS W. *World Population Data Sheet.* Washington, DC: Population Reference Bureau, 1985.

HAUPT, ARTHUR, and KANE, THOMAS T. *Population Handbook.* Washington, DC: Population Reference Bureau, 1980.

HOWELLS, WILLIAM H. "The Distribution of Man." In *Biological Anthropology: Readings from Scientific American.* San Francisco: W.H. Freeman, 1975.

JONES, HUW R. *A Population Geography.* New York: Harper and Row, 1981.

KNIGHT, C. GREGORY, and WILCOX, R. PAUL. *Triumph or Triage? The World Food Problem in Geographical Perspective.* Association of American Geographers Resource Paper No. 75–3. Washington, DC: 1976.

LEAKEY, L.S.B., and GOODALL, VANNE MORRIS. *Unveiling Man's Origins.* London: Methuen, 1969.

McEVEDY, COLIN, and JONES, RICHARD. *Atlas of World Population History.* Harmondsworth, Middlesex, England: Penguin Books, 1978.

MAULDIN, W. PARKER. "Population Trends and Prospects", *Science* 209, no. 4452 (1980): 148–57.

"Modern Man: Mid-East Origins." *Science News* 115 (1979): 132.

POPULATION REFERENCE BUREAU. "U.S. Population: Where We Are; Where We're Going." *Population Bulletin* 37 (1982).

WOLF, JOSEF. *The Dawn of Man.* New York: H. N. Abrams, 1978.

ZIMOLZAK, CHESTER E., and STANSFIELD, CHARLES E. *The Human Landscape: Geography and Culture.* Columbus, OH: Charles E. Merrill Publishing Co., 1979.

3
The Elements of Cultural Geography

THE CONCEPT OF CULTURE
CULTURAL PROCESSES
ARTIFACTS
SOCIOFACTS
MENTIFACTS

This transmitting tower of a metropolitan TV station reaches 469.4 meters (1,540 feet) skyward. With its effective transmitting radius of about 80.5 kilometers (50 miles), the station broadcasts nearly 20,340 square kilometers (8,000 square miles).

In the preceding chapter, we reviewed some important aspects of population distribution and characteristics. The emphasis was on origins, races, numbers of people, and on how those numbers are changing, particularly with respect to the earth's ability to feed and provide other resources for the rapidly increasing total. We noted that the physical environment exerts climatic and other physical controls that, to some extent, condition settlement patterns. Although human ingenuity has dramatically increased food productivity, the physical environment does present limits—as yet far from being reached—on the amount of energy available to people via food supply. To survive, humans must adapt to the earth's environment, although in small ways, we can modify the environment to fit our needs. Within limits we can change land uses and heat or cool indoor spaces. In general, however, we are powerless to control the broader forces of nature—the distribution of land and sea, the endowment of soils, and patterns of climate.

Although the emphasis of this book is on the human aspects of geography, it is important to appreciate that all human activities occur in the context of the planet's physical environment. We frequently see examples of human adaptation to the physical world as we observe activities and landscapes. Building materials may reflect locally available stone, clay, or lumber. Architecture may demonstrate responses to climate. Agriculture is acutely sensitive to variations in climate, soils, and slopes. Cities and regions may experience growth because of their physical amenities—climate or scenery. Industries have historically located in response to the availability of minerals such as coal and iron ore. The location of mining, including extraction of oil and gas, depends directly on where those resources are located. Our emphasis

CHAPTER 3 THE ELEMENTS OF CULTURAL GEOGRAPHY

on human geography, then, is a matter of curricular convenience, not an ideal reflection of reality.

This chapter is a preface to the field known as cultural geography. Broadly defined, cultural geography is synonymous with human geography. Historically, cultural geography was more narrowly described. Carl O. Sauer (1889–1975), the father of modern cultural geography, said that cultural geography dealt with "those elements of material culture that give character to area" (Sauer, 1931). In recent decades, however, the scope of cultural geography has broadened. Today, we can say that most definitions of cultural geography would at least include analysis of language, religion, material culture, and some aspects of agriculture.

In this chapter we will review some of the commonly accepted components of cultural geography and then move to more detailed treatments of specific topics. In the next few chapters, we will try to answer the following questions:

- What are the patterns of world languages and religions, and how did these patterns evolve? (Chapters 4 and 5)
- What elements of material culture allow the delineation of culture areas? (Chapter 6)
- What cultural patterns are identifiable in the United States and how do they relate to U.S. culture regions? (Chapter 7)

Chapters 4 through 7 are more oriented toward the traditional view of cultural geography, while later chapters may be considered representative of the contemporary view of cultural geography as a perspective to help us understand social, economic, and political patterns.

THE CONCEPT OF CULTURE

A good place to begin answering the general and specific questions we have raised is with consideration of the concept of *culture*. To some persons, culture is a very narrow concept, thought of as having to do with the fine arts—music, painting, ballet, and so forth. This leads to comparative evaluations of cities—New York City has a lot of "culture," Amarillo has less. In this book, and in other discussions of the geography of culture, the term has a much broader meaning. There is no one "right" definition, and there are at least as many definitions of culture as there are geographers who write about it. Here are two examples:

Culture . . . is the sum total of historically learned human behavior and ways of doing things (Spencer and Thomas, 1978, p. 1).

A specific culture is the total way of life of a people (Broek and Webb, 1968, p. 25).

Culture, then, is an all-embracing concept. In effect, all the things we do and say—with the exception of a few instinctive acts, such as eating, drinking, blinking, and mating—are culturally conditioned. The language we speak, the religion we practice, the foods we eat, the styles of our homes, the sports we play and watch—all are *learned* behaviors, and can be referred to as *cultural elements,* or *traits*.

One classification scheme divides these cultural elements into three types.

1. Artifacts
2. Sociofacts
3. Mentifacts

Artifacts are objects or systems that supply our goods and services—tools, factories, housing, and so forth. Such cultural elements are also referred to as *technology*. *Sociofacts* are interpersonal arrangements—the family, education, the way we raise our children, and others. These elements also may be called *social organization*. *Mentifacts,* as the name implies, are mental constructs having to do with such relatively abstract phenomena as language, religion, astrology, superstition, and the arts (Zelinsky, 1973, p. 73).

CULTURAL PROCESSES

A cultural system involves the working of several cultural processes on the cultural elements. Consideration of the processes helps us understand how the cultural elements interact with one another and with the physical environment, causing change in the system. According to geographers Joseph Spencer and William Thomas (1978, p. 4), four processes work on the elements of culture to create the conditions that maintain or change a cultural system:

1. Discovery
2. Invention
3. Evolution
4. Diffusion

Discovery, according to Spencer and Thomas, "is the way in which mankind learns about the physical world." Finding out, for example, that coal or oil burns or that disease is caused by some particular virus is the kind of activity that may be properly regarded as a discovery.

Invention "is the human act of creating something new that does not occur naturally in the physical/biotic world." Inventions may include abstractions such as nations and states, as well as obvious things such as aluminum, steel, and automobiles.

Evolution is the cumulative process of change over time. Like material objects, institutions may experience evolution, as in the case of changes in laws or modifications in forms of government over time. Many of you are aware of the rapid evolution of the calculator within your lifetime—from a bulky, often noisy device to a small, silent, highly efficient machine. And the automobile shrinks in response to the energy crunch—that's evolution, too.

Diffusion is a spreading process, allowing cultural elements, discoveries, inventions, or evolutionary changes to move across the earth's surface—between individuals, between cities, between regions, and even between continents. The spread of the English language concurrently with the spread of British control in the course of empire-building is one example. Another is the diffusion of various plants (Chapter 10), including wheat, rice, and corn, as farmers found that they could produce these crops outside their areas of origin. Many innovations (technological improvements) have been transferred from one place to another by diffusion processes, including, in agriculture, such developments as hybrid corn and "miracle" rice, as well as improvements in farm machinery and agricultural chemicals. (For further discussion of diffusion, see Chapter 8.)

ARTIFACTS

It is important to understand that cultural processes interact with one another, and with the physical environment. A change brought about by one process may result in the modification of a cultural element, which in turn triggers new changes brought about by other processes. Consider, for example, the *invention* of television as an artifact. Countless prior discoveries and inventions in electronics (vacuum tubes, switches, etc.) and other fields were needed to make the TV concept practical. Mass ownership of TVs could not have happened without low prices made possible by mass production techniques in industry—techniques which themselves were developed and refined prior to the invention of TV. Less obvious, but no less critical, was the invention of centrally generated electricity—no wall outlet, no picture!

Evolution of TV technology led to the availability of color, and more recent development has brought home videotape recorders and big-screen home TV. The *diffusion* process was directly related to the availability of TV signals, that is the locations of TV transmitters and their power. This in turn was affected by the physical geography of areas, since TV signals are FM-type, which can be received only on a "line of sight" from transmitters. Areas "behind" hills or mountains may be cut off from transmissions, and with respect to the TV medium, isolated. The process of diffusion eventually led to more or less complete coverage of populated areas (Figure 3–1).

We can also talk about the automobile as another example of cultural interactions. As with TV, many prior innovations were necessary before the automobile, powered by the internal combustion engine, was feasible. These inventions—such as the wheel—that cumulatively made automotive transportation a possibility can be traced to antiquity. *Evolutionary* advances were needed in metallurgy, fuel chemistry, and mechanical and electrical engineering. Various materials, such as rubber, glass, and paint, had to be synthesized. Not least, relatively sophisticated social and economic organization was needed before there was an effective demand for motor vehicles and the ability to manufacture and market them. A hunting and gathering society, with little *division of labor,* or specialization in jobs, would find motor vehicles of little practical value. Even if they could be built and maintained, lack of paved roads would make them ornamental rather than functional machines. In the last decade we have seen quite vividly how cultural, economic, and technological factors interrelate with respect to automobile size, shape, and fuel economy. The American automobile industry was slow to adjust to rising fuel prices, and sales of traditional large cars slumped, to be replaced by smaller, more economical, better-made imports. Now U.S. automobile makers struggle to compete in the new technologies of fuel efficiency, microcomputer systems, and robotics. Many other artifacts that we take for granted today depended for development on advances in basic and applied sciences.

The degree of interdependence among cultural elements increases as technology becomes more sophisticated. This means that *vulnerability* increases. Electrical failures, for example, instantly shut down urban functions, and may have disastrous social consequences, such as looting, quite apart from mechanical difficulties and general inconvenience. This realization that electricity is so crucial to the way of life in more developed nations has led to confronta-

CHAPTER 3 THE ELEMENTS OF CULTURAL GEOGRAPHY

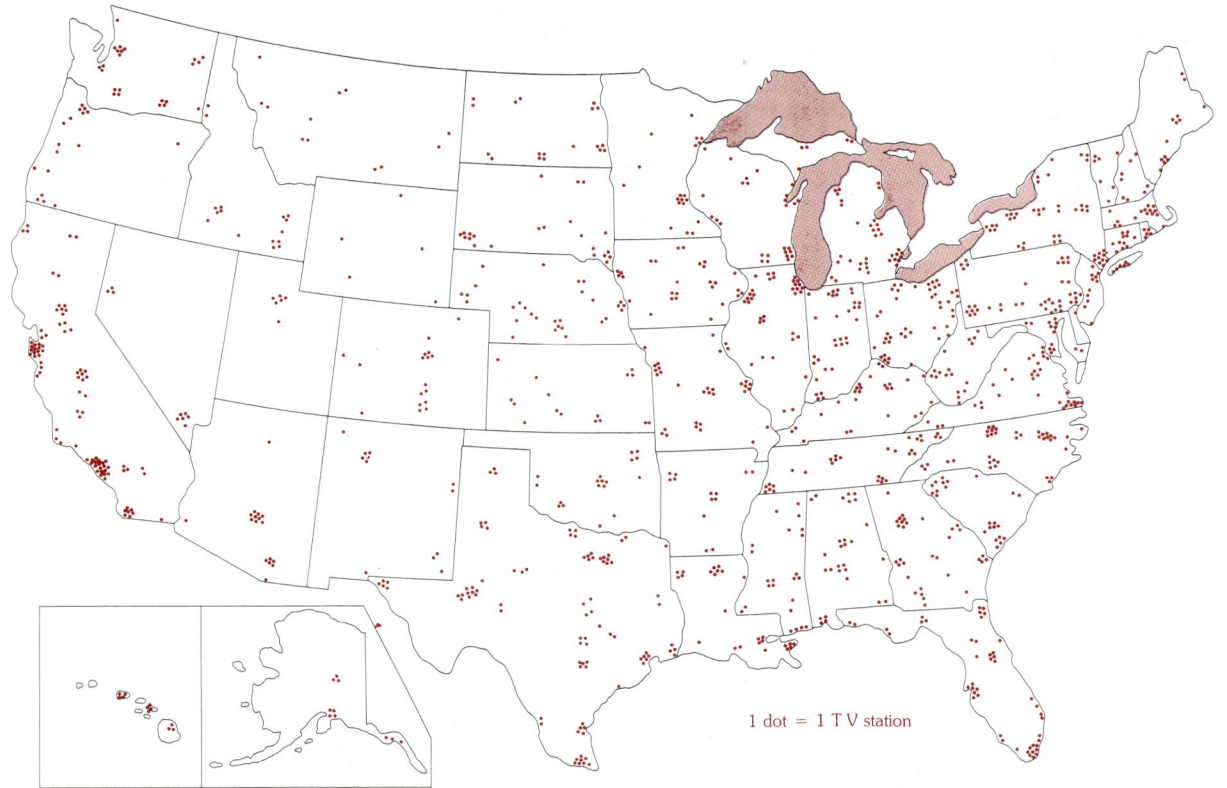

FIGURE 3–1 Commercial and public TV stations in the United States, 1979. (Data from *Broadcasting*, 1979, pp. B-85–B-14.)

tions over future supplies, whether they are to be based on coal, nuclear, or other sources.

Television, the automobile, and electricity are examples of the artifacts in cultural systems. (For a more detailed discussion of artifacts, see Chapter 6.) What about sociofacts and mentifacts?

SOCIOFACTS

The scope of sociofacts is extremely broad, encompassing as it does family organization, political behavior, and other institutions and systems. One fundamental aspect of social organization, however, involves the determination of the rules or laws by which we live. Laws, whether formally codified or passed verbally from one generation to another, are a necessity in any society. Lawmaking is a political process, one that involves the interplay of groups and individuals and struggles for power. Laws, in the broadest sense, include criminal and civil statutes, as well as a host of regulations promulgated by agencies such as the Federal Aeronautics Administration or the Federal Trade Commission. Local ordinances and codes (relating to building and zoning, for example) also are laws, in the sense that they constrain behavior. Is there a discernible pattern of laws on a global scale?

Geojurisprudence

In an exercise in what he called *geojurisprudence*, Ernest Easterly (1977) pointed out the importance of evolutionary processes in the development of laws in particular areas. As different population groups have become dominant, whether through migration, invasion, or other means, such groups have added a new "layer" to the laws already existing in the area in question. Among the world's legal systems, Easterly identified two principal groups—the *Occidental* (Euro-American, Western) and the *Socialist/Communist*. The Occidental group is divided into several families, and certain distinctions also are recognized within the Socialist/Communist group.

Occidental Group In the Occidental Group of geojurisprudence, we find distinctions among Anglo-American Common Law, Romano-Germanic Civil Law, and Nordic or Scandinavian Law.

Anglo–American Common Law is based primarily on the decisions of judges in combination with written statutes and long-standing customs. The legal systems of the United States, Canada, and some former British colonial territories are rooted in English common law (Figure 3–2).

In *Romano–Germanic Civil Law,* legislation is considered more important than judicial decisions. Essentially, it was felt that this would be more democratic than a system oriented to judicial decision making, in which the interests of the ruling classes might be of more concern than those of the mass of the people. As its name suggests, the system is of Roman origin, and it tends to dominate in continental Europe and in areas that have been colonized by such powers as Spain, France, and the Netherlands. This has had the effect of splitting the Americas, with the Romano–Germanic family dominating Latin America, and the Anglo–American family in North America, a pattern that clearly reflects diffusion processes linked to migration (Figure 3–2).

The *Nordic (Scandinavian)* family of law, although akin to German law, is sufficiently different to be classified separately (Figure 3–2).

Socialist/Communist Group The fundamental purpose of what is basically Soviet law is quite different from that of the Occidental group. In the latter, the emphasis is on resolving conflicts, while in Soviet law there is more concern with reinforcement of the broader goal of implementing the objectives of a socialist society. Another striking difference is the lack of separation between legislative and judicial branches of government in Soviet law; in the Soviet Union, for example, both are incorporated in the Supreme Soviet. Chinese law is part of this group, but there are differences compared to the Soviet approach.

Processes in the Development of Laws in the U.S. The development of laws in the U.S. illustrates cultural processes at work. We have noted that the legal system of the U.S. is rooted in English common law. Laws reflect the values of those who write them. The underlying rationale for the existence of laws and regulations is the maintenance of order and defense of the ruling elite, whether it be capitalist, socialist, or otherwise oriented. Laws arise, then, from complex interactions among religious and political philosophies and various institutions charged with drafting and enforcing legislation. Laws impose values on a society. When that society is broadly in agreement with the laws, they tend to work. When laws meet the opposition of substantial segments of the population, the result may be revolution or anarchy. In the 1980s, for example, we have seen the breakdown of laws in Iran, Poland, and Northern Ireland.

The values embodied in laws vary over time in response to changing attitudes in society. In the 1980s, we see conservative forces attempting to introduce school prayer and to limit or abolish abortion in the United States, while liberals campaign to legalize marijuana. The shades of political and religious opinion found in the modern U.S. could be encountered among early immigrants, too. Granted, the issues were different, but one of the underlying questions was still whether individuals should be allowed more or less freedom to behave as they wished. Other questions centered then, as they do now, on appropriate punishments for behaviors universally regarded as unacceptable: murder, rape, burglary, robbery, and so forth. Legislators who turn to religion for guidance may be confused by religious interpretations that are often ambiguous and contradictory. In the Islamic world, religion and government are closely interwoven and there is no separation of church and state. Laws relate rather directly to the edicts of the Koran, the holy book. In the U.S., however, church and state are formally separated so that religious values become incorporated into laws more indirectly.

Economic as well as religious values have been injected into our legal framework. The underlying assumption of our *civil* law, which governs the relations of citizens to each other (and which is *not* concerned with punishments), is the validity of *private property* and *property rights.* This is not the case under socialist law.

Apart from federal law, which applies equally to all the territories of the United States, there are substantial place-to-place variations in state and local laws and regulations.* Harries and Brunn (1978) describe how these differences in statutes have come about. They organized their interpretation of the geography of statutes around three themes: *regional social philosophy, spatial rights,* and *geographic variation in statutes.*

Regional Social Philosophy

Regional differences in laws can be traced to the values of the groups that settled each region. This settlement was itself a complex process, as new migration streams interacted with established settlers to modify the regional or local consensus on what con-

---

*We will not concern ourselves here with place-to-place variations in *enforcement* of laws, discussed in Chapter 9.

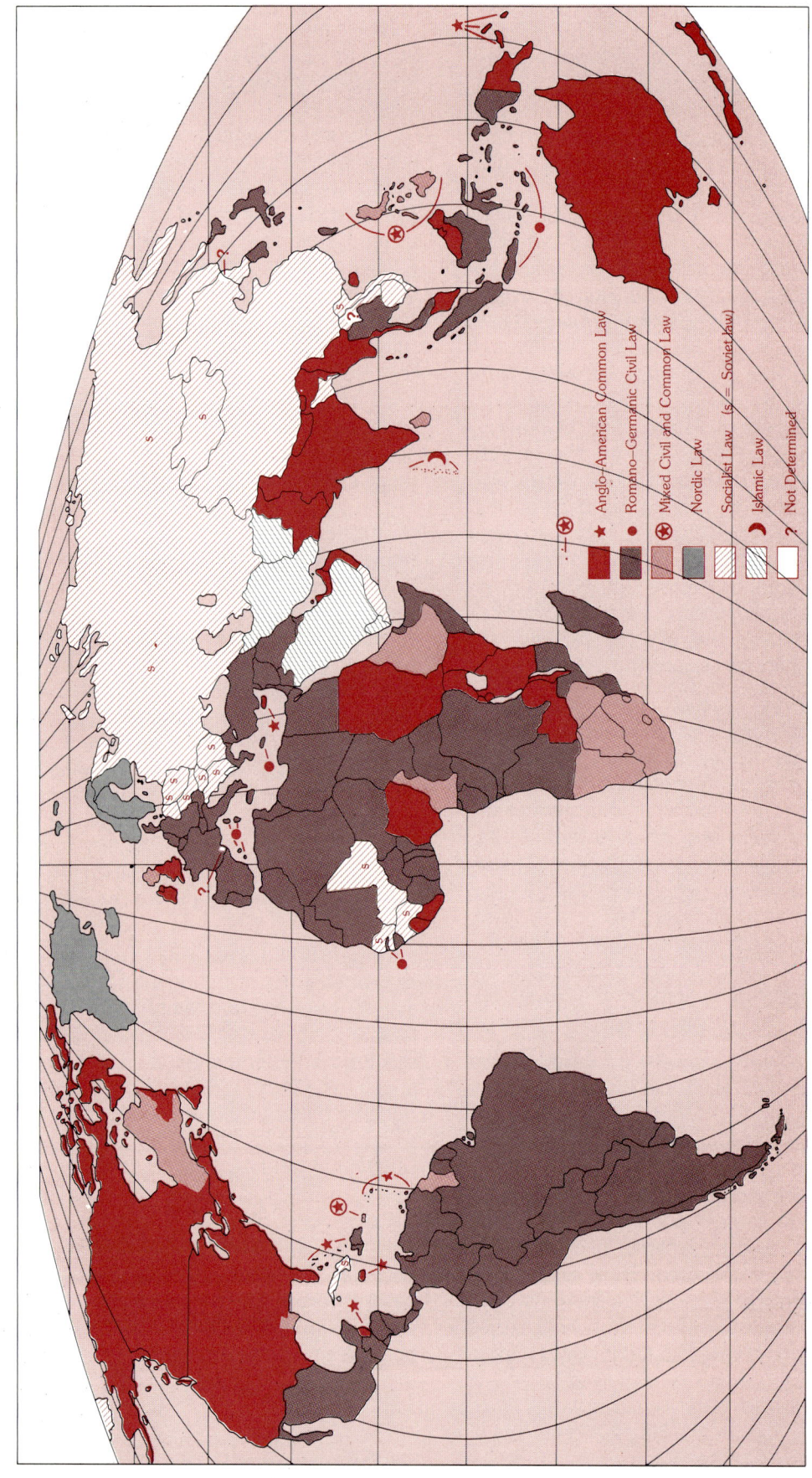

FIGURE 3–2 Major legal systems of the world as of January 1, 1976. (Reprinted from *Geographical Review* 67 [1977], with permission of the American Geographical Society.)

stituted acceptable behaviors. Regional social philosophies are like layers of a cake, with each new layer modifying the "flavor." This layering is an ongoing process, happening now as you read this page. The political scientist Daniel Elazar has interpreted political cultures of the United States, with the aid of a three-part classification, into *individualistic, moralistic,* and *traditionalistic.*

Individualistic political culture emphasizes the interests of the individual and minimizes governmental intervention in private affairs. The government role is seen primarily as the encouragement of private enterprise. Politics tends to be professional, and corruption in political life tends to be tolerated.

Moralistic political culture tolerates government intervention for the general welfare of the people. Political corruption is less tolerated than in the individualistic culture. Politics is seen as an activity for dedicated amateurs, a public service devoid of private gain.

Traditionalistic political culture emphasizes the importance of family and social ties in a small, elite "establishment" group. The traditionalist culture tends to be closed to outsiders and inward-looking. In some respects, this culture is preindustrial, as it excludes, or prefers to exclude, mass participation in the governing process. Government in this culture tends to defend the status quo and is unlikely to take initiatives (Elazar, 1966, pp. 86–94).

Figure 3–3 shows the political cultures across the United States. The moralistic culture was spread across the northern tier of states by the Puritans, their descendants, and those of similar views, including Scandinavians and Mormons. The midsection of the country was settled by more individualistic British and Germans whose influence also spread westward, mixing with moralistic cultures as it did so, and eventually reaching Northern California. The South came to be based on a plantation-oriented agrarian economy utilizing slaves. This economy lent itself to a traditionalist culture dominated by an elite landed gentry. Each of these cultures has left its imprint on state and local laws, since judges, district attorneys, attorneys general, and legislators are usually elected. Their

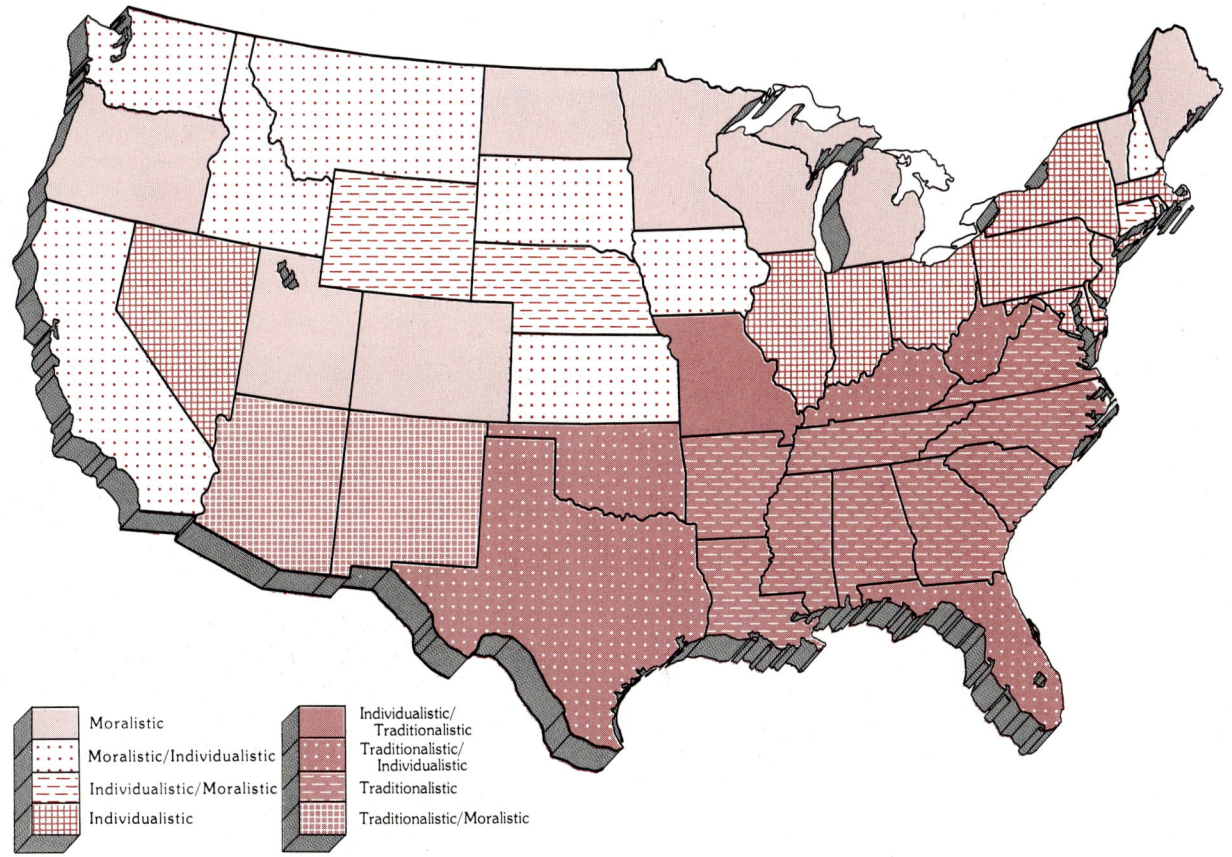

FIGURE 3–3 Dominant political cultures by state. (Figure 5.4, p. 135 "Dominant Political Cultures by State" from *American Federalism: A View From the States,* Third Edition by Daniel J. Elazar. Copyright © 1984 by permission of Harper & Row, Publishers, Inc.)

CHAPTER 3 THE ELEMENTS OF CULTURAL GEOGRAPHY

FIGURE 3–4 "Wet" and "dry" areas in Arkansas. (From Stanley D. Brunn, *Geography and Politics in America* [Harper and Row, 1974], p. 203.)

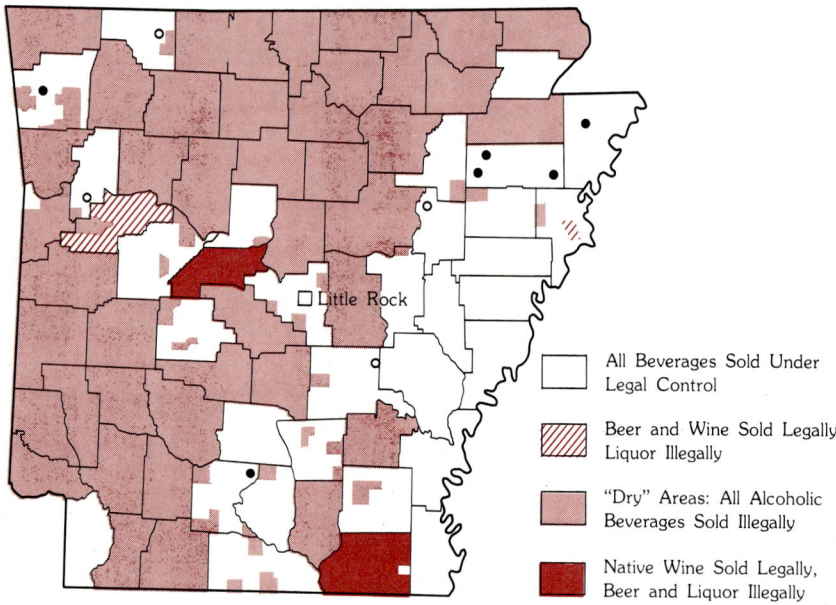

collective values broadly mirror those of the electorate. Legislation, as well as its interpretation and enforcement, also reflects the regional or local value system.

Spatial Rights

Laws apply to specific territories, whether the entire nation (federal law), or individual states, counties, or municipalities. Acceptable and unacceptable behaviors are defined, therefore, by the locations in which we find ourselves. In this sense, individuals have *spatial rights*, or rights that vary from place to place. Furthermore, *interpretations* of laws differ *within* jurisdictions so that federal laws may be interpreted differently in the North compared to the South, and Illinois state law may be interpreted differently in Northern Illinois compared to Southern Illinois.

Geographic Variation in Statutes

Local variations are illustrated by intrastate variations in liquor regulation (Figure 3–4), and we find similar intrastate patterns with respect to the legality of parimutuel betting and prostitution. Nevada law permits the licensing of brothels, except in counties exceeding 200,000 in population. Only Clark County (Las Vegas) is legally excluded by this limitation (Ley, 1974, 1981), as we see in Figure 3–5.

Local ordinances and covenants often affect many conditions, such as the spacing of buildings and whether nonwhites could be residents of various subdivisions. (This form of discrimination was struck down as unconstitutional.) The interaction between economics and local political culture can influence the urban landscape, as we see in this scenario based on a factual example. The minimum lot size in residential subdivisions in Homeville is 6,000 square feet. Minimum front, back, and side setbacks for dwellings are also specified in the city building code. Home sales slow down as a result of a sluggish economy and high interest rates. Developers pressure the city council to reduce the minimum lot size so as to reduce the land component in the cost of dwellings and to permit higher density of homes. The city concurs, reducing the minimum lot size to 5,000 square feet and reducing setback requirements. Street paving standards are also relaxed at about the same time. Thus a change in local regulations affected the urban landscape, part of *material culture* (Chapter 6). In theory, each city in the United States can prescribe different criteria for the spacing of dwellings, except where state law may have preempted the issue.

There are numerous variations in law at the state level. Criminal penalties vary substantially, not only in length but also in certainty, since some states have mandatory minimum sentences while others do not.

In U.S. law, then, the attitudes of migrants have become enshrined to define acceptable conduct in specific geographic areas. Cultural processes interact to fashion a vital component of our cultural geography. The geography of laws, like other aspects of cultural geography, is dynamic. Laws tend to change slowly, however, and many today are irrelevant, unenforced, or unenforceable. Meanwhile, laws to regulate new conditions or behaviors often lag behind reality. We will discuss the geographies of social processes and social problems in Chapters 8 and 9, and much of the rest of the book discusses, directly or indirectly, the processes leading to the geography of sociofacts.

MENTIFACTS

The two principal topics that fall under the rubric of mentifacts, or mental, abstract phenomena, are *language* and *religion*. These topics are the subjects of Chapters 4 and 5, so we will discuss them only briefly here.

Language is the key element in cultural geography because it allows the transmission of abstract ideas and facilitates the maintenance and development of toolmaking technology. Language, combined with demonstration, is the means by which the making and uses of tools are explained. Without language, material culture as we know it could not exist. Language has been called a "storehouse of culture," as groups of people use it to maintain and pass on their culture, in written or spoken words. Language helps us identify cultural regions through the classification of dialects. These dialects and colloquial word usages can make communication almost impossible *even in the same language.* You have only to introduce a Texan to a "Geordie" (someone from the Newcastle-Upon-Tyne region of northeastern England), and the fun begins. The Geordie has a good chance of understanding the Texan, because the Texas dialect, or accent, is familiar to British TV watchers and moviegoers, but the Texan has little chance with Geordie English! When you consider, again with reference only to English, the very distinct modes of speech *within* the United States, Canada, England, Scotland, Wales, Ireland, Australia, South Africa, and other English-speaking areas, you can begin to appreciate the level of complexity on a world scale.

The pattern of languages is so complex that related languages have been grouped together in families. The classifications are mapped in Figure 4–4 and discussed in Chapter 4. Chapter 4 also explains the historical geography of the English language. English evolved and diffused as a result of complex interactions of peoples who came into contact through invasions and migrations. It was partly sheer historical accident that English became the principal language of North America. If the cultural processes of the last few hundred years had gone just a little differently, you might be reading this book today in a Native American language or in French, Spanish, or Chinese!

Language and culture are often intertwined. Aspects of culture are often reflected in language; for example, Eskimos have many words for *snow* and *seal.* Urban dwellers may have several words for streets; rural dwellers may not. Some cultures have no words for certain elements from other cultures, and simply borrow the foreign words. When the idea of educating very young children was adopted in U.S. schools, there was no word for it, so the original German—*Kindergarten*—("child garden") was borrowed. The original words have been retained to name many ethnic foods. "*Spaghetti*" is a more convenient label than, say, "long, stringy, white stuff." You will be able to think of other examples.

As Chapter 4 illustrates in greater detail, it is impossible to separate interconnections among language and other cultural traits such as political, eco-

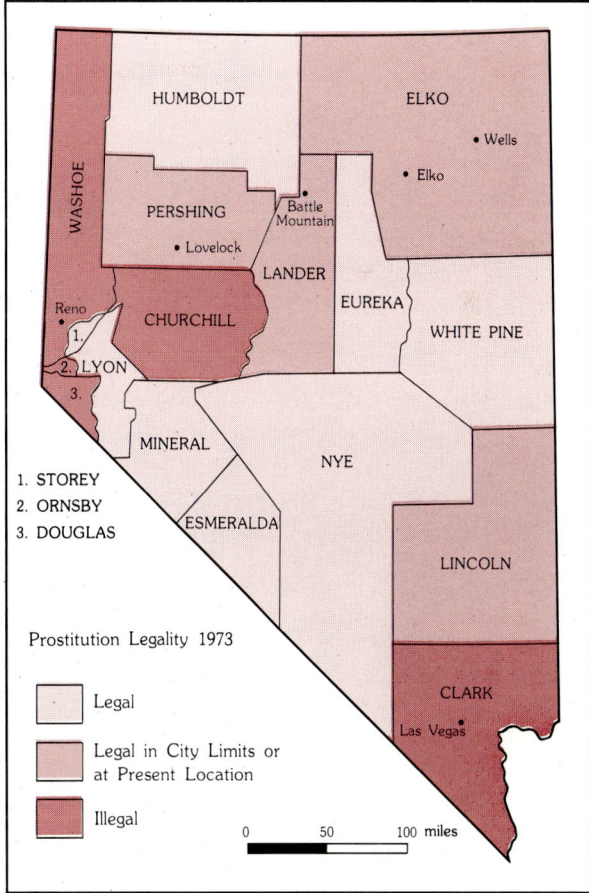

FIGURE 3–5 Legal and illegal prostitution in Nevada. (From Richard Symanski, "Prostitution in Nevada," *Annals,* Association of American Geographers 64:3 [Sept. 1974], p. 360.)

nomic, and religious systems. The presence of several languages in a country (*multilingualism*) may be a source of political tension, including pressures to redraw political boundaries to coincide with the limits of language groups, as has been the case with French in Canada and Welsh in Wales. Religion and language are inseparable when a religion adopts an official language for its rituals, as in Catholicism (Latin) and Islam (Arabic). Languages used for trading illustrate the tie to economic systems. Pidgin English is used in the Orient, for example, and Swahili is a well-known trading language in East Africa. A language used for trade is known by the generic term *lingua franca,* so called because of a trading language developed in Medieval Europe by the Franks, the people of France.

As we will see in Chapter 5, *religions,* like the world's languages, are numerous and complex. As with the processes affecting languages, religions have undergone invention, evolution, and diffusion. Religions were invented in the sense that they were often identified with the teachings of key people—Jesus, for example, or, in the case of Islam, the prophet Mohammed. Evolution has occurred when new sects or dissenting groups have sprung up to become subdivisions of the main religion, or when a religion has accepted some aspects of another religion to gain converts. Thus, Christianity can be divided into three major branches (Figure 5–1) and into numerous familiar denominations—Baptists, Presbyterians, Episcopalians, and so forth. Diffusion has taken place in the course of migrations, missionary activities, and conquests, with the superimposition of the foreign religion on the native religion.

We find, then, that Christianity is dominant in Europe and in the Americas populated by people of European origin. Note, however, that people of Spanish and Portuguese heritage (Catholics) dominate in Latin America, whereas northern Europeans (Protestants) have been the major influence in North America. The third great branch of Christianity—Eastern Orthodox or Eastern Rites—survives in eastern and southeastern Europe and the Soviet Union, though its survival has been jeopardized behind the Iron Curtain.

Like Christianity, Islam had its origins in the region known as the Middle East, only a few hundred years after the beginning of Christianity. Also like Christianity, Islam evolved and diffused spatially. While Christianity spread mainly northward, Islam diffused to the east and south, becoming dominant in the Arab world (including northern Africa) and eastward into Iran, Afghanistan, Pakistan, and southeastern republics of the Soviet Union. Islam attempted to penetrate northward, but met resistance from Christianity.

In the 1980s, the geographic impacts of religion are clear as we observe events in the Middle East, often triggered by religious factors, which can directly influence the way of life of many people. In Islam, the division between church and state, which is a cornerstone of U.S. life, is unknown; religion and government merge in a way that allows the direct participation of government in religious life and vice versa. In the United States, the so-called Moral Majority has attempted to fuse politics and religion in the hope of ensuring the election of public officials sympathetic to Moral Majority positions on issues.

The influence or lack of influence of religion may profoundly affect our ways of life and the environments of the societies in which humankind lives. The presence or elaborateness of churches (Figure 3–6), religion-related land cultivation patterns, street layouts, the use of colors, cemeteries, place names, ta-

FIGURE 3–6 Shinto Shrine in Honshu, Japan, dating from the eighth century. Two thousand stone lanterns (left) and 1,000 bronze lanterns are lighted on festive occasions. (Photo courtesy of Robert E. Cramer, the National Council for Geographic Education, and the Great Plains National Instructional Television Library.)

boos on foods, drinks, or work, and various ties between religion and political and economic systems all vary among cultures (Sopher, 1967). Significantly, these religious influences affect us whether or not we are religious. For example, the *Protestant work ethic* influences the value we place on working hard for a living and contrasts to the more leisurely pace of other cultures, and reminds us that the influence of religion may be much stronger than we realize. (For further discussion of religion, see Chapter 7).

CONCLUSION

Any discussion of the geography of human activity relates directly or indirectly to cultural geography as defined by Carl Sauer: "those elements of material culture that give character to area."

The geographies of humans and of the physical world are inseparable; indeed the geography of religion underscores this unity, for people in most regions demonstrate concern for the physical world as well as for human beings. According to Judeo-Christian theology, for example, humanity and the earth were both created by God, and man was given the role of steward, a role that has been used to justify protective postures toward the environment (Glacken, 1967, Chapter 4).

Values imparted by religion, education, the economic system, and other sources ultimately determine how people interact with the physical environment. Will this interaction be exploitive, with humans taking more out than they put back, or will they strive for a more harmonious relationship with nature? These rhetorical questions remind us that culture embraces much more than the few elements discussed in this chapter; culture also encompasses the values and attitudes that determine human use of the earth, war and peace, and all other interactive processes.

KEY WORDS

artifacts
culture
diffusion
discovery
evolution
geojurisprudence
individualistic
lingua franca
material culture

mentifacts
moralistic
multilingualism
political culture
regional social philosophy
sociofacts
spatial rights
technology
traditionalistic

REFERENCES

Broadcasting: 1979 Yearbook Issue. Washington, D.C.: Broadcasting Publications, 1979.

BROEK, JAN O. M., and WEBB, JOHN W. *A Geography of Mankind.* New York: McGraw-Hill, 1968.

EASTERLY, ERNEST S. "Global Patterns of Legal Systems: Notes toward a New Geojurisprudence." *Geographical Review* 67 (1977): 209–20.

ELAZAR, DANIEL. *American Federalism: A View from the States.* New York: Thomas Y. Crowell, 1966.

GLACKEN, CLARENCE J. *Traces on the Rhodian Shore.* Berkeley, Calif.: University of California Press, 1967.

HARPER, R., and SCHMUDDE, T. *Between Two Worlds: An Introduction to Geography.* Boston: Houghton-Mifflin, 1978.

HARRIES, KEITH D., and BRUNN, STANLEY D. *The Geography of Laws and Justice.* New York: Praeger, 1978.

SAUER, CARL O. "Cultural Geography," in *Encyclopedia of the Social Sciences* VI (1931): 621–623. Reprinted in: Philip L. Wagner and Marvin W. Mikesell, *Readings in Cultural Geography.* Chicago: University of Chicago Press, 1962.

SOPHER, DAVID E. *Geography of Religions.* Englewood Cliffs, N.J.: Prentice-Hall, 1967.

SPENCER, J. E., and THOMAS, W. L. *Introducing Cultural Geography.* New York: John Wiley, 1978.

SYMANSKI, RICHARD. "Prostitution in Nevada," *Annals,* Association of American Geographers, 64 (1974): 357–77.

SYMANSKI, RICHARD. *The Immoral Landscape: Female Prostitution in Western Societies.* Toronto: Butterworth, 1981.

ZELINSKY, WILBUR. *The Cultural Geography of the United States.* Englewood Cliffs, N.J.: Prentice-Hall, 1973.

Retrospektive ÖSTERREICHISCHES FILMMUSEUM Wien Viennale 1973

DER AMERIKANISCHE WESTERN
1898–1960

4
Geography of Language

THE NATURE AND USE OF LANGUAGE
WORLD LANGUAGE PATTERNS
HISTORICAL GEOGRAPHY OF THE ENGLISH LANGUAGE
MULTILINGUALISM
BILINGUALISM
PLACE NAMES

This poster for a foreign film festival at London's National Film Theater shows how languages are interrelated.

What is language? Why does it vary from place to place? How does it relate to other elements of culture? What is the world pattern of languages and how are they related? These are some of the questions we will deal with in this chapter. Language may be thought of as a genuinely universal element of culture. Everyone has language, not always in written form, but at least as a verbal means of communication.

THE NATURE AND USE OF LANGUAGE

The term *language* is somewhat ambiguous. The most general meaning is the ability of people to communicate via speech. The word is also used to mean a "standard," "official," or literary language used, for example, in government documents. A third meaning applies to a group of related *dialects*, more or less mutually comprehensible. English and Spanish are languages in this sense. What makes dialects mutually intelligible is that they have similarities in *phonology* (sounds), *grammar* (rules of construction), and *lexicon* or *vocabulary* (words). As the box "Brooklynese" shows, Brooklyn English is a colorful blending of dialects from many sources. Non-Brooklynites may have trouble with Brooklynese at first, but eventually one adapts by learning the variations in pronunciation. What thus seems at first to be a different language is actually a dialect.

How and where did language originate? These questions cannot be answered with any degree of certainty. We can trace the recent development of certain languages, such as English, in some detail, but the broader question of how and where language first emerged as a medium of communication is quite obscure. One line of reasoning suggests a link between toolmaking and language. Only humans are able to *make* complex tools (as opposed to simply using objects picked up in the environment) and to use language. Language may have been necessary for the maintenance and development of toolmaking technology. It was through some kind of language that one person explained to another how to make a tool and how to use it. Archaeological evidence suggests that some early members of the family of mankind, the hominids, had tools, and therefore probably had language, too. If this suggestion is true, it means that language is several million years old—ancient from our perspective, but very young in

BROOKLYNESE

Ya got dese guys. Dey live in Brooklyn wit dere mudduhs and fadduhs, see? People tink dey tawk funny.

Nah, says Margaret Mannix Flynn. It ain't funny. It's wunnerful.

Mrs. Flynn has listened to thousands of people in Brooklyn, and as a lecturer at the Department of Speech of Brooklyn College, she's put together a study of the dialects and accents of the borough that calls itself the nation's fourth largest city.

"Most people believe that coming from Brooklyn is some kind of joke," the Brooklyn native says.

"It always gets a laugh—you know, the guy in the World War II movie who is played by William Bendix and says he is from Flatbush. . . . He always says 'Toity-toid Street and Toid Avenue,' and 'woik' for 'work,' and 'earl' for 'oil.'"

First of all, she says there is no Brooklynese. There's a New York dialect that is found throughout the metropolitan area.

That changing, living dialect is the culmination of wave upon wave of immigration, starting with the Dutch and continuing right up to today's influx of Russian Jews, Mrs. Flynn says.

"Very few places have the rich cultural diversity of Brooklyn," and thus Brooklyn dialect is especially rich, says Mrs. Flynn.

"We learn to speak from the people around us," Mrs. Flynn said in a recent interview. "Say you have a second-generation Italian child. All around him, he hears relatives who speak an Italian dialect.

"But then he's 3 years old, and he goes out to play. He may meet an Irish-American kid or a Jewish-American kid, and he adopts some of the way they speak. Before you know it, his speech is a conglomerate."

And so it goes. New Englanders who came to Brooklyn after the Revolution changed "mother" to "mothah"; the Germans changed "where" to "ver" and "so" to "zo"; the Eastern Europeans added a melody that made declarative sentences sound like questions; the Italians made the word "last" sound like "le-ast."

The Irish changed "going" to "goin" and "this" to "dis." Mrs. Flynn says the Irish spoke an archaic form of English because of their isolation; the early part of this century marked the arrival of blacks, who had been similarly isolated and made similar changes in Brooklyn speech.

Even now, Mrs. Flynn says, Brooklyn's new immigrants are changing the speech of the borough. Puerto Ricans make "ship" sound like "sheep" and "very" sound like "berry." And West Indian, Oriental, and Russian Jewish newcomers also are having their effect, she says.

"Brooklyn is not a peculiar place where people speak a peculiar language," Mrs. Flynn says. "Brooklyn really represents a multi-national heritage. I think we deserve a little respect."

Source: The Associated Press. Used with permission.

terms of the geological time scale (Greenberg, 1968, pp. 4–6).

This view of language makes it the most fundamental element of culture, for without it, the technology of toolmaking could not be passed from person to person or from generation to generation. Language is thus not only a medium of communication, but also a kind of storehouse of culture, an efficient means by which human groups transfer and maintain the core concepts of their culture, verbally or in writing. Language also serves to identify social status, since dialects, or accents, can indicate level of education or membership in certain social groups.

We know relatively little about the historical geography of languages. Only a few have ancient written records, and even these go back only a few thousand years—a small fraction of their total history. It is not known with certainty whether language was invented once, and then diffused (spread), or whether it was invented many times in different places. Whatever the origin, the result is today an extraordinarily complex array of languages, numbering perhaps as many as 5,000.

Studies show that language is inseparable from other aspects of culture, and may also correlate with people's genetic characteristics. Topographic barriers can isolate peoples, particularly in areas that lack communication and transportation systems. This isolation contributes to genetic differentiation as well as divergence of language and of other cultural attributes. The Yanomama Indians of southern Venezuela and northern Brazil, for example, are an isolated group occupying some 150 villages. Research found that the linguistic divergence of seven language areas of the Yanomama related to genetic variations, and it was suggested that the Yanomama dialects had undergone divergence for about 1000 years (Spielman et al., 1974). This is not to suggest, of course, that a particular language is itself a genetic or inborn trait, but rather that, over a long period of time, the changes experienced by isolated groups—including changes in language—tend to set those groups apart from others. They do not exchange cultural traits with other groups to any significant degree, and changes tend to be generated internally. Each group goes its own linguistic way and thus diverges, or separates, from the others. Isolation and divergence are hardly typical of the modern world, in which migration, travel, and worldwide communication systems lead to the more or less constant interactions of cultures, albeit within a framework of political and social constraints.

American English provides a good example of a language with substantial variation in regional dialects as well as a continuous supply of influences for change in the form of large flows of immigrants. Linguists (scientists who study language) have done a great deal of work in *linguistic geography*, mapping variations in dialect and lexicon to improve our understanding of the processes of language change. Harold B. Allen, for example, prepared a linguistic atlas of the Upper Midwest on the basis of interviews with 206 informants between 1947 and 1956. This work enabled the preparation of maps such as that in Figure 4–1, which shows the eastern boundaries of certain western terms. These boundaries are known as *isoglosses*, from Greek words meaning "equal" *(iso)* and "language" *(gloss)*, which separate places with different language characteristics. In Figure 4–1, *trail, ranch, corral,* and *range* are probably familiar to most readers. *Soogan* is the term for a cowboy's saddle-roll comforter. *Hay flats* are low-lying grasslands or meadows. *Bunch* refers to a small pile of hay in a field, while *honyocker* was a term of insult applied by cattlemen to homesteaders who plowed and fenced the rangeland (Allen, 1973, p. 133). Note that these terms are intimately tied to the local environment, and would have no utility in a city or even in a different rural setting, as the isoglosses themselves suggest.

Another major research effort in linguistic geography was a study of the Eastern U.S. done by Hans Kurath, who, like Allen, prepared numerous maps of regional language variations, including that shown in Figure 4–2, which illustrates place-to-place differences in terms for *doughnut.* Maps such as those in Figures 4–1 and 4–2, in combination with others, allow identification of linguistic regions like those illustrated in Figure 4–3. This kind of work has given us a much more complete view of language areas. It had been thought that American dialects could be reduced to three: New England, Southern, and the remainder, but the "remainder" is much too complex to be characterized by one general label, and, as we see in Figure 4–3, Kurath has identified "Midland" speech, which differs from Northern and Southern. Kurath concludes that regional dialect differences among educated Americans originated in regional differences in Standard English in Britain (Kurath, 1971, p. 20; see also Marckwardt, 1958, Chapter 7, and Kurath, 1972).

A number of influences have helped make American English different from native English, including the Indian languages, as well as French, Spanish, Dutch, and German, all of which contributed new terms. About fifty words, including *chipmunk, skunk, hominy,* and *moccasin,* are of Indian origin. French has contributed nearly as many, in-

CHAPTER 4 GEOGRAPHY OF LANGUAGE

FIGURE 4–1 Eastern limits of western terms in the Upper Midwest. (Selected from THE LINGUISTIC ATLAS OF THE UPPER MIDWEST, Vol. I, edited by Harold B. Allen [© copyright 1973 by the University of Minnesota; reprinted by permission of Gale Research Company], University of Minnesota Press, 1973, p. 134.)

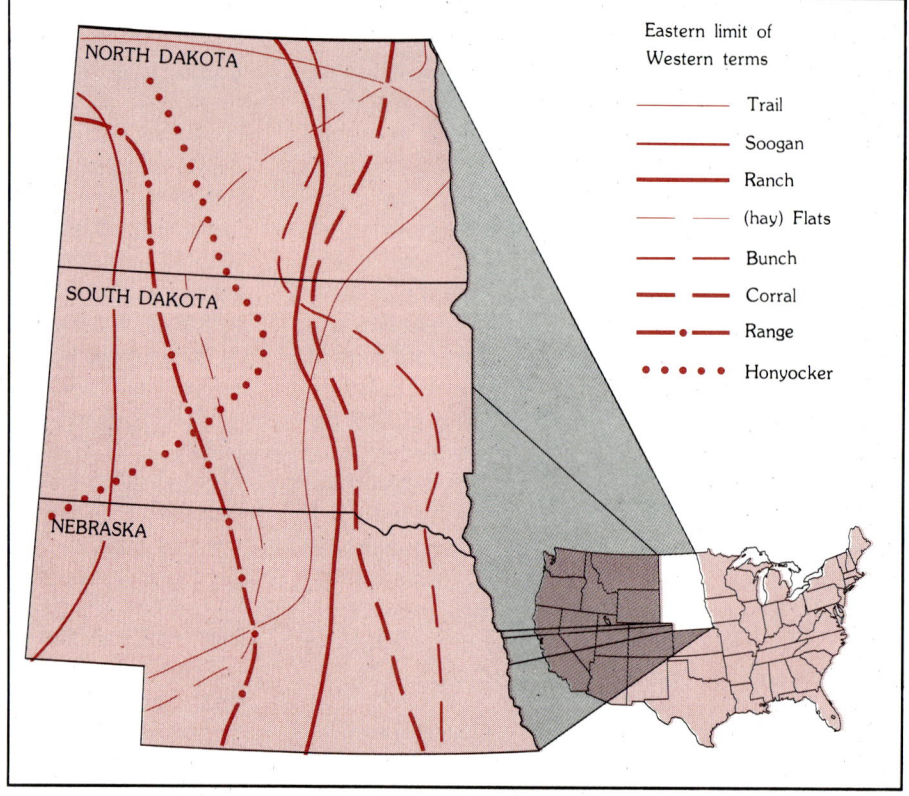

cluding *pumpkin, chowder, bayou, levee, cent, dime,* and *rotisserie.* Nearly 100 words in American English were borrowed from Spanish, such as *marijuana, bronco, patio,* and *pueblo,* as well as all the well known terms applied to Mexican food and drink. From Dutch we took *cole slaw, cookie, waffle, boss, dope,* and *Yankee,* among others. German examples include *delicatessen, frankfurter, hamburger, semester,* and *seminar* (Marckwardt, 1958, Chapter 3).

Differences between American English and native British English have also occurred because words once current in native English have died out in England but were retained in American English. *Druggist* is an example, having been replaced by *chemist* in England by about 1800. In other cases, new meanings developed in the U.S. but were never adopted in England. An example is *fraternity;* originally applied in England to religious orders and trade guilds, the term was used in America for a literary society at William and Mary College. The connection with the concept of fraternity was that one of the pledges members took was to eternal brotherhood. The term fraternity was then used for other, similar organizations, and was complemented later by *sorority* for comparable women's groups. These institutions, and the terminology relating to them, are unknown in England (Marckwardt, 1958, pp. 103–4).

WORLD LANGUAGE PATTERNS

As in the case of other complex phenomena, one helpful approach to understanding languages involves *classification,* the sorting of languages into major families (Figure 4–4). The principle behind this scheme is that languages similar to each other in terms of grammar, vocabulary, and phonology should be grouped together on the assumption that they share common origins. Thus we see that English and Spanish, the dominant languages of the Americas, belong to the *Indo-European* family.

Indo-European Languages

English is regarded as a member of the *Germanic* subfamily, and there are indeed many similarities between English and German (Table 4–1, p. 70). The Indo-European languages have ancient origins. Around 2000 B.C., languages that were variants of Indo-European were being spoken in a belt from Europe to India.

The historical geography of Indo-European is sketchy because its varieties were not written down until they had already evolved over millenia. In the period before Christ, there is documentary evidence of only four language groups: Hittite, Indo-Aryan, Greek, and Italic. Altogether about a dozen branches

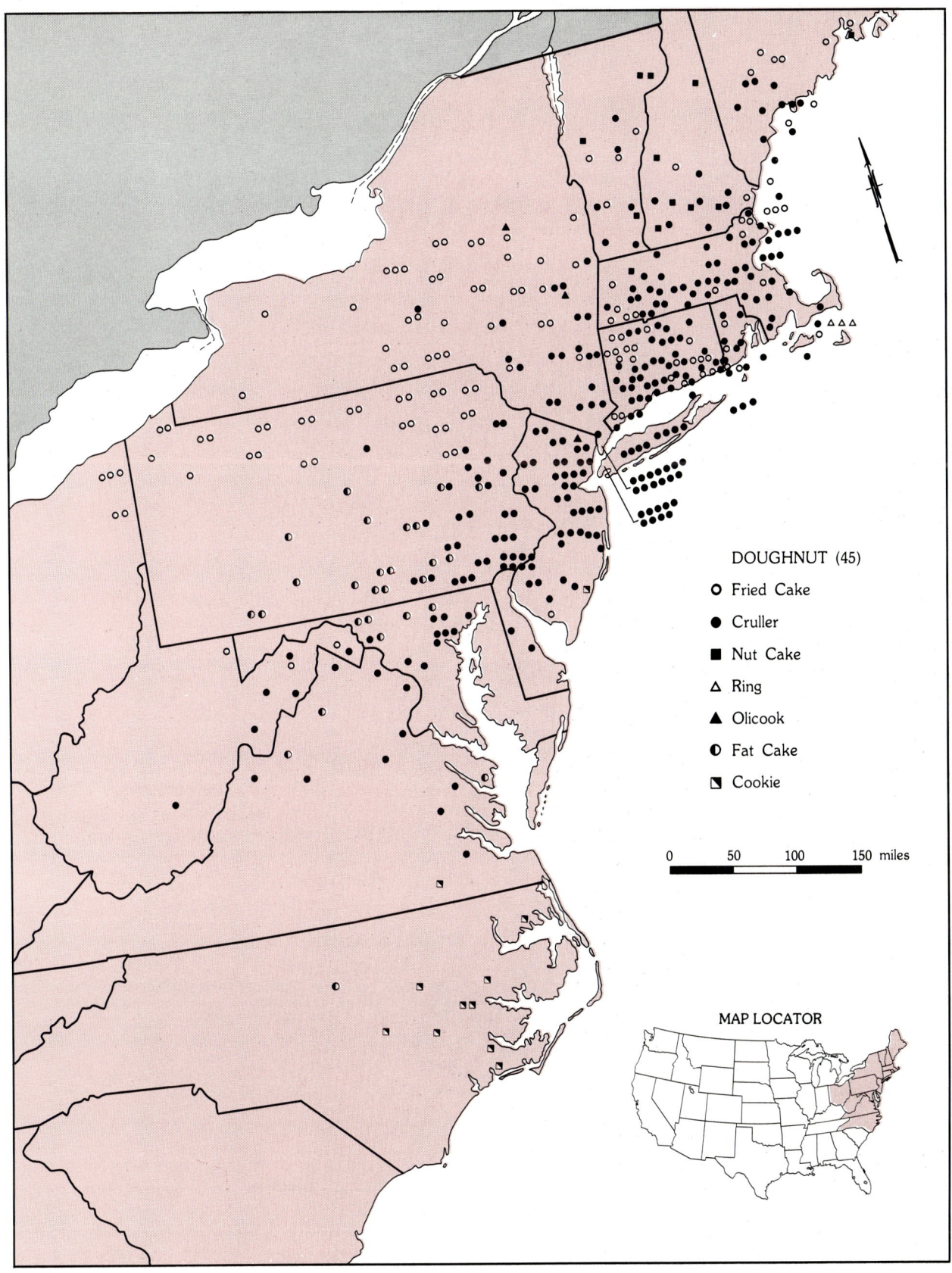

FIGURE 4–2 Regional variations in terms for "doughnut" in the Eastern United States. (From Hans Kurath, *A Word Geography of the Eastern United States* [Ann Arbor, MI: University of Michigan Press, 1949], Fig. 120.)

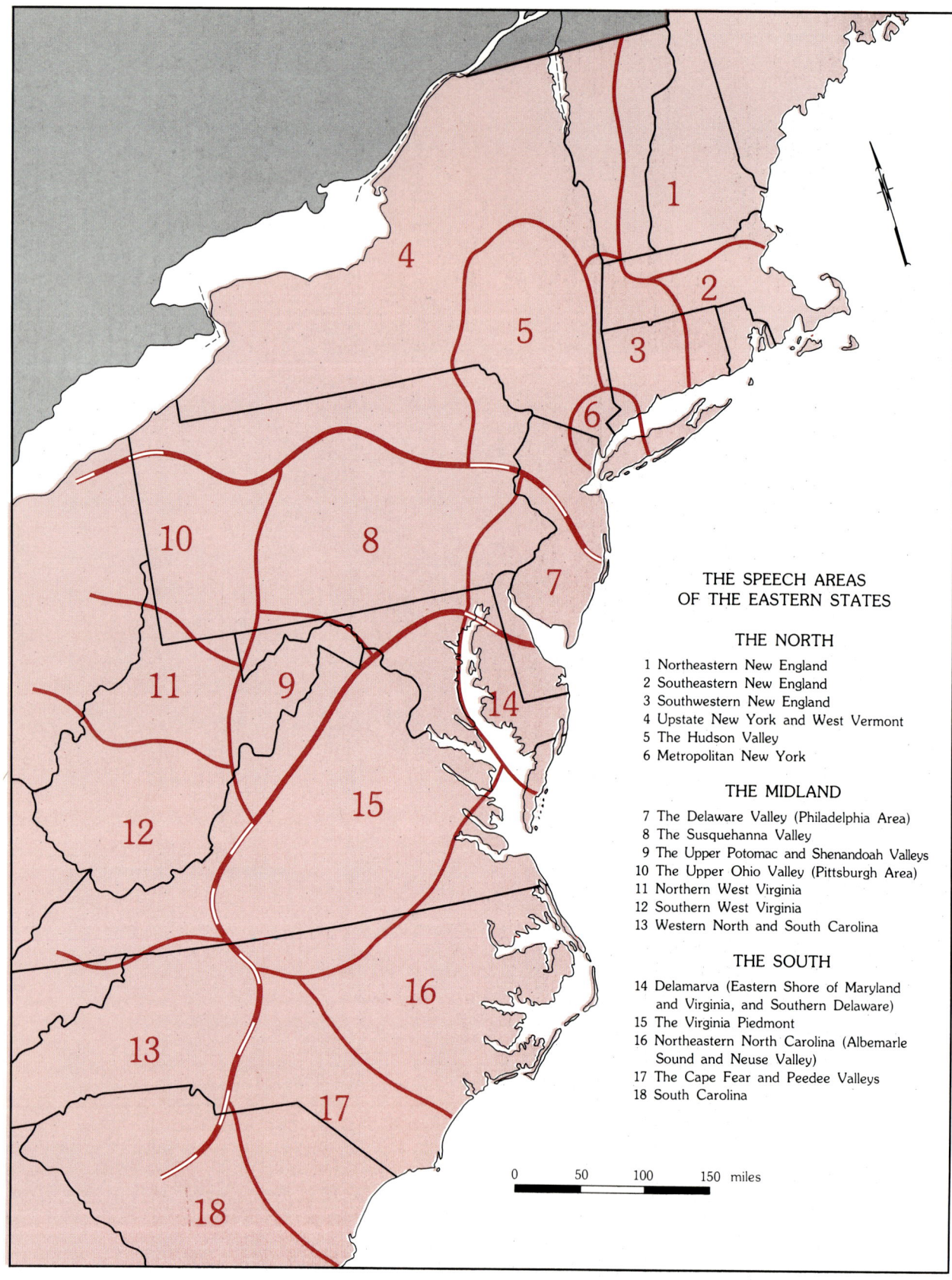

FIGURE 4–3 The speech areas of the eastern states. (From Hans Kurath, *A Word Geography of the Eastern United States* [Ann Arbor, MI: University of Michigan Press, 1949], Fig. 3.)

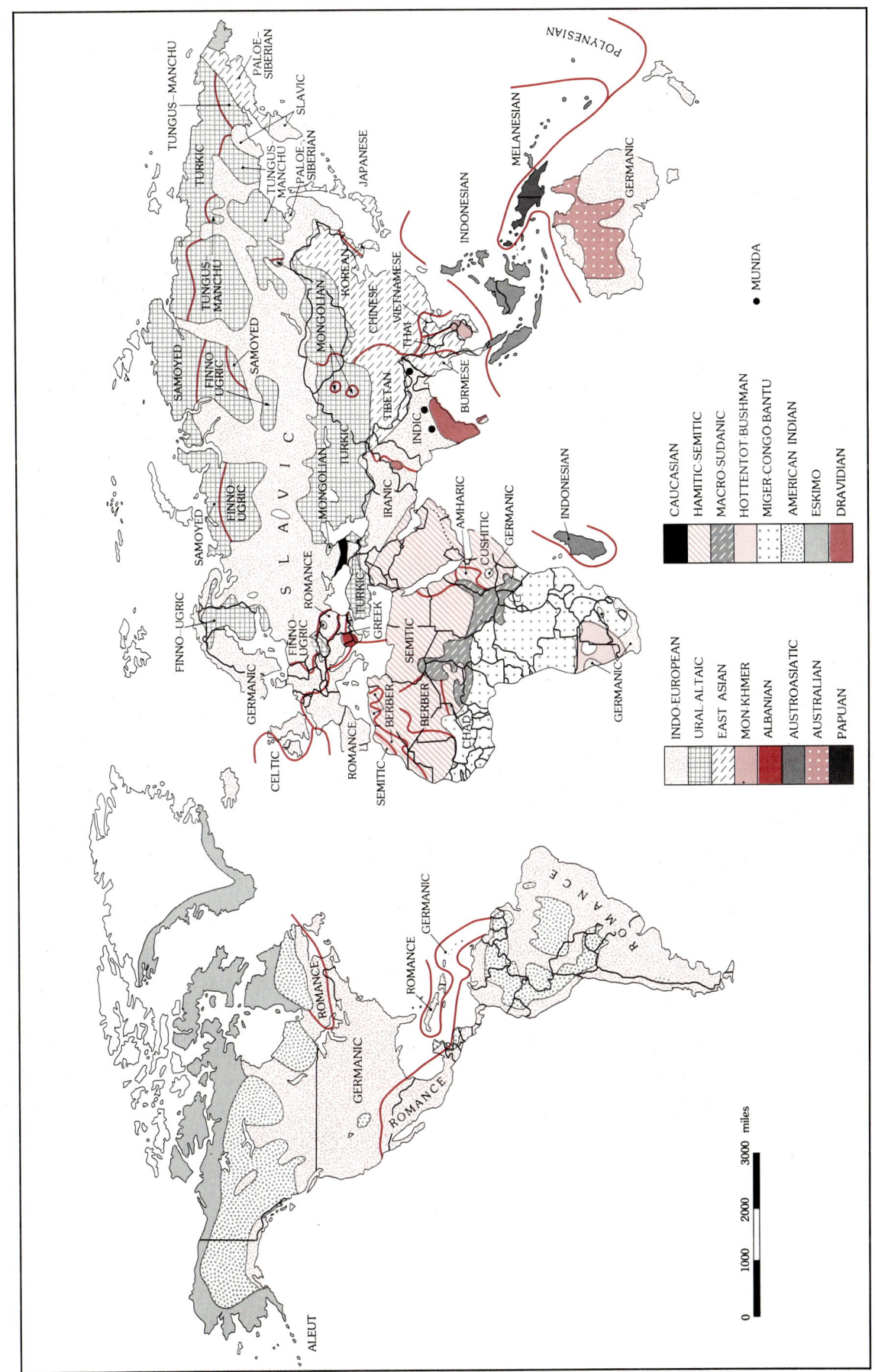

FIGURE 4–4 Language families of the world. (From Jan O. M. Broek and John W. Webb, *A Geography of Mankind*, 3rd ed. [New York: McGraw-Hill, 1968], pp. 100–101, Fig. 5–1.)

TABLE 4–1 Similarities in English and German vocabulary

English	German
dumb	dumm
blind	blind
(girl) cousin	die (the) Kusine
next year	nächstes Jahr
friend	der (the) Freund
to weigh	wiegen
swine	das (the) Schwein
wasp	die (the) Wespe
loud	laut
grass	das (the) Gras
weather	das (the) Wetter
cold	kalt

of Indo-European have been recognized. These include *Hellenic* (Greek, ancient and modern); *Italic*, from which Latin, the basis of the Romance languages, is derived; *Celtic, Baltic, Slavonic,* and *Germanic*. Celtic is found in the fringes of northwestern Europe, where the Celtic peoples were pushed by various invaders. The Celtic languages are Gallic and Cornish (both extinct), Welsh, Breton (northwestern France/Brittany), and the Gaelic of Ireland and Scotland. Baltic includes Prussian, Lettish, and Lithuanian. Russian is subsumed by the Slavonic group, while English, Dutch, and the languages of Scandinavia (except Finnish) are Germanic (Wolff, 1971, p. 28).

Spanish How did Spanish, a major language of the Indo-European family, become, with English, the other principal language of the Americas? As a Latin language, the beginnings of Spanish are traceable to the evolution of Latin and its relatives. Latin was, from perhaps the sixth century B.C., the language of what is today the Italian "compartment" (district) of Latium, including Rome. Roman military successes spread the Latin language as they spread the Roman Empire, some two thousand years ago. Latin then became the language of education and business in subjugated areas. Eventually, local languages died—particularly in cities—and Latin dominated. This happened in Iberia (Spain and Portugal). In each region, Latin took on its own special character, influenced by local pronunciation and vocabulary. The Latin of Iberia became unique, replacing perhaps two local languages, Iberian and Celtic.

In the eighth century, the Arabs invaded Spain, and the influence of Arabic permeated "Iberianized" Latin, but Germanic invasions, elsewhere influential, had little effect. Arabic words such as *wadi* (water) are found in names such as *Guadalquivir* (great river), and many other borrowings occur in vocabularies that deal with irrigation, crafts, and business.

In the tenth century, Castile, a province in central Iberia, led the Christian Reconquest of the peninsula. Castilian then became an influential language, and its written form was fixed in the thirteenth century. Divergence from the other Romance languages of Iberia, Catalan and Portuguese, continued. The next step was the conquest and exploration of the Americas by speakers of Castilian (Spanish) and Portuguese (Wolff, 1971, pp. 173–84).

In terms of numbers, English and Spanish are the most important of the Indo-European languages, with about three-quarters of a billion speakers. Hindi, Russian, Bengali, and Portugese are also numerically significant.

Other Language Families

The East Asian, also known as Sino-Tibetan, languages account for over a billion people. The principal language is Chinese, with over three-quarters of a billion speakers. None of the other East Asian languages, including Japanese, Cantonese, Korean, Wu, Vietnamese, and Thai, approach the importance of Chinese.

Non-Indo-European Indian languages of the Dravidian family (Telegu, Tamil, Kannada, and Malayalam) have about two hundred million speakers, while the Hamitic-Semitic family languages count some two hundred million. Other language families are numerically less important.

HISTORICAL GEOGRAPHY OF THE ENGLISH LANGUAGE

English, a member of the Indo-European language family, belongs to the Germanic subfamily. This means that English is more similar to the Germanic languages than to any others, a fact that may surprise students who have attempted to learn German (see Table 4–1). Although English is Germanic, it has other important linguistic roots shared by other Indo-European languages. In the mists of antiquity, peoples called the *Keltoi*, or Celts, occupied much of Europe north of the Alps, from Spain to the Danube, and it was recorded in the sixth century B.C. that most of the inhabitants of Britain spoke Celtic. Latin, the language of the Roman invaders, was added to the mix of languages some 2,000 years ago. Then, in the fifth century A.D., precursors of English were introduced by invading tribes from North Germany—the Jutes, Saxons, and Angles. (The dialect of the Angles was *aenglisc*, from which our word *English* comes.) The general term used to describe the language of the tribes is *Teutonic*. The Teutonic language contained only about 2,000 words, compared to about a quarter of a million in modern English. It evolved into the Germanic languages of today, including German, English, Dutch, Flemish, and the Scandinavian languages (except Finnish).

"Old English" appeared in writing in the ninth century. It was a very Germanic language, containing the sound indicated by an umlaut over vowels, as in *ü*, where the *u* is pronounced like the vowels in *food*. This sound remains in German, but English speakers have difficulty with it. Old English contained almost no Celtic, but some Latin; otherwise it was totally Germanic. Perhaps a quarter of the Old English vocabulary survives today.

Beginning at the end of the eighth century, Old English was strengthened by Danish raids on the east coast of England. Some 1,400 place names in northeastern England have Danish elements, such as the suffix *-by*, meaning village or farm (Derby); *-thorpe*, meaning hamlet (Scunthorpe); and *-toft*, meaning estate (Lowestoft). The Norman invaders in 1066 introduced new linguistic complexity as they spoke Flemish as well as French (Wolff, 1971, pp. 157–67). Further evolution has occurred over the last thousand years, illustrated by reference to fourteenth-century Middle English, in which the poet Chaucer wrote. A few lines from *The Nun's Priest's Tale* in the original and the modern equivalent will give you the general idea:

"Hoo!" quod the knyght, "good sire namoore of this;
  ("Ho!" cried the knight, "no more, sir, of this stuff!)
That ye han seyd is right y-nough, y-wis,
  (What you have said is certainly enough)
And muchel moore; for litel hevynesse
  (And more besides; a little heaviness)
Is right y-nough to muche folk, I gesse. . . ."
  (Will do for most of us, as I should guess. . . ")

Celtic, Latin, Teutonic, and French all contributed to the development of English. Today, the remaining Celtic languages have been pushed back into the western and northern hills and peninsulas of Britain and France—into Britanny, Wales, Ireland, and Scotland. Latin is a "dead" language in the sense that it is not used for day-to-day communication among significant numbers of people. To what extent have the various roots of English contributed to today's vocabulary? The simple sentence in Table 4.2 shows several origins. Old English (presumably mainly Teutonic in origin) dominates, but French and Latin are represented, along with a Celtic language, Gaelic.

MULTILINGUALISM

When several substantial fractions of the people in a nation adhere to different languages, the condition is known as *multilingualism*. There is no formula for determining when a nation is multilingual and when it is not. All nations are multilingual in the sense that they contain people whose native language is not the dominant one. The key question, however, is whether there are enough speakers of additional languages to constitute a significant social and political force. As we have already noted, language, religion, and ethnicity are often closely linked. When we refer to a group's speaking a particular language, there is a good chance that we are referring to an entire cultural complex involving acute group consciousness and pride, and very likely sensitive to outside attempts to modify that culture through control of language or religion.

Nationalistic objectives and those of individual linguistic groups may be at odds. Nationalism calls for national consciousness and identity, ease of communication, and cohesion among regions. Nationalism in this sense is a *centripetal* force, pulling toward the center, keeping the nation together. Multilingualism, on the other hand, fosters regional diversity and independence, acting in a *centrifugal* manner, tending to pull apart, or resist, pressures for a national perspective. At stake here is political power—multilingualism makes it harder for national leaders to manipulate nonconforming linguistic areas. While many nations are to some extent multilingual, the problems associated with multilingualism are illustrated vividly in the Soviet Union and India, which bear some linguistic resemblance to each other. Both have many languages, several language groups, and a *lingua franca*, or general communication language, that is Indo-European (Matthews, 1951, p. 1).

The Soviet Union

It is difficult to appreciate the role of language in the Soviet Union without first understanding the vast size of that country. The Soviet Union is 8.6 million miles^2 (22.3 million km^2) compared to the U.S. area of 3.7 million miles^2 (9.6 million km^2), or 2.3 times larger. The Soviet population is also substantially larger—270 million compared to 232 million in the U.S. These facts emphasize the isolation of Soviet regions and the vast distances involved in communication and transportation. When one realizes that Soviet

CHAPTER 4 GEOGRAPHY OF LANGUAGE

TABLE 4–2 Origins of Words in a Sentence

Sentence (Reading Down)	Original Word	Linguistic Origin
Cultural	cultūra	Latin
patterns	patron	French
cannot	cunnan (to know)	Old English
be	beon	Old English
	bin	German
	bi	Gaelic
understood	understandan	Old English
	with (against)	
without	withutan	Old English
	utan (outside)	
knowing	cnawan	Old English
	kna	Old Norse
	noscere	Latin
	gignoskein	Greek
something	sum	Old English
	thing, thinc	Old English
about	on butan	Old English
the	the	Old English
geography	gē (earth)	French
	graphē (description)	Latin
	graphein (to write)	Greek
of	of	Old English
	af	Dutch
	ab	German
	ab	Latin
	apo	Greek
language	language, langue	French
	lingua (the tongue)	Latin

territory is also, on the average, much farther north than U.S. territory, with correspondingly more severe winters, one sees that the problems of interaction are further compounded.

In this geographic context, we find about 200 languages divided into six groups—Uralian, Altaic, North Caucasian, South Caucasian, Indo-European (Slavic), and Paleoasiatic, shown in Figures 4–4 and 4–5. The first five language groups are genetically related, but the Paleoasiatic group, scattered over the far eastern U.S.S.R., combines both related and unrelated languages. The number of speakers of the

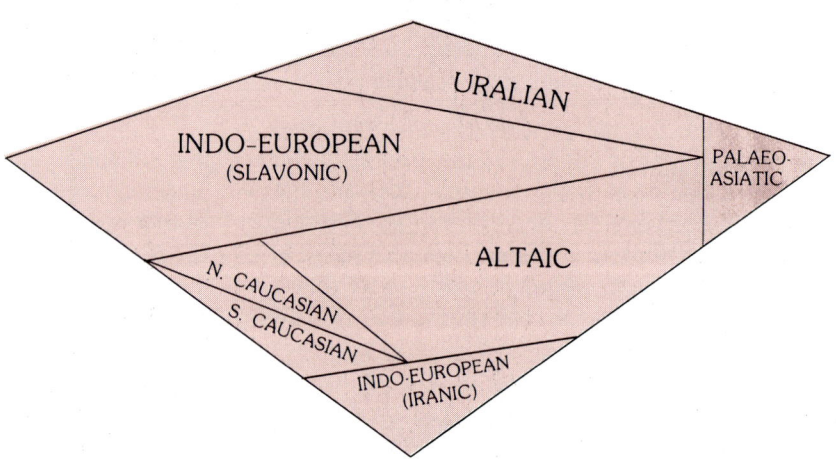

FIGURE 4–5 Diagrammatic map of language stocks in the U.S.S.R. (Adapted from W. K. Matthews, *Languages of the U.S.S.R.* [Cambridge: Cambridge University Press, 1951], Fig. 1, p. 2.

various languages varies from almost none (for example, the Altaic language *Orok*), to many millions, such as the Altaic *Kazakh* and the Indo-European *Russian* and *Ukranian* (Matthews, 1951).

Following the 1917 Revolution, the official attitude toward the national languages was tolerant. Language development was fostered, dictionaries were written, and the Latin alphabet was encouraged. This policy changed in the 1930s, when the role of the majority language (Russian) became more prominent at the expense of the minority languages. The Cyrillic alphabet was promoted at the expense of the Latin. The major minority languages were still maintained, however, in the media, official communications, grade school instruction, and technical documents. Complicating consideration of Soviet multilingualism is the extent to which contacts occur between Russian speakers and minority speakers, as well as the attitudes of minority members themselves toward their own ethnic groups. Some are extremely loyal to the ethnic group and its culture, while others are more willing to accept adoption of the majority ways—a process called *Russification*. Ethnic identification, including language, is particularly difficult to maintain when people move away from their own nations. City dwellers, even within their own nation, are more likely to be Russified than rural folk (Silver, 1974, pp. 101–2). The situation is further complicated by variations in attitudes among subgroups such as the young or the elderly.

In general, it seems that the role of the Russian language in Soviet life will become increasingly dominant (Figure 4–6). Indications of this probability include increasing attention to teaching Russian, the link between knowledge of Russian and career mobility, the publication of major works in Russian, and the tendency to create administrative units using economic rather than ethnic boundaries (Ornstein, 1968, pp. 134–37).

India

While India is less than one-seventh the size of the Soviet Union, it is nevertheless impressive in its linguistic diversity and sheer size of population. It is estimated that the 714 million people of India speak 1,652 different mother tongues. Most of these languages, however, are not numerically significant, and twelve regional languages are the mother tongues of about 95 percent of the people. Hindi is easily the most important, spoken by perhaps 20 percent. In order of number of speakers, the other major languages are Telegu, Marathi, Tamil, Bengali, Gujarati, Kannada, Malayalam, Oriya, Rajasthani, Punjabi, and Assamese. These major languages belong to the Indo-Aryan and Dravidian language families (Figure

FIGURE 4–6 Crowds on Nevsky Prospekt, Leningrad's main thoroughfare. (Photo by Charlotte Kahler.)

CHAPTER 4 GEOGRAPHY OF LANGUAGE

FIGURE 4-7 The linguistic geography of India. (From NATIONAL COMMUNICATION AND LANGUAGE POLICY IN INDIA by Baldev Raj Nayar. Copyright © 1969 Frederick A. Praeger, Inc. Reprinted by permission of Praeger Publishers.)

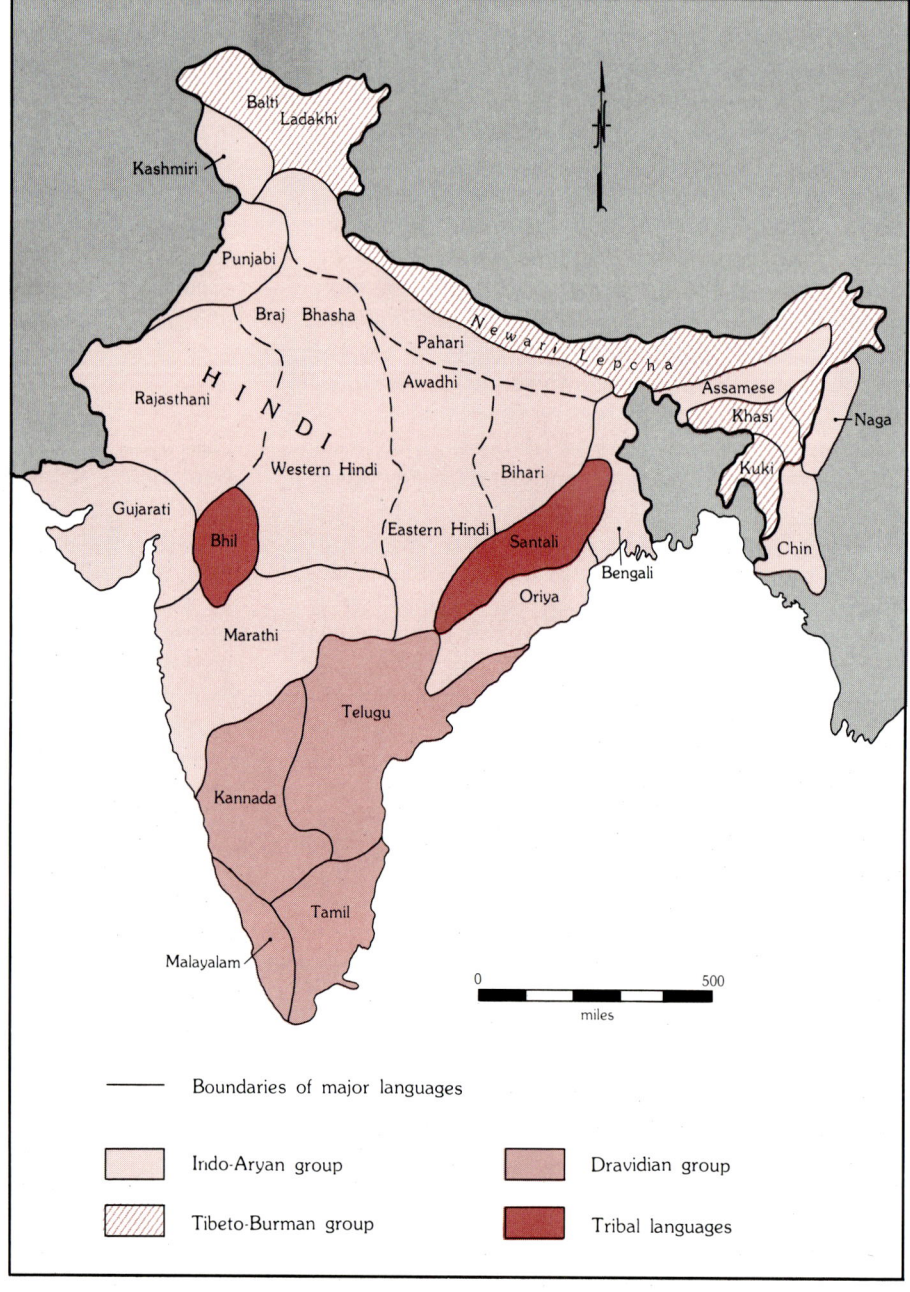

4-7). Both Indo-Aryan and Dravidian languages have been strongly influenced by Sanskrit, one of the original Indo-Aryan languages. Despite the existence of several major languages, India is in a sense mono- rather than multilingual, in that the overwhelming majority of people—perhaps 95 percent—are monolingual.

India's language problem is reinforced by the concentration of the principal languages into compact regions, which are themselves the states of a political federation. Each language has a rich history and unique written form, or script, so that language is often the focus of intense loyalty. This regional loyalty makes the strengthening of Indian national identity more difficult (Nayar, 1969, p. 27).

Beginning in 1837, during the period of British colonial rule in India, the English language became the official language of national administration, as well as the language of higher education. English became a *lingua franca,* or "link" language, among the regions of India, but only for a small elite. Of the major Indian languages, Hindi became dominant partly because it was the language of the open northern plains that facilitated human mobility and interaction, including the historical Aryan settlement of the region. Physical geography thus played a role in the development of language geography. Muslim dominance in India in the thirteenth century led to the imposition of Persian as the official language, which persisted until it was displaced by English in 1837. Over time, Hindi and Persian mingled, yielding a Persianized Hindi called Urdu. Urdu became the language of the Muslim elite.

As the Indian independence movement grew, so did the issue of the adoption of an official Indian language. The great leader Mahatma Gandhi wanted a language that would be easy to learn and usable in political, economic, and religious affairs. He selected Hindi as fitting these criteria. When India became independent in 1947, however, it proved difficult to formulate a national language policy. Although Hindi is more or less intelligible over much of India, it is feared that it could be used as an instrument of political control, in much the way that Russian is used in the exercise of centralized political control in the Soviet Union. In practice, India has two *lingua francas*, Hindi and English; English is used in higher education and diplomacy, for example, while Hindi is used much more broadly (Nayar, 1969, Chapter 2).

BILINGUALISM

The dividing line between bilingualism and multilingualism is fuzzy, to say the least. Often, what is described as multi- or bilingualism may be little more than pluralism, the existence of multiple languages. Although many languages may exist side-by-side, few people may speak more than one. Bilingualism is distinguished from multilingualism by emphasis on two languages. We will consider two examples: Canada (English and French) and Belgium (Walloon and Flemish).

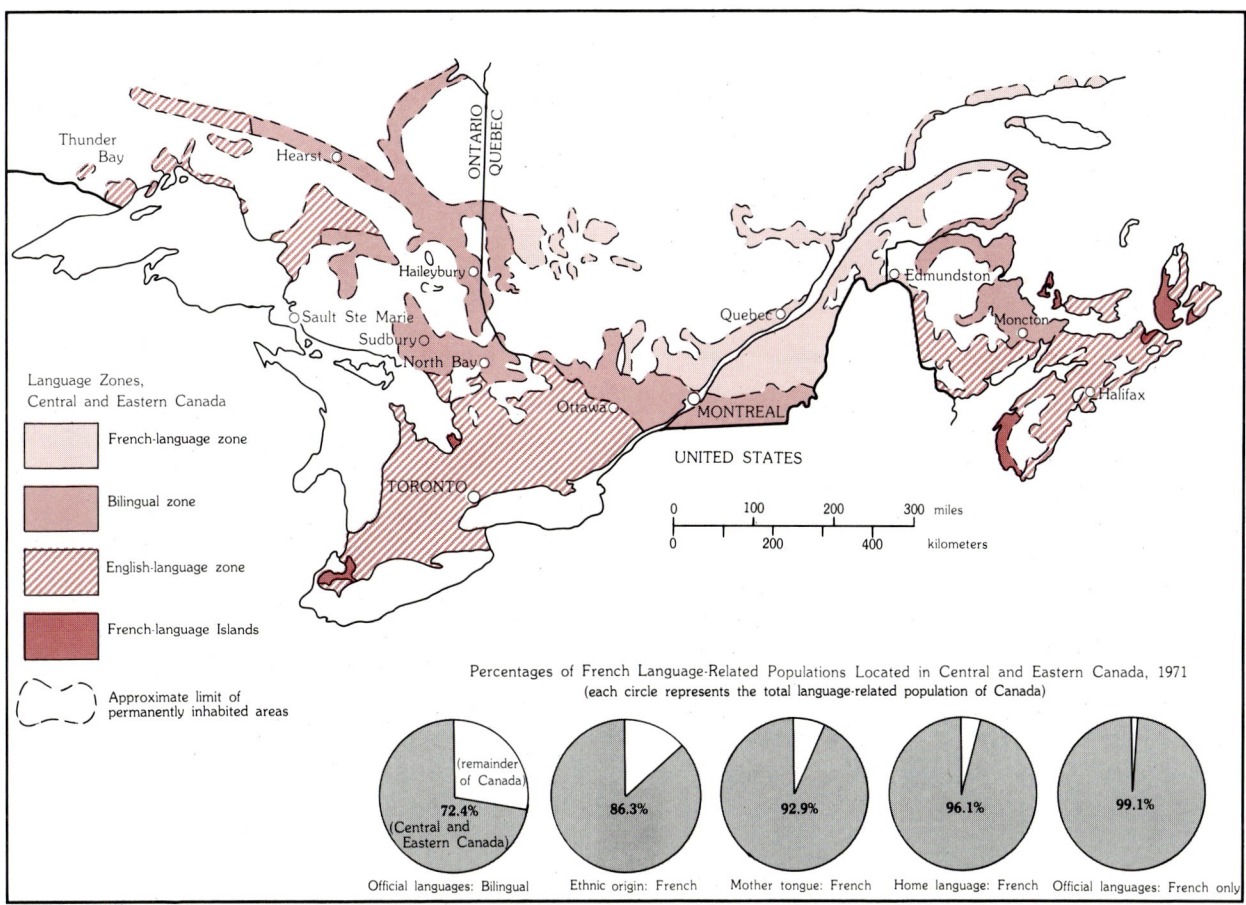

FIGURE 4–8 Language zones of French language population, Central and Eastern Canada, 1971. (From D. G. Cartwright, "The Designation of Bilingual Districts in Canada Through Linguistic and Spatial Analysis," *Tijdschrift voor Economische en Sociale Geografie*, 68 [1], 1977:16–29.)

FIGURE 4–9 Canada is a bilingual country; both English and French are official government languages. (Photo by Sybil Shelton, © Peter Arnold, Inc.)

Canada is described officially as a bilingual country, but one geographer suggests that it is really divided into two separate regions, each with its own language (Barrett, 1975, p. 125). The French-speaking province of Quebec and the rest of the country are merged via a linguistic "shatter zone," or bilingual belt (Figure 4–8). Canada became formally bilingual in 1969 with passage of the Official Languages Act, which declared English and French official languages for parliamentary and Canadian government use (Figure 4–9). The act also established procedures for setting up bilingual districts, to be reviewed after each population census (Cartwright, 1977). Bilingualism in Canada varies according to locational and demographic factors. Urban residents are about twice as likely as those in rural areas to be bilingual. In recent decades, people with English as their mother tongue have become more bilingual (that is, more able to speak French), while bilingualism has declined among those of the French mother tongue. The extent of bilingualism is affected in subtle ways by sex roles and occupational structure. As French-speaking women have increased their participation in the labor force, opportunities and pressures favoring bilingualism have increased. Although the French speakers are more bilingual overall, people with English as their mother tongue have become more bilingual (Lieberson, 1970, Chapter 4).

French is gradually losing ground as a Canadian language, however, declining from 28.08 percent of the total population in 1961 to 26.86 in 1971. (There was an absolute increase in the size of the French mother-tongue population, from 5.1 million to 5.8 million, but this was not enough to offset a proportionately larger increase in the English group.) The relative decline of French has been attributed to a rapid drop in the birthrate in Quebec province. If current trends continue, the role of French will erode further, even in Quebec, which is presently 80 percent French (Barrett, 1975).

Belgium is dominated by Dutch (Flemish) in Flanders in the north and French (Walloon) in Wallonia in the south. Flemish and Walloon are the official languages; however, a 1963 law established four linguistic regions—French, Dutch, German, and the capital city of Brussels, located in the Flemish area, but with officially bilingual status. About 55 percent of the population speak Dutch, 44 percent French, but less than 1 percent German (Figure 4–10).

Emotions between the language provinces run high. In the nineteenth century, French was used in government, the courts, and education. The Flemish reacted by starting a nationalist movement. Political

PLACE NAMES

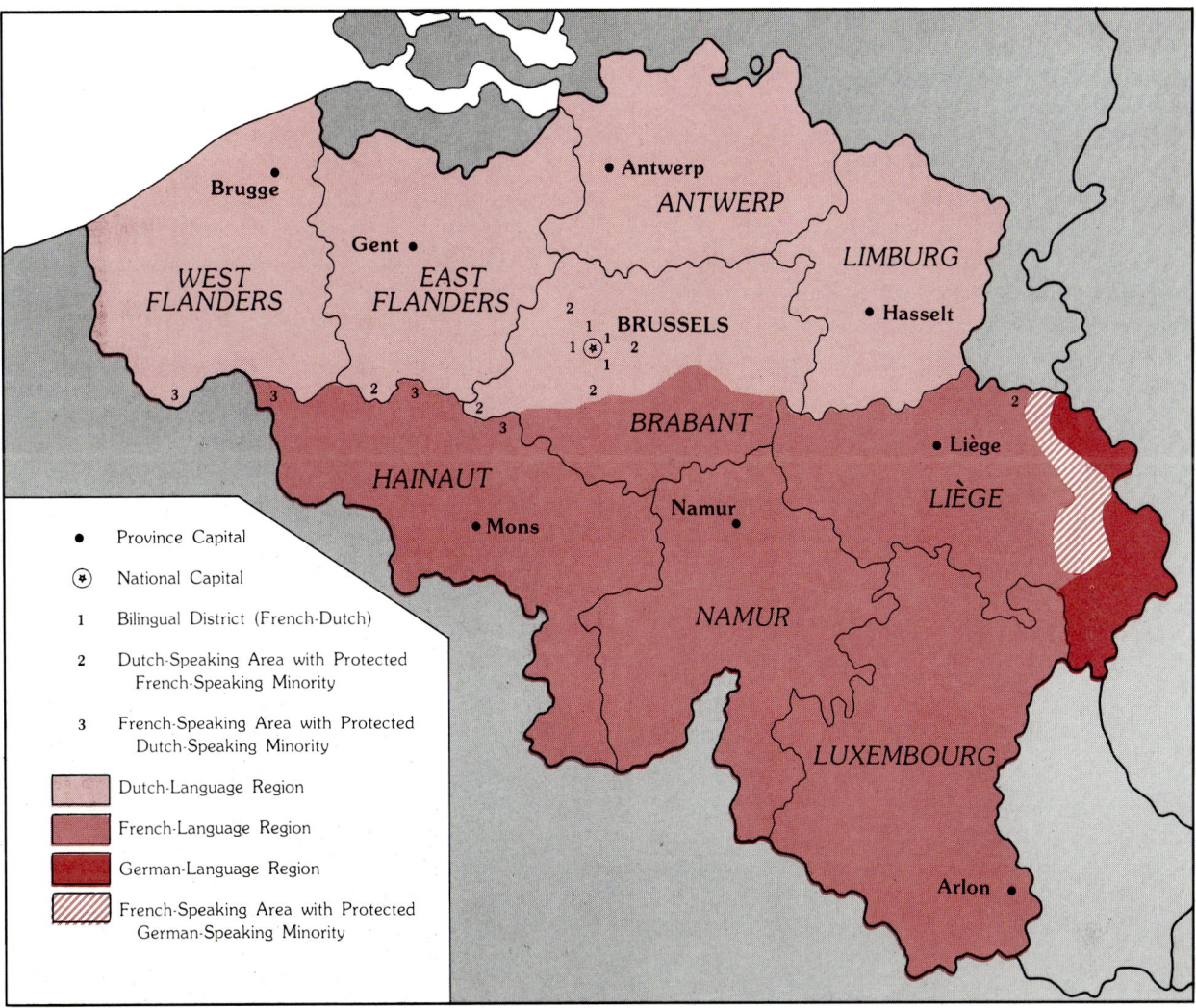

FIGURE 4–10 Linguistic areas in Belgium. (From Eugene K. Keefe et al., *Area Handbook for Belgium* [Washington, D.C.: U.S. Government Printing Office, 1974], p. 77.)

polarization has continued to the present, with Flanders as the stronghold of conservatism, and Wallonia of socialism. In the 1970s, the trend was toward regional autonomy, as the linguistic areas sought greater independence.

Canada and Belgium are representative of the kinds of problems that occur in bilingual nations. Conflict between linguistic groups is really part of a broader struggle for dominance by a particular culture, symbolized by language. Similar emotions are often expressed through the medium of religion.

PLACE NAMES

Most of us take place names for granted, but they often have a good deal to tell us about those who settled in an area. The frequent repetition of Old World place names in the New World suggests that migrants have an emotional attachment to the places they have left behind, and, if the opportunity arises, will use those names again to name settlements or features of the natural landscape. The seemingly simple process of moving into an area and naming places is in reality, however, much more complex. In North America, the native peoples were overwhelmed by masses of immigrants, and we often forget that the Indian population already had names for natural features and settlements—names that were sometimes retained but more often swept away by the newcomers who did not understand Indian languages.

The naming of places was not without conflict, as groups vied with each other to attach their pre-

77

ferred name to a place. Most place names in the New World are a recent phenomenon associated with the huge immigrations of the last couple of hundred years. In the Old World, place names usually have much deeper roots. Many European names, for example, can be traced to the Roman conquests, although the original Roman names have often changed or been abandoned altogether over the centuries since Roman occupation. The modern names of three early Roman capitals in Britain—Canterbury, Chelmsford, and St. Albans—are unlike their Roman names—*Durovernum Cantiacorum, Caesaromagnus,* and *Verulamium*. On the other hand, the name London is a recognizable derivative of the Roman *Londinium Augusta,* as are Valencia *(Valencia Edetanorum)* and Minorca *(Minorca insula)* in Spain.

Place names, or *toponyms,* often have two parts: the general, or *generic,* and the specific, or *genetic.* The generic part tells us what kind of feature is being named—city, village, lake, hill, creek, river. The genetic part tells the origin of that particular name. New York City implies that there was an "old" York (which there was, in northeast England). Washington, D.C., indicates that the District was named in

BODY (BAWDY?) LANGUAGE

Not all communication is verbal or written. Considerable numbers of messages are transmitted by means of body movements and hand signals. Different cultures and even subgroups within the same culture may place different meanings on similar movements or signs. In a book called *Gestures,* Morris and his co-workers (1979) have catalogued twenty key gestures for which they gathered data in forty locations across Europe. The gestures include the *fingertips kiss, cheek screw, forearm jerk, chin flick, ear touch,* and *palmback V-sign.* Some of the gestures are widely used in the United States, but at least one American gesture, the obscene raised middle finger, was not included among the twenty regarded as more important in Europe. This suggests that the U.S. has some signs that are unique and others that are imported or modified from other sources. Interestingly, gestures, like toponyms, have generic and genetic, or specific, meanings. The *temple tap,* for example—the touching of the temple lightly with the forefinger—has two opposite generic meanings: craziness and intelligence. Examples of specific meanings might be: "Fool!" or "Brilliant!" The *cheek screw,* involving rotating the forefinger against the center of the cheek, may mean "good," "crafty," "crazy," or "effeminate." The map below shows how the geography of gestures may vary. As the map shows, the meaning "good" is common in Italy, but more or less unknown elsewhere in Europe. The meaning "crafty" was also unique to Italy. "Crazy" was found only in Germany, and "effeminate" was a Spanish interpretation. Like other cultural elements, gestures have boundaries based on political, topographic, cultural, linguistic, and religious obstacles that prevent diffusion (Morris et al., 1979, pp. 247–65).

commemoration of George Washington. One researcher suggests that place names may be classified into several types, including names that are *descriptive, possessive, commemorative, euphemistic,* and *manufactured* (Stewart, 1954). Examples of descriptive names include Hot Springs, Arkansas; Great Sandy Desert, Oregon; Great Divide Basin, Wyoming; and Quartzite, Arizona. Possessive names indicate ownership or association of individuals with places. Most Finnish place names in Minnesota, for example, are possessive, such as Paavola Creek, Heikkala Lake, and Kaunonen Lake (Kaups, 1966, p. 387). Commemorative names incorporate the names of people or places, such as New York, New Orleans, Baltimore (Lord Baltimore), Pennsylvania (William Penn), and many saints' names where Hispanic influence is strong in the southwestern and western U.S. (San Francisco, Santa Barbara, San Diego). Euphemistic names are designed to attract settlers with the use of optimistic or positive words, such as Paradise, California; Hopedale, Massachusetts; Sun City, Arizona, and Greenbelt, Maryland. Manufactured names are made up to suit some particular pupose; for example, El Segundo ("the second"), California,

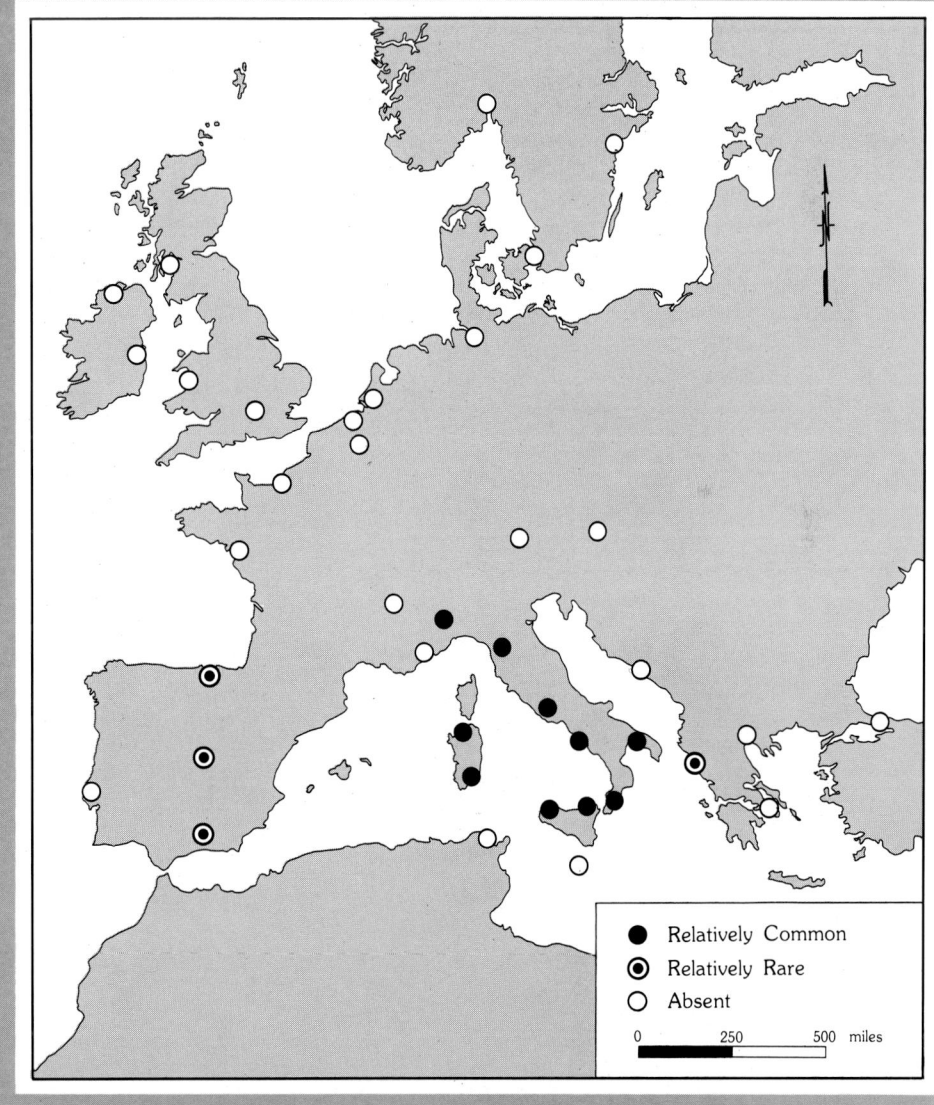

The geography of the cheek screw. (From Desmond Morris, Peter Collett, Peter Marsh, and Marie O'Shaughnessy, *Gestures: Their Origins and Distribution* [New York: Stein and Day, 1979]. Reprinted by permission.)

was so named by the Standard Oil Company when it located its second California refinery there in 1917. To these types, we may lightheartedly add *onomatopoeic* (Whizbang, Oklahoma), *exclamatory* (Eureka! California), and *biokinetic* (Bug Tussle, Oklahoma) names.

While regional dominance of toponyms of English, Spanish, French, or other linguistic origins are predictable in various American regions, Zelinsky (1967) draws attention to the phenomenon of classical place names in the U.S., an oddity in view of the fact that there was no direct connection between the classical world and North America. Classical elements are embedded in American culture in personal names, architectural styles, and in other ways. No other region of the world colonized by Europeans, however, has anything approaching the classical influence of toponyms found in America.

Zelinsky recognized three related processes in the spread of classical place names: expansion diffusion over short distances (see Chapter 8); transfer of the idea of classical place names with pioneer settlers; and the more or less instantaneous acceptance of the idea via rapid communication among members of the elite. Some 424 different names were found to have been applied to 3,095 places. Overall it is estimated that about two percent of American political units, such as townships or counties, and settlements had classical names (Figure 4–11).

Place names, like other aspects of human culture, are temporary labels applied to the physical and human landscape by dominant culture groups. The rapid erasure of Indian toponyms in North America illustrates how quickly place names may change under new conditions. In Canada (which actually is an Indian name, derived from the Huron-Iroquois *kanata*), even English translations of Indian names were not always acceptable. Thus Regina, the capital of Saskatchewan, commemorated Queen Victoria, because the translation of the Sioux *waskana* or Cree

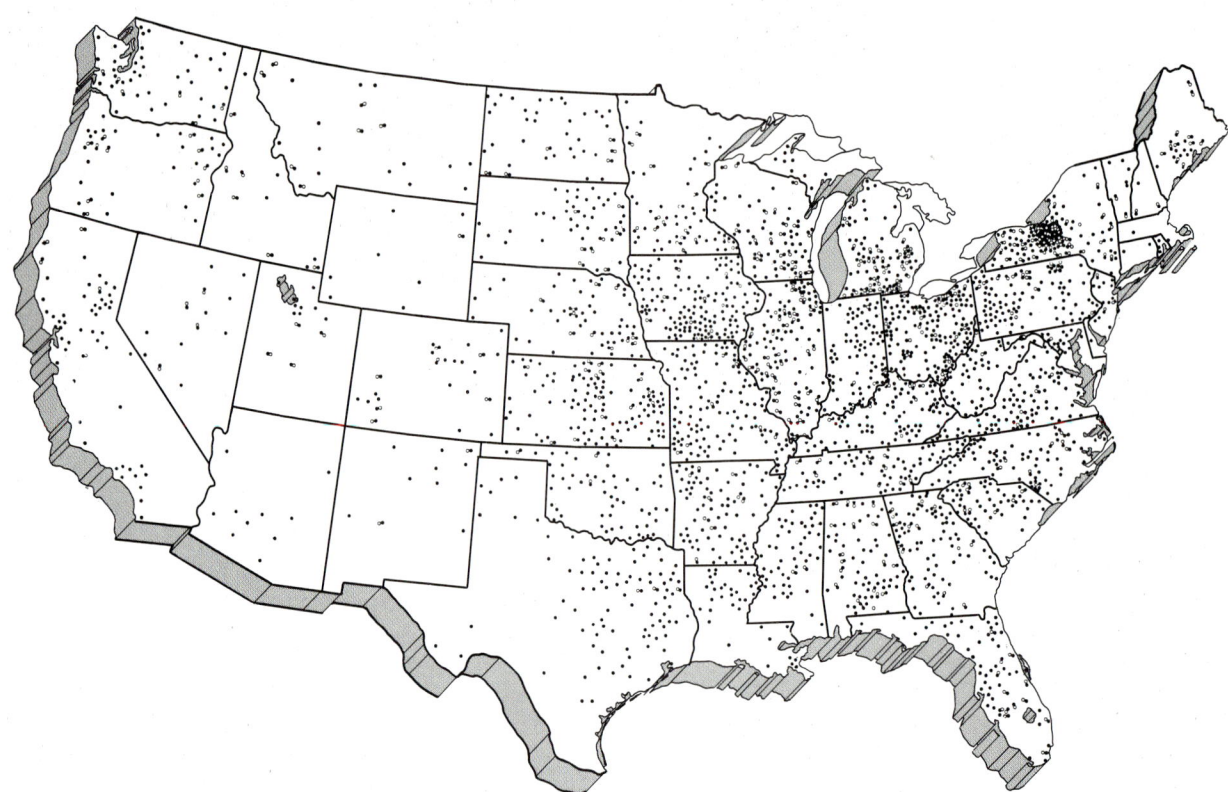

- Independant Adoption
- Local Duplication

FIGURE 4–11 Adoption of classical town names in the U.S., 1880–1890. (From Wilbur Zelinsky, "Classical Town Names in the U.S.," *Geographical Review,* 57 [1967], p. 483.)

oskunew names as "Pile of Bones" offended the sensibilities of immigrants. Strange-sounding Medicine Hat, another translation, survived (Rayburn, 1967, pp. 204–6).

Whether or not we recognize the cultural influences associated with place names depends to a considerable extent on the scale at which we view the landscape. If we look at a small-scale atlas map, we may entirely miss cultural imprints that appear only on large-scale maps. Kaups illustrated this phenomenon in Minnesota, where no counties, cities, or larger lakes and rivers have Finnish names; Finnish names are found entirely at the local level (Kaups, 1966, p. 397). The importance of studying place names lies in their role as an expression of dynamic cultural processes.

CONCLUSION

Language is the most fundamental element of culture, acting as a medium of communication and a repository of information. Geographic variations in languages are striking. People who may appear quite similar physically and in dress, and who may live quite close to each other, may not understand one word of each other's language and may therefore be almost entirely unable to communicate. Language is emotionally charged, for it is the medium of expression of literature and of patriotic feelings in the form of pledges of allegiance, oaths of loyalty, college songs, and national anthems. The association between language and ethnic or national pride is reinforced by the adaptation of languages to specific cultures, through the development of special words or phrases to meet the needs and preferences of the group. These words and phrases may not have an equivalent in any other language.

Language is an instant basis for recognizing other people with a common or related cultural heritage. For small ethnic groups with a unique language, that tongue becomes an identity symbol and may be the focus of struggles to win recognition of the language in schools, government, and business affairs. Language may become synonymous with nationalism, and the fortunes of a particular language will rise and fall with the political power of a particular ethnic group. Major languages, such as English and Spanish, maintain or enhance their importance through association with aggressive, expanding cultures.

Population increase among speakers makes a language more influential, and colonization spreads language with the rest of the invading culture. Languages also maintain their usefulness by accommodating technological change through the invention of new vocabularies or the adaptation of existing words, such as "chip" and "memory" in the case of computerese. Languages, like other elements of culture (including nonverbal language) are constantly changing. As Middle Eastern oil and Japanese electronic and other products have assumed importance, so has the need to know Arabic and Japanese increased. Perhaps, in future centuries, the great languages of today will fade to obscurity, or one may emerge as a world *lingua franca*.

KEY WORDS

bilingualism
centrifugal
centripetal
dialect
generic
genetic
gestures
grammar
Indo-European
isogloss

language
lexicon
lingua franca
linguistics
multilingualism
phonology
Russification
toponym
vocabulary

REFERENCES

ALLEN, HAROLD B. *The Linguistic Atlas of the Upper Midwest,* Vol. 1. Minneapolis: University of Minnesota Press, 1973.

BARRETT, F. A. "The Relative Decline of the French Language in Canada: A Preliminary Report." *Geography* 60 (1975): 125–29.

CARTWRIGHT, D. G. "The Designation of Bilingual Districts in Canada Through Linguistic and Spatial Analysis." *Tijdschrift voor Econ. en Soc. Geografie* 68 (1977): 16–29.

DE CARVALHO, C. M. DELGADO, "The Geography of Languages." In Philip L. Wagner and Marvin W. Mikesell, *Readings in Cultural Geography.* Chicago: University of Chicago Press, 1962.

GREENBURG, JOSEPH H. *Anthropological Linguistics.* New York: Random House, 1968.

KAUPS, MATTI. "Finnish Place Names in Minnesota: A Study in Cultural Transfer." *Geographical Review* 56 (1966): 377–97.

KURATH, HANS. *Studies in Area Linguistics.* Bloomington, Ind.: Indiana University Press, 1972.

KURATH, HANS. "The Origin of the Dialectical Differences in Spoken American English." In Juanita V. Williamson and Virginia M. Burke, eds., *A Various Language: Perspectives on American Dialects.* New York: Holt, Rinehart and Winston, 1971.

LIEBERSON, STANLEY. *Language and Ethnic Relations in Canada.* New York: John Wiley, 1970.

MATTHEWS, W. K. *Languages of the U.S.S.R.* Cambridge: Cambridge University Press, 1951.

MARCKWARDT, ALBERT H. *American English.* New York: Oxford University Press, 1958.

MORRIS, DESMOND, PETER COLLETT, PETER MARSH, and MARIE O'SHAUGHNESSY. *Gestures: Their Origins and Distribution.* New York: Stein and Day, 1979.

NAYAR, BALDEV RAJ. *National Communication and Language Policy in India.* New York: Frederick A. Praeger, 1969.

ORNSTEIN, JACOB. "Soviet Language Policy: Continuity and Change." In Erich Goldhagen, ed., *Ethnic Minorities in the Soviet Union.* New York: Frederick A. Praeger, 1968.

RAYBURN, J. A. "Geographical Names of Amerindian Origin in Canada." *Names* 15 (1967): 203–15.

SILVER, BRIAN. "The Impact of Urbanization and Geographical Dispersion on the Linguistic Russification of Soviet Nationalities." *Demography* 11 (1974): 89–103.

SPIELMAN, RICHARD S., ERNEST C. MIGLIAZZA, and JAMES V. NEEL. "Regional Linguistic and Genetic Differences Among Yanomama Indians." *Science* 184 (1974): 637–44.

STEWART, GEORGE R. "A Classification of Place Names." *Names* 2 (1954): 1–13.

WOLFF, PHILIPPE. *Western Languages A.D. 100–1500.* New York: McGraw-Hill, 1971.

ZELINSKY, WILBUR. "Classical Town Names in the United States: The Historical Geography of an American Idea." *Geographical Review* 57 (1967): 463–95.

5
Geography and Religion

Religion is an important aspect of human psychology and behavior. Religious beliefs can influence the way people speak, dress, eat, educate their young, plan their families, arrange time, punish criminals, and cultivate land—to cite but a few examples. In a more general sense, religion may affect people's world view—how they perceive their relationship to other peoples and to the earth environment. This chapter outlines some of the principal themes in the relationship between religion and human geography.

WHAT IS RELIGION?

In the narrowest view of religion, individuals take the position that the only true religion is their own. This view is the essence of *bigotry*, utter intolerance for any belief that is not one's own. A broader view typically contains several key concepts. Religion includes a set of *beliefs* which may explain the *universe* in terms of powers of a supernatural being or a god. Religion frequently involves *rituals*, and may prescribe a *moral code* to guide the behavior of its adherents. The broadest or most general view of what constitutes religion, a kind of "minimum definition," is that of *belief in spiritual beings* (Tylor, 1958).

Why do religions exist? What purposes do they serve? There is little doubt that early *homo sapiens* developed a powerful curiosity about the meanings of life and death and events. Why were there war, famine, flood, plague? Could such events be attributed to a hidden force? One view holds that religion was a product of fear and the need for self-preservation. Others think religion arose from magic, while some think religion and magic arose simultaneously. Yet another perspective regards religion as having arisen instantaneously, at the creation (Braden,

WHAT IS RELIGION?
TRADITIONAL RELIGION
THE MAJOR RELIGIONS
RELIGION AND SPATIAL PROCESSES

Modern monuments to Christianity: Crystal Cathedral at Garden Grove, California, and City of Hope Medical Center at Oral Roberts University, Tulsa, Oklahoma.

1954). Scholarly interpretations, however, generally adhere to the evolutionary perspective—that religions developed differently in different places at different times. Some had a single god; some had many. Others had no god as such, but were still based on belief in spiritual beings.

It is no exaggeration to say that humans are incurably religious, in the sense that every society, no matter how ancient or, in Western eyes, primitive, reveals evidence of some kind of religious activity. In spite of the rise of "rational" science, religion remains an extremely powerful force in American society and elsewhere in the world. One has only to consider the debate surrounding the proposed Constitutional amendment (introduced in 1982) to encourage voluntary prayer in schools in America, to appreciate how passions can be aroused by religious issues.

TRADITIONAL RELIGION

Several characteristics distinguish a traditional from a modern religion, including:

- Belief in powers or spirits and in people's ability to communicate with the spirits and affect their attitudes toward people
- Inclusion of magic, ceremony, and ritual in religious affairs
- The concept of life after death
- The concepts of *mana, tabu,* and *fetish* (Braden, 1954, pp. 29–30; Bradley, 1963, pp. 13–15)

Traditional and modern religions clearly overlap. References to the "the Holy Spirit" or the "the Holy Ghost" are prominent in Christian liturgy, as is the concept of "life after death." Ritual, too, is prominent in modern religion. Traditional and modern religions also have their professionals, whether called shamans, medicine men, priests, or pastors. The difference between traditional and modern religions is in part a matter of degree of emphasis on supernatural explanations for everyday phenomena. Modern society, for example, explains weather events in terms of the science of meteorology, while a traditional society would be more likely to find explanation in *mana*, a universal force that causes things to happen. Mana (a Melanesian word) would be seen as the cause of earthquakes, fire, flood, disease. Such phenomena are seen to have lives of their own. Scientific explanation and remedies are not available, so mana must be controlled. One way of doing this is through the use of *tabu* (usually *taboo* today), a Polynesian word denoting some object or action that is to be avoided. A person might bathe in a particular stream and then die; the stream might then be designated as tabu. A group might assemble in a particular place to appeal to the spirits for an end to floods; more floods follow, so the place might become tabu. A related concept is the *fetish* (based on the Portugese word *feitico* meaning "made" or "created"). Fetishism referred to the belief that spirits could be controlled. Perhaps a spirit could be persuaded to reside in a rabbit's foot or cow's horn. The modern equivalent might be a charm bracelet. The general purpose of the fetish was to ward off evil. Today, a fetish has come to refer to any idea or object that is the subject of intense devotion—"she made a fetish of tennis," or "for him, losing weight became a fetish." Various forms of *magic* have also been used in attempts to control mana.

Animism

Derived from the Latin word *anima* (soul), animism is the belief that material objects and animals, as well as people, have souls. The human soul is seen as a wispy, shadowy image of the individual, capable of moving from place to place and of life after death. Sleep is interpreted as the temporary departure of the soul; death occurs when the soul leaves permanently. It is thought that this concept developed, at least in part, from the interpretation of dreams in which we seem to visit other places. Since our material possessions may accompany us in our dreams, it is not unreasonable to assume that they also have souls or spirits that enable them to lead a dual existence (McDougall, 1911). There are many variations on the theme. In some societies, breath was considered synonymous with the soul. The Seminole Indians in Florida, for example, had a custom of holding a newborn infant over the mother's face if the mother died in childbirth, to receive her parting spirit (Tylor, 1958, p. 17).

Animistic rites associated with death have had disastrous consequences for some societies. Quite commonly, individual possessions would be buried with the dead so as to provide them with comfort in the afterlife. This idea extended to warriors' horses with the Pawnee and Comanche Indians, and in Patagonia in southern Argentina, it was customary to bury with the dead *all* their ornaments and weapons and *all* livestock, making it virtually impossible for wealth to accumulate (Tylor, 1958, p. 56).

Where is animism found in the world today? As Figure 5.1 shows, traditional religions, including animism, are practiced for the most part in relatively in-

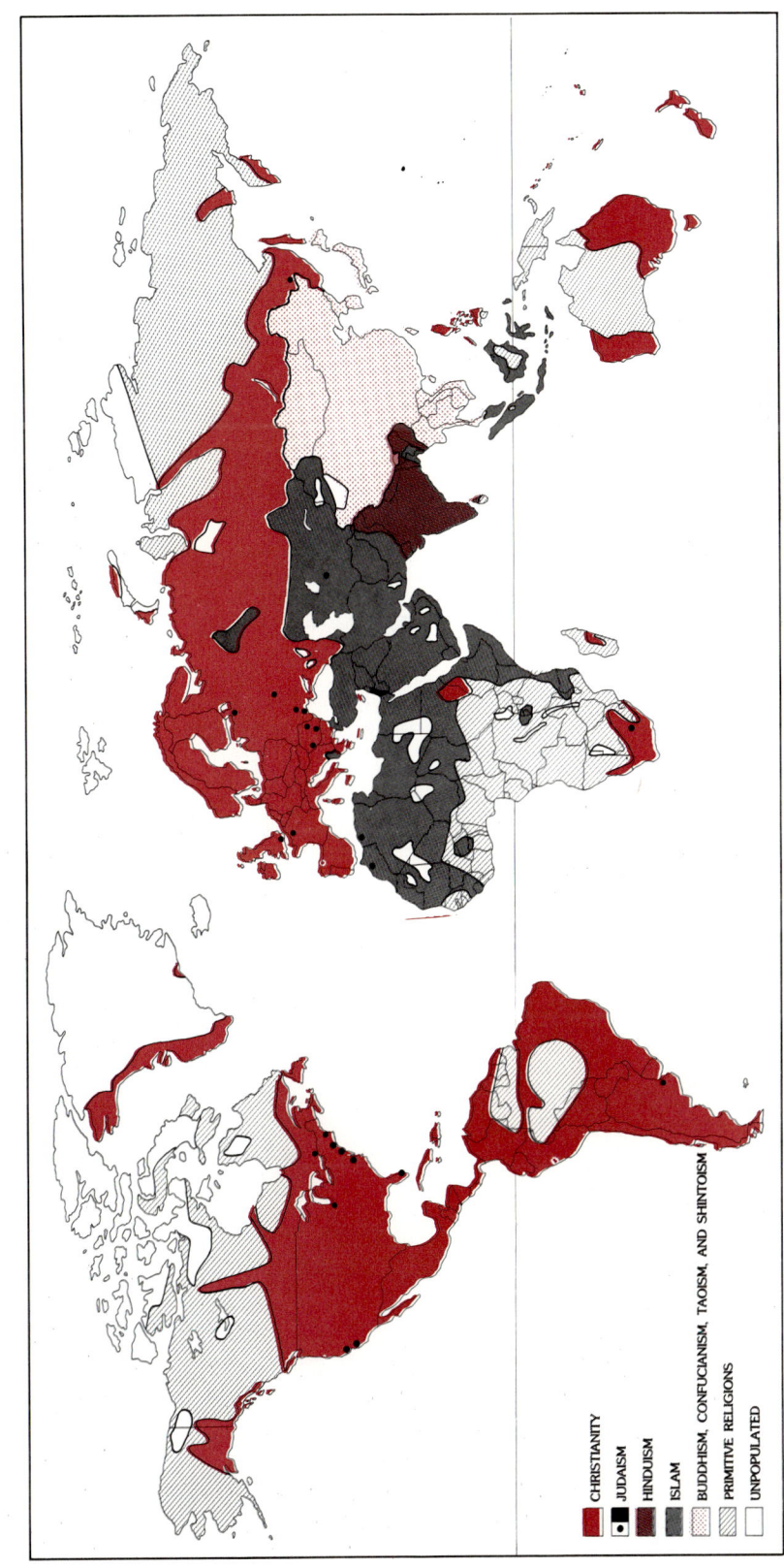

FIGURE 5–1 World pattern of religions. (From R. Harper and T. Schmudde, *Between Two Worlds: An Introduction to Geography* [Houghton-Mifflin, 1978]).

accessible continental interiors, and in the northern margins of North America, and in Asia. Traditional religions, sometimes called "primitive," are generally outside the urban and metropolitan realms. They are the religions of isolated, largely subsistence-based peoples who are cut off from participation in market economies and from contact with "outside" cultures. If they were to have contact with other cultures, it might include aggressive proselytizing by missionaries. Figure 5–2 shows a *shaman,* or medicine man, invoking the supernatural.

A word of caution about the term "primitive" in this context: it is tempting to interpret the word to mean "inferior." Such an interpretation, however, is *ethnocentric*—rooted in the belief that our own culture is inherently superior. Primitive religions are primitive in the sense that they are relatively unsophisticated. We cannot claim that the adherents of so-called primitive religions obtain any less satisfaction or usefulness from their religious practices than people belonging to more sophisticated faiths. Indeed, when we look at the extent to which superstition and the occult are given credibility in the modern world, we see quite a widespread tendency for people to cling to primitive beliefs. People may hold primitive beliefs even while they concurrently adhere to an "advanced" religion.

Considering traditional or primitive religions helps us understand the origins of religious beliefs.

As we consider the geography of several major world religions, we must realize that they are regarded as major because of either their large number of adherents or their critical role in the development of other religions. We cannot overlook the fact that the development of today's major religions owes a debt to earlier religious culture. Whether we consider the evidence of religious observances among Neanderthal people a hundred thousand years ago, or the *polytheism* (belief in many gods) of ancient Egypt, Greece, and Rome, a cumulative heritage leaves its marks on contemporary religions. Geographical processes, particularly migrations, diffusion of religious ideas, and the relationship between people and the physical environment, have played an important role in this cultural imprinting. The environment has often served as a source of religious belief, as when people sought explanations for the regularity of bountiful floods on the Nile or relief from devastating natural hazards.

Zoroastrianism: Example of a Predecessor

To understand the evolution of Judaism and Christianity, it is useful to refer to the faith called *Zoroastrianism,* which had a profound influence on religions that developed later. Founded in Iran by Zoroaster around 500 B.C., Zoroastrianism has com-

FIGURE 5–2 A *shaman* conducts a primitive religious ceremony. (Photo by Jacques Jangoux, © Peter Arnold, Inc.)

pletely disappeared from Iran (Persia) and survives with a few adherents called Parsis (Persians), most of whom live in the Bombay area in India.

Iran was inhabited by one of two streams of Indo-European peoples (Aryans) who had separated around the Caspian Sea about 2,000 B.C. One stream occupied an area including parts of Iran; the other went on to India. This geographical separation led to the development of distinctly different cultures, including religions (Noss, 1974, pp. 336–37).

In Iran, Zoroaster was disgusted by the barbaric behavior of nomads, and taught that men should practice sedentary farming. Thus religion had a direct impact on the geography of land use. Zoroastrianism was diffused partly through Zoroaster's success in converting an Aryan king, Vishtaspa, in eastern Iran. Vishtaspa energetically spread the faith, and his support led, over a period of about twenty years, to the firm establishment of Zoroastrianism in Iran. Regional lifestyle, featuring the conflict between fighting nomads and peaceful farmers, is reflected in the deities of Zoroastrianism. Ahura Mazda, the chief deity, was the force for good; Angra Mainyu, the god of evil, was comparable to the Christian concept of the devil. The unique appeal of Zoroastrianism was its monotheism (based on one principal god) and its incorporation of moral law coming from that god (Noss, 1974, p. 340).

Following its successful establishment in Iran, Zoroastrianism diffused throughout southwest Asia, helped by the military conquests of believers such as Darius and Xerxes. Indeed, had it not been for the defeat of Xerxes on the Mediterranean island of Cyprus, Zoroastrianism might be a major world religion today. The territorial influence of the Persians shrank in the fifth and fourth centuries B.C., when Alexander the Great overthrew them. Zoroastrianism in some form persisted until Moslem conquest in 651 A.D., when the last of the Persian Sassanid rulers was defeated. This defeat initiated outmigration by Zoroastrians, who moved, in stages, to India, where they were tolerated by the Hindus. Those who remained in Iran were persecuted historically (Noss, 1974, pp. 344–53), and are presumably in difficulties again in the 1980s given the fundamentalist Moslem regime in Iran.

Although numerically minuscule today, Zoroastrianism had a profound influence on Judaism and hence on Christianity. It is thought that the Judaic concepts of Paradise and Hell, and the Christian concept of Resurrection came from Zoroaster, as did all of Jewish *eschatology*, or doctrines relating to death and afterlife (al Fārūqī and Sopher, 1974, p. 137).

THE MAJOR RELIGIONS

Judaism

Like Zoroastrianism, Judaism also developed in the source region of urban society—southwest Asia. The Holy Land of Judaism was Palestine, located in an area of constant conflict and cultural exchange. The location of Palestine has had a good deal to do with its historical experience. Egypt was to the southwest, with its population concentrated in the Nile Delta. Egyptian military excursions to the east involved crossing the Sinai Desert and Palestine. To the east of Palestine lay the productive valleys of the Tigris and Euphrates Rivers, the core of the Fertile Crescent, also known as Mesopotamia ("the land between the rivers"). This region attracted invaders and also produced conquests, some of which were directed toward Palestine. To the north of Palestine were Syria, Lebanon, and Asia Minor, or Anatolia, today the nation of Turkey. This region was the home of the Hittite kingdom, which could threaten Palestine. Activities in the three regions—Egypt, Mesopotamia, and Asia Minor—had a profound impact on Palestine, which was likely to act as a buffer in good times and to be overrun in bad. The name *Palestine* was derived from its being the home of the Philistine people. This name, originally applied to the southwestern part of the region, became the label for what the Old Testament refers to as "the land of Canaan" or "the land of Israel" (Anderson, 1966, pp. 7–8).

Just as some roots of Judaism are found in Zoroastrianism, others can be traced to nomadic Arab religions, including: honoring stones thought to signify deities, sacrificing animals and pouring their blood over stones, and a preference for animal sacrifices rather than vegetable offerings. These elements were found in early Judaism, which was tribal and polytheistic (Braden, 1954, p. 164).

Around 2000 B.C., Semitic tribes, the Hebrews (derived from *Ibri*, meaning "to cross over," suggesting nomadism), including Abraham as one of their leaders, established themselves in Palestine, probably pushed from the east by the threat of invasion. These peoples also called themselves *Israelites*, based on a legend that the tribes had descended from one ancestor, Jacob, also known as *Israel* (Bradley, 1963, p. 25). Palestine was selected because Abraham was promised a permanent home there by El-Shaddai, a god in whom he put all his faith. Threatened by famine, the Hebrews migrated southwest to Egypt about 1600 B.C. Egypt was a reasonably hospitable place for the Israelites until about 1300 B.C. when the pharoah Ramses II enslaved them and forced them to help build public works. This enslavement terminated with another migration, the Exodus, led by Moses, at a time when the Egyptians were too distracted by other threats to devote adequate manpower to stopping the Israelites. Moses was responsible for changing Judaism from polytheism to monotheism—the idea that there is one god, Yahweh, apparently synonymous with Abraham's El-Shaddai. Tradition has it that the Exodus led to Mt. Sinai where Moses obtained the moral code, known to us as the Ten Commandments, in communion with Yahweh. Then, again according to tradition, the Israelites wandered for forty years, and then invaded Canaan (Palestine).

Through a drawn-out and complex process of conquest and immigration, the Israelites eventually dominated Canaan, beginning a phase of interaction between religion and physical and human environments. The Canaanites were well-established farmers, while the Israelites were seminomadic. In northern Palestine, more suited to agriculture, the Israelites tended to adopt some Canaanite religious practices. In the south, however, more suited to pastoralism, Israelite shepherds had no need for the spirit lore of the farmers, and tended to cling to "pure" Judaism (Noss, 1974, p. 370; Anderson, 1966, p. 43). Thus Judaism came to be modified through the interaction between religious culture and regional physical geography.

The historical geography of Judaism has been characterized by persecution and migration. Nebuchadnezzar took Jerusalem in 597 B.C., and the destruction of the city was completed in another attack by the Babylonians in 586 B.C. The inhabitants of Jerusalem were deported in what has been called the *Babylonian Exile*. Later in the sixth century B.C., the Jews were able to return to Jerusalem, following Nebuchadnezzar's defeat by the Persians. It was during this Persian period that Judaism was influenced by Zoroastrianism. Greek and then Roman influence followed Persian, as Palestine was subjected to a continuing regional tug of war between rival powers. Friction between Romans and Jews led to war in 66 A.D., resulting in the out-migration of the Jewish people. This wave of migration was one of several referred to as the *Diaspora*, or dispersion, the forced spread of Judaism outside Palestine. The Diaspora came about mainly because the Jews were inflexible in their faith, and usually refused to compromise with the religions of neighboring groups, who often reacted by persecuting Jews.

In the Middle Ages, Jews were often treated more tolerantly by Muslims than by Christians. Jews would not accept the Christian claim that Jesus was the Messiah, and thousands of Jews died rather than repudiate their faith during the Crusades. Relationships with Muslims were generally more friendly, partly because of cultural and ethnic similarities. Many Jews migrated from Babylonia to Spain in the tenth and eleventh centuries, when there was persecution by the Turks. In Spain, the Moors were tolerant of the Jews, and during the tenth to thirteenth centuries Jewish culture enjoyed its *Golden Age*.

Jews became the objects of massacre or expulsion in various areas of medieval Europe because their secretive religious services provoked people to suspect perverse motives. The massacres, or *pogroms*, began in Germany and spread through Europe. The southern European Jews fled eastward to Turkey, Syria, and Palestine. Northern European Jews concentrated in and around Poland, where they spoke Yiddish, a dialect of Hebrew and German (Figure 5–3). Where Jews remained in cities, they were often forced to live in segregated areas known as *ghettos* (Noss, 1974, pp. 408–9). In reaction to further pogroms, including the killing of six million Jews by the Nazi regime in Germany between 1939 and 1945, the Zionist movement developed. Zionism expresses the view that the best hope for the Jewish people lies in a return to their homeland, Palestine. By 1947, when the United Nations created Israel, nearly 650,000 Jews had migrated to Palestine. Israel's population is currently about four million, and the world's Jewish population is concentrated in the U.S., Europe and the Soviet Union, and Israel. By far the largest concentration of Jewish population is in the U.S., where almost half the world's Jews live (Figure 5–4).

Christianity

Christianity developed as an offshoot of Judaism, which was itself influenced by the cultures of Egypt, Babylonia, Canaan, Persia, and Greece. The incorporation of the Jewish Old Testament in the Christian scriptures is clear recognition of the link with Judaism. Christianity developed in the political context of bitter resentment against the role of Rome. The Jews, beset by greater difficulties, lived in constant hope that their Messiah (Hebrew, "anointed one") would come to deliver them from seemingly constant fear and oppression. It was relatively easy for any individual to claim to be the Messiah, and many had, in fact, made such a claim, developed a following,

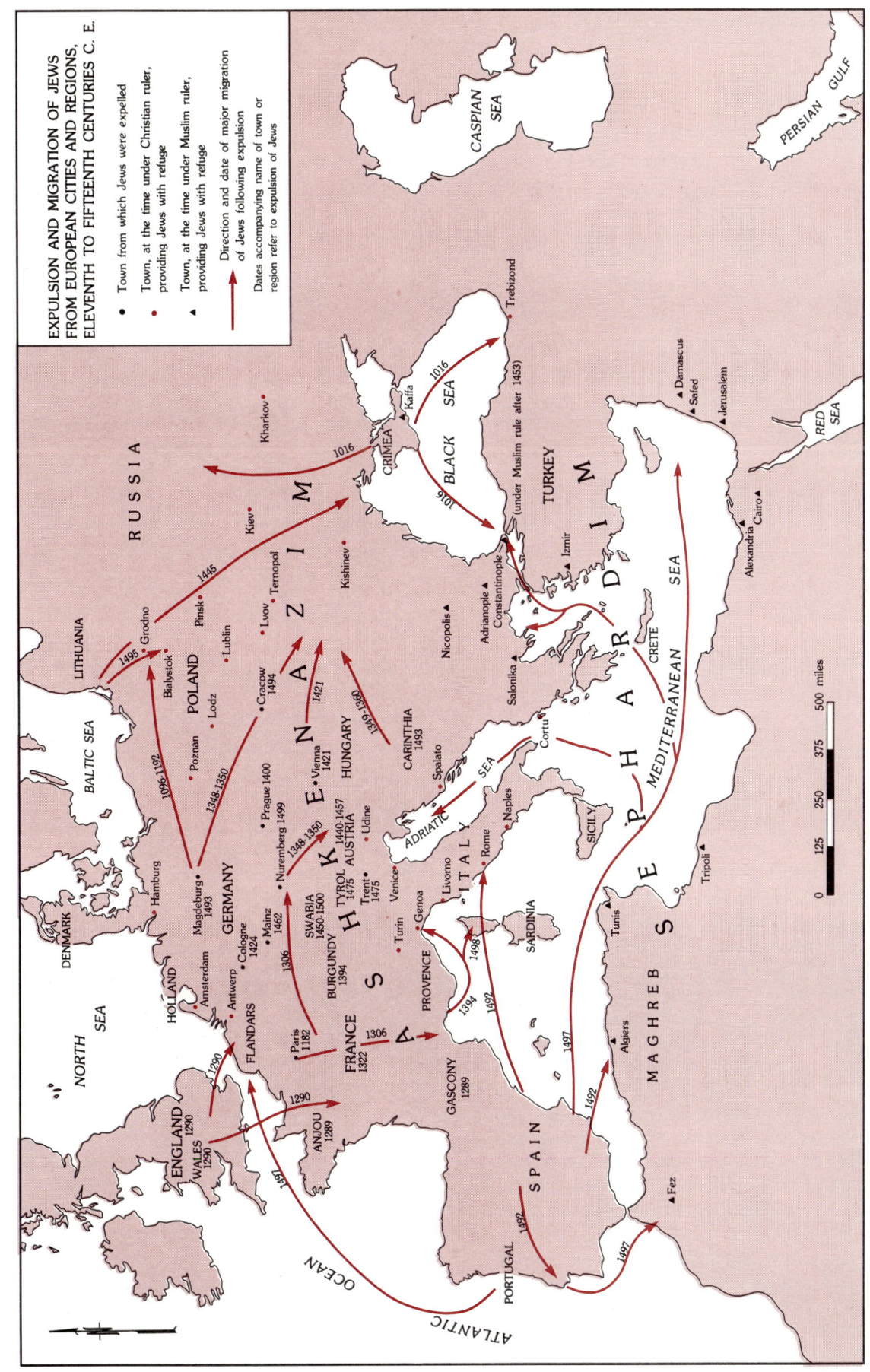

FIGURE 5–3 Expulsion and migration of Jews from European cities, 11th–15th centuries A.D. (From al Fārūqī and Sopher, eds., *Historical Atlas of the Religions of the World* [Macmillan, 1974], pp. 148–49.)

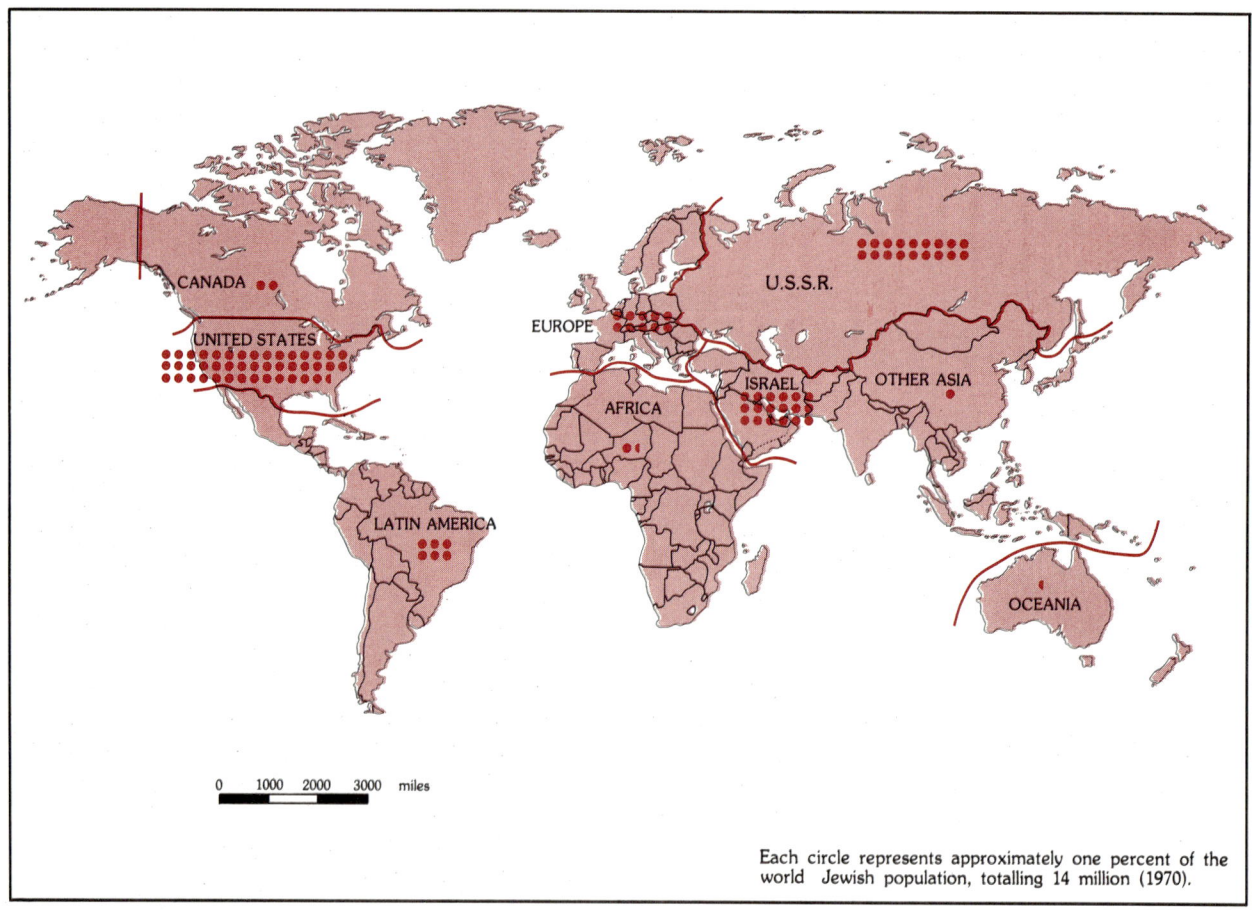

FIGURE 5–4 World Jewish populations by major regions. (From al Fārūqī and Sopher, eds., *Historical Atlas of the Religions of the World* [Macmillan, 1974], p. 156.)

Each circle represents approximately one percent of the world Jewish population, totalling 14 million (1970).

and proclaimed their opposition to Rome. They were duly crushed. It was in this environment, about 28 A.D., that John the Baptist preached that the Kingdom of God was at hand. Jesus became a follower of John, and, after John's arrest, continued teaching the idea that salvation was imminent. Jesus was apparently an effective public speaker and teacher, and his preaching attracted large audiences. The Jewish establishment resented his radical teachings, which led eventually to his crucifixion, about 30 A.D. This was followed by his disciples' claims that Jesus had been resurrected, proving that he was the Messiah. In this belief lies the fundamental difference between Christians and Jews. The former regard the Messiah as having come, while the latter do not recognize this claim (Bradley, 1963, p. 50).

Christianity now began its rapid spread beyond Palestine, particularly as a result of Paul's missionary efforts. His first journey took him to Cyprus and Asia Minor, then to Macedonia, in modern Greece. A third trip followed more or less the same route, and a final journey, as a prisoner, took him to Rome (Fig. 5–5). These journeys facilitated the *diffusion* or spread of Christianity. Diffusion tended to be of the *expansion* and *hierarchical* types. (Chapter 8 further explains the diffusion concept.)

Expansion diffusion occurred through contact between neighboring peoples. Hierarchical diffusion involved successful establishment of Christianity in large commercial centers, followed by spread to nearby smaller places. The diffusion of Christianity received a strong stimulus with the end of Roman opposition at Constantine's accession in the fourth century. He made Christianity the imperial state religion, and, until the decline of the Roman empire, the full power of the Roman state was behind Christian efforts. Figure 5–6 illustrates the spread of Christianity, showing the early nucleus in Macedonia, or Asia Minor, Palestine, and then penetration into Italy, Gaul, and Spain. Virtually all of western Europe and parts of southwest Asia had come under Christian influence by 600 A.D. Eastern and northern Europe

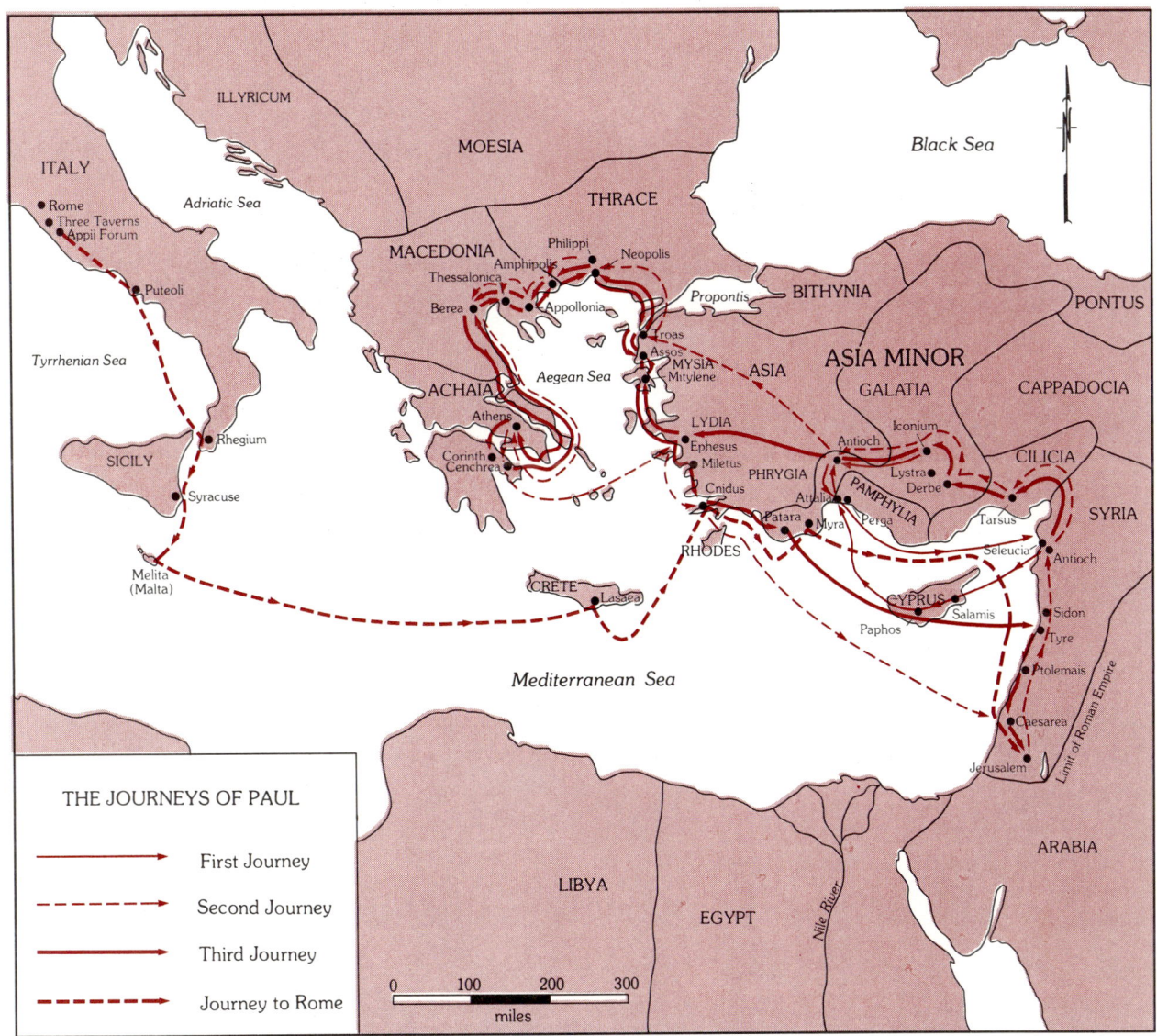

FIGURE 5-5   The journeys of Paul. (From John B. Noss, *Man's Religion*, 6th ed. [Macmillan, 1974], p. 457.)

followed into the Christian realm by the thirteenth century. From the early days of the church, one of the principal means of maintaining Christian influence was through the establishment of monasteries. Monastic orders were frequently active in missionary work, thus promoting the diffusion of Christianity.

Christianity is regarded as a missionary religion and, as such, has the characteristics of *universality, continuity,* and *adaptability* (Bradley, 1963, p. 55). *Universality* means that anyone can participate in the religion, and it must have strong intrinsic appeal. *Continuity* implies that a successful missionary religion must be rooted in cultural tradition that provides cohesion as the religion spreads. *Adaptability* means that Christianity had to recognize the uniqueness of places, peoples, and local cultures. It had to admit some modification to allow it to blend in with the local culture without alienating people by forcing on them seemingly radical ideas.

By the eleventh century, the Catholic ("universal") Church had split into the Roman Catholic Church in the west and the Eastern Orthodox Churches, centered in Constantinople. With the conquering of Constantinople by the Muslims and the end of the Byzantine Empire (1453), church power moved to Moscow and further development of Christianity in Muslim lands was curtailed (Bradley, 1963, p. 62). Christianity was affected by other

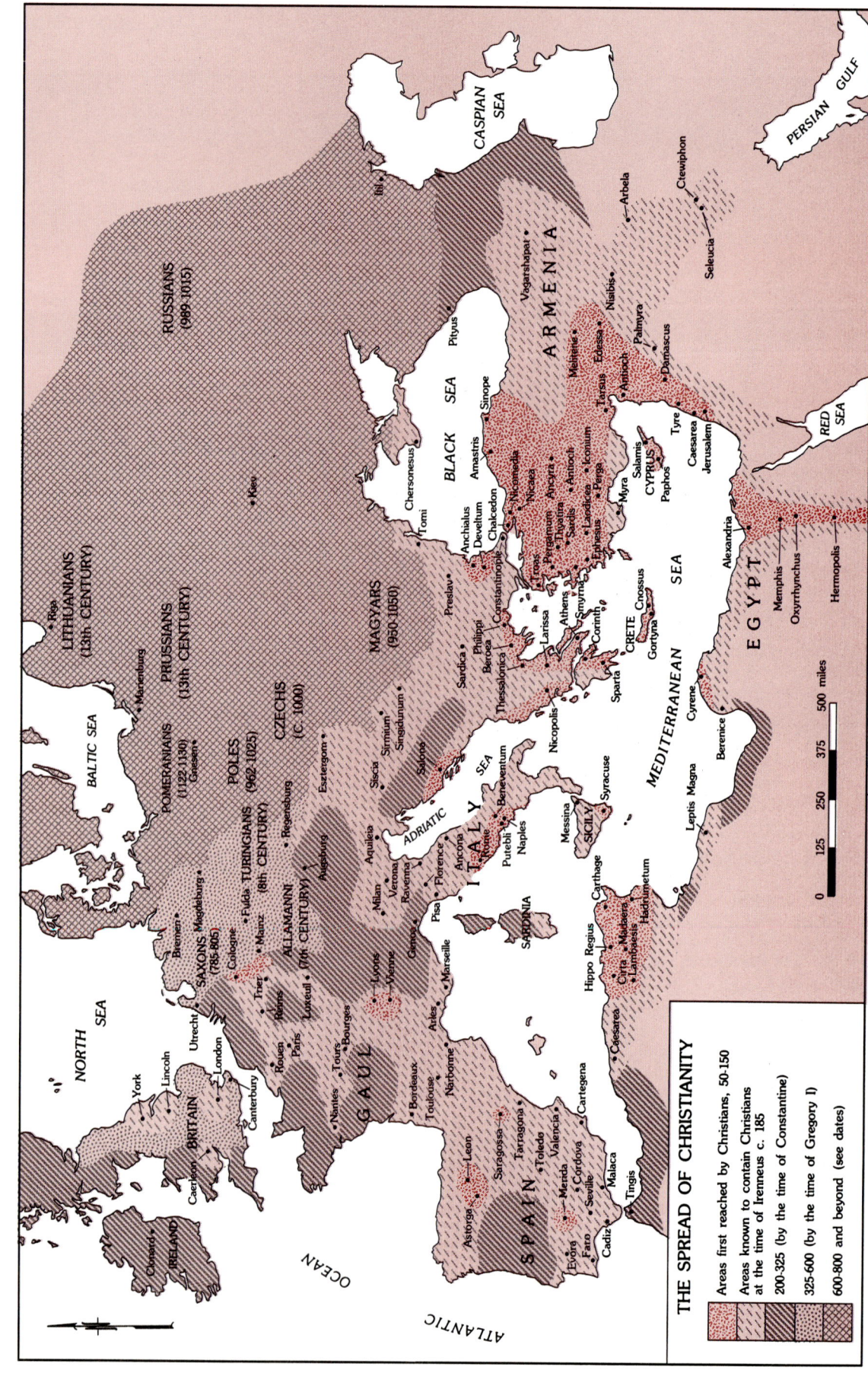

FIGURE 5–6 The spread of Christianity. (From John B. Noss, *Man's Religion*, 6th ed. [Macmillan, 1974], pp. 452–53.)

changes. The fifteenth century saw the *Renaissance,* a new interest in learning. Ideas could spread rapidly through the use of the new technology of printing. Reform movements gathered momentum in the Church in the sixteenth century, when *protestants* (those who protested the current state of affairs) initiated the *Reformation,* in which Martin Luther in Germany and John Calvin in Switzerland were central figures. Just as Christianity had a place of origin and a pattern of diffusion, so did the Protestant Reformation movement, as shown in Figure 5–7.

The diffusion of Christianity received tremendous impetus from the voyages of exploration and subsequent colonization. Catholic influence was strong as early exploration of the Americas was sponsored by Catholic nations, Spain and Portugal. British and Dutch colonization were major factors in the spread of Protestant Christianity. Today, 600 million people in the Americas are nominally Christian; the majority of these are Catholics. (We will discuss religion in the United States in greater detail in Chapter 7.)

Islam

Although Christianity and Judaism were successfully propagated in several regions, the Arabian Peninsula was left relatively untouched. The Arabs were generally polytheistic, worshipping local or tribal gods. Animism was universal, though some Arabs had been converted to Judaism or Christianity. This complex mix of religious orientations was reinforced by the diversity of the region's physical and social geographies.

Muhammed, the founder of Islam, came into this environment in 570 A.D. He was born in Mecca, a long-standing center of religion and pilgrimage, where worship was based primarily on animistic respect for a stone, a black meteorite. Muhammed reacted against certain religious practices, such as polytheism, animism, and burying female babies alive. He began to advocate acceptance of one God, a suggestion with economic and political ramifications that generated opposition. If there were only one God, the economy of Mecca would suffer since it was based on the worship of a number of gods and goddesses. Furthermore, if Muhammed were a prophet, and claimed spiritual leadership, this position might lead to political control. Muhammed received his religious knowledge in a series of revelations, compiled in the holy book of Islam, the Koran.

Persecution in Mecca led Muhammed to try elsewhere, initially in the city of Taif, southeast of Mecca. Failing there, he established himself in Medina, about 200 miles (320 km) north of Mecca. After years of conflict between the Muslims and Meccans, Mecca was defeated. By the time of Muhammed's death in 632 A.D., Islam had diffused throughout Arabia, though with varying degrees of acceptance. The seventh century A.D. saw the expansion of Islam beyond Arabia. Syria, Palestine, and Egypt were followed by the conquest of Spain after a push through North Africa. About half of France was actually occupied before Muslim forces were defeated at the Battle of Tours (732 A.D.) After the domination of Iraq, Persia, and Asia Minor, Muslims made incursions eastward into China, India, and the East Indies (Figure 5–1).

By the ninth century, the empire had begun to decline, a process in which the harrassment of the Christian Crusades between the eleventh and thirteenth centuries played a role. From the eleventh century, the power of Islam centered on Turkey, and Muslim influence spread again, with the expansion of the Ottoman Empire, until World War I. The history of Islam, like that of other religions, has been marked by disagreements and divisions. Islam is divided into many sects, of which the *Sunni* and *Shiite* dominate. The more numerous Sunnis accept leadership from among followers of Muhammed, while the Shiite, who are dominant in Iran, regard Muhammed's son-in-law, Ali, as his true successor. Conflict in Islam has taken on global political and economic importance because of the massive oil reserves in the Arab world and Iran. The war between Iran and Iraq in the 1980s has given rise to the fear of a wider conflict that could draw in other Muslim nations in the region, perhaps threatening world petroleum supplies. The 600 million people of Islam are under constant stress as the pressures for economic development conflict with traditional religious values. External influences, such as the use of alcohol and tobacco, modern banking practices (with what are, to Muslims, usurious interest rates), women's liberation, and rock music are among the sources of tension. Thus the geography of economic development may be strongly influenced by the geography of religious belief.

Hinduism

The term *Hindu* derives from the name of the Indus River located mainly in what today is Muslim Pakistan. A Hindu was one who lived in the region of the Indus but was not a follower of Islam. What makes Hinduism so different from many other religions is its extraordinary diversity. It has no creeds or central authority and includes great extremes of belief and practice. Like other religions, Hinduism has ancient roots. Up to about 1500 B.C., the dominant people

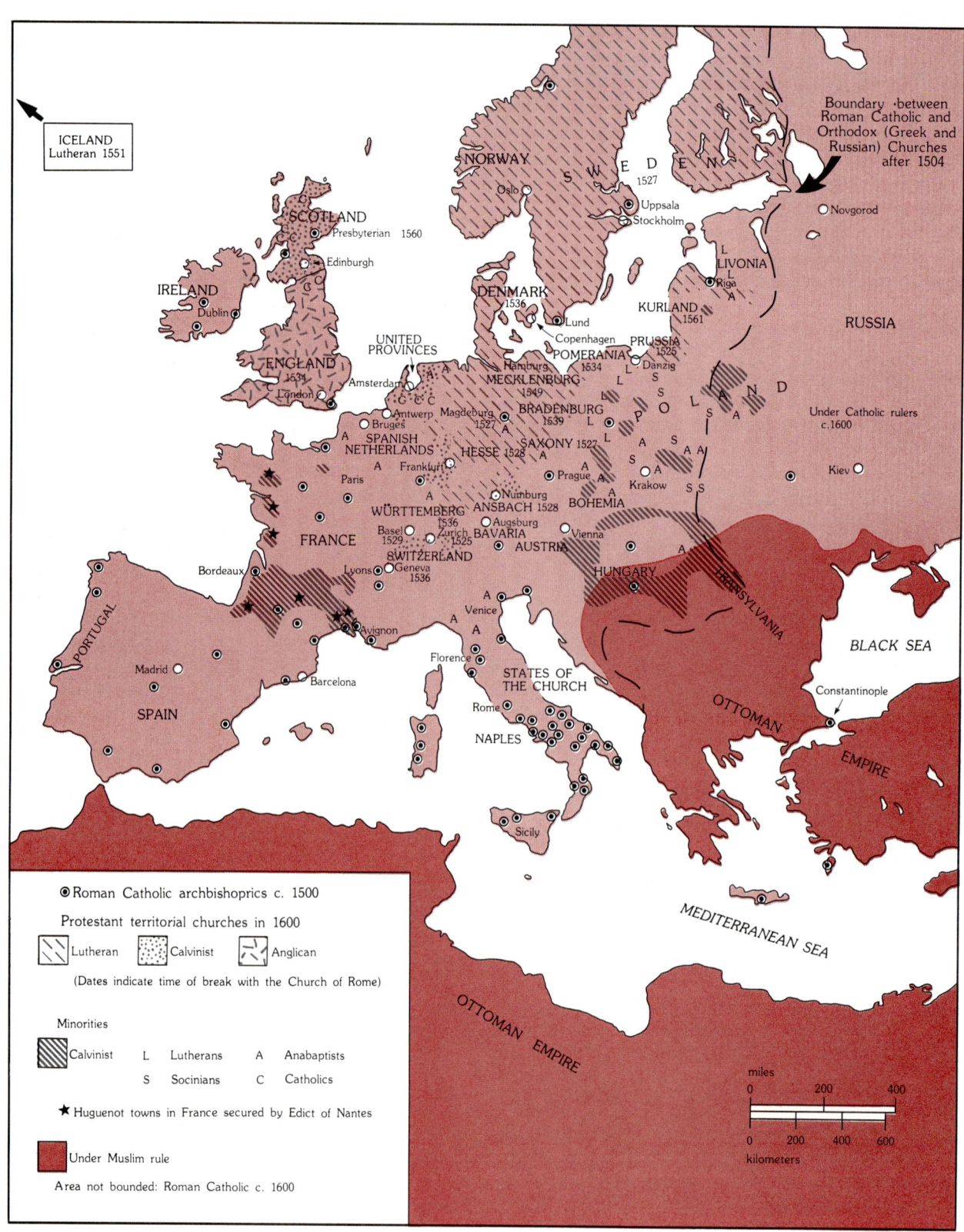

FIGURE 5–7 The Church of Rome and the Protestant Reformation. (From al Fārūqī and Sopher, eds., *Historical Atlas of the Religions of the World* [Macmillan, 1974], p. 225.)

of India were black, relatives of the black Dravidians of today's southern India. These folk were gradually replaced as the dominant group by light-skinned Aryan (Iran) people who invaded from the northwest. The Aryans brought religious practices and materials with them, including a massive, complex literature contained in four main parts known as *Vedas,* meaning "knowledge." Of the four Vedas, the most important was Rig Veda, a collection of over a thousand hymns. Aryan religion was characterized by ancestor worship, complex ritual and mythology, and polytheism, elements of which were retained in Hinduism.

An early development in this religion was the rise of a class of hereditary priests called *Brahmans,* and by about 500 B.C. it was possible to identify four major social groups, called *varnas* (Sanskrit for "color"): the Brahmans (priests), Kshatriya (nobles), Vaisyas (commoners), and Shudras (slaves). The Shudras were black, and provide an early example of racial discrimination. These social groups formed the basis of the *caste system,* which has evolved into castes or classes for thousands of occupations as well as for racial and ethnic groups. An important element of Hinduism is the concept that one may move to a higher caste through a process of rebirth. This caste system, which involves the utter rejection of "outcastes" or "untouchables," has only recently begun to decline. Despite legal reform, change has been slow, just as it has been with respect to racial and ethnic discrimination in the United States.

Between about 800 and 300 B.C., new interpretations of the Vedas emerged—the *Upanishads* (translatable as "sitting with a teacher")—which led to trends toward *asceticism,* or self-denial, and away from ritual (Noss, 1974, pp. 96–97). The Upanishads provided classical Hinduism with its foundation. Because of the dominance of the Brahman class, Hinduism had become exclusive, leading to reactions in the forms of *Jainism,* based on thorough asceticism, and *Buddhism.* Both were founded by members of the Kshatriya class (Bradley, 1963, p. 94).

In the first millennium A.D., the influence of the Vedic gods declined and new cults and philosophies emerged, to be modified into more or less final form over the next thousand years. Over time, three gods gradually emerged to take over the functions of many local gods: *Brahma,* the Creator; *Shiva,* the Destroyer; and *Vishnu,* the Preserver. However, these gods are not the only gods of Hinduism.

In reality, the average Indian is highly polytheistic and appeals to local gods on an "as needed" basis. The population geography of India helps to explain this situation. The population of India is today only 22 percent urban, and the majority of the 714 million people is dispersed in hundreds of thousands of villages. Urbanization, through which standardized ideas could perhaps have been imposed on the people, has been a weak force. In a crisis, people are much more likely to appeal to local gods than to Shiva or Vishnu. When we appreciate that India is not only a rural nation, but also one of numerous languages, it is not surprising that religious uniformity, or even an approximation of uniformity, is missing.

Unlike Christianity, Judaism, and Islam—which spread through a combination of conquest, missionary activity, and forced migration—Hinduism has remained confined primarily to India, where about 85 percent of the people (over 600 million) are adherents. In a sense, the geography of Hinduism is a product of the ancient Aryan invasions, and the pattern has not changed since the Aryan conquest of India was completed. Since that time, Hinduism has evolved from Vedic religion to coexist with many local practices that are animistic relics of the spiritual activity that existed prior to the Aryan invasions. India's relative isolation has probably contributed to her unique religious evolution.

One of the most extraordinary aspects of Hinduism, with profound implications for the way of life in India, is the veneration of cows. There are an estimated 200 million cows in India, a ratio of about one cow to every four people. The Vedas contained material on cow worship, although there was no Vedic prohibition of cattle slaughter. Eventually, however, the sacredness of cattle became established, probably by a combination of reasons: the association between cows and the god Krishna, the fact that invading Muslims slaughtered cattle, and adherence to the concept of nonviolence (Hinnells and Sharpe, 1972, pp. 119–21). Cows have a role in Hindu rituals, and one belief is that cows can guide people to the afterlife. Cow dung is used for many purposes, including fuel, medicine, and as an ingredient in building materials. The sacredness of cattle in India has frequently drawn criticism from observers in other nations on the grounds that many cattle are poorly fed and that resources used to keep cattle alive could be better used to feed the Indian people. Yet food avoidance is a common phenomenon around the world—for example, Muslims avoid pork and pork products, and meatless Fridays are part of Catholic tradition (see Simoons, 1961).

Buddhism

Christianity and Buddhism share two major characteristics. Both are missionary religions diffused over vast areas from an initial point of origin, and both are offshoots of an earlier religion—Judaism was the parent of Christianity while Buddhism sprang from Hinduism. The effect of Buddhism in Asia has been comparable to the influence of Christianity in Europe, the Americas, and elsewhere.

The founder of Buddhism was Gautama, the Buddha, born in what is today Nepal, on the northeastern edge of India, about 560 B.C. As a young man, Gautama set out on a six-year period of extreme asceticism. From this experience, the Four Noble Truths emerged: *suffering*, such as birth, illness, death; the *cause of suffering*, desire; *cessation of suffering*, attained by terminating desire; and the *Noble Eightfold Path* leading to the end of suffering. The eight points may be likened to commandments, such as "right speech" and "right conduct," leading, if observed properly, to *nirvana*, or freedom from the constant cycle of rebirths and their associated suffering (Bradley, 1963, p. 112). This approach is also known as the *Middle Path*, meaning a midcourse between complete self-denial, as found in Jainism, on one hand, or total self-indulgence on the other. In contrast to the religions we have already discussed, Buddhism had no important place for a god. Salvation was to come from self-discipline and concentration rather than through appeals to deities.

The diffusion of Buddhism was quite limited until the Indian emperor Asoka became a convert in the third century B.C. Asoka promoted Buddhism in every possible way, including support of missionary activity in India and abroad. About this time, *Theravada* Buddhism, which stressed the notion that only a few have access to nirvana, was dominant. This form has also been called *Hinayana*, or the "lesser way," by those critical of it (Smith, 1951, Chapter IX). Then, between about 100 B.C. and 100 A.D., another movement developed known as *Mahayana*, or "greater way," characterized by the doctrine of *bodhisattvas*, or "future Buddhas," meaning that there are many Buddha-like people available as earthly helpers. Through this philosophy, Buddhism was able

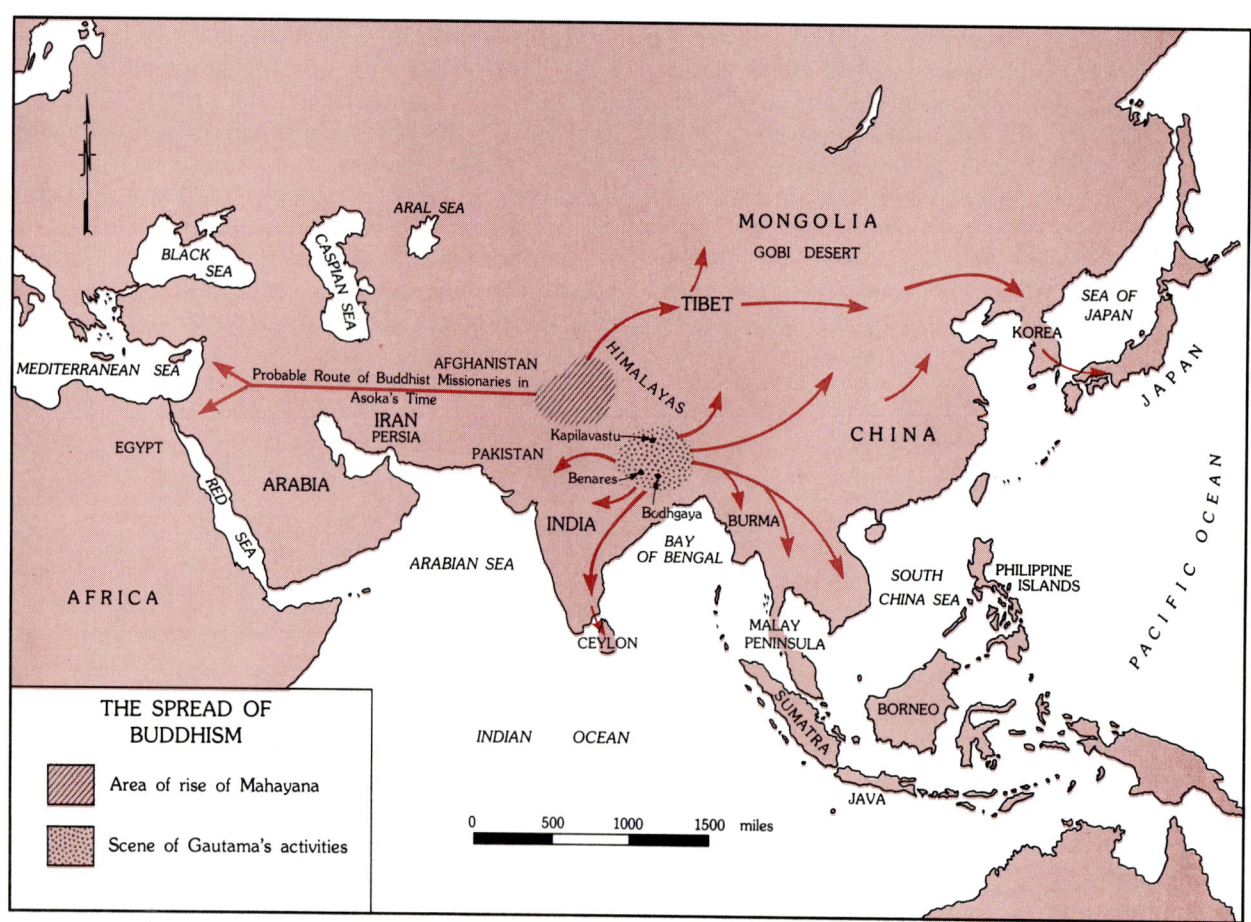

FIGURE 5–8 The spread of Buddhism. (From John B. Noss, *Man's Religions*, 6th ed. [Macmillan, 1974], p. 140.)

to offer wider appeal and to accommodate various local deities (Robinson, 1970, p. 49; Bradley, 1963, p. 117). This was the form of Buddhism introduced into China, Korea, Tibet, and Japan (Figure 5–8). In China, Buddhism diffused along silk trade routes, and, until the third century A.D., most adherents were foreigners. Early Buddhism was an urban phenomenon; foreigners clustered in the cities for commercial purposes. Under diverse cultural influences, different strains of Buddhism developed in north and south China, until Buddhism in China reached its zenith in the ninth century (Smith, 1968, Chapter 10).

By the seventh century A.D., Buddhism had begun to decline in India, and had virtually disappeared by the thirteenth century. The decline is attributed to its absorption into Hinduism, in combination with persecution by Hindus and invading Muslims. Had Buddhism not spread to other countries, it might have been extinct by now (Braden, 1954, pp. 127–28). In recent decades, Buddhism in India has experienced renewal, in part through official encouragement by the Indian government. Today, Buddhism is a major world religion, often mixed with other influences. There are no accurate counts of the number of Buddhists; one estimate suggests between 150 and 500 million, located in significant numbers in most regions of the world except Africa (al Fārūqī and Sopher, 1974, pp. 179–83).

RELIGION AND SPATIAL PROCESSES

Our review of major religions and their historical geography reveals that the geography of religions, like many other distributions in human geography, is an outcome of *stochastic*, or chance, processes interacting with a set of underlying conditions, including regional physical geography, urbanization, military conquest, migration, and the influence of some strong personalities who were able to persuade others to their beliefs. Many other strong personalities, most likely with equally plausible beliefs, failed to exert significant influence because circumstances were unfavorable. Had people and places interacted a little differently, Christianity, for example, might today be a mere footnote in religious history rather than a powerful universal religion. We can say the same for other religious or philosophical movements.

Because so many values are rooted in religious beliefs, the geography of religion is a major part of general human geography. The changes humans have made on the surface of the earth, whether in patterns of urbanization, agriculture, or industry, would be different today if patterns of religious belief had been substantially different. Attitudes would differ on a host of subjects—birth control, the status of women, human relationships to the natural world, the work ethic, modes of dress and diet, punishments for crimes, and so on. We can divide religious impacts on human geography into two broad overlapping categories: *landscape influences* and *sociopolitical influences*.

Landscape Influences

Geographer David Sopher suggests that religion is expressed in the landscape both positively and negatively. Positive expressions include sacred structures, land-use patterns, cemeteries, plants and animals, and place names. Sacred structures vary greatly in size and elaborateness, ranging from the ornate tem-

FIGURE 5–9 Storefront church on Main Street in the Los Angeles black community.

ple, cathedral, or mosque to the humble village shrine or storefront church (Figure 5–9). Even seemingly primitive structures, such as Stonehenge, must have involved extraordinary effort, given the technological and political skills available. Land-use patterns have been found to reflect religious views, as in the case of the Dogon people in Mali, where field patterns represent the belief that the world formed as a spiral. The necessary space for cemeteries varies greatly by religion depending on burial practices. Buddhists have dispersed plants, such as the Indian *bo* tree, into Sri Lanka and Japan. Religious place names are quite common, particularly in Catholic areas, where places are often named after saints (Sopher, 1967, pp. 24–34). Religious influences also appear in urban design (Vance, 1977, Chapter 2).

Negative expressions of religion include taboos against food and work. We have already touched on food taboos in our discussion of Hinduism. Work taboos vary in intensity from place to place and from religion to religion. For example, many Christians work on Sundays in retailing and in essential services such as medicine. In contrast, Orthodox Jews observe their Sabbath rigidly. For Muslims, the Sabbath does not disrupt normal activities. Other taboos prohibit certain kinds of work; in the practice of Jainism in India, agriculture is objectionable because it may involve killing insects (Sopher, 1967, pp. 35–41; see also Glacken, 1967, and Tuan, 1974).

Sociopolitical Influences

Religious influence in social and political affairs is usually inseparable from ethnic, racial, and linguistic factors. Christians, for example, are mostly caucasoid, and speak English, Spanish, or other European languages. Islam is associated with the Arab world, and Hinduism with India.

The role of religion in the life of a nation and in its relationship to its neighbors is nowhere more influential than in Israel. The 1980s represent the fourth decade of conflict over Israel, going back to 1947, when the United Nations voted to divide Palestine into Jewish and Arab states. Israel was established in 1948, but immediately found itself at odds with its Arab neighbors. Major conflicts occurred again in 1956, 1967, 1973, and 1982, when Israel invaded Lebanon to suppress the Palestine Liberation Organization. Israel came into existence as a refuge for Jews who have traditionally been persecuted almost everywhere they have settled. In contrast to its predominantly Muslim, Arabic-speaking neighbors, Israel is based on Judaism, the Hebrew language, and the concept of Zionism. Zionism pervades Israeli policy, both domestic and foreign, and makes it virtually impossible for Israel to become a binational state that would include Jews and Palestinians.

Although in the United States most media attention focuses on the international implications of Zionism, it has significant internal influences in Israel. The National Religious Party has periodically enjoyed a powerful position in the Israeli parliament, particularly during the administration of fundamentalist Prime Minister Menachem Begin. Fundamentalists have tightened restrictions on postmortem examinations, made it easier for women to avoid military service for religious reasons, grounded airplanes of El Al (the Israeli airline) on the Sabbath, promoted automation of industrial plants to minimize Sabbath work, and restricted abortion. Some liken the attitude of fundamentalist Jews toward women to the intolerance and chauvinism in fundamentalist Islam and Christianity. You may recall that the Equal Rights Amendment providing equal rights for women would probably have become part of the U.S. Constitution had it not been for opposition from Southern states where fundamentalist Christianity prevails.

The relative strength of religion in the government has profound implications for the geography of Israel and its region. Internally, development projects tend to favor Jewish rather than Arab communities and resources tend to be allocated inequitably. Territorial claims are often based on religious justifications. In nations with strong religious influences in the government, official policies are often likely to express religious doctrine. Indeed, the government may be accepted as an institution for promoting religion, and the values inherent in the religion then become the official values of the nation, with important implications for foreign relations, development policy, and daily life.

Another example of bitter ongoing conflict rooted in religious differences is that of Northern Ireland, where some 2,000 people have died in violence since the mid-1960s.

CONCLUSION

We can now formulate several broad generalizations about the geographical patterns of religion and its related culture. First, southwestern and southern Asia were the source regions, or hearths, of today's dominant world religions. Christianity, Judaism, and Islam diffused from their points of origin to influence vast areas. That southwest Asia was the hearth of these religions is partly attributable to the fact that the region was also the hearth of urban civilization, in which ideas travel quickly. Hinduism, with roots in

RELIGION IN NORTHERN IRELAND

The most obvious characteristic that distinguishes protagonists in Northern Ireland's violence is their religion. Although the conflict is not about theology or religious practice, church affiliation is frequently the best indicator of political, economic, educational, and social distinctions within the community. Northern Ireland's one million Protestants generally support union with Britain, whereas the half-million Catholics usually favor membership in an enlarged Irish Republic. The war that consolidated the Plantation of Ulster was won by a Protestant claimant to the British throne (William III) against a deposed Catholic monarch (James II). Ironically, papal sympathies lay with William.

Ulster Protestantism is now an amalgam of several denominations infused with strong fundamentalist evangelical tendencies. A long line of fiery, articulate, and often intolerant clerics have helped to fuel sectarian outbursts that usually coincide with midsummer parades by the Orange Order or by related groups commemorating the victories of King William III and the Protestant ascendancy. The bloody sectarian attacks following such parades and the Catholic counterdemonstrations have been a common feature of Belfast life in almost every decade during the past 150 years. Ulster Catholicism is an equally intense and devout faith, although Catholic clergy have been more hesitant than Protestants to involve themselves directly in political action. As one of the few Irish institutions to weather seven centuries of British rule without debasement of principles, the Catholic Church has a powerful emotional appeal for its followers. Protestants and Catholics are both ardent churchgoers and supporters of foreign missionary work. Neither group makes much effort to convert the other, a circumstance that highlights the entrenched divisions within Northern Ireland.

Public responses to violence and mutual distrust heighten the isolation of both communities. Residential areas, schools, sports, and cultural activities are usually segregated by religion. When Northern Ireland is peaceful, segregation wanes; during violence, it is accentuated. Recent geographical research documents a rapid and widespread pattern of residential resegregation after the Belfast street riots of the late 1960s. In such circumstances, religious ghettos afford a sense of security that one does not feel in integrated neighborhoods. Conversely, these ghettos are easily subject to surveillance and control by vigilante or paramilitary organizations and susceptible to containment by government security forces. Antagonism and suspicion breed unchecked in segregated areas. Catholics view Protestants as mean, dour, and stubborn oppressors of civil rights who, in the name of Christian piety, frown on Sunday drinking and entertainment but who are ready to conduct pogroms on slight provocation. The stereotyped Protestant image of Catholics is no more positive. Catholics are regarded as superstitious, priest-ridden, unlearned, and seditious, conniving to overthrow democratic government and establish a theocratic state.

Northern Ireland Protestants fear that union with the Irish Republic, whether by peaceful or violent means, will lead to the extinction of their way of life. The working class looks with trepidation at the high Catholic birthrate and the Republic's small, declining Protestant minority. Middle-class observers oppose absorption into a state where education, hospital care, and public welfare are chiefly controlled by Catholic clergy, where censorship of the press and the other media is openly practiced, where divorce is unobtainable, where contraception is banned, and where most children of mixed marriages are reared as Catholics.

Source: James K. Mitchell, "Social Violence in Northern Ireland," *Geographical Review*, 69, no. 2 (April, 1979): 182–84.

the beliefs of the migrant Aryans, did not spread significantly outside India, but it spawned Buddhism, which diffused widely in Asia.

Second, the world's major religions owe debts to each other. Particularly obvious are the foundations of Christianity in Judaism and Buddhism in Hinduism.

Third, religious culture is spatially dynamic. Religions move with migrants, like a piece of luggage, or are implanted by missionaries. To gain acceptance, beliefs have often been adapted to local conditions. Changes like these, over long time periods, can evolve into religious beliefs and practices that are quite different from the pure, or original, form.

Fourth, religion and the physical environment are interrelated. Early religious beliefs often developed as "explanations" for natural phenomena, such as seasonality or catastrophic floods. Religious views influence how we interact with the physical world, sometimes determining whether our approach is adaptive or exploitive. Furthermore, the diffusion pattern of religions has been affected by topographic and other physical barriers. It has been suggested, for example, that Islam was unable to significantly penetrate Africa south of the Sahara because of the missionaries' dependence on camels as their mode of transportation and the camels' susceptibility to insect pests and diseases of the humid tropics.

Fifth, religion may be directly or indirectly involved in national and international affairs. Political leaders often seek the counsel of religious leaders; this interaction can have far-reaching effects if the religious leaders successfully advocate their views on specific issues such as welfare, birth control, or nuclear disarmament. The role of religion is particularly clear in some conflict situations, as in the Catholic-Protestant conflict in Northern Ireland or the tension between Judaism and Islam around the eastern Mediterranean (see Smith, 1970).

KEY WORDS

Animism
asceticism
Babylonian Exile
Brahmans
caste
Diaspora
diffusion
eschatology
ethnocentricism
Fertile Crescent
fetish
ghetto
Golden Age
mana
Mesopotamia

monotheism
moral code
nirvana
pogrom
polytheism
Reformation
Renaissance
ritual
stochastic
tabu
universe
varnas
Vedas
world view
Zionism

REFERENCES

AL FĀRŪQĪ, ISMA'ĪL RAGI, and DAVID E. SOPHER, (eds.) *Historical Atlas of the Religions of the World.* (New York: Macmillan, 1974.

ANDERSON, G. W. *The History and Religion of Israel.* London. Oxford University Press, 1966.

BRADEN, CHARLES S. *The World's Religions: A Short History.* Nashville, Tenn.: Abingdon Press, 1954.

BRADLEY, DAVID G. *A Guide to the World's Religions.* Englewood Cliffs, N.J.: Prentice-Hall, 1963.

GLACKEN, CLARENCE J. *Traces on the Rhodian Shore.* Berkeley: University of California Press, 1967.

HARPER, R., and T. SCHMUDDIE. *Between Two Worlds: An Introduction to Geography.* Boston: Houghton-Mifflin, 1978.

REFERENCES

HINNELLS, JOHN R., and ERIC J. SHARPE. *Hinduism.* Newcastle-Upon-Tyne: Oriel Press, 1972.

MCDOUGALL, WILLIAM. *Body and Mind: A History and Defense of Animism.* London: Methuen, 1911.

NOSS, JOHN B. *Man's Religions,* 5th ed. New York: Macmillan, 1974.

ROBINSON, RICHARD H. *The Buddhist Religion: A Historical Introduction.* Belmont, Calif.: Dickenson, 1970.

SIMOONS, FREDERICK J. *Eat Not This Flesh.* Madison, Wisc.: University of Wisconsin Press, 1961.

SOPHER, DAVID E. *Geography of Religions.* Englewood Cliffs, N.J.: Prentice-Hall, 1967.

SMITH, D. HOWARD. *Chinese Religions.* London: Wiedenfeld and Nicolson, 1968.

SMITH, DONALD EUGENE. *Religion and Political Development.* Boston: Little, Brown, 1970.

SMITH, F. HAROLD. *The Buddhist Way of Life.* New York: Hutchinson's University Library, 1951.

TUAN, YI-FU. *Topophilia.* Englewood Cliffs, N.J.: Prentice-Hall, 1974.

TYLOR, EDWARD BURNETT. *Religion in Primitive Culture.* New York: Harper and Row, 1958.

VANCE, JAMES E. *This Scene of Man.* New York: Harper and Row, 1977.

6
Material Culture

Material culture refers to the material objects created by humans that can be identified as distinct to particular cultures. These objects include most anything people make for their home life, economic activities, or for their quest for enjoyment. Their architecture, burial grounds and arenas, fences and barns, and personal tools and instruments are all objects of material culture.

Students of culture have established criteria to identify items of material culture. The item must be something that can be seen either on the landscape or in the home. Items must be numerous enough to be classified and counted so that any regional differences can be analyzed. The items must also have been made by humans, not by some natural occurring feature.

To classify items in material culture, one usually identifies: (1) the *use* of the object (2) the *material* from which it is made (3) its *design* (4) all of these criteria. The objects may not always be used specifically to identify differences from place to place in culture. Different types of houses in the same town, for example, may reflect different time periods or economic strata, rather than different cultural influences. The emphasis in this chapter is on the place-to-place differences in the use, design, and materials of objects that humans construct.

ARCHITECTURE
BORDERS, WALLS, AND FENCES
MONUMENTS, BURIAL SITES, AND SHRINES
OTHER ITEMS OF MATERIAL CULTURE

ARCHITECTURE

The most obvious items of material culture are the buildings people construct. Architecture is the design and construction of shelters for both humans and their domestic animals, as well as the structures they build for economic, religious, political, and entertainment purposes. Architectural styles can be identified

The Quetzalcoatl Pyramid, about 60 miles (97 km) southeast of Mexico City. (Photo by Robert Buchbinder.)

CHAPTER 6 MATERIAL CULTURE

by both time and location. The remains of structures built centuries ago indicate both the stage of development of the culture and its areal extent.

Cultures in all parts of the world are distinguished by their architecture. Buddhist temples are readily distinguished from Chinese pagodas, and Egyptian pyramids are different from those of the Aztec and Mayan empires. Simpler structures such as houses are just as easily distinguished, and we can discover the source of current architectural influences by looking at the older styles.

Ancient Architecture

We trace influences on western architecture to the ancient Greeks. Their basic rectangular style of constructing buildings differed from the more rounded styles common to the east and throughout Asia. Greek architecture has been divided into three periods (Figure 6–1). The oldest style, the *Doric*, is named after the people from Doris, a region of ancient Greece. Doric architecture is noted for its simplicity of form, and is identified most easily by the columns that were used both for decoration and to hold up the roofs of the buildings.

The middle period of Greek architecture is the *Ionic*, named after people from the Ionia region. The Ionic style is more elaborate than the Doric, identified by the ornamental scrollwork at the tops of the columns. The third and most recent period of ancient Greek architecture is the *Corinthian*, named for the people of Corinth. Corinthian architecture is characterized by elaborate carvings of leaves and vines at the tops of the columns, which are more slender than the earlier versions and are fluted.

Romanesque architecture, or the style of architecture used by the ancient Romans, is characterized by its design and materials as well as its location. Ro-

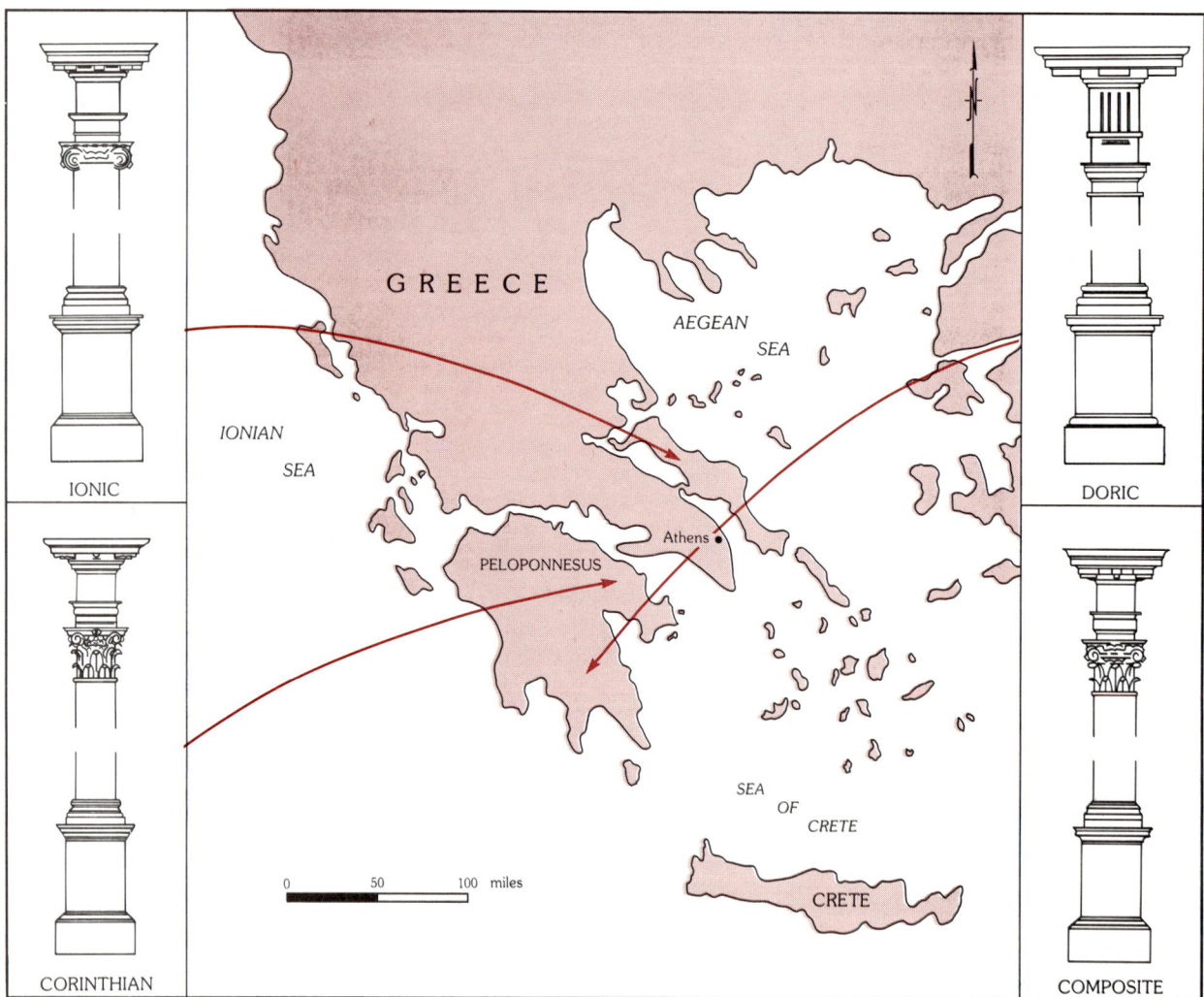

FIGURE 6–1 Distribution of architectural styles in ancient Greece.

man architecture is identified by its rounded arches and thick, massive walls. The Romans used large square-cut pieces of rock as well as much brick and concrete. Many of the massive buildings have withstood the test of time and can be found throughout the Mediterranean region today.

The Romans duplicated the famous colosseum in Rome throughout southern France, eastern Spain, and north Africa. The Roman colosseum in Arles, France, used today as an arena for bullfights, has remained intact and functional for 2000 years. The Roman colosseum at El Djem in Tunisia (Figure 6–2) is a tourist attraction, because it remains the largest structure for miles around the city. Centuries ago these structures, and many like them, were built for entertainment, but today are physical evidence of a culture that once existed in that region. Today we can measure the extent of the Roman empire by the remains of structures the Romans built.

The Greek and Roman architectural influences traveled westward through France and England to the United States. Today we see Doric columns on libraries and government buildings, and even some of our homes are adorned with Romanesque doorways. The Greek and Roman influences were particularly strong, however, on medieval architecture.

Medieval Architecture

The Goths, Germanic tribes of northwest Europe, conquered most of the Roman Empire during the 3rd to 5th centuries. We use their name to describe a type of architecture, *Gothic*, developed in western Europe between the 12th and 16th centuries (late medieval period). As with the Romanesque, the Gothic architecture is distinctive; instead of round arches, the medieval craftsmen developed pointed arches, and used them extensively. Gothic architecture is also characterized by steep roofs, flying buttresses, and arch-topped vaults.

Cathedrals Foremost among the Gothic structures of northwest Europe are the medieval cathedrals. These huge, towering structures were built in specific locations designated as seats of church power. Districts called *dioceses* were under the jurisdiction of a bishop, and each diocese included numerous *parish* churches. The bishops were territorial magnates with almost regal powers because they were the overseers of land belonging to the Crown. They surrounded themselves with knights and built numerous fortified castles in their dioceses. Many of the bishops also owned their own land. The bishops' estates and revenues were commensurate with the size of their diocese. A bishop's throne is a *cathedra*; thus a cathedral was built to house the bishop's throne.

Originally only a limited number of cathedrals could be built because of people's limited incomes. Also, a somewhat uniform spacing of cathedrals occurred because each diocese could have only one cathedral. Near the end of the medieval period and at the time of the Reformation (16th century), there were only nineteen cathedrals in England. As the population increased and became wealthier, and as

FIGURE 6–2 Roman colosseum at El Djem, Tunisia.

church reform brought redistricting of dioceses, new cathedrals were built. Today, there are more than forty major cathedrals in England, some of which were built as late as the 20th century (Figure 6–3).

Although no two medieval cathedrals are exactly alike, builders followed a somewhat standard plan or style. All the medieval cathedrals in England, for example, are built in the shape of a cross with the main axis running east to west. The altars are on the eastern ends so the congregations face east. The western parts of the main axes usually terminate with imposing facades flanked by twin towers. There is very little regional variation in the basic style of English medieval cathedrals.

Gothic architecture in France, on the other hand, is notable for the variation in provincial styles. In the north and the region around Paris, cathedral architecture is distinctly French. The cathedrals in England were built with square corners, whereas the French style was to round the east and west ends of the main axes. The roofs were therefore more arched than the English versions. In Alsace and Lorraine and other regions close to Germany, the French style was more German in particular details. Toward the south of France, the architecture took on a distinct Romanesque flavor. In Arles, for example, one can visit both a 2000-year-old Roman colosseum as well as a medieval cathedral built in the French Gothic style. Further to the south, the cathedrals of France took on a Spanish influence with greater use of bricks (Figure 6–4).

Castles Fortresses had been used as homes and military strongholds for centuries before the medieval period, the 12th to 16th centuries, but that time period is noted as the great castle-building age. In England, the original castles were built by the Norman conquerers after 1066, but were constructed almost entirely of earth and timber. The Norman architects erected large mounds of earth called *mottes* to artificially raise a fortress above the surrounding countryside. A ditch dug around the base of the motte became known later as a *moat*. On top of the mound or motte they usually built a dirt palisade topped with a wooden fence to enclose a yard called a *bailey* and later a *keep*. The buildings inside the bailey were made of wood also, and usually consisted of a few dwellings, workshops, and one large hall for meals and meetings. Baileys varied in size from about an acre up to six or eight acres, large enough for gardens and cattle pens (Figure 6–5).

Of about a hundred castles built in England before medieval times, all have since vanished, except for the six or seven that were made of stone. Only the mounds remain, and most of those have been covered over by later castle-builders. The motte-and-bailey type of construction, however, set the scene for medieval architects. Over three hundred castles were built in England during the 12th century alone, and construction continued through the Middle Ages. Many of the castles were destroyed during local feuds and civil wars; some were replaced, others were not.

Castles were built for defense against foreign enemies, civil wars and local feuds, or uprisings of discontented subject populations. All aspects of construction, then, were for defensive purposes. A mound or high point is easier to defend than flat land, so medieval architects retained the motte. Instead of a wooden fence, however, the bailey was enclosed with huge rock and masonry walls. Protection of the castle wall included towers called *bastions* and large gatehouses called *barbicans*. The towers were built outward from the wall so that defenders could fire through loopholes built into the base of the wall. The gatehouse held the *portcullis* (iron gate) and the machinery for raising and lowering the

FIGURE 6–3 Salisbury Cathedral in England.

FIGURE 6–4 Entrance to the harbor at Marseilles, France.

bridge across the moat. Most of the buildings inside the castle walls were also constructed of stone, thus the entire castle grounds, including walls, towers, gatehouses, and dwellings combined to make an imposing structure. All castles are unique, but most of them contain the essential parts mentioned here (Figure 6–6).

After cathedrals, the medieval castles are the most prominent features of the European landscape. Their distribution in the various regions, however, is irregular and difficult to understand. In some areas they are numerous; in others, it is a long distance between castles. During the Civil War in England (1644–46), castles were systematically destroyed. In other areas, poor land and low population densities accounted for the lack of castles. In some places, castles were restricted where the church or crown opposed them. The castles that were built in strategic defensive locations, such as along seacoasts, at critical fords and passes, and at junctions of main roads, have tended to remain intact because they were taken over for national defense rather than destroyed. These economic and political conditions resulted in an extremely complex geography of castles.

Houses and Cottages Today, one rarely finds structures other than castles and cathedrals built during the Middle Ages; houses simply were not built to the massive proportions of a cathedral or with the ten-foot-thick walls of a castle. But we do find many examples of medieval home styles, some of which are original structures. Three distinct types dot the English countryside: manor houses, timber-frame houses and barns, and thatched-roof cottages.

The manor house, which evolved from castles, first appeared as a stone-built house in England during the last few years of the 12th century. During the medieval period, they were the typical homes for knights, who were lower in status than the castle-

FIGURE 6–5 Launceston Castle in Cornwall, England, is an example of motte-and-bailey construction.

dwelling barons but modeled their homes after the castles. Manor houses are of standard form and thus easily recognizable. They are plain, rectangular buildings, with high-pitched roofs. Inside, the main feature is a large hall in the middle of the house with kitchen quarters on one side and sleeping quarters on the other. The crude, barnlike structures of the early Middle Ages gave way to finer, more elaborate buildings that stand today as examples of English Gothic architecture. The large, central hall remained a dominant feature of the medieval manor house.

Timber-frame buildings began to appear in Great Britain during the medieval period and are now characteristic features of many parts of the English and Welsh countrysides. These buildings also are called *half-timber* and *black-and-white* houses. Timber-frame buildings are unique and intricate. They were erected by joining together prefabricated frames, then filling the areas between the timbers with bricks, stones, flint, or lath and plaster. The fill materials and designs created an interesting regionalism, because each part of the country used local materials and provincial designs.

The best type of medieval farmhouse was roofed with clay tiles, but poorer farmers had to make do with a thatched roof. These unique houses were referred to as *cottages*. A thatch of straw or reeds was placed on a roof with a very steep pitch. The steeper the pitch, the more weatherproof the roof. Most thatched roof buildings did not have gables, so the wind could not raise the thatch and allow moisture to get under it. Making a good weathertight thatch became a craft, and a well-constructed thatched roof lasted as long as wood shingles. Again, local materials and designs created regional differences in thatched-roof buildings, many of which still exist in England today (Figure 6–7).

Colonial Architecture

The colonial period in Europe is marked by advances in home construction. The craftsmanship that had gone into the design and construction of castles and cathedrals was turned toward private homes. As times changed, barons and bishops lost their power, and the common people turned their attention to their homes and schools.* Renaissance architecture in England is referred to as the *Classic* period, separated from the Gothic period by a transitional stage called *Tudor*. Table 6–1 outlines the dates of the different architectural periods. We see from the table that the Classic period consists of many styles, from Elizabethan to Victorian. All the styles mentioned in the table can be seen in England today, and most have been replicated in the United States.

Colonial people took the architectural styles of their homelands with them to their new homes. In

FIGURE 6–6 Examples of medieval castles in the United Kingdom: (A) Shrewsbury, (B) Harlech, (C) Warwick.

---

*For example, many of the buildings at both Oxford and Cambridge Universities were constructed during the 16th century, although some go back to the 12th century.

FIGURE 6–7 An English cottage with thatched roof.

the United States, therefore, the colonial tradition includes not only the English styles, but also Spanish, French, Dutch, Swedish, and German, as well as others. Additions to traditional styles of local materials and new ideas produced a rich variety of house types in the United States.

Log Cabins The log cabin era of architecture in the United States can be called the "fireplace" era. The house plan of the log cabin began with the fireplace, and a room was built around it. The fireplace was the central feature because it provided both warmth from the cold winters and a place to cook. Chimneys for the large fireplaces became a distinctive part of the building and controlled the plan of the house. The tradition of a fireplace with a distinctive chimney has carried over into the plans of modern American homes.

The concept of making a house from logs came to America with the Swedish and German settlers around 1700. It was much easier to construct than the English frame house and, by the time of the American Revolution, had become the typical American dwelling from Maine to Tennessee. Brick, stone, and closely articulated frame houses were constructed, but only by the wealthy. In New England, the roof of the cabin had a steep pitch, a tradition retained from the thatched-roof construction in England. Further south and west, the roof pitch became less extreme. Regional differences can also be seen in types of chimneys, primarily because of available local materials, but there are design differences as well. In Maine and New Hampshire, for example, we find single-spire rock chimneys, whereas in Massachusetts, multiple-spire brick chimneys were more common. Greater use of chimney tops and pots distinguish the chimneys of the middle states and the South from those in New England (Figure 6–8).

The first architectural change in the one-fireplace, one-room log cabin became known as the *saddlebag* house. Pioneer house builders found they could accommodate growing families by adding another room to the chimney-end of the cabin. The fireplace was then in the middle of the house and served both rooms. Some builders added a room onto the end of the cabin away from the chimney to create a *double-pen* house. Usually, the rooms were not connected, each having one door to the outside. Other builders separated the rooms entirely, but put a roof over the separations to create a breezeway. These houses became known as *dogtrot* houses, because the open passageway was used as a dogrun. Other rooms were added in various styles to the original one-room cabin, but the builder always had to consider the location of the fireplace or add an entirely new one.

Buildings such as barns, wash houses, bake ovens, corn cribs, and toilets were also of log construction. Few examples remain today, but their appearances varied geographically in accordance with differences in terrain, available materials, and local styles, some of which we will consider later (Figure 6–9).

Early Frame Houses There are early American wood-frame houses in all parts of the country, but

TABLE 6–1 Periods and Styles of English Architecture

Date	Style
– 43	Pre-Roman
43– 446	Roman
446–1100	Saxon
1100–1190	Romanesque
1190–1485	Gothic
1485–1603	Tudor
1603–1880	Classic (See below)

Classic Period of English Architecture

Date	Style
1558–1603	Elizabethan (and Tudor)
1603–1625	Jacobean
1603–1649	Early Stuart
1649–1660	Commonwealth
1660–1689	Late Stuart
1689–1702	William and Mary
1702–1714	Queen Anne
1714–1830	Georgian
1811–1830	Regency
1837–1880	Victorian

Note: Dates overlap because more than one style appeared concurrently.
Source: Adapted from A. H. Gardner, *Outline of English Architecture* (New York: Charles Scribner's Sons, 1946), p. 115.

the traditional colonial type is found only in New England. One facet of construction unique to New England is the second-story overhang. Sometimes the overhang goes all around the house; sometimes it appears on only the ends or sides. Other features, such as small doorways, are found only in Eastern Massachusetts; *Dutch doors* are found in New York and Pennsylvania. (Only the wealthy used *double doors*.) These early houses were made of pine that was allowed to weather, and had high-pitched roofs similar to the older thatch houses. Shingles or boards were smoothed down with drawing knives, and the shingles were put on the house according to the phase of the moon. Putting shingles on during a dark or shrinking moon phase, it was believed, would cause them to curl and loosen.

Wood-frame houses were the next step up from log cabins, and were the preferred homes for most common people. Bricks, however, were used extensively from early in American history. Bricks were made in Virginia as early as 1612, and by 1650, Massachusetts had three brick factories. Some of the most famous buildings from the Revolutionary War era are of red brick. Stone buildings were also erected, but use of cut stone was limited to the vicinity of a local quarry because of the cost of transportation. Both brick and stone show evidence of regional differences. The texture and color of brick depends on the constituents of the local clay, which vary with location. Types of available stone also vary geographically. The colonists found granite in Massachusetts, marble in Vermont, *trap-rock* or slate in Pennsylvania, and limestone in many places. The construction results give ample opportunity to study the regional variations in color and texture of materials as well as the styles of old buildings in America (Figure 6–10).

Traditional American Houses Waves of new settlers across the United States took their home construction ideas with them—an example of relocation diffusion that we will discuss in Chapter 8. The log cabins (Figure 6–11) were the first to appear, fol-

FIGURE 6–8 The elaborate chimney pots of Hampton Court Palace were adapted to American architectural styles and building materials in parts of the United States.

A. PREPARATION OF LOGS FOR HOUSE CONSTRUCTION
   (1) NON—HEWN LOGS

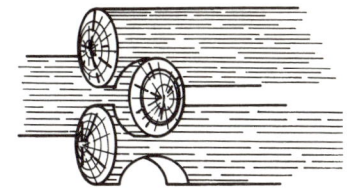
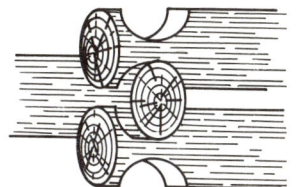

SADDLE NOTCH—TOP ONLY   SADDLE NOTCH—BOTTOM ONLY   SADDLE NOTCH—TOP AND BOTTOM

   (2) HEWN LOGS

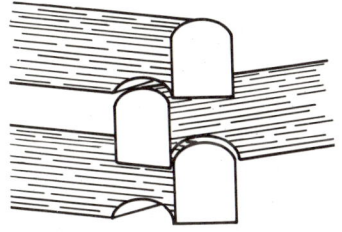
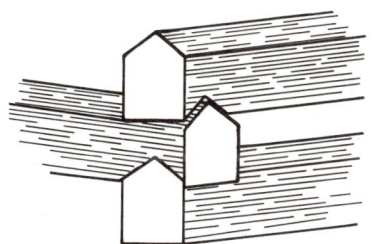
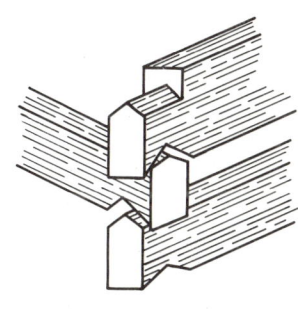

SADDLE NOTCHED   REGULAR V-NOTCH   INDENTED V-NOTCH (OR DOVE—TAIL)

B. TYPES OF LOG HOUSE CONSTRUCTION
   (1) ONE ROOM CABINS (FLOOR PLANS)

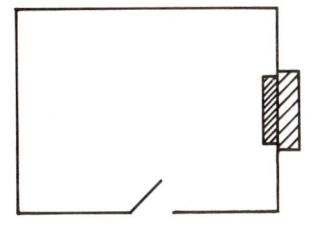
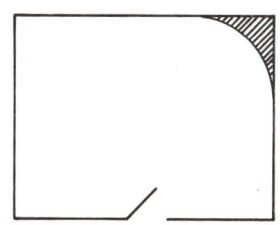

GABLE END FIREPLACE   GABLE END FIREPLACE, EXTERIOR CHIMNEY   CORNER FIREPLACE

 LOCATION OF FIREPLACES

   (2) MULTIPLE ROOM COTTAGES (FLOOR PLANS)

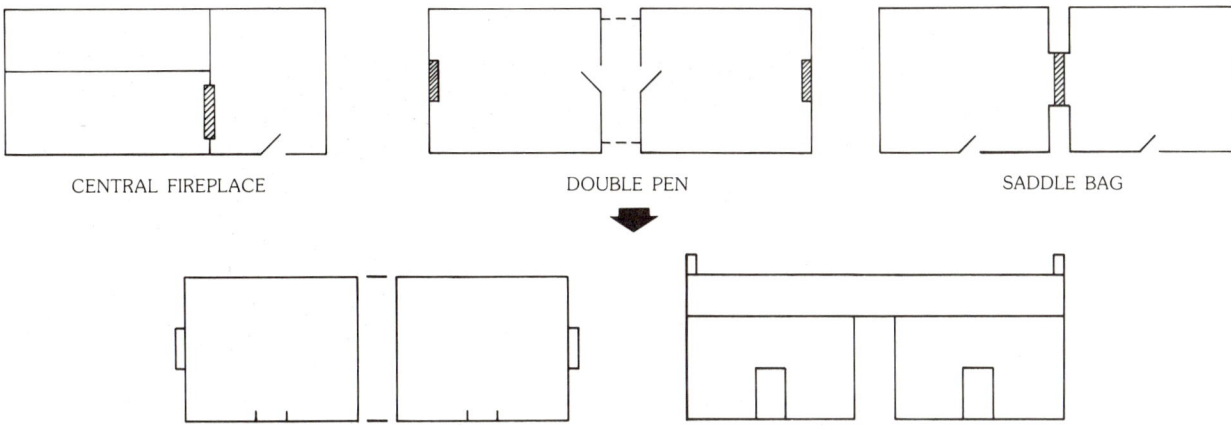

CENTRAL FIREPLACE   DOUBLE PEN   SADDLE BAG

DOG TROT

FIGURE 6–9 (a) Logs used in house construction; (b) types of construction for one-room and multiple-room houses. (Adapted from Rooney, Zelinsky, and Louder, eds., *This Remarkable Continent* [Texas A & M Press, 1982].)

CHAPTER 6 MATERIAL CULTURE

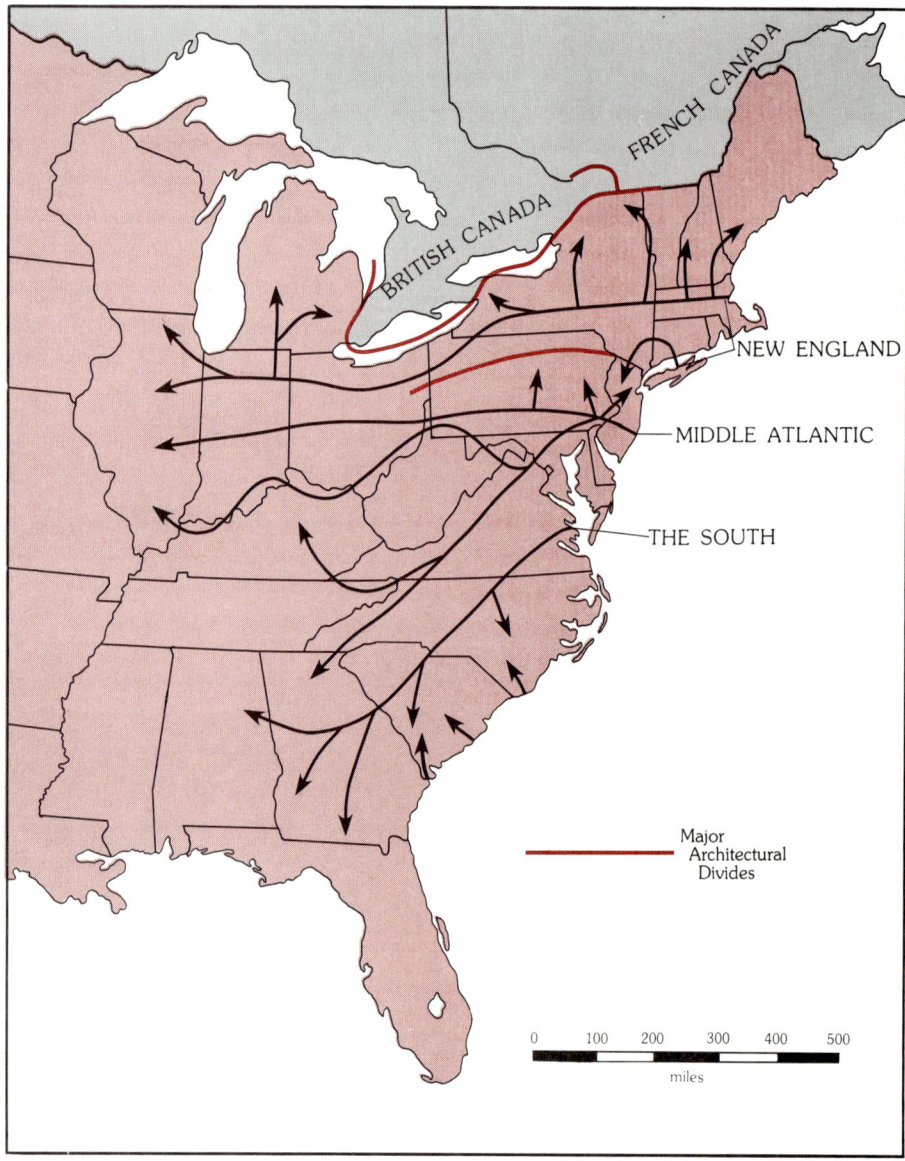

FIGURE 6–10 Diffusion of house types in the United States. (From Rooney, Zelinsky, and Louder, eds., *This Remarkable Continent* [Texas A & M Press, 1982].)

lowed by wood-frame construction, and then brick and stone. When settlement reached the plains, where trees were not available, the settlers constructed *sod houses*. Then, in the Southwest and West, the Spanish influence became prominent, characterized by the use of *adobe* bricks, flatter roofs made of tile, and arched doorways. Early Spanish buildings can be seen today, and the line of missions through California, built by the Spanish missionary Father Junipero Serra, epitomizes that style. Spanish and Mexican political influence in the United States was limited, but the architectural style has been lasting, appearing in thousands of homes and buildings from Texas to California.

The westward movement of people and their house types ran into other environmental and cultural influences. In the South, for example, periodic flooding in the lowland delta areas created the need for a raised house. The *tidewater cottage* evolved from this need. It was similar in construction to the wood-frame houses, but was raised as much as six feet above the ground on a brick or stone superstructure. The dogtrot house was also used in the South, because the breezeway was found to be functional in the warmer climate. Besides the environment, distinct cultural factors became prominent in the South. The Louisiana *Creole* house shows French influence, as do many of the large plantation mansions.

Blacks in America also influenced house styles, and the premier example is the *shotgun* house. Of African design, this style was brought by slaves to

FIGURE 6–11 A log cabin in Oklahoma.

Louisiana. The house is characterized by being only one room wide and numerous rooms long. Front and back doors as well as all internal doors align with each other, so that it is theoretically possible to shoot a shotgun through the house from front door to back without hitting any walls. In Africa, the style promoted cooling in the house; in the United States, it fit the long lots used in the South. This house style diffused up the Mississippi and Ohio Valleys, and can be found today in cities such as Louisville, Kentucky (Figure 6–12).

Traditional American houses or *folk houses* were constructed from memory. Builders began with an image of what they had seen at an earlier place and time; using local materials and their own innovations, they created unique house types. In each settlement area, one sees influences from the culture that settled it. Modern American homes combine these influences; looking around a modern suburban housing development, one can see black-and-white houses copied from Gothic England, roofs without gables from the thatched-roof design, red-tile roofs and thick walls from the Spanish influence, and examples of nearly every other design we have mentioned. (See also Chapter 7.)

BORDERS, WALLS, AND FENCES

In Chapter 15, our discussion centers on the significance of boundaries on the lives of humans, but here we will explore another aspect of boundaries—the design and construction of the barriers themselves. All walls and fences are designed either to keep people or animals inside an area or to keep intruders out.

Ancient Borders

One of the oldest surviving human-built structures is a barrier designed to keep invaders out. The Great Wall of China is truly a remarkable feat of construction. It is the only structure made by humans that has been observed by astronauts in space. The wall is 1200 miles long in a straight line, but with all its windings, uphill and down, even over a mountain peak, it is more than 1500 miles in actual length. It was begun more than 2000 years ago, in 212 B.C., and completed a few years later.

The first emperor of the combined area of China, Shih Huong Ti, used thousands of troops to construct the Great Wall. They repaired, joined, and extended a series of isolated earthern walls constructed earlier by local rulers. The purpose of the wall was to provide protection against the barbarian tribes of central Asia. The nomadic tribes, living in areas of marginal rainfall, often raided the stockyards and granaries of the sedentary Chinese when the rains failed to provide grass for their own herds. After the Great Wall was built, the emperor garrisoned it with troops and waged war on the barbarians.

The Wall was constructed of cut rock and mortar. It is 25 feet wide and 30 feet high. Every few hundred feet there are watch towers made of the same material that rise another 15 feet above the top of the wall. Troops could march along the top of the wall, protected by *parapets* built along the top,

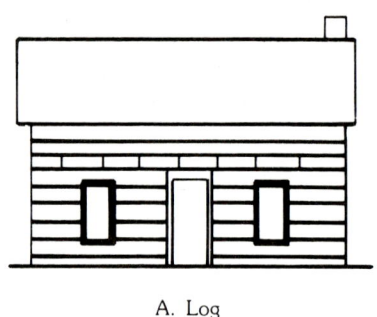

A. Log

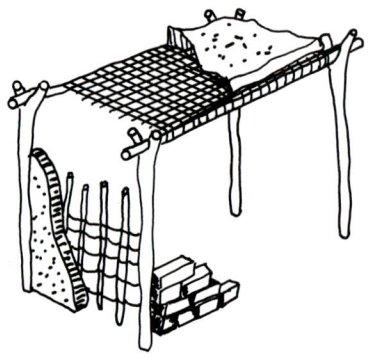

B. Adobe

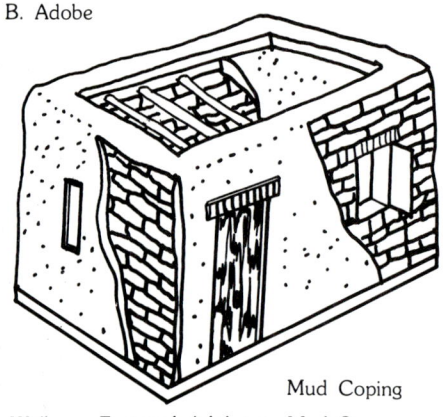

Mud Coping

Walls — Exposed Adobe or Mud Stucco

C. Creole

Creole House Types of Lower Louisiana

D. Shotgun House

FIGURE 6–12 Traditional American house types: (a) log cabin; (b) adobe; (c) Creole; (d) shotgun. (Adapted from Rooney, Zelinsky, and Louder, eds., *This Remarkable Continent* [Texas A & M Press, 1982].)

BORDERS, WALLS, AND FENCES

FIGURE 6–13 The Great Wall of China. (Photo © Peter Arnold, Inc.)

or they could fire at the enemy through loopholes. The rocks used in construction were from local quarries, so the wall generally matches the color of the terrain. The rocks were tediously cut to uniform size so that they resemble large bricks. Most of the original wall remains, and many parts of it are still in perfect condition. The Great Wall of China is an incredible monument of the human desire to build barriers (Figure 6–13).

Although the Great Wall is the longest and most famous structure built as a political border, other "great" walls have been built for that purpose. The Romans, for example, are noted for the walls they built along their borders. Some sections of one Roman wall are still visible today in England, where it is known as Hadrian's Wall, after the Roman emperor who ordered it built in 122 A.D. Great Britain had no natural barriers, like the Rhine, Danube, or Euphrates, to mark the frontier of Roman control, so the purpose of Hadrian's Wall was to make a permanent and obvious barrier to mark the northern extent of Roman territory in Britain. It was built to separate the inhabitants into Romans and Britons on the south and barbarians in the area of Scotland on the north.

Hadrian's Wall reached from sea to sea across northern England, from Wallsend-on-Tyne to Bowness-on-Solway, a distance of 73 miles. Another section ran for 40 miles down the west coast from Bowness. The original height of the wall, constructed of cut limestone blocks and mortar, was about 15 feet, with a six-foot parapet on top. Small forts, called *mile castles*, were built every mile, with two watchtowers spaced between each pair of mile castles. Large forts, occupied by as many as 1000 Roman soldiers each, were also built at regular intervals along the wall.

The original wall that Hadrian ordered was completed in eight years, but was abandoned, reoccupied, partially destroyed, and rebuilt numerous times until the Romans withdrew from Britain at the end of the fourth century. After the Romans left England, most of the wall was destroyed so as to use the limestone blocks for other construction projects. Today,

117

only short stretches of the wall remain, but they are enough to indicate the enormity of the undertaking.

Hadrian's Wall marks the ancient boundary between England and Scotland, and another visible structure marks the boundary between England and Wales. A great running earthwork known as *Offa's Dyke* stretches for 149 miles (240 km) from Chepstow on the south to Prestatyn in the north. Offa was the first ruler to be called King of the English, and in 784 A.D. he ordered his subjects to construct a barrier between themselves and the Welsh. The Dyke is an earthen bank, ditched usually on the west side, but sometimes on both sides. It is about six feet (2 m) above ground level, and about sixty feet (18 m) wide. The Dyke runs through difficult terrain, but is aligned throughout to allow visual control to the west, toward Wales (Figure 6–14).

The principal purpose of the Dyke was to mark the frontier between England and the Welsh kingdoms, to control trade and other interaction across the border, but it was obviously an ineffective barrier. About 80 miles (130 km) of the Dyke are still visible today. The remainder has been destroyed during the centuries since it was built by natural erosion, plowing, road building, and housing developments. In the village of Llanymynech, however, some houses are built on the Dyke itself, and the English-Welsh border passes directly through the middle of a small hotel. The hotel bar is divided by a line painted on the wooden floor.

The largest earthwork in the world built before mechanical help is another ancient boundary in Nigeria. The total length of the structure has been estimated at 8000 miles. The earth boundary surrounded the Benin Empire in the Bendel state. The structure has been only partially surveyed, and is now eroded nearly beyond recognition.

Modern Borders

International boundaries today are rarely fenced for their entire length. If barriers are constructed, they are usually located only at strategic points along the border, such as where roads or railroads cross, at mountain passes, and between cities or within a city. The most famous political barrier today is the Berlin Wall (see Fig. 15–16). Where political friction is less, the barriers are also less formidable. The Mexican-U.S. border, for example, is fenced in twin-city areas such as Nogales, Arizona/Nogales, Mexico and El Paso, Texas/Juarez, Mexico, but the ten-foot chain-link fence does not compare to the Berlin Wall.

European countries are more likely to fence their borders than countries anywhere else in the world.

During the 1930s, France spent huge sums to build an elaborate chain of steel-and-concrete underground fortifications along its borders with Germany. The *Maginot Line,* named after the French Minister of War at the time construction started, was intended to protect France from invasion by German troops, but it proved useless against the tanks of the German Panzer divisions during World War II. Remnants of the Line can be seen today, as many of the abandoned bunkers are still intact (Figure 6–15).

Germany also constructed a line of defense during the Second World War. The *Siegfried Line* or *West Wall* defense system ran from the Swiss border to the Netherlands. The 450-mile system was made of five rows of concrete antitank barriers laid out in a zig-zag fashion. Concealed pillboxes, troop shelters, and command posts were spread out behind the barriers. This defensive system was supposed to slow down enemy assaults until reserve forces could mount a counterattack. As with the Maginot Line, the Siegfried Line also proved ineffective in stopping the Allied invasion. Many of the concrete antitank barriers are still apparent in West Germany's farmlands.

Walled Cities

For many centuries it was customary to build defensive walls around cities. From the time cities came into being until the close of the medieval period, city dwellers felt the need for an outer wall to protect not only the city dwellers but also the farmers who lived near the cities. They needed protection from invading armies, marauding barbarians, and outlaw bands. Because most political units were small, as with the city-state, the cities were the focal points of entire regions. There is a close relationship between the rise and fall of empires and the rise and fall of cities.

City walls went out of fashion for two unrelated reasons. First, after the Middle Ages, cities began to grow rapidly. The added population settled outside the city walls, and this sprawling growth left the wall as a midtown relic. Second, with the invention of casting methods for iron that allowed the manufacture of large guns, city walls were found to be vulnerable. Despite their formidable appearance, the rock and mason walls could not withstand continuous bombardment of cannonshot. No walled cities were built in the United States, because by the time of settlement walls were useless for defense.

In many cities today, from Britain through Europe, north Africa, and the Middle East, we find evidence of walls. In some cities, three or four walls

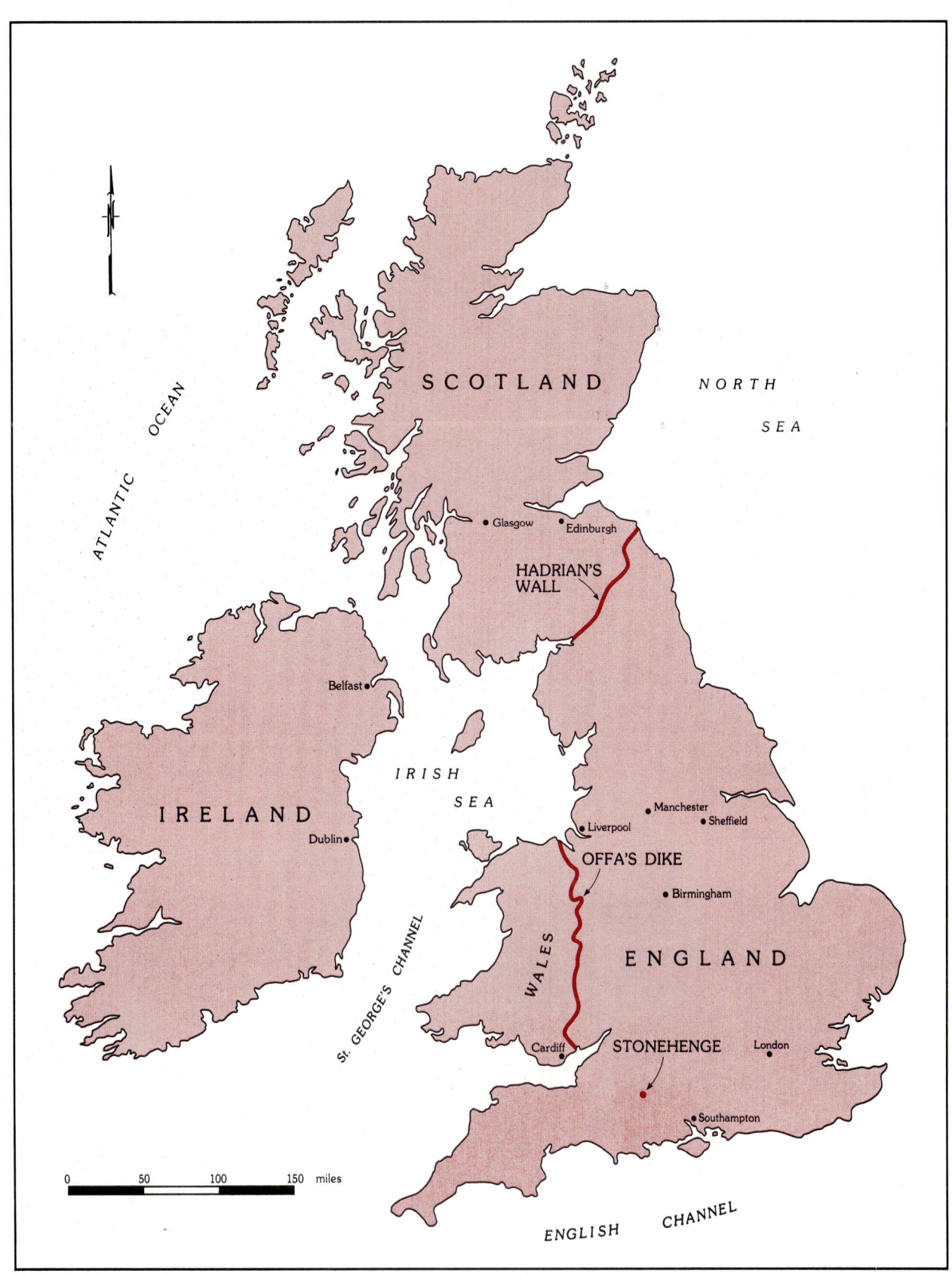

FIGURE 6-14 Site of (a) Hadrian's Wall, marking the ancient boundary between England and Scotland; (b) Offa's Dyke, a barrier between the English and the Welsh.

CHAPTER 6 MATERIAL CULTURE

FIGURE 6–15 This marker in Belgium shows the furthest extent of the German invasion during the Battle of the Bulge in World War II.

mark a city's historical spread. In other places, entire medieval walls remain, surrounded by the larger new city. Some towns retain street patterns suggesting the outline of a wall, although the actual wall has long since been removed. Other walls and partial walls have become parts of buildings. City walls are an obvious relic, but a fascinating part of the world's material culture (Figure 6–16).

Walls and Fences

Since the beginning of human history, property owners have built various types of barriers to protect their property. The Old Testament abounds with accounts of walled gardens and fields. The ancient Britons and Gauls were skilled in the use of wattles and mud walls. They learned about hedging, stonework, and

FIGURE 6–16 This wall in Tunisia is a remnant of medieval times.

FIGURE 6–17 Garden walls, like this one in Spain, are still part of the landscape in European countries.

brickwork from the Romans. The French herb gardens of the Middle Ages were surrounded by stone walls and tunneled hedges, as were the private British gardens of the same era.

Gardens were the first parcels of private property to be fenced. The Romans built public works such as Hadrian's Wall to protect the empire, but large stretches of the empire itself were unfenced and unbounded. Thus, homeowners had to build walls to protect their gardens from both domestic and wild animals. Similar situations continued in northwest Europe through the Middle Ages. Castles and cities were walled, but the fields were not fenced. Gradually, garden walls were extended to become long fences surrounding entire fields (Figure 6–17).

Wall and fence designs and materials vary considerably. The basic materials are stone, wood, and wire, but other materials such as concrete, earth, and live vegetation have been used. Individual walls and fences can also be made of a combination of materials (Figure 6–18).

Live vegetation fences are the least common type, especially in the United States. In England, however, miles and miles of fields are fenced with hedge. Sometimes the uncut hedge grows to 25 or 30 feet, turning narrow roads into virtual tunnels. *Hedgerow* fences are also common in France and Belgium, and caused considerable problems for the invading American army in World War II. Privet, box, locust, fuchsia, laurel, hawthorn, and cacti have also been used as live fences. In drier areas like North Africa, miles of prickly pear fences have been established. In the United States, midwestern farmers used hedgerow fences until about 1850, and some of these old hedgerows can still be seen.

Early American farmers in the Plains region also made fences of sod. Strips of sod about 16 inches (400 mm) wide, 32 inches (800 mm) long, and 4 inches (100 mm) thick were cut on either side of the fence line. By making nine cuts on either side of the fence line, 18 layers of sod could be used to make a fence about 6 feet (2 m) tall. Sod fences are subject to erosion, and none remain today.

Stone fences are more complicated to build than sod fences and last much longer. Building *dry stone fence,* especially, needs much practice. This fencing was made from boulders and rocks cleared from fields, and the varying-sized stones were fitted together without mortar. The fence required no foundation, and it moved gently with land movement such as frost action. Dry stone fences are found today in parts of England and in New England, where the soil was strewn with rocks.

Stone fences made with mortar and brick walls are much alike. Both stone and brick have been used as fencing material for centuries, and last a very long time, as seen in the case of China's Great Wall. Thus, one can still find many examples of these old structures. Constituents of the rock material and of the clay used for the bricks give a unique quality to each wall that reflects the area where it is located. Mortared stone fences are common in New England, where the field rocks were used, and segments of a brick wall built by Thomas Jefferson remain today on

FIGURE 6–18 This wall in Stratford-upon-Avon in England combines several durable materials.

the campus of the University of Virginia. Adobe bricks were used for walls in the American southwest, and some 250-year-old structures are still standing. Tile "roofs," often placed over adobe walls to help preserve them from erosion, are common today throughout the Mediterranean region (Figure 6–19).

Wood is a much more flexible fencing material than stone or brick, so there is more variation in the styles of wood fences than in mortared fences. The first all-wood fences in North America were the *palisades* surrounding early Indian villages. They were constructed by setting poles close together to form a continuous wall or barrier. The tops of the poles were sharpened to a point to make it difficult to climb over the fence and to prevent decay. Later, the French and English settlers used similar techniques to enclose their forts with *stockades*. *Split rail* fences originated in early Virginia, and were used in the wooded areas for many years. Unique construction of split rail fences creates a zig-zag formation giving rise to the term *snake fence,* also known as a Virginia fence.

A great variety of all-wood fences have been built. Some have been built entirely of tree stumps, from dried brush, and from stake and willow wicker. Poles with the bark removed have been used for pole fences, and swan boards for board fences. Picket fences originated and are still common in the Southeastern U.S., and horizontal board fences are common in the Southwest where they are used for cor-

FIGURE 6–19 The "roof" on this fence prevents damage from erosion.

rals. Because they are attractive and economical, wood fences are popular with suburban homeowners today in all parts of the U.S.

When American settlers moved westward out of the forests and into the prairies, they needed a new type of fencing material. The lack of trees made split rail fences impossible, so some people used hedgerows and sod fences. The godsend to prairie farmers, however, was the innovation of *barbed wire*. Along with the steel plow and steel windmill, fences made of steel wire not only helped settle the prairies, but also made the region uniquely American.

Barbed wire was patented in 1874 by Joseph F. Glidden, a farmer who lived near DeKalb, Illinois. Glidden barely beat one of his neighbors with the patent, as both farmers were working on the idea. Between 1874 and 1892, nearly 1000 barbed-wire designs were submitted to the U.S. patent office. Within ten years of the Glidden invention, over 200 million pounds of barbed wire were being sold annually, and by 1886, nearly 1.5 million miles (2.3 million km) of barbed wire had been manufactured by 50 companies. The wire with the thorn changed the open prairie into an enclosed pasture (Figure 6–20).

Barbed wire is not effective in controlling hogs, so Midwestern farmers invented other types of wire fences. Hog farmers use an eight-strand *woven wire* fence, and add one or two strands of barbed wire on top to stop cattle from reaching over it. This fence type was common in the mixed farming areas of the Midwest. The *chain-link* fence is a tougher version of a woven wire fence used by suburban homeowners as well as for barriers around military and industrial installations.

People always need some way to separate their domains from each other. Borders, walls, and fences are obvious and important but little-studied aspects of material culture.

BARBED WIRE COSTS

This table shows the amounts and cost of materials needed to construct a barbed wire fence, at 1982 prices in a small, midwestern prairie town.

Materials	Amounts				
Area to be enclosed (in acres):	1	10	40	80	160
Length of boundary (in rods; rod = 16 ft):	60	165	330	495	990
Weight of wire (in pounds):	67	183	365	547	730
Cost of wire (dollars):	$19	51	102	153	204
Cost of three strands of wire (in dollars):	$57	153	306	459	612
Number of posts needed:	60	165	330	495	990
Cost of posts (in dollars):	$495	1361	2723	4084	8167
Staples needed (in pounds):	3.75	10.3	20.6	41.2	82.4
Cost of staples (in dollars):	$ 2.63	7.21	14.42	28.84	57.68
TOTAL COSTS:	$554.63	1521.21	3042.42	6084.84	12,169.68

At today's prices, it would cost $12,169.68 to enclose a 160 acre (65 ha) homestead with a three-strand barbed wire fence. The cost does not include materials for gates, special corner posts, tools, or labor. You can calculate the cost of fencing the 600,000 acre (243,000 ha) King ranch in Texas.

CHAPTER 6 MATERIAL CULTURE

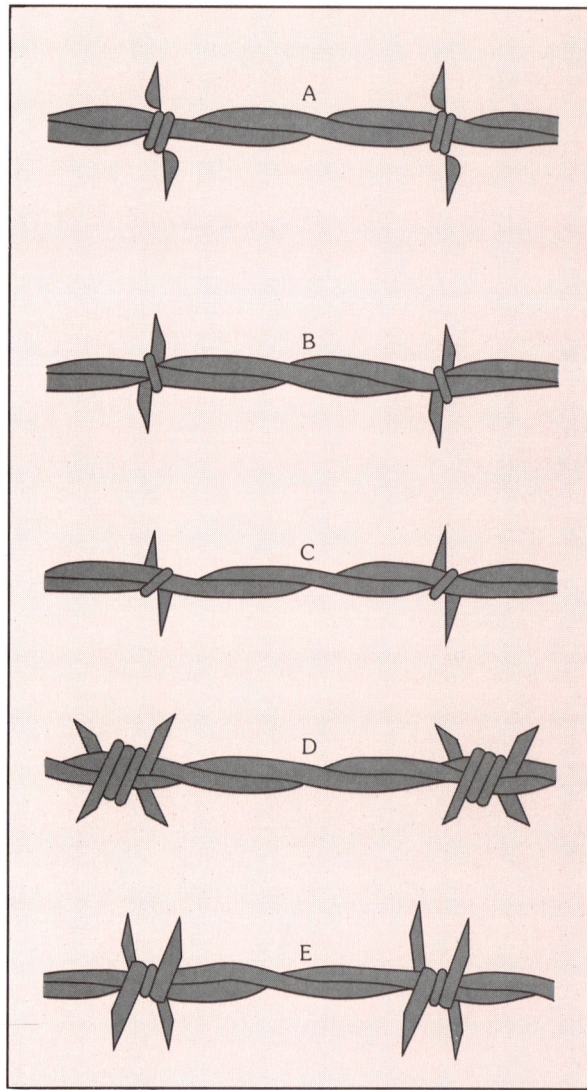

FIGURE 6–20 Various types of barbed wire.

MONUMENTS, BURIAL SITES, AND SHRINES

Humans have left their imprint on the environment in many seemingly strange ways. What appears strange to one culture, however, can be awe-inspiring and wonderful to another. It is also difficult sometimes for people from one culture to understand the purpose of a structure built by another. Huge amounts of time, effort, and money have gone into the construction of some structures, many of which have endured for centuries. Shrines are places endowed with a sacred character, usually because of some historical event that occurred there. Monuments are constructed to keep alive the memory of a person or event, but have no particular religious significance. Burial sites vary with cultural and geographical conditions.

Ancient Structures

Some of the world's ancient structures are quite mysterious. The remains of a 20-foot-high stone tower, for example, have been excavated from the walls of ancient Jericho. The tower was built about 5000 B.C., but its purpose is unknown. Even more mysterious is the circular arrangement of rocks on the Salisbury Plain in Southern England (Figure 6–21). Each rock in the monolithic structure of Stonehenge weighs over 50 tons. We do not know for certain how the rocks were moved and why the structure was built. Built about 2200 B.C., Stonehenge is dwarfed in size by the pyramids of Egypt.

The oldest of the Egyptian pyramids is the *Djoser Step Pyramid*, built about 2650 B.C. The tallest is the *Great Pyramid of Cheops* (2580 B.C.) at 481 feet (147 m). The Great Pyramid covers slightly over 13 acres and contains 2.3 million limestone blocks weighing an average of 2.8 tons each. Nonmechanical construction was tedious and difficult: the cut rocks were pulled up temporary dirt inclines by teams of men. The pyramids were built by the Egyptian Pharoahs as royal tombs.

The largest pyramid, and largest monument ever constructed, is the *Quetzalcoatl* pyramid located southeast of Mexico City. It is only 177 feet (60 m) tall, but covers 45 acres. It contains 4.3 million yards^3 of building material (3.3 million meters^3) compared to the 3.4 million yards^3 (2.6 million meters^3) for the Pyramid of Cheops. The oldest pyramid in Mexico dates from about 800 B.C., but Quetzalcoatl was built in the sixth century A.D. The New World pyramids were more like shrines than tombs. The largest tomb in the world was built for a Japanese emperor in the fifth century A.D. Located south of Osaka, it measures 1600 by 1000 feet (488 × 305 m) and is 150 feet (46 m) high.

Modern Monuments

Some of the most magnificent structures in the modern world are monuments. Victory in battle is one common reason for building a monument. The tallest statue in the world is an enormous female figure called *Motherland* located near Volgograd, U.S.S.R. The concrete figure, 270 feet (82 m) tall, was built to commemorate the Battle of Stalingrad of World War II. The tallest column in the world is a concrete and limestone structure located near Houston, Texas. At 520 feet (158 m) tall, it was built to commemo-

MONUMENTS, BURIAL SITES, AND SHRINES

FIGURE 6–21 Stonehenge, on England's Salisbury Plain.

rate the battle of San Jacinto in 1836. The *Arc de Triomphe* in Paris was built in memory of the French soldiers who died in World War I (Figure 6–22). The *Nelson Monument* at Trafalgar Square in London celebrates the 1805 naval battle in which Lord Nelson's fleet defeated Napoleon's fleet at the Straits of Gibraltar. Many other cities have monuments to celebrate famous battles.

The world's tallest monument is the *Gateway Arch* in St. Louis, Missouri (Figure 6–23). The stainless steel arch, 630 feet (192 m) tall, was built to commemorate the westward expansion after the Louisiana Purchase of 1803. One of the most famous monuments in the world is the 150-foot-tall (46 m) bronze statue called *Liberty Enlightening the World*—more familiarly, the *Statue of Liberty*. The Goddess of Liberty, holding a torch in an upraised hand, stands in New York harbor, and has welcomed millions of immigrants to the United States. Another famous monument in the United States is Mount Rushmore, where the faces of Presidents Washington, Lincoln, Jefferson, and Theodore Roosevelt are carved into the 6040 foot (1841 m) peak.

Cemeteries

Ancient and modern burial sites are visible aspects of human material culture that have allowed us to study many things, such as settlement patterns, epidemics,

FIGURE 6–22 The *Arc de Triomphe* in Paris, a monument to France's World War I dead.

FIGURE 6–23 Gateway Arch in St. Louis. (Photo courtesy of Missouri Division of Tourism.)

architecture, and wars. The style and material of grave markers, their inscriptions, and the location of the graves can reveal information about the people who constructed them. A simple wood marker in Boot Hill cemetery near Tombstone, Arizona, contains this message: "Here lies Lester Moore, Shot in the chest with a 44, no Les, no more." The laconic epitaph indicates the lackadaisical attitude of frontier Arizonans toward violent death.

A solemn atmosphere, on the other hand, surrounds the Great Wall of the Missing at the U.S. Military Cemetery in Cambridge, England, where over 5,000 names are inscribed (Figure 6–24). On the Vietnam Memorial in Washington D.C., about ten times as many are memorialized.

A similarly solemn atmosphere prevails at Little Big Horn, Montana; Vicksburg, Mississippi; Arlington, Virginia; and the other U.S. military cemeteries throughout the world. Every burial site in the world, whether an Indian mound in Wisconsin or the mausoleum at the Taj Mahal at Agra, India, can be a source of information about material culture.

Shrines

Shrines of three great world religions are located in the Middle East. Christians look to Bethlehem in Israel as the birthplace of Jesus Christ. Jews cherish the Wailing Wall in Jerusalem, and Moslems worship at the Kaaba in Mecca. Shrines may be the most difficult item of material culture to understand by nonbelievers of the faith that worship them. The *Kaaba*, for example, is a cube-shaped building draped with a black cloth that protects a small, black meteorite. Moslems believe the stone was given to Abraham by the Angel Gabriel, and it is the holiest shrine in their religion. It is the dream of every one of the 500 million believers of Islam to worship at the shrine. Indeed, nearly one-half million Moslems from more than 50 nations visit Mecca to pray at the shrine every year.

The largest shrine to Buddha is the Shwe Dagon Pagoda near Rangoon, Burma, although the remains of a 1,000-foot (305 m) long reclining Buddha have been found near Bamiyan, Afghanistan that date from the 3rd century A.D. The oldest shrine known dates from 6500 B.C., and was uncovered at Jericho in the Israeli-occupied area of the West Bank of Jordan. This small stone pillar is believed to have been used by a fertility cult. Many Hindus make an annual pilgrimage to the Ganges River, which is a type of shrine to them. Shrines as divergent as a small meteorite and a large river are as sacred as human-made objects.

MONUMENTS, BURIAL SITES, AND SHRINES

FIGURE 6–24 U.S. Military Cemetery, Cambridge, England.

U.S. MILITARY CEMETERIES IN EUROPE AND AFRICA

Cemetery	Location	Graves	Missing*
WORLD WAR I			
Aisne-Marne	Belleau, France	2,288	1,060
Brookwood	Brookwood, England	468	563
Flanders Field	Waregem, Belgium	368	43
Meuse-Argonne	Romagne, France	14,246	954
Oise-Aisne	Fere-en-Tardenois, France	6,012	241
St. Mihiel	Thiaucourt, France	4,153	284
Somme	Bony, France	1,844	333
Suresnes	Seine, France	1,541	974
	Totals:	30,920	4,452
WORLD WAR II			
Ardennes	Neupre, Belgium	5,319	462
Brittany	St. James, France	4,410	498
Cambridge	Cambridge, England	3,811	5,125
Epinal	Epinal, France	5,255	424
Florence	Florence, Italy	4,402	1,409
Henri-Chapelle	Belgium	7,989	450
Lorraine	St. Avold, France	10,489	444
Luxembourg	Luxembourg City	5,076	370
Netherlands	Margraten, Holland	8,301	1,722
Normandy	St. Laurent, France	9,386	1,557
North Africa	Carthage, Tunisia	2,841	3,724
Rhone	Draguignan, France	861	293
Sicily Rome	Nettuno, Italy	7,862	3,094
	Totals:	76,002	19,572

*Missing are those whose remains were never recovered.
Source: *American Memorials and Overseas Military Cemeteries* (Washington, D.C.: The American Battle Monuments Commission, 1977).

OTHER ITEMS OF MATERIAL CULTURE

This discussion has centered on immovable items of material culture, but hundreds of other objects can be used to study culture. Coins, for example, have been used for centuries, and contain valuable information about the people who made them. Hand tools, musical instruments, stamps, books, furniture, and kitchen utensils and many other items reflect the time and place of human activities. Spatial diffusion of items such as cowry shells for money, or iron nails, or banjos, or styles of tombstones can help explain current cultural patterns.

Other nonmovable objects of material culture that we could have included are great commercial buildings, like the Sears Tower in Chicago, the Boeing 747 plant in Everett, Washington, or the largest building in the world, the Ford Parts Redistribution Center in Michigan, and office buildings such as the World Trade Center in New York and the Pentagon in Arlington, Virginia. Arenas like the Superdome in New Orleans and the largest stadium in the world (207,000 seats), the *Strahov* in Prague, Czechoslovakia, demonstrate the human quest for entertainment and games. The great dams and bridges of the world are phenomenal features of the material culture landscape. The old, wooden, covered bridges of northeastern U.S. are especially interesting.

CONCLUSION

Human occupancy of the earth leaves its traces in many forms. The use of objects, construction materials, and design, and the diffusion (spread) of objects help to describe various cultures at different times. Some designs used today have ancient origins. Migrants diffused ideas from one place to another. Other structures are based on innovations in material use and improved engineering skills. Because most structures reflect the local environment, we find geographical variation with similar design principles.

KEY WORDS

adobe
bailey
barbed wire
barbican
bastion
black-and-white house
chain-link fence
covered bridges
Creole house
diocese
dogtrot house
Doric
double-pen house
drystone fence
Dutch door
folk house
half-timber house
hedgerow
Ionic
keep
mile-castle
moat
palisade
parapet
parish
portcullis
saddlebag house
shotgun house
snake fence
sod house
split-rail fence
stockade
tidewater cottage
trap-rock
Tudor
woven wire

REFERENCES

ARTHUR, ERIC, and DUDLEY WITNEY. *The Barn.* Toronto; M. F. Feheley, 1972.

BASTION, ROBERT W. "Indiana Folk Architecture." *Pioneer America* 9:2 (1977): 115–36.

BRANDT, LAWRENCE R., and NED E. BRAATZ. "Log Buildings in Postage County Wisconsin: Some Cultural Implications." *Pioneer America* 4:1 (1972) 29–39.

REFERENCES

BRAUN, HUGH. *Old English Houses*. London: Faber and Faber, 1962.

BUMPUS, T. FRANCIS. *The Cathedrals of France*. London: T. Werner Laurie, 1927.

COOK, G. H. *The English Cathedrals*. London: Phoenix House, 1957.

EKBLAW, K. J. T. *Farm Structures*. New York: Macmillan, 1914.

GARDNER, A. H. *Outline of English Architecture*. New York: Scribner's, 1946.

GORDON, HAMPDEN. *A Key to Old Houses*. London: John Murray, 1955.

JORDAN, TERRY H. "Log-Corner-Timbering in Texas." *Pioneer America* 8:1 (1976): 8–18.

KNIFFEN, FRED B. "Why Folk Housing?" *Annals of the Association of American Geographers* 69:1 (1979): 59–63.

———. "The American Covered Bridge." *Geographical Review* 41 (1951): 114–23.

———. "Louisiana House Types." *Annals of the Association of American Geographers* 26 (1936): 179–96.

———. "Folk Housing: Key to Diffusion." *Annals of the Association of American Geographers* 55:2 (1965): 549–77.

KNIFFEN, FRED B., and GLASSIE, HENRY. "Building in Wood in the Eastern United States." *Geographical Review* 56:1 (1966): 40–66.

MARTIN, GEORGE A., ed. *Fences, Gates and Bridges*. Chicago: Orange Judd, 1909.

MEYER, DOUGLAS K. "Diffusion of Upland Folk Housing to the Shawnee Hills of Southern Illinois." *Pioneer America* 7:2 (1975): 56–66.

MONTELL, WILLIAM LYNNWOOD, and MICHAEL LYNN MORSE. *Kentucky Folk Architecture*. Lexington, Ky: Univ. of Kentucky Press, 1976.

OMAN, CHARLES. *Castles*. New York: Doubleday, Page, 1926.

ROBINSON, ETHEL FAY, and THOMAS P. ROBINSON. *Houses in America*. New York: Viking Press, 1936.

ROONEY, JOHN F., JR., WILBUR ZELINSKY, and DEAN K. LOUDER, eds. *This Remarkable Continent*. College Station, Texas: Texas A&M Press, 1982.

ROTH, LELAND M. *A Concise History of American Architecture*. New York: Harper and Row, 1979.

SHURTLEFF, HAROLD R. *The Log Cabin Myth*. Glouster, Mass.: Peter Smith, 1967.

SYMONS, E. J. *Fences*. New York: McGraw-Hill, 1958.

WACKER, PETER O. "Folk Architecture as an Indication of Culture Areas and Cultural Diffusion." *Pioneer America* 5:2 (1973): 37–47.

WILSON, EUGENE M. *Form and Change in Folk Houses*. Man and Cultural Heritage: 1974.

ZELINSKY, WILBUR. "The Log House in Georgia." *Geographical Review* 43 (1953): 173–93.

7

Selected Topics in the Cultural Geography of the United States

DIVERSITY AND PATTERN IN RACE AND ETHNICITY
RELIGION
THE URBAN SCENE
PASTIMES
CULTURE REGIONS

The Watts Tower in Los Angeles, built by Sabotino Rodia, symbolizes the richness and variety of immigrants' contributions to U.S. culture.

The richness and diversity of world culture patterns is matched in the United States, which offers many examples to illustrate the working of cultural processes. Of the many possibilities, we have chosen a few topics to provide a glimpse of the tip of the cultural iceberg, with the hope of whetting your appetite for further independent explorations.

The discussion is organized as follows: first, we emphasize the importance of the relationship between culture, race, and ethnicity by considering several spatial patterns that have grown out of the cultures associated with racial or ethnic groups. Then, we will discuss religion—a powerful force in U.S. life (particularly in view of the emerging political consciousness of the fundamentalist religions)—in terms of the geography of various denominations and the processes leading to these patterns. Third, we will present some examples of the imprint of culture on the urban landscape. Pastimes then become our theme, for it is clear that sports, recreation, hobbies, and other leisure-time activities are elements of our cultural environment and reflect its place-to-place variation. Finally, the concept of the culture region is applied to the United States to show how geographers divide a nation into areas with recognizable cultural characteristics.

DIVERSITY AND PATTERN IN RACE AND ETHNICITY

The peopling of the United States is a never-ending process. Folks have come in steady streams and in massive waves, voluntarily and involuntarily, from almost every region of the earth. The earlier inhabitants—American Indians—have been slaughtered, dispossessed, moved around, and generally oppressed so completely that they are, today, a minority group torn between resurgent pride and utter despair.

Strictly speaking, the distinction between *race* and *ethnicity* is not very useful, because the concept of a "pure" race, owing to the historical mingling of the world's population groups, is virtually meaningless. On the other hand, people do react to one another partly on the basis of superficial physical characteristics such as skin color. The relatively low status of blacks in the United States comes from the consistent and strong tendency for whites to discriminate against them in many ways, particularly in employment and housing. In fact, the concepts of race and ethnicity are blurred and overlap in many respects.

Many persons make the mistake of attributing culturally-based behavior patterns to the biological characteristic of race. For example, blacks in the United States are prominent in some sports (football, baseball, basketball), but almost entirely absent from others (tennis, golf, swimming). It is tempting, then, to draw the conclusion that blacks are adapted by *race* to the first group of sports. However, the sports in the second group tend to be activities of the more affluent, and blacks, who are generally poorer than whites, have, with a few exceptions, been denied access to such activities.

What many interpret to be a racial pattern, then, is really a cultural or ethnic one. We see this again in the 1980s with the emergence of soccer as a major U.S. sport. Most players are white foreigners, brought in from major soccer-playing nations. The gradually increasing number of U.S. professional soccer players is also overwhelmingly white, a product of white middle-class families seeking an alternative to the expenses and injuries associated with U.S. football. Soccer is not a sport of the black ghetto, and is not likely to become one in the near future, since the great sports personalities of the ghetto have succeeded in *American* sports. In contrast, soccer is *the* football-type game in the Spanish-speaking United States, because it is *the* game in the "root" nations, including Mexico, Puerto Rico, and Cuba. There are some parallels in the case of ice hockey, also.

It is useful to relate the terms *race, culture,* and *ethnicity,* because population groups are identifiable on the basis of a combination of these characteristics. Persons of similar physical appearance, language, religion, dietary preferences, and socioeconomic status often prefer to live close to one another, on the grounds that friends and neighbors will have common concerns and interests, and will be able to communicate them. This is not to say that black or other ghettos necessarily are preferred by the residents of such areas; most ghettos are the result of exclusion by the majority, forcing minority members together.

Racial antagonisms have tended to sort people racially; if there were no such conflicts, the racial distribution of the population might be a random pattern, with cultural and socioeconomic considerations dominating, as they already are in many areas.

To summarize, an ethnic group is a group of people of the same race or national origin who also share a common cultural heritage. *Culture* and *ethnicity* are thus broad labels generally understood to incorporate racial characteristics.

A statistical summary of racial groups in the United States shows that blacks are by far the most numerous of the minority races, followed by Indians, Chinese, Filipinos, and Japanese (Table 7–1). Ethnic identification (Table 7–2) shows that race and ethnicity overlap, in that some labels appear in both Tables 7–1 and 7–2. In Table 7–2, people were counted twice if they said in the 1980 Census that they belonged to more than one ancestry group. English, German, and Irish are the most frequent ethnic identifiers used by Americans.

Current Patterns

Racial and ethnic groups can be mapped to indicate the regions where we can expect to find evidence of their cultural influence. The six maps of the United States in Figure 7–1 show the regional concentrations of the five principal minority racial groups and a major ethnic group—persons of Spanish (language) origin. The distribution of blacks (Figure 7–1a) shows the persistence of the "Black Belt" in the South. This pattern is a relic of the geographic distribution of the

TABLE 7–1 Racial Groups in the United States, 1980

Group	Total (thousands)
White	188,341
Black	26,488
American Indian	1,418
Chinese	806
Filipino	775
Japanese	701
Asian Indian	362
Korean	355
Vietnamese	262
Other	6,998

Source: U.S. Department of Commerce, Bureau of the Census, *Statistical Abstract of the United States: 1981* (Washington, D.C.: U.S. Government Printing Office, 1981), p. 32.

slave population. Although the importance of blacks in the South persists, many blacks have migrated with the expectation of economic opportunities in metropolitan areas outside the South, so that today about half the black population lives elsewhere. Large-scale movement of blacks from the South began during World War I and accelerated after it. In the three decades from 1940–1969, about 1.5 million blacks left the South each decade. In the 1970s, a new pattern developed, of black movement *to* new employment in the South approximately equaling outmigration (U.S. Department of Commerce, 1979). The cultural influence of blacks would be expected to be greatest in the South and in the inner-city ghettos of metropolitan areas in the North and West.

The map of American Indians in Figure 7–1b is almost the converse of the map of blacks. Apart from southern California, regions without blacks tend to be areas with Indians. The Indian population today has a primarily western distribution; as of 1980, the most populous Indian states were California (201,000), Oklahoma (170,000), Arizona (153,000), New Mexico (106,000), and North Carolina (65,000). Many Cherokees remained and fought in North Carolina rather than travel the "Trail of Tears," a forced march to Indian Territory—today called Oklahoma. Substantial Indian populations are found in many other states, of which Alaska, Washington, South Dakota, Texas, and Michigan rank highest.

The cultural influence of Indians is generally weak in metropolitan settings but strong in regions where reservations are prominent or where Indians are the dominant population group. The distribution of the Indian population can be explained through a combination of voluntary historical migration processes and involuntary resettlement mandated by the federal government.

Two states, Hawaii and California, overwhelmingly dominate the distribution of Japanese (Figure 7–1c). Each has a Japanese population approaching a quarter of a million. These concentrations originated in the nineteenth century with the inmigration of Japanese farm laborers. The only other states with significant populations are Washington, New York, and Illinois, with some 20,000 each. Where they are numerous, Japanese–Americans have had quite a strong impact on cultural patterns, perhaps most conspicuously as retail merchants, farmers and horticulturalists, and restaurateurs. Buddhist churches are also prominent, along with distinctive, religiously-influenced gardens and architectural styles. Fellows points to the Sawtelle district of Los Angeles as a case study in Japanese cultural influence, illustrated by the distribution of Japanese Buddhist gardens shown in Figure 7–2 (Fellows, 1972, pp. 152–63).

The Chinese population (Figure 7–1d) is concentrated particularly heavily in California (170,000), where the original attraction was the prospect of work in gold mines and railroad construction. New York and Hawaii also have substantial communities (81,000 and 52,000, respectively). One of the most distinctive cultural marks created by the Chinese is the Chinatowns we find in several large metropolitan areas (most notably in San Francisco). Even outside Chinatowns, Chinese people are also noted for their excellent restaurants. Chinese contributions to the English language also should not be overlooked. *It is important, however, to avoid identifying ethnic groups on the basis of such stereotypes, for their contribution to American society is, in reality, a diverse and vital one which stereotypes can in no way adequately represent.*

The distribution of Filipinos (Figure 7–1e) resembles that of the Chinese and Japanese populations,

TABLE 7–2 Selected Ethnic Groups in the United States, 1980*

Group	Total (thousands)
English	49,598
German	49,224
Irish	40,166
French	12,892
Italian	12,184
Scottish	10,049
Polish	8,228
Mexican	7,693
American Indian	6,716
Dutch	6,304
Swedish	4,345
Norwegian	3,454
Russian	2,781
Spanish/Hispanic	2,687
Puerto Rican	1,444
Chinese	894
Filipino	795
Japanese	791
Cuban	598

*Note: Ethnic origin is based on self-identification of someone's origin or descent. Covers persons who reported single and multiple ancestry groups. Persons who reported a multiple ancestry group may be included in more than one category. This double counting explains some inconsistencies between Tables 7–1 and 7–2.

Source: U.S. Department of Commerce, Bureau of the Census, *Statistical Abstract of the United States: 1984* (Washington D.C.: U.S. Government Printing Office, 1983, p. 42.

CHAPTER 7 SELECTED TOPICS IN THE CULTURAL GEOGRAPHY OF THE UNITED STATES

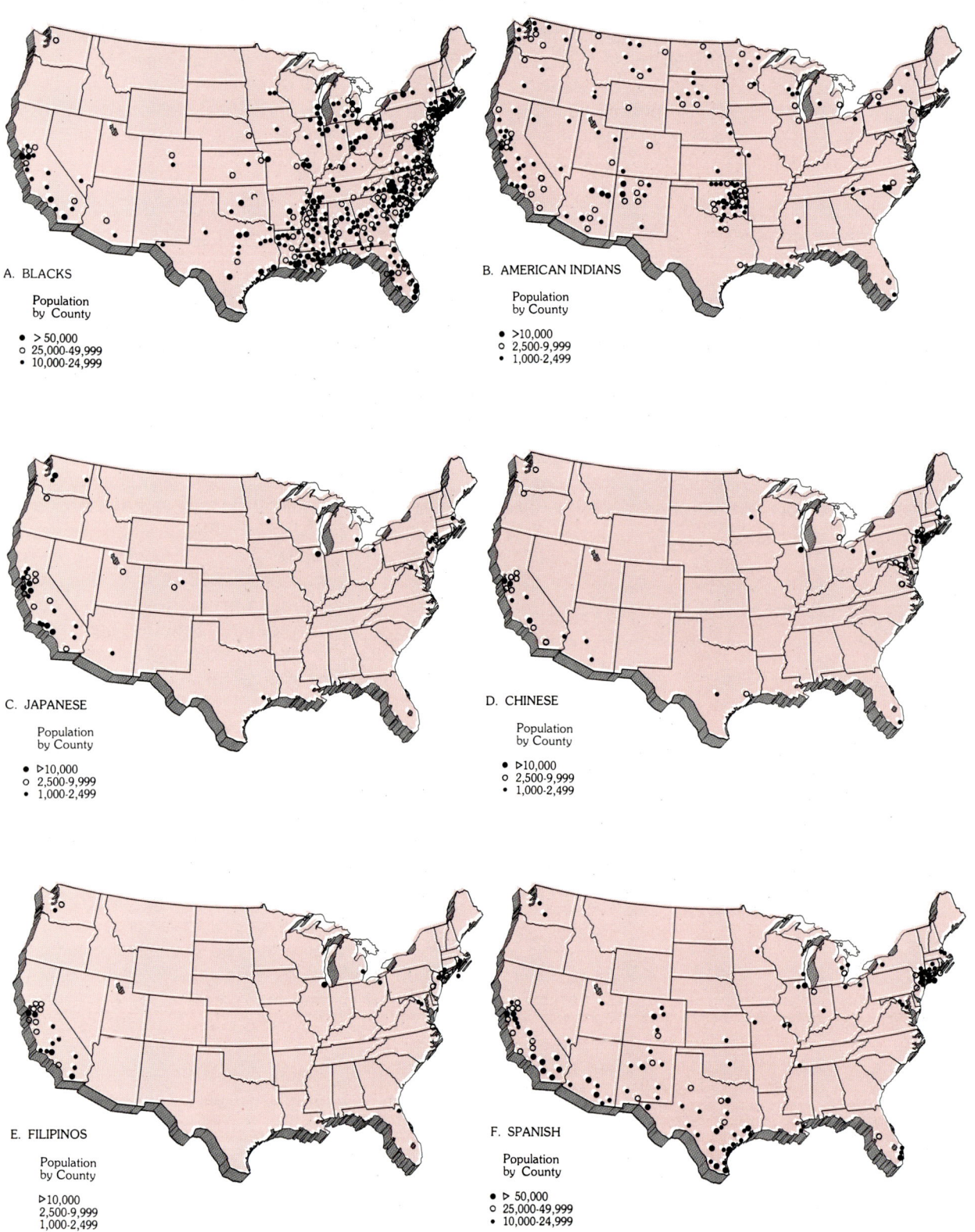

FIGURE 7–1 Ethnic groups in the United States. (Based on 1970 Census of Population data.)

DIVERSITY AND PATTERN IN RACE AND ETHNICITY

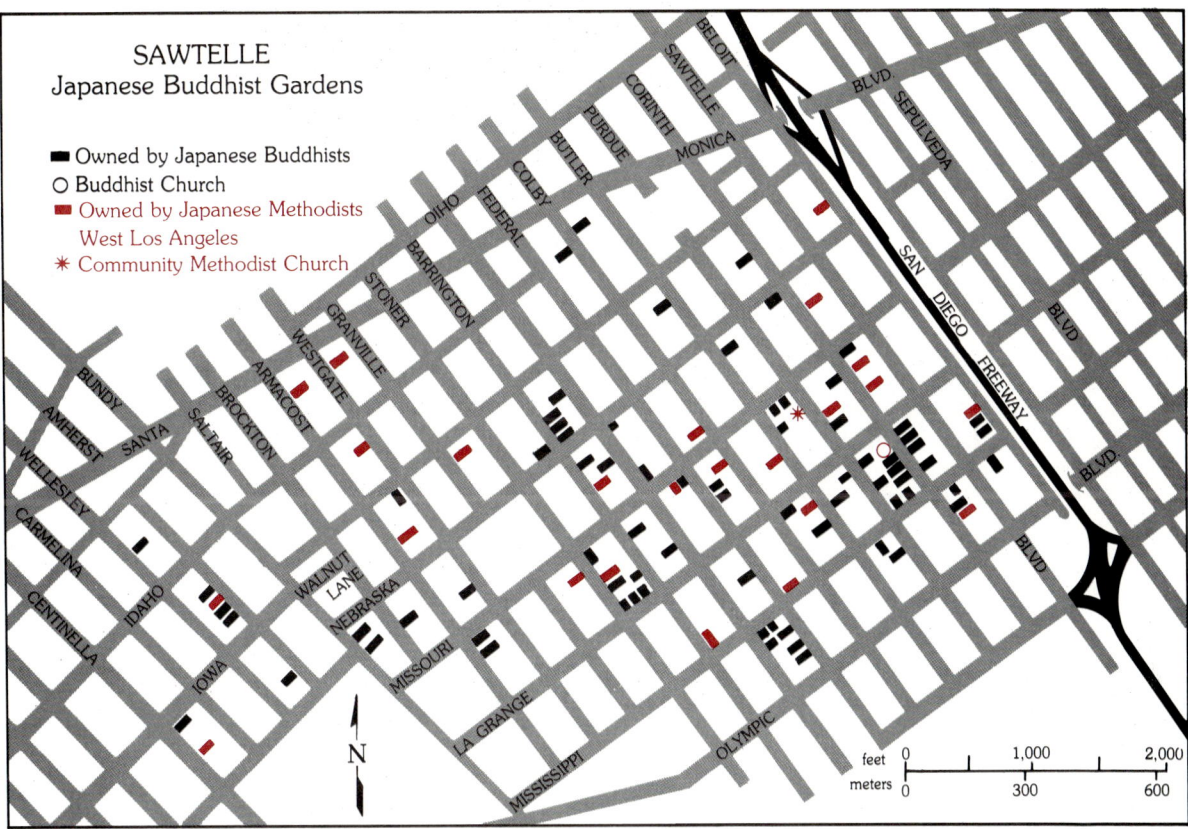

FIGURE 7–2 Japanese Buddhist gardens in the Sawtelle district of Los Angeles. (From Donald K. Fellows, *A Mosaic of America's Ethnic Minorities* [John Wiley, 1972], p. 156. Reproduced by permission of Donald K. Fellows.)

especially with regard to the dominance of California, which accounts for 40 percent of all Filipino–Americans (139,000), compared to 39 percent of all Chinese and 36 percent of all Japanese. Indeed, early Filipino immigration, like early Japanese immigration, consisted mainly of farm laborers going to Hawaii and California. Hawaii (94,000), New York (14,000), and Illinois (13,000) are other major nodes. The pattern is changing somewhat, however, as Filipinos are one of the most rapidly growing ethnic groups in the United States. Unlike some other ethnic groups, Filipinos do not form conspicuous cultural islands in U.S. cities, perhaps because individual clusters were never large enough to be locally dominant. San Francisco's "Manilatown," for example, has largely dispersed because of outmigration and urban renewal (Allen, 1977).

Persons of Spanish heritage constitute another large minority group, classified as ethnic rather than racial (Table 7–2 and Figure 7–1f). This group is also referred to as Hispanic, and often erroneously as Mexican–American. The people have diverse origins, ranging from descendants of persons who settled in North America prior to the establishment of the United States to recent Cuban immigrants, and including many Mexicans, and others from Central and South America. Cultural links between these peoples are based on language and religion but extend into other realms, including distinctive dietary preferences.

The regional distribution of the Hispanic people shows a major concentration in southwestern states, with California (more than 3.5 million) and Texas (over 2.5 million) being dominant (*see* Nostrand, 1970; 1979). These states are in areas of former Spanish settlement, and are also adjacent to Mexico, the source of many immigrants. Metropolitan areas in the Northeast also have Hispanic communities, and Florida—particularly Miami—has become a center for Cuban immigration, with over 100,000 people arriving there in 1980 alone.

You should bear in mind that the patterns shown in Figure 7–1 are only a fraction of all the maps that could be displayed to illustrate possible cultural influences by racial or ethnic groups. Zelinsky (1973), for example, shows patterns of Scandinavians, Germans, Italians, Slavs, Irish, Jews, and Franco–Americans (pp. 30–31).

The Rural Frontier

Of crucial importance in understanding the depth of the cultural influence of various racial and ethnic groups that have occupied the United States is the concept called the *doctrine of first effective settlement.* In Zelinsky's words:

> **Whenever an empty territory undergoes settlement, or an earlier population is dislodged by invaders, the specific characteristics of the first group able to effect a viable, self-perpetuating society are of crucial significance for the later social and cultural geography of the area, no matter how tiny the initial band of settlers may have been (1973, p. 13).**

To illustrate this statement, Zelinsky goes on to point out the importance of British immigrants in the United States, and of French immigrants in Canada, in the first major wave of immigration between 1607 and 1700. The next two waves (1700–1775 and 1820–1870) were still strongly British, and it was not until after 1870 that British elements became numerically less significant. As shown in Table 7–2, the British easily outnumbered other identifiable ethnic groups. It is not surprising, then, that the English language, British place names, sports (U.S. football, for example, is descended from rubgy football), and various borrowings in legal and governmental institutions, architecture, art, literature, and other fields can be traced to British roots.

A stranger to the United States, upon learning these facts, would not be surprised that the northeastern states are called New England, or that the names (New) York, Boston, Portland, Manchester, Worcester, Taunton, Warwick, Weymouth, Cambridge, Northampton, and many others are also the names of English towns. Predictably, the parts of the United States closest to Britain seem to have the strongest British imprint in names and speech, and perhaps in other more subtle ways.

The most desirable eastern seabord areas tended to be occupied early by British immigrants, so those who arrived later were more likely to leapfrog to the interior regions (Figure 7–3). This process is illustrated by the concentration of Germans in the Upper Midwest, Scandinavians in the north-central states, Italians in California, and Slavs in the area north and northwest from Kansas (Zelinsky, 1973, p. 26).

How could feelings of ethnic community and shared cultural heritage persist in areas of relatively sparse settlement? A major reason is the very strong tendency to keep farms within families through the inheritance process, perpetuating the family name and the culture. Even today, urban children have no hope of growing up to be farmers. Farming is a closed occupation, available only to those who inherit a family farm or, increasingly, those who manage a farm for a corporation. (Such a corporation may itself be the family farm in corporate form.) Rural cultural communities, then, have remained stable not only because of the sheer numbers of immigrants, but also because of this intense geographic persistence of the family farm.

Although many rural areas have a distinct and persistent cultural character, we must also consider the dynamic nature of U.S. society—a dynamism that constantly rearranges people and modifies both urban and rural cultures. Sometimes the changes are traumatic upheavals, like the Dust Bowl conditions and the westward travels of the "Okies" (Oklahomans) immortalized by John Steinbeck in *The Grapes of Wrath.* This migration to California meant that Bakersfield, California, and some other communities suddenly assumed an "Okie" character, with the superimposition of speech patterns and country music preferences that have, in part, persisted into the 1980s. Other changes are more subtle—persistent rural-to-urban migration, the yearly decline in the number of farms (37,000 lost in 1984), and the continuing sprawl of cities into previously rural habitats. (For additional discussion of the migration process, *see* Chapter 8.)

The Urban Frontier

One of the most striking ways in which racial/ethnic identity has been preserved and impressed on host areas has been through the development of urban ghettos. These communities have acted like conduits through which some groups have passed on their way to *acculturation* (the adoption of cultural traits of another group). Tragically, this melting pot concept has worked for some groups but not for others. Although we hear a lot about the black ghetto, or Chinatown, or Little Italy, we rarely, if ever, hear reference to Little England or Little Scotland. The United States is an English-speaking nation, at least in the sense that most public bodies deliberate in English, which is also the language of most schools and most literature. This has meant that English-speaking white immigrants have found it relatively easy to move between jobs and places of residence. Non-English-speaking people have had more difficulty, needing to stay in a hospitable community of others

FIGURE 7–3 Spread of settlement in the Middle West indicated by isopleths for 18 persons per mile at each census between 1820 and 1900. (Reproduced by permission from *Annals of the Association of American Geographers* 62 [June 1972]:261.)

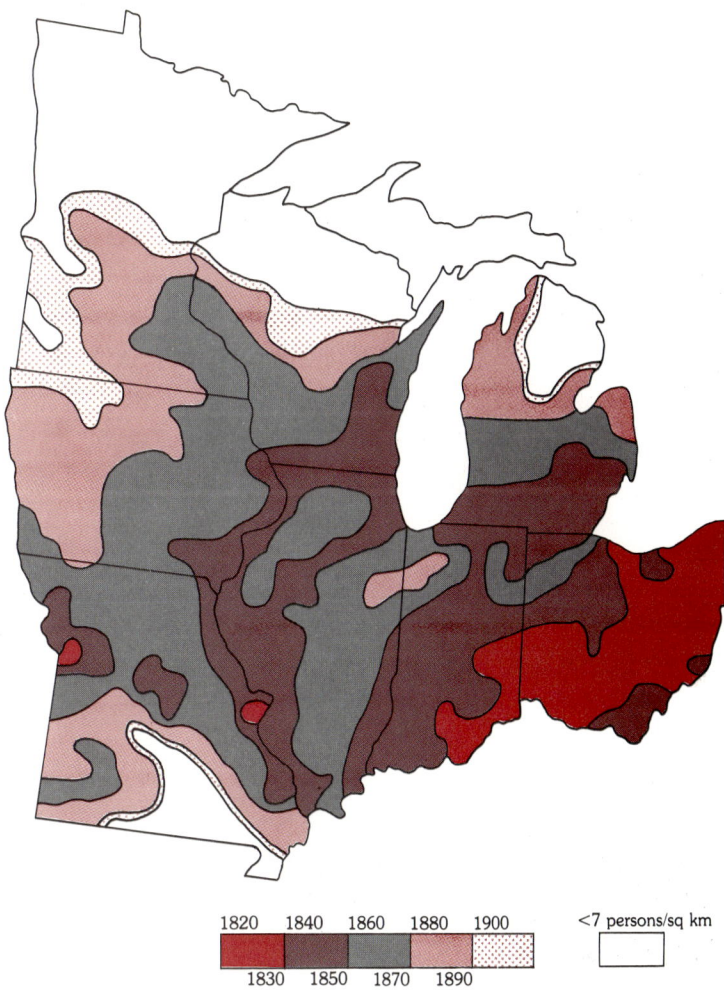

with similar background so as to learn the new language and make other cultural adjustments. Ethnic ghettos came into existence partly to meet these kinds of needs, serving as permanent homes for many but way stations for others who sought to move on to broader opportunities.

While acculturation has been reality for white ethnic groups, though at differing rates depending on the group, racial groups have had a much more difficult experience. For them, the melting pot has been in many respects an impossible dream. For example, the emancipation of black slaves eventually led to increased mobility, but it also meant exchanging one poor lifestyle for another as blacks moved from rural squalor to urban squalor. The experiences of racial groups have differed, but there is much validity to the idea that "progress" has often meant exchanging one difficult environment for another.

One shocking example (not to be compared in overall significance with the suffering of urban blacks) was the forced evacuation of all Japanese, U.S. citizens as well as aliens, from the West Coast, and the disruption of Alaskan natives, after the Japanese attack on Pearl Harbor. Interestingly, although Japanese and Alaskans on the West Coast were seen as a security threat, Germans and Italians on the eastern seaboard were not.

Urban ghettos formed by racial/ethnic groups have been persistent. European immigrant groups formed ghettos on the edges of urban central business districts in the nineteenth century to take advantage of a large and diverse pool of unskilled jobs available within walking distance (Ward, 1968; 1971). There were, in effect, two frontiers; the urban ethnics established territory in ports of entry and other major metropolitan centers, while their rural cousins moved the agricultural frontier westward.

Racial ghettos evolved in the early 1900s, initially in northern cities. Blacks have remained highly segregated and, in contrast to European immigrants, have not experienced much reduction in segregation as their economic status has improved (Roof, 1979,

THE STORY OF MICHAEL A CHILD OF THE WATTS RIOT

The rat crouched in the corner and fixed Michael with its eyes, shining like lumps of wet coal in the light from the living room lamp. It twitched its nose, then flared its nostrils. Suddenly, the rat began to move.

It crawled forward, slowly at first, the black of its eyes turning bluish-purple in the changing light. It darted into a run, skittering across the rug, and Michael could see pink on the bottoms of its feet. It headed straight for him.

He reached for a pack of Winstons on the coffee table and hurled it. Then a pencil.

Both missed.

Michael, 4, scrambled onto the couch. The rat, big as an alley cat, kept coming. It would feel cold, Michael thought, when it touched him. He crawled to the far end of the sofa.

At the last minute, the rat ducked under it.

For a long five minutes, Michael sat absolutely still. Then he ventured down, dropped to his knees and looked under the couch. He could see not a single gray-brown hair. The rat was gone.

But it stays etched as Michael's earliest vivid memory of his hometown. Watts, where 15 years ago tomorrow the black populace, its belly full of rats and poverty and insult and neglect, touched off the nation's first major race riot of the 1960s, a conflagration that scarred Watts forever. The ghetto would never be the same.

Yet it is.

In their all but hopeless, violent protest, a few in Watts exacted a great cost from many: 34 persons lost their lives; 1,032 were injured; 200 buildings were destroyed; another 400 were burned and looted. But the price brought too little in return.

Men in Watts still can't find jobs. Women in Watts are still on welfare. Housing in Watts is still inadequate.

There is still too little recreation. There are still too many drugs. Transportation is still poor. Low-price, wide-choice, close-in shopping is still scarce. Police are still distrusted. Gangs are still at war.

Indeed, their weaponry has improved. They have traded rocks and pipes for knives and guns.

Sometimes, to Michael and others who represent Watts' future, the institutions of law and justice, which normally keep communities from becoming chaos, seem to operate inconsistently at best; capriciously, at worst.

As a result, trust in those institutions is still shaky.

And the ghetto is still tense. The static that turned a drunk-driving arrest into a riot 15 years ago still can turn an innocent water fight into a pitched battle with flashing steel, barking pistols—and the police.

Watts is a community, not a riot.

It harbors the educated and uneducated, criminals and noncriminals, poor people and some who are making it, some people with bars on their windows and others without.

But the story of Watts since 1965 still is a story of trying to stop what the McCone Commission, which investigated the riot, called a "spiral of failure."

Source: Richard E. Meyer, "The Story of Michael. A Child of the Watts Riot," *Los Angeles Times*, 10 August 1980, Part 1-A; p. 1. Copyright, 1980, *Los Angeles Times*. Reprinted by permission.

p. 1). In many ghettos, the persistence of concentrated poverty linked to race has resulted in what has been called a "culture of poverty"—a cyclical process of unemployment, poverty, low levels of educational attainment interlaced with attitudes and values that have evolved from a variety of sources, including welfare regulations, discrimination in housing and employment, and the need to survive in an environment of extreme hostility—what one study refers to as "negative utopia" (Rabinovitz and Siembieda, 1977, p. 36). The feeling of the ghetto was conveyed well in "The Story of Michael," an article in the *Los Angeles Times* on the occasion of the fifteenth anniversary of the Watts riot.

Clearly, much of what may be considered a *cultural* difference between ghetto and suburb is actually based on *economic* differentiation, and it seems that cultural and economic factors are often blended together in a complex fashion. A study of Los Angeles based on data from the black, Hispanic, and majority "Anglo" communities showed that differences in the functional organization of retail and service activities could indeed be linked to both cultural and economic forces (Harries, 1971). Activities such as professional and financial services (as defined by the federal government in its Standard Industrial Classification), which are oriented toward higher-income clients, were sparse in the minority communities (Figure 7–4). Vacancies were high, particularly in the black community. Two interarea differences that appeared to be based substantially on cultural factors were the prominence of personal service establishments in the black area and of food stores in the Hispanic (predominantly Mexican–American) zone (Figure 7–5). The category "personal services" includes such functions as laundries, cleaners, beauty and barber shops, and funeral homes, and the major difference came from the fact that shoe-shine parlors were found *only* in the black area, and they were numerous. The high frequency of food stores in the Hispanic sample was related to the survival of small corner ("Mom 'n Pop") groceries as well as *tortillerias* (bakeries specializing in tortillas), and the virtual absence of supermarkets.

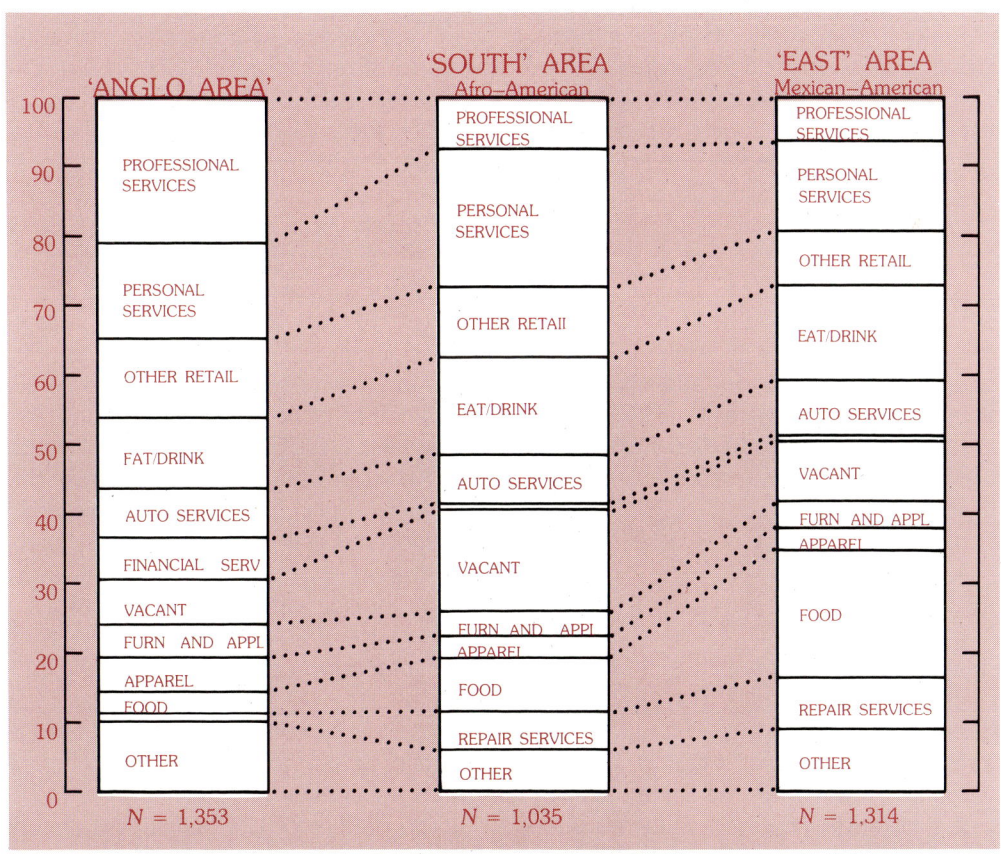

FIGURE 7–4 Functional variation in retail and service activity in Los Angeles ethnic areas. (Reproduced by permission from *Annals of the Association of American Geographers*, 61 [1971]:739.)

FIGURE 7–5 The ethnic dimension of retailing as it appears on a building in Hispanic East Los Angeles.

What could account for this absence of supermarkets, in view of their dominance elsewhere? Catering to Mexican–American food preferences is more costly for supermarket chains, in addition to which the proximity and intimacy of the neighborhood store and its Spanish-speaking clerks make the corner stores attractive. Furthermore, the small stores may allow customers to buy on credit. In short, the small stores are more "comfortable" for the community even though consumers probably pay higher prices than they would in larger stores (Harries, 1971; see also Wong, 1977; and Schmidt and Lee, 1978).

There is a rich literature on the geography of minority groups in U.S. cities, much of which contains information on cultural processes. For additional discussions, look at Davis and Donaldson (1975), Ley (1974), and Peach (1975). We also find important contributions in the literature of sociology and urban history.

RELIGION

Religion is a major cultural component, a phenomenon often linked to ethnic identity. There is much validity to stereotypes that portray Irish and Hispanic–Americans as Catholics, for example,—most are, at least nominally. Religion in the United States is something of a paradox, however. Churches are numerous, with some 341,000 reported in 1983, or one church for every 674 persons. Furthermore, churches are generally recognized as political forces to be reckoned with, particularly in view of the rapid growth of political consciousness and influence among evangelical groups, especially Southern Baptists. On the other hand, as Zelinsky notes, religious conviction in the United States is shallow, and "traditional theological concerns scarcely ever enter the average citizen's head" (1973, p. 95). Churches are essentially social centers, and the clergy are at least as much social workers as they are theologians. Contrast the social orientation of U.S. religion, if you will, to the fervent zeal of Islam in Iran, where church decrees touch virtually every aspect of life. The link in the United States between fundamentalist religion, patriotism, and conservative politics (the Moral Majority) tends to confirm Zelinsky's assertion that "Americanism has, in a most fundamental sense, become the true religion of Americans" (1973, p. 95).

Whether or not you accept Zelinsky's somewhat controversial suggestion, you can probably agree that Americans are fairly loyal to their churches and that large sums of money are invested in church buildings and activities. Less obvious, perhaps, is the fact that religious regions can be delineated, although not all can be explained easily. The major forces in the development of religious regions have been *colonization* and *migration*. Religion has usually been a piece of "cultural baggage" that migrant groups have carried with them and used as a tool to maintain cultural identity—a tool comparable in importance to native language.

The pattern of U.S. religions is shown in Figure 7–6. Here, the areal extent of a religion does not necessarily correspond to the numerical importance of that region. Catholic regions, for example, cover about as much territory as Baptist areas, but the

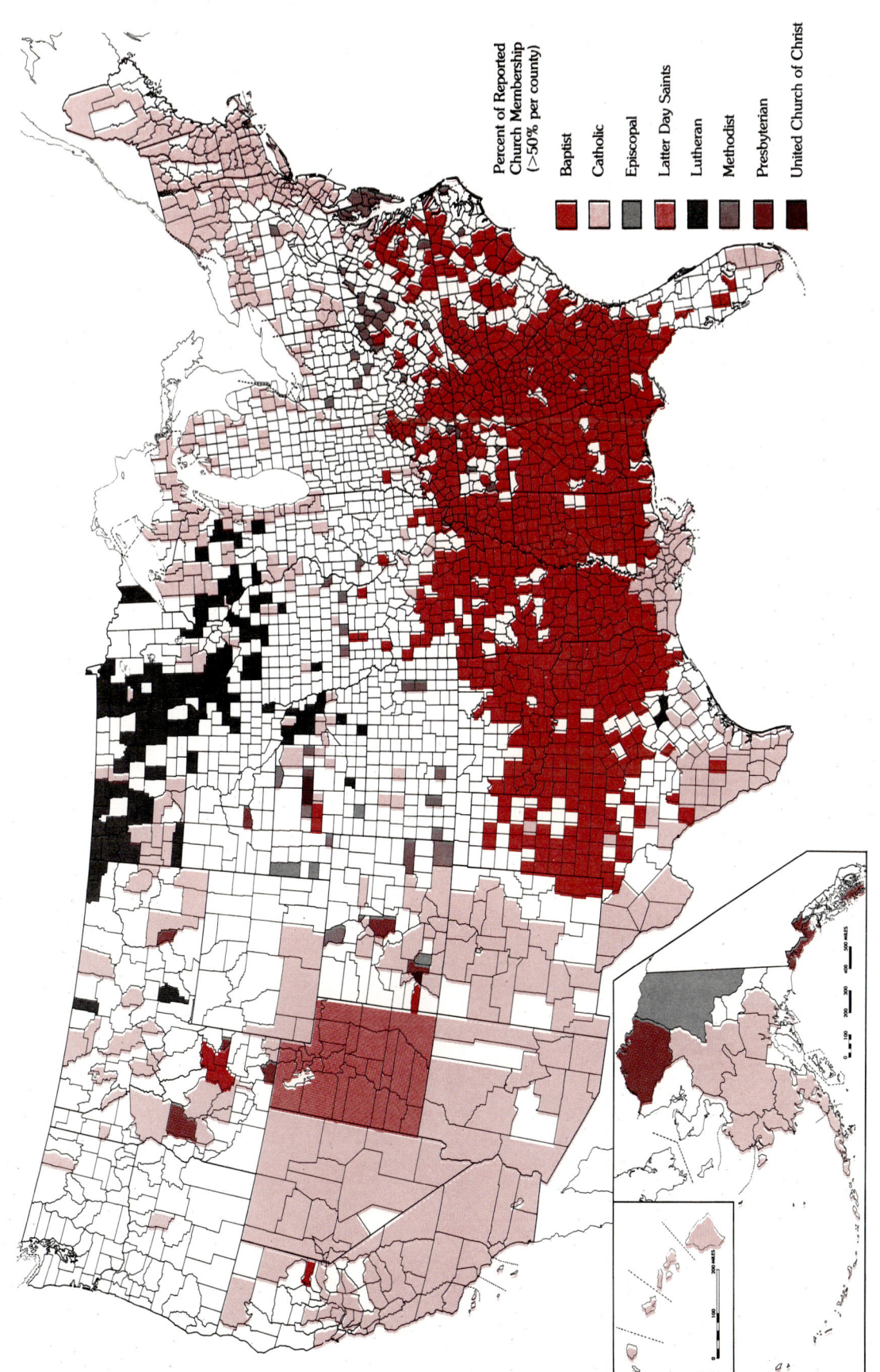

FIGURE 7-6 Major U.S. religious denominations by county, 1971. (From Glenway Research Center, Washington, D.C., 1971. Adapted by permission.)

Catholic church claimed a membership of about 52 million, compared to some 14 million in the Southern Baptist Convention. Similarly, areas of Mormonism far exceed those dominated by Methodists, yet the Methodist churches claim some 10 million members, three times the membership of the Mormon church (also called the Church of Jesus Christ of Latter-day Saints).

Why are there so many Christian sects in the United States? The answer lies partly in the fact of the nation's religious freedom—anyone who so wishes can start a new denomination. This process is facilitated by the lack of an established or state religion. Furthermore, Christianity was already fragmented when it arrived in the United States, brought by immigrants who had adapted the religion to their needs in their native lands.

Groups concentrated in fragmented urban communities are particularly slighted by the type of map in Figure 7–6, which is based on denominations that claim at least 50 percent of all church members in a given county. Jewish congregations, for example, claim nearly six million members, roughly half the total for the Southern Baptist Convention, but they are usually religious minorities in the counties where they reside.

One of the best examples of the impact of religion on the culture of a region is the Mormon church in the West (Meinig, 1965). Mormonism had its roots in New England. Church founders Joseph Smith and Brigham Young were from Vermont, and Smith organized the church in 1830 in western New York State. However, attempts to establish permanent communities were not initially successful, as the Mormons moved to Ohio, then to Missouri, and then to Illinois, where a mob murdered Smith in 1844. Having failed to establish settlement at the frontier, the Mormons decided to go beyond it, choosing the Salt Lake Valley, where Brigham Young, in 1847, uttered the immortal words "This is the place"—commemorated with an impressive memorial (Figure 7–7).

Although Salt Lake City was the focus of Mormon activity, a vast realm of Mormon domination was hoped for—an area called "Deseret," reaching from the Continental Divide in the east to the Pacific coast in the west (Meining, 1965, p. 199). Later, non-Mormons (whom Mormons called "Gentiles") infiltrated the Mormon area when railroads, mines, and other economic activities opened up the West. In Salt Lake City, the influence of both Mormons and Gentiles was reflected in the development of a dual central business district, marked by the Mormon Hotel Utah and Temple Square to the north and the Gentile Hotel Newhouse to the south (Meinig, 1965, p. 212). The Mormon landscape is unique in other respects, too. Mormon towns, compared to non-Mormon, generally have wider streets, distinctive architecture, unpainted buildings and fences, centralized barns and other farm buildings, and additional conspicuous features, such as hay derricks (Francaviglia, 1970, pp. 59–60).

In his analysis of the Mormon culture region, Meinig (1965) used the concepts of *core, domain,* and *sphere* to describe the nature and extent of the region. The *core* was the Salt Lake City area, along the front of the Wasatch Mountains, and including the city of Ogden. Salt Lake City is not only an economic center but also a religious focus, containing as it does the Mormon Temple and the large adminis-

FIGURE 7–7 Salt Lake City memorial to Brigham Young's famous phrase, "This is the place."

trative offices of the church. About 40 percent of the Mormons in the United States are located in this core area.

The *domain,* where Mormon culture is dominant, but with less intensity, covers most of Utah and spills over into neighboring states (Figure 7–8). The *sphere* of Mormonism, where influence is peripheral, extends on a roughly north-south axis, from Idaho and Oregon into northern Mexico. In addition, there are significant metropolitan nodes on the Pacific coast, and it is anticipated that eventually more Mormons will live in California than in Utah, due to natural population increase and migration (Meinig, 1965, p. 220).

It would be misleading to claim that there is likely to be, in any randomly selected location in the United States, strong physical evidence of the presence or dominance of a culture of religion. The influence of religion is generally more subtle, but nevertheless real. Faithful Catholics will heed papal exhortations against birth control and abortion, for example, and affect the *demography* (population structure) of Catholic communities. And, like any political lobby, the so-called Moral Majority of conservative evangelicals may exert influence out of proportion to its numbers. This influence tends to represent regional attitudes, particularly those of the South and Midwest, and is another example of the role of religion in the cultural geography of the United States.

THE URBAN SCENE

Cities in the United States, like cities in other nations, are cultural expressions. The layout of streets, the design and spacing of structures, and controls on land use and building materials are all the result of a complex process of human interaction, including the application of differing values. If you travel through several nations, you will notice that cities *look* different. Just exactly what is different is not always obvious, but there are differences. Americans visiting Europe for the first time often remark on how the cities appear to be compressed and crowded versions of their U.S. counterparts. Many Europeans, on the other hand, are impressed by the towering skylines of U.S. metropolitan areas, by the large number of detached single-family residences, and by the fact that cities are so spread out that few Americans ever seriously consider walking to work or to shop. Despite these differences, U.S. and European cities are all basically European in style.

Although economic considerations are crucial in determining whether a given parcel of land will be developed, and for what use and at what intensity (Chapter 11), other characteristics of cities are outcomes of more complex processes that interweave economic, social, political, cultural, and other factors in ways that determine the function and form of urban areas. The cultural component under consideration here is particularly relevant to a number of topics, including street patterns, architecture, and art.

Horvath presents an unusual perspective on street patterns by regarding them as *automobile territory* or *machine space,* defined as "any area that is devoted to the movement, storage, or servicing of automobiles" (1974, p. 169). When we consider cities from this viewpoint, the extent to which automobiles dominate the territory is indeed astonishing (Figures 7–9 and 7–10), and Horvath shows how an area may be progressively taken over by machine space (Figure 7–11). Our willingness to allow this takeover is an expression of our devotion to the free-

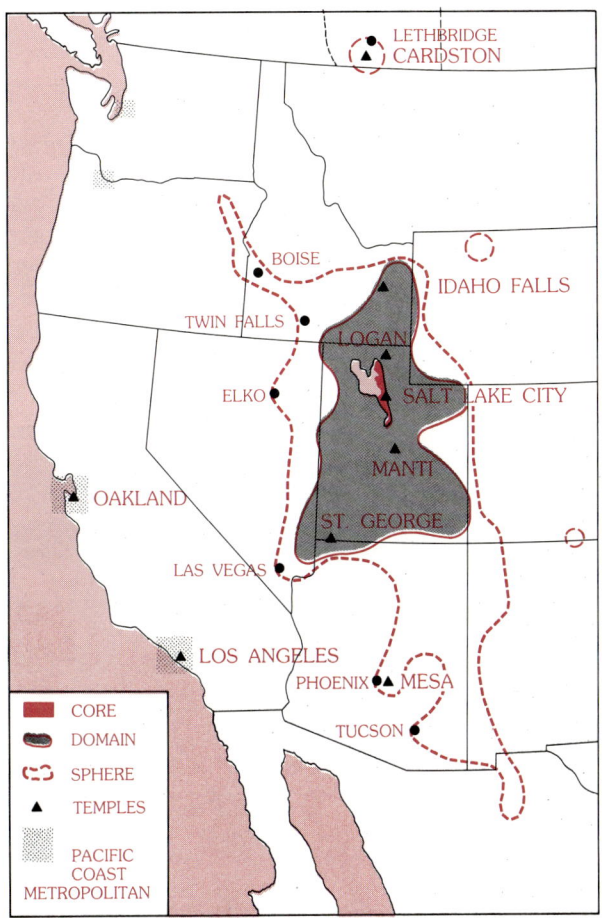

FIGURE 7–8 The Mormon culture region. (Reproduced by permission from *Annals of the Association of American Geographers* 55 [June 1965]:214.)

FIGURE 7–9 Machine space at ground level in downtown Detroit, 1971. (Adapted from *Geographical Review* 64 [1974], with permission of the American Geographical Society.)

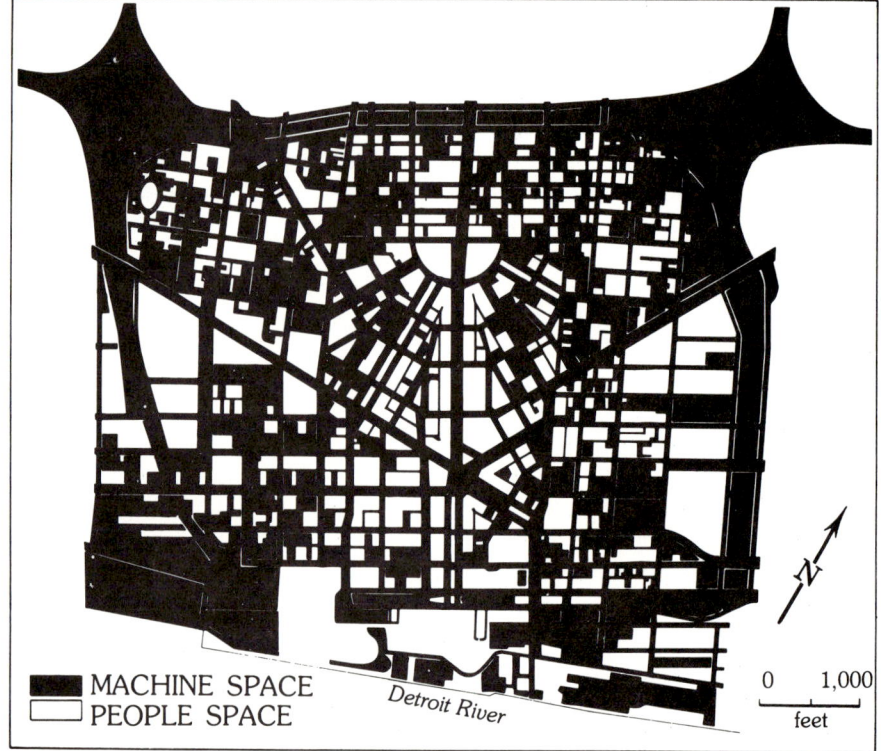

dom offered by the automobile, and our corresponding unwillingness, historically, to support public transportation systems.

Street patterns are also cultural indicators in an historical context. In Pennsylvania, for example, Pillsbury (1970) found two major kinds of street patterns—nongeometric and geometric. The state was then regionalized on the basis of these patterns, and it was found that central and western Pennsylvania were dominated by geometric plans. The southeastern portion was mainly nongeometric, as were the northern counties, while the southwestern region was mixed. Furthermore, street pattern boundaries were found to coincide approximately with other cultural indicators such as speech, religion, and house type (Figure 7–12). Pillsbury views these patterns as

FIGURE 7–10 Machine space in downtown Kansas City, Missouri.

THE URBAN SCENE

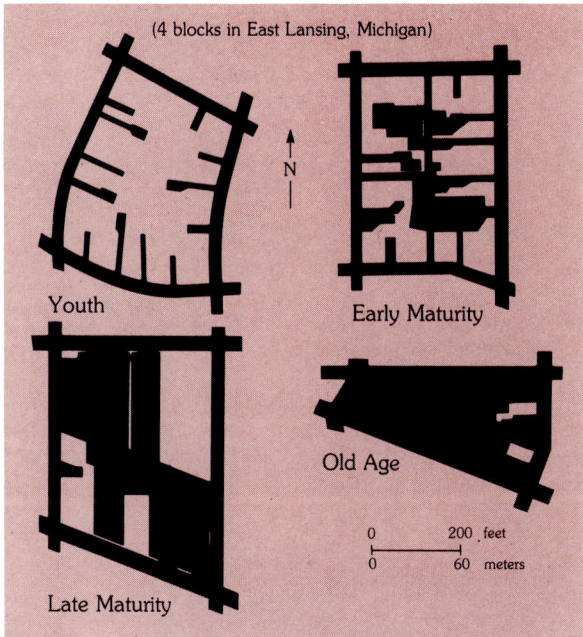

FIGURE 7–11 Stages in the expansion of automobile territory. (Adapted from *Geographical Review* 64 [1974] with permission of the American Geographical Society.)

products of the impact of forms various national groups imported.

Similarly, urban architecture is a cultural indicator. Early house styles were imported by migrants and were generally adaptations of European designs. Homes built by the wealthy in major cities became trend-setters, and their styles spread hierarchically, from larger cities to smaller, throughout the United States (Bastian, 1975, p. 166). This kind of foreign introduction has occurred periodically throughout U.S. history. The California bungalow, for example, is an expression of British colonial influence, as it was a style traditionally used by the British in India and Africa, where, as in California, the attraction was often the prospect of a mild climate and "easy living." Also in California, an outbreak of château building (patterned after a style from the Normandy region of France) was attributed to architects who had been captivated by the style while serving in World War I (Rubin, 1977). According to Rubin (1979), commercial building design in the United States owes much to amusement zones (midways) in late nineteenth-century world's fairs. In general, the expression of cultural preferences in the landscape of urban architecture is modified by various limitations, including

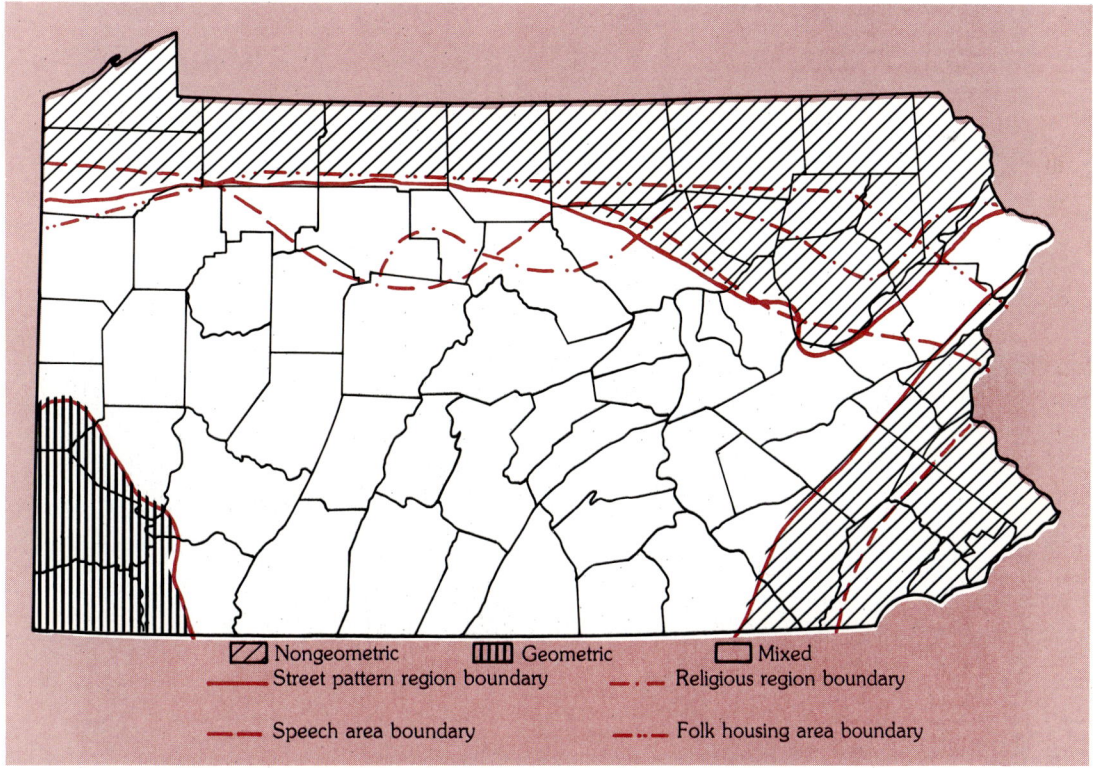

FIGURE 7–12 Comparison of street pattern regions and other cultural indicators in Pennsylvania. The observed patterns are related to topography. (Adapted by permission from the *Annals of the Association of American Geographers* 60 [1970]:442, 444.)

145

costs, city regulations, and what Rubin calls "aesthetic ideology"—the definition of good or bad taste according to critics, scholars, corporations, the media, politicians, and others.

Another aspect of urban culture that has achieved a great deal of notoriety is the form of self-expression called *graffiti*, the marking of public places, usually with spray paint. To many, graffiti may seem to be only mindless vandalism; however, there are distinct geographical variations in styles and applications (Figure 7–13). Spectacular murals in the Mexican–American community in East Los Angeles have become a recognized art form. In New York City and some other eastern metropolitan areas, "bubble" lettering has turned subway cars into mobile art galleries. In small towns, on the other hand, graffiti are generally uninspired or obscene, or both. But graffiti are more than splashes of paint on unguarded walls. Ley and Cybriwsky (1974) have shown that graffiti may be markers to delineate gang territories. In Philadelphia, they found that graffiti became more aggressive toward the edges of "turfs." Graffiti, then, may be regarded as anonymous staccato messages, many of which we can interpret, and from which we can learn something about the attitudes of social groups.

PASTIMES

Just as language, religion, and ethnic origins vary regionally in the United States, so can we distinguish

(a)

(b)

FIGURE 7–13 "Formal" graffiti decorate the perimeter of a construction site in Arne Street, London (a); and random graffiti on the wall of a spillway in the rural U.S. Midwest (b).

patterns with respect to other cultural phenomena, including pastimes such as sports and music. For example, Pillsbury (1974) points out that, although stock-car racing is scattered all over the United States, major-league racing is restricted to four basic regions—the piedmont of the Carolinas and Virginias, a Wisconsin–Indiana belt, southern New England and upstate New York, and central and southern California. The importance of the South as a stock-car region is thought by some to be an outgrowth of moonshine running, an activity that taxed driving skills to the utmost. Another interpretation is that the South, historically a poor region, was never very receptive to "fancy" sports cars. Although stock-car racing is not uniquely southern, the pattern of residences of leading drivers is indicative of the strong role the South has had in the development of the sport (Figure 7–14).

Rooney (1974; 1980) developed distinctive patterns in sports geography. He presents a variety of spatial perspectives of football, basketball, and baseball. Some of Rooney's most interesting maps relate to regional surpluses and deficits of major college talent in various sports. In football, for example (Figure 7–15), New Jersey produced nearly four times as many players as its programs could use. Pennsylvania and Florida produced more than twice as many. In contrast, Wyoming, Colorado, and New Mexico produced less than half their requirements. Rooney uses such data in combination with other information to suggest various reforms and conference realignments in collegiate athletics (1980).

In the realm of music, distinctive regional arrangements have been identified with respect to rock and bluegrass. According to Ford (1971), rock grew out of a combination of black rhythm and blues and white country and western. The *hearths,* or roots of the elements, that went into rock are found in Appalachia, the Mississippi Delta, and various metropolitan areas (Figure 7–16).

Diffusion processes led to the spread of rock music, and the simultaneous decline of some rock centers such as Philadelphia and the emergence of new ones such as Los Angeles and Detroit. New groups like the Beach Boys added distinctive regional flavor, and foreign influence, like that of the Beatles, was superimposed. Eventually, U.S.-style rock music became a worldwide phenomenon.

Another sound that exhibits distinct regional patterns is the bluegrass variety of country music. Country music itself is a kind of British ethnic music—a combination of English–Scottish–Irish ballads transplanted to the United States in colonial times—that soaked up and expressed the American experiences of the immigrants and their descendants. The bluegrass variant has been attributed to Bill Monroe in Kentucky in the 1930s (Carney, 1974, p. 34). Bluegrass performers tend to originate in the Kentucky–Tennessee–Virginia–North Carolina region (Figure 7–17), but diffusion processes, including radio, have stimulated interest in other regions. Carney (1979) discusses other aspects of the geography of music.

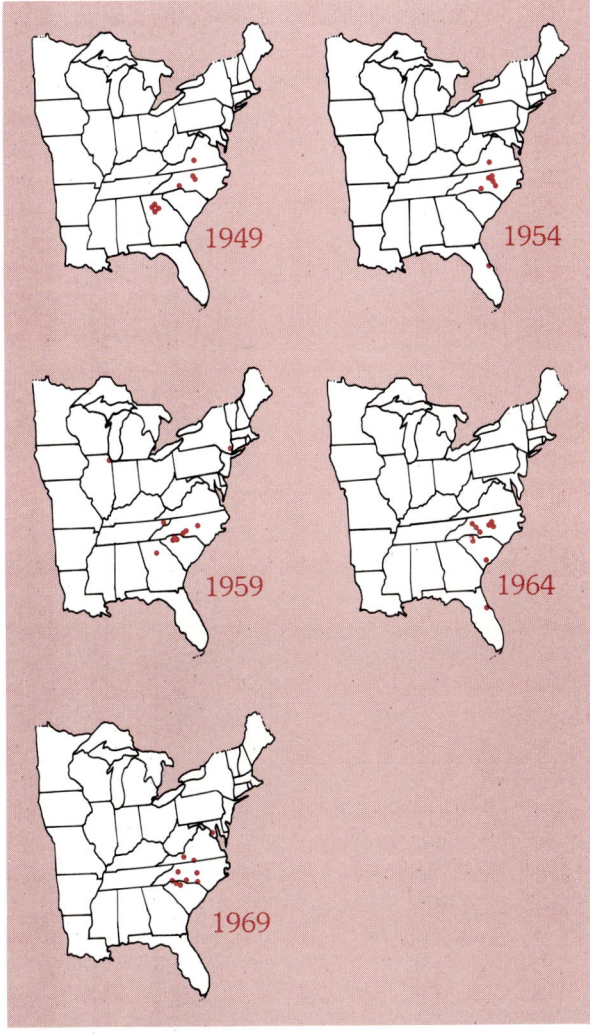

FIGURE 7–14 Leading NASCAR Grand National drivers by residence, 1949–1969. (Adapted from *Journal of Geography* 37 [January 1974]:39–47.)

CULTURE REGIONS

So far in this chapter, we have discussed a variety of significant elements of U.S. culture. Is it possible to make any sense out of the complex patterns? The boundaries on a map of cultural regions depend on

CHAPTER 7 SELECTED TOPICS IN THE CULTURAL GEOGRAPHY OF THE UNITED STATES

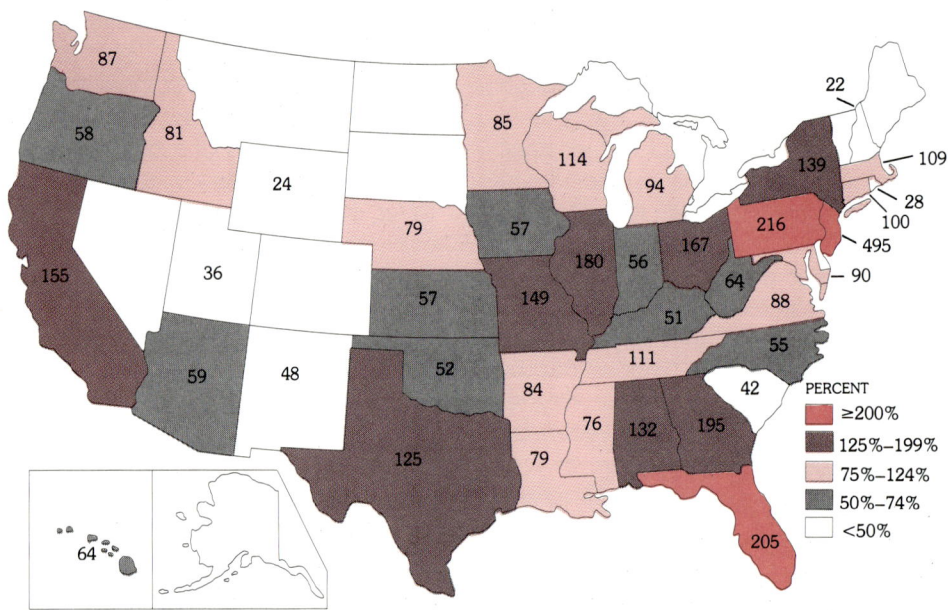

FIGURE 7–15 State surpluses and deficits of college football talent. Numbers show the percentage of its own needs that each state supplies. Based on 1971–72 and 1976–77 rosters. (Adapted from *The Recruiting Game* by John F. Rooney, Jr., by permission of University of Nebraska Press. Copyright © 1980 by the University of Nebraska Press. All rights reserved.)

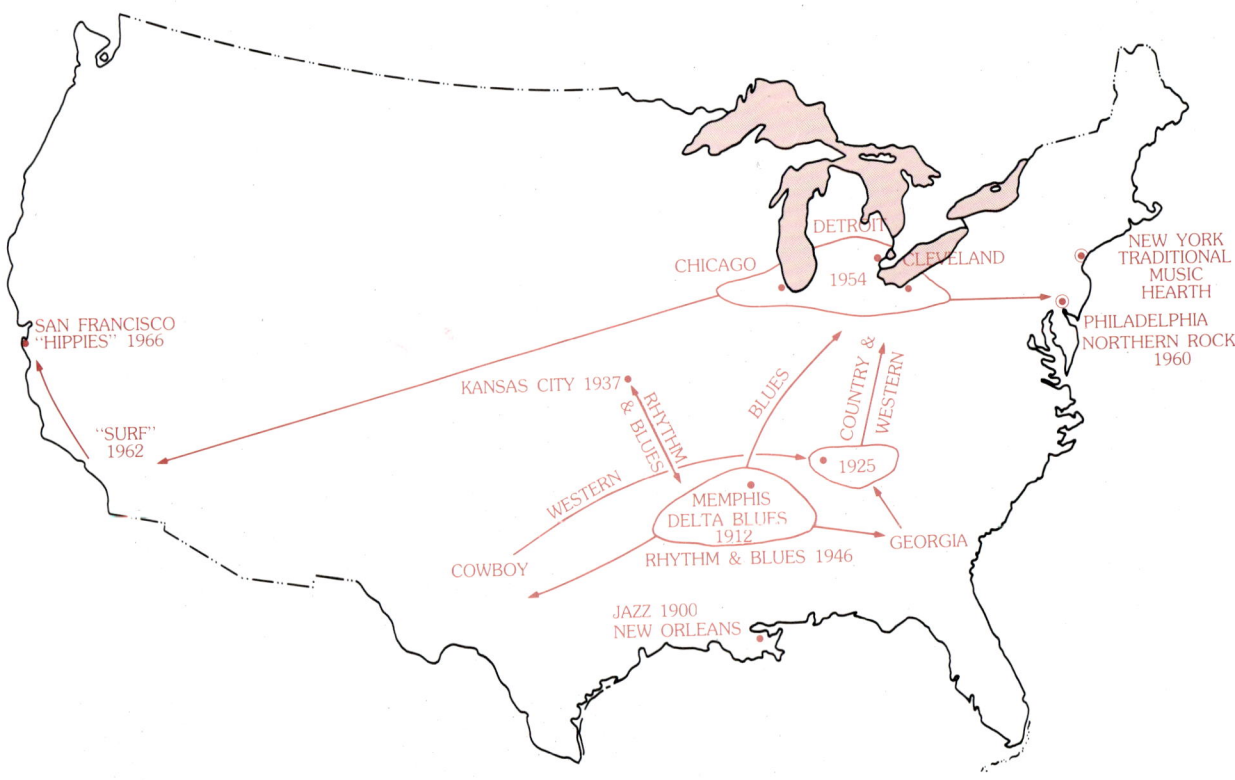

FIGURE 7–16 Geography of rock music. (Adapted from *Journal of Geography* 70 [1971]:460.)

148

CULTURE REGIONS

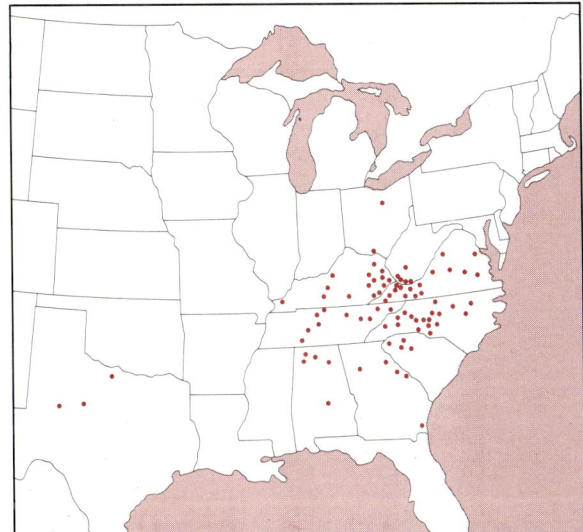

FIGURE 7–17 Distribution of bluegrass music performers' birthplaces (adapted from: George O. Carney, "Bluegrass Grows All Around," *Journal of Geography* 73 [1974]: 37).

the criteria used, so it is not surprising that there are differences among maps. Here we present just three of many possible examples to illustrate the cultural regionalization of the United States.

Building on Zelinsky's doctrine of first effective settlement, Gastil (1975) developed a map with 13 major regions and various subregions, districts, and subdistricts (Figure 7–18). The subdivisions of the major regions were based on factors such as differences in people's ethnicity and the extent of urban hinterlands.

Whereas Gastil's map had 13 regions, Zelinsky's had only 5 (Figure 7–19), which Zelinsky explained in terms of the three "European" eastern-seabord regions—"New England," the "Midland," and the "South." The Middle West is seen as an outgrowth of these three, and the rest of the continental area is classified as the "West." Although Zelinsky categorizes the "West" as a major region, he expresses reservations about the existence of a "genuine, single, grand Western culture region" (1973, p. 129). In fact, he states that all the western population clusters have in common is "cultural mixing" (Europeans, Mexicans, and Asians) and "newness."

The two maps in Figures 7–18 and 7–19 are based on "formal" data sources such as censuses and various prior studies. Another approach to mapping regions uses "informal" data and is based on how people perceive their own areas (Figure 7–20), yielding what are called *vernacular regions.* Zelinsky (1980) identifies such regions on the basis of regional

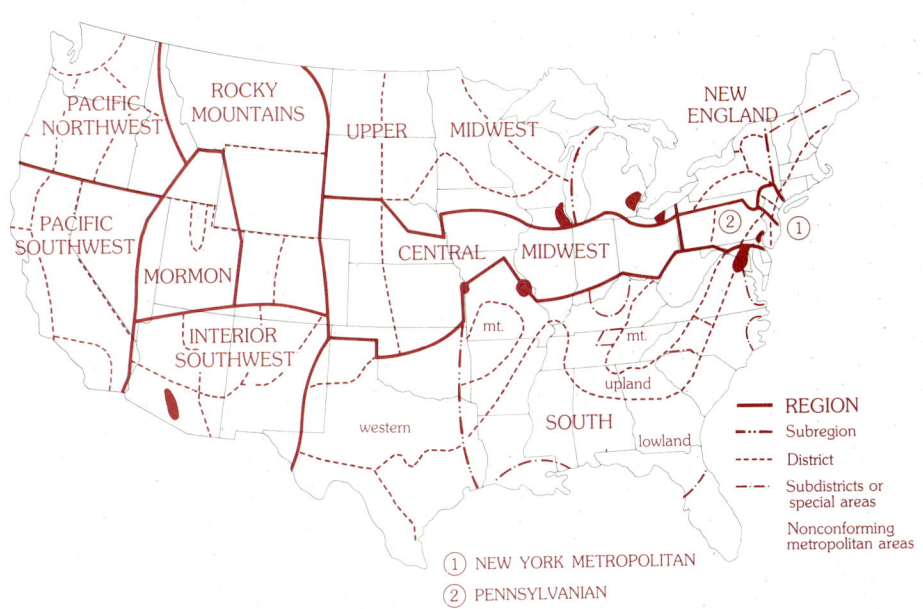

FIGURE 7–18 Gastil's 13 United States cultural regions. (Adapted from Raymond D. Gastil, *Cultural Regions of the United States.* Copyright © 1975 by the University of Washington Press.)

149

CHAPTER 7 SELECTED TOPICS IN THE CULTURAL GEOGRAPHY OF THE UNITED STATES

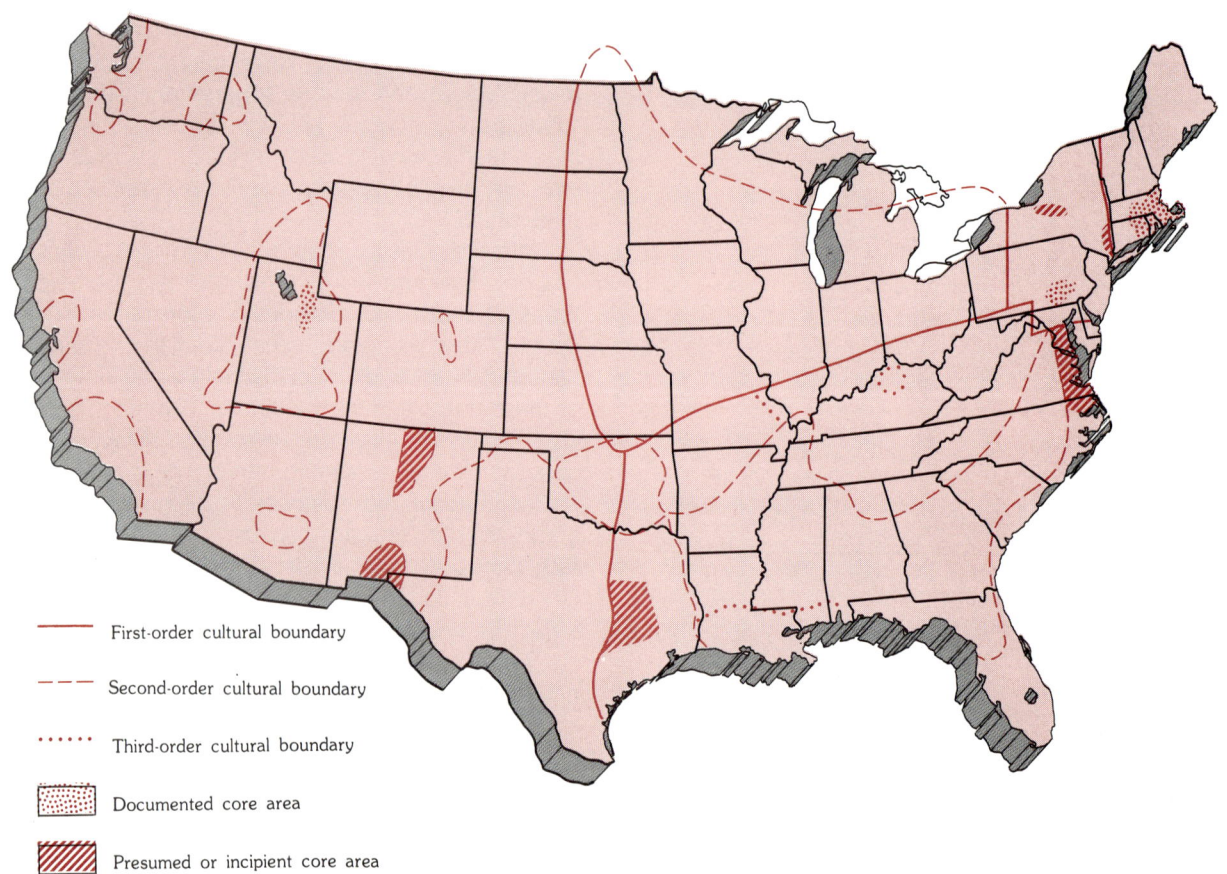

FIGURE 7–19 Zelinsky's 5 United States cultural regions. (Adapted from Wilbur Zelinsky, THE CULTURAL GEOGRAPHY OF THE UNITED STATES, © 1973, pp. 118–119. Reprinted by permission of Prentice-Hall, Inc., Englewood Cliffs, N. J.)

FIGURE 7–20 "Coon ass," the vernacular for "Cajun," reflects this car owner's pride in his regional and ethnic affiliation.

and locational terms found in telephone books; the generalized pattern is shown in Figure 7–21. While the number of major regions in Figure 7–21 is comparable to that in Figure 7–18, there are significant differences in the maps. In Figure 7–21, much of the "West" remains undifferentiated, with subregional identity emerging only in relation to the "Pacific Northwest," "Pacific," and "Southwest." The differences between these maps illustrate the complexity of culture and the difficulties involved in mapping cultural phenomena, as well as the fact that maps are influenced by the perceptions of their makers. (For a related discussion of cultural regions, you might want to look at Joel Garreau's *The Nine Nations of North America* [1981].)

CONCLUSION

This chapter provides a basis for understanding and appreciating the richness and diversity of cultural

CONCLUSION

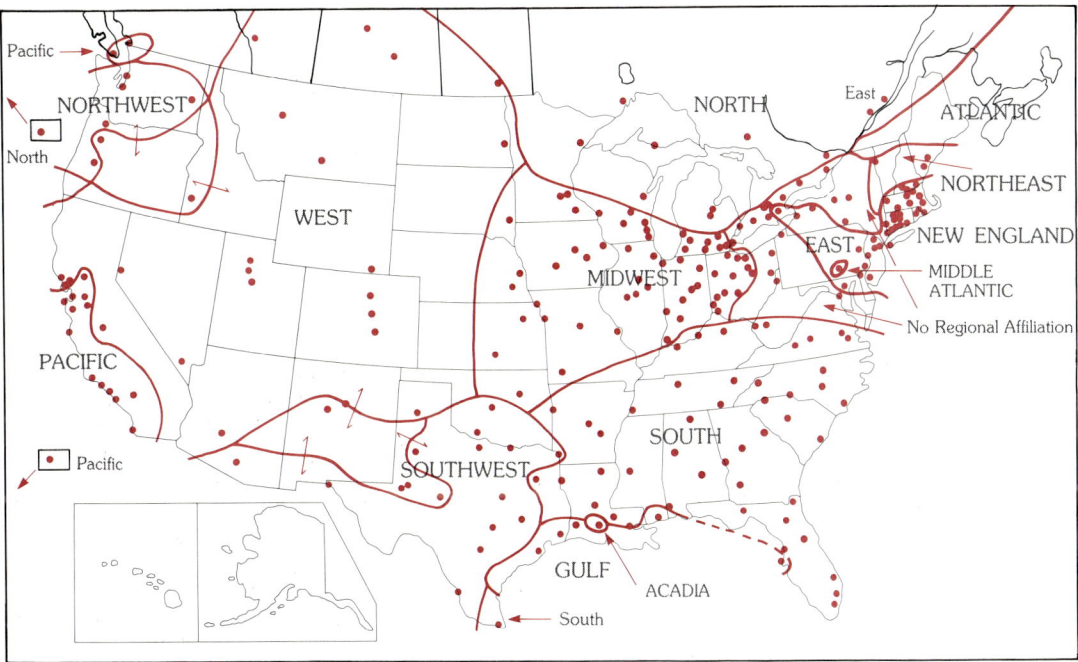

FIGURE 7–21 Vernacular regions of North America as indicated by metropolitan businesses. (Adapted by permission from the *Annals of the Association of American Geographers* 70 [March 1980]:14.)

patterns in the United States. Initially, we reviewed the interrelated concepts of race and ethnicity in the U.S. context. While many peoples of diverse origins have been assimilated into American culture through adoption of the language and other cultural traits, many signs of ethnicity are still obvious, such as the adherence of Hispanic–Americans and Irish–Americans to Catholicism. Furthermore, blacks have never been assimilated in the same way as white ethnics. Because of discrimination against various groups, the melting pot has not always come up to expectations.

We have seen the role of religions in U.S. life and the extraordinary diversity of religious sects. The Mormon church illustrates how a particular religion can become dominant in a region. The city is a cultural phenomenon, with street layouts, the presence or absence of sidewalks, land-use patterns, architectural styles, and even graffiti all as expressions of human tastes, preferences, and perhaps frustrations. Many of these attitudes have been "imported" by immigrants, then adapted to the U.S. scene.

Even pastimes in the United States have a distinct cultural imprint. Baseball, football, basketball, stock-car racing, country music, jazz—all either originated in the United States or are heavily modified versions of imports. American football, for example, today bears little resemblance to the rugby football from which it was derived.

There are several versions of U.S. culture regions; as shown by the maps, there is no agreement among geographers on exactly how the United States should be divided culturally. All that is established with certainty is that there are cultural divisions; how the lines are drawn depends ultimately on the criteria used and the judgment of the individual who applies the criteria.

CHAPTER 7 SELECTED TOPICS IN THE CULTURAL GEOGRAPHY OF THE UNITED STATES

KEY WORDS

acculturation
core
culture region
demography
doctrine of first effective settlement
domain
ethnic group
ghetto
graffiti
hearth
machine space
race
sphere
vernacular region

REFERENCES

ALLEN, JAMES P. "Recent Immigration from the Philippines and Filipino Communities in the United States." *Geographical Review* 67 (1977): 195–208.

BASTIAN, ROBERT W. "Architecture and Class Segregation in Late Nineteenth-Century Terre Haute, Indiana." *Geographical Review* 65 (1975): 166–79.

CARNEY, GEORGE O. "Bluegrass Grows All Around: The Spatial Dimensions of a Country Music Style." *Journal of Geography* 73 (1974): 34–55.

———, ed. *The Sounds of People and Places: Readings in the Geography of Music.* Washington, D.C.: University Press of America, 1979.

DAVIS, GEORGE A., and DONALDSON, O. FRED. *Blacks in the United States: A Geographic Perspective.* Boston: Houghton Mifflin Co., 1975.

FELLOWS, DONALD K. *A Mosaic of America's Ethnic Minorities.* New York: John Wiley & Sons, 1972.

FORD, LARRY. "Geographic Factors in the Origin, Evolution, and Diffusion of Rock and Roll Music." *Journal of Geography* 70 (1971): 455–64.

FRANCAVIGLIA, RICHARD V. "The Mormon Landscape: Definition of an Image in the American West." *Proceedings of the Association of American Geographers,* vol. 2, 1970, pp. 59–61.

GARREAU, JOEL. *The Nine Nations of North America.* Boston: Houghton Mifflin Co., 1981

GASTIL, RAYMOND D. *Cultural Regions of the United States.* Seattle, Wash.: University of Washington Press, 1975.

HARRIES, KEITH D. "Ethnic Variations in Los Angeles Business Patterns." *Annals of the Association of American Geographers* 61, (1971): 736–43.

HORVATH, RONALD J. "Machine Space." *Geographical Review* 64 (1974): 167–88.

LEY, DAVID. *The Black Inner City as Frontier Outpost: Images and Behavior of a Philadelphia Neighborhood.* Association of American Geographers Monograph Series No. 7. Washington, D.C., 1974.

LEY, DAVID, and CYBRIWSKY, R. "Urban Graffiti as Territorial Markers." *Annals of the Association of American Geographers* 64 (1974): 491–505.

MEINIG, D. W. "The Mormon Culture Region: Strategies and Patterns in the Geography of the American West, 1847–1964." *Annals of the Association of American Geographers* 55 (1965): 191–220.

MEYER, RICHARD E. "The Story of Michael: A Child of the Watts Riot." *Los Angeles Times,* 10 August 1980, Part 1–A (supplement, 12 pp.).

NOSTRAND, RICHARD L. "The Hispanic—American Borderland: Delimitation of an American Culture Region." *Annals of the Association of American Geographers* 60 (1970): 638–61.

———. "Spanish Roots in the Borderlands." *Geographical Magazine* 52 (1979): 203–9.

REFERENCES

PEACH, CERI. *Urban Social Segregation.* New York: Longman, 1975.

PILLSBURY, RICHARD. "The Urban Street Pattern as a Culture Indicator: Pennsylvania, 1682–1815." *Annals of the Association of American Geographers* 60, (1970): 428–46.

———. "Carolina Thunder: A Geography of Southern Stock Car Racing." *Journal of Geography* 37 (1974): 39–47.

RABINOVITZ, FRANCINE F., and SIEMBIEDA, WILLIAM J. *Minorities in Suburbs.* Lexington, Mass.: Lexington Books, 1977.

ROOF, WADE CLARK. "Race and Residence: The Shifting Basis of American Race Relations." *Annals of the American Academy of Political and Social Science* 441, (1979) 1–12.

ROONEY, JOHN F. JR. *A Geography of American Sport.* Reading, Mass.: Addison-Wesley Publishing Co., 1974.

———. *The Recruiting Game.* Lincoln, Nebr.: University of Nebraska Press, 1980.

ROONEY, JOHN F., Jr., WILBUR ZELINSKY, and DEAN R. LOUDER (Editors), *This Remarkable Continent: An Atlas of United States and Canadian Societies and Cultures* (College Station, Texas: Texas A&M University Press, 1982).

RUBIN, BARBARA. "A Chronology of Architecture in Los Angeles." *Annals of the Association of American Geographers* 67 (1977): 521–37.

———. "Aesthetic Ideology and Urban Design." *Annals of the Association of American Geographers* 69 (1979): 339–61.

SCHMIDT, CHARLES G., and LEE, YUK. "Impacts of Changing Racial Composition upon Commercial Land Use Succession and Commercial Structure." *Urban Affairs Quarterly* 13 (1978): 341–54.

THERNSTROM, STEPHEN, ed. *Harvard Encyclopedia of American Ethnic Groups.* Cambridge, Mass: Harvard University Press, 1980.

U.S. DEPARTMENT OF COMMERCE, Bureau of the Census. *The Social and Economic Status of the Black Population in the United States, 1790–1978.* Washington, D.C.: U.S. Government Printing Office, 1979.

WARD, DAVID. "The Emergence of Central Immigrant Ghettos in American Cities: 1840–1920." *Annals of the Association of American Geographers* 58 (1968): 343–59.

———. *Cities and Immigrants.* New York: Oxford University Press, 1971.

WONG, CHARLES CHOY. "Black and Chinese Grocery Stores in Los Angeles' Black Ghetto." *Urban Life* 5 (1977): 439–64.

ZELINSKY, WILBUR. *The Cultural Geography of the United States.* Englewood Cliffs, N. J.: Prentice-Hall, 1973.

———. "North America's Vernacular Regions." *Annals of the Association of American Geographers* 70, (1980): 1–16.

8
Social Processes

SOCIAL SPACE
AGGREGATION AND BEHAVIOR
BASIC CONCEPTS IN HUMAN SPATIAL INTERACTION
INTERACTION THROUGH MOVEMENT
INTERACTION THROUGH COMMUNICATION

This scene in central Boston symbolizes the social pathologies of many inner-city areas.

Social geography is about people—how and why they are arranged geographically, how and why they interact (make contact with one another), how and why they move, and how and why various conflicts and inequities arise out of observed patterns of people and their interactions and movements. Social geography, like other branches of geography, touches on other disciplines and on other facets of geography.

Any discipline or subdiscipline that attempts to develop explanations of human behavior is always complex and often, despite researchers' best efforts, disappointing in its ability to predict how people will behave. Social geography shares the complications and frustrations of its most closely related fields—sociology, psychology, and cultural geography. The challenges center on the unpredictability of human behavior, which is compounded by the "chemistry" involved when people of diverse age, ethnicity, class, and race are brought together in cities or other settlements.

In this chapter we will deal with how social geography views the world via concepts of social space and methods of social geography. Then we will focus on the perception process, and next on the controversial topics of density and crowding. The latter part of the chapter deals with various forms of interaction, including interaction through movement (journey to work, journey to shop, and social trips), migration processes and patterns, and interaction through communication.

SOCIAL SPACE

In Chapter 1, you read about the concepts of relative and absolute distance and location, which imply the existence of absolute and relative space. *Absolute space* locates objects with reference to an *x-y* coordinate system. *Relative space* measures location with reference to other objects—person A is three yards (2.7m) from person B. Now we will introduce another way of thinking about space.

In discussing some of the basic concepts of social geography, it is useful to be able to refer to the idea of *social space*. Just as we can measure distance in units of length or time or in terms of the dollar cost of traveling a unit distance, so can we refer to space in different ways. This, in effect, enables us to look at our environment selectively, to see limited aspects of the complexity of reality. Social space, then, may be regarded as a composite of areas of human interaction. The following scheme (Buttimer, 1969, pp. 420–21) has several levels of social space. *Personal space*, which we will cover in more detail later in the chapter, refers to the immediate environment of individuals. If you are in a crowd—at a concert, for instance—your personal space may be very limited. If you are alone in a wilderness, you may feel that your personal space stretches from horizon to horizon. *Familial space* refers primarily to the home—the context in which domestic relationships developed. *Neighborhood space* includes the geography of day-to-day movements—visits to neighborhood stores or parks, for example. Neighborhood space has been subdivided into three types: (1) the *social acquaintance neighborhood*, including only the few streets in the vicinity of your residence; (2) the *homogeneous neighborhood*, consisting of homes of similar quality, perhaps equivalent to a subdivision; and (3) the *unit neighborhood*, a wider area with stores, churches, and schools. In some cities, the terms *district* or *community* may be the rough equivalent of the unit neighborhood (Lee, 1968; see also Porteous, 1977, Chapter 4). *Economic space* refers to spatial patterns of (weekly) interaction with workplaces. *Urban-regional space* includes the area within which a person might travel farther, but less frequently. What gives these terms special meaning is that they link common institutions or areas (family, neighborhood, etc.) to both space and time.

Social space differs from simple geographic space (area) in that it includes implications about human behavior that cannot be captured adequately through consideration of geographic space alone. As social space, for example, a blue-collar neighborhood has a profoundly different pattern of human movements and interactions than an upper-class neighborhood. A map of social class areas in the city gives us little useful information unless we realize we are looking at different social spaces.

Extremes may serve to illustrate. On a map, there is nothing particularly remarkable about the location or extent of the city of Beverly Hills, California, or the major black community of South Los Angeles (often called *Watts*). But when these areas are considered as social spaces, the differences are striking. In Beverly Hills, land use in residential areas is rigidly controlled; in South Los Angeles, it is not. Standards of health, housing, nutrition, education, and public safety are all high in Beverly Hills, but not in South Los Angeles. Residents of Beverly Hills *are* the power structure—through their contributions to political campaigns and their corporate and professional strength, they influence outcomes in society. South Los Angeles residents do not influence outcomes, except negatively by being seen as a "problem" to be placated periodically by allocations of funds or new programs. Beverly Hills residents have essentially unlimited mobility—their wealth enables them to go where they please. The mobility of blacks in South Los Angeles is severely limited. High unemployment means that job searching is an important activity, but jobs may be available in areas where blacks are not welcome to live or where the available housing within reasonable commuting distance is too expensive. *De facto* residential segregation is thus reinforced.

Social space, then, is a concept that carries with it a package of interrelationships based on observations of *conditions* and *spatial interactions* in our society. *Social space*, like other technical jargon, is a kind of shorthand term—it means a lot more than you might think at first glance, and you have to learn quite a bit about society before you grasp all the subtleties of the concept.

AGGREGATION AND BEHAVIOR

How do social geographers go about their work? What methods or approaches do they use? Social geographers consider people from two main points of view. One approach involves *aggregate data*. For instance, if we want to represent the income level of individuals in one neighborhood of a city, we might use the *median family income*, a measure from the Census of Population (Figure 8–1). If we wish to compare this city with other cities, a single statistic is derived to represent the entire city. The same might apply to states or nations. Aggregate data, then, are

FIGURE 8–1 Computer processing is often the only practical way to deal with the massive amounts of data contained in census files.

"summed up," reducing a lot of detailed information to one value. For example, after a test, your instructor might tell you that the average (mean) grade for 100 students was 72 percent. That is an aggregate statistic. In reality, it is possible that no student actually received a score of 72 percent, but that statistic is a useful *generalized* measure of how students scored, particularly as a basis for comparison with other groups.

Studies based on aggregate data are often criticized on the ground that it is unreasonable to use data representing *groups* of people—all the people in a neighborhood, for instance—to say things about *individuals* in the neighborhood. To use the test score example, you would be treated as though you had an average score (72 percent) whether you did or not.

The other major point of view of social geography focuses on data at an *individual* or *behavioral* level. The reasoning behind this is that if people's interactions are going to be studied and discussed, then people should be looked at as individuals, which includes gathering data on them as individuals. This approach, it is felt, gives a more detailed picture of social geography, enabling identification of "micro" processes in society. In the test example, each student's grade would be studied individually to make detailed comparisons.

Both the aggregate and individual approaches have advantages and disadvantages. The main advantage of the aggregate method is that, because of censuses, a comprehensive set of information is available on neighborhoods, cities, counties, states, and other political subdivisions. On the other hand, although a large number of data are available, information about many aspects of social geography is not included. Censuses (and other conventional data sources) rarely provide information about people's attitudes or about special problems such as crime or health care. In addition, the use of grouped data to represent individuals is not entirely satisfactory. The aggregate approach is most useful for making broad, general comparisons among areas, while avoiding the implication that all people in the areas are the same as the aggregate statistics would suggest. Aggregation is often the only practical way to analyze large areas since the individual approach is often quite expensive.

The individual-level approaches help us understand processes in small areas. The major disadvantage is that survey research must be done through interviews, questionnaires, or some other related technique. Such survey research is expensive and time-consuming (Figure 8–2), and it is not usually practical to repeat individual-level studies in several cities because of the high costs.* Also, making generalizations about individual-level data may mean a return to aggregation. Used appropriately, however, generalization is a powerful means of dealing with large quantities of diverse information.

Both of these approaches, aggregate and individual, are useful and necessary. In the rest of this chapter, and in Chapter 9, you may find it helpful to think about whether the various studies we will dis-

*Note that the census is an example of survey research, as it is administered mainly by mailed questionnaires. But since the anonymity of census respondents is protected by law, census data, in practice, must be dealt with as aggregate data.

CHAPTER 8 SOCIALL PROCESSES

FIGURE 8–2 This geography graduate student is conducting a survey dealing with urban travel behavior.

cuss have used an aggregate or an individual approach. If you can identify the approach employed, you will better understand the discussion and be able to consider it more critically.

BASIC CONCEPTS IN HUMAN SPATIAL INTERACTION

Four key concept clusters form the basis for explanation of spatial interaction: (1) perception, (2) density, crowding, and personal space, (3) the movements of people, and (4) communication. These concepts deal with several of the principal geographic aspects of our social existence.

Perception

The concept of perception is complex, and we will introduce it here only briefly. The dictionary definition of the word includes such words as "cognition" (the act or process of knowing), "understanding," and "apprehending with the senses." In the most general sense, perception refers to knowing something, particularly through sight, hearing, touching, or smelling. For example, if you are stuck in traffic on 34th Street for an hour, you might say (among other things!) that you *perceive* 34th Street to be a busy one—the traffic congestion was a sensual experience. However, if you learn vocabulary in a foreign language course, you would not say that you *perceive* the words you have learned.

In geography, *perception* generally relates to understanding of the environment. Perception provides us with a grasp of *psychological space,* the bundle of *mental maps* and images we carry around in our heads and that guide us in our hometown, in the campus community, and to some extent around our state and nation. These maps and images may also condition our behavior in some ways. This psychological space is inseparable from the idea of social space—in fact, our social space is usually a subset of our psychological space. Indeed, we may have good mental maps of places we have never been and may never go. New York City images appear so frequently in the media that almost all of us have either an image or a mental map of the city, whether we have visited there or not. This is also true of the moon, and of Mars and other planets brought into the realm of our perception by the Voyager space project. In these cases, it is precise to say that our perception has changed. Before the moon landing in 1969, most of us perceived the moon as only a bright orb in the night sky. Other planets, such as Venus, were perceived as stars. Now we have seen close-up images and our perception has been revised drastically, as demonstrated in Figure 8–3.

A hierarchical scheme, or model, helps us understand where the perceived environment fits in relation to other kinds of environments (Figure 8–4). At the top of the perceptual hierarchy is the whole world (to which should be added other parts of the solar system). This is the *geographical environment.* The *operational environment* is the smaller realm that influences human behavior more directly. The *perceptual environment* is that part of the operational environment of which people have some awareness. The *behavioral environment* is the environment directly associated with individual human reactions (Saarinen, 1969, p. 5).

What people perceive to exist or happen is in many respects at least as important as what does exist or happen. If people perceive a threat of crime, for example, they may change their behavior to avoid the perceived threat, whether or not crime is much of a real hazard. Similarly, criminals may react to a perceived threat of being caught; some have been known to move from one police department jurisdiction to another to avoid "hard-nosed" law enforcement.

The interaction between perceptions and behavior is to some extent bound up with our values, beliefs, and traditions as a society or an ethnic group. Indeed, we "process" many perceptions and classify them as "good" or "bad." A heavy storm with large quantities of precipitation and a threat of floods and mudslides is usually perceived as bad, but not inevitably. It can be argued that we perceive a stormy, flood-producing situation as bad as a consequence of our inappropriately occupying vast areas of floodplains. If we had adapted our development patterns

BASIC CONCEPTS IN HUMAN SPATIAL INTERACTION

FIGURE 8–3 This photograph of Saturn was taken from *Voyager 1* in October, 1980, from a distance of 34 million kilometers (21.1 million miles). The marks just below the south pole represent Dione, one of Saturn's inner satellites. (Photo courtesy of NASA.)

more carefully to the natural environment, we might rejoice in flooding as an essential process, generously supplying a vital resource, instead of fearing it as a threat to public safety and welfare. Our exploitive use of the physical environment, then, leads us to evaluate our perceptions differently than if we had an adaptive approach.

From the geographer's point of view, environmental or space perceptions may be looked at from three broad approaches: (1) the *structural* approach, (2) the *evaluative* approach, and (3) the *preference* approach (Downs, 1970, pp. 70–81).

Structural Approach The structural approach considers those perceptions that help us relate to and navigate in the environment we occupy. The best-known research dealing with perceptions of this type was done by Lynch (1960), who was interested in finding out how urban residents perceive their cities. People were asked to draw sketch maps of Boston, Jersey City, and Los Angeles; from these maps, Lynch produced composites, such as those in Figures 8–5 and 8–6.

Lynch used the concepts of *legibility* and *imageability* to suggest how people develop perceptions of spaces. The city was said to be legible (readable) if its various areas could be recognized and arranged in an understandable way. The city was imageable if it contained buildings or areas that an observer would remember easily. Thus, the Sears and Hancock buildings in Chicago, Central Park in New York, and the Civic Center complex in Los Angeles are imageable. A tract of identical homes or a commercial strip of fast-food franchises might not be. Apart from these concepts, Lynch used a clear scheme for analyzing the contents of the city maps. This consisted of five elements:

1. *Paths* are travel corridors, whether streets, highways, subway lines, or sidewalks.
2. *Edges* are barriers or boundaries between areas. Examples would be a break in land use between a residential and an agricultural or industrial area, or railroad tracks that form a boundary between neighborhoods of differing social classes.
3. *Districts* have certain unifying characteristics that make them recognizable. Entertainment districts such as Times Square and Sunset Strip and Bourbon Street are well known. Districts also could involve industrial activities (e.g., New York's garment district), or commercial or other uses. Every city has a central business district, for example.

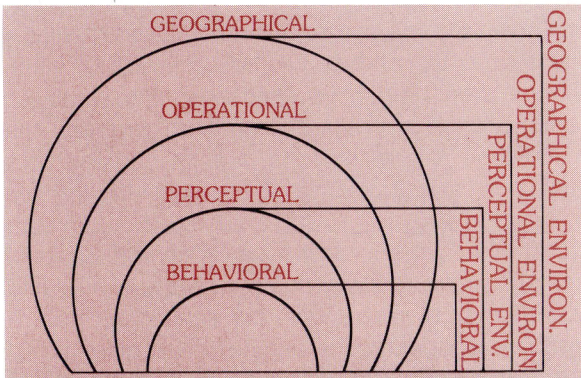

FIGURE 8–4 Hierarchy of environments. (Adapted from T. F. Saarinen, *Perception of Environment* Association of American Geographers, Resource Papers for College Geography no. 5 [1969]:6. By permission.)

159

CHAPTER 8 SOCIAL PROCESSES

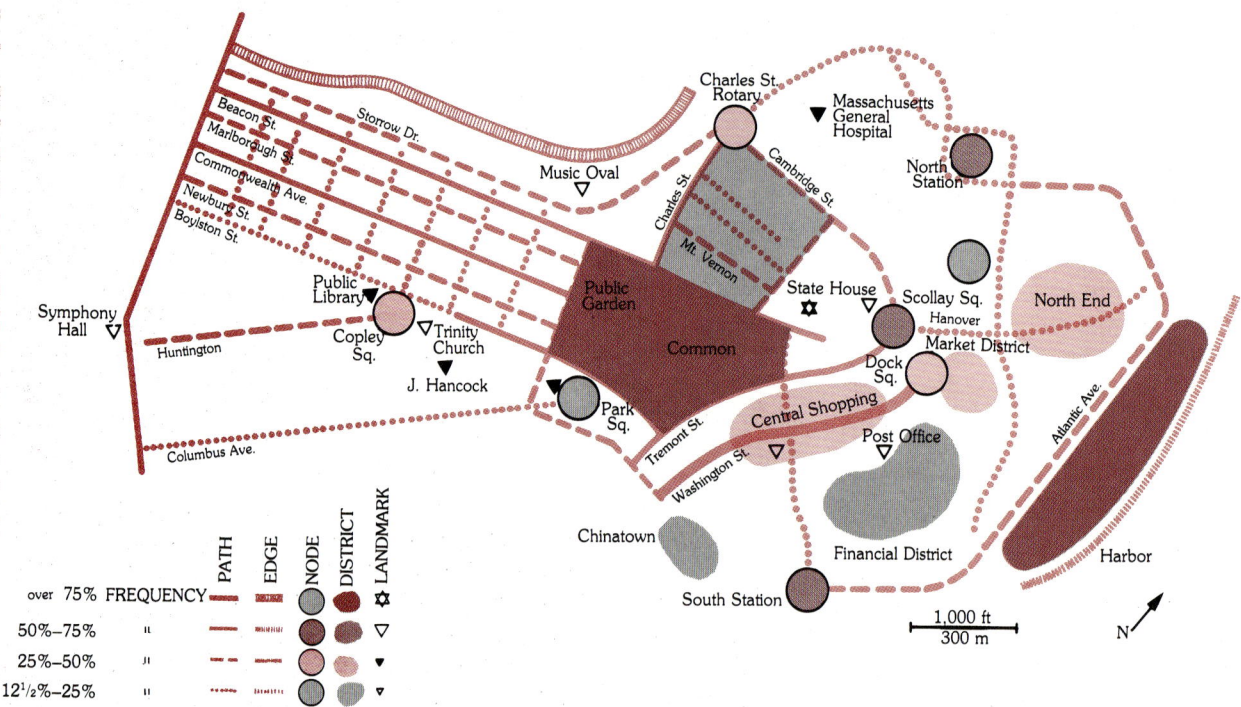

FIGURE 8–5 Composite image of Boston based on sketch maps. (Adapted from *The Image of the City* by Kevin Lynch by permission of The MIT Press, Cambridge, Massachusetts. Copyright © 1960 by Massachusetts Institute of Technology and the President and Fellows of Harvard College.)

4 *Nodes* are points of convergence, where *paths* cross. A major intersection is a node. A node also can be a center of activity or interest, such as a library, courthouse, or monument.

5 *Landmarks* help people orient their mental maps. Landmarks may be nearby—for example, commercial signs, billboards, or tall buildings clustered downtown—or distant, such as a mountain or tower on the horizon (Lynch, 1960, pp. 47–48).

Lynch approached the perception of the city from the viewpoint of an urban designer; he wanted to understand the process by which people "read" cities so that he could help design cities that are more easily comprehended by the people who live in them.

Evaluative Approach The basis of the evaluative approach is that people use their perception of the environment in their decision-making processes. Perception, then, may be translated into action, or behavior. Much of the work that has been done under this heading refers to *hazard perception,* and relates to the way people perceive natural and artificial hazards, including floods, fires, droughts, air pollution, earthquakes, noise, and tornadoes.

Each year, usually in January or February, television viewers are subjected to the annual mudslide and "flood test" from Los Angeles. When asked what they will do following the annihilation of their homes, survivors inevitably reply that they will build again on the same spot. This attitude was typified by a victim of the Santa Barbara, California, fire on July 1977, which destroyed about 230 homes (Figure 8–7). She was quoted as saying: "We're going to start over. This is part of life's condition" (*Newsweek,* 8 August 1977, p. 27). This type of reaction suggests that, even though people may understand there is a real chance their house will be destroyed by some phenomenon in the physical environment, ties to the home location are very strong, and generally, the heart seems to rule the mind. This phenomenon is a subject of investigation in dissonance theory (see Adams, 1973).

Another aspect of the perception of environmental hazards is that people who are exposed to hazards may wish to move, but cannot because of economic considerations. Air pollution, noise pollution near airports, and odor pollution near meatpacking plants are examples of such situations.

Preference Approach The preference approach to perception is used to find out what places or areas

BASIC CONCEPTS IN HUMAN SPATIAL INTERACTION

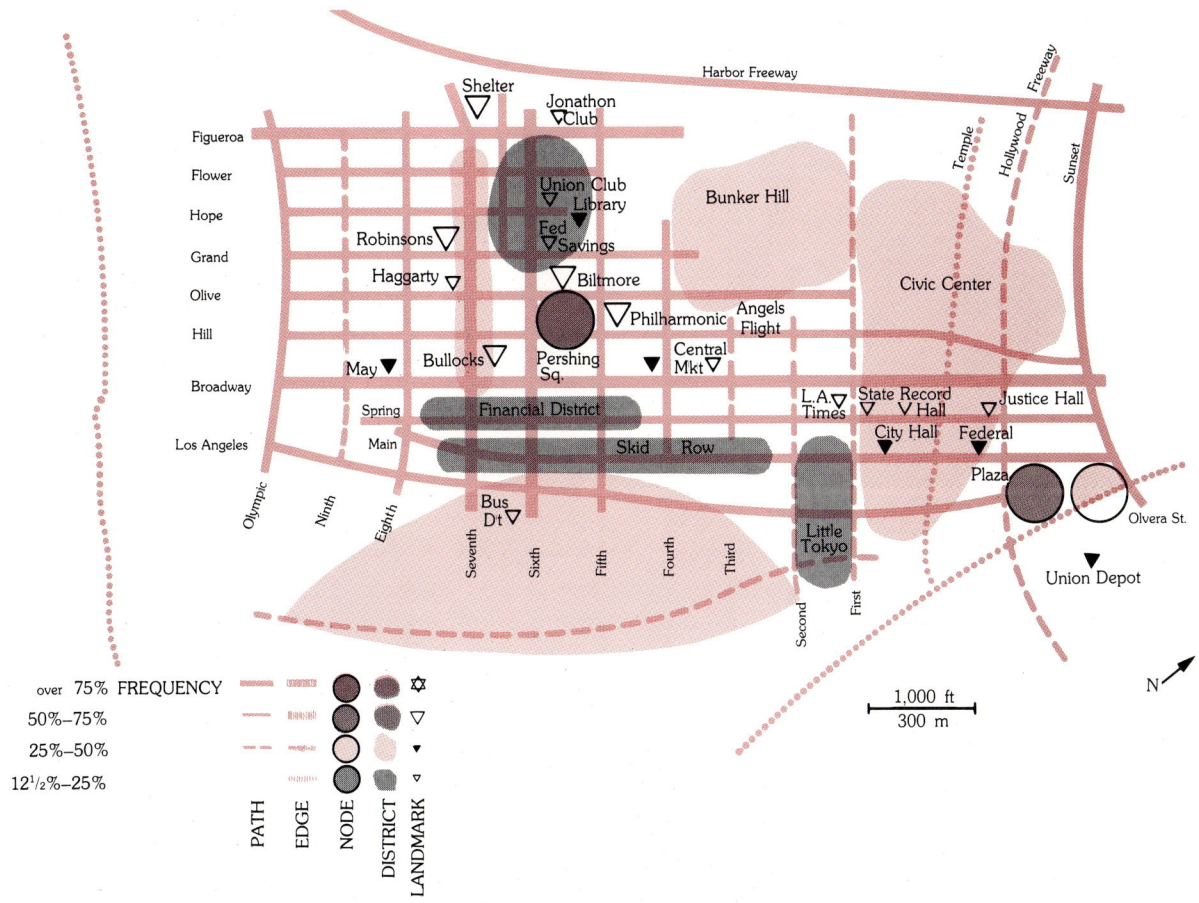

FIGURE 8–6 Composite image of Los Angeles based on sketch maps. (Adapted from *The Image of the City* by Kevin Lynch by permission of the MIT Press, Cambridge, Massachusetts. Copyright © 1960 by Massachusetts Institute of Technology and the President and Fellows of Harvard College.)

people prefer or dislike in some way. Gould (1969) asked freshman students at four universities—University of California at Berkeley, Alabama, Minnesota, and Pennsylvania State—to rank-order the 48 contiguous states according to their own preferences. Maps were produced to show the general residential desirability of the United States as seen from each of the four states (Figure 8–8). How do we interpret the

FIGURE 8–7 This is all that remains of a home destroyed in Santa Barbara, California, in 1977's "box kite" blaze, when sparks from a box kite touching high-voltage lines set off the fire.

161

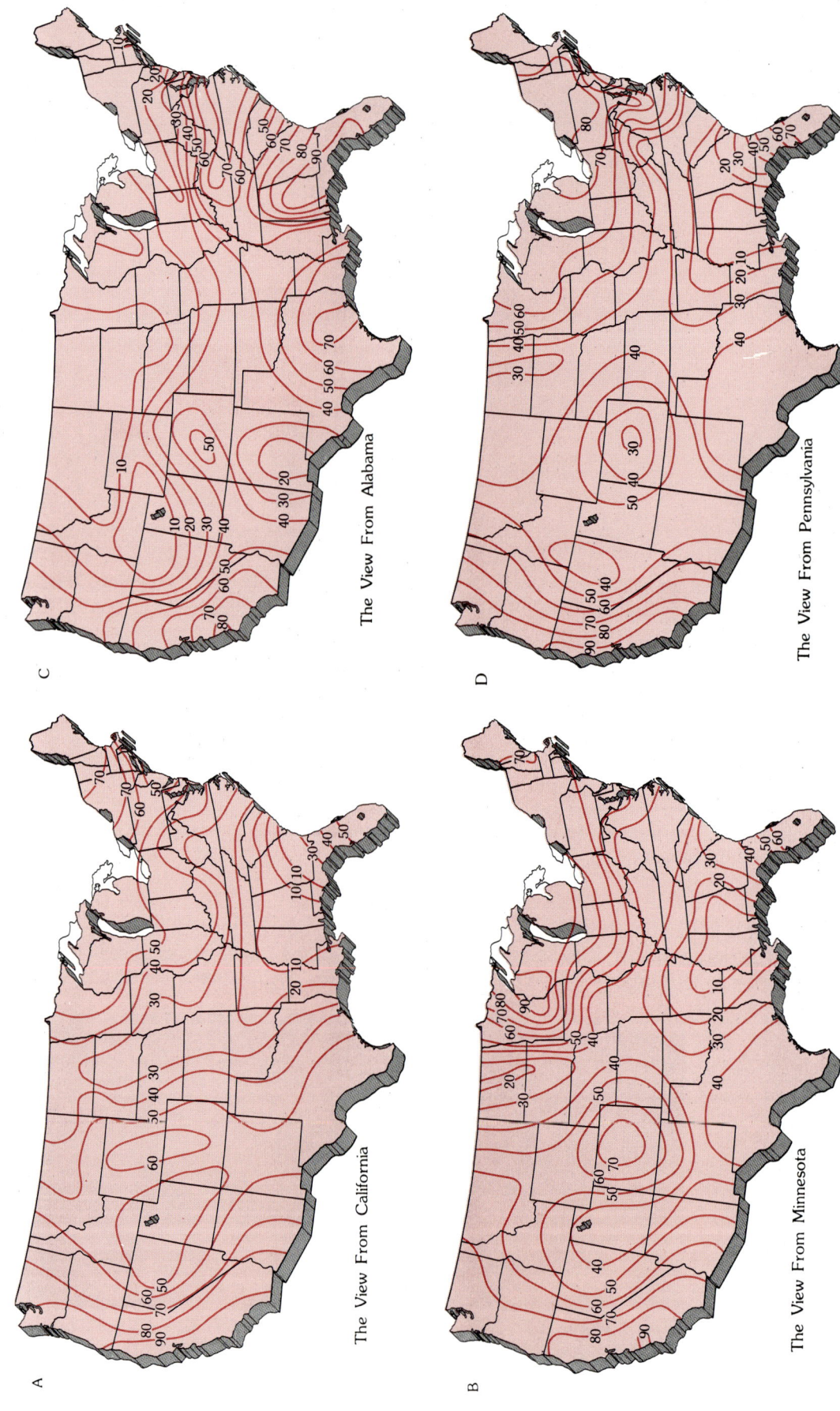

FIGURE 8–8 Perceptions of the United States from several vantage points. (Adapted from Peter R. Gould, "On Mental Maps," [1966], by permission of the author.)

maps? In Figure 8–8a, the view from California, data values are shown in two ways: first at the approximate center of population of the state, and second as *isolines*, which Gould gives the special name *isopercepts*. The numbers are percentages related to the highest preference score. The value 100.0 means that the area so labeled was most desirable; the 50.0 isoline, running from Texas to Montana, delineates the area that was half as desirable as the California coastal region. As shown in Figure 8–8a the desirability "surface" tends to decline eastward, and the Northeast tends to score better than the Southeast. Alabama scored 0.0, meaning that the California students regarded it as the "least desirable" other state.

The view of Minnesota students was similar to that of California students, except that the "home" state scored highest (Figure 8–8b). Both maps have a high West Coast ridge, and what Gould called the "Utah perceptual basin," the "Colorado high," and the "Dakota sinkhole."

Pennsylvania State students were unusual in that they preferred coastal California to their own state (Figure 8–8c). Otherwise, the view was similar to that from California and Minnesota.

The view from Alabama was quite different (Figure 8–8d). Alabama was most preferred, as might be expected. Outside the South, California and Colorado scored quite high. The least preferred states were the Dakotas, and Gould drew attention to the unexplained "New Mexico sinkhole," showing that state to be less desirable than any neighboring state.

Gould pointed out the *applications* of research on such mental maps or sets of preferences. Many businesses and industries locate where they do because of the geographic preferences of key decision makers. Certainly, people's decisions about whether to move to other states are influenced by their perceptions of a variety of environmental factors, including economic and political conditions.

Mention of the economic and political environments reminds us that there are many *invisible* landscapes that may be every bit as important as visible ones in people's decision-making processes. One suggestion is that we live in an *information environment*, and that our *location* determines how much and what kind of information we get about the world (Gould, 1975).

Density, Crowding, and Personal Space

In many respects, people are delicate creatures and should be handled with care. The day-to-day conditions under which we live and work can have important effects on our physical and mental well-being. Although there are influences on us that derive from many conditions in the home and workplace, the emphasis here will be on a fundamental issue that has perplexed social scientists and others for decades—population density and its near relative, crowding.

There is a widespread belief that high density is bad, that it tends to be associated with slums, crime, and a variety of social problems. Similarly, low density is generally regarded as good—it implies space for kids to play, fresh air, sunlight, and lack of congestion.

These preconceptions bear closer examination. First, density and crowding must be differentiated. *Density* is a physical concept, informing us that there are so many persons per acre, square kilometer, or square mile. Detroit, for example, had 357 km^2 (138 mi^2) of territory and 1,511,336 people in 1970. The density formula is $\frac{p}{a}$ where p is the population and a is the area. Substituting, we get

$$\frac{1,511,336}{357} = 4,233 \text{ persons per km}^2$$

$$\left(\frac{1,511,336}{138} = 10,951.7 \text{ persons per mi}^2\right)$$

We can say, then, that Detroit had a population density of about 11,000 persons per square mile (more than 4,000 per km^2).

Density, a physical measure, should not be confused with crowding, which is a psychological phenomenon. We *feel* crowded (or uncrowded). Even under conditions of very high density (at a football game, say), we may not feel particularly crowded because we know the situation is temporary. But we may feel crowded in an apartment or dormitory room, even though the density is much lower, because we perceive the situation to be more permanent. Under what conditions do you feel crowded?

Although it may seem like a contradiction, in residential areas it is possible to have high density without crowding, or crowding without high density. A common standard for detached single-family dwellings sets a minimum lot size of 560 m^2 (6,000 ft^2). With 4,047 m^2 (43,560 ft^2) to the acre, this means about seven households per acre. Consider a high-rise luxury apartment building on a typical city block, about 300 × 300 ft (90,000 ft^2 or 8,400 m^2) or some 2 acres. If half the block is taken up with parking, landscaping, sidewalks, and so on, the building covers about an acre. In a 20-story building, there would be hundreds of apartments, producing a high *density* per acre. But it is unlikely that the apartments are crowded in terms of *persons per room,* a common measure. Thus, we have high density but low crowding.

Now, consider a city block in a ghetto consisting of single-family dwellings, which is usually the case in the South and West. There may be only 12–15 housing units on a city block, but families may be large, and the persons-per-room count may be high, indicating crowded conditions. Here, then, is the other side of the paradox—low density coexisting with crowding.

Many of the negative feelings people have about density and crowding have grown out of studies showing that animals become stressed when they are overcrowded. Animals have problems with feeding, reproduction, and other aspects of behavior, and start to behave eccentrically, becoming aggressive or passive, or abandoning their offspring, for example. Such findings about animal behavior were generalized to apply to people in the urban riots of the second half of the 1960s. It was hard to resist a line of cause-and-effect reasoning; many said that because crowded animals often became aggressive, it therefore should be expected that people crowded into ghetto slums would react similarly.

There is, however, no evidence to support this point of view. In reality, people do *not* behave just like rats or lemmings. The history of human settlement patterns suggests that people usually have lived under fairly high-density, crowded conditions. In fact, many of us are probably living today under less dense, less crowded conditions than people have typically enjoyed at any time in history. Middle-class suburbs in U.S. cities help confirm this suggestion.

In his study of neighborhood density, Baldassare (1979) reviewed the relationship of density to physical health, mental health, "satisfaction with life," and "happiness." He could establish no connection between persons per room, persons per residential area, and satisfaction with physical health, mental health, and life. There was some indication that people living at high neighborhood densities generally were less happy, but this tie was weak. Overall, Baldassare felt that higher densities can actually help organize complicated social groups, through increased interaction. Also, unlike animals, humans are able to adapt to crowded condiditons. It probably is oversimplifying too much, however, to say that statistical findings or generalizations on density apply equally to all people. Mothers and children in crowded homes may be more vulnerable, and the same may be true of certain poor, elderly, and physically or mentally handicapped individuals. In general, though, Baldassare was able to say that "household crowding leads to mild family problems and no serious disruptions" (p. 205).

Another important point of view Baldassare advanced was that space is a resource. By this, he meant that people value space not only as land but also as personal space—private or semiprivate area that can be used for activities ranging from sex to studying. Generally, more powerful people have more personal space of higher quality, while weaker people have less and of lower quality. Students, the poor, the old, children, and the handicapped are relatively powerless and must struggle for space. This struggle is often complicated by the fact that space for special groups ideally should be modified to meet the needs of those groups. We find a vivid example in the need to remove architectural barriers that hinder the use of space by persons in wheelchairs. For these people, a building that is inaccessible may as well not exist. At the other extreme is the legendary executive washroom—personal space elevated to a status symbol.

This point about space as a resource illustrates that the concepts of density and crowding are really much more complex than one might think at first. Our perception of space, and therefore to some extent our perception of what is crowded and what is not, depends in part on what we have been accustomed to. This in turn may be a cultural phenomenon, depending on the nation we live in or the ethnic group to which we belong. One researcher describes a hierarchy of personal territories relating to Americans in social situations (Hall, 1966). This scheme would have to be modified in other cultures where standards are different. Just as criteria of appropriate interpersonal spacing differ among cultures, so do perceptions of crowding. To many rural Americans, low-density suburbs are crowded, yet to Europeans, U.S. cities seem very spread out (see also Chapter 15).

As we said, the popular view of high density and crowding is that they are bad. One alternative interpretation we mentioned shows that density and crowding probably have negligible effects on some important aspects of human behavior. Another view that complements this perspective is that "crowding by itself has neither good effects nor bad effects on people but rather *serves to intensify the individual's typical reactions to the situation*" (Freedman, 1975, pp. 89–90). For example, if you do not like people with objectionable body odor or halitosis, your displeasure will be most intense if you are compelled to occupy a small space with them (in an elevator, say, compared to a large room). If, on the other hand, you like handsome men or beautiful women, your enjoyment is likely to be intensified by closer contact (at a party, perhaps, compared to observation across a street or large room).

Freedman tested his *intensity theory* with several experiments. In one, individuals were asked to read short speeches to a group. The situation was set up so that some groups would only praise the speaker, however well or badly the speaker did. Other groups were to be entirely negative in their comments no matter how good or bad the speaker was. Then, both positive and negative situations were varied between small and large rooms. It was found that positive comments were more positive and negative comments more negative in the crowded conditions. Other experiments varied the basic conditions somewhat, but the findings still confirmed the intensity theory.

Freedman, a social psychologist, agreed with Baldassare, a sociologist, that crowding and pathology (ill-health) are not related. This conclusion challenges the popular ideas not only that density and crowding are bad, but also that there are human feelings of *territoriality* related to shortage of space. This is not the same as saying that humans have no feelings of territoriality. What it does say is that our feelings of territoriality with respect to, say, our homes, do not vary appreciably with the size of our home or of the lot on which it sits (Figure 8–9). Freedman summed up by stating that "the common lore that crowding is bad will take a long time to change" (1975, p. 105).

You may have some difficulty accepting the suggestion that high density and crowding are not necessarily bad—and actually may be good—because you probably can think of numerous situations that are unpleasant because of overcrowding. Bear in mind that the comments made here refer to *general* conditions rather than to isolated instances. Few students quit drinking beer because of an occasional hangover. One usually copes with hangovers by learning to live with them or by limiting maximum beer intake. By and large, this is how we cope with high density or crowding—we *adapt* movement patterns, schedules, and interpersonal relationships as far as possible to minimize negative impacts. Leaving the ball game before the final whistle or getting to the cafeteria late or early to avoid the rush are simple everyday examples of such adaptation.

INTERACTION THROUGH MOVEMENT

Events and activities in people's lives almost always involve movement—journeys to work, social trips, moves to new homes across town or in another city or nation. There are trips for health care, and trips for recreation. People flee from disaster and flock to opportunity. Some people take trips they would prefer to avoid—to jail or prison or to fight in a war. For others, a trip is a phenomenal achievement—climbing Mount Everest, crossing the Atlantic in a balloon, sailing singlehanded around the world, or going to the moon. Even after we die, we make more trips—to the mortuary and cemetery or crematorium. Movement, then, is a key part of human existence. People are peripatetic—always active, moving about. Even in sleep, people are not still.

We can divide discussion of movement into two major approaches. First, we can consider journey or trip behavior, movement that tends to follow a daily

FIGURE 8–9 A homeowner may express territoriality with signs.

or weekly rhythm. We will focus on trips to work, to shop, and to social activities, with some consideration of differences that have been observed in movement patterns based on people's social characteristics. Then we will consider longer-distance movement in the context of discussion of the migration process.

The Journey to Work

Work trips have profound impacts on the social and economic life of cities. Before the streetcar, when commuting was limited to walking distance, cities were close-knit and crowded. Improvements in transportation helped cities to sprawl, and meant eventually that people could easily live in one city but work in another. Residential segregation was promoted as the automobile allowed dissimilar ethnic groups to separate, and the dichotomy developed between *inner city* and *suburb* (see Ward, 1971, Chapter 5).

How far do workers travel today, and how do distances vary by modes of transportation? Table 8–1 summarizes the general characteristics of the journey to work in the United States. The information in distance traveled by each mode (type) of transportation, together with the data on numbers of people, is important for developing national policies and plans with respect to energy. These data, in combination with other data on time spent traveling and on people's places of origin compared to their destinations yield useful information on preferences with respect to residential locations.

Table 8–1 is worth reviewing in some detail. As with any complex table, you should first study the title and the column and row headings to find out exactly *what* the table is telling you and *how* that information is provided. Are the numbers counts of people, percentages of people, or what? When you are satisfied that you are able to interpret the table, read on.

For all workers, the largest single distance category, with about 22 percent of commuters, is 5 mi–9 mi. When the data are broken down for particular types of transportation, the 5 mi–9 mi category is the single largest for automobile or truck trips as well as for public transportation overall. When public transportation is broken down, the 3 mi–4 mi and 5 mi–9 mi classes have approximately the same proportions for buses or streetcars. For subways or elevateds, the 5 mi–9 mi and 10 mi–14 mi distances are comparable in terms of numbers of travelers. For railroads, the longer distances become much more important (about 46 percent over 25 mi), whereas taxicabs were used mainly for short distances (about 46 percent in the 1 mi–2 mi class). As one would expect, bicycling and walking involve short distances (averages of 1.4 mi and 0.1 mi, respectively). Motorcyclists have a pattern similar to automobile drivers, but with a slightly shorter average distance (7.5 mi compared to 9.0 mi).

Other important facts about the journey to work have been outlined in a federal report (U.S. Department of Commerce, 1979, p. 1):

- In 1975, the average commuting trip in the United States was 9 miles long and took about 20 minutes.
- About 65 percent of U.S. workers drove to work alone. Nineteen percent used carpools and 6 percent used public transportation. Of people living

TABLE 8–1 Means of transportation by distance to work, for the United States, 1975

Means of Transportation	Total* (thousands)	Percentage Distribution by Distance to Work							
		Total	1 mi	1 mi–2 mi	3 mi–4 mi	5 mi–9 mi	10 mi–14 mi	15 mi–24 mi	25 mi or more	Mean
All workers*	70,816	100.0	12.3	16.0	17.2	21.6	13.5	12.3	7.1	8.5
Automobile or truck	61,657	100.0	8.1	16.3	17.9	22.9	14.1	13.1	7.6	9.0
Drive alone	47,188	100.0	8.7	16.9	18.8	23.5	13.8	12.1	6.0	8.3
Carpool	14,470	100.0	6.0	14.4	15.0	20.7	15.0	16.0	12.8	11.4
Public transportation	4,587	100.0	2.8	14.3	21.3	24.1	16.9	13.5	7.0	9.1
Bus or streetcar	2,958	100.0	3.1	18.0	26.1	25.7	15.2	8.7	3.3	7.1
Subway or elevated	1,124	100.0	1.3	5.6	15.8	28.2	26.0	18.7	4.2	10.1
Railroad	387	100.0	—	2.1	0.8	3.9	8.3	39.8	45.7	24.3
Taxicab	118	100.0	18.6	45.8	22.0	11.0	3.4	—	—	2.4
Bicycle	432	100.0	41.4	43.1	10.0	4.2	1.6	—	—	1.4
Motorcycle	285	100.0	11.2	19.3	17.2	19.3	15.8	12.6	4.6	7.5
Walk only	3,645	100.0	91.4	8.3	0.2	0.1	—	—	—	0.1
Other	210	100.0	27.1	31.4	8.1	19.0	10.0	3.8	—	3.9

*Excludes workers with no fixed place of work and persons who worked at home. All workers were at least 14 years old.
Source: U.S. Department of Commerce, 1979, p. 8

and working in central cities, 16 percent used public transportation.
- At least two-thirds of the people living in suburbs drove to work alone.

These facts have important implications for energy policy and urban planning. Vast amounts of energy could be saved by reducing the average trip distance, changing driving habits to increase carpooling, and increasing dependence on public transportation. But adjustments are extremely difficult, since so much money already has been invested in the way cities are presently laid out. City-planning efforts should be directed toward intensification of land use to discourage urban sprawl and reduce average commuting distances. This would involve a process known as *infilling,* the seeking out and developing of vacant land in otherwise developed areas. Such lots are usually easily served by utilities because connections are nearby. Thus, there are dollar savings not only in energy costs but also in costs of land development.

People who live in suburbs and commute to central cities to work travel almost 12 miles each way, 3 miles farther than the average, or 6 miles farther per day. Since about eight million workers in this category drive to work, this means 48 million "above average" miles traveled daily. At 20 miles per gal, this translates into 2.4 million gallons of gas, or over $3.2 million at $1.35 per gallon. Converted into an annual total, based on 250 working days per year, the total is $810 million, or the price of 10,125 homes worth $80,000 each. We can think of this as a kind of premium or tax that people pay to live in suburbs.

The Journey to Shop

The length and frequency of shopping trips depend in part on whether people live in urban or rural environments, and also on factors such as age, economic status, and the kinds of goods and services being purchased.

The most frequently shopped-for goods, such as groceries and gasoline, usually involve short trips on the order of a mile or two. These trips are short not only because of people's desire to save time but also because of the perishability of some of the materials (dairy products and frozen foods) and because increased distance costs more in gasoline. Indeed, time can be a more important factor than distance; for example, a shopper may prefer to take the freeway to a more distant store instead of driving to a closer store that would take longer to reach because of stoplights.

Although prices do vary among supermarkets, there is not usually a sufficient difference to make it worth driving long distances to get the price advantage. Less frequently purchased durable items, such as cars and appliances, however, may repay more extensive searching for a better price, for a preferred model, or for both. Long "shopping" trips also might be expected for visits to specialized physicians. For metropolitan residents, the search for a medical specialist may involve driving less than 10 miles, whereas rural residents may have to drive hundreds of miles to get the same service.

Therefore, we can say that most shopping trips (and related trips such as service-seeking journeys) are short, and relatively few are long. This is typical of several types of "journey" behavior, and has been called the *distance–decay* concept (Figure 8–10). For the most part, people prefer to minimize the effort and cost involved in travel. For example, we will see in Chapter 9 that the journeys of criminals to their crimes have a similar pattern.

What is the importance of this descriptive information about shopping behavior? For all practical purposes, most individuals—and particularly the disadvantaged—are "prisoners" of their neighborhoods. People tend to rely on nearby facilities, whether or not they are the best in the community, because of the general inconvenience and dollar cost of seeking alternatives. For blacks and other minorities, a real cost is involved. Grocery stores in minority areas tend to charge higher prices than elsewhere, and minority area residents in effect are forced to pay those prices because of their inability to reach practical alternatives.* Taking the argument a step further, it could be said that limitations on interaction (mobility) have the practical effect of making the poor even poorer.

For a different approach to the interpretation of shopping behavior, see the discussion of *central place theory* in Chapter 11, the *hierarchy* concept in Chapter 13, and the discussion of Figure 7–4.

Social Trips

Trips to visit friends and relatives form another important category of interaction. Knowledge about patterns of social trips can help in planning transpor-

---

*Research has shown that there is an *inverse relationship* between the size of food stores and their prices. In other words, the *smaller* the store, the *higher* the price. Food stores in minority areas tend to be small because they are located in older neighborhoods where supermarkets were never built, owing to lack of vacant land and the lesser attraction of poorer customers.

CHAPTER 8 SOCIAL PROCESSES

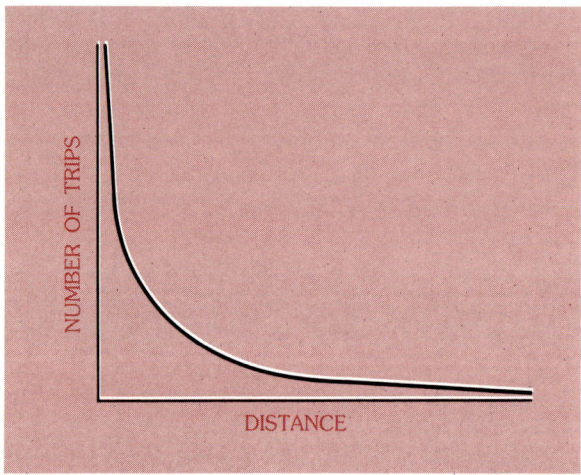

FIGURE 8–10 This typical distance–decay curve illustrates that many more trips are short-distance rather than long-distance.

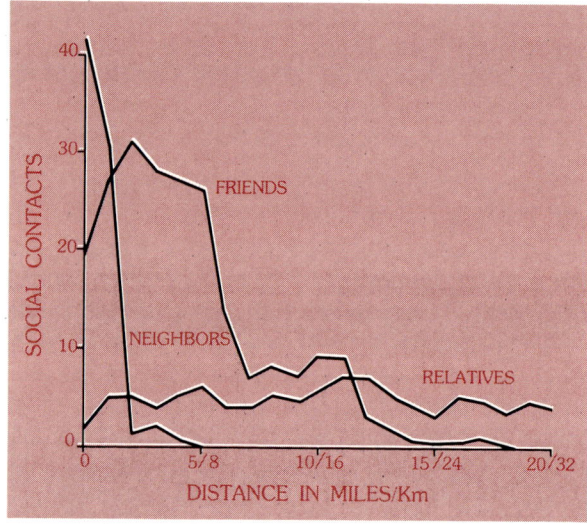

FIGURE 8–11 The relationship of social interaction to distance. (From Frederick P. Stutz, in *Economic Geography* 49 [1973]:139.)

tation systems. If street and highway networks are set up in such a way that neighborhoods are split or blocked off (by freeway embankments, for instance), social relationships may be affected adversely.

In a study of social *interaction fields* in San Diego, California, it was found that social trips could be divided into three kinds—trips involving *friends, neighborhood interactions,* and *relatives* (Stutz, 1973, pp. 137–38). Trips to neighbors were shortest, those to relatives longest. Travel to friends came closer to approximating the "typical" distance-decay curve illustrated in Figure 8–10. Figure 8–11 shows the relationship between number of social contacts and distances for each of the three types of social trips.

People seem to do a kind of *cost/benefit analysis* with respect to their social trips, evaluating both the likely rewards and the costs of social interaction. On the cost side, there are factors of time, gasoline, risks of highway accidents, and entertainment costs at the destination. Benefits include the pleasures of socialization, enjoyment associated with entertainment, and the satisfaction of perhaps promoting longer-term relationships, such as marriage. The greatest benefits are derived from making contact with people of similar background. Therefore, people often are willing to pay a higher price to make such contacts (Stutz, 1973, p. 142). This process of comparing costs and benefits, whether social or economic, undoubtedly occurs with respect to other kinds of travel behavior, too. This is not to say that travel behavior is always perfectly reasoned out (we all make mistakes and errors of judgment), but it is likely that costs and benefits do match up in a general way.

Social Characteristics and Interaction

It is reasonable to suggest that social interaction will be influenced by the characteristics of the people in particular areas. Are the individuals old, young? Rich, poor? Male, female? Black, white? Each characteristic may affect how people relate to one another socially and geographically. The poor, a category that usually includes minority people, tend to have restricted interaction fields compared to the more affluent. This may have important ramifications for the educational development of ghetto children, who grow up with restricted mental maps and therefore are less able to relate to various human and physical phenomena than the children of the more affluent.

It has been shown that social trips are most numerous in the 20–24 age category, with a secondary peak in the 65–69 bracket. These flows relate to mate selection processes and to postretirement, respectively. Interestingly, social trips decline in relative importance as income increases. It has been suggested that poorer people substitute social visiting for other, more expensive activities (Stutz, 1976, pp. 7–8).

Marital status may also relate to patterns of social interaction. A study of 114 married couples in the Mar Vista community of Los Angeles revealed substantial differences in the extent of the areas that were significant to husbands (a larger area) compared to wives (a smaller area). There were also directional biases. Wives' trips tended to be restricted to northerly directions from the study area, while husbands' trips showed more directional variety.

These differences were explained in terms of the husbands' greater mobility as a result of their participation in a greater variety of occupations and activities compared to wives. The northerly directional bias of wives' trips related to the socioeconomic status of surrounding areas. Locations to the north held more social contacts because of their similarity to Mar Vista (Everitt, 1976).

Such differences may tell us something about family structure and about women's roles in society. The traditional emphasis on wives' domesticity has tended to restrict their activity spaces. For example, the cost of commuting 40 miles per day for a (presumably female) secretary will constitute a larger percentage of her income compared to a (presumably male) corporate executive. As women continue, in increasing numbers, to enter occupations that were previously male strongholds, the economic impact of gender is gradually being reduced.

Migration Processes and Patterns

Migration is what most people refer to as moving, as in "We are moving across town" or "I'm moving to Pennsylvania." The word *migration* is preferred in academic discussion because it is much more specific than *move*. A residential migration generally involves a degree of permanence. Households in particular, in contrast to individuals, may need years to recoup the costs—which may be economic, social, or psychological—of migrating. Migration may be as short as moving to the house next door or as distant as relocating from Vietnam to Arkansas. Historically, migrations of peoples have had profound impacts on many nations. In fact, the migration process was influential before nations as we know them existed. The peopling of North America by migration across the then-existing land bridge between the Soviet Union and Alaska is a case in point.

Processes What has stimulated migration? Why have people been prepared, in some cases, to give up an entire way of life—job, family, friends, cultural traditions—to venture into a new and often essentially unknown environment?

The most fundamental reason for migration is a belief that the move will result in some advantage that the person or family does not presently enjoy. Often, this perceived advantage is monetary—the prospect of a job rather than unemployment, or of a *better* job. Some people migrate for social or political reasons, to avoid persecution or reprisal when major changes occur within the home nation. Migrations out of Hungary (1950s), Cuba, and Vietnam were partially of this type (see Chapter 16). Others migrate primarily out of a sense of adventure, a motivation to "see the world." Frequently, reasons for migration are mixed, and many migrants combine economic objectives with hopes for a beneficial change in lifestyle. The sense of adventure may be present whether the migrant wants it or not, and "adventure" will often become surprise, shock, or fear.

A useful approach to understanding migration is to think in terms of *push* and *pull* factors. Push factors—for example, unemployment, famine, political factors—make people dissatisfied with their home area. Pull factors help migrants decide exactly *where* they will go. Which of the possible destinations is most attractive? Costs of relocation (i.e., distance), whether or not family or friends are already there, job opportunities, government policies with respect to immigration (if the move is to another country), and numerous other factors are all relevant. That there are emotional as well as economic and other considerations often makes it difficult for migrants to make choices. Indeed, many people refrain from migrating because the prospect of leaving family and friends and the comfort of a familiar culture or location is not sufficiently compensated for by the prospect of economic or other gains.

One process that has been shown to be important as a pull factor in migration, and which also relates to overall processes of social interaction, is the gravitational pull of larger cities. Based on analogy to the physical law that the gravitational pull of a body is proportional to its mass, the *gravity model* of migration states that larger cities will attract more people, and will also attract people from longer distances, than small cities. The same can be said of large shopping centers, large medical complexes, and large events in show business and sports. The gravity concept is a simplified way to express the attraction of the economic and social opportunities of large population centers.

As we have suggested, people normally go through a cost/benefit analysis, however primitive, to help in their decision-making process. In the context of migration, this will be true whether the move is around the world or across the city. The simple flowchart model in Figure 8–12, for example, shows how people might structure their cost/benefit analysis in the process of searching for a new home. Once the decision to seek a new home has been made, formal or informal criteria are developed as a basis for making comparisons in the marketplace (more bedrooms, bigger kitchen, etc.). Then, vacant units are sought and evaluated. Finally, a decision is made as to whether to move or stay.

CHAPTER 8 SOCIAL PROCESSES

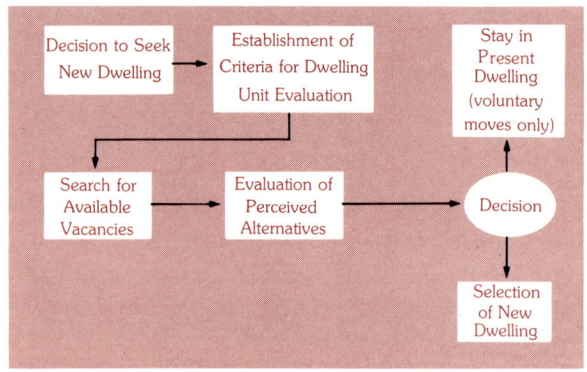

FIGURE 8–12 Elements an individual considers in selecting a new residence. (From E. G. Moore, *Residential Mobility in the City,* Association of American Geographers, Resource Papers for College Geography no. 13 [1972]:13. Reprinted by permission.)

The basis for a more detailed understanding of the migration process at one level—between U.S. states—has been compiled by the U.S. Census Bureau. Data were obtained through the Annual Housing surveys of 1974, 1975, and 1976, involving interviews with 62,000–64,000 occupants of housing units in each year. Table 8–2 shows the percent breakdown of responses for specific reasons for moving. Clearly, job-related reasons are dominant, with "job transfer" and "new job or looking for work" accounting for about half the households or persons. If all the employment-related reasons are combined, between 55 percent (households) and 59 percent (persons) are accounted for. Other important reasons for household moves are, in order of importance, "to be closer to relatives," "to attend school," "wanted change of climate," and "entered or left U.S. Armed Forces."

Migration patterns, like other kinds of social interaction, vary with population characteristics such as age, sex, and economic status. For example, the peak age for interstate migration is 23; females are less likely than males to move for employment reasons; and persons with college educations are more likely than those without to move between states (Long and Hansen, 1979, pp. 8–13). In addition, it has

TABLE 8–2 Reasons for moving

Reason for Move	Percentage of Households	Percentage of Persons	Reason for Move	Percentage of Households	Percentage of Persons
Employment			Other		
Job transfer	23.8	27.6	Neighborhood overcrowded	0.4	0.4
Entered or left U. S. Armed Forces	4.8	4.9	Change in racial or ethnic composition of neighborhood	0.2	0.1
Retirement	3.4	3.0			
New job or looking for work	23.6	23.4	Wanted better neighborhood	1.1	1.1
Commuting reasons	1.0	0.9	Wanted to own residence	0.9	1.0
To attend school	5.4	3.9	Wanted lower rent or less expensive house	0.8	0.8
Other	2.4	2.6	Wanted better house	0.3	0.4
Family			Displaced by urban renewal, highway construction, or other public activity	0.1	0.1
Needed larger house or apartment	0.8	1.1			
Widowed	0.7	0.3			
Separated	1.2	1.2			
Divorced	1.0	0.8	Displaced by private action	0.3	0.4
To be closer to relatives	7.5	7.1	Schools	1.0	0.9
Newly married	1.6	1.4	Wanted to rent residence	0.2	0.1
Family increased	0.1	0.1	Wanted residence with more conveniences	0.2	0.1
Family decreased	0.1	0.1			
Wanted to establish own household	1.6	1.2	Natural disaster	0.1	0.1
			Wanted change of climate	5.1	4.8
Other	2.7	2.8	Other	5.5	5.4
			Not reported	2.1	1.7
			Interstate migrants (*thousands*)	5,843	16,332

Note: Responses given by heads of household moving between states in 12 months preceding 1974, 1975, and 1976 annual housing surveys.
Source: Long and Hansen, 1979, p. 6

been shown that the likelihood of residential moves differs among nations. Figure 8–13 shows that the peak age for moving is around 20–24 in all four countries, but moves are more likely in the United States. During a lifetime, a person in the United States will make about 13 moves, compared to 8 in Britain, and 7 in Japan (Long and Boertlein, 1976, p. 14).

Patterns In recent history, migrations of peoples have happened in several fairly distinctive patterns:

- There has been massive migration out of Europe, particularly to the United States, but also to Central and South America, Canada, South Africa, Australia, New Zealand, and other nations. People were pushed by adverse economic conditions at home and pulled by the opportunities (real or imagined) in the destination nations. The United States received 40 million immigrants between 1880 and 1914. A distinctive feature of world migration patterns has been that many Europeans have migrated, but fewer Asians.
- In the Americas, particularly, a stage in the migration and settlement process involved the "filling in" of open space, that is, an increase in rural population.
- In the twentieth century, particularly, rural areas have contributed to massive rural-to-urban migration in developed and developing nations alike. This migration pattern has hastened *urbanization.*
- More recently, there has been a movement from cities to suburbs. This process is called *suburbanization.*
- In the United States, amenities have become an important factor in migration decision making. Such factors as climate, scenery, recreational opportunities, and the general quality of life are increasingly influential considerations. The growth of the Sunbelt states relates in part to this trend and also to labor costs. The South traditionally has resisted the influence of labor unions, which has meant lower wages compared to the non-South.

Migration processes continue to be a major element in social interaction in the United States. Most of us are aware of the importance of intraurban migration (moves within cities) and of interurban and interstate movement patterns. At the international level, a great deal of attention is paid to unusual or illegal migrations—flows across the U.S.–Mexican border, Vietnamese refugees, the Haitian boat people, and recent waves of Cuban refugees. We should emphasize, however, that some of the more traditional migration flows into the United States continue, as shown in Figure 8–14. The pattern of location of new immigrants in the period 1961–1970 shows the importance of relatively few states (particularly California, New York, and Texas) as receivers of foreign immigrants.

The contribution of immigration as a factor in population growth should not be overlooked. If the United States were to maintain a condition of zero population growth (see Chapter 2), all future population increase would consist of immigrants, who would contribute several million persons per decade (Carlson, 1973, p. 11).

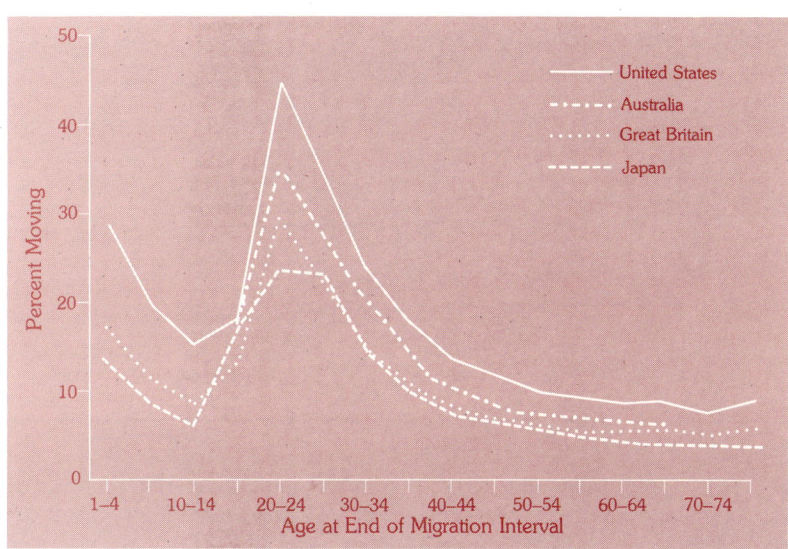

FIGURE 8–13 Percentage of population residentially mobile during one year in Australia, Great Britain, Japan, and the United States, by age, around 1970. (From Larry H. Long and Celia G. Boertlein, *The Geographical Mobility of Americans: An International Comparison* [1976], p. 13.)

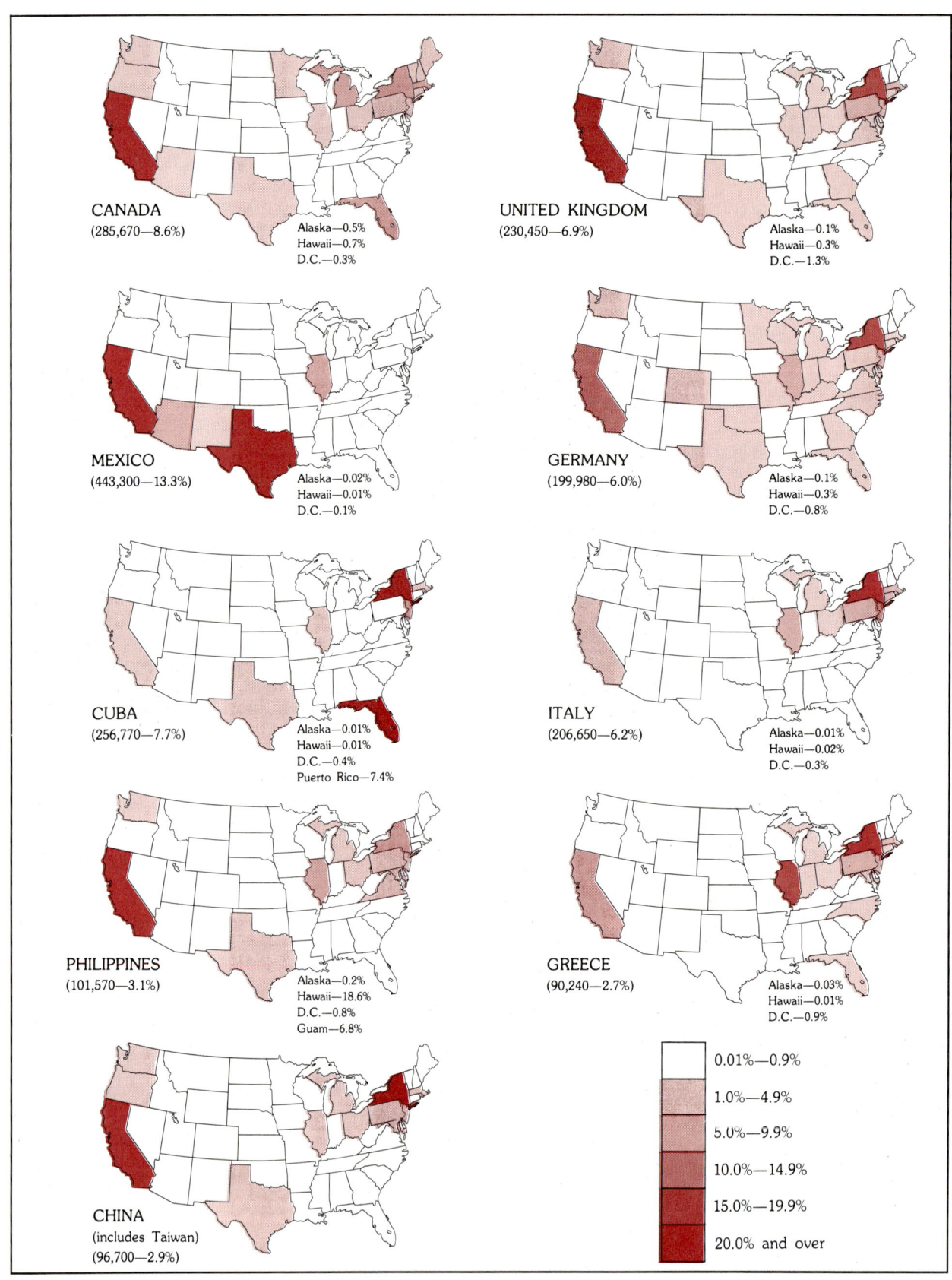

FIGURE 8-14 Immigrants admitted to the United States, by specific countries of birth and state of intended permanent residence, 1961-1970. (Adapted from *Journal of Geography* 72 [1973]:17.)

Since the impacts of migration can strongly affect neighborhoods, states, and nations, it is important to understand migration processes and monitor migration patterns. Understanding and monitoring enables us to anticipate consequences and plan for them. It has been shown, for example, that the availability of jobs alone may not attract people to cities—people have become more discriminating in choosing environments in which to live. Cities that wish to enjoy sustained economic growth may have to pay as much attention to environmental amenity development as to the provision of jobs (Long and Hansen, 1979, p. 28).

INTERACTION THROUGH COMMUNICATION

Movement of people contributes to social interaction. Another way interaction can occur, with or without the movement of people, is through communication, which takes many different forms. Face-to-face conversation, mail, radio, and all forms of telecommunication (television, telephone, telegram) are obvious examples. Is there a geographical dimension to communication that contributes to our understanding of social interaction processes?

Communication is indeed influenced by geographical conditions such as distance, direction, and the relative locations of cities and other settlements. Although distance is still an important influence, improvements in the efficiency of telecommunications in recent decades have reduced its significance. A direct-dial, "off-peak" phone call to Tokyo, Japan, for example, is $2.53 for the first minute. To Dublin, Ireland, or London, England, the cost is $1.25.

Increasing numbers of people, at least in the United States, are able to communicate telephonically with many distant nations at reasonable cost, thus expediting business links and the maintenance of social ties. Similarly, the adoption of cable TV systems has meant that many smaller cities have been able to receive varied programming from multiple metropolitan centers, in addition to the capability of generating local programs within the cable system itself.

Two concepts that relate closely to the process of interaction through communication are *information field* and *diffusion*. The concept of information field is related to the idea of mental maps: an information field is really a subset of a mental map. To ask a person to map the city in which he or she lives would provide a mental map or image. If we then ask the person to map the locations of all homes selling for less then $50,000, we are asking for an information field. A mental map is acquired through *familiarization* with an area, whereas information is obtained through a *communication* process supplemented by familiarization.

The way people acquire information about the real estate market illustrates the concept of information field. The information that home purchasers need to make a sound decision is found in many places—newspapers, realty offices, friends, and "for sale" signs posted outside homes. Newcomers to a city are at the greatest disadvantage—they have no large network of social contacts and are unfamiliar with neighborhoods. The best source for newcomers is often the realtor's Multiple Listing Service (MLS), which can be expected to provide unbiased information about housing vacancies. In a study of Minneapolis, Minnesota, Palm (1976) examined three questions relating to realtors' information fields: (1) Do MLS realtors cover the whole market in their listings? (2) Do realtors' perceptions of vacancy patterns conform to reality? (3) Do realtors vary in their recommendations of areas for certain types of home buyers?

It was found that realtors' *awareness spaces* (areas with which they were familiar) varied greatly. Realtors specialized, and even MLS realtors were unlikely to provide newcomers with data on the entire city. Information from more than 250 realtors produced general agreeement about the locations of vacancies at particular price levels. But in practice, people deal with only a few realtors, not 250. When the recommendations of individual realtors were reviewed, there was a strong local bias—realtors tended to suggest locations closest to their offices, regardless of social class or family type (Figure 8–15).

These findings have important practical implications for home buyers. Minneapolis is a relatively homogeneous physical environment, yet realtors' information is quite localized. In a more physically complex area such as Los Angeles or New York, realtors' information fields are probably even more fragmented. Ranges of hills, rivers, and highways may "fracture" the area. Home buyers are at a distinct disadvantage, because they suffer a "second-generation" loss of information, acquiring imperfect knowledge of the realtors' imperfect knowledge (Palm, 1976, p. 280).

As this example shows, the characteristics of information fields have an impact on one facet of spatial behavior—where people move, and why. The information field concept applies just as well to decisions about where to go to school, where to seek a job, where to look for the most rewarding

CHAPTER 8 SOCIAL PROCESSES

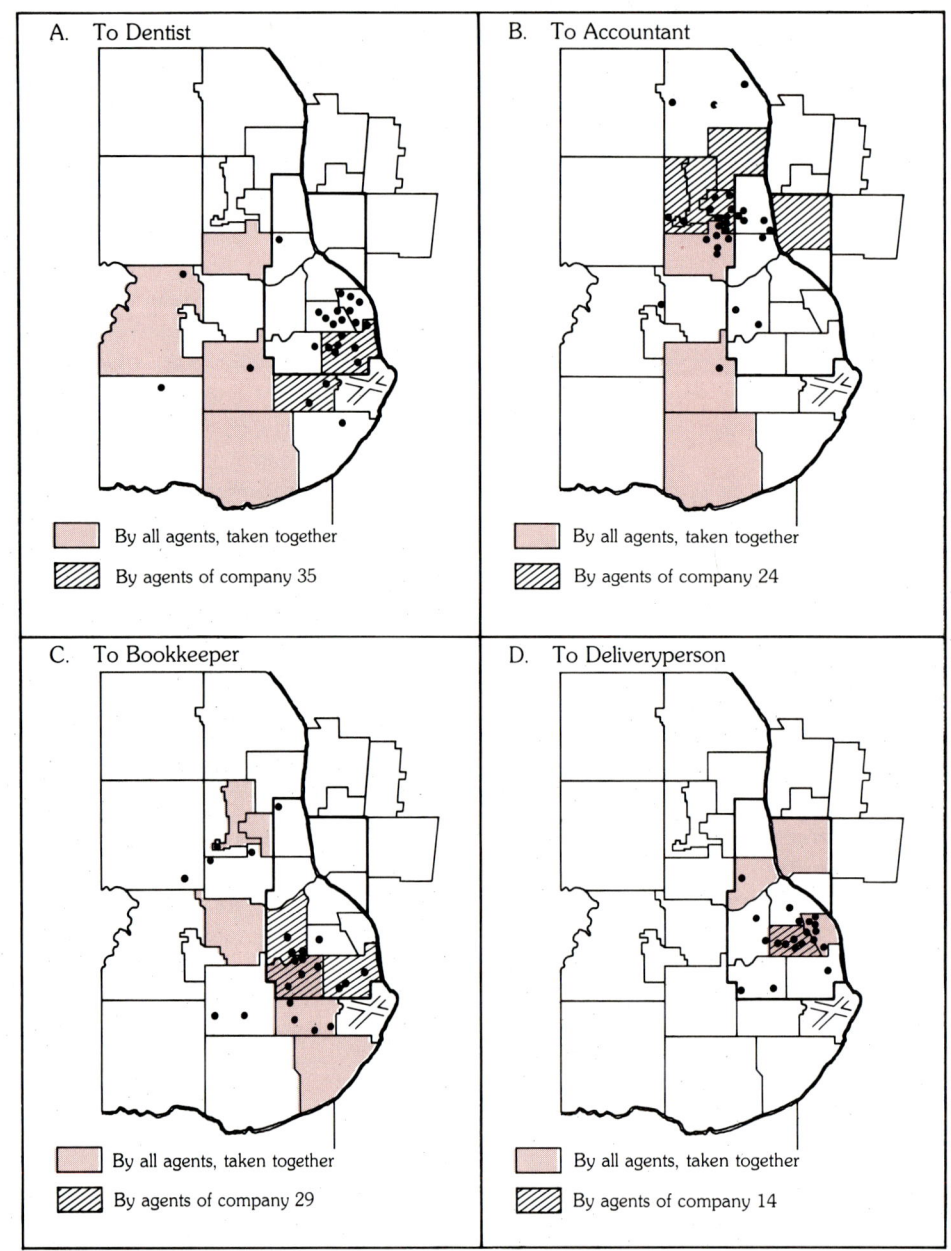

FIGURE 8–15 Spatial bias in information fields among Minneapolis realtors. Dots represent individual homes that realtors recommended. (Adapted from *Geographical Review* 66 [1976] with permission of the American Geographical Society.)

social contacts, and so forth. To make this concept work for us, we need to ask, with respect to our own locational decision making, if we have a reasonably complete information field as a basis for making our decision.

Another particularly useful concept in learning about the geography of communication is *diffusion*. *Diffusion* means "spreading" and is quite a general concept. We speak of the diffusion of a disease or the diffusion of a plant or animal species. For exam-

ple, an article in a popular gardening magazine explained how the cabbage white butterfly *(Pieris rapae)* was accidentally shipped to North America in a cargo ship about 1860. After colonizing Quebec, the butterfly *diffused* west and south, reaching Iowa and Missouri by 1878. By 1880, every state was host to *Pieris* (Berenbaum, 1979). We can also refer to the diffusion of information, including ideas and innovations. This topic is particularly important because it may tell, in effect, what the geographic pattern of

INTERACTION THROUGH COMMUNICATION

diffusion will be. It may also be possible to determine how long it will take for new ideas to catch on in industry, agriculture, medicine, education, or other fields. That information, in turn, may help with predictions about the productivity of cities and regions, and of society as a whole.

Research shows three underlying regularities in the diffusion of innovations (Brown and Cox, 1971):

1 **The S-Curve.** This curve, also called a *logistic curve* which can be diagrammed as a normal (bell-shaped) curve (Figure 8–16), shows the *temporal* (time-related) dimension of the diffusion process. The "innovators" start out with a new idea that is first accepted by the "early majority," who are followed by the "late majority." Those who adopt the innovation last are the "laggards." The S shape occurs when cumulative percentage is plotted on the vertical axis.

2 **Neighborhood Effect.** The neighborhood effect is the application of the distance–decay concept to the diffusion process. Simply stated, the adoption of an innovation is most likely closest to lo-

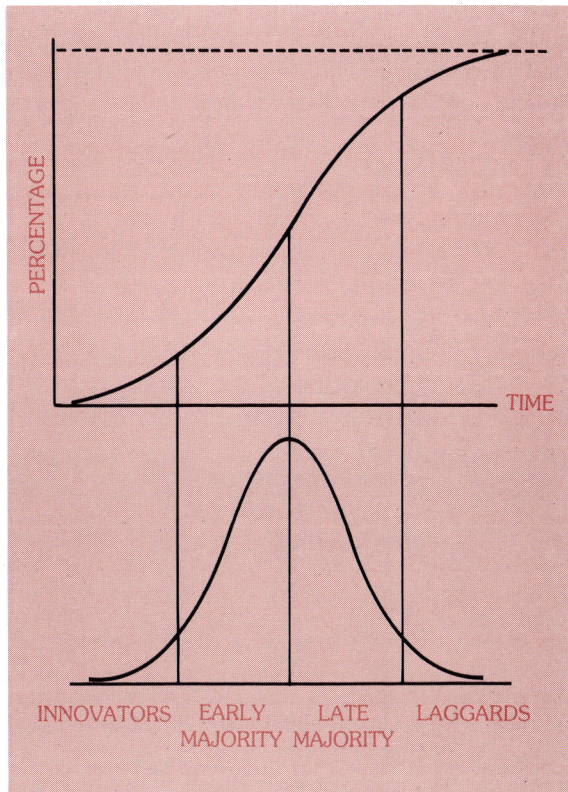

FIGURE 8–16 S-shaped and normal curves illustrating diffusion of innovations. (Adapted by permission from P. Gould, *Spatial Diffusion*, Association of American Geographers, Resource Papers for College Geography no. 4 [1969]:19.)

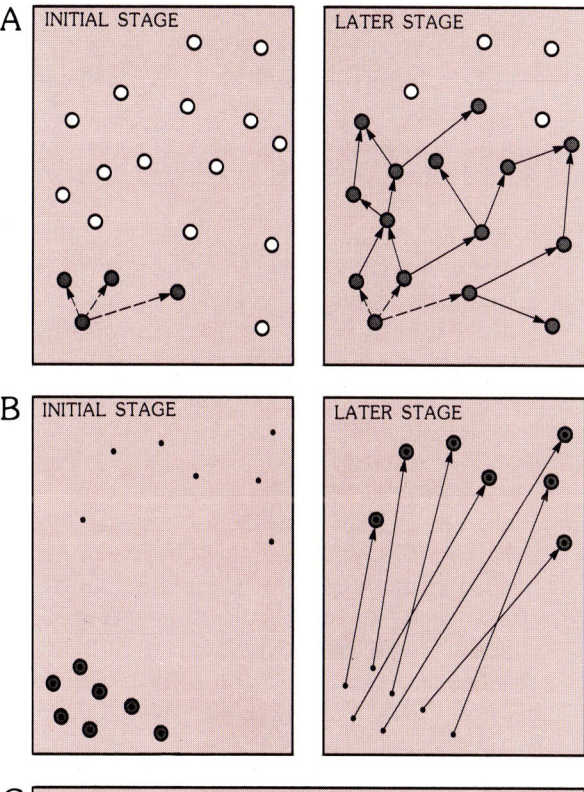

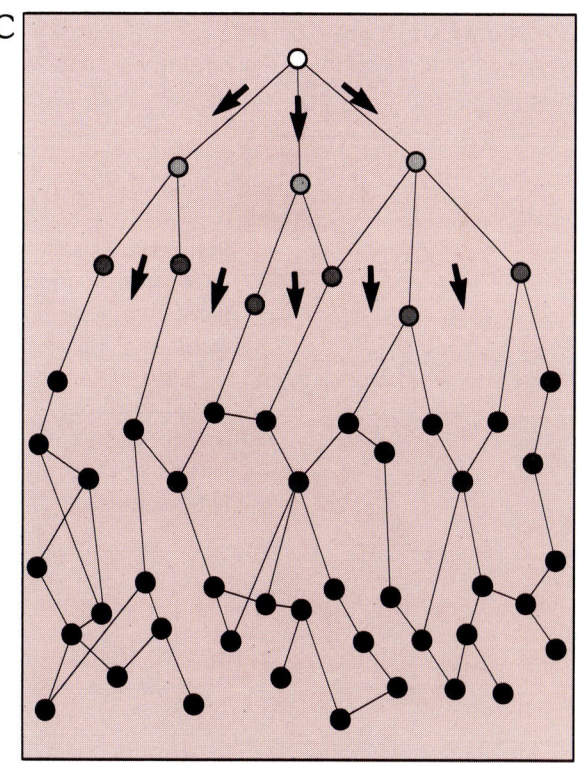

FIGURE 8–17 Diffusion: (a) expansion; (b) relocation; (c) hierarchial. (Adapted with permission from P. Gould, *Spatial Diffusion*, Association of American Geographers, Resource Papers for College Geography no. 4 [1969]:4, 6.)

cations where adoption has already occurred. Two kinds of diffusion—*expansion diffusion* (Figure 8–17a) and *relocation diffusion* (Figure 8–17b)—can be considered in the context of this neighborhood effect. Expansion diffusion can be illustrated by the spread of the innovation of urbanization from Mesopotamia and Egypt to southern, and eventually northern, Europe. Relocation diffusion involves the movement of the phenomenon being diffused. For example, a language might be introduced to a new area by relocation of the people who speak it, with subsequent diffusion following the expansion process. In either expansion or relocation diffusion, closer locations are more likely to be affected than locations farther away.

3 **Hierarchical Effect.** The hierarchical effect states that the more important places people go to get needed goods and services (central places) will adopt innovations earliest, and diffusion will occur down to less important places (Figure 8–17c). This has also been called the *short-circuit effect,* because it may overpower the neighborhood effect.

Numerous studies of diffusion processes have demonstrated these three regularities. For further examples, refer to Gould and White (1968), Gould (1969), and *Economic Geography* (October 1974; July 1975).

CONCLUSION

Social geography deals with the arrangement, interaction, and movement of people. The concept of social space refers to the areas within and between which humans act out their existence as social animals. Of the processes of perception, crowding, movement, and communication, each has a bearing on how we interact with others—that is, our social behavior. Each process is actually made up of a complex of subprocesses. Movement, for example, involves several *types* of movement, each of which may be regarded with different levels of priority by different population groups. One category of movement—migration—cannot be separated from the cultural factors considered in the two previous chapters. Social behavior is clearly related to cultural patterns. Similarly, the diffusion of new ideas can be intimately tied to aspects of culture—the emphasis given to the quality of education, the sophistication of information systems, and the effectiveness of media. One final point—those who best understand social and cultural processes will best understand social problems.

KEY WORDS

awareness space
cost-benefit analysis
crowding
density
diffusion
distance-decay
information field
intensity theory
interaction field

isoline
mental map
migration
perception
personal space
social space
spatial interaction
survey research
territoriality

REFERENCES

ADAMS, ROBERT L. A. "Uncertainty in Nature, Cognitive Dissonance, and the Perceptual Distortion of Environmental Information: Weather Forecasts and New England Beach Trip Decisions." *Economic Geography* 49 (1973):287–97.

BALDASSARE, MARK. *Residential Crowding in Urban America.* Berkeley, Calif.: University of California Press, 1979.

BERENBAUM, MAY. "The Cabbage White Butterfly: An American Success Story, Unfortunately." *Horticulture* 57 (1979):42–46.

BROWN, LAWRENCE A., and COX, KEVIN R. "Empirical Regularities in the Diffusion of Innovation." *Annals of the Association of American Geographers* 61 (1971):511–59.

REFERENCES

BUTTIMER A. "Social Space in Interdisciplinary Perspective." *Geographical Review* 59 (1969):417–26.

CARLSON, ALVAR W. "Recent Immigration, 1961–1970: A Factor in the Growth and Distribution of the United States Population." *Journal of Geography* 72 (1973):8–18.

COX, KEVIN R., and ZANNARAS, GEORGIA. "Designative Perceptions of Macro-Spaces: Concepts, a Methodology, and Applications." In Roger M. Downs and David Stea, eds. *Image and Environment*. Chicago: Aldine Publishing Co., 1973, pp. 162–78.

DOWNS, ROGER M. "Geographic Space Perception: Past Approaches and Future Prospects." In C. Board, R. J. Chorley, P. Haggett, and D. R. Stoddart, eds. *Progress in Geography*. Vol. 2. London: Edward Arnold, 1970, pp. 65–108.

EVERITT, JOHN C. "Community and Propinquity in a City." *Annals of the Association of American Geographers* 66 (1976):104–16.

FREEDMAN, JONATHAN L. *Crowding and Behavior*. San Francisco: W. H. Freeman & Co., 1975.

GOULD, PETER R. "On Mental Maps." Michigan Inter-University Community of Mathematical Geographers Discussion Paper No. 9, 1966. Reprinted in Roger H. Downs and David Stea, eds. *Image and Environment*. Chicago: Aldine Publishing Co., 1973, pp. 182–220.

———. *Spatial Diffusion*. Association of American Geographers Resource Paper No. 4. Washington, D.C., 1969.

———. "Acquiring Spatial Information." *Economic Geography* 51 (1975):87–99.

GOULD, PETER R. and R. R. WHITE, "The Mental Maps of British School Leavers", *Regional Studies* 2 (1968):161–182.

HALL, EDWARD T. *The Hidden Dimension* (Garden City, N.Y.: Doubleday, 1966)

JORDAN, TERRY G. "Perceptual Regions in Texas." *Geographical Review* 68 (1978):293–307.

LEE, T., "The Urban Neighborhood as a Socio-Spatial Schema", *Human Relations* 21 (1968):241–268.

LONG, LARRY H., and BOERTLEIN, CELIA G. *The Geographical Mobility of Americans: An International Comparison*. Current Population Reports, Special Studies Series P–23, No. 64. Washington, D.C: U.S. Government Printing Office, 1976.

LONG, LARRY H., and HANSEN, KRISTIN A. *Reasons for Interstate Migration*. Current Population Reports, Special Studies Series P–23, No. 81. Washington, D.C.: U.S. Government Printing Office, 1979.

LYNCH, KEVIN. *The Image of the City*. Cambridge, Mass: M.I.T. Press, 1960.

MOORE, E. G. *Residential Mobility in the City*. Association of American Geographers Resource Paper No. 13. Washington, D. C.: Commision on College Geography, 1972.

PALM, RISA. "Real Estate Agents and Geographical Information." *Geographical Review* 66 (1976):266–80.

PORTEOUS, J. DOUGLAS, *Environment and Behavior: Planning and Everyday Urban Life*. Reading, Mass.: Addison-Wesley, 1977.

SAARINEN, THOMAS F. *Perception of Environment*. Association of American Geographers Resource Paper No. 5. Washington, D.C.: Commission on College Geography, 1969.

STEEL, RICHARD, and GRAM, D. "The Box Kite Blaze." *Newsweek*, 8 August 1977, pp. 25–27.

"STUDIES IN SPATIAL DIFFUSION PROCESSES: I. Empirical." *Economic Geography* 50 (1974).

"STUDIES IN SPATIAL DIFFUSION PROCESSES: II. Conceptual." *Economic Geography* 51 (1975).

STUTZ, FREDERICK P., "Distance and Network Effects on Urban Social Travel Fields." *Economic Geography* 49 (1973):134–144.

_____. *Social Aspects of Interaction and Transportation.* Association of American Geographers Resource Paper No. 76–2. Washington, D.C., 1976.

U.S. DEPARTMENT OF COMMERCE, Bureau of the Census. *The Journey to Work in the United States: 1975.* Current Population Reports, Special Studies P–23, No. 99. Washington, D.C.: U.S. Government Printing Office, 1979.

WARD, DAVID. *Cities and Immigrants: A Geography of Change in Nineteenth Century America* (New York: Oxford University Press, 1971).

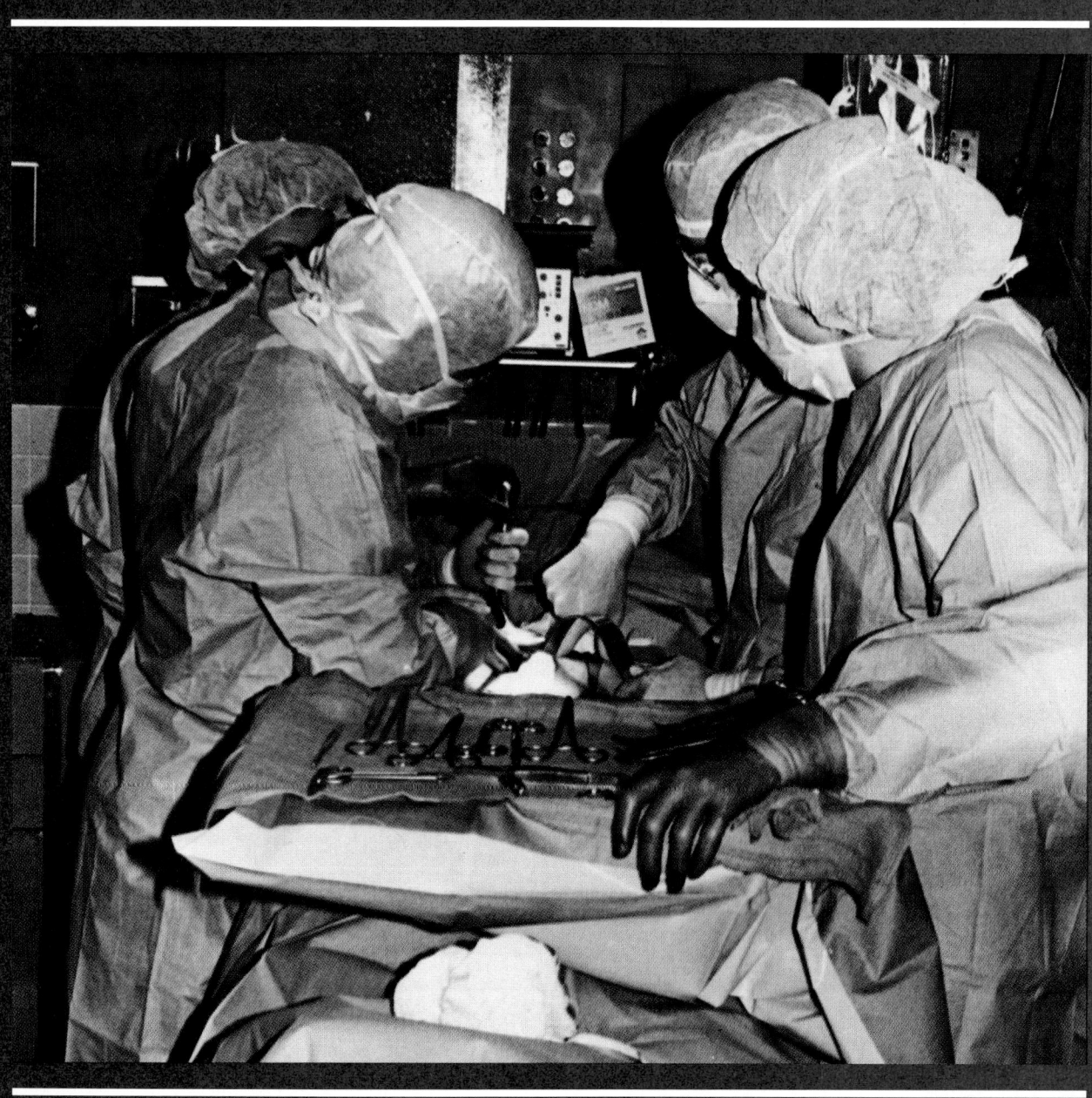

9
The Geography of Social Problems

HEALTH AND DISEASE
CRIME AND JUSTICE

Medical facilities are unevenly distributed; big cities may be well served, and large rural areas may have no facilities.

Whether a nation's economy is based on capitalism, socialism, or is mixed, its citizens are subject to geographical variations in *life chances*—the bundle of opportunities, obligations, and events that translates into the way people live their lives. In some locales, infants are seemingly born with silver spoons in their mouths, their mothers' conditions carefully monitored through prenatal care, and the children watched over with minute attention. In other places, whether developing nation or inner-city ghetto, pregnancy and birth may be serious life-threatening situations because of poor nutrition, care, and counseling. In a neighborhood served by adequate emergency services, a heart attack may mean survival and years added to a productive life; if emergency services are inadequate, the heart attack may mean death.

Similarly, the chance event of *where* you live may determine the likelihood that you will be victimized by crime. Rates of crime vary among nations, among regions in nations, and among cities and neighborhoods. Ironically, those who are least able to bear the economic or emotional costs of crime victimization are often most likely to be victimized. The burglary of a white family in the suburbs is an unpleasant event with emotional ramifications, but the monetary value of lost possessions is probably covered by insurance. When the poor are "ripped off," inadequate or nonexistent insurance may mean they cannot replace the stolen items. Work time lost because of physical injuries suffered during crimes also has greater impact on the poor in both absolute and relative terms.

Just as the incidence of crimes varies from place to place, so does the system of laws and the manner in which laws are administered. In the United States, each state has enacted laws that supposedly meet the test of being *constitutional;* that is, they are consistent with the U.S. Constitution. But this setup allows wide discretion in terms of what acts are defined as crimes and what penalties are prescribed. Within limits, cities and counties are free to enact ordinances and penalties dealing, typically, with traffic control, building design, zoning, and public health. Generally, traffic laws are enforced vigorously, whereas building code violations are not. This unequal enforcement creates a pattern of discrimination based on geography and social class. Tenants who live in older housing, usually in the inner city or close to older university campuses, are more likely to be victimized by building code violations—unvented heaters, inadequate electrical wiring, sewer backup, and so forth. In effect, unequal enforcement acts to the benefit of landlords and to the detriment of tenants. Equal enforcement is unlikely, because landlords have clout at city hall, and tenants usually do not.

In education, another critical realm of social concern, opportunities, in both quantity and quality, are constrained by locational considerations. Some states have high-quality public school systems with relatively well-paid and well-qualified staffs; some do not. Variations in funding levels among school districts in the same state may be substantial, thus producing clear differentials in educational opportunity. States with weak systems of higher education produce inferior teachers, who in turn contribute to inferior public school education. Freedom of movement from one state to another tends to perpetuate inequalities, as the best-educated and most capable individuals from poor states are drawn to wealthier areas by prospects of greater opportunities. These inequalities, then, are difficult to overcome.

Another controversial process with social impact is the disbursement of federal funds for a massive variety of purposes, including agricultural subsidies, defense contracts, unemployment benefits, and university research. For example, in 1984, state and local governments received almost $98 billion in federal aid. In some states, per capita taxes paid *to* the federal government exceed per capita expenditures *by* the federal government; this is the case in New York, Pennsylvania, Illinois, and California. In other states (Missouri, the Dakotas, Oklahoma, and much of the South and West) the reverse is true. A state like New York, then, is subsidizing a state like Oklahoma, which may be regarded as a state on "welfare," supported in part by federal revenue surpluses from other states. This kind of income redistribution may be fair and reasonable if the funds are used to promote economic development or somehow alleviate the difficulties of the poor. In reality, need is often secondary to political considerations—agricultural subsidies may increase when the vote of farmers is needed, a large federal public works project such as a dam may be authorized to win the support of a powerful contractor, and so forth. This political influence-peddling is not purely a product of the capitalist world; rather, it seems to be a consequence of human nature, about as likely under socialism as under capitalism (see Smith, 1979, pp. 342–43).

Social problems of universal concern are obvious. What may be more subtle is that the impact of social problems varies greatly according to the status of the affected population. Health problems, for example, particularly relate to the young and the old. Educational problems have an impact on the young, but have a greater impact on youth who are poor or black or non-English-speaking or handicapped. The location of a new military base or other facility reduces the local pool of unemployed, just as closing such a facility increases unemployment. Therefore, these social problems should not be thought of as abstract, vague concepts. In reality, they touch us directly or indirectly as individuals, and the degree to which we are affected often depends on where we are located.

To illustrate this spatial dimension in social problems, and simultaneously put to work some of the concepts discussed in Chapter 8, we will consider two significant problems with particular reference to U.S. society: the issues of health and criminal justice. Not everyone would rank these as their two primary concerns, but few would dispute the suggestion that they are general problems in virtually all nations.

HEALTH AND DISEASE

At any geographic scale, the level of health relates to human happiness and has major economic impacts. Unhealthy people lose time from school and work, and the productivity of the economy suffers. The direct and indirect costs of illness are enormous. But why look at health questions from a geographical perspective? There is overwhelming evidence that diseases are often patterned spatially. *Communicable* diseases (e.g., smallpox) have been linked to characteristics of climate, vegetation, insect species, water quality, and various other environmental factors. *Chronic* diseases (e.g., cancer) have been related to such factors as water quality and the nature of bedrock (Pyle, 1976, p. 95). The fears expressed by residents of the Love Canal, New York, area in relation to the health effects of chemical contamination dra-

LOVE CANAL

"For sale, 82 chemicals. You dig 'em." This hand-made sign hanging on the porch of a home at Love Canal in Niagara Falls in upstate New York symbolized the frustration of Love Canal homeowners. In the late 1970s, they found that their homes had been built over a chemical waste dump. In the 1890s, William T. Love had attempted to construct an industrial complex that would use water from the Niagara River channeled through a canal. The project was unsuccessful, and a half-mile section of canal remained unused until the 1940s, when it was bought by the Hooker Chemical Co. In the 1940s and early 1950s, the canal was used as a chemical waste dump. Some 22,000 tons were disposed of. In the 1950s, the school board assembled land around Love Canal for a school, including the Hooker site, which the company sold to the board for $1. The deed for the land included a stipulation that Hooker could not be held liable for damages. A school was built, and around it a residential subdivision.

By 1978, chemicals were seeping into the basements of homes, and the area was evacuated in the summer of that year, following claims by residents that miscarriages and birth defects were occurring at unusually high rates. An informal survey of the outcomes of pregnancies for calendar year 1979 indicated that only 2 births of 12 were normal. Love Canal earned the dubious distinction of being the first place to be designated a disaster area as a result of a man-made disaster.

By 1980, the federal government had decided to help relocate 710 families (New York State had evacuated and compensated 239 families in 1978). Unlike in a natural disaster, which is limited in duration, the fear and anxiety associated with Love Canal could go on for generations as people worry about the effects of possible genetic damage on themselves, their children, and their grandchildren. Soon after a study (later discredited) by the Environmental Protection Agency showing chromosome change in about a third of 36 people tested, Lois Gibbs, president of the Love Canal Homeowners Association, stated that people were "very, very frightened, almost panicked."

The health effects of the contamination and of the stresses associated with fear are extremely difficult to assess. According to Holden (1980), "although no one has yet come up with the unassailable evidence that chemicals from the dump site have been making people sick, there is enough to convince people that they are being poisoned and that the authorities are more interested in soft-pedaling the problem than in protecting the public's health" (p. 1242).

The costs associated with cleanup and relocation will run into hundreds of millions of dollars. The costs in human health, both physical and mental, are incalculable. At a time when it has become very fashionable to criticize the federal government for overregulating business activities, it is worth reflecting on the fact that Love Canal was caused by *lack* of regulation—Hooker Chemical claims its disposal methods were perfectly legal given the rules that existed when it was dumping.

Other Niagara Falls dump sites pose additional problems, including the discovery of carcinogenic sludge at the city's water treatment plant about 180 m (600 ft) from another Hooker dump. Numerous stories of chemical contamination are coming in from around the nation. The destruction of 30,000 cattle plus many other farm animals as the result of polybrominated biphenyl (PBB) contamination in Michigan is one of the more notorious examples. The United States has yet to develop policies and procedures that adequately address this mounting problem.

matically illustrated the impact on a specific community from disease, or from the *perceived* fear of disease, or, in the Love Canal case, from genetic damage. Vinyl chloride contamination of a dump and its environs in Islip, New York (on Long Island), led to a comparable outcry, and the area was dubbed "Love Canal South." Other chemical waste problems come to light with frightening frequency.

Dramatic situations like Love Canal make headlines periodically. More subtle are the long-term links between lifestyle (diet, exercise patterns, smoking and drinking habits, etc.) and health, between health and conditions in the workplace, and between health and the natural environment, including patterns of epidemics of infectious diseases. All these factors have geographic components. Lifestyles do vary from nation to nation and region to region. Low levels of heart disease in the Orient as compared to the western world are thought to be linked in part to dietary differences. Hazards presented by the workplace are often highly concentrated on a regional or local basis, as subsequent discussion of cancer patterns will show. Not only are workers directly affected, but industrial emissions to air and water can also have an effect on the health of those who are not directly involved in industrial processes. Epidemic patterns are closely tied to spatial patterns, including travel behavior, settlement geography, and population density. The worldwide spread of flu, for example, has been shown to relate to intercontinental travel patterns.

Just as disease has a strong spatial dimension, so does health care. We might ask whether doctors and hospitals are geographically distributed so as to match the population distribution. How far must people travel to reach medical facilities? Is the arrangement of community health agencies convenient to the majority of the people? How far must people travel to reach highly specialized facilities? Are the limited number of trauma centers (for high-quality emergency care) accessible to the maximum number of people in the minimum amount of time? These are the kinds of geographic questions one can ask about health-care personnel and facilities and imply a strong concern about inequalities in the supply of health care.

Inequalities are inevitable, but tend to be more extreme in the United States, where the health industry is organized primarily for profit and secondarily to supply health care. Many people were surprised to learn that among the thousands of Cuban refugees admitted to the United States in the massive 1980 influx, "the incidence of disease . . . was lower than for the U.S. public as a whole" (Alpern et al.,

1980, p. 25). Although the Cuban economy is weak, Cubans apparently have had access to basic health

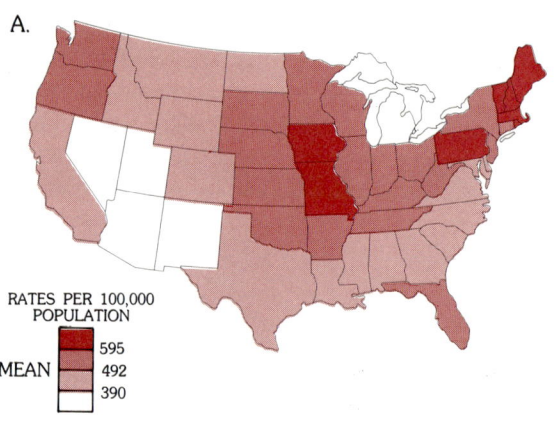

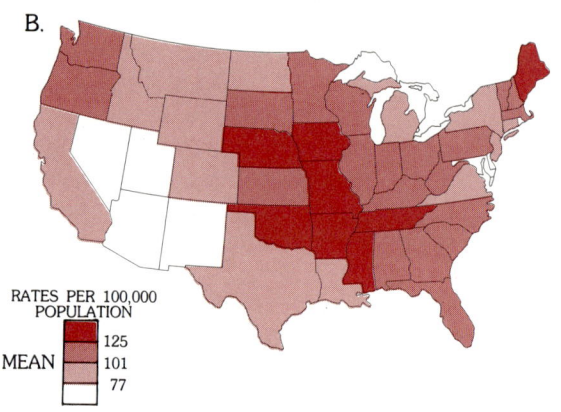

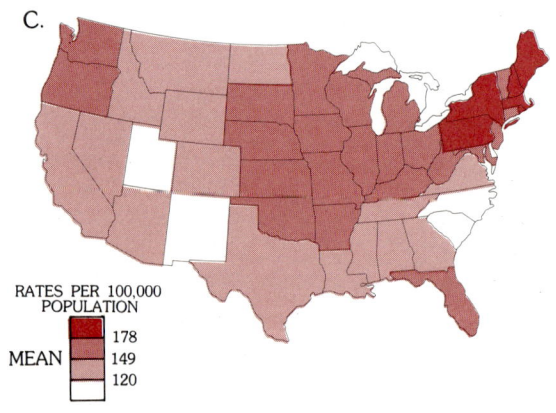

FIGURE 9–1 Distribution of (a) heart disease; (b) cancer; (c) stroke, 1967. Class intervals are on standard deviations of each disease rate. (Adapted from Gerald F. Pyle, *Heart Disease, Cancer, and Stroke in Chicago* [1971], pp. 58, 59.)

care, of which one result is the lowest infant mortality rate in Latin America. In general, the highest health levels (measured by indicators such as life expectancy and infant mortality) tend to occur in nations with more public control over health-care provision (Smith, 1979, pp. 256–57).

Health and disease may be considered from two perspectives: first, we can consider the patterning of disease and knowledge of patterns in the search for causes; and second, we can consider geographic methods for allocating health-care resources.

Mapping Disease and the Search for Causes

The three most common causes of death in the United States are heart disease, cancer, and stroke (Figure 9–1). The maps in Figure 9–1 are based on the number of occurrences of these diseases per 100,000 persons. These rates are the usual way of expressing the incidence of phenomena that affect people. One must be careful in interpreting these maps, however, since no adjustment is made for the age of the population. In other words, we would expect that an older population would have a higher incidence of these diseases, so to some extent, the maps show where the elderly population is located. If age were the only significant factor, however, all three maps would be the same, at least in terms of the ranking of states. That the maps are markedly different suggests the involvement of causal factors other than age.

Heart disease has been shown to correlate with race, sex, and occupation, as well as age. More urban environments tend to have higher rates than less urban areas. Cigarette consumption and water hardness also have been shown to relate to heart disease. Climate is a significant factor in death from stroke; winter blood pressures tend to be higher (Pyle, 1971, pp. 41–45). The *Atlas of Cancer Mortality for U.S. Counties* (1975) has shown dramatically how maps may be used to suggest *etiologic* (Latin *aetiologia,* "determining the cause of something") factors. Numerous cancers have excessively high mortality rates in the industrialized Northeast. According to the *Atlas:*

> It is nearly certain that industrial exposures have produced the striking geographic clusters of bladder cancer in males [Figure 9–2]. Of the 21 counties in New Jersey, 18 have bladder cancer rates in the highest decile of male rates for all U.S. counties. Indeed, the rate for Salem County, New Jersey (16.1 per 100,000 population) ranks highest among all American counties with a white population of at least 10,000. In Salem County, approximately one-fourth of the work force is employed in chemical and allied industries, and workers exposed to chemicals such as 2-napthylamine are known to be at increased risk of bladder cancer [Mason et al., 1975].

Stomach cancer is linked to ethnic factors such as diet. In the north-central states, where people of Austrian, Soviet, and Scandinavian ethnicity are concentrated, rates are elevated for both males and females (Figure 9–3). The nations of origin also have elevated rates. High rates of skin cancer in the South are striking, and probably relate to excessive exposure to ultraviolet light. In other words, climate may be a key factor (Figure 9–4).

The diffusion process discussed in Chapter 8 has often been observed in the study of infectious diseases. Knowledge of disease diffusion is useful for predicting how a disease is likely to spread and in what kind of time frame. The dreaded Black Death (bubonic plague), for example, spread across Europe in the fourteenth century from southeast to northwest, taking about 2 years to move from the Mediterranean coast to northern Britain and Scandinavia. Millions died (Pyle, 1979, pp. 127–28). Another well-documented diffusion pattern involved the spread of cholera in the United States in the nineteenth century. Cholera is an acute intestinal disease with extremely unpleasant symptoms, including diarrhea and physical collapse. If the sickness is not treated within 24 hours, death is likely. Cholera spreads mainly by contact with victims, whether they are dead or alive. Transmission also occurs via water contaminated with infected human feces, food, and flies. In the nineteenth century, there was a series of *pandemics* (worldwide outbreaks) of cholera, each of which impacted North America with *epidemics* (local outbreaks). Three epidemics occurred—in 1832, 1849, and 1866—but the disease diffused differently each time because of differences in the pattern of settlement, population density, and transportation networks (Figure 9–5). Pyle (1969) explains it this way:

> In 1832, contact with the natural environment was close, transportation was crude, and the urban hierarchy had not yet evolved. In 1849, the disease moved down the evolving hierarchy in two ways, thus reflecting more control over the environment and some integration of the urban system since 1832. The 1866 epidemic shows a completed hierarchy. City size was a prime factor in the spread of cholera over space and through time. Differences in spread of the epidemic were

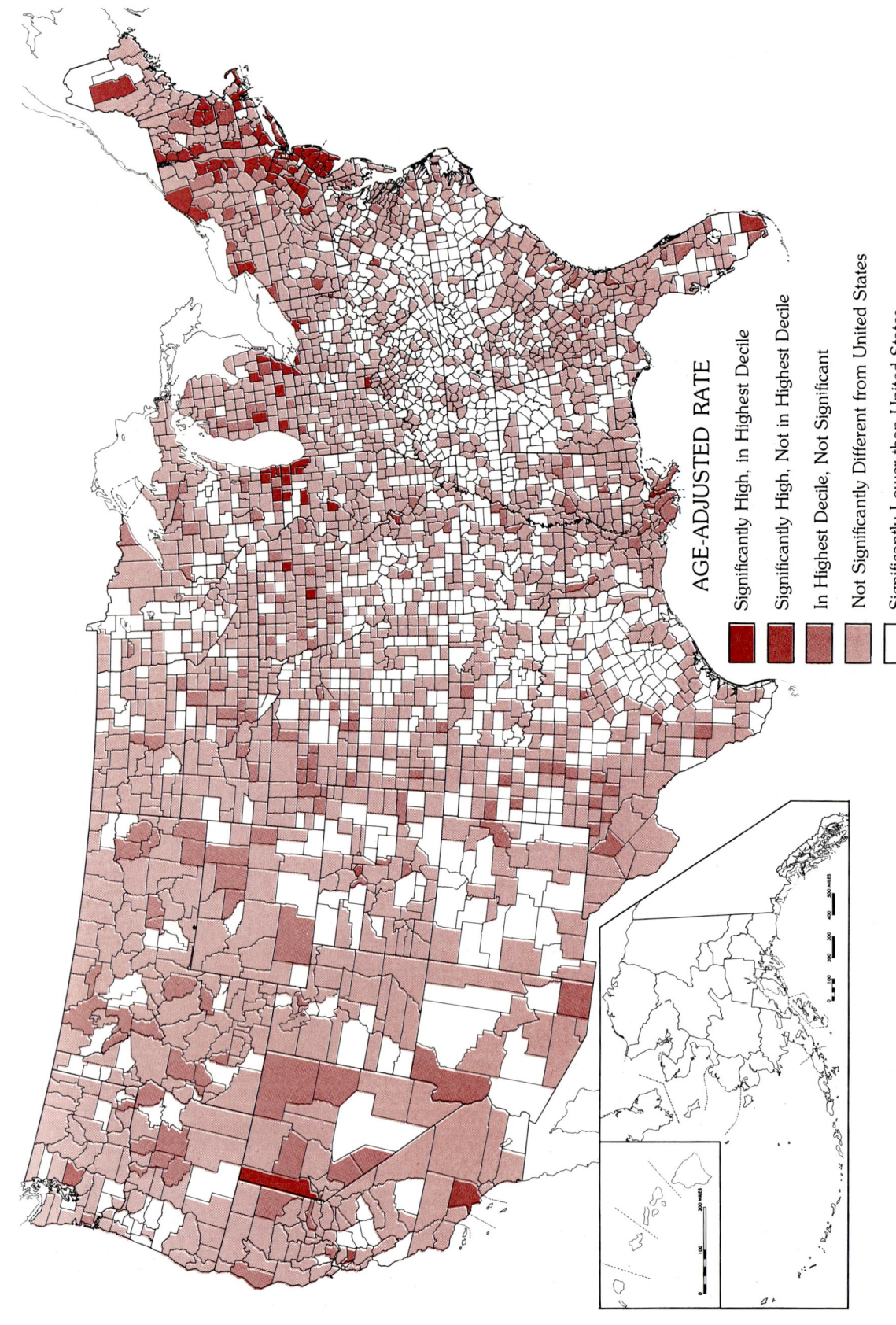

FIGURE 9–2 Bladder cancer mortality for white males, by county, 1950–1969. (From Mason et al., 1975, p. 18.)

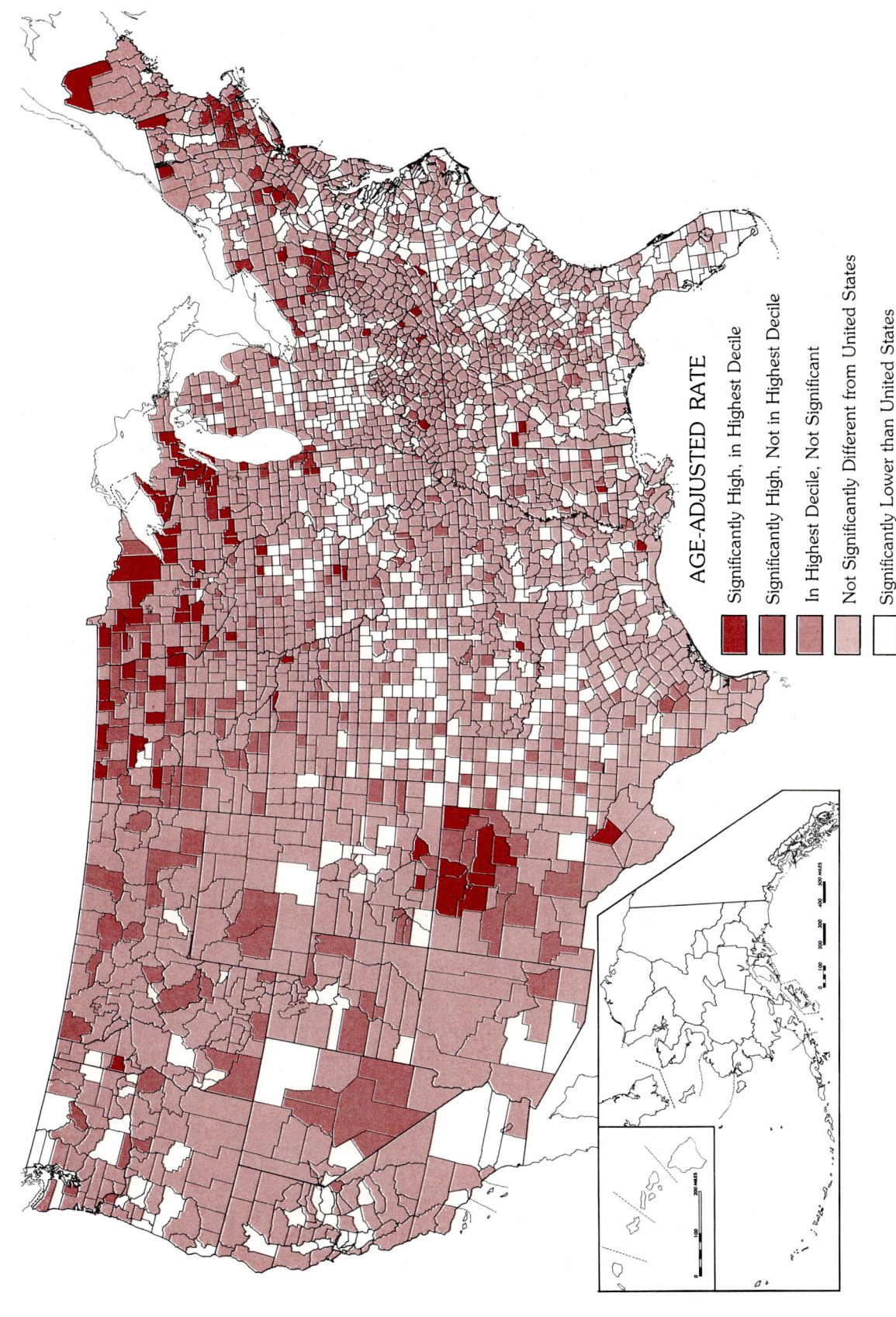

FIGURE 9–3 Stomach cancer mortality for white females, by county, 1950–1969. (From Mason et al., 1975, p. 5.)

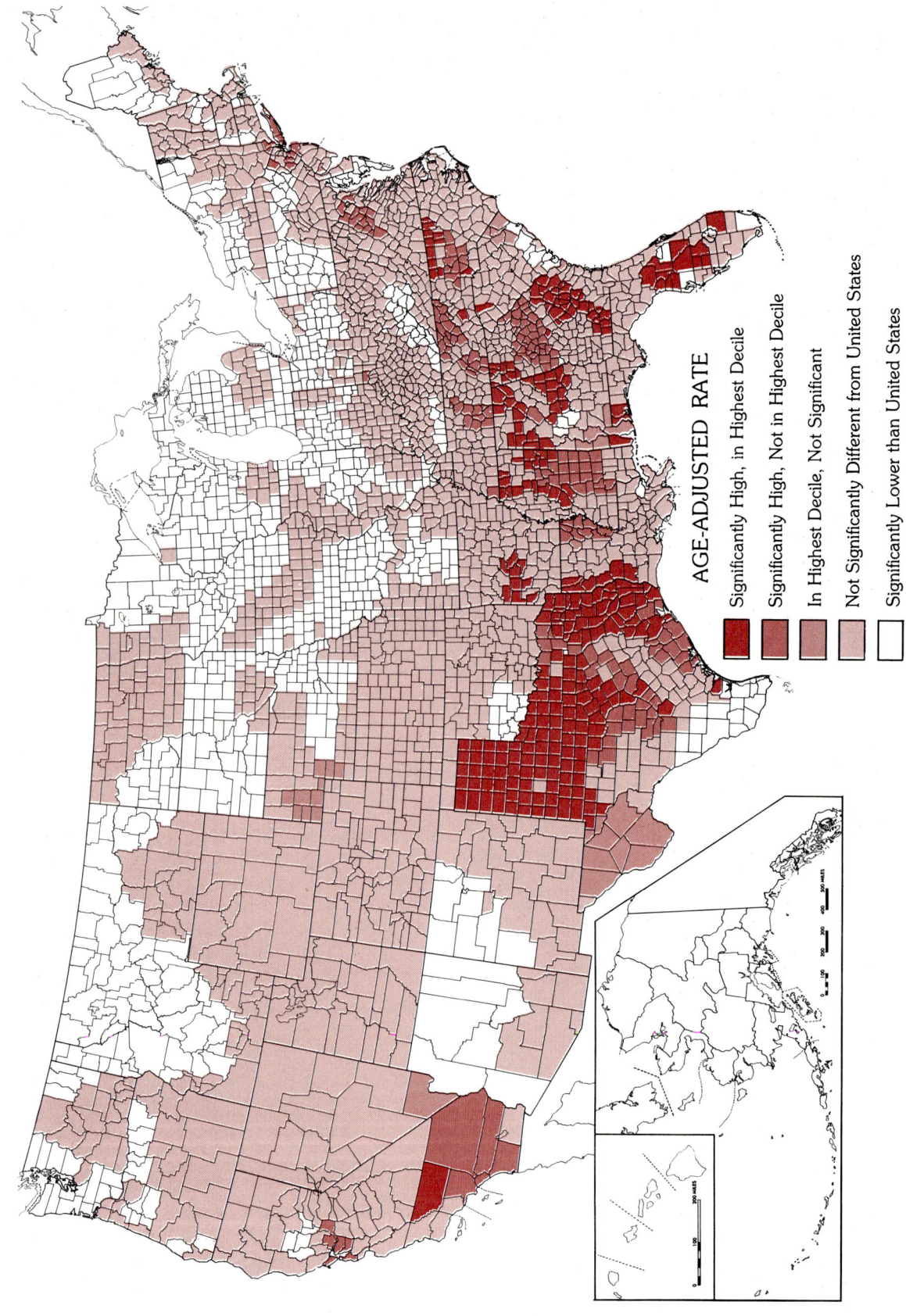

FIGURE 9–4 Cancer mortality due to melanoma of the skin for white males, by state economic area, 1950–1969. (From Mason et al., 1975, p. 4.)

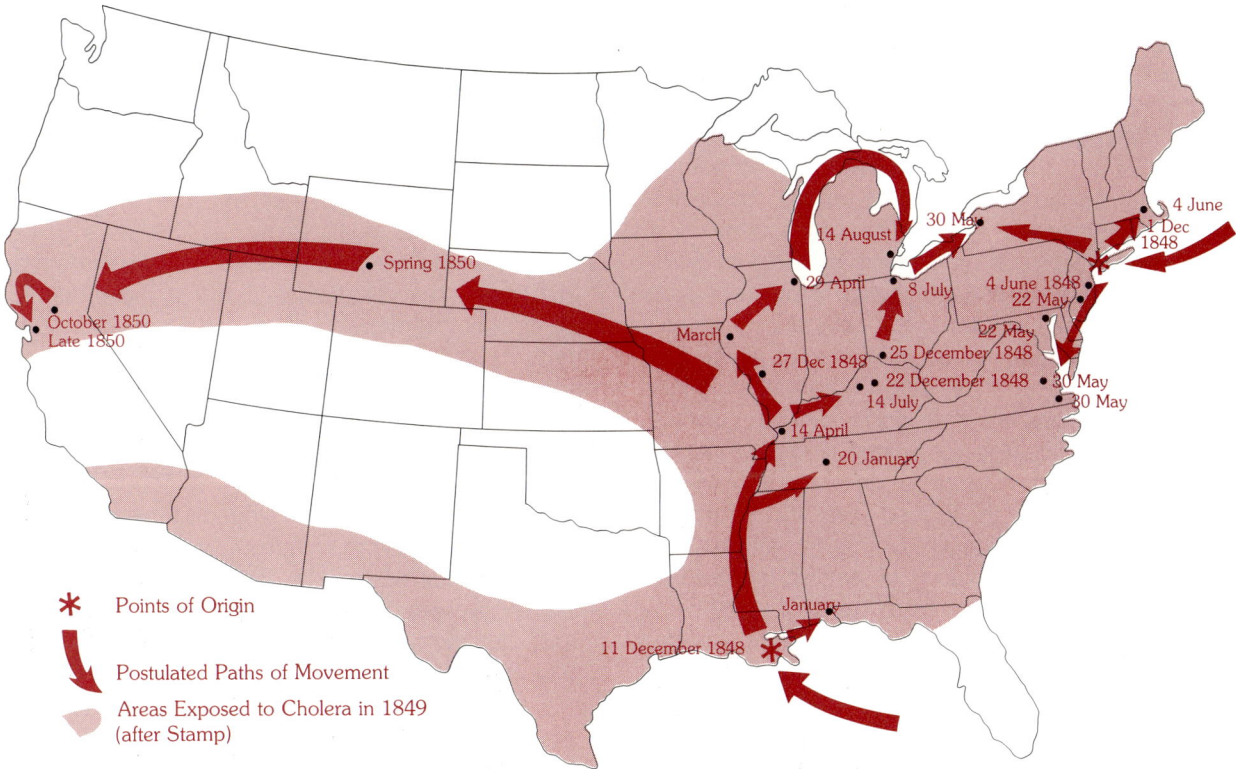

FIGURE 9–5 Movement of cholera, 1848–1849. (Reprinted by permission from G. F. Pyle, "The Diffusion of Cholera in the United States in the Nineteenth Century," *Geographical Analysis,* Vol. 1 [January 1969], pp. 59–75. Copyright © 1969 by the Ohio State University Press. All rights reserved.)

thus related to a changing transportation and urban environment. (p. 74)

Although such historical reconstructions are interesting, health data have improved greatly in the twentieth century, and it is now possible to create diffusion patterns more easily and with more direct application to current problems. (See Chapter 8 for discussion of diffusion processes.)

Influenza outbreaks have been the subject of a good deal of research. One study of the 1957 pandemic showed how influenza spread through Britain, where 7,000 deaths were attributed to the disease. Port cities were seeded most heavily, and the disease diffused outward from them. A typical epidemic process was traced: a few people infected initially, then a *threshold* or "take-off" level triggering geometrical increase (2, 4, 8, 16, 32, 64, . . .), then a falling off as already infected people, who had resistance to the disease, interrupted transfer of infection to those not yet victimized. Ethnic factors were involved in the diffusion process. Not only was the epidemic thought to have been introduced by Pakistani visitors, but Pakistanis customarily visit the sick, do not ventilate their homes, wear many clothes, and live under high-density conditions—all circumstances that tend to promote influenza (Hunter and Young, 1971). Maps of influenza or other infectious disease diffusion patterns can help with health planning by suggesting potential allocation of health-care resources.

Mapping diseases not only helps us understand which geographic areas are most severely affected (and provides clues about how patterns may change), it also helps identify factors linked to disease. In an extended discussion of *disease ecology,* Pyle (1979, Chapter 4) shows that links between disease and environment are numerous and significant. For example, Burkitt's lymphoma, a disease characterized by tumorous masses around the jaw, is *endemic* (locally prevalent) in Africa around the equator. The disease seems to be related to the pattern of insect *vectors* (transmitters), which in turn is related to patterns of climate and topography.

Goiter, involving swelling of the thyroid gland in the neck, has been endemic in many parts of the world, including the Pacific Northwest and St. Lawrence River region (Schiel and Wepfer, 1976, p. 116). The geochemical environment is thought to be closely linked to the disease, with iodine deficiency playing a strong role. Interestingly, goiter is prominent in areas that experienced Pleistocene glaciation, where soil is thin and chemicals have been washed out.

Malaria occurrence is climate-related; the disease migrates northward in summer and southward in winter with seasonal movements of the sun. Schistosomiasis, a serious world health problem, occurs mainly at lower latitudes and is caused by a worm's entering the human body, by means of either contaminated drinking water or skin perforation. Again, natural conditions correlate closely with the disease. In North America, diseases related to the natural environment include California encephalitis (mosquitoes), Rocky Mountain spotted fever (ticks), and rabies (transmitted by the bite of infected animals).

In general, the *etiology* of disease is incredibly complicated—what most of us think of as one disease may be in reality a complex of interrelated diseases, each with a unique set of causative factors. Understanding the spatial distribution of diseases is only part of the picture, and specialists from a variety of disciplines must cooperate in developing an understanding of this intricacy. As societies have become more complex, the distinction between natural and man-made environments has become blurred, further confusing the search for environmental links to diseases. This point reinforces the more general argument that we have made repeatedly throughout this book—that physical and human environments are deeply interwoven, whether we consider disease patterns, locations of cities, or a host of other economic and social activities.

Patterns of Health Care

Health expenditures in the United States have steadily increased as a proportion of gross national product, from 4.5 percent in 1950 to 10.8 percent in 1983. Per capita health care costs stood at $1,459 in 1983, an increase of about tenfold since 1960. The price index for physicians' services went from 100 in

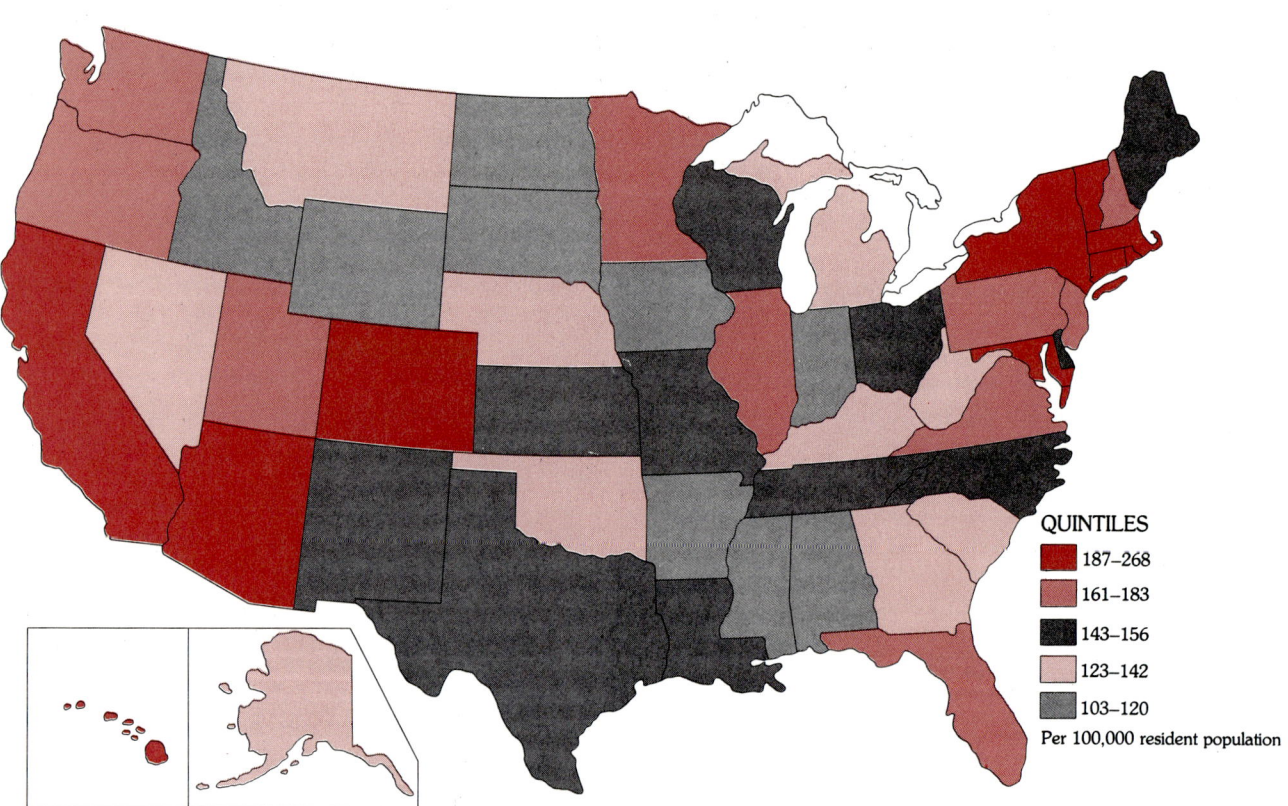

FIGURE 9–6 Physician-to-population ratios, 1981, excluding doctors of osteopathy and federal physicians.

1967 to 377 in 1984; hospital rooms went to an index value of 662 from the same base. Despite these massive increases in cost and the increasing allocation of resources to health care, the United States has substantial inequities in provision of services. The number of physicians per 100,000 population varied in 1981 from highs of 277 in Massachusetts, 271 in New York and 270 in Maryland, to lows of 107 in Idaho, 108 in Mississippi, and 116 in South Dakota (Figure 9–6).

From a purely economic view, physicians behave rather irrationally. One might expect them to locate where their services are needed most—where they could maximize their number of patients. In reality, physicians tend to locate in urban areas where physician-to-patient ratios are already highest. Locational factors such as availability of medical facilities and of professional colleagues for consultation, lower workloads facilitated by partnership arrangements, and urban amenities all help promote a polarized distribution of physicians, with many in the affluent parts of cities and few in rural or poverty areas.

Just as there are major inequalities in the availability of physicians, so the availability of health facilities, measured at the state level in terms of hospital beds per 1,000 population, is also highly uneven (Figure 9–7). At the local level, the distribution of emergency facilities may mean the difference between life and death (Figure 9–8). Overall, the United States has a highly developed health care system that has failed to respond systematically to needs (Pyle, 1974, p. 155). In spite of dazzling new techniques and wonder drugs, infant mortality in the last two decades has declined little, and life expectancy has not increased much. De Vise (1973) condemns the system as separate and unequal, by which he means that people have been classified for health care purposes:

> If you are either very poor, blind, disabled, over 65, male, white, or live in a middle- or upper-class neighborhood in a large urban center, you belong to a privileged class of health care recipients, and your chances of survival are good. But, if you are none of these, if you are only average

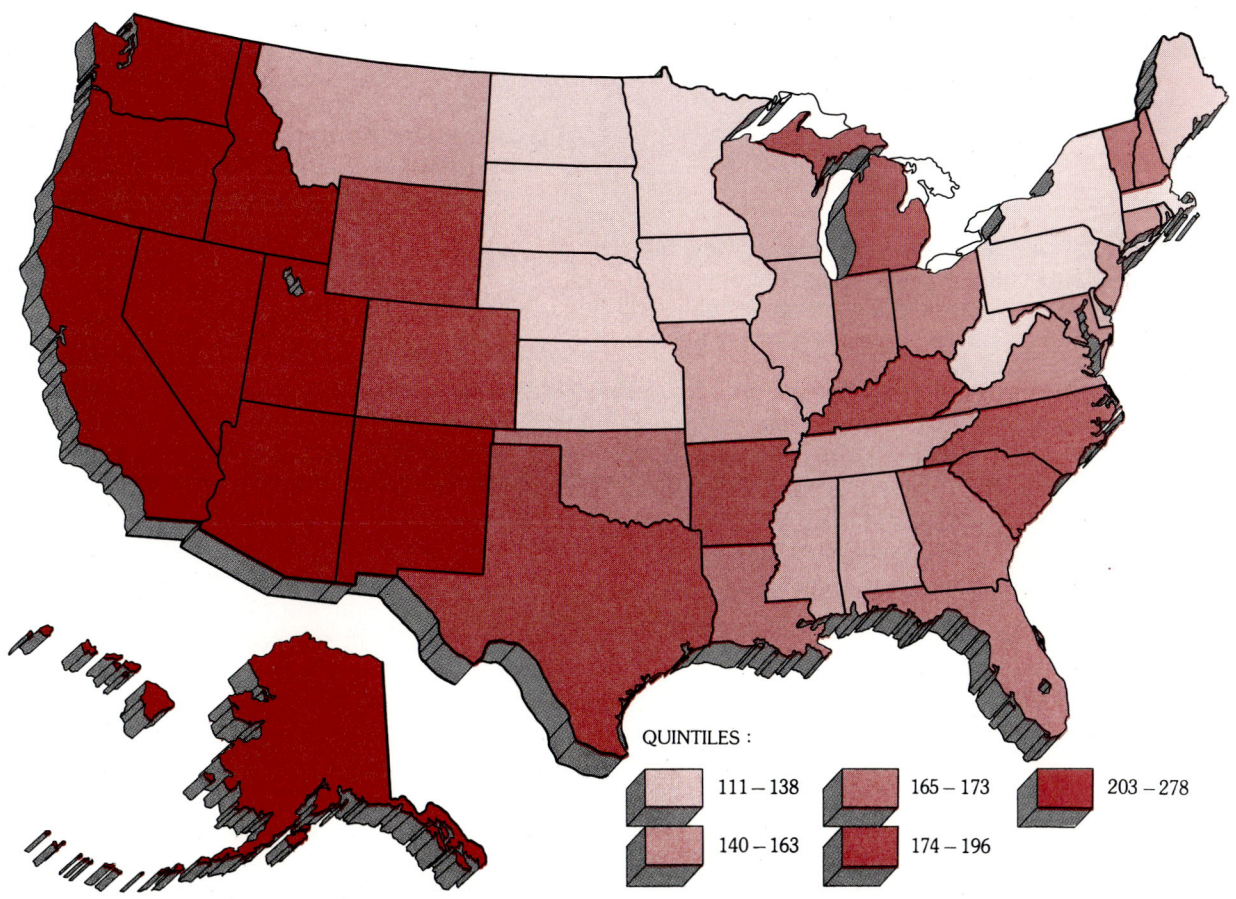

FIGURE 9–7 Hospital beds per 1,000 population, 1979. (Data from U.S. Department of Commerce, 1981.)

CHAPTER 9 THE GEOGRAPHY OF SOCIAL PROBLEMS

FIGURE 9–8 Ideally, ambulance response times should be short and emergency facilities should be equipped to deal with a wide range of problems. (Photo courtesy of Rick Bellatti, the Stillwater *News-Press*.)

> poor, under 65, female, black, or live in a low income urban neighborhood, small town, or rural area, you are a disenfranchised citizen as far as health care rights go, and your chances of survival are not good. (p. 1)

The poor performance of the United States in international health care comparisons suggests that we have much to learn from the organization of care in other nations. That the politics of medicine will allow introduction of innovative organizational changes to help reduce geographical inequalities is doubtful, however.

CRIME AND JUSTICE

Disease and crime have several characteristics in common—both are unpleasant for the victims, both cost a vast amount of money, both are inevitable, and both vary greatly in seriousness. For example, at the "mild" end of the disease seriousness scale, it may be difficult to determine whether a person is sick; at the other extreme, the patient dies. A similar parallel can be drawn to crime. Law enforcement agencies ignore many "mild" crimes to the point that the law becomes a "dead letter" and is not enforced at all. This tends to be true of laws relating to such situations as "Sabbath breaking" or the use of obscene language. In Oklahoma, for example, state statutes specify that a crime occurs:

> if a person shall utter or speak any obscene or lascivious language or word in any public place, or in the presence of females, or in the presence of children under ten years of age, he shall be liable to a fine of not more than one hundred dollars, or imprisonment for not more than thirty days, or both [State of Oklahoma, 1978, p. 85].

This law, enacted in 1910, is unenforced, as are laws preventing the sale of most goods and services on Sundays. At the other end of the crime seriousness scale, as with disease, the victim dies. The point is that crime, like disease, is a complex phenomenon. When politicians talk about "reducing crime," the statement has about as much meaning as "reducing disease." Which one? By how much? Where will efforts be concentrated?

A statistic that helps us understand the enormity of the crime problem in the United States is that, by the year 2000, about a million people will have been homicide victims, *in this century alone*. Perhaps 25 million Americans will have been victims of serious assaults. (If you have trouble visualizing a million people, think of 20 football stadiums, with 50,000 seats each, filled to capacity.) What makes a geographical perspective useful is that (again, as with disease) there are sharp place-to-place variations in crime occurrence, and in law enforcement and judicial processes. Professionals in law enforcement are appointed and trained according to different criteria, and they operate according to different procedures in different states (Figure 9–9). Judges are elected in some states and appointed in others. Pay scales in law enforcement and justice vary greatly (Harries, 1974, Chapter 5). In this section, we will consider regional variations in crime and justice, patterns at the urban/suburban levels, and some of the factors most commonly associated with the occurrence of crime.

Regional Variation

The most dramatic and most important regional pattern of crime in the United States is a concentration of high homicide rates in southern states. This south-

CRIME AND JUSTICE

FIGURE 9–9 Borrowing a tradition of Western gunfighters, who put a notch in their pistol grips to record their victims, Louisiana state troopers note recoveries of stolen vehicles.

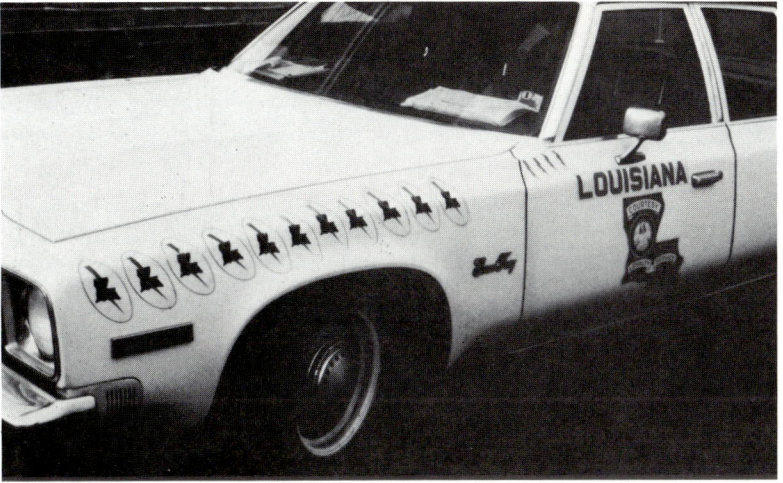

ern homicide region is an extremely persistent phenomenon that has appeared with little variation since official statistics began to be kept in the 1930s. In fact, the region may have seen more relative change in the last decade than in the previous half century. The map in Figure 9–10 actually suggests some decay of the southern homicide region compared to earlier years. (For further discussion of this pattern in an historical context, see Harries, 1985.) High homicide rates in the South help give the United States an exceptionally high homicide rate compared to other "advanced" nations. Compared to a U.S. rate of 8.3 homicides per 100,000 people in 1983, recent rates in some other countries were: England and Wales,

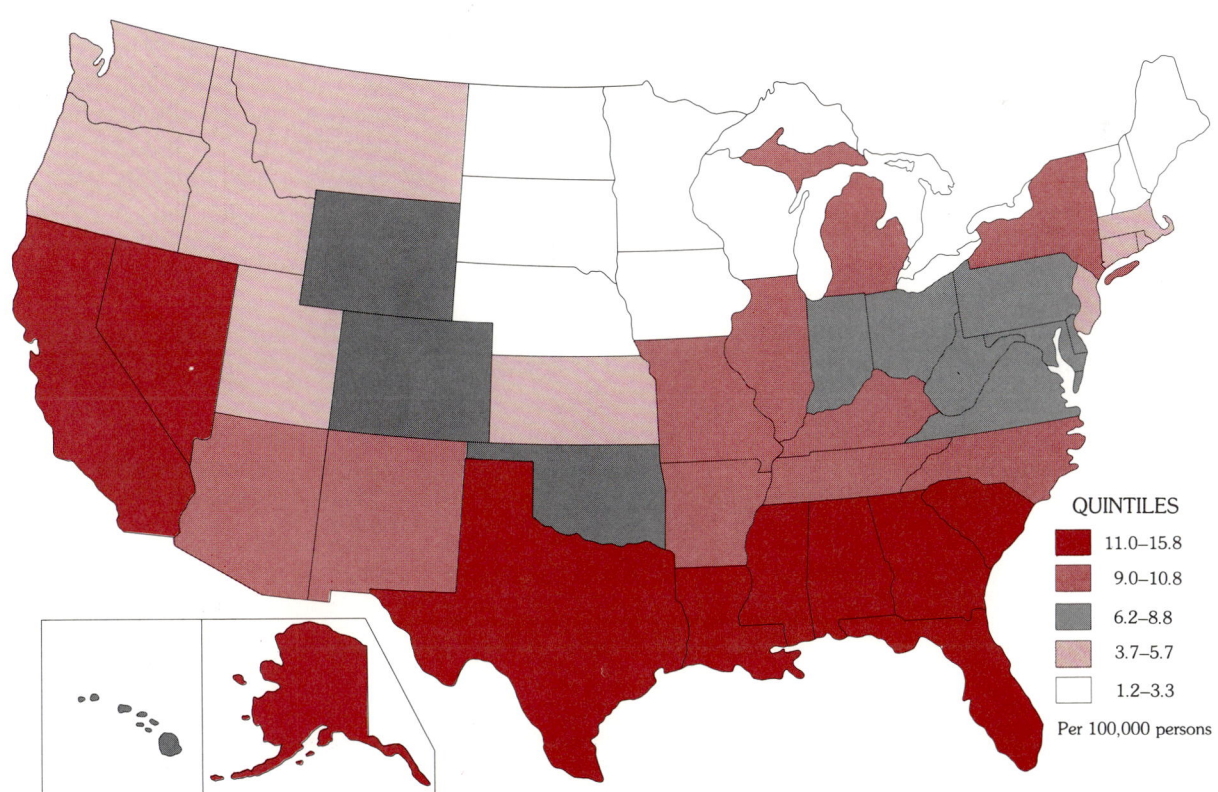

FIGURE 9–10 Regional homicide pattern, 1983.

193

0.8; Scotland, 1.6; West Germany, 1.2; Australia, 1.9; Japan, 1.0; Canada, 2.7; France, 1.0; and Israel, 1.3.

Interestingly, Northern Ireland (13.6) is to Britain as the South (10.4) is to the U.S.—a more violent region in an otherwise less violent nation. In Northern Ireland, causes relate to social and political unrest between minority Catholics and majority Protestants. Like blacks in the United States, Catholics in Northern Ireland have been an oppressed minority, and recent violence there has been partly a response to that oppression.

What about the causes of the southern homicide belt in the United States? Scholars have generally offered two kinds of explanation, one focusing on a cultural interpretation, the other on economic factors. The cultural approach states that southerners carry among their traditions and values an inclination toward violent behavior. For example, in an argument between spouses, southerners are more likely to act out their aggression, and to do so with firearms (Table 9–1). This dominance of firearms in the South is even more pronounced with respect to serious assault, a crime similar in its intent to homicide. High rates of assault in the South suggest that homicide rates would also be high, regardless of the level of firearm ownership; firearms make it more likely that an assault will become a homicide. This tendency toward violence in the South is seen, in part, as the product of an historically rural region, where values associated with individualism, slavery, and rigid racial segregation, have promoted violence partly through the persistence of social control of blacks by violent means. The interaction of values and economically marginal conditions, the argument goes, has reinforced a thread of violence in Southern culture (Hackney, 1969; Gastil, 1971; Curtis, 1975).

The economic argument suggests that poverty is really better than culture as an explanation of southern violence, with poverty measured via such factors as infant mortality, education, literacy, and so forth (Loftin and Hill, 1974). Both the cultural and economic arguments are quite convincing, but in reality, it is unlikely that either explanation is complete in itself. It is more probable that cultural and economic factors are interwoven to provide a complex of conditions and attitudes that favors the violent resolution of interpersonal conflicts. Interestingly, nonsouthern states from time to time exhibit high homicide rates. It is likely that such states as California and Illinois (Figure 9–10), for example, have had sufficient impact by migration from the South that their homicide rates have become elevated. (For more extended discussions, see Harries, 1974; 1980.)

Geographical variations in the processes of justice are also apparent at the regional level. One pattern that is particularly apt to draw attention is the geography of executions (Figure 9–11). The most obvious test of fairness of a pattern of punishment is whether the severity of crimes committed is paralleled by comparably severe punishments. The execution map in Figure 9–11 does reflect, in a general way, the geography of homicide, with the greatest concentration in the South. If you look carefully at Figures 9–10 and 9–11, however, you may recognize an important inconsistency that suggests major inequities in the dispensation of justice. Figure 9–10 shows homicide data on the basis of *rates*—occurrences per 100,000 persons. Figure 9–11 shows *frequencies* of occurrence, that is, absolute numbers. Why is it that the rather small-population states in the South, even with their high homicide rates, have executed many more offenders than large-population states where there have been more homicides? Georgia, for example, with about 5 million people, has some 600 homicides per year. California, with about 22 million, has around 2,500 homicides. Yet according to Figure 9–11, Georgia has executed 366,

TABLE 9–1 Percent distribution of weapons used in murder, 1982

Regions of United States	All Weapons	Firearms	Knife or other cutting instrument	Other Weapon (Club, poison, etc.)	Personal Weapon*
Northeast	100.0	52.2	24.7	12.6	10.5
North Central	100.0	60.6	19.5	13.8	6.2
South	100.0	65.8	18.8	10.4	5.1
West	100.0	55.1	23.1	14.8	7.0
Total	100.0	60.2	20.9	12.3	6.7**

*Personal weapons are hands, fists, feet, etc..
**Any discrepancies in totals are due to rounding.
Source: Federal Bureau of Investigation, *Uniform Crime Reports, 1982* (Washington D.C.: U.S. Government Printing Office, 1983)

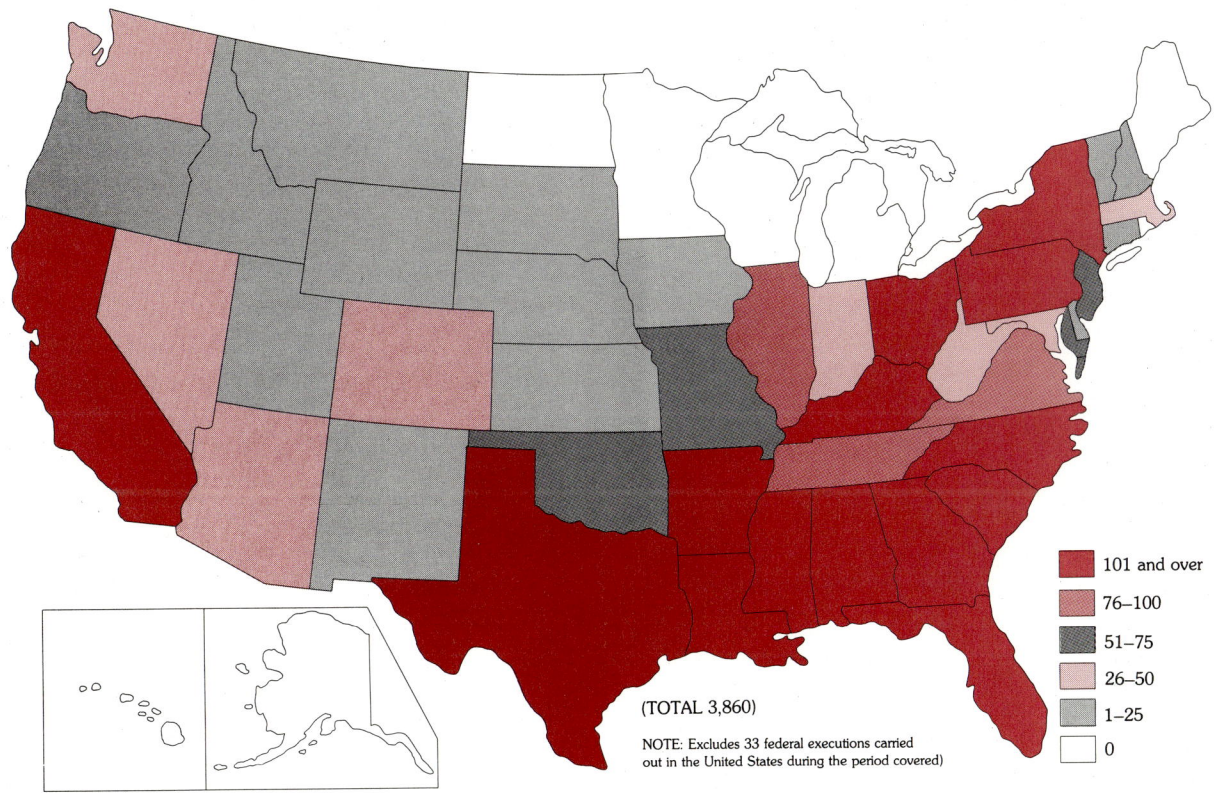

FIGURE 9–11 Number of executions by state, 1930–1977. (From U.S. Department of Justice, *Capital Punishment, 1977*, p. 9.)

California 292. In fact, in the 1930–1977 period, Georgia executed almost 10 percent of the total put to death.

One might reasonably argue that it is unfair to compare *current* data on population and homicides to *historical* data on executions. Yet, even if prisoners under sentence of death in a recent year are considered, it is by no means the states with most homicides that have most prisoners under sentence (Figure 9–12). Indeed, New York state, with some 2,000 homicides, had no one on death row.

The gross regional inequities in capital punishment were recognized in 1972 in the *Furman* v. *Georgia* U.S. Supreme Court decision, and many states have been compelled to revise their death penalty statutes. The states still have substantial discretion—some have never had the death penalty, while others use it for several offenses (e.g., murder, rape, armed robbery, sexual battery), thus increasing the likelihood that capital sentences will be handed down.

Even when we consider the more general pattern of imprisonment, there is little relationship between rates of serious crime and imprisonment rates, by states (Figure 9–13). As in the case of capital punishment, the South is more punitive as a region. It has about a third of the population of the United States, and about a third of the nation's serious crime; however, about half of the state prisoners sentenced to at least a year were imprisoned in the South. In terms of number of prisoners held, Texas ranked first nationally, with over 22,000, more than much more populous states such as California and New York. The highest rate of incarceration was in South Carolina.

The Johnson decision in 1976 in Alabama ruled that prisoners in that state suffered cruel and inhuman incarceration in violation of the Eighth Amendment of the U.S. Constitution. As a result, there has been a general increase in the level of national concern about jail and prison conditions, and a number of states have been under federal court orders to reduce prison overcrowding. It has been shown that many of the prisoners in maximum security institutions pose no physical threat to society. When this information is combined with the fact that there is no convincing evidence that imprisonment has a deterrent effect, it is difficult to justify the long-term incarceration of any but those who would pose a threat of violence if released (Figure 9–14).

CHAPTER 9 THE GEOGRAPHY OF SOCIAL PROBLEMS

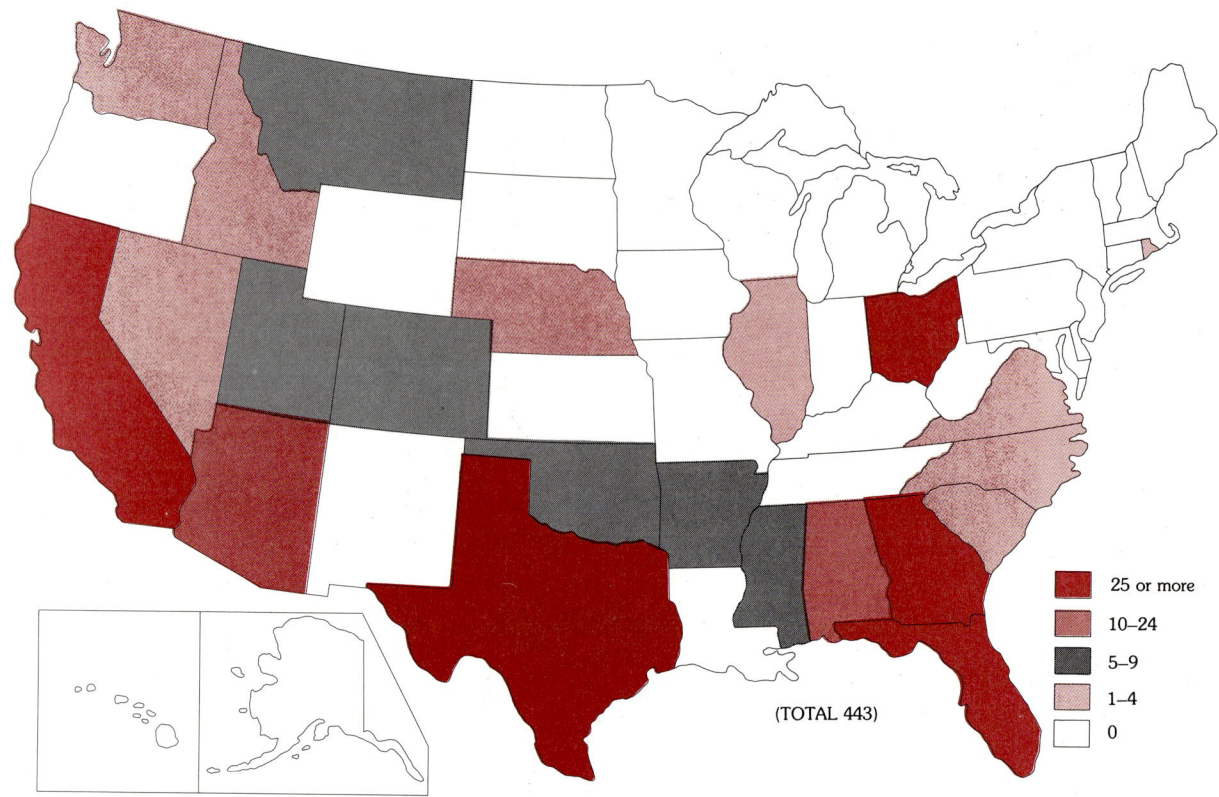

FIGURE 9–12 Prisoners under sentence of death, by state, December 1977. (From U.S. Department of Justice, *Capital Punishment, 1977*, p. 5.)

In reality, the criminal justice process is a kind of geographical Russian roulette. In one jurisdiction a relatively minor offense may lead to years in the state penitentiary; in another, a serious crime may not be punished severely. Studies show that a factor in prison riots is unequal sentencing for similar crimes. What is at best a chancy process becomes more so when you consider the patchwork of variations in state laws and the interplay of social and political factors such as race, the ambitions of prosecutors, and the attitudes of jurors, all of which vary from place to place.

Of the many examples we could cite of such interplay, one of the more recent and devastating involved the acquittal of four white police officers who had been accused of the beating death of Arthur McDuffie, a black insurance salesman, in Miami, Florida. The trial was moved from Miami to Tampa, where the pool of prospective jurors contained few blacks, and an all-white, male jury was selected. In the violence that followed the acquittal in May 1980, 16 people died, 400 were injured, and about $200 million worth of property damage was done. Observers described Miami as having a dual system of justice: one for whites, another for blacks. Tensions were heightened by the allocation of resources to the massive immigration of Cubans (technically illegal aliens) and the rejection of the (black) Haitian boat people. The event seemed to be a replay of the urban ghetto violence of the 1960s, when the first major event was the so-called Watts riot in 1965, also triggered by a law enforcement incident. In December, 1982, Miami was the scene of yet another outbreak of violence, provoked by the fatal wounding of a black youth by a white police officer.

Even a superficial look at criminal justice processes at the regional level suggests that there is a good deal of truth to the aphorism "It's not what you do but where you do it." One may argue with some force that lawbreakers really do not deserve fair treatment—in breaking the law, they are accepting the chance that they will be treated unfairly. This is a point many readers will agree with; unfortunately, the inequities are not without a price. Sentence disparity—the unequal punishment of similar offenders for similar offenses—was identified as "a primary source of tension and bitterness within the walls" at the Attica Prison in New York, where 43 people died in the "bloodiest one-day encounter between Americans since the Civil War" (New

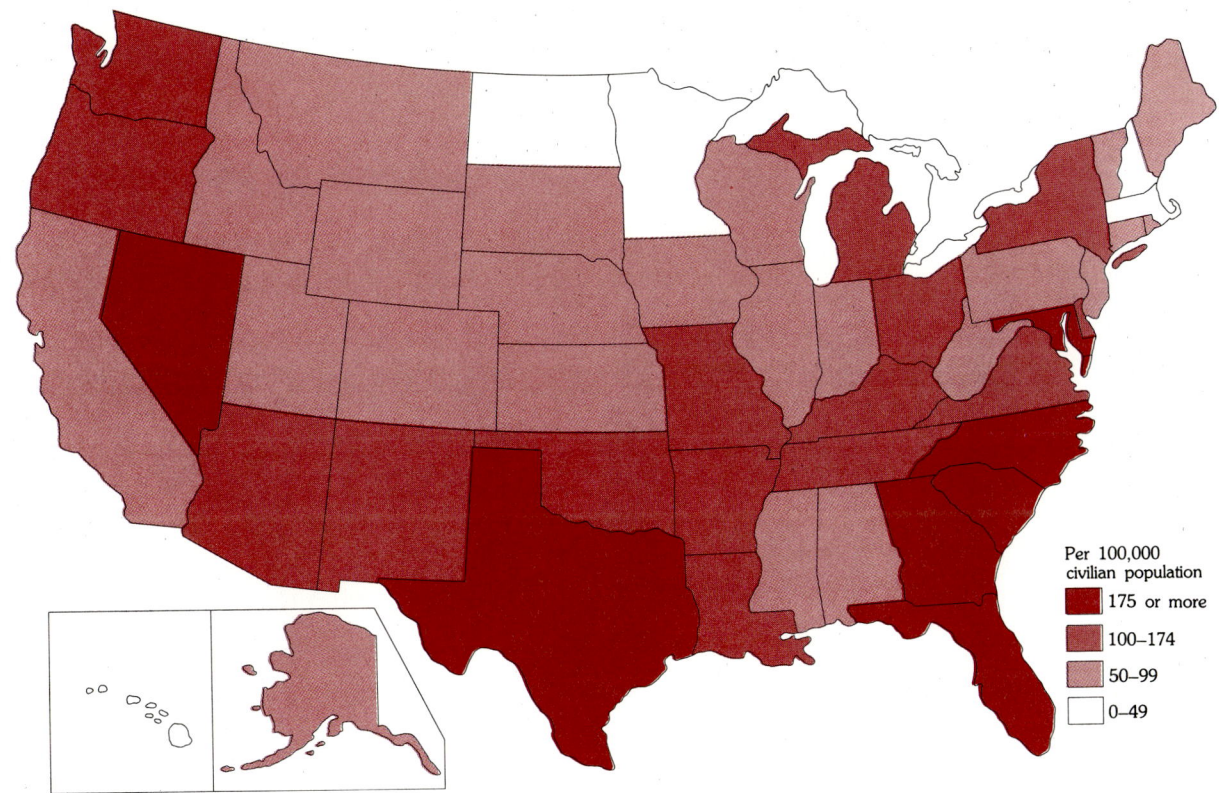

FIGURE 9–13 Number of sentenced state prisoners per 100,000 population, December 1977. (From U.S. Department of Justice, *Capital Punishment, 1977*, p. 4.)

York State Special Commission on Attica, 1972, pp. xi and 93).

Urban, Suburban, and Rural Crime

Are there differences in crime rates among urban, suburban, and rural settlements? One approach to answering this question is to consider how *opportunities* for crime vary in different areas. Clearly, if there are no people, there can be no crime, whether or not there are opportunities. On the other hand, if an area is crowded with people there are many opportunities for crime. In theory, each person could commit a crime upon all other persons in a group. With five people, each could commit four crimes (it is unlikely that each person would victimize himself), so there is the theoretical possibility that $(n^2 - n)$ crimes could occur, where n is the number of people. Substituting, we get $(5^2 - 5) = 25 - 5$, or 20. And, if you punch in on your pocket calculator some large numbers for the population, the results get so big that the display cannot handle them. These large totals can be regarded as examples of crime potential—what *could* happen, but what we hope will not.

The concept of crime opportunity is more complex than the idea of potential crime, but both are interrelated. Opportunity involves interaction not only between people but also between people and property. Various environmental conditions—levels of economic status of population groups, age, sex, traffic patterns, time of day, and others—also may react with opportunity.

FIGURE 9–14 Signs like this one often appear along highways near prisons.

CHAPTER 9 THE GEOGRAPHY OF SOCIAL PROBLEMS

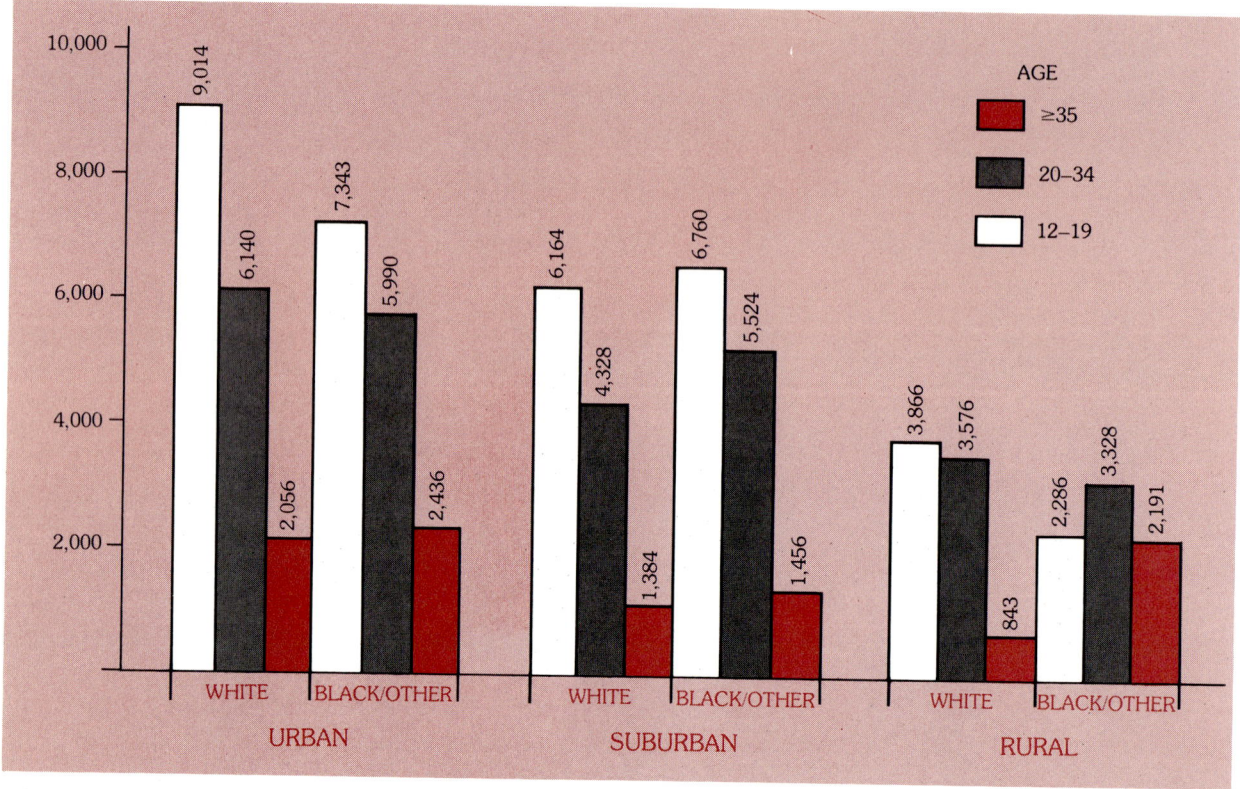

FIGURE 9–15 Estimated rates, per 100,000 persons 12 years of age or older, of personal violent victimization, by race, age, and extent of urbanization. (Adapted from Gibbs, 1979, p. 47.)

If you consider the characteristics of urban, suburban, and rural environments, you may conclude that opportunities for crime are generally greater in cities and suburbs, and less in rural areas. Evidence suggests that your conclusion would be correct, particularly with respect to violent crime (Figures 9–15 and 9–16). *Urban* is defined here as the central or "name" city of metropolitan areas (see *SMSA* in the Glossary); *suburban* is the remainder of metropolitan counties; and *rural* is any area outside SMSAs. Figure 9–15 shows the levels of violent victimization by race, age, and extent of urbanization, and indicates the declining gradient of victimization outward from the central city. Points of interest are that the 12–19 age group dominates all categories except rural black victimization. The 35-and-over age group is consistently least victimized, regardless of race.

Personal theft victimization reveals a less clear gradient from urban to rural (Figure 9–16). That blacks are victimized differently from whites is shown by the much smaller difference between the two lowest age categories for blacks as compared to whites. It has also been shown that "high concern" crimes (violence by strangers and burglary) are more prevalent in urban rather than suburban or rural households. Furthermore, such crimes prevail in black rather than white households, and are more likely among households with incomes less than $7,500 rather than over $15,000 (U.S. Department of Justice, 1982, p. 2).

Analysis of victimization data leads to several other general conclusions. Males are more likely to be victimized than females, and married people are victimized less than those who are single. The poor suffer the greatest impact of violent crime, while the more affluent experience greater theft victimization (Gibbs, 1979, p. 11). Each of the population characteristics varies geographically and contributes to sharp place-to-place differences in crime rates.

Crime Factors

We must be careful to avoid excessive analogy between disease and crime. While a physician may be able to say with some certainty that a child contracted rabies because he was bitten by a rabid dog, such a positive diagnosis is virtually impossible for criminal activities, just as it is for many diseases. As

CONCLUSION

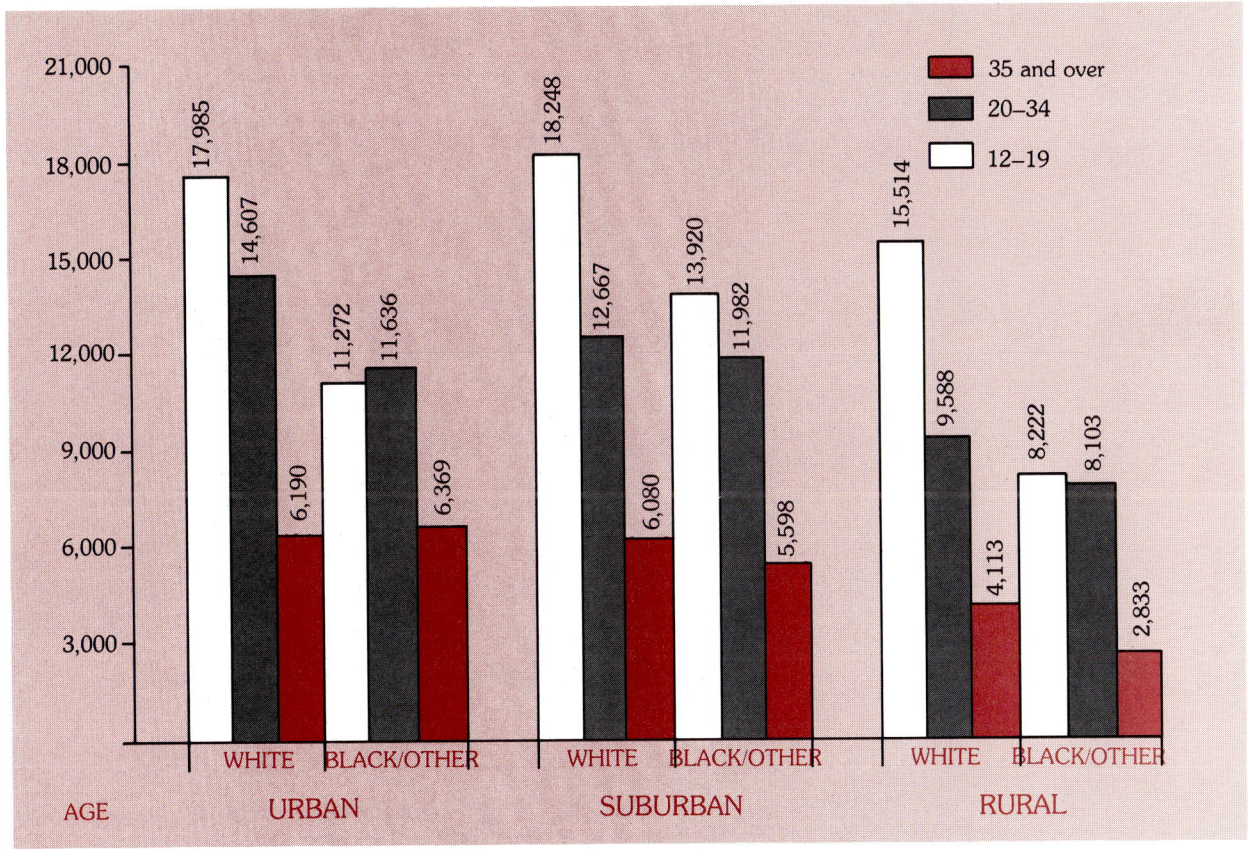

FIGURE 9–16 Estimated rates, per 100,000 persons 12 years of age or older, of personal theft victimization. (Adapted from Gibbs, 1979, p. 48.)

we have seen, rates of victimization tend to be higher in urban areas, but we cannot say that urbanization *causes* crime—at least not with enough certainty to be able to predict levels of crime purely on the basis of levels of urbanization. What *can* be said, at least in a geographic context, is that certain conditions seem to be *associated* with higher levels of crime. These conditions are:

1. Low socioeconomic status (including unemployment)
2. Minority population
3. Proportion of youthful males
4. Crowded housing (as distinct from high population density)
5. Proximity to offender residence areas (Harries, 1980, p. 90)

There is considerable overlap in this list; for example, minority people are likely to have low socioeconomic status. So the conditions should not be thought of as separate influences, but rather as members of an interrelated "bundle" which, together, *tend* to be indicators that high levels of crime are likely. (See also Baldwin, 1979; Georges-Abeyie and Harries, 1980.)

CONCLUSION

This brief overview of the problems of health and criminal justice shows that both have strong geographical components—both problems vary enormously from place to place. Returning to the example of birth at the beginning of the chapter, it is not unreasonable to suggest that *place* of birth and early upbringing is probably the single most important characteristic in determining an individual's life chances. Birth and childhood in a ghetto slum mean insurmountable odds against a healthy, safe, economically stable existence. The odds are much worse for someone born in a developing nation.

Elsewhere in this book, particularly in Chapter 14, we will explore various elements of lifestyle and living conditions, to help you understand the complex interrelationships in the living environment and to help you make your own locational decisions.

CHAPTER 9 THE GEOGRAPHY OF SOCIAL PROBLEMS

KEY WORDS

ecology
endemic
epidemic
etiology
geometrical increase
   (progression)

pandemic
percentile
polarized
rate
sentence disparity
threshold

REFERENCES

ALPERN, DAVID M.; BUCKLEY, JERRY; SMITH, VERN E.; WILLENSON, KIM; and McGUIRE, STRYKER. "Carter and the Cuban Influx." *Newsweek,* 26 May 1980, pp. 22–28.

BALDWIN, JOHN. "Ecological and Areal Studies in Great Britain and the United States." In Norval Morris and Michael Tonry, eds. *Crime and Justice: An Annual Review of Research.* Vol. 1. Chicago: University of Chicago Press, 1979, pp. 29–66.

CURTIS, LYNN A. *Violence, Race, and Culture.* Lexington, MA: Lexington Books, 1975.

DE VISE, PIERRE. *Misued and Misplaced Hospitals and Doctors: A Locational Analysis of the Urban Health Care Crisis.* Association of American Geographers, Resource Paper No. 22. Washington, D.C. 1973.

FBI. *Uniform Crime Reports,* 1983. Washington, D.C.: U.S. Government Printing Office, 1984.

GASTIL, RAYMOND D., "Homicide and a Regional Culture of Violence." *American Sociological Review* 36 (1971):412–27.

GEORGES-ABEYIE, DANIEL E., and HARRIES, KEITH D., *Crime: A Spatial Perspective.* New York: Columbia University Press, 1980.

GIBBS, JOHN T., *Crime against Persons in Urban, Suburban, and Rural Areas: A Comparative Analysis of Victimization Rates.* Analytic Report SD-VAD-7. Washington, D.C.: U.S. Government Printing Office, 1979.

HACKNEY, SHELDON., "Southern Violence." *American Historical Review* 74 (1969):906–25.

HARRIES, KEITH D., *The Geography of Crime and Justice.* New York: McGraw-Hill Book Co., 1974.

———. *Crime and the Environment.* Springfield, Ill.: Charles C. Thomas Publishers, 1980.

———. "The Historical Geography of Homicide in the U.S., 1935–1980." *Geoforum* 16 (1985):73–83.

HARRIES, KEITH D., and BRUNN, STANLEY D. *The Geography of Laws and Justice.* New York: Praeger Publishing, 1978.

HOLDEN, CONSTANCE. "Love Canal Residents under Stress." *Science,* vol. 208, no. 13 (1980), pp. 1242–44.

HUNTER, JOHN M., and YOUNG, JOHNATHAN C., "Diffusion of Influenza in England and Wales." *Annals of the Association of American Geographers* 61 (1971): 637–53.

LOFTIN, COLIN, and HILL, R. H. "Regional Subculture and Homicide: An Examination of the Gastil–Hackney Thesis." *American Sociological Review* 39 (1974): 714–24.

MASON, THOMAS J.; McKAY, FRANK W.; HOOVER, ROBERT; BLOT, WILLIAM J.; and FRAUMENI, JOSEPH F. Jr. *Atlas of Cancer Mortality of U.S. Counties: 1950–69.* Washington, D.C.: U.S. Department of Health, Education, and Welfare, 1975.

NEW YORK STATE SPECIAL COMMISSION ON ATTICA. *Attica.* New York: Bantam Books, 1972.

PYLE, GERALD F., "The Diffusion of Cholera in the United States in the Nineteenth Century." *Geographical Analysis* (1969):59–74.

REFERENCES

———. *Heart Disease, Cancer, and Stroke in Chicago.* Chicago: University of Chicago Department of Geography Research Paper No. 134, 1971, pp. 41–45.

———. "The Geography of Health Care." In John M. Hunter, ed. *The Geography of Health and Disease.* Chapel Hill, N.C.: University of North Carolina Department of Geography, 1974, pp. 154–84.

———. "Introduction: Foundations to Medical Geography." *Economic Geography* 52 (1976):95–102.

———. *Applied Medical Geography.* New York: John Wiley & Sons, 1979.

SCHIEL, JOSEPH B. Jr., and WEPFER, ANITA JOAN. "Distributional Aspects of Endemic Goiter in the United States." *Economic Geography* 52 (1976):116–26.

SHANNON, GARY W., and DEVER, G. E. ALAN. *Health Care Delivery: Spatial Perspectives.* New York: McGraw-Hill Book Co., 1974.

SMITH, DAVID M. *Geographical Perspectives on Inequality.* New York: Harper & Row Publishers, 1979.

STATE OF OKLAHOMA. *Oklahoma Criminal Laws.* Oklahoma City, Okla.: Department of Public Safety, 1978.

U.S. DEPARTMENT OF COMMERCE, Bureau of the Census. *Statistical Abstract of the United States: 1979.* Washington, D.C.: U.S. Government Printing Office, 1979.

U.S. DEPARTMENT OF COMMERCE, Bureau of the Census. *Statistical Abstract of the United States: 1985.* Washington D.C.: U.S. Government Printing Office, 1984.

U.S. DEPARTMENT OF JUSTICE, *Bureau of Justice Statistics Bulletin.* Washington D.C.: U.S. Government Printing Office, 1982.

U.S. DEPARTMENT OF JUSTICE. *Capital Punishment, 1977.* National Prisoner Statistics Bulletin SD–NPS–PSF–S. Washington, D.C.: U.S. Government Printing Office, 1979.

10
Economic Geography: Primary Production

PRINCIPLES OF PRIMARY PRODUCTION
GEOGRAPHY OF AGRICULTURE
TYPES OF AGRICULTURE
EXTRACTIVE INDUSTRIES
GEOGRAPHY OF FORESTRY
GEOGRAPHY OF FISHING

Hong Kong, the major port between Shanghai and Singapore has an excellent deep-water harbor. (Wolfgang Kaehler, Photography

The general topic of this chapter is economic geography, with a focus on *primary production*. Economic geography is the study of the spatial variations in economic activity. Primary production is the first economic step that humans take in utilizing the earth's resources. Thus, our concern here is with the location and distribution of such things as farming, mining, fishing, and lumbering—the *primary* production activities.

Economic activity includes all human behavior related to the production, exchange, and consumption of things that have value. Items of value can be either *goods* or *services,* as long as somebody will pay for them with either cash or through trade for other things of value. The values of goods and services are fixed according to the prices people are willing to pay for them. People are generally willing to pay more when items are scarce; thus, the price of something is a function of its *supply*.

When people work, they do so to produce something of value. Production is the initial phase of economic activity. Generally, we categorize occupations into four broad levels of production. The first, *primary production,* includes activities such as farming, mining, fishing, and lumbering, through which humans take things of value directly from the earth. These activities are usually restricted to places that have appropriate conditions. For example, most farming is carried on where the soil and climate conditions will allow, and mining must be done where minerals are found. Humans deal constantly with the physical environment in the primary production stage of economic activity.

The next level is *secondary production,* in which economic activities include the work that is done to change items from primary production into new items that have greater value than the originals. The log from a tree, for example, is cut from the forest during primary production (lumbering industry), but the log increases dramatically in value after it is transformed into a piece of furniture. The transformation process always adds value to an item. This process is called *manufacturing,* the most common type of secondary production.

The *tertiary production* stage of economic activity includes all the work involved in moving, selling, and trading the goods produced at either the primary or secondary stages. Thus, all the people connected with transportation, as well as all those involved in wholesale and retail trade, are tertiary economic workers. Besides movers and sellers, tertiary production also includes all the people involved in *services.* The service industries include occupations that are *professional* (teaching, medicine, law), *financial* (banking, real estate, insurance), *semiskilled* (plumbing, painting, barbering), and many others. (We will discuss secondary and tertiary production in Chapter 11.)

The final stage of economic activity, *quaternary production,* is defined as all activities that are nonprofit oriented. These activities include occupations that are of value, and sometimes great value, but are not of direct service to somebody else. A research scientist is an example of someone whose occupation is in the quaternary production stage.

Production at all levels is equated with the work people do, and any expenditure of work or money that increases the value of goods or services is classified as production. Therefore, *exchange* is part of the production process. Exchange involves increasing the value of something by changing either its location or its ownership or both. A bushel of wheat, for example, is worth much more in a grain elevator in Minneapolis than in the wheat field in North Dakota. Between the field and the elevator, not only does the location change, but ownership may have changed two or three times. Exchange can occur at any level of production, or among levels.

The final stage in the sequence of economic behavior is *consumption.* The purchase and use of basic necessities—food, clothing, and shelter—are part of economic consumption. The purchase and use of all so-called "consumer goods," including automobiles, washing machines, and television sets, are also part of consumption. Geographical consumption patterns vary because people have different preferences. We can identify regions where people prefer one type of food over another, certain types of houses over others, and particular styles of clothing over other styles. Not only do sales of retail goods vary from one place to another, but services in some areas are unheard of in other areas.

PRINCIPLES OF PRIMARY PRODUCTION

Compared to the other sectors of production, primary activities are unique in that they are tied to specific locations or regions. In agriculture, appropriate climate and soils must be available. In mineral extraction, forestry, and fishing, production can occur only where the resource is found. In general, primary production is dominated by four factors: the physical environment, economic factors, cultural factors, and political factors.

The Physical Environment

Physical geography is critical in primary production. Tropical crops such as coffee, tea, and bananas cannot be grown economically outside the tropical regions. Temperate, or middle-latitude crops such as oats or barley, will not thrive in the humid tropics. Similarly, soils must be suitable for the crop under cultivation. Certain kinds of livestock do better in warm climates than in cool, while others do better in cool climates.

Mineral deposits are widely but not randomly distributed across the earth. Some countries are rich with minerals, while others must import most of their needs. The petroleum wealth of Saudi Arabia and Kuwait is great, but other countries such as Uruguay, Ethiopia, and Thailand consume far more than they produce.

The location of forestry is determined by the geography of tree species. This can be modified by human intervention in the long run, as cut trees are replaced by new plantings. In the near term, however, forestry is limited by the trees that are available in the world's forests.

Commercial fishing depends on the geography of ocean ecology, which varies from year to year, with changes in ocean currents and temperatures. Crabs became scarce in the Pacific Ocean off the west coast of North America in the mid-1980s, because of a warming of the water that disturbed the crabs' food chain. Off the east coast of the United States, attempts have been made to enrich marine ecosystems by creating artificial reefs made of old tires, barges, and other scrap materials. But in general, various species of fish have their own favored marine environments and fishermen must go to them.

Economic Factors

The economic factors involved in primary production are similar to those in the other sectors of economic activity. Production is normally a response to demand. If demand increases but supply does not, prices tend to rise, but if supply increases and demand does not, then prices go down. In the primary sector, lag times in production in response to demand changes may be very long. In response to an increase in the demand for oranges, for example, growers plant more orange trees, but the new trees do not bear fruit for several years. Also, primary activities, especially agriculture, are subject to losses from natural disasters such as frosts, floods, droughts, and damaging winds. Mineral resources, with the exception of water, are generally nonrenewable; therefore, most minerals become more and more scarce. Prices of these nonrenewable commodities are destined to rise in the long term.

Cultural Factors

The crops and livestock grown by farmers and ranchers, the minerals extracted by miners, the trees felled by foresters, and the fish caught by fishermen are subject to people's tastes and preferences. Dairy products are staples in the diets of North Americans and Europeans, but not of many Africans and Asians. Rice is the staple cereal in East and South Asia, but in the Americas, wheat and corn are more popular. Beef is the staple meat in the United States, Argentina, and Australia, but is much less important in most of the remainder of the world, partly because beef production is an inefficient use of animal feed. Religion prohibits human consumption of cattle in India, and of hogs in Moslem countries. The precise mix of primary activities in a given region, then, is the result of a complex interaction among tastes, technology, economics, religion, and politics.

Political Factors

Politics influences primary production just as it does the other sectors of economic activity. Governments protect their farmers, for example, by guaranteeing prices, paying farmers not to produce (so as to prevent oversupply), and supporting research. The complex structure of tariffs, duties, and quotas that limits freedom of trade is really a political device to protect industries. Presently, a conspicuous example of political influence in primary production is the Organization of Petroleum Exporting Countries (OPEC), which attempts to control the world price of oil. OPEC was able to control oil prices because its member nations control so much of the world's production of petroleum.

GEOGRAPHY OF AGRICULTURE

In the context of agriculture, geographers have designed more specific ways to conceptualize the factors associated with why things are located where they are. These *space models* illustrate the relationship among forces that act on the processes of location on the landscape.

Von Thünen

The first space model for explaining the location of economic activities was designed during the 1820s by Johann Heinrich von Thünen (1783–1850). Von Thünen lived on the flat agricultural lowlands of northern Germany, near the city of Rostock in the former state of Mecklenburg. Von Thünen, a landowner and farmer, was concerned with the economics of crop production. He had observed that crop production tended to occur in definite patterns around settlements. These land-use patterns consisted of concentric zones similar to a target, with the settlement located at the "bull's eye" (Figure 10–1).

Von Thünen explained the causes for the recurring circular patterns in his book, *The Isolated State*, published in 1826. His ideas are important to geography students because they deal with explanations of why things are located where they are. His methods are also significant because we can apply them to other areas and other types of studies. Rather than merely describing what he saw, von Thünen devised a model to explain the world in which he lived

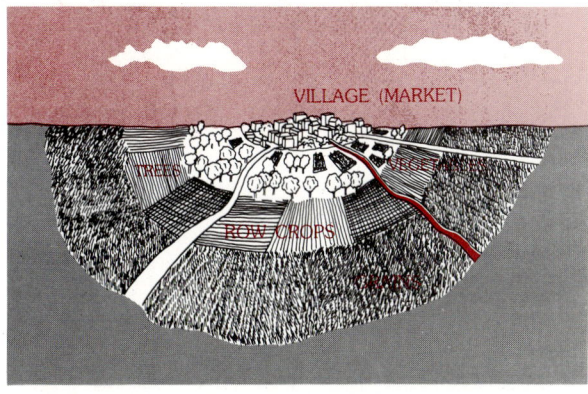

FIGURE 10–1 Schematic representation of the northern German landscape as von Thünen described it.

CHAPTER 10 ECONOMIC GEOGRAPHY: PRIMARY PRODUCTION

FIGURE 10–2 A view of the actual German landscape that von Thünen attempted to explain in his model. (Photo courtesy of German Information Center, New York.)

(Figure 10–2). In the process, he provided a foundation for future geographical models and explanations.

Von Thünen's Model

A *model* can be defined as an idealized representation of reality. A globe is a type of model that approximates the world. It is a *physical* model because it has some of the physical properties of the real thing; it is spherical and indicates the locations of land and water. By necessity, however, most of the earth's characteristics, such as soil, rock, water, hot interior, and atmosphere, are not reproduced. Although most of the actual earth materials do not appear on a globe, it remains a valuable aid to learning especially as far as locations are concerned. To learn about the locational characteristics of an agricultural economy, von Thünen also had to eliminate a lot of "real" things, which he did by constructing an imaginary landscape (Figure 10–3).

Von Thünen formulated his model economy by constraining most of the myriad factors that affect agricultural production. He based the constraints on a series of assumptions; for example, a regional economy is intricately tied to the national economy of the state in which it operates. National recessions, inflations, wars, and other things that affect the state also affect the region. Von Thünen eliminated this tie by assuming an *isolated state,* an area with a completely independent economy, consisting of one market city and the agricultural region surrounding it. Then, to eliminate place-to-place differences in physical factors such as soil and climate, von Thünen assumed a *uniform plain.* This assumption ensured that crop yields per hectare (2.471 acres) would be equal at all places on the model landscape and that transportation costs would be strictly a function of distance, since movement on a uniform plain would be equally easy in any direction. Von Thünen also assumed only one mode of transportation, the most common of the time, the horse and wagon.

Von Thünen's isolated landscape was further restricted by economic considerations. The single mar-

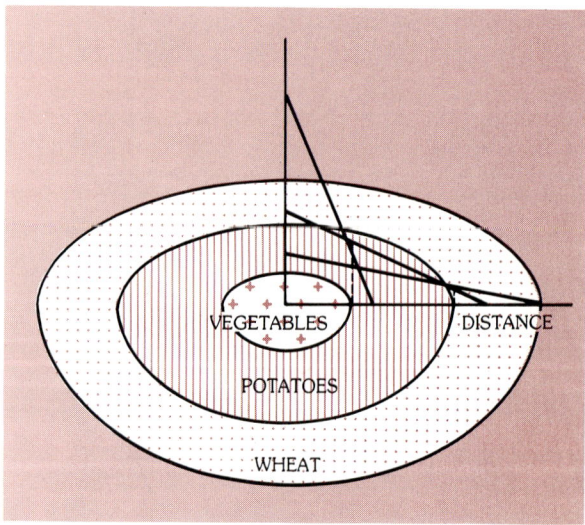

FIGURE 10–3 Von Thünen's hypothesis of the landscape around a market town.

ket city on the homogeneous surface of the isolated region was assumed to be the only market for surplus goods produced by farmers, and the city received no products from areas outside the isolated region. Thus, to make a profit, the farmers had to adjust to the demands of their single market. They also had to pay the transportation cost for getting their products to the market.

Over a period of time, the prices paid to farmers tend to stabilize. Thus, the distance from the market city that a particular crop can be grown becomes fixed, and a *transport gradient* is created. When other crops are added to the model, transport gradients are created for each. Consider, for example, three crops: vegetables, potatoes, and wheat (Figure 10–4). Vegetables have the highest market price of the three crops, but also cost the most to produce and transport (because they spoil quickly). Wheat, on the other hand, costs the least to produce and can be shipped without spoiling, so it can be grown at a greater distance from the market. Potatoes occupy an intermediate position in terms of price, production costs, and transportation cost. The three crops' transport gradients reflect the different conditions of each.

After creating the transport gradients for various crops and establishing the distances from the market at which crops can be grown for a profit, one can rotate the model around the vertical axis. The rotation creates the pattern of land use described in Figure 10–3. The resulting concentric zones of production are called *Thünen rings*. By relaxing some of the assumptions he had used in the original model, Von Thünen went on to explain how the perfectly round concentric zones are distorted in reality. For example, if other modes of transportation such as railroads or waterways were available to the farmers, the symmetry of the production rings would be altered according to the transport cost of each mode. Or, if the fertility of the land were not uniform, production would certainly be affected, and the rings would reflect the differences. Von Thünen also discussed the effects of a second market, such as a small town. Other real-world factors could be included to recreate an actual landscape. Although the von Thünen model cannot be applied directly to today's geography of agriculture, it is still a good example of a spatial model and helped to lay the foundation for later, more sophisticated models.

TYPES OF AGRICULTURE

People in agriculture deal primarily with animals or with crops, and are either primarily subsistence producers or commercial producers. Generally, people who deal mostly with animals are called *herders,* and those who deal with crops are referred to as *farmers.* *Subsistence* producers are those who use nearly everything they produce to satisfy their own basic needs for food, clothing, and shelter. *Commercial* producers generate a surplus which they trade or sell to obtain their basic needs. We classify these divisions of labor in agriculture into four activities:

- Subsistence herding
- Subsistence farming
- Commercial herding
- Commercial farming

The categories overlap because some agriculturists are both herders and farmers, but the four categories are a convenient framework for studying most types of agriculture.

The most primitive economic activity is subsistence by *hunting and gathering*. People who live in this fashion hunt animals and gather wild fruit and other naturally-occurring edible materials. They do not grow domestic crops or animals for their food supply. Few people today exist entirely by hunting and gathering, but occasionally a primitive tribe is discovered. The Xeta tribe of the Serra dos Dourados mountains of interior Brazil, who were not discovered until 1956, knew nothing about agriculture. The

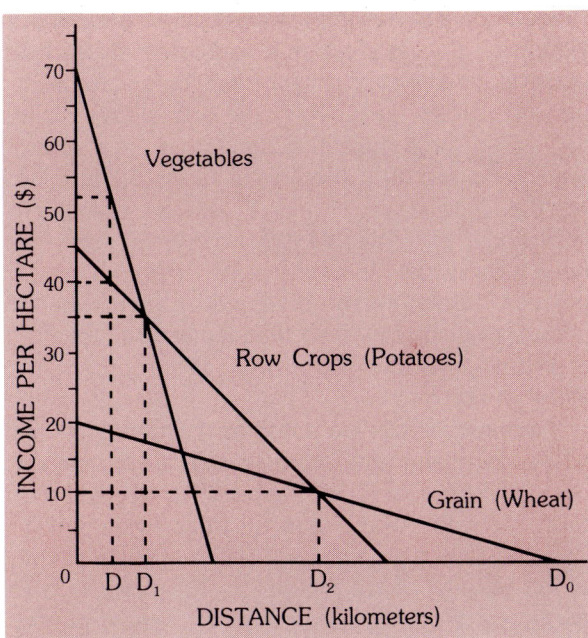

FIGURE 10–4 Von Thünen's two-dimensional model for three crops.

CHAPTER 10 ECONOMIC GEOGRAPHY: PRIMARY PRODUCTION

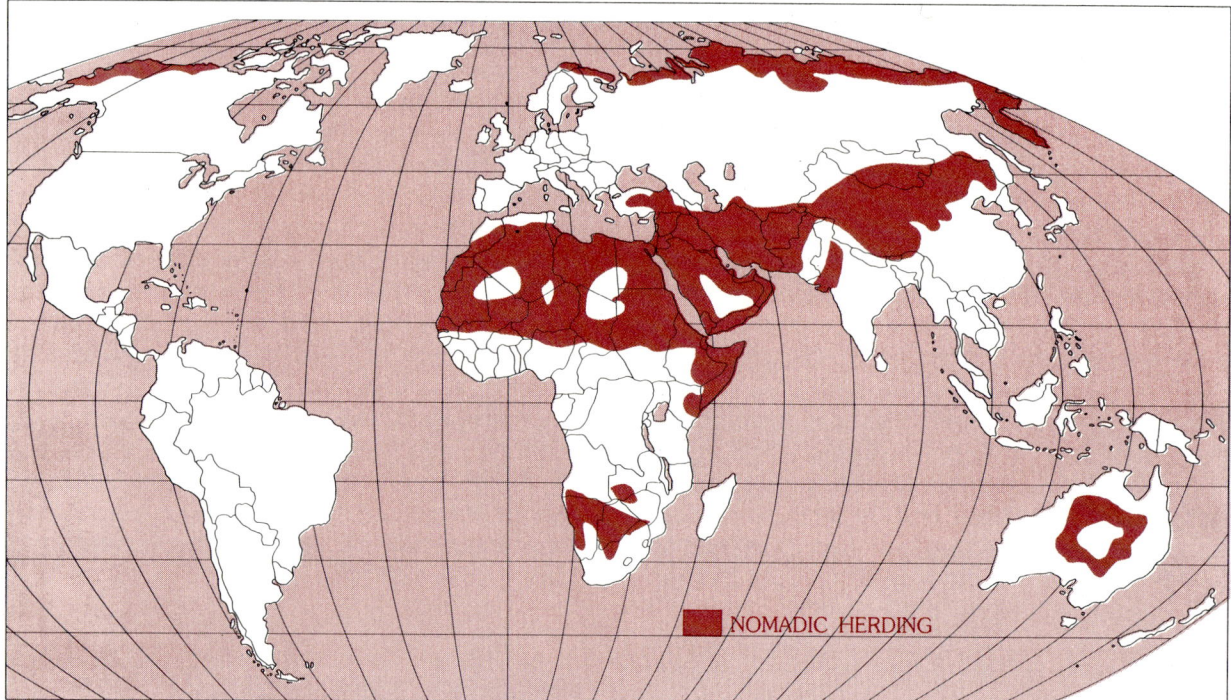

FIGURE 10–5 Areas of the world where nomadic herding is the major economic activity.

Tasaday tribe in the Philippines was not found until 1971. The first contact with the Tasadays was by helicopter, and the primitive people thought the machine was a giant insect. The Tasadays also did not grow any animals or crops. Other than these isolated groups, subsistence by hunting and gathering has all but disappeared. It is significant, however, in that it represents the once-universal condition of human adaption to the environment, discussed in Chapter 2.

Subsistence Herding

Subsistence herding is much more widespread than hunting and gathering. In fact, the combined areas where subsistence herding is the predominant economic activity make up the largest economic region on earth (Figure 10–5). The places are either hot and arid or very cold; the harsh climatic conditions support only sparse vegetation. (For example, compare the locations of subsistence herding on the map in Figure 10–5 with the ET, BW, and BS climate areas on the climate map in Appendix A.) The lack of vegetation limits the number of animals that can be accommodated, which in turn limits the number of people that can survive in these regions. Thus, subsistence herding occurs over large portions of the earth, but only a few people are involved in the activity.

The Bedouin tribes of Saudi Arabia and North Africa are subsistence herders. These nomadic people usually cluster in clans, and the clans migrate from place to place according to their animals' needs for water and forage. The animals, primarily goats, sheep, and camels, supply the Bedouins' basic needs (Figure 10–6). They use milk and a variety of milk products, as well as meat, for food. They make clothing and shelter (tents) from the animal hair, wool, and skins. They make tools and toys from animal bones, and even use the animal refuse for burning. Yet the Bedouins also take advantage of modern technology; they listen to radios made with state-of-the-art transistors, and carry water to their herds in Mercedes trucks. Wealth is judged by the number of animals a person owns, so the animals are protected as diligently as other types of wealth in other parts of the world.

Nomadic people are noted for being rugged and independent, and both characteristics are fostered by where and how they live. The harsh climate and constant search for food makes for tough, lean people. Their constant movement and self-contained lifestyle lead to feelings of independence. These people tend to ignore political boundaries during their migratory cycles. Thus, loyalty to a specific country is irrelevant to them, but they are fiercely loyal to clans, tribes, and sometimes to particular regions. Governments

TYPES OF AGRICULTURE

FIGURE 10–6 This Bedouin is milking his camel in the open desert. Besides providing milk, camels are also beasts of burden to the Bedouins.

do not like to have people wandering back and forth across borders, but attempts to force the nomads to settle in one place have met stiff resistance. Transition from a nomadic culture to a sedentary lifestyle is nearly complete, however, in Mongolia and parts of China and the Soviet Union. It is occurring, but more slowly, in North Africa and Southwest Asia.

Subsistence Farming

Like subsistence herding, subsistence farming is a primitive economic activity in large areas of the world. Unlike subsistence herding, however, many people are involved in the activity. Subsistence farming predominates primarily in rainy, tropical areas, especially the Af-type climates. The three major regions include one in the Western Hemisphere, one in Africa, and another in Southeast Asia (Figure 10–7). The warm, moist conditions in these three regions encourage plant growth, whereas they cause meat and animal products such as milk to spoil quickly. The environmental conditions are therefore more favorable for plants than for animals as the major source for food, clothing, and shelter.

Subsistence farmers live in close accord with their environments, and any changes in environmental conditions cause changes in the human adaptations to them. For example, in some hot and wet areas (especially the Af climatic regions), farmers must use *shifting cultivation,* also called *slash-and-burn* agriculture, because they must cut down and burn the large trees that grow naturally so as to plant their crops. The heavy rains that produce the large trees also cause the soil to lose fertility within three or four years after the trees have been removed. Thus, the farmers are forced to abandon their clearings every few years, and move to other areas to maintain satisfactory crop yields. Over time, the tropical rainforest becomes patterned with small clearings in various stages of recovery. It takes about 50 years for a cleared area to return to its natural state. Unusually large areas are needed to support only a few people.

Although primitive, shifting cultivation is still the prevailing form of agriculture in many parts of the world, involving an estimated 50 to 200 million people, mostly in Brazil, central Africa, and the large islands of Southeast Asia, including Java, New Guinea, Borneo, and the Philippines.

Shifting cultivation creates a nomadic way of life. Every three or four years, the home, family, and everything of value must be moved to a newly cleared part of the rainforest. *Semishifting agriculture,* on the other hand, is conducted in areas with more favorable physical conditions, such as higher elevations where it is not so hot, and along coastal plains and river valleys where it is also cooler and there are fewer tall trees. Semishifting agriculture is similar to shifting agriculture except the farmers maintain their homes in one place. They do, however, shift their plantings from one clearing to another just as in shifting agriculture. This activity creates small farm villages, and supports a greater density of population. Although it is slightly more sophisticated than shifting cultivation, farmers use slash-and-burn techniques and primitive tools.

CHAPTER 10 ECONOMIC GEOGRAPHY: PRIMARY PRODUCTION

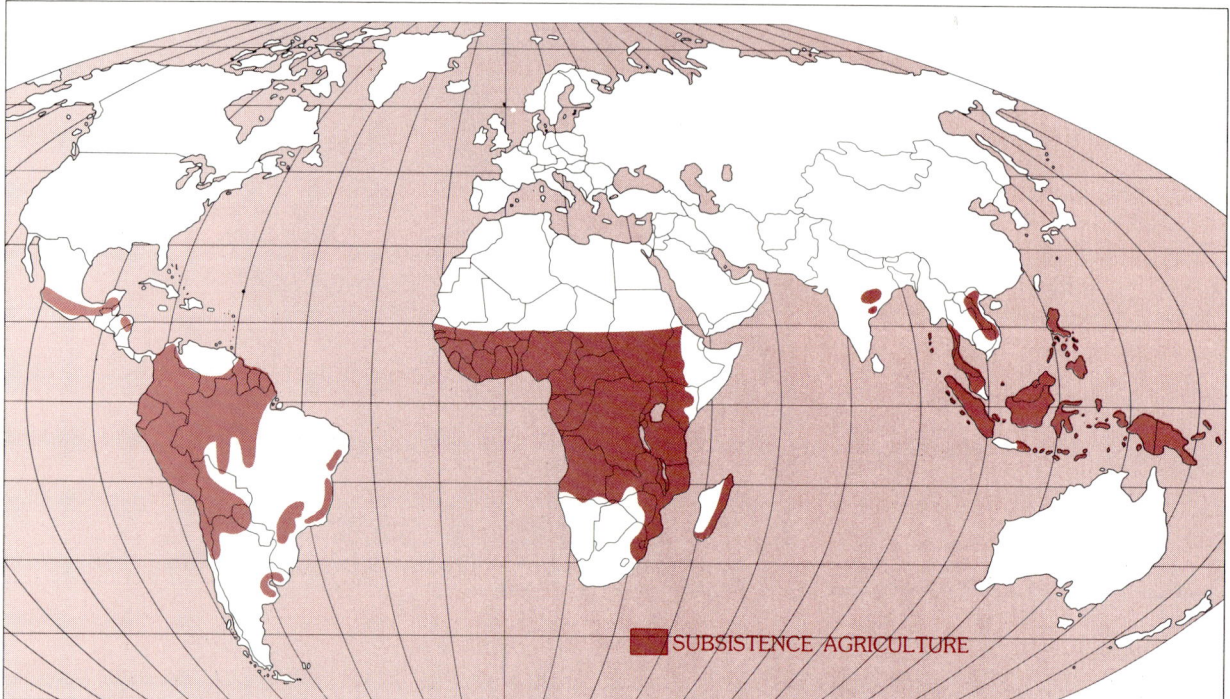

FIGURE 10–7 Approximate areas of the world where subsistence agriculture is the major economic activity. (Data from U.S. Department of Agriculture, Foreign Agricultural Service.)

The most advanced type of subsistence agriculture is *sedentary subsistence farming*. To be successful at this type of agriculture, farmers must know how to replace soil nutrients. Although their methods are unsophisticated by today's standards, sedentary subsistence farmers have learned to use fertilizers and sometimes they know enough about crop rotation to help preserve the precious soil. Shifting cultivators merely use what nature provides, but sedentary farmers take care in preparing and caring for the soil, selecting and planting the best seeds, killing weeds, and harvesting. Even with the extra care and diligence, however, sedentary subsistence farming does not produce much surplus for sale. Most of these people augment their meager circumstances by using, selling, and trading naturally-growing items they gather from the forests (Figure 10–8).

Subsistence farming may seem remote and irrelevant today, yet it was not long ago that most people in the United States were involved in this type of agriculture. Even now, the occupation of farming ranks number one in the world based on the number of people involved in it. This means that about half the people of the world are subsistence farmers. Many of these people live in the heavily populated areas of southern and eastern Asia, and we do not usually see them or think of them in the parts of the world where farmers make up only a small percentage of the population.

Subsistence farmers today live much the same as their ancestors did thousands of years ago. Their food preferences remain stable over time, and they cultivate plants that were domesticated from wild plants found locally. Obviously, there is regional variation in the types of crops; maize (corn) is the leading grain in the Western Hemisphere, rice is the staple of southeast Asia, and millet (a cereal grass) is most common in Africa. All three of these plants originated in the areas where they are now the leading subsistence crops (Figure 10–9). Maize was first domesticated in Mexico, rice in Thailand, and millet in Uganda.

Subsistence farmers enhance their meager diet with specialty crops such as peanuts and beans, which, along with tomatoes, originated in the highlands of Peru, but are now grown in lowland tropical areas worldwide. Bananas and sugar cane, domesticated on the islands of southeast Asia, have been transplanted to most of the world's tropical areas. Two root crops grown throughout the subsistence farming areas are yams and cassava (manioc). Local varieties of yams were domesticated separately in Asia, Africa, and the Americas; cassava, on the other hand, is native to Colombia. It is a shrub with tuberous roots, and produces a much higher yield of carbohydrates and calories than either maize or rice. Cassava is second only to yams as a food source per unit of land, but unlike yams, it is also a cash crop, used to make industrial starches and tapioca. In addition, cassava is more tolerant to drought than yams, and resists insects and disease better than yams. These qualities led to rapid diffusion of cassava cultivation throughout the tropical world.

Commercial Herding

Livestock ranching and dairy farming are the two major commercial herding activities (Figure 10–10). As in subsistence herding, animal husbandry is the primary concern of commercial herders, who most often use sheep and cattle. The major products are wool, hides, meat, and milk. The herds are protected with painstaking care against theft, parasites, disease, and thirst and hunger. Natural food and water supplies for the animals are usually augmented by feed purchased from or grown by local farmers. Owners also provide water from wells rather than force their animals to search for it. The animals and animal products are sold, providing the major portion of the herders' income.

One finds several similarities between nomadic herding and commercial livestock ranching. Both activities take place in dry regions (see especially the BS-type climate areas on the map in Appendix A). Lack of precipitation in these semiarid regions makes it difficult to grow cultivated crops on a sustained basis; however, many species of grass have adapted to the dryness, and have grown naturally for thousands of years. But the carrying capacity of the land for dryland grazing is low, so several acres are needed to support each animal, and large herds need hundreds of acres. Both the lack of crop agriculture and the need for large tracts of land contribute to low human population densities in the commercial grazing regions. On the other hand, there are several major differences between nomadic herding and livestock ranching: (1) the two activities occupy different locations in the world; (2) livestock ranching is sedentary rather than nomadic; (3) livestock ranching is commercial rather than subsistent; and (4) nomadic herding has survived from ancient times, whereas livestock ranching is only about 200 years old.

Every continent except Europe contains extensive areas of semiarid (BS) and arid (BW) climate regions where livestock grazing is the predominate economic activity, shown in Figure 10–10 and Appendix A. The most important areas are western North America, eastern and southern South America, southern Africa, the southern part of the Soviet Union, and Australia. These regions were settled more recently than the nomadic herding regions, and settlement occurred only after some technological innovations were made. The most important technical advances were the invention of barbed wire and improvements in the windmill. Barbed wire was the first cheap and effective barrier for containing cattle, and windmills assured a constant supply of water in arid regions. Together, the two devices permitted a sedentary way of life for the livestock herder. Other advances have come in the breeding and medical care of animals. Breeding is oriented toward the development of dis-

FIGURE 10–8 A subsistence farm in the tropical rainforest of Costa Rica.

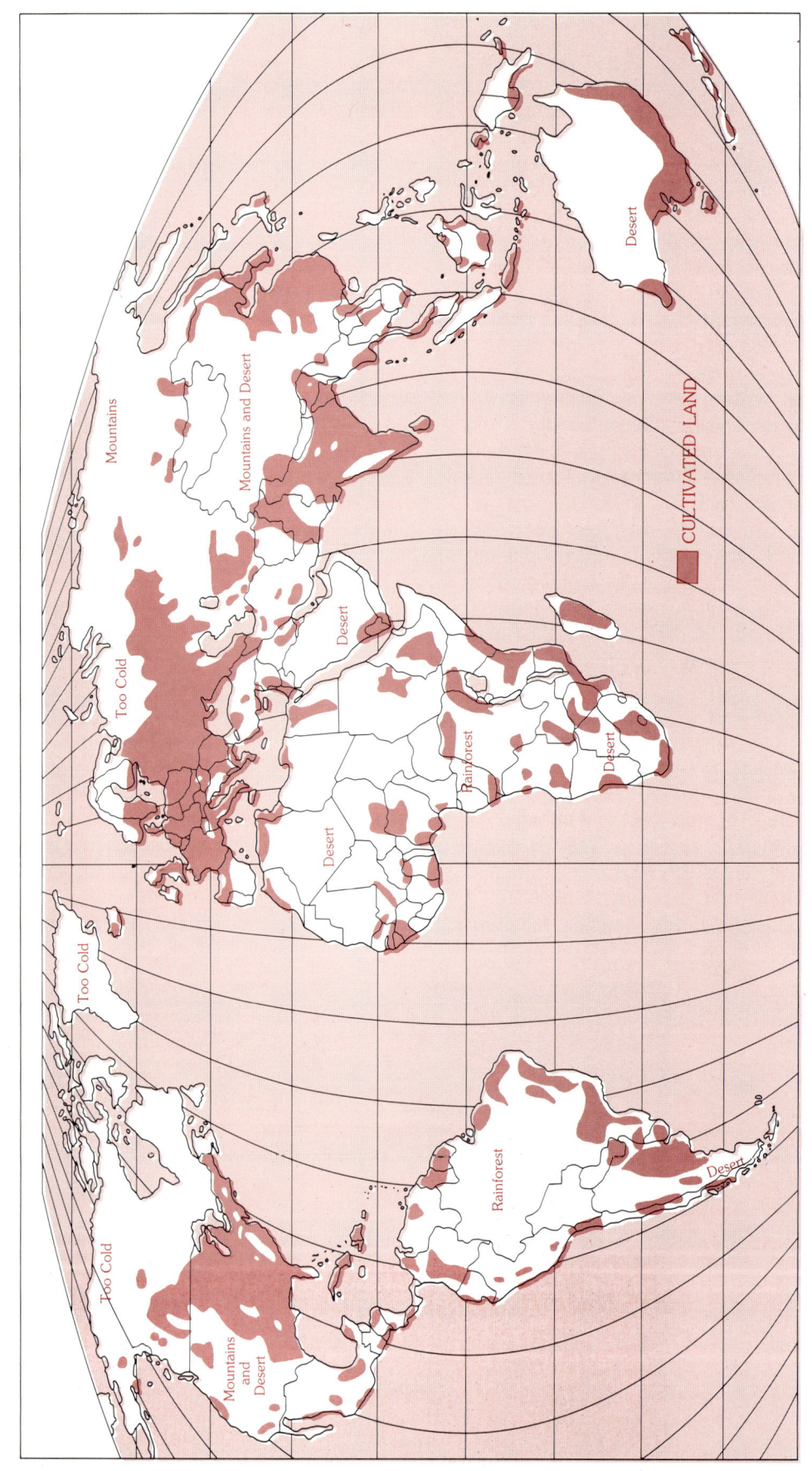

FIGURE 10–9 Approximate areas of cultivated land in the world (see also Figure 16–14, p. 360). (Data from U.S. Department of Agriculture, Foreign Agricultural Service.)

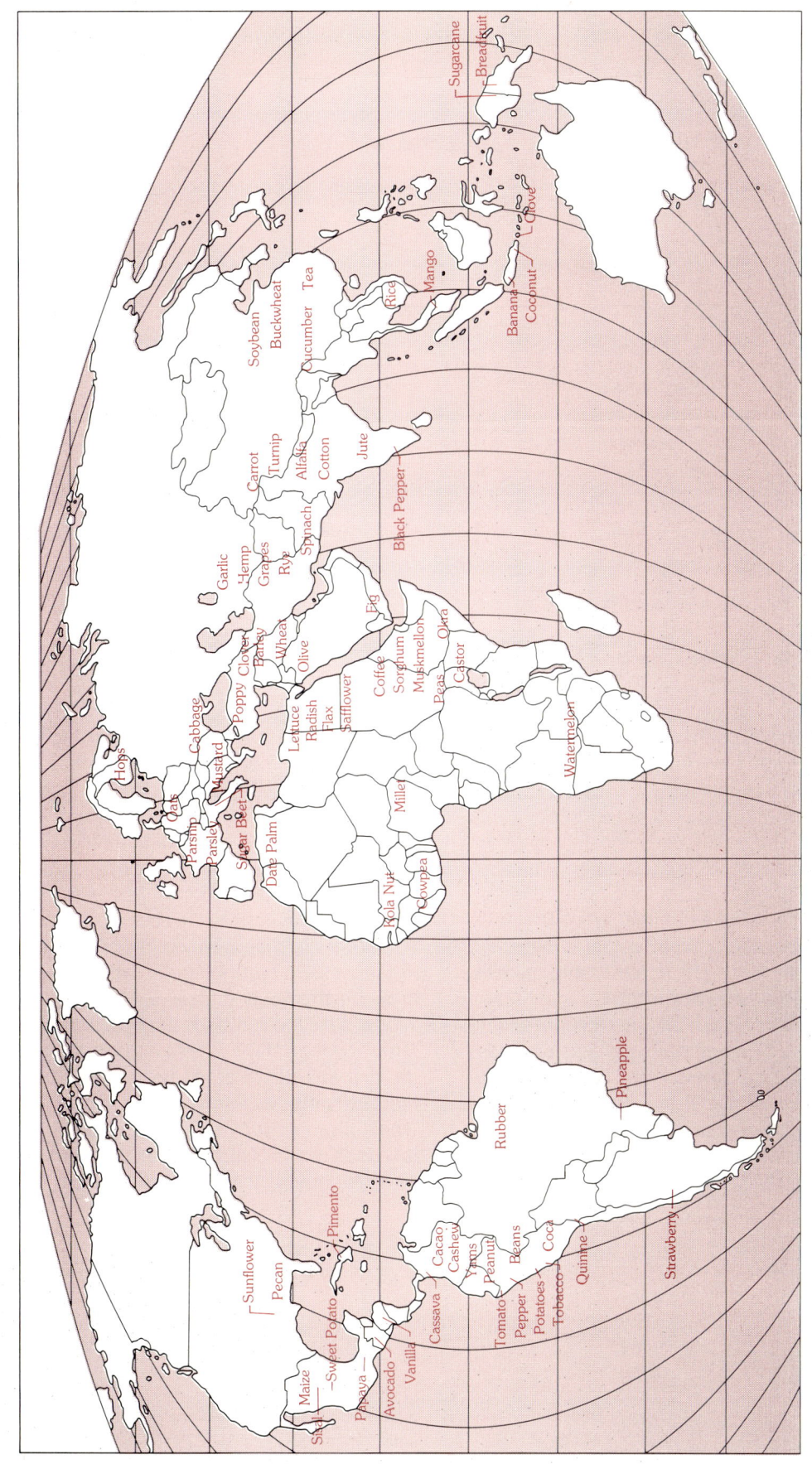

FIGURE 10–9 Places where the world's major crops were first domesticated. (Data from U.S. Department of Agriculture, Foreign Agricultural Service.)

CHAPTER 10 ECONOMIC GEOGRAPHY: PRIMARY PRODUCTION

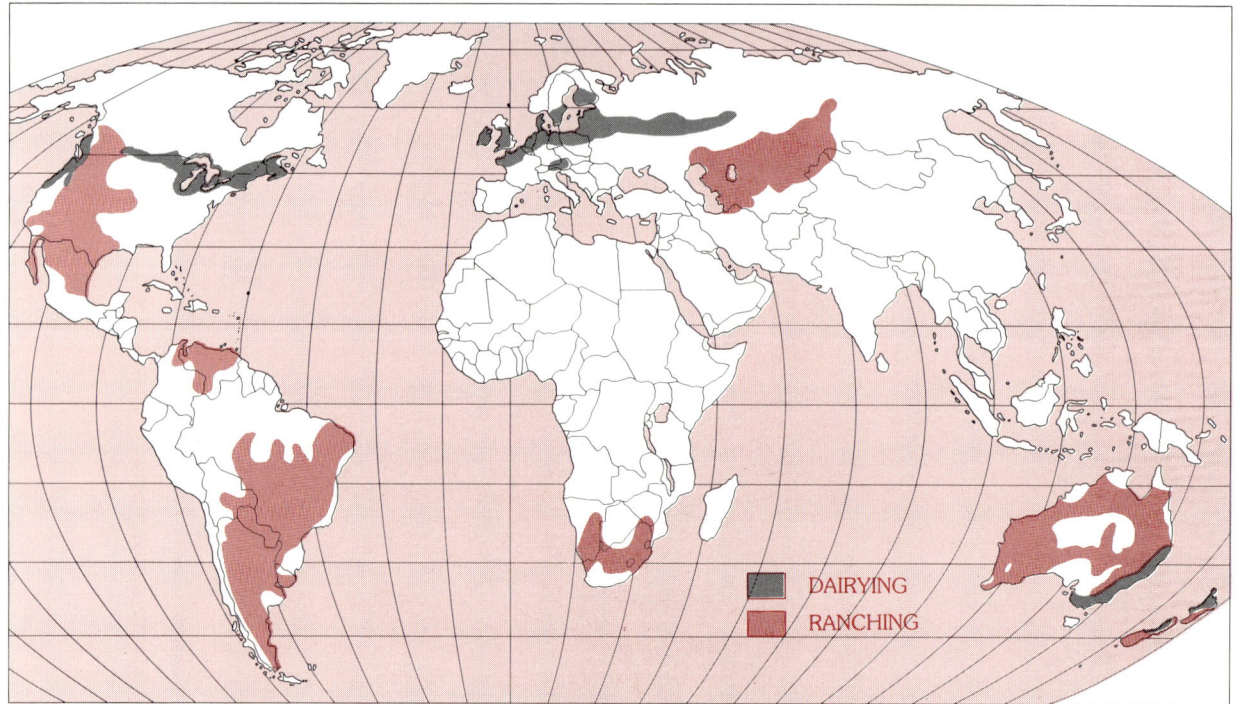

FIGURE 10–10 Areas where commercial herding (ranching and dairying) is the major economic activity.

ease-resistant hybrids, with an emphasis on rapid weight gain for cattle and long wool growth for sheep.

Cattle, sheep, and goats all were domesticated about 11 or 12 thousand years ago in southwest Asia. The general region of domestication runs from Syria and Turkey on the west, through northern Iran, and into the Turkestan area of the Soviet Union on the east. All present breeds of cattle, sheep, and goats derived from those first domesticated animals. Table 10–1 shows present world totals.

The 274 breeds of cattle can be categorized into two general types. The *Bos indicus* breeds are those that have adapted to tropical and subtropical regions. Most cattle of the *Bos indicus* breeds have prominent humps on their backs just above the shoulders. One of the most common is the zebu, shown in Figure 10–11. The *Bos taurus* breeds include those that have adapted to higher latitudes. The most common of these humpless breeds used for beef production in the United States and Australia are the Aberdeen Angus and Hereford. As indicated by their names, both breeds originated in Great Britain. The only beef cattle developed in the United States are the Santa Gertrudis from the King Ranch in Texas.

Domestic sheep, as well as cattle, first appeared in the western hemisphere in 1493, when Columbus brought them on his second voyage to the New World. Later, colonists brought sheep with them to Jamestown in 1609. Sheep and goats were probably the first animals to be domesticated, and remain the most versatile in terms of the variety of foods on which they can survive and the types of environmental conditions in which they exist. Sheep are raised in every country of the world, from tropical to polar re-

TABLE 10–1 Domestic Animals of the World

Types of Animals	Number of Breeds	World Total (in millions)	Leading Country (% of world)
Cattle	274	950	India (30%)
Sheep	800	850	Australia (18%)
Hogs	312	450	United States (13%)
Goats	62	350	India (17%)

Source: H. H. Cole and Magnar Ronning, eds., *Animal Agriculture* (San Francisco: W. H. Feeman, 1974), p. 39.

FIGURE 10–11 Tropical zebu cattle.

gions, in humid and dry areas, and on mountains and plains. There are more breeds of sheep than there are of cattle, goats, and pigs combined, because they have been bred to withstand so many different conditions. In west Africa, for example, sheep have no wool, and some breeds have hair similar to goats.

Modern sheep used for commercial purposes are classified as either wool breeds or meat breeds. The wool breeds are descendants of the *merino*, which originated in Spain prior to 1700. Countries that now produce the most sheep are located primarily in the southern hemisphere: Australia, New Zealand, South Africa, Argentina, and Uruguay. Wool breeds are classified according to the grade of their wool: fine, medium, long, or coarse. Meat breeds all originated in England: Hampshires are the leading breed for market lambs, and Shropshire and Southdown are raised for mutton as well as wool. The number of sheep in the United States in 1980 was just under 10 million, a decline from a high of 52 million in 1940. The decrease is due to the greater use of synthetic fibers as a substitute for wool. By comparison, New Zealand has over 7 million head of sheep, and Australia has about 155 million. The sheep population in Australia is 12 times the human population.

Commercial goat breeds for non-milk-producing purposes include the Angora and cashmere. Angora goats originated in Turkey, and cashmeres came from Tibet. Goat hair, known as *mohair*, is used to manufacture brushes, carpets, felts, cords, upholstery materials, and fabrics for light summer suits. The United States, Turkey, and South Africa are the leading producers of mohair, with Texas producing about 95 percent of the U.S. total. Cashmere goats produce a fine wool used for sweaters, shawls, suits, and hats. Most of the world's cashmere comes from Tibet and northern India.

Milk was a subsistence product through most of history, but for the last 100 years, most of the world's supply has come from commercial dairy farms. Commercial herders who specialize in milk production sell it for use as: (1) *fluid market milk,* to be consumed directly; and (2) *manufactured milk products,* such as butter, cheese, cottage cheese, yogurt, and ice cream.

World milk production occurs in different places than does livestock ranching. Dairy herds must be more closely supervised than beef cattle. Because they must be milked twice a day, they must be kept in smaller pastures, otherwise the daily herding for milking would be impossible. Greater rainfall produces a lusher grass cover; thus smaller pastures can support many more head of cattle than pastures in dry regions. Also, milk is "market oriented" (see Chapter 11), so dairies tend to locate near large urban areas and other heavily populated regions. The three major milk-producing areas are northwestern Europe, north-central United States, and southeastern Australia. Numerous other pockets of high production exist throughout the world, especially around the large urban centers.

Numerous breeds of dairy cattle have been developed, but dairy buffalo, goats, and sheep also produce milk (Table 10–2). Other animals, such as camels, yaks, llamas, and even horses, are used for subsistence milk production, although dairy cattle are by far the best producers. One large Holstein cow

TABLE 10–2 World milk production

Region	Total milk Production (10^6 metric tons)	Cow	Goat	Sheep	Buffalo
North America	62	99	1	—	—
Central America	6	96	4	—	—
South America	19	91	8	1	—
Europe	151	94	2	3	1
Asia	50	50	6	6	38
Soviet Union	85	98	1	1	—
China	3	100	—	—	—
Africa	13	76	11	5	8
Oceania	14	100	—	—	—
Total	403	91	2	2	5

Note: Values for animal types in percentages of total production.
Source: U.S. Department of Agriculture 1980 estimates.

can deliver over 18,000 kg (40,000 lb) of milk per year. Using the same amount of feed, it would take at least 10 goats to produce as much milk as the one cow, and more human labor would be required to milk the ten goats. Holsteins are the most popular dairy breed in the United States because of their large production capabilities.

Because of their large populations and large areas of cool climates (especially the Dfa-type climates), the Soviet Union and the United States are the world's leading milk producers. The economy of New Zealand, however, is more closely tied to commercial dairying than that of any other country. Dairy products account for nearly one-third of New Zealand's exports. Some countries, and even specific regions within countries, have become known for cheese making. Like wine, a wide variety of cheeses can be produced, depending on the mold or bacteria used in the process. Regions have developed reputations for producing particular types of cheese. The most popular varieties produced in the United States are Cheddar, Swiss, Italian, brick, Limburger, and blue. As some of the names indicate, the recipes originated in European countries.

Commercial Farming

Commercial crops depend upon the physical environment, especially climate. The two broad categories of world crops based on climatic conditions are *tropical crops* and *middle-latitude crops*. Tropical crops include all the commercially-grown plants that originated in tropical environments; that is, between about 25 degrees north and south latitudes. Examples include bananas, sugarcane, coffee, cacao, rubber, jute, and pineapples. Middle-latitude crops are those such as corn, wheat, barley, oats, and sorghum. The United States, for example, is primarily a middle-latitude country. Commercial bananas are not grown in this country, so they must be imported from tropical countries in Latin America. On the other hand, the United States is a world leader in the production of wheat, which is exported to many other countries.

Commercial agriculture is characterized by specialization. A commercial farmer usually produces only one type of crop. Specialization allows farmers to save money, time, and energy, because they need only one type of planting and harvesting equipment and only one type of expertise. The traditional *mixed farming* regions of the United States are changing to one-crop commercial agriculture. Specialization does not mean exclusivity, however. A significant number of auxiliary animal and crop products are grown in most specialized regions. The major part of a farmer's income is from one crop, but secondary products allow full utilization of the land and are necessary for effective crop rotation.

Wheat is the world's most important commercial crop. More rice is produced than wheat, but rice is used more as a subsistence crop than is wheat, especially in Asia (see Figure 10–12). The other major commercial grains are corn, barley, soybeans, and oats (Table 10–3). The United States is the world leader in production of many of these cash grains; for example, the United States produces more corn *and* soybeans than all other countries of the world combined. Most of the wheat is consumed as food by humans, whereas commercial corn and oats serve as animal feed. Soybeans are used for products that feed both humans and animals.

Wheat is the oldest known domestic crop. The first type was domesticated from wild grass along the river valleys of ancient Mesopotamia (modern

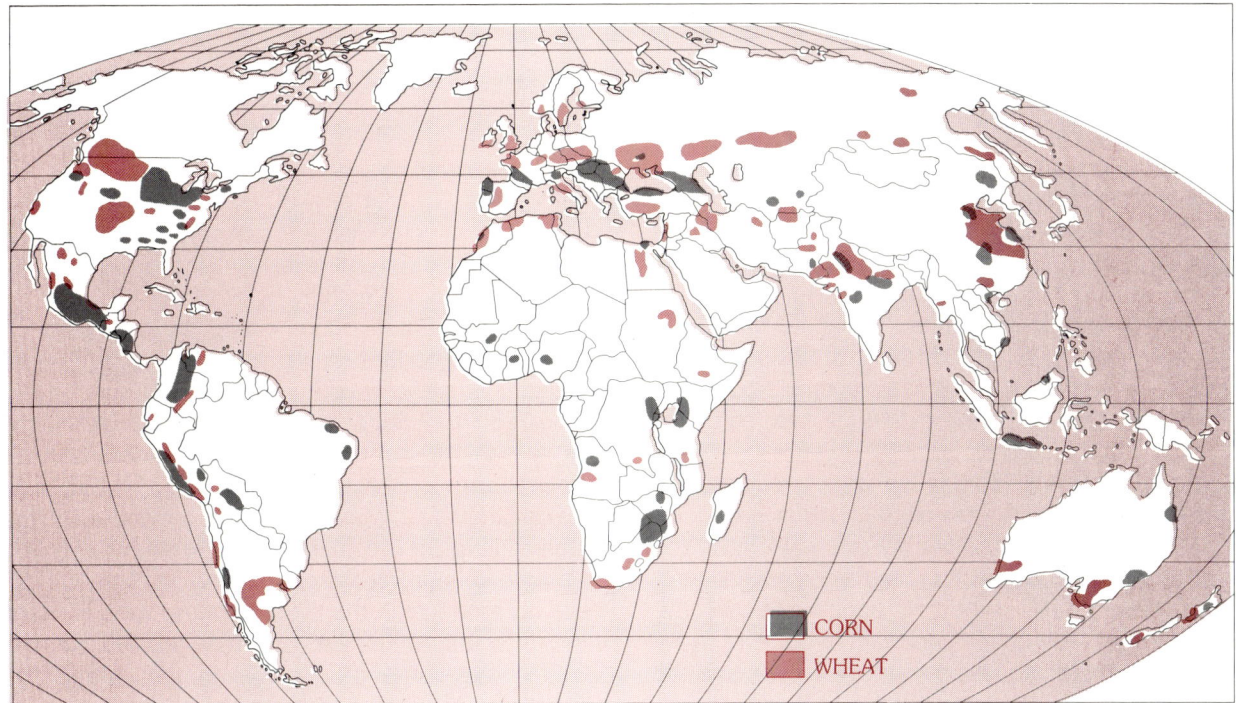

FIGURE 10–12 The major wheat- and corn-growing areas of the world.

Iraq), and its success led to other forms of agriculture. Many species of wheat have been developed, but all are of two basic types: *soft wheat* and *hard wheat*. Soft wheat is grown in more humid areas than is hard wheat, and because of a higher water content, the soft variety spoils more quickly than the hard. The ideal wheat climate has a cool, moist spring (for early growth), followed by a hot, dry summer (for maturation). Most of the wheat produced and exported is hard wheat, primarily because of its resistance to spoilage, but also because it is better than soft wheat for making bread. Soft wheat flour does not rise well with yeast, so it is used to make unleavened foods such as crackers and spaghetti.

Wheat is also designated *winter wheat* or *spring wheat*. Winter wheat is sown in the fall; the seeds sprout before cold weather arrives, and the small plants lie dormant over the winter. This gives the wheat a head start in the spring and allows early summer maturation. Spring wheat, on the other hand, is sown in the spring and matures in late summer or fall. Usually, winter wheat yields are much greater than those of spring wheat, but winter wheat can be grown only in areas where the winters are not severe enough to kill the small wheat plants. In the United States, central Kansas marks the transition between the winter wheat belt to the south and the spring wheat belt to the north.

TABLE 10–3 Commercial crop production and exportation

Crop	World Production (10^6 metric tons)	Percentage Produced in United States	World Exportation (10^6 metric tons)	Percentage Exported from United States
Rice	352	2	8	25
Wheat	350	17	73	44
Corn	322	50	61	71
Barley	144	6	13	4
Soybeans	59	58	19	79
Oats	47	17	2	13

Source: U.S. Department of Agriculture, Foreign Agricultural Service, 1976.

Corn is an original North American crop. The plant was domesticated in Mexico, and the United States has been the world's leading producer ever since the Indians helped the colonists plant their first crop. Corn is the world's most efficient plant for converting the sun's energy into food. It ranks second to wheat in acreage among cash crops in the world. It is grown in every state except Alaska, but does best where there is a frost-free period of at least 120 days. Corn likes lots of sunshine, and needs 40–50 cm (15–20 in.) of rain during the growing season. The Corn Belt region of the United States is the largest area of the world for profitable corn production. The factors that make the region ideal for corn are: (1) favorable temperatures, (2) generous, well-distributed rainfall, (3) level to gently rolling land, and (4) deep, medium-textured soils that have high moisture-holding capabilities. Iowa usually leads the nation in corn production, followed closely by Illinois. The United States produces about one-half the world's corn, but other important producing areas are the southern Ukraine in the Soviet Union and the Danube Valley and Hungarian Plain in Europe.

Other Commercial Crops Other crops important to world commercial agriculture are raised where the climates or soils are not suited to rice, corn, or wheat. For example, barley is a hardy grain that requires only a short growing season. The Soviet Union is the leading producer partly because so much of its territory has short summers (see the D climate areas on the map in Appendix A). Oats are grown as a secondary crop in the Corn Belt, usually in areas that are too cool and wet for good corn. Rye and sorghum are cultivated where it is too dry for successful wheat production. Soybeans, however, are grown as a cash crop and compete successfully with corn in the Corn Belt and with cotton in the Mississippi Valley. In addition, soybeans are a legume, which means they replenish the soil with nitrogen. Soybeans, therefore, are ideal for *crop rotation,* especially with corn, because corn uses a lot of nitrogen. Crop rotation is the process of "rotating" crops from one year to the next within the same field.

Cotton is similar to soybeans in that it is economically competitive with other crops in both irrigated and unirrigated regions. Cotton requires a long, hot growing season, however, so its growth is confined to the southern part of the United States. The Soviet Union and China have both surpassed the United States in cotton production during the last twenty years. As with wool, synthetic fibers have replaced cotton fabrics to a large extent. Texas accounts for over one-fourth the cotton produced in the United States. The location of textile mills and fabricating plants are influenced by the location of the growth of cotton, as we will discuss in Chapter 11. Mississippi is the second leading cotton producing state. Most of the cotton grown in Texas is irrigated, whereas that grown in Mississippi is not. The Old South still produces a lot of cotton, but the new irrigated fields of west Texas, Arizona, and California are competing successfully for the crop.

Sugarcane and sugar beets, both sources of sugar, are important commercial crops grown under entirely different environmental conditions. Sugarcane requires temperatures above 20°C (70°F) and more than 130 cm (50 in.) of rainfall annually. (This includes the Af climates and the warm, humid margins of the Cfa climates. Refer to Appendix A.) The sugarcane plant originated in New Guinea, but is now grown in tropical areas worldwide. Hawaii is the leading producer in the United States, but significant amounts also come from Louisiana and Florida. The leading sugarcane producing countries are Brazil, Cuba, and India. Sugar beets, originally from Italy, prefer a Mediterranean type climate (the Csa types on the climate map), but will grow well in the cooler, drier, middle latitude areas. California is the leading sugar beet producing state. The world's leading producer is the Soviet Union, which cultivates about three times as much as France, its nearest competitor.

Farmers grow vegetables commercially throughout the world, but there is wide variation in the types they grow. Many vegetables are important as pure subsistence crops, and nearly all farmers, and many nonfarmers, set aside a small plot of land for a vegetable garden. People who live on large collective farms in the Soviet Union are allowed to grow vegetables for their own use. This subsistence and semi-subsistence production is impossible to show on a world map; however, vegetables grown on a strictly commercial basis do have some spatial patterns. White potatoes, for example, require sandy soil and cool weather, having originated under those conditions in the Lake Titicaca region of Bolivia and Peru. Today, white potatoes are grown in the same kinds of regions as sugar beets, and as with sugar beets, the Soviet Union is the world's leading producer. In the United States, the leading potato producers are Maine, Idaho, and North Dakota. People in the middle latitudes, especially in the northern hemisphere, eat four to five times as many white potatoes as people who live in more tropical locations. Within Europe, for example, northern Europeans are potato eaters, but the southern Europeans get their starch from pasta and bread. In the tropical areas, rice and cassava are the potato substitutes.

Vegetables are perishable, which dictates patterns of production for most of the world. In the Less Developed Countries, vegetables are grown near urban markets, because they must be sold before they spoil. Since producers cannot afford refrigeration, transportation is limited to relatively short hauls. In many parts of the world, producers haul vegetables to market every day, and much of the hauling is done by draft animals or by human power. Outdoor vegetable markets are common in every city of the world, except in the United States and Canada, although even in these two countries, they are making a comeback because of the emphasis on natural food consumption. Growing vegetables near urban areas is called *truck farming*, and is generally a seasonal activity.

Refrigeration and rapid transportation have changed truck farming in the United States and Canada. California produces over one-third of all vegetables in the United States, and the major market is the urbanized northeastern part of the country. A year-round flow of fresh vegetables goes from California (and Arizona, Texas, and Florida) to the northeastern markets, including Canadian cities. Canning, dehydration, and freezing processes supplement fresh vegetables. Vegetables are also grown in greenhouses during the off-season. All these techniques, however, are restricted to the wealthy nations, those that can afford the high-cost alternatives to traditional truck farming.

Tree products such as fruit and nuts are important commercially, but as in the case of vegetables, areas of production are widely scattered. Some general patterns do exist, however. In the United States, the west coast, Texas, and Florida predominate, although there are pockets of production along the shores of the Great Lakes and in other parts of the Northeast. Fruits produced in the United States, in order of total value, are oranges, apples, grapes, peaches, grapefruit, plums, pears, lemons, cherries, and apricots. As one can see, the list contains citrus grown in semitropical areas, grapes from Mediterranean-type areas, and the more hardy, cold-climate varieties such as apples. In international trade, fruits are more important than vegetables. The United States and northern European countries are the major importers, especially of tropical fruits such as olives, bananas, and pineapple. Although no bananas grow in the United States, they are the most common fruit eaten in this country.

Tobacco and beverage crops such as coffee, tea, and cocoa are important primary products grown commercially. Areas of production and consumption differ for each of the four crops. North Carolina and Kentucky rank first and second in tobacco production in the United States, where tobacco is grown on about a quarter of a million farms. About 800,000 acres of tobacco were harvested in the United States in 1980, accounting for domestic use as well as nearly $1 billion of export sales. At the same time, the United States imported about one-third that amount to blend with domestic tobacco to produce various brands of cigarette and pipe tobaccos. After the United States, Turkey, Bulgaria, and Greece are the largest exporters of tobacco, and Great Britain, West Germany, and the Soviet Union are the leading importers.

The three beverage crops, coffee, tea, and cacao, are generally produced in tropical and semitropical countries and consumed in the temperate regions. Brazil accounts for about one-third of the coffee that enters world trade, and the United States is the leading consumer. Coffee is produced also in Colombia (second to Brazil), and in many central African nations. About 60 percent of the coffee grown enters world trade (Figure 10–13). Only less than half the tea produced enters world trade, and Asia accounts for over 90 percent of that. India and Sri Lanka produce about half the total world-marketed tea. Other producers consume much of what they grow. In terms of the amount of tea they import, major countries are Great Britain, the United States, the Netherlands, West Germany, and France. Africa leads the world in the production of cacao, where Ghana alone accounts for about one-third the world's total. The leading cacao importers are the same as those for tea.

Coffee and tea come from bushes, but the beans are used from the coffee plant and the leaves are used from the tea plant. Neither type of plant can tolerate low temperature, and both need more moisture than corn or wheat. Moist tropical climates are needed for all three beverage crops. (See the Af-type climate areas on the world climate map in Appendix A.) The rich volcanic soils and sloping hillsides of Sri Lanka are ideal for the tea plant. The slopes allow plenty of sunlight to reach each plant. Cacao, on the other hand, is a tree product (Figure 10–14). The cacao pods grow from the trunk and branches of the cacao tree, and grow to about the size of cantaloupes. The cacao beans form inside the pods. The beans, about the size of a teaspoon, are a rich, dark brown in color, in contrast to the white fiber inside

FIGURE 10–13 Coffee growing on steep slopes in Costa Rica.

the cacao pod (Figure 10–15). All three beverage crops are labor intensive; that is, harvesting requires much hand labor. The round, dark brown coffee beans must be handpicked, because the beans on one plant ripen at different times. Tea leaves and cacao pods are also handpicked. Thus, beverage crops have common features even though they grow in different parts of the world.

World patterns of animal and crop production are influenced to a large extent by the physical environment. Remember, however, that human behavior also dictates where things are produced. Variations in cultural patterns affect animal and crop production. Religion, for example, plays a role in what types of animals people raise in certain parts of the world. Moslems do not eat swine, so few hogs are produced in North Africa and the Middle East. Hogs do not tolerate the desert heat well, anyway, but religion bars their existence more than the heat. Hindus are forbidden to kill cattle, thus India has more cattle than any other country in the world. Cows, although not actually worshipped as deities, are treated with respect. Consequently, millions of weak, skinny cattle wander the village streets, blocking traffic, entering homes, and competing with humans for space and forage. These and other cultural factors contribute to the spatial aspects of agriculture.

Each commodity in agriculture is important in its own way, either locally or for world trade. Many crops are vitally important as part of the human food supply. Our purpose here has been to introduce some of the major commodities, and to indicate the close link between agriculture and the physical and cultural environments. Regardless of human sophistication in the realms of art, music, and machines, we remain dependent upon the physical environment for our food. The cultural environment, in turn,

FIGURE 10–14 Cacao pods growing on the trunk of a cacao tree near a tropical rainforest.

EXTRACTIVE INDUSTRIES

FIGURE 10–15 A cacao pod split into two pieces reveals the seeds from which cocoa is obtained.

affects patterns of food production. Unfavorable food supply conditions can lead to hunger, malnutrition, and even starvation.

EXTRACTIVE INDUSTRIES

The extractive industries are those primary economic activities geared toward "extracting" valuable commodities from the earth's crust. Humans have found to be useful or valuable a vast array of materials that lie buried in the rock under the earth's surface, and have developed a number of methods to extract these materials. We will mention only the most prominent materials, methods, and locations.

As a result of past geological factors, mining and drilling operations are unevenly distributed over the earth's surface. Other factors, such as richness of the deposit, ease of extraction, location of the market, and transportation costs, also dictate the location of mines and wells. The value of the product is also important in terms of locations of facilities. For example, diamonds and platinum can be mined for profit regardless of where they are found, but gravel and brick clay cannot. In other words, diamonds have a very high *specific value,* whereas that for gravel is very low. The specific value of an item is its value per unit of weight.

We can group extractive industries into three general categories of activities. The extraction of *fuels,* which includes mining or drilling for the energy materials such as coal, oil, and natural gas, is the most important from an economic standpoint. Mining of *metals* such as iron, copper, and tin, is next in importance. Extraction of *nonmetals,* such as sand and gravel, ranks third in economic importance, but first in the volume and weight of material removed from the earth's crust.

The Fuels

Coal The energy materials are usually referred to as *fossil fuels,* because they are the remains of plants and animals that existed during a former geological time. Giant forests of ferns and some trees covered a large portion of the earth's surface during the height of the Carboniferous period, about 300 million years ago. Warm, moist climates existed for about 65 million years. During that time, the forest plants captured solar energy, and when they died, toppled over and sank into mud and swamps. The dead plants were thus sealed off from insect attacks, and from oxygen that would have caused them to decay. Finally, erosion filled in the swamps with layer upon layer of sediments. The plants became fossilized, but retained the energy they had received from the sun. These fossilized plants are now mined as a mineral, specifically *coal.* Approximately 20 feet of original plant matter produces about a 1-foot seam of coal, and some coal seams are 400 feet thick. Great amounts of coal are produced from deposits throughout the world.

Three grades of coal are mined: (1) lignite, (2) bituminous, and (3) anthracite. These grades are based primarily on hardness; lignite is the softest and anthracite the hardest. Vegetation that falls and sinks into mud turns into *peat* first. Peat is forming today, but will lie for centuries, changing only slightly. The overburden of sediment eventually compresses peat into lignite, a low-grade brown coal with a woody texture. Under further compression, lignite changes into bituminous coal, which is a relatively hard, black coal. Bituminous coal is the most abundant type. Finally, additional pressure caused by crustal movements of the earth changes bituminous coal into the hard, black anthracite type. Very little anthracite coal has been found.

Although we find coal in many places on earth, only six countries account for over 80% of coal production (Figure 10–16). In order of production, they are the United States, the Soviet Union, China, Poland, Great Britain, and West Germany. The United States is not only the largest producer, but also leads the world in coal exporting. The steel industries of Japan, western Europe, and South America, and the electric utility companies in Canada use the exports of *coking coal* (bituminous). The United States has the best position in world markets because of its high-quality coal, the large seams in which it is found, and its advanced mining technology.

Petroleum Like coal, petroleum is of organic origin, and the thick, greenish-black crude oil retains the solar energy that was captured millions of years ago. It is rather widely distributed in the upper strata of the earth's crust. Historically, petroleum was used to coat walls and hulls of ships, but its real prominence began with the development of gasoline engines. The first commercial oil was produced from a well near Ploesti in Rumania in the late 1850s, but soon after that, the United States became the unrivaled leader in both production and consumption. Annual oil production in the United States went from 500,000 barrels in 1860, to 63 million in 1900, to 442 million in 1920, to over 1 billion barrels in 1940. This upward trend has continued, but not as dramatically as during the first one hundred years. At first, the United States supplied the petroleum-deficient areas of the world by exporting huge amounts of oil. During the 1950s, however, U.S. domestic consumption began to increase more rapidly than production. By 1970, despite the annual production of 3.1 billion barrels of crude oil, the United States had not kept pace with consumption and had to rely on imported oil. That trend continues today, and is the source of myriad economic and political problems.

Alaska is the leading producer of crude oil in the United States. Texas had been the leader for the past 70 years, and still leads in total petroleum production (including natural gas and natural gas condensates), but the great Alaskan discovery started to pay off on June 20, 1977 when oil began to flow through the trans-Alaskan pipeline, running from the North Slope oil field near Prudhoe Bay to the Pacific port of Valdez. By 1980, Alaska had overtaken Texas in production of crude oil. Other leaders in oil production are Louisiana, California, and Oklahoma. Most of the leading oil producing areas also produce natural gas, because both products often come from the same well. The major exception occurs when oil is obtained from shale and tar-sand. These potential sources of crude oil are being developed slowly, however, because of high costs.

Since World War II, the major areas of consumption of petroleum products have not changed, but the major production areas have altered dramatically. The shift has been from the Western Hemisphere to the Eastern Hemisphere, largely because of the discoveries in the Middle East. Iraq was the first country of the region to claim an oil discovery. The find was made in 1935, and production began the same year. Three years later, large quantities were discovered in Saudi Arabia, and the same year Kuwait was found to lie over huge pools of oil. Today, the Persian Gulf region possesses about 65 percent of the total known reserves; tiny Kuwait alone has about 15 percent of the world's supply. The major area of oil production may shift back toward the Western Hemisphere, however, since recent discoveries in Mexico led to estimates of *potential* reserves nearly twice those of the entire Persian Gulf region. Mexico is not a member of the Oil Producing and Exporting Countries (OPEC) organization, so it can set its own prices on exported oil. Bolivia, Colombia, and Ecuador recently began oil exportation, and the United States has imported oil from Venezuela since 1948. The Latin American production of crude oil could eventually challenge that of the Middle East.

Other areas of petroleum production are the Soviet Union, the North Sea, Africa, and Indonesia (Figure 10–17). Soviet oil and gas comes from three major areas: (1) along the shores of the Caspian Sea, (2) the region between the Volga River and Ural Mountains, and (3) western Siberia. The Soviet Union has

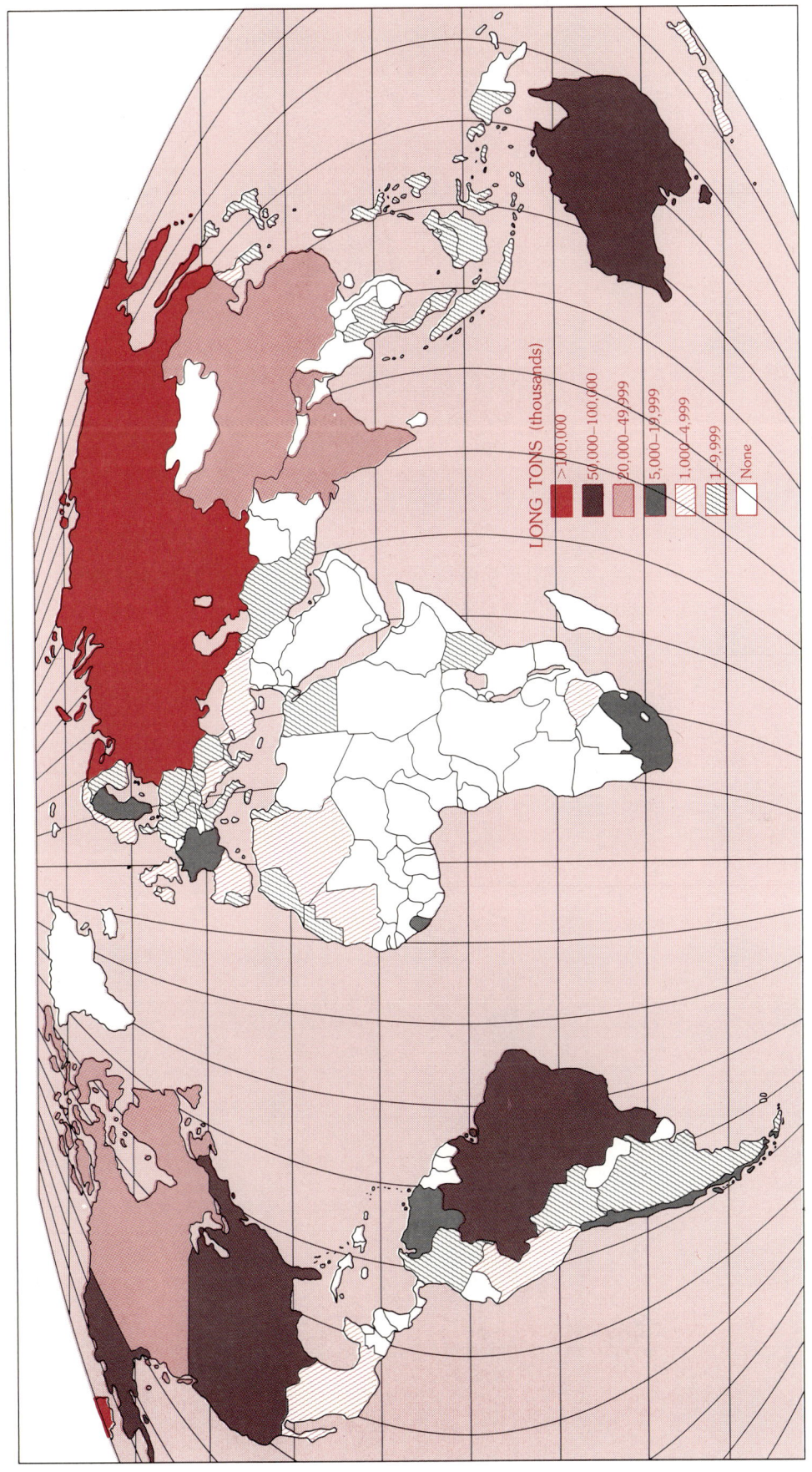
FIGURE 10–16 Worldwide iron ore production, with figures in long tons. (A long ton equals 2,240 lbs.)

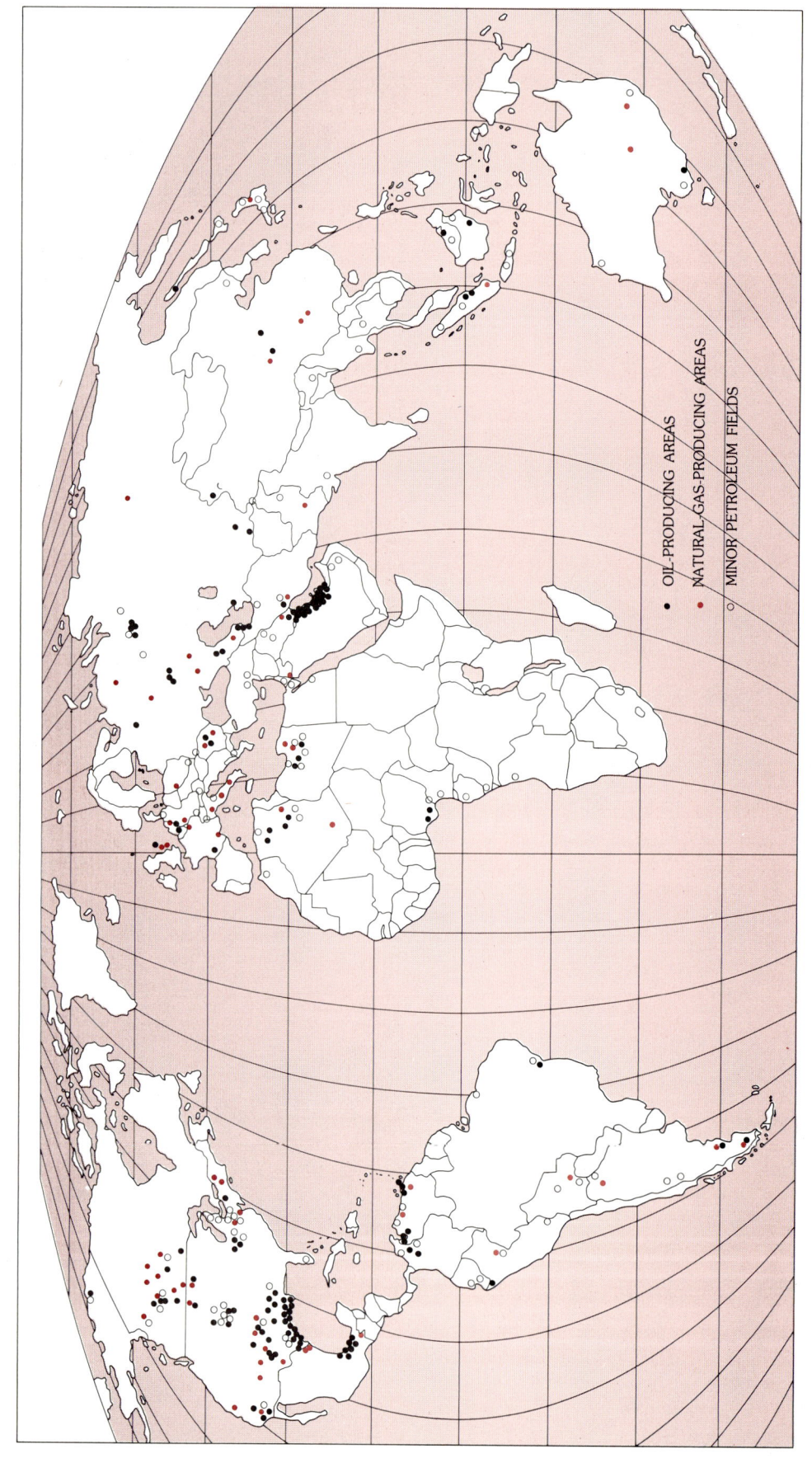

FIGURE 10–17 Worldwide petroleum and natural gas fields.

the world's largest known natural gas reserves and has built pipelines from the oil fields to the population centers. At present, the Soviets are self-sufficient in oil, and comfortable enough with their reserves to begin exporting. Construction of a pipeline from Soviet petroleum regions to western Europe was started in 1983.

The North Sea has recently become a major petroleum production region. It was divided in 1958 into economic zones controlled by Great Britain, Norway, Denmark, West Germany, and the Netherlands. Significant oil and gas discoveries have led to Great Britain's self-sufficiency in oil. The Netherlands has become the world's leading exporter of natural gas. Western Europe, however, must still import over 90 percent of its petroleum supply. Gasoline prices at the pumps in most European countries remain high in comparison to those in the United States.

The major oil countries in Africa are Libya and Algeria north of the Sahara, and Nigeria, Gabon, and Angola south of the desert barrier. Nigeria is the world's 7th leading oil country and is the United States' largest supplier. The 1980 estimates were that Indonesia has about 10 billion barrels of crude oil reserves. Oil export earnings have made that country's economy one of the most stable in the world. Indonesia produces about the same amount of crude oil annually as Louisiana, and, like that state, much of its oil comes from off-shore wells.

Besides the fossil fuels, energy is also generated through hydroelectric stations and nuclear plants. The United States leads the world in generation of electricity by hydroelectric means, but France leads the world in the percentage of electricity generated by nuclear power stations. There are about 50 hydroelectric plants in the United States with capacities over 150,000 kW each, and about 75 nuclear reactors with an average capacity of about 500,000 kW. The Soviet Union is second to the United States in total production of electricity. Other areas of the world, especially central Africa, have tremendous potential for hydroelectric production, but as yet it has not been developed.

Metals Production

Iron is the most important metal. The discovery of uses for iron completely changed civilization, as will be apparent from the discussion of the Industrial Revolution in Chapter 11. The Iron Age began about 3,500 years ago when the pure metal was obtained from meteorites. After discovery of methods for its extraction from ores, iron became increasingly available for arms, tools, and eventually machines. Throughout the centuries, iron increased in importance, especially when it was discovered that a stronger metal could be made by combining pure iron, through heat, with certain alloy metals. The stronger metal, of course, is *steel.* Steel is the basic, indispensable metal of our current civilization. And, iron mining, along with its companion, coal mining, is a prime indicator of a country's material progress.

Metals are categorized as: (1) *base metals,* (2) *alloy metals,* (3) *monetary metals,* and (4) *minor metals* (see Table 10–4). Each of the 22 metals listed in the table has its own geography of production. Some of the source areas are listed. Many important metals are found in close proximity to each other; for example, lead and zinc are usually found together, as are gold and silver. For simplicity, we will discuss only iron ore.

Iron ore, one of the most common elements in the earth's crust, is mined in many locations. The world's leading producing areas have changed dramatically over the last few decades. In 1950, the United States produced about one-half the world's steel, and most of the iron ore (80%) came from the Lake Superior district. For many years, the Mesabi, Cuyuna, and Vermillion ranges in Minnesota, the Gogebic in Wisconsin, and the Menominee in Michigan were the world's most prolific iron ore producers. By 1980, however, the United States was, for several reasons, mining less than 10 percent of the world's iron ore. First, the rich iron deposits around Lake Superior began to give out during the 1950s, making imported ore more important each year. The United States now imports over half as much as it mines. Second, even though it became common to recycle scrap iron, increased mining activity in other parts of the world did the most to change the pattern of world production. The decline in the primary production of iron ore in the United States had reverberations through the steel industry, an example of secondary production (see Chapter 11).

The Soviet Union is now the world's leading iron ore producer, with over twice the amount of the second leading country, Brazil. Both Brazil and Australia were insignificant producers in 1950, but are among the world's leaders today. The United States ranks fourth behind these three countries. Canada ranks fifth in the world and, along with Venezuela, is a major supplier of iron to the United States. Iron ore is a major commodity for world trade, especially since the developing nations (such as China, India, and Liberia) have increased the output of their mines, and countries such as Brazil, Canada, and Australia produce much more than they require for their own use.

CHAPTER 10 ECONOMIC GEOGRAPHY: PRIMARY PRODUCTION

TABLE 10–4 Metals, their uses, and production areas

Metal	Common, Ore*	Major Uses	Major Producers (In Order)
Base			
Aluminum	Bauxite	Alloys, airplanes	Australia, Guinea, Jamaica
Copper	Bournonite	Electrical industry	United States, Chile, Soviet Union
Lead	Galena	Batteries, gasoline	Japan, Soviet Union, Canada
Zinc	Hemimorphite	Die castings	Japan, Canada, United States
Tin	Cassiterite	Containers, solder	Malaysia, Soviet Union, Bolivia
Iron ore	Hematite	Steel	Soviet Union, Brazil, Australia
Alloy			
Chromium	Chromite	Hardens steel	Soviet Union, South Africa, Albania
Manganese	Pyrolusite	Required in steel	Soviet Union, South Africa, Brazil
Molybdenum	Molylbdenite	Strengthens steel	United States, Canada, Soviet Union
Tungsten	Wolframite	Hardens steel	China, Soviet Union, Canada
Vanadium	Descloizite	Strengthens steel	South Africa, United States, Soviet Union
Nickel	Niccolite	Stainless steel	Canada, Soviet Union, Cuba
Monetary			
Gold	Gold	Money, jewelry	South Africa, Soviet Union, Canada
Silver	Silver	Photographic film	Canada, Peru, Soviet Union
Platinum	Platinum	Automobiles	Soviet Union, South Africa, Canada
Minor			
Antimony	Stibnite	Pewter, type	Mexico, United States, Canada
Bismuth	Bismuthinite	Alloy, medicine	West Germany, United States, Bolivia
Cobalt	Cobaltite	Blue dye, medicine	Sweden, Poland, Norway
Magnesium	Magnesite	Alloy, photography	United States, Soviet Union, West Germany
Mercury	Cinnabar	Thermometers	Soviet Union, China, Spain
Titanium	Ilmenite	Aircraft, paint	Norway, Switzerland, United States

*Most metals are found in more than one ore. For example, antimony occurs in a native state but is very rare. It is, however, contained in about 55 minerals. The most familiar is stibnite. The word *stibnite*, in fact, derives from the Latin name for antimony, *stibium*, which means "that which marks."
Source: Shaub, 1975.

Nonmetallic Mineral Production

Of the many nonmetallic minerals, some are excavated in huge quantities throughout the world, while others are much less common. The nonmetallic minerals are classified according to their use. For example, *fertilizer* minerals include nitrogen, phosphate, and potash. Nitrogen, which is extracted from the atmosphere, is found everywhere on earth. In order, the United States, Morocco, and the Soviet Union rank as leading world phosphate producers. Canada, the Soviet Union, and the United States are the major potash producers. Both the United States and the Soviet Union are well endowed with not only the necessary minerals, but also with the lesser ones.

Other nonmetallic minerals include those used for *construction*. These are also found nearly everywhere on earth, and hence are mined as close as possible to the place of consumption. (In Chapter 11, we will talk about "weight loss" in manufacturing.) Loose materials such as sand and gravel, as well as solid rock such as granite, marble, and limestone, are all important for construction. Cement is made from gypsum and limestone and mixed with sand and gravel, so the cement industry also belongs in this category.

Ornamental stones and *gems* also come from the earth's crust. Diamonds are usually thought of as gems, but actually about 80% of all diamonds that are mined go to industrial uses, such as for saw blades and drill bits. South Africa is by far the most important diamond producing country in the world. Other gems include emeralds, rubies, sapphires, pearls, and opals, and there is a geography of production for each.

GEOGRAPHY OF FORESTRY

Wood is one of the world's most important raw materials, used for numerous products by every society regardless of the level of development. Wood is a primary product because timber is taken directly from the woodlands where the trees grow. Mills,

GEOGRAPHY OF FORESTRY

where logs are processed into boards, plywood, shingles, and wood pulp, also represent primary forms of economic activity. We usually find these primary wood factories in forest regions, because logs are difficult to transport, and because only about three-fourths of each log is used for lumber. This 25% loss in sawdust, bark, and odd-shaped remnants is called the *weight loss ratio*. (This ratio is important in all manufacturing processes because it dictates the location of factories, and will be discussed in Chapter 11.) The weight loss ratio for trees has decreased through time as new uses have been found for the parts that were once thrown away. In 1900, only about one-third of each tree became a useful product; by 1950, about one-half of each log was used; and soon the entire tree will be utilized.

Trees are considered natural vegetation even though many species have been moved from their natural habitats. Today, forests grow on about one-third of the earth's land surface, and many species have adapted to many variations in natural conditions.

Soil and climate are the two most important general factors that affect tree growth. Some trees require sour (acid) soil, while others require sweet (alkaline) soil, but a tree species exists for nearly every gradation of soil between sour and sweet. Variations in climate, especially in amounts of sunshine and precipitation, are more critical for tree growth than are variations in soil. Cold and lack of moisture are the specific conditions that limit tree growth. Some trees need large amounts of direct sunlight, and some will not grow at all in direct sun. All trees require at least 100 frost-free growing days during the year. Some trees must have copious amounts of moisture; others need only small amounts. The general rule is that tree growth requires at least 50 cm (20 in.) of rainfall each year. Varying conditions in the environment produced hundreds of kinds of trees that have adapted to the conditions. In the United States alone, for example, there are 1,182 species.

It is somewhat easier to discuss the multitude of tree species by categorizing them. Trees are either *needleleaf* or *broadleaf*, and either *evergreen* or *deciduous*. For commercial purposes, they are classified further as *hardwoods* and *softwoods* (see Table 10–5). The difference between needleleaf and broadleaf is in the structure of the leaf. Needleleaf trees have leaves shaped like needles (long and slender), while broadleaf trees have leaves shaped like fans. The difference between evergreen and deciduous trees is in when they lose their leaves. All trees discard their leaves, but evergreen trees lose theirs a few at a time, so the loss is not noticeable, and they appear *ever* green. Deciduous trees, however, drop their leaves seasonally, and nearly all at the same time. Table 10–5 shows examples of particular types of trees.

Most of the world's trees are found in three belts running from west to east and located primarily in the Northern Hemisphere (Figure 10–18). These belts are associated with three distinct climate regions. The northernmost belt runs from Scandinavia through the Soviet Union and Canada and is known as the *taiga* (see Dfc- and Dfd-type climates on the climate map in Appendix A). The taiga contains a continuous stand of *conifers*, needleaf, evergreen trees that produce cones. Several species of spruce are found, but there are also fir, cedar, pine, and hemlock. The second world belt is located in the temperate region just to the south of the taiga (see the Dfa and Cfa climates) and runs through the eastern United States, Great Britain, central Europe, and eastern Asia. This belt contains deciduous trees such as oak and maple. The third belt of forests is located along the equator in South America, Africa, and Southeast Asia (see the Af- and Am-type climates) and contains the tropical hardwoods that are broadleaf evergreens.

Farmers, loggers, fires, and insects have reduced the forests in the United States from over a billion acres in 1800 to about three-fourths that amount. Fortunately, conservation practices and disease control have brought a recent balance between cutting and growth, and forest expansion is expected. World patterns (Table 10–6) indicate that most lumber manufacturing (sawn wood and paper) takes place in the industrial nations of Europe and North America, whereas shipment of raw logs is carried on by developing countries in Africa, Latin America, and the Far East.

Humans have decimated the world's forests for thousands of years. We know that 3,000 years ago Lebanon was covered by great cedar forests, and the Sahara is believed to have been a great forest at one time. The temperate forests have been cut relent-

TABLE 10–5 Categories of trees

	Needleaf	Broadleaf
Deciduous	Larch (Soft)* Tamarack (Soft) Bald Cypress (Soft)	Oak (Hard)* Maple (Hard) Cottonwood (Soft)
Evergreen	Fir (Soft) Pine (Soft) Spruce (Soft)	Teak (Hard) Ebony (Hard) Mahogany (Hard)

*"Hard" and "Soft" refer to hardwood and softwood.

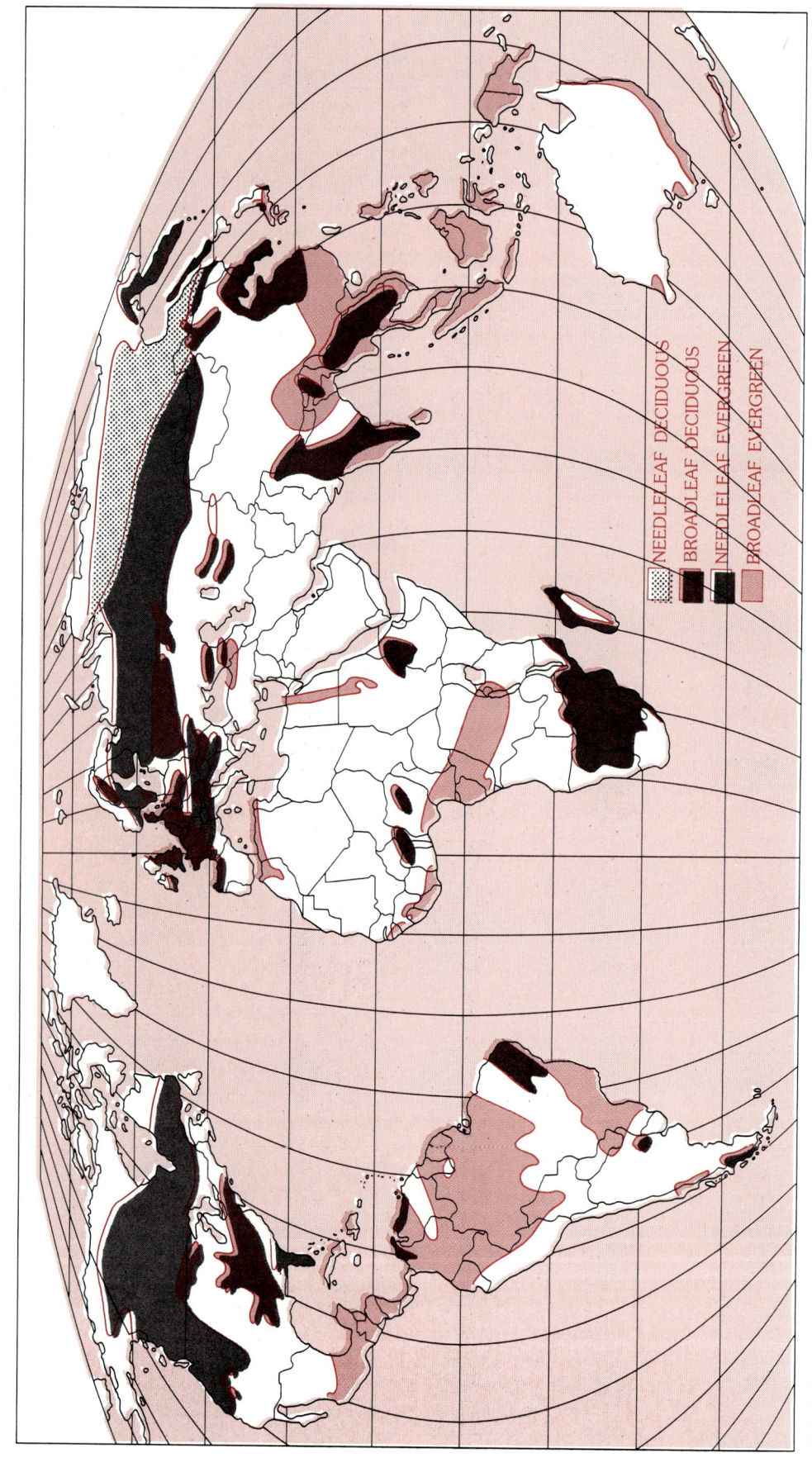

FIGURE 10-18 Worldwide major forest areas.

TABLE 10–6 Exports and imports of sawnwood, logs, and paper

Region	Exports			Imports		
	Sawnwood	Logs	Paper	Sawnwood	Logs	Paper
Africa	1.3	6.4	—	2.3	0.3	0.8
Latin America	2.1	—	0.2	2.2	0.1	1.7
Far East	9.0	37.4	0.9	3.5	47.3	2.1
Eastern Europe, Soviet Union	14.0	9.8	1.4	4.5	0.7	1.8
Western Europe	24.3	4.6	13.9	37.6	13.2	12.3
North America	34.8	15.3	10.9	29.9	2.3	6.9
Other	0.7	0.2	0.4	5.9	0.9	0.8
Totals	86.2	73.7	27.7	85.9	64.8	26.4

Note: Units are 10^6 m^3.
Source: Food and Agriculture Organization of the United Nations, 1979, pp. 104–5.

lessly to make room for farms, roads, and cities. This clearing of forests may turn out to be the most brutal human impact on the physical environment. The recent removal of tropical rainforests to make room for plantations could have alarming consequences. It is estimated that as much as 30% of the world's oxygen supply is produced by the trees of the Amazon rainforest alone. Removal of the tropical forests could therefore be more devastating to human life than any other event, including war, pollution, and famine.

GEOGRAPHY OF FISHING

Commercial fishing is a primary economic activity, because the product is gathered directly from the earth's waters. Most commercial fishing is conducted by corporate fleets with sophisticated electronic equipment. The world catch of about 75 million metric tons annually is not large in comparison to the production of other foodstuffs, and the total number of people involved in full-time fishing is not great. In some parts of the world, however, fish are a primary part of people's diets, and in some countries, fishing constitutes a major portion of labor activity.

The most important fishing areas in the world's oceans are found where certain factors of the physical environment predominate. Shallow water and water mixing are important for the growth of plankton. Fish feed on the plankton. Shallow water allows sunlight to penetrate the water so that photosynthesis occurs, and water mixing causes nutrients for food to be stirred up from the ocean floor. Shallow water is found where *continental shelves* extend many miles offshore, and mixing occurs where warm and cold ocean currents meet and where underwater landforms cause upwelling. The Grand Banks area, off the coast of Newfoundland, has been an important commercial fishing region because the water there is shallow and because that is where the cold Labrador Current meets the warm Gulf Stream. The Peru Current off the west coast of South America causes considerable upwelling, which is the environmental basis for the coastal fisheries in Peru and Chile. A warm and cold current meet in the Pacific Ocean near Japan, giving that area a wealth of fish.

Commercial fishing is largely a cold water activity, because colder regions are where ocean current mixing occurs, and fish congregate in schools. Because tropical fish do not swim together in groups (schools), single species cannot be caught in large numbers. Furthermore, tropical fish contain more oil than coldwater fish, which makes them less attractive as human food. The large commercial fleets, therefore, sail toward the colder regions. In the north Atlantic Ocean, cod, herring, and haddock are the main catches off northwestern Europe, while cod, haddock, and flounder are common off northeastern North America. In the Pacific Ocean, salmon and halibut are the main catches off northwestern North America, and cod, herring, and salmon off northeast Asia. Tropical fishing is an activity of small fleets and independent fishermen. These commercial catches include shrimp in the Gulf of Mexico, sponges in the Mediterranean, tuna in the Pacific off California, and menhaden off Peru. Because of their high oil content, many tropical fish are used for making fish oil. What remains after the oil is extracted, is used as fish meal for fertilizer and animal feed.

Commercial fishing has changed in recent decades, both in how people use the fish and in which countries catch the most fish. There has been a dramatic shift from using fresh and cured fish to freez-

CHAPTER 10 ECONOMIC GEOGRAPHY: PRIMARY PRODUCTION

TABLE 10–7 Utilization of fish for human consumption

	1960	1970	1980	Change 1960–1980
Fresh	53	43	38	−15
Frozen	11	25	30	+19
Canned	12	15	18	+6
Cured	24	17	14	−10
Total	100	100	100	

Note: Numbers represent percentage of world catch.
Source: Food and Agriculture Organization of the United Nations, 1975, p. 18.

ing and canning (see Table 10–7). The change reflects a change in technology, especially in greater use of refrigeration by underdeveloped countries.

Because of a combination of its physical and cultural factors, Japan has been the leading fishing nation for many years. The Japanese islands are small but densely populated. The Japanese cannot afford to "waste" land by raising meat animals, so they depend on fish as a major source of protein. Also, because Japan is located between two ocean currents, fishing has always been good near the islands. Today, however, Japan's enormous demand for fish cannot be supplied from its coastal waters, so Japanese fishermen roam the world's oceans. The traditional Japanese diet had been low in meat and dairy products, but this is changing as western foods become more popular.

Except for Japan, rankings of the leading fishing nations have changed considerably over the last few years (Table 10–8). The order and composition of the list will continue to alter as the underdeveloped nations increase their catches, and as the influence of the fishing agreements from the *Law of the Sea* conferences take effect. The Exclusive Economic Zones (EEZs) established for coastal countries have caused cutbacks in some national fishing efforts. For example, the Soviet Union increased its fish catch dramatically from 1960 to 1970, but has shown very little increase since then (Table 10–8). Also note the decrease in Peru's catch. Both of these changes are at least partially related to the establishment of EEZs. Part of the Peruvian decline may result from a combination of overfishing and an ecological change in coastal waters. Many coastal states place restrictions on fishing in their waters by other nations to protect their natural environments.

CONCLUSION

The primary production activities of agriculture, extractive industries, forestry, and fishing are basic to human needs for food, shelter, and clothing. Primary economic activities are closely tied to the physical environment. Various types of agriculture depend on the types of soils and climates in different parts of the world. Mining must be carried on at the locations of the mineral resources; lumbering depends on where the trees grow; and fishermen must follow the fish. Thus, location factors are important in each type of primary economic activity.

The primary economic activities are common to all countries. Regardless of a country's degree of sophistication in terms of modern inventions and industry, every society is still tied to the earth with regard to basic items for food, shelter, and clothing. Some countries have more expertise at growing or extracting certain commodities, and some countries are favored with certain climates and soils, which gives rise to international trade. Commodities that grow only in tropical areas find their way to the temperate regions, and the return flow of goods is equally important. In this way, humans take advantage of place-to-place differences in the natural environment. A large part of world trade is made up of primary products and the remainder of products associated with secondary economic activity.

TABLE 10–8 Leading fish-catching countries

1979 Rank	Country	1979 Catch (10^3 tons)	Percent change From 1970	Percent change From 1960	1960 Rank
1	Japan	10,733	0.4	73.3	1
2	Soviet Union	9,352	0.9	206.6	4
3	China	7,740	1.5	54.2	2
4	Norway	3,562	30.6	122.9	6
5	United States	3,102	7.2	10.9	5
6	India	2,540	16.5	119.2	7
7	Peru	2,530	−23.5	−28.4	3
8	South Korea	2,419	24.2	607.3	19
9	Denmark	1,807	6.9	211.0	15
10	Thailand	1,778	12.3	708.2	28

Sources: Food and Agriculture Organization of the United Nations, 1979, p. 100; 1960, p. 73.

KEY WORDS

- alloy
- anthracite
- base metal
- bituminous
- broadleaf tree
- coking coal
- commercial dairy farming
- commercial producer
- conifer
- consumption
- continental shelf
- deciduous tree
- evergreen tree
- exchange
- hard wheat
- hardwood tree
- imperfect knowledge
- Law of Sea conferences
- lignite
- livestock ranching
- manufacturing
- merino
- minor metals
- mixed farming
- mohair
- monetary metal
- needleleaf tree
- peat
- photosynthesis
- plankton
- primary production
- quaternary production
- school (of fish)
- secondary production
- sedentary subsistence farming
- shifting cultivation
- slash-and-burn agriculture
- soft wheat
- softwood tree
- space model
- specific value
- spring wheat
- subsistence producer
- taiga
- tertiary production
- truck farming
- von Thünen
- weight-loss ratio
- winter wheat
- zebu

REFERENCES

ALDRICH, SAMUEL R., and LONG, EARL R. *Modern Corn Production.* Cincinnati, Ohio: F & W Publishing, 1965.

BERGER, JOSEF. *The World's Major Fiber Crops: Their Cultivation and Manuring.* Huber, Zurich: Centre d'Étude de l'azote, 1969.

CAMERON, EUGENE N. *The Mineral Position of the United States,* 1975–2000. Madison, Wis.: University of Wisconsin Press, 1973.

COLE, H. H., and RONNING, MAGNAR, eds. *Animal Agriculture.* San Francisco: W. H. Freeman & Co., 1974.

FARB, PETER. *The Forest.* New York: Time, Inc., 1961.

FOOD AND AGRICULTURE ORGANIZATION OF THE UNITED NATIONS. *Yearbook of Fisheries Statistics.* 1960.

_____. *Expanding the Utilization of Marine Fishery Resources for Human Consumption.* FAO Fisheries Report No. 175, 1975.

_____. Svanoy, Norway, *Forest Resources in the Asia and Far East Region.* FAO Commodity Report, Rome, 1976.

_____. *Forest Resources in the European Region.* FAO Commodity Report, Rome, 1976.

_____. "Forestry Products." *FAO Community Review and Outlook, 1977–1979.* Rome, 1979.

NATIONAL COAL ASSOCIATION. *Coal Data.* Washington, D.C., 1976.

PARK, CHARLES F. JR, and FREEMAN, MARGARET C. *Earthbound: Minerals, Energy, and Man's Future.* San Francisco: Freeman, Cooper & Co., 1975.

RICARDO, DAVID. *The Principles of Political Economy and Taxation.* New York: E. P. Dutton, 1912.

ROUSE, JOHN E. *World Cattle.* Norman, Okla.: University of Oklahoma Press, 1976.

SCOTT, WALTER O., and ALDRICH, SAMUEL R. *Modern Soybean Production.* Cincinnati, Ohio: The Farm Quarterly, 1970.

SHAUB, BENJAMIN M. *Treasures from the Earth: The World of Rocks and Minerals.* New York: Crown Publishers, 1975.

SOBEL, LESTER A., ed. *World Food Crisis.* New York: Facts on File, 1975.

STREYFFERT, THORSTEN. *World Timber: Trends and Prospects.* Stockholm: Almquist & Wiksell, 1958.

SUTULOV, ALEXANDER. *Minerals in World Affairs.* Salt Lake City, Utah: University of Utah Press, 1972.

SYMONS, LESLIE. *Agricultural Geography.* New York: Frederick A. Praeger, 1967.

WARREN, KENNETH. *Mineral Resources.* New York: John Wiley & Sons, 1973.

WARTENBURG, CARLA M. *Von Thünen's Isolated State.* (Translated from Johann Heinrich von Thunen, *Der Isolierte Staat.*) New York: Pergamon Press, 1966.

11
Economic Geography: Secondary and Tertiary Economic Activity

MANUFACTURING
PRINCIPLES OF INDUSTRIAL LOCATION
ORIGIN OF MANUFACTURING
LIGHT INDUSTRY
HEAVY INDUSTRY
HIGH TECHNOLOGY INDUSTRY
TERTIARY ECONOMIC ACTIVITY
PRINCIPLES OF RETAIL LOCATION
RETAILING

Sparrows Point steel mill, Baltimore, Maryland. (Photo courtesy of Bethlehem Steel Corporation.)

Most of the accumulated knowledge in economic geography concerns production. The focus of Chapter 10 was on primary production, where human energy, time, and cost are concentrated on growing products or taking resources directly from the earth. Here, the emphasis is on secondary and tertiary production. Secondary production includes the economic activities involved in converting products from the primary production phase into intermediary or finished goods, usually through some type of *manufacturing*. Tertiary economic activities differ from primary and secondary production activities in that no material item is produced. Work in the tertiary economic stage involves control, movement, sales, and use of the goods produced during the primary and secondary stages.

The *service industries* are also part of the tertiary sector of the economy. Service activites include government, finance (banking, real estate, insurance), the professions (teaching, medicine, law), utilities, recreation, motels and hotels, and retail and wholesale trade. Tertiary activities, then, include all the services for which people are willing to pay. The emphasis in this chapter will be on retail trade. Retailing, or providing goods for customers, is a tertiary economic activity. Millions of items are sold through thousands of retail outlets every day. The focus here is on the basic human needs of food, clothing, and shelter.

MANUFACTURING

Five essential features define manufacturing:

1 The process must *change the form of goods*.
2 The process must be accomplished through *division of labor*, that is, assignment of workers to particular jobs.

3. The operations must be carried on in *factories*, not in homes or fields. Thus, farming, handicrafts, and construction are excluded.
4. The factory must turn out a *uniform product*.
5. *Machinery* driven by some form of *power* must be used in the process.

These criteria define the modern concept of manufacturing. Goods are produced by processing or combining materials through an assembly-line operation in a factory that uses power-driven machines from which uniform products evolve. This modern operation is a product of historical development.

Another approach to the study of manufacturing is to classify industries into categories based on (1) the type of factory, (2) the raw materials used, and (3) the goods produced. Industries can be categorized according to whether they are light or heavy, or require high technology. In *light industry*, for example, factories use comparatively light-weight machinery. A light industry might also be one that requires only small amounts of raw materials, as in textile manufacturing and food processing. *Heavy industry*, on the other hand, uses large, heavy machines that consume huge amounts of raw materials. Processing metals, especially iron and steel, and manufacturing large vehicles, such as cars, trucks, buses, and trains, are examples of heavy industry. *High technology* industries can be either light or heavy, but have an added dimension that requires specialized knowledge and skills. The manufacture of calculators and computers is a relatively light industry, for example, but the design of their microchips and circuit boards requires special knowledge. The manufacture of aircraft and space shuttles is a heavy industry, but also requires specialized electronic skills as well as many others. A large part of the costs in high technology industries goes into research.

PRINCIPLES OF INDUSTRIAL LOCATION

The focus of secondary production is the *factory*. It is the place that receives the raw materials, the place where the raw materials are changed into more useful commodities, and the place from which the finished products are shipped to the customers. Factories, therefore, are links between the raw materials and the markets (customers). The geography of manufacturing concerns the locations of factories. They do not appear on the landscape randomly or haphazardly; certain principles or *location factors* influence the decision as to where a new factory is built.

The most important location factors are the source areas for raw materials and locations of the markets. The raw materials and markets are usually separated by some distance, and some factories may have numerous sources of raw material and/or numerous markets. Thus, the transportation costs of raw materials or finished products or both must be considered when deciding where to construct a factory. Other things can also influence the location of a factory; for example, a source of labor is important. Factory location might be influenced not only by an available source of labor, but by whether the labor is cheap or expensive. Factories also need energy supplies, and some need much more fuel or power than others. Local terrain is a consideration in factory location decisions, as are state and local taxes. In some cases even city zoning laws are important (see Chapter 13). Some states try to attract industry with tax incentives and other breaks. Because research is so important to some industries, they try to locate near universities. Financial capital is important, so some factories are located according to where the owners can obtain loans. Finally, some factories are located where they are simply because the founder lived at that location. Location factors thus include all the influences on the decision to place a new factory.

The four essential requirements for a factory to operate include *raw materials, energy supply, labor supply,* and *market*. Most places do not offer the best of these four elements, however, so industries must choose among various locations that each provide some of the requirements. As a general rule, the best location for a plant is at the point where transportation costs for raw materials and finished products are minimal. Although owners might deviate from this location to take advantage of a site with low labor costs or one with low energy costs, transportation costs are usually the prime locational factor, and the orientation of an industry determines which of the transport costs is most critical.

From the four factory requirements and the orientation of factories, one can derive general patterns of industrial location. For example, in a *resource oriented* factory, the cost of transporting raw materials is the dominant control, and the factory would locate as close as possible to the source of raw materials. Resource-oriented factories include those involved in the initial cleaning, sorting, and separating of mineral ores, petroleum, lumber products, and food crops.

Copper ore, for example, produces only about two tons of concentrate for every 100 tons of mined ore. The concentrating mills are located as near the mines as possible, because it does not make sense to transport large amounts of waste material.

The second type of factory location takes into account factories that are _market oriented_. It costs more to transport finished products than raw materials. If no weight is lost in the manufacturing process, the factory will locate near the market. Markets always have a strong pull on the location of factories. Market oriented factories are large commercial bakeries, breweries, soft drink bottling plants, and any other factory that sets a premium on location near its customers over other factors.

A _power oriented_ factory will be located near a dam, coal field, oil field, or other place that offers an abundance of energy. An example of a power oriented industry is the processing of aluminum. To produce one ton of aluminum requires about 25,000 kilowatt-hours of electricity, enough to service an eight-room house for ten years. Because of the need for huge amounts of electricity, the first aluminum mill in the United States was located at Niagara Falls (Figure 11–1). It was cheaper to transport the bauxite (aluminum ore) to the source of power (the Falls) than to transport the power. More recent aluminum mills are located in the regions of the Pacific Northwest, the Southeast, and the Gulf Coast, where large amounts of power are available from hydroelectric dams or natural gas fields.

The fourth type of factory is _labor oriented_. The need for skilled labor can be a strong pull on the factory location decision, but sometimes the pull is for cheap labor rather than skilled labor. Many manufacturers make parts in the United States, but maintain assembly plants in Mexico or some other country to take advantage of the cheaper labor supplies in those countries. The parts are sent to the Mexican plants where they are assembled into finished products, which are shipped back to the the United States to be sold. The decreased cost of labor offsets the extra shipping charges. The familiar phrase, "Made in the U.S.A.," has been replaced on many products with "Assembled in Mexico" or "Assembled in Taiwan." This kind of manufacturing usually involves

FIGURE 11–1 Niagara Falls.

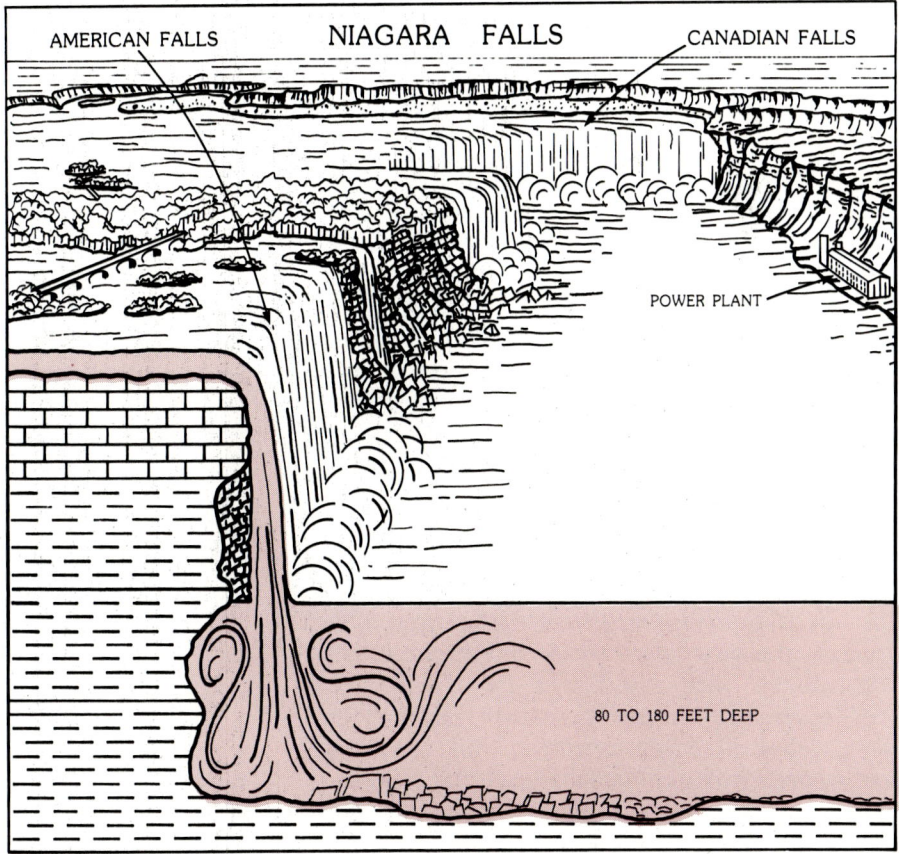

small, lightweight items with a high specific value, such as electronic equipment.

Agglomeration oriented industries need to cluster together. Some industries agglomerate into particular cities and regions because they can help each other; for example, a supply of specialized labor builds up when more than one factory locates in one place. The factories can use each other's transportation facilities and other support services. Many of the factories may use the same suppliers and even the same markets. Almost all big industrial plants spawn a group of smaller plants that do business with only the main plant. Probably the best example of an agglomeration oriented industry is automobile manufacturing. Plants that specialize in glass, rubber, and plastics usually locate close to the large automobile plants, and the smaller factories make parts the larger plants need.

ORIGIN OF MANUFACTURING

Manufacturing began as an auxiliary occupation. Farmers and shopkeepers used their spare time to make handcrafted items such as brooms or knives to sell or trade to their neighbors and friends. Everything that was made was an individually handcrafted item. Manufacturing was done by hand in the home to meet local needs. It took many centuries for specialists to evolve who obtained their livelihood from the manufacture and sale of uniform, machine-made, products. The most dramatic changes began to occur in Europe near the end of the Middle Ages, which historians date between 500 and 1450 A.D.

The first change in manufacturing occurred with the concept of *specialization*. Specialization appeared when local communities and small regions became known for particular products. For example, farm products such as cheese and wine took on regional flavors. People exchanged goods produced in one region for goods from other areas. The exchanges first took place at regional fairs and markets, but eventually direct trade began among regions. Thus, local product specialization led to trade, which led to further specialization in the work itself. To promote the industry of a given place and to protect the specialized workers, local associations called *craft guilds* were established. The guilds eventually began to regulate wages, fix prices, determine work conditions, and inspect quality of workmanship. The guilds became strong locally and finally came to hold monopolies on the products of particular regions.

The craft guilds gave way slowly to *livery companies,* which were responsible for developing the business of manufacturing into a capitalist system. The livery companies were not as provincial as the guilds. Their traders secured the raw materials from one or various regions and marketed the finished products in yet other places. They began to demand more and more control over the manufacturing process. They discovered they could control manufacturing most efficiently by putting a number of workers in one building and subdividing the work among them. Assembling workers in one place and *division of labor* among them led inevitably to the factory system of production. These ideas were important steps on the road to industrialization.

After the Middle Ages, trade rapidly increased. The Crusades had just ended, and those travels allowed the people of northwest Europe to glimpse products from other lands, especially the Middle East. The Age of Exploration began as a search for new raw materials and new markets. Because it was an island and dependent on shipping, England became the world's leader in exploration, colonization, and trade. The creation of a larger resource base and large market allowed a greater division of labor in England than in other European countries. People with special skills or training began to devote full time to their callings in exchange for money they could use to purchase their needs. The increasing amounts of trade and division of labor, then, were the crucial steps that led to the Industrial Revolution.

Industrial Revolution

The turning point in the human endeavor to produce uniform, quality goods in quantity occurred with (1) the *invention of machines,* and (2) the use of *inanimate energy for power.* These two events occurred somewhat simultaneously during the eighteenth century. Simple machines such as the potter's wheel, waterwheel, and windmill had been used since ancient times, but true machines were products of the Industrial Revolution. The revolution had no definite beginning, and has never really ended; however, historians usually date it from about 1750 to 1850, because that is the period of most rapid change.

The first real machines were invented in England for use in the textile industry. For centuries, making garments was tedious, time-consuming work. The fiber had to be cleaned, brushed or combed, and then spun into thread. The thread was woven into cloth, the cloth was dyed, and finally, clothes were sewn together from the cloth. Each step was a slow hand process. Spinning wheels helped relieve some of the tedium in making thread from fiber, but even they were hand operated. During the first half of the eighteenth century, England's population began to increase rapidly. Its trade also took on new significance at about the same time. The demand for textile products and the supply of raw materials from trade led to significant inventions. The machines that were invented not only increased textile production dramatically, they forecast modern industrialization (Table 11–1).

The textile machines were first run by water power, but the invention of the steam engine in 1769 changed the power source to coal. This change was probably the most significant of the era, because it led to a host of other inventions. The search began for sources of fuel and for metals to make both engines and machines. New ways were invented to process metals. Western Europe, especially England, was soon far ahead of the remainder of the world in all facets of industrialization.

LIGHT INDUSTRY

The industrial nations lead the world in all aspects of manufacturing, including light industries. Industrialization began with the light industries, and each country usually goes through that step on its way to further industrial development. Today, nearly every country in the world has some light industry, and the textile industry is the most widespread type of manufacturing. Factories for production of cotton cloth are worldwide. In fact, some of the least-developed nations are world leaders in the production of textiles: India, South Korea, Paraguay, Bangladesh, Burma, Kenya, and the Dominican Republic rank among the world's leading producers of cotton yarn.

Another form of light industry is the slaughter of animals for human consumption. This industry is also found in most countries of the world. Slaughterhouses are local factories, however, because unlike textiles, meat is highly perishable. Cotton yarn can be stored for months and then shipped long distances, but meat must be consumed within a short time or refrigerated. The less-developed countries generally cannot afford refrigeration; thus, meat processing is a continuous operation, performed near the place where the meat is to be consumed. Some less developed countries do export meat products, with the importer paying for transporation and refrigeration. Third World countries that are leading meat producers include Nigeria and Pakistan (beef and veal), Egypt and Turkey (poultry), Zaire and Vietnam (pork), Ethiopia, Sudan, and Haiti (mutton and lamb), and Somalia, Libya, and Mongolia (other fresh meats). Of course, the industrialized nations are by far the world's leading meat producers, but the point is that meat processing is a widespread light industry.

Light industry appears in the less developed parts of the world for a number of reasons. Manufacturing processes in these industries are relatively simple, requiring little skilled labor. The machines are nearly automatic and require little maintenance. Local raw materials and cheap labor are available in almost all cases, and the demand for the products is universal. The major problem comes in purchasing the machines, but because nearly every Third World country trades with a modern industrial nation, long-term arrangements can usually be made to purchase the necessary machinery.

Industries that have become widespread throughout the world have certain things in common: they supply products that have universal demand; they use local raw materials; the manufacturing processes are simple; and automatic machinery can be used, or cheap labor is abundant, or both. Besides textiles and meat processing, other Third World industries are the manufacture of footwear

TABLE 11–1 Eighteenth-century inventions that led to the industrial revolution

Year	Invention	Inventor	Country	Use
1709	Furnace	Darby	England	Burned coal to smelt iron
1732	Spinning Machine	Wyatt	England	Non-hand spinning of cotton
1733	Flying Shuttle	Kay	England	Speeded up weaving
1767	Spinning Jenny	Hargreaves	England	Multiple thread spinning
1769	Water Frame	Arkwright	England	Improved spinning
1769	Steam Engine	Watt (Scottish)	England	Power source
1779	Spinning Mule	Crompton	England	Automatic spinning and winding of thread onto spindle
1784	Furnace	Cort	England	Wrought iron from raw coal
1785	Power Loom	Cartwright	England	Weaving with power
1793	Cotton Gin	Whitney	U.S.A.	Separated cotton fiber from seed

CHAPTER 11 ECONOMIC GEOGRAPHY: SECONDARY AND TERTIARY ECONOMIC ACTIVITY

TABLE 11–2 Number of manufactured products that enter world trade by country, 1980

Fewer Than 50		50–200	200–300	350–500	More Than 500
Afghanistan	Laos	Angola	Algeria	Austria	France
Albania	Lebanon	Argentina	Australia	Brazil	Germany (W)
Bahamas	Lesotho*	Bangladesh	Belgium	Czech.	Japan
Bahrain	Liberia	Bolivia	Bulgaria	Denmark	UK
Barbados	Libya	Burma	Canada	Finland	USA
Belize	Luxembourg	Cameron	Chile	Hungary	USSR
Benin	Malawi	China	Colombia	Italy	
Bhutan*	Maldines	Cyprus	Ecuador	Poland	
Botswana	Mali	Dom. Rep.	Germany (E)	Portugal	
Burundi	Mauritania	Egypt	Greece	Spain	
Cape Verde	Mauritius	El Salvador	India	Sweden	
Cent. Afri. Rep.	Mongolia	Ethiopia	Indonesia	Turkey	
Chad	Namibia	Ghana	Korea (S)	Yugoslavia	
Comoros*	Nauru*	Guatemala	Mexico		
Congo*	Nepal	Iceland	Netherlands		
Costa Rica	Nicaragua	Iran	Norway		
Djiboute*	Niger	Iraq	Peru		
Dominica	Onam*	Ireland	Philippines		
Equatorial Guinea*	Papua N. G.	Israel	Romania		
	Qatar	Ivory Coast	South Africa		
Fiji	Rwonda	Jamaica			
Gabon	Saint Lucia*	Madagascar			
Gambia	Saudi Arabia	Malaysia			
Grenada*	Seychelles*	Malta			
Guinea	Sierra Leone	Morocco			
Guinea Bissau*	Somalia	Mozambique			
Guyana	Surinam	New Zealand			
Haiti	Swaziland	Nigeria			
Honduras	Tonga*	Pakistan			
Jordan	United Arab Emirates	Panama			
Kenya		Paraguay			
Kiribate*	Upper Volta	Senegal			
Komchat	Vanuatu*	Singapore			
Korea (N)	Yemen	Sri Lanka			
Kuwait	Yemen (S)	Sudan			
		Switzerland			
		Syria			
		Tanzania			
		Thailand			
		Trinidad			
		Tunisia			
		Uganda			
		Uruguay			
		Venezuela			
		Vietnam			
		Zaire			
		Zimbabwe			

*Fewer than 10.
Source: *UN Yearbook, 1979/80.*

(sandals, shoes, and boots), brewing and distilling alcoholic drinks, and mixing and bottling soft drinks. These countries are also involved in milling flour and initial preparation of other foodstuffs, and almost every country also makes its own cigarettes and other tobacco products (see Table 11–2).

HEAVY INDUSTRY

The Industrial Revolution moved into full swing with the advent of the iron industry. Iron smelting in factories for commercial use is a *heavy industry* whose roots lie far back in history.

The Iron Age began some time between 4000 and 1500 B.C. The metal was first obtained from meteorites, and discovery of its uses was probably repeated in different places. Because it was rare, its first use was ornamental. The birthplace of true iron smelting was the southern slopes of the Caucasus Mountains between the Black and Caspian Seas (now the state of Georgia in the U.S.S.R.), from which the innovation spread into Anatolia (western Turkey) about 1600 B.C., and into Palestine by 1400 B.C. The seafaring Phoenicians took the idea to the Greeks, who in turn passed it on to the Romans. The Phoenicians also originated the iron industry in early Spain, where the Catalan region led the world in iron making for centuries. By 800 B.C., the concept of making forged iron tools reached England, probably by way of northern France through the Celtic invasion. By the time of the Roman conquest of England (43 A.D.), iron was being used for swords, daggers, knives, awls, shears, sickles, hoes, and other agricultural tools (Figure 11–2).

After ancient times, the first important advance in iron smelting was the Catalan forge developed in northern Spain during the 9th century. The Catalan forge was similar in some ways to the modern blast furnace and was important because it was the first forge with enough capacity to produce iron on a commercial basis. The first true blast furnace evolved

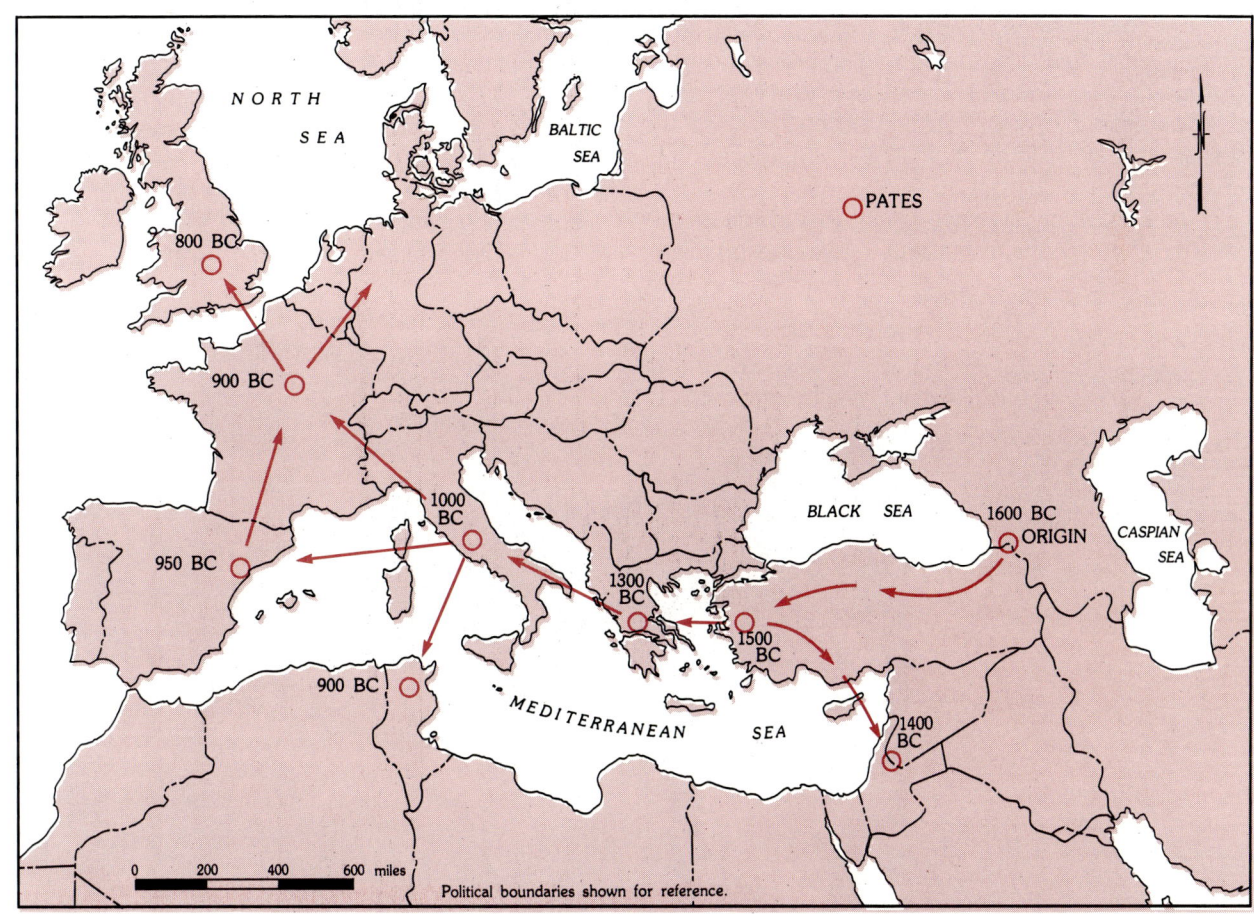

FIGURE 11–2 Diffusion of iron use.

gradually, but finally appeared in eastern Belgium during the last few years of the 14th century. The new invention spread rapidly, and by 1450 many blast furnaces existed, not only in Belgium, but also in Germany and France. The idea reached England by 1496, and soon England became a leader in making cast-iron cannons and bells. The busiest iron center in England was a heavily forested region south of London known as the Weald. Wood made into charcoal fueled the early blast furnaces, and the forests of the Weald were virtually destroyed by the iron makers. What wood they did not use went into shipbuilding.

As England's forests were being depleted, charcoal became steadily more expensive. Consequently, the English iron industry shrank to insignificance, and England went from iron exporting to importing. Raw coal had been tried as a fuel in iron smelting, but during burning it gave off a chemical (sulfur) that nearly ruined the iron. This problem was not solved until the middle of the 18th century, when Abraham Darby, an English Quaker, discovered how to make *coking coal* by preheating raw coal to burn off the sulfur and other impurities. First accomplished in 1709 at the Darby ironworks in Coalbrookdale, the process gave new life to the English iron industry. Output of iron doubled from 1750 to 1775, and doubled again by 1800. Coal production increased at similar rates, and all the charcoal-fueled furnaces disappeared by 1800 (Table 11–3).

The Coalbrookdale region, just west of the present city of Birmingham, became the world's premier iron making area. It became known as the *Black Country*, because smoke and soot covered nearly everything, vegetation died, and the countryside took on a black hue. The world's first iron bridge was erected near Coalbrookdale in 1779. Still in use today, the 100-foot span over the Severn River is a tribute to its builder, Abraham Darby (Figure 11–3).

Location of Heavy Industry

Heavy industries are not found throughout the world in the way that light industries are. The heavy industries are dependent upon iron and steel manufacturing, and that is done in only certain places. The spread of heavy industry is conditioned by a number of factors. The major geographical factor is the location of coal deposits with respect to the location of iron ore deposits, but there are other economic and political influences as well. The nature and number of its people, its overall economy, its political system, and the degree of ocean commerce all affect a country's rate of entry into the field of heavy industry. Most of continental Europe's industrial regions developed later than those in England, and many developed even after heavy manufacturing in the United States had become well established.

Europe. Belgium and France were the first countries in Europe to become industrially developed. The people in Belgium had developed iron making techniques along with the British, and their seaboard location allowed ocean commerce. Also, the rivers of

FIGURE 11–3 The first iron bridge, Coalbrookdale, West Midlands, England.

HEAVY INDUSTRY

TABLE 11–3 Nineteenth-century inventions related to the iron and steel industries

Date	Invention	Inventor	Country	Use
1831	T-Rail	Stevens	USA	First all-iron rail for railroads
1839	Babbitt Metal	Babbitt	USA	Reduces friction in bearings
1856	Steel	Bessemer	England	First blast-furnace production of steel
1861	Furnace	Siemans (German)	England	First open-hearth making of steel
1865	Chromium Steel	Bour	USA	Very strong steel
1866	Reversing Mill	Romsbottom	England	Basis for iron rolling mills
1873	Barbed Wire	Glidden	USA	Agriculture
1884	Manganese Steel	Hadfield	England	Strengthens steel
1891	Four-High Mill	Potter	USA	For rolling armor-plate
1891	Steel Alloy	Harvey	USA	Increased flexibility of steel

Belgium allowed access to inland resources, of which coal was plentiful and of excellent quality for making steel. Belgium's steel industry dates from shortly after that in England, and Belgium began to specialize in iron and steel products. France had similar advantages to Belgium in ocean commerce, river access to the interior, and deposits of iron ore, but the French did not have the well-located, high quality coal. France overcame the early problems, however, and has become a world leader in production of iron and steel. Based on their steel production, both Belgium and France are highly industrialized nations. (Table 11–4 lists the world's top iron and steel producers.)

Germany, Italy, and Austria, until the 1860s, were each made up of a collection of ministates. All the ingredients for manufacturing—regional and world trade, regional division of labor, and regional variations in resources—were missing. Industrial development in these countries was retarded by political handicaps. After these ministates had developed into three nation states, industrial development occurred rapidly. Germany, with a disciplined and

TABLE 11–4 World's ten top iron and steel producers

Country	1970	1975	1980
Pig iron for making steel:			
1. USSR	75,649	93,795	111,000
2. Japan	65,736	84,870	82,831
3. USA	79,861	69,979	76,419
4. China	22,000	32,000	36,730
5. West Germany	31,119	28,265	33,483
6. France	17,476	16,071	17,724
7. UK	15,839	11,265	12,432
8. Brazil	3,298	7,053	11,594
9. Italy	7,579	11,051	11,043
10. Belgium	10,718	9,068	10,776
			(World Total = 519,501)
Crude steel ingots:			
1. USSR	108,736	141,344	149,099
2. USA	119,309	105,817	123,695
3. Japan	91,884	101,269	110,618
4. West Germany	44,315	39,746	45,495
5. China	18,000	29,000	34,480
6. Italy	16,998	21,568	24,023
7. France	23,319	21,078	23,006
8. UK	27,720	19,574	21,068
9. Poland	11,276	14,017	18,845
10. Canada	11,024	12,808	15,855
			(World Total = 720,519)

Source: *U.N. Statistical Yearbook, 1979/80.*

CHAPTER 11 ECONOMIC GEOGRAPHY: SECONDARY AND TERTIARY ECONOMIC ACTIVITY

highly competent people, eventually became an industrial giant. Heavy industry in Europe, then, spread from England eastward into Belgium and France, and eventually on into Germany and Italy.

Most of Germany's iron and steel facilities today are located in the lower Rhine district known as the Ruhr. The area became important for steel production because of its high-grade *bituminous* coal. The Ruhr industrial region, a triangular area about 35 miles wide and 60 miles long, is crisscrossed with a maze of canals, railroads, and navigable rivers for moving raw materials and finished products cheaply. The steel industry spawned hundreds of other industries, and today the region is one of the most heavily industrialized in the world. Major cities are Essen, Dusseldorf, and Cologne, but the entire region is a vast metropolitan area, home to millions of people who work in the hundreds of factories. Another important heavy industry area of Germany is the Saar district near the Luxembourg and French borders. The Saar is important for iron and steel, but not nearly as industrialized as the Ruhr.

North America At the same time that northwest Europe was becoming industrialized, the world's other great heavy industrial region began to develop. The area of the northeastern United States and southeastern Canada was colonized by Europeans, especially the British. These people brought their standards of production and consumption with them when they came from the old countries. In North America, they found a vast array of high-quality raw materials. Through the adoption of techniques learned in the Industrial Revolution and the invention of new methods, the region eventually far surpassed the Old World in many manufacturing techniques (Table 11–5).

The North American manufacturing belt epitomizes the concept of a large, diverse, heavy industry region. The area produces about 17 percent of the world's pig iron (ingots of nearly pure iron), 20 percent of its steel, and 27 percent of its passenger cars. The region also produces every item that requires manufacturing through heavy industry and, like the Ruhr, provides low-cost water transport on large rivers and the Great Lakes. Raw materials can be moved relatively cheaply; for example, iron ore is moved from the Lake Superior district (see Chapter 10) and from Labrador to the manufacturing centers completely by water. Coal is transported from the Appalachian coal fields by water, and the necessary alloy metals are imported from foreign sources through the St. Lawrence seaway. These materials are combined with local limestones at dozens of steel mills along the lakefronts at Chicago, Detroit, Cleveland, and Buffalo, or on the riverfronts at inland locations such as Pittsburgh. About 90 percent of the steel produced comes from the main manufacturing belt, even though there are steel mills in 35 states. America has more steel making capacity than today's demand requires. Cheaper imported steel has caused many plants to operate well below capacity and oth-

TABLE 11–5 American inventions of the 20th century

Year	Invention	Inventor
1900	Crawler tractor	Holt
1903	Airplane	Wright Brothers
1903	Bottle machine	Ownes
1911	Air conditioning	Carrier
1911	Gyrocompass	Sperry
1913	Electron tube	Langmuir
1913	Radio receiver	Alexanderson and Fessenden
1913	X-ray tube	Coolidge
1922	Radar	Taylor and Young
1925	Circuit breaker	Hilliard
1927	Talking movies	Warner Brothers
1927	Television	Farnsworth
1928	Radio beacon	Donovan
1928	Teletype	Morbrum and Kleinschmidt
1929	Coaxial cable	Espensched
1930	Nylon	Carothers
1934	Launderette	Cantrell
1939	Computer	Aiken et al.
1939	Helicopter	Sikorsky
1947	Transistor	Shockley, Brattain, and Bardeen

ers to close down entirely. The Sparrows Point mill shown at the beginning of the chapter operated at a peak employment of 30,000 in 1959, but had declined to 8,800 workers by 1986.

Asia Other heavy industry areas of the world did not become important until much later than those in Europe and North America. The Japanese economic awakening occurred during the late 19th century, but its rapid industrial expansion did not begin until after 1900. Japan did not have raw materials like those in North America and Europe, but its island location, cheap labor supply, and large market encouraged it to develop anyway. Japan's industry began with textiles, using raw materials produced on the islands. The country moved on to heavy industries, but they developed slowly until raw materials were imported in large quantities. Today, Japan is the world's second leading producer of iron and third leading producer of steel (Table 11.4). Japan's crude steel production increased from about seven million metric tons in 1950 to over 100 million metric tons in 1980, although the country has few iron ore deposits within its national boundaries. Japan relies heavily upon imported raw materials, exported finished products, and its great shipping capabilities.

Japan's industrial regions are near the major port cities, especially Yokohama, Tokyo, and Osaka. The country is so productive that it is often plagued by huge *trade surpluses;* that is, it exports much more than it imports in terms of monetary value. Japan's major trade partner is the United States.

The political climate in the Soviet Union before the Bolshevik Revolution in 1917 and 1918 was not conducive to industrialization. The country, therefore, did not start industrializing until the Bolshevik-led planned economy came into effect around 1920. Industrialization occurred rapidly, however, because vast amounts or raw materials were found, a large home market existed, and the country could copy what was working in other industrialized countries. The Soviet Union did not have to suffer through the "trial and error" stage of industrialization.

Today, the Soviet Union leads the world in production of both iron and steel, surpassing the United States in production of both commodities. The capacity for production is far greater in the United States than in the Soviet Union, but the United States began to rely more heavily on imported steel during the 1970s. Much of that imported steel comes from Japan. The largest concentration of steel mills in the Soviet Union is in the Ukraine, a Soviet state directly north of the Black Sea. The city of Donetsk is the "Pittsburgh" of the Soviet Union, but the region also extends westward through the cities of Rog and Zaporozhe. Other important steel producing locations in the Soviet Union are in and near the cities of Chelyabinsk and Magnitogorsk along the Ural Mountains, and at Novosibirsk in the Kuznetsk Basin.

In the Soviet Union, the state owns all legal economic enterprises. The production and movement of commodities is closely controlled and carefully planned. Fortunately for planners in the Soviet Union, many raw materials lie in close proximity to each other. The location factor helped the country in its drive for industrial expansion by minimizing the cost of transporting heavy raw materials. Also, the Soviet Union is extremely rich in natural resources. Besides iron and steel production, it leads the world in oil production, so it not only has the stuff for heavy industry, it is also self-sufficient in energy. Because the Soviet Union lags behind the United States in producing consumer goods, its heavy industry will probably remain second to the United States for some time, despite its huge steel production.

Other Heavy Industry Areas of the World As we have noted, heavy industry includes the production of iron and steel and depends upon it; thus, access to iron ore and coal is important to develop heavy industry. Political circumstances also play a role in the location of heavy industry. A well-developed iron and steel industry, however, is the initial and most crucial phase for establishing other heavy industries. Many of the developing nations are beginning to concentrate on their iron and steel industries. You can see from Table 11.4 that China and Brazil are among the top ten producers of pig iron, and that China is the fifth-largest steel producer in the world; this suggests that these countries could soon become recognized as industrial nations.

The iron and steel industries in both China and Brazil are relatively new. Brazil's output of pig iron increased three and one-half times during the 1970s, from 3.3. million metric tons in 1970 to 11.6 million metric tons in 1980. China's steel output during the same period nearly doubled. These and other countries, such as India and Australia, are notable for recent increases in iron and steel production, but although production is strong in some areas, there are not vast regions of heavy industry like those in northeastern North America, the Ruhr, and the Ukraine.

HIGH TECHNOLOGY INDUSTRY

The early lead the United States established in the light and then the heavy industries gave this country a technological advantage as well. The key to high technology is research, and the early use of machinery helped free manpower for research. Obviously, it was not that simple—the economy, the educational system, the political system, and many other factors played a part—but factory-trained people did become available. Then, one industry fed upon another as new and better machines were invented. With each step, more people were released from hand labor to become scientists and engineers. The people of the United States became research-minded almost from the nation's beginning. Industrial growth occurred because many elements came together in the same place at the same time: vast amounts of resources, a free market, available capital, an increasing market size, and skillful and inventive people.

Machine Tools

The definition of "high technology" has changed through time. In early America, the use of machines in manufacturing was a technological breakthrough, and constituted the high technology of that time. The most important early inventions, besides those associated with iron and steel production, were the machines that were used to make other machinery. These *machine tools* include all the devices used for changing iron and steel ingots into gears, wheels, rods, wire, and other precisely-shaped metal parts needed to manufacture machinery. Metal-working machines are used to shear, press, and roll the ingots into sheets and plates of solid metal. Other tools are used to grind, drill, stamp, punch, and turn the raw metal. The number of different types of machine tools exceeds 200, and that figure does not include the multitude of recent inventions such as robot welders and computer-guided equipment.

The leading countries in metal fabricating and machine making are those that have well-developed iron and steel industries, but other essential ingredients include the availability of large amounts of investment capital and a skilled and inventive labor force. Most countries do not have the necessary prerequistites to become even marginally involved in machine-tool manufacturing, so only a few countries are involved in the industry, and there is a great deal of variation among them. You can see from Table 11.6 that the United States is among the top five countries in production of all eight types of machine tools listed, and ranks first for half of them. The Soviet Union probably ranks high in all eight categories also, but that country is reluctant to release its production figures. The other leading countries are West Germany and Japan.

Chemicals

In the United States, mass production of automobiles gave a tremendous boost to the oil industry, which led in turn to the *petrochemical industry*. The chemical industry, then, is another example of a high technology industry spinning off from a heavy industry. Besides gasoline and lubricating oils, the petrochemical industries turn out a large variety of products, including ethylene glycol for making antifreeze, ethylene oxide for use in detergents, rubber, and plastics, and other chemicals for making explosives, res-

TABLE 11–6 Major machine tool producers, 1980*

Drilling		Stamping		Grinding		Turning (Lathes)	
1. USA	46,043	1. Spain	8,395	1. USA	107,304	1. China	58,000
2. Japan	43,516	2. E. Germany	5,979	2. W. Germany	41,116	2. Japan	28,429
3. W. Germany	19,934	3. W. Germany	625	3. Denmark	33,694	3. USA	19,666
4. UK	12,871	4. USA	599	4. China	20,000	4. UK	17,615
5. Poland	5,451	5. Japan	482	5. Czech.	14,166	5. Bulgaria	7,634

Milling		Cutting		Pressing		Binding & Drawing	
1. USA	15,480	1. Japan	72,801	1. USA	26,077	1. W. Germany	87,720
2. China	12,000	2. USA	69,495	2. Japan	16.350	2. USA	58,859
3. Japan	9,231	3. W. Germany	33,997	3. W. Germany	12,783	3. UK	30,941
4. W. Germany	8,908	4. UK	10,705	4. UK	4,485	4. Japan	30,369
5. UK	5,146	5. Bulgaria	3,664	5. Denmark	3,240	5. France	3,320

*Data do not include USSR.

Source: *UN Statistical Yearbook 1981.*

ins, textiles, fertilizers, insecticides, cellophane, and brake and transmission fluids.

The use of petroleum-based chemicals led to development of the general chemical industry, which transforms raw materials of all sorts into new materials for a vast array of consumer goods. The raw materials are both *organic*—wood, coal, cotton, and petroleum—and *inorganic*—minerals, sea salts, and atmospheric gases such as nitrogen and neon. Chemical products unheard of only 20 years ago are now part of everyday life in the technically advanced nations. One example is the degree to which polyester has replaced natural fibers in clothing.

The United States is by far the world's leading producer of chemical products. The chemical industries in Europe and Japan are closing the gap, however. As recently as the late 1950s, the United States produced over one-half the world's output of chemicals, but by 1980 only about one-third the world total. The major world producers are the high technology countries, of which eight produce over three-fourths of all chemicals.

Computers

High technology includes the manufacture of computers as well as a multitude of electronic components for all sorts of devices. Super-technology parts are used in airplanes and missile guidance systems, lasers, and satellite communications, as well as in domestic commercial items such as automobiles and washing machines. The hearts of these devices are *microchips,* which are miniature integrated circuits. A chip the size of a small fingernail can contain as many as 256,000 memory functions, and miniaturization continues. Memory chips are made of *silicon,* a nonmetallic chemical element more abundant in nature than any other element except oxygen.

The core area for the high technology electronics industry in the United States is "Silicon Valley," located south of San Francisco between San Jose and Palo Alto (Figure 11–4). The computer and microelectronic industries have grown rapidly, and other centers of production have sprung up, but Silicon

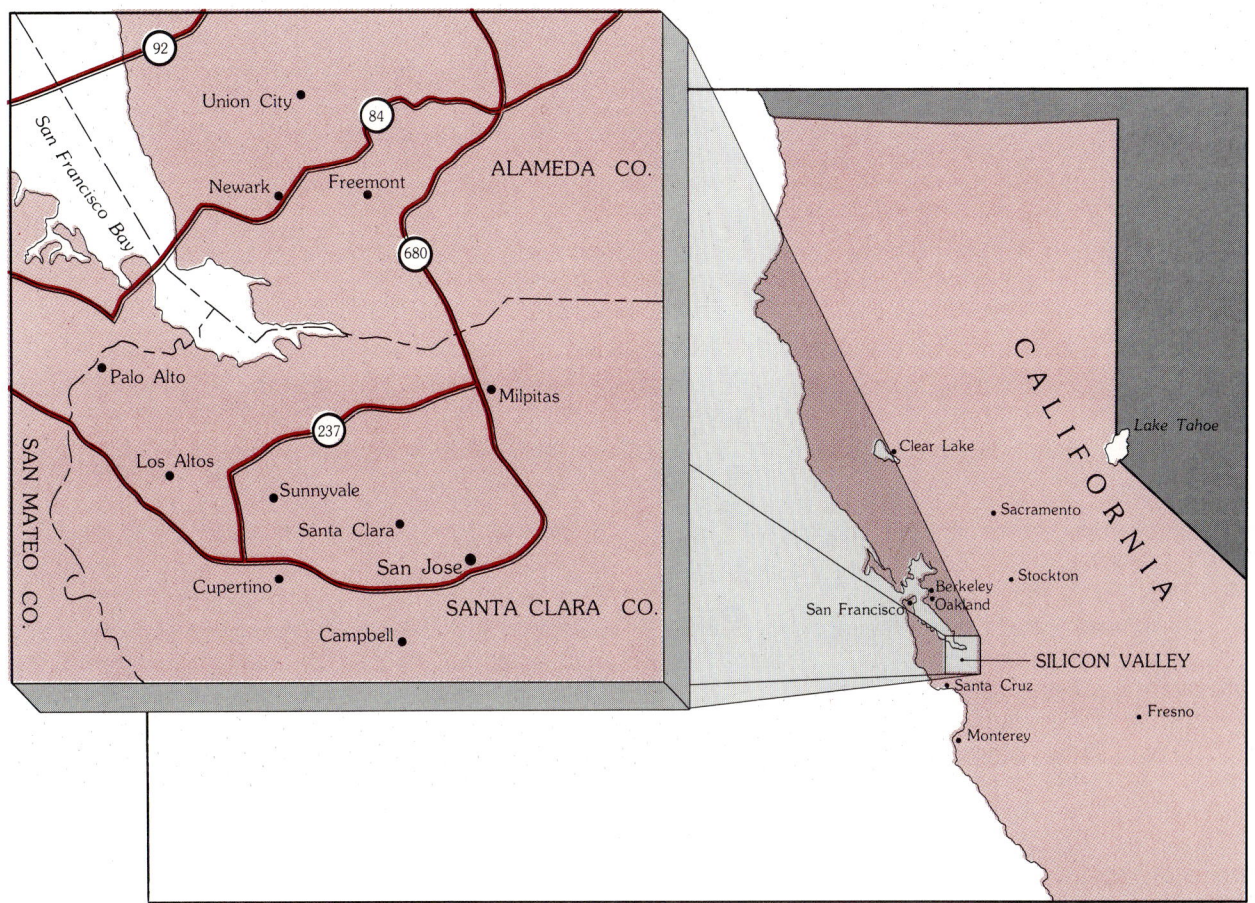

FIGURE 11–4 California's Silicon Valley.

CHAPTER 11 ECONOMIC GEOGRAPHY: SECONDARY AND TERTIARY ECONOMIC ACTIVITY

MULTINATIONAL CORPORATIONS

The concept of seeking profits overseas is an old one. The British, Dutch, and French East India Companies, for example, were established in the seventeenth century. So was the Hudson's Bay Company, founded to earn profits for English businessmen through the exploitation of Canadian resources. Modern multinational corporations, however, are manufacturers rather than trading companies. They are considered to have started with the overseas activites of the Singer Sewing Machine Company in 1867. Multinationals did not become a significant force on the world scene until after World War II, when an era of rapid multinational growth began.

What are multinationals and why do they go overseas? Multinational corporations are companies with operations in more than one country; the larger examples operate in numerous nations. They are profit-seeking and regard overseas operations as profitable ventures that contribute to higher dividends for shareholders in the home country. Overseas operations may be justified for several reasons:

1. **Increased profitability** The "territory" of the firm, and hence markets, volumes, and profits, can be expanded enormously by operating globally. The extension of operations is as natural and useful as corporate expansion from New York into Pennsylvania or from California into Oregon. Territorial expansion may allow manufacturing plants to be closer to markets or raw materials. It is not economically feasible, because of the high cost of transportation, to export soft drinks to China from the U.S. The solution is to locate manufacturing plants in China. The U.S. population is only about a quarter of a billion, out of a world population approaching 5 billion. Overseas operations permit direct access to vastly enlarged markets.
2. **Access to cheap labor** Part of this rationale is the avoidance of trade unions. Taiwan, for example, offers an hospitable environment for corporations because the government suppresses trade unions and labor unrest is extremely unlikely because there is a general lack of human rights.
3. **Avoidance of trade restrictions** Restrictions would reduce sales if finished goods were exported. Japanese car manufacturers have been building

Valley remains the world's leading area for production of super-electronics. Activities ranging from warfare to washing clothes now require machines that are controlled by computers.

The United States has led the world in production of large, general-purpose computers since their common use began about thirty years ago. The world's largest manufacturer of data processing equipment is the International Business Machines (IBM) Corporation. A recent facet to the computer industry is the manufacture of personal computers, designed for small office operations and home use. The leading microcomputer companies are IBM and Apple, but numerous brands share the American market.

The international computer market has been dominated by firms from the United States. National governments in other high-technology countries have responded by becoming involved in their own computer industries to encourage local competition with American imports. The Japanese government directed the merger of six of its major computer companies and backed the group with financial assistance. British and German companies that received assistance from their governments have produced impressive new computer equipment. European computer consortia have also been established. These competitiors have slowed American exports in computer equipment, but American technological advances, extensive marketing, and large, installed

HIGH TECHNOLOGY INDUSTRY

plants in the U.S. to sidestep pressure for harsher restrictions on Japanese imports.

4 **Pollution havens may allow lower production costs** Pollution havens are countries in which pollution controls are lax and production costs can be minimized because companies need not have expensive control devices and safety measures. Industrial accidents in LDCs, like that which caused the deaths of over 2,000 people next to a Union Carbide plant in Bhopal, India, in 1984, have prompted greater international concern about the safety of all industrial operations.

5 **Host countries may subsidize operations** Some host countries are so anxious to promote economic development that they offer loans, grants, tax relief, or other forms of assistance to attract companies. An example was the now-defunct de Lorean sports car company, attracted to Northern Ireland by British government subsidies. Such assistance may not be available in the "home" country and may offer a competitive advantage.

Conflicts between Multinationals and Host Countries Multinationals and their host countries often find themselves at odds over conflicting objectives. In simple terms, multinationals strive to maximize profits by allocating resources as efficiently as possible at the *global* level, which may mean periodically shutting down plants. Nationalistic feelings are often offended by such actions, and local leaders may lose political control as a result of significant economic activities. Some corporations have become embroiled in local or national politics in host countries so as to ensure survival of a political climate receptive to the company's continued presence. But multinationals do employ large numbers of workers, an important factor to all nations with unemployment problems.

The Largest Multinationals In 1980, the ten largest multinationals as measured in foreign sales in billions of dollars were: Exxon ($57); Mobil ($27.4); Texaco ($26); Ford Motor Company ($19.1); Standard Oil of California ($17.5); General Motors ($16.8); IBM ($12.2); IT&T ($11.6); Gulf Oil ($11.1); and Engelhard Minerals ($9.8).

Source: *Forbes,* July 8, 1980.

---

bases have helped the United States maintain the lead in computer sales.

Transportation Equipment

Although the automotive, airplane, and aerospace industries fit the description of heavy industry, the technological expertise they require places them in the high-technology category. Only the United States and the Soviet Union have ongoing programs for space travel. Many less-developed countries produce their own automotive equipment, but production is generally limited to assembly plants because developing nations simply cannot afford the research for designing and producing automobiles or airplanes from scratch. The entire continent of Africa is devoid of automotive, airplane, and aerospace industries that manufacture items from scratch. Some African countries do produce automotive products in assembly plants, but the parts are manufactured in other countries. Generally, the parts, as well as finished products, come from countries that once held political control of the country in which assembly takes place. Most of the cars in Tunisia, for example, are manufactured in France. The major exception to this rule is Japan's entry into the African market with their small, fuel-efficient cars, and Japanese products are seen nearly everywhere in Africa.

Automotive Industry The automotive industry epitomizes the modern manufacturing process. Factories convert a multitude of raw materials into the 15,000 parts needed to make a single car, then the parts are assembled into a finished product. The work of assembling the parts is done through the division of labor in factories. The parts (and finished products) are so uniform that any single part can be replaced without affecting the finished product. Power-driven machines are used in the manufacturing process, and in many of the new factories, much of the actual work is done by robots.

The functional use of the ideas of division of labor, standardized and interchangeable parts, and low-cost, high-volume production we attribute to the Michigan automotive pioneers, Ransom E. Olds and Henry Ford. Their success brought other manufacturers to the Detroit area. The Big Three in American car manufacturing—General Motors, Ford, and Chrysler—have headquarters in or near Detroit. About 45 percent of the auto workers in the U.S. live in the Detroit area, and the Big Three manufacture 90 percent of all American automobiles. Some dispersal of automobile manufacturing plants has occurred in the U.S., but Michigan remains the core region.

Automotive manufacturing originated in the United States, but the industry has changed dramatically since Henry Ford set up the first assembly line. The location of the industry has changed considerably during the last few years. In 1960, all the automobile manufacturers in the world produced about 13 million passenger cars, and firms in the United States accounted for about half that total. By 1980, the total number of cars produced had risen to over 31 million, but U.S. companies made only about 25 percent of that total. During the twenty-year period, Japan jumped from a lesser producer to the world's second leading manufacturer. The small, fuel-efficient Japanese cars became popular in the United States, especially after the 1972 Arab oil embargo that triggered higher fuel costs. Japanese exports to the United States accounted for much of that country's production increase, but Japan also sells to many other countries. On the other hand, the British automobile industry declined significantly during the twenty years. British trade names such as MG, Jaguar, and Triumph have been displaced on the American market by names such as Toyota, Honda, Suzuki, Nissan, and Isuzu. Other international trends include the significant increases in car manufacturing in Brazil, Spain, and the Soviet Union. Germany, France, and Italy have also increased their automotive production, but because they have not tapped the huge American market in the same way as the Japanese, their production has not increased as dramatically (Table 11–7).

Airplane Industry A higher order of technology is required for the airplane industry than for automobile manufacturing, because airplanes are technically more complicated than cars. Scientists and engineers, therefore, make up a larger proportion of the airplane industry's workforce than that of the automotive industry. Proportionately more money goes into research for making airplanes than for automotive vehicles. Only the most technically advanced countries can produce aircraft; ironically, however, Japan and West Germany, two of the most technically advanced nations, produce very few aircraft. Airplane manufacturing was restricted in both countries by the conditions of surrender after World War II. On the other hand, the Soviet Union, which lags in many technical areas, is the world's leading producer of military aircraft. Politics obviously plays a role in the aircraft industry.

TABLE 11–7 Leading countries in production of passenger cars

		Production (Thousands)	
Country	1980	1960	% Change
1. USA	8,434	6,675	+26.4
2. Japan	6,176	165	+3,643.0
3. W. Germany	3,943	2,830	+39.3
4. France	3,730	1,136	+228.4
5. Italy	1,481	596	+148.5
6. USSR	1,314	158	+852.2
7. Spain	1,071	*	—
8. Canada	988	326	+203.1
9. UK	897	1,353	−33.7
10. Brazil	568	*	—

*Data not available.
Source: *U.N. Yearbooks 1960 & 1980.*

In the United States, the federal government is the single largest customer of the aircraft industries, so the industry is affected by yearly changes in the military budget. Just as in Japan and the Soviet Union, politics is the guiding force. Civilian aircraft production in the United States, however, is the uncontested world's leader. Companies such as Boeing, Lockheed, and McDonnell-Douglas provide aircraft for most of the world's airlines. Annual sales average between 10 and 15 billion dollars, with the largest purchases coming from the United Kingdom, Canada, Japan, France, and West Germany. As in the computer industry, however, European consortia are beginning to challenge the dominance of American aircraft imports into Europe. American companies are meeting the challenge with more advanced technology and by opening new markets in countries such as Brazil, Mexico, India, and Korea.

Seattle, San Diego, Los Angeles, and Wichita are the centers of the U.S. aircraft and aerospace industry. More than half the aerospace workers live in the Pacific Coast region. The combined industries, including both aircraft and missile production, are among the largest in the United States in terms of numbers of employees. Rapid changes occur in an industry that went from Lindbergh's first transatlantic flight in 1927 to Armstrong's first walk on the moon in 1969 in only 42 years. Research is a vital part of the industry, because only the companies that keep pace with rapid changes will survive.

TERTIARY ECONOMIC ACTIVITY

Tertiary occupations include all the work that humans do for each other for a price or wage. This kind of work forms the "service industry." When somebody pays a neighbor's child to mow the lawn, the child is performing a service for a price. The person who mows the lawn is a production worker in the sense that his ability to work has value. People are willing to pay for a multitude of services, but some services are more critical to a nation's economy than are others.

The professional services of teaching, medicine, and law relate to the people's education, health, and welfare, and are probably the most critical services performed in a country. The service industries also include transportation workers, however, as well as governmental and financial workers. Generally, the services include everything people could do for themselves, but are willing to pay somebody else to do. As a nation progresses from underdeveloped to developed, more and more people enter the service industries. In an underdeveloped society, for example, people build their own homes, cut their own hair, and generally do all the things that people in more highly developed countries pay to have done for them. The spatial distribution of the demand for services is dictated by purchasing power, productivity level, and even culture.

Service industries tend to concentrate in urban areas because people who live in or visit cities need many types of services. Taxicab drivers, police officers, hotel workers, gas station attendants, grocery workers, retail sales clerks, and druggists, as well as many others, all perform useful services. The ratio of service workers to production workers varies from city to city depending on the cities' major functions; for example, resort cities such as Phoenix and Miami have a greater proportion of service workers among their populations than do industrial cities such as Houston and Cleveland. All cities worldwide provide goods and services for smaller towns and the surrounding rural areas, putting service jobs among the world's leading occupations.

PRINCIPLES OF RETAIL LOCATION

Walter Christaller, in the 1930s, developed one of the first geographical theories on the location of retailing. The most important ideas from his original model are the concepts of *threshold* and *range*. Christaller defined "threshold" as the minimum level of demand needed to sustain a particular good or service. Demand is expressed in terms of the number of people who live in the market area. The "range" of goods and services is a function of the distance people will travel to purchase them. A refrigerator has a greater range than does a carton of milk, because people will travel much farther to purchase a refrigerator than they will to purchase milk. All retail goods and services can be assigned an *order* that indicates its range. Low-order goods are those that are low priced and bought frequently; high-order goods are higher priced and purchased less frequently. Using the two concepts of threshold and range, one can determine the size, spacing, and number of retail outlets needed to satisfy an area's demand (Figure 13–15).

In rural areas where the population is evenly distributed, as in intensive farming regions, a series of small towns develop. The towns tend to be spaced at equal distances from one another, and retail stores in these towns carry only low-order goods. Superimposed upon the network of small towns is a network of larger towns, also spaced equally distant from one another but farther apart than the small towns. The stores in the larger towns carry everything those in the smaller towns carry, plus numerous higher-order goods. The trade area, and consequently the threshold, for the higher-order goods is larger than that for the lower-order goods, because the larger towns are farther apart than the smaller ones. The hierarchy of towns continues to the next larger places that are farther apart and carry yet higher-order goods. At the top of the hierarchy are the largest cities in the region, located approximately equal distances apart, that carry the region's greatest variety of goods and services. Christaller called the towns and cities *central places,* and his theory is referred to as the "Central Place Model."

The central place concept can apply to the arrangement of retail outlets in a city as well as those in rural areas. Small neighborhood grocery stores sell only a few items, but are located only a couple of blocks apart. Larger groceries are farther apart, and carry a much larger inventory of goods. Small shopping centers are next in the hierarchy, and then the large shopping centers. Retail outlets are farther apart at each level, and they offer more goods than outlets in the previous level. Cities usually have only one "downtown" shopping area, but even there, types of shopping outlets are located according to the distances between them and the number of goods and services each offers. Thus, threshold and range factors are considerations in the initial decision as to where to locate a new retail store.

Besides threshold and range, many other factors enter into the geography of retailing; for example, interstore relationships, sales methods, corporate policy, local preferences in brands of goods, parking, and location of major streets and highways are influential in determining the location of a retail store. Some stores cluster naturally, while others operate better when separated. In spite of all the influences on the location of shopping areas, they usually co-vary most closely with population density. The second most important factor is the location of the downtown, followed closely by the location of major highways. Thus, the important considerations in the location of a city's major shopping areas are population, competition, and access.

RETAILING

Retailing is defined as the sale of goods or articles individually or in small quantities directly to the consumer, as opposed to *wholesaling,* which involves selling relatively large quantities of goods, especially to retailers.

Grocery Stores

Food is the most common retail purchase, so there are more grocery stores and restaurants than any other type of retail outlet. Food stores account for slightly over one-quarter of all retail sales in the United States, but have become fewer and larger over the last few years. There were 446,350 grocery stores in 1940, but by 1980, the number was down to fewer than 150,000. The selling area of these stores totaled about 10,000 acres; stretched into a single aisle, that area would reach from New York to Los Angeles and back to Pittsburgh. Table 11–8 ranks the ten largest retail grocery chains in the United States in terms of annual sales.

Besides its own vast market, the United States is also the largest food exporter in the world. About one-sixth of the world's agricultural exports are shipped from this country. The U.S. exports crops from one out of every three acres of farmland to other nations, including more than half the production of rice, wheat, soybeans, and cattle hides; more than one-third the tallow and cotton; and more than one-fourth the tobacco and feed grain.

TABLE 11–8 Ten top grocery chains of the U.S.

Rank	Store Name	Founded	Headquarters
1	Safeway	1915	Oakland, CA
2	Kroger	1883	Cincinnati, OH
3	A & P	1869	Montvale, NJ
4	Winn Dixie	1925	Jacksonville, FL
5	American Stores	1891	Philadelphia, PA
6	Lucky Stores	1931	Dublin, CA
7	Southland (7-Eleven)	1927	Dallas, TX
8	Grand Union	1935	East Paterson, NJ
9	Malone & Hyde	1907	Memphis, TN
10	Jewel	1899	Chicago, IL

RETAILING

TABLE 11–9 Top ten fast food chains in U.S.

Rank	Restaurant	Number of Stores
1	McDonald's	5,500
2	Kentucky Fried Chicken	5,300
3	Burger King	2,155
4	International Dairy Queen	4,800
5	Wendy's	1,410
6	Pizza Hut	3,710
7	Big Boy	1,060
8	Hardee's	1,125
9	Tastee Freez	2,025
10	Arby's	1,000

Source: *Restaurant Business,* March, 1981

Restaurants According to total retail sales, the restaurant industry is the third largest industry in the United States. The 360,000 eating establishments in this country employ about 4 million people, making restaurant work the most common occupation in the United States. Restaurant meals represent about one-third the amount Americans spend for food, of which one-fifth goes to fast-food restaurants.

Restaurant franchises are generally associated with the fast-food eating places; the world's leading fast-food franchise by far is McDonald's. The figures associated with this restaurant chain are staggering, and change daily. For example, the company sells a billion hamburgers every three months, and purchases more eggs, more potatoes, and more fish than any other company in the United States. The products are sold in more than 5,500 restaurants in all 50 states and many foreign countries. (Japan alone has more than 200 McDonald's.) For every fast-food dollar Americans spend, about 20 cents goes to McDonald's.*

The McDonald brothers opened the first McDonald's restaurant on old Highway 66 in San Bernardino, California and established the major concepts that have since become world famous,

*Restaurant Business 14 (March 1, 1979): 25–37.

including the golden arches, cleanliness, and uniformity of products. Ray Kroc purchased the operation in 1954, and turned it into the rapidly growing chain. The first McDonald's franchise restaurant opened in 1955 at Des Plaines, Illinois, near Kroc's hometown of Chicago. Five years later, there were 250 McDonald's restaurants; ten years later, there were ten times that number. Table 11–9 ranks in terms of sales the top ten franchise restaurants in the United States.

Besides the hundreds of American fast-food restaurants in countries around the world, there is a Coca-Cola bottling plant in China and a Pepsi Cola plant in the Soviet Union. The two companies are the leading soft drink producers in the United States, where the annual per capita consumption is about 36 gallons. The most common drink in the United States as late as 1965 was milk, followed by coffee and beer, but today Americans drink more soft drinks than any other beverage. Coke has about 1,500 bottling plants, and it is sold in 135 countries; Pepsi is sold in 126 countries.

Clothing The largest retailers in the world are stores that sell "soft goods," primarily clothing. At least the stores began as outlets for clothing, but most of the largest have expanded their inventories to include everything from television sets to motor oil. Sears, with headquarters in Chicago, is the world's largest retailer. The 900 Sears stores, located in all 50 states, Canada, Mexico, Spain, and South America, sell about $25,000 worth of goods every ten seconds. Sears started as a mail-order business, and catalog sales still account for about 15 percent of the firm's business. Mail-order sales in the United States exceed $25 billion annually, and clothing is the most popular category purchased through the mail. Table 11–10 lists the five largest retailers.

The world's first department store was the *Bon Marché* in Paris, France. French law had forbidden the sale of more than one kind of merchandise in a shop, but the *Bon Marché* owners defied the law during the 1850s and began selling a variety of

TABLE 11–10 Five largest retailers in the U.S.

Rank	Store	Founded	Headquarters
1	Sears	1886	Chicago, IL
2	K-Mart	1897	Troy, MI
3	J. C. Penney	1902	New York, NY
4	F. W. Woolworth	1879	New York, NY
5	Montgomery Ward	1890	Chicago, IL

Source: *Chain Store Age,* June 1980.

TABLE 11–11 Five leading department stores in U.S.

Rank	Store	Location
1	Macy's	New York
2	Hudson's	Detroit
3	Broadway	Los Angeles
4	Bamberger's	New Jersey
5	Marshall Field	Chicago

Source: *Stores,* July 1980.

items. They also encouraged shoppers to browse with no obilgation to buy. These ideas were the foundation for the great department stores of today. By 1900, the *Bon Marché* had become the greatest department store in the world. The large American chain stores eventually surpassed the *Bon Marché,* but the original store is still in Paris occupying the same location where it started. Besides the *Bon Marché* stores in France, there are 27 in the United States, run by the Allied Stores chain. The five leading department stores in the United States, according to annual retail sales, are listed in Table 11–11.

The average regional shopping center in the United States has at least one major department store, and most have two or three, usually located at opposite ends of the mall. A regional shopping center occupies between 30 and 50 acres of land, and relies on a threshold population of 150,000 customers. Companies that operate retail stores employ more than 14 million Americans.

Particular clothing brands sold by the retail stores of America include many famous names. The number-one apparel maker is Levi Strauss & Co. of San Francisco, which makes all types of clothes, but is most famous for the blue jean pants known as "Levis." Levi produces one out of every three pairs of pants sold, for an annual total of about 150 million pairs. Levi operates about 130 manufacturing facilities in the United States, with the heaviest concentration in Texas. The Levi trademark is registered in 150 countries, and foreign manufacturing plants are operating in Australia, Argentina, Belgium, Brazil, Britain, Canada, France, Mexico, Hong Kong, and the Philippines.

The second ranking jeans company in the United States, and number one in women's jeans, is the Blue Bell Co. of Greensboro, North Carolina. The company started out making suspendered bib overalls, but got into the jeans business after World War II with their Wrangler brand. The company has 108 manufacturing plants, located mostly in the cotton-producing states of the Old South; 25 plants are in North Carolina.

The world's largest shirtmaker is the Cluett Co. of New York. Before 1921, men's shirts did not have attached collars, and Cluett made the starched collars. That was all the company made, and at one time they advertised 400 different collar styles. During World War I, American soldiers became used to wearing shirts with the collars attached, so Cluett began making the new type of shirts. The Cluett Company's brand name is Arrow. Then Sanford Cluett, a nephew of the company's founder, invented a way to compress cotton fabric so that it would not shrink after washing. The "Sanforized" Arrow shirts became popular, and Cluett has retained its position as the number-one shirtmaker. Table 11–12 ranks the top clothing manufacturers in the United States.

Fifteen thousand companies make clothing in the United States, but the amount of imported clothing doubled between 1965 and 1975. The average American clothing manufacturing plant has about 100 employees, and about 80 percent of all American clothing workers are women.

Shelter A third basic human need, along with food and clothing, is for shelter. Many large companies provide both the structures themselves and the hundreds of items—appliances, plumbing materials, and fixtures—that go into American homes. Housing companies are not as well known as food and clothing companies, because they are mostly regional

TABLE 11–12 Five largest clothing manufacturers in the U.S.

Company	Most Famous Brand Name	Item with Number-One Rank
Blue Bell	Wrangler	Women's jeans
Cluett	Arrow	Men's shirts
Hart, Schaffner & Marx	Society	Men's clothing
Levi Strauss	Levi's	Apparel and pants
Melville Corp.	Thom McAn	Shoes

Source: American Apparel Manufacturers Association, 1980.

TABLE 11–13 Five largest home construction firms in the U.S.

Rank	Company	Headquarters	Homes built
1	U.S. Homes	Houston, TX	12,000
2	Centex	Dallas, TX	10,000
3	Ryan Homes	Pittsburgh, PA	8,500
4	Lincoln	Dallas, TX	8,000
5	Weyerhaeuser	Tacoma, WA	6,000

Source: *Professional Builder*, July 1981.

rather than national firms. Table 11–13 lists the top five home builders in terms of number of houses built.

You will notice in Table 11–13 that most of the largest builders are located in the areas where the population is growing rapidly. Migration into Texas and the West has created a demand for new housing. One of the largest home builders in the United States does not appear on the table, because the list is for only one year. The Kaufman-Broad Company of Los Angeles, however, has provided homes for over 100,000 American families.

The names of companies that supply materials from which the homes are built are more familiar than the builder's names, as you can see in the list of the largest building supply companies in the United States in Table 11–14. Notice how the most familiar company names are those that have been in business for a long time, and are national companies that provide materials to builders across the United States. Most of the companies manufacture numerous products, but the product listed in the table is the one for which each company is most famous.

Nearly every home in the United States (99.9 percent) has an electric iron, a toaster, and a television set. Other appliances are less common, but not by much; for example, 85 percent of all American homes have a color television set, 75 percent have clothes washers, and 60 percent have clothes dryers. Making the millions of home appliances has kept manufacturers busy, and the sale of these types of items has had a tremendous effect on the American economy. Of the long list of manufacturers, some of the most prominent are Black & Decker, General Electric, Scovill, Singer, Sunbeam, Whirlpool, and Zenith.

CONCLUSION

The locations of secondary activities (manufacturing) are dependent upon a number of factors, of which one of the most important is the cost of transportation. Types of manufacturing include: (1) the light industries, (2) the heavy industries, and (3) the high technology industries. Light industries are found in nearly every country of the world, but heavy industries are located only where an abundant supply of raw materials can be obtained cheaply. The major raw materials for heavy industries are iron ore and coal. The location pattern of high technology industries is similar to that of heavy industries, but more limited. Research is a major component of the high technology industries.

Tertiary activities relate to retail trade—those that provide that basic human needs for food, clothing, and shelter.

TABLE 11–14 Largest building supply companies in the U.S.

Company	Headquarters	Founded	Products
American Standard	New York, NY	1881	Plumbing
Armstong	Lancaster, PA	1860	Flooring
Crane	New York, NY	1855	Plumbing
Johns-Manville	Denver, CO	1858	Asbestos
Jim Walter	Tampa, FL	1946	Building materials
Kohler	Kohler, WI	1873	Plumbing
Lowe's	North Wilkesboro, NC	1946	Lumber
U.S. Gypsum	Chicago, IL	1901	Gypsum
Wickes	San Diego, CA	1854	Lumber

Source: *Professional Builder*, July 1959.

CHAPTER 11 ECONOMIC GEOGRAPHY: SECONDARY AND TERTIARY ECONOMIC ACTIVITY

KEY WORDS

agglomeration-oriented factories
bituminous coal
Catalan forge
central places
chain store
clothing industry
coking coal
computers
division of labor
fast-food
heavy industry
high technology
housing industry
Industrial Revolution
labor-oriented factories
light industry
livery companies
machine tools
manufacturing
market-oriented factories
microchips
order of goods
petrochemicals
power-oriented factories
range of goods
raw materials
resource-oriented factories
retailing
secondary production
service industries
silicon
Silicon Valley
tertiary production
threshold of goods
trade surpluses
uniform product
wholesaling

REFERENCES

ALEXANDER, JOHN W. *Economic Geography.* Englewood Cliffs, N.J.: Prentice-Hall, 1963.

ALEXANDERSSON, GEORGE. *Geography of Manufacturing.* Englewood Cliffs, N.J.: Prentice-Hall, 1967.

BERRY, BRIAN J. L. and GARRISON, WILLIAM L. "Functional Bases of the Central Place Hierarchy," *Economic Geography* 34 (1958):145–54.

BERRY, BRIAN J. L., and GARRISON, WILLIAM L. "A Note on Central Place Theory and the Range of a Good," *Economic Geography* 34 (1958):304–11.

BERRY, BRIAN J. L., BARNUM, H. G., and TENNANT, R. J., "Retail Location and Consumer Behavior." *Papers and Proceedings, Regional Science Association,* vol. 4 (1962):65–106.

CHRISTALLER, WALTER. *Central Places in Southern Germany.* Translated by Carlisle Baskin. Englewood Cliffs, N.J.: Prentice-Hall, 1966.

ESTALL, ROBERT C., and BUCHANAN, R. O. *Industrial Activity and Economic Geography,* 3rd ed. London: Hutchinson, 1973.

FAY, C. R. *Great Britain: From Adam Smith to the Present Day,* 5th ed. London: Longman, Green, 1950.

HECOCK, RICHARD D., and ROONEY, JOHN F. "Towards a Geography of Consumption." *Professional Geographer* 20 (1968):392–95.

HOOVER, E. M. *The Location of Economic Activity.* New York: McGraw-Hill, 1948.

ISARD, WALTER. "Some Locational Factors in the Iron and Steel Industry Since the Early 19th Century." *Journal of Political Economy* 56 (1948):203–17.

ISARD, WALTER, and SCHOOLER, E. W. *Location Factors in the Petrochemical Industry.* Washington, D.C.: Office of Technical Services, Area Development Division, U.S. Department of Commerce, 1955.

JOHNSON, PETER S. *The Economics of Invention and Innovation.* London: Martin Robertson, 1975.

KARASKA, GORDON J., and BRAMHALL, D. F. *Locational Analysis for Manufacturing: A Selection of Readings.* Cambridge, Mass.: MIT Press, 1969.

McCARTY, HAROLD H., and LINDBERG, JAMES B. *A Preface to Economic Geography.* Englewood Cliffs, N.J.: Prentice-Hall, 1966.

MOSKOWITZ, MILTON, KATZ, MICHAEL, and LEVERING, ROBERT, eds. *Everybody's Business: An Almanac.* San Francisco: Harper & Row, 1980.

PRED, ALLEN. "Some Locational Relationships Between Industrial Inventions, Industrial Innovations, and Urban Growth." *East Lakes Geographer* 2 (1966):45–70.

WEBER, ALFRED. *Theory of the Location of Industries.* Chicago: University of Chicago Press, 1909.

12
Rural Settlement Patterns

PRINCIPLES OF SETTLEMENT AND LAND USE
ANCIENT SETTLEMENT PATTERNS
RURAL SETTLEMENT IN THE MIDDLE AGES
MODERN RURAL SETTLEMENT
RANGE AND TOWNSHIP
RURAL SETTLEMENT IN THE UNITED STATES

Rice terraces in Indonesia's Upper Solo River basin. (WFP photo by P. Sutcliffe.)

Observation of the landscape reveals differences between patterns created by nature and those created by humans. We can usually attribute gently curved landform features and jumbled patterns of vegetation to natural phenomena, although there are exceptions to this rule. Some fault lines (cracks in the earth's crust) make straight lines on the earth's surface. Many rocks break along planes (cleavages) that create smooth, flat surfaces. And, various types of landforms appear to be flat and regular, while others have sharp angles and points. Generally, however, straight lines and uniform patterns are associated with human activity.

Rural settlement implies agricultural use of the land, noted for its square corners, straight lines, symmetry, and balance. Farmers prefer to build their homes and divide their fields so as to give themselves the best advantage for working and protecting their individual plots of ground. Long, straight rows for crops require less wasted energy in turning draft animals or machines than do short rows. Many disruptions, however, keep farmers from using the land in the most ideal way. Physical conditions, such as landforms, rivers, soil conditions, and climate, affect the location of crops, fields, and buildings. Other factors, such as economic and political conditions as well as a region's history, also affect patterns of land use, causing variation in the types of rural settlement patterns from place to place.

In the geography of rural settlement, some landscape patterns have developed over centuries of continuous human occupation, while others are comparatively recent. Land tenure, which means "who owns the land," also affects its use, and use of the land creates patterns. We will examine these and other land-use factors, such as population density (Chapter

2), social processes (Chapter 8), agriculture (Chapter 10), and politics (Chapter 15).

PRINCIPLES OF SETTLEMENT AND LAND USE

The ideal shape for a farm would be a circle, with the farm buildings at the center of the circle. This shape would give the farmer a number of advantages. It would minimize the cost of external fencing, for example, and would allow equal access and minimum distance to all fields on the farm. The farm's perimeter could be protected with equal ease in all directions. Fields could be laid out in pie-shaped wedges, and crops could be rotated in waves, going around the circle from one year to the next. Why, then, do we rarely see circular farms?

The most obvious drawback to circular farms is that groups of them would not fit together without overlaps or void areas between them. Also, road systems to connect circular farms would have to be curved. If the farmstead is in the middle of the farm, the farmer would have to maintain his own road or driveway to the periphery, and a circular fence around the outside would be more difficult to build than a straight-line fence. Also, it is easier to plant, cultivate, and harvest most crops by moving in a straight line, and it would obviously be difficult to divide a circular land area into straight-line fields. Thus, although circular farms may at first seem the best, they are actually impractical.

For row crop farming, long narrow fields would be best, because they would minimize the turns at the ends of rows. Crops, time, and energy are lost every time draft animals or machines have to be turned around; thus, the longer the rows, the better. On the other hand, long, narrow fields would require long, narrow farms. The linear shape creates other types of problems, as well; for example, what would be the best location for the farm buildings on a linear farm, and what would be the least complicated placement of crops on long, narrow land holdings?

Newly settled farm areas are usually laid out with square farms. Square plots have been found to be the most practical from both the standpoint of the farmer's daily activities and the state's need to construct and maintain roads in the area. Most of the United States was laid out in a square land-use pattern, but other newer areas have also used that pattern. For example, the Dutch polders, where new land is claimed from the sea, are laid out in square plots. Where land has been consolidated, as in West Germany, the new regions are constructed with square plots of land. And, in the Brazilian rainforest, where trees are removed so that crops can be grown, the newly cleared land is plotted in squares.

Farmstead Location

Even on square plots of land, farmers must decide where to locate their farm buildings. They try to minimize the distance from farmstead to fields as well as from the buildings to roads and telephone and electric lines. These problems are illustrated in Figure 12–1. In the example, a square mile of land is divided into four farms, each 160 acres in size. In farm A, the farmstead is located in the middle of the plot of land. The distance from the farm buildings to the fields is minimized, but the distance to the public road is a quarter of a mile, and it could be expensive to maintain a driveway that long. And, if the farmer has to pay for access to other services, the buildings' location may not be the best. The farmer would have to weigh the cost of daily journeys to his fields against the cost of access to public services and road maintenance.

The farmstead in example B is located so that the driveway maintenance cost is minimized, but half the farm lies more than one-quarter mile away from the farm buildings. The farmstead in example C is located so that three-fourths of the farm is more than one-quarter mile away from the farm buildings. This example is the least practical from the standpoint of minimizing the daily trip to the fields; however, the location's advantage is that farmsteads could cluster at the crossroad corner.

Clustering is a historical factor brought about by the early settlers' need for protection and for cooperation with work. A small group of farmers had a distinct advantage against marauders, while the lone farmstead was more open to attack. Farm groups could do seasonal work such as harvesting grain much easier and quicker than could the lone farmer. Today, farmers do not need the cluster arrangement for protection or for cooperative work, but they do find social advantages in living close together.

The farmstead location in example D of Figure 12–1 is a compromise between those in examples A and B. The idea is to minimize both the distance from the farmhouse to the fields and the length of the driveway. All four examples in Figure 12–1 appear in the midwestern farm country. Although historical factors are important, even newly settled land does not have haphazard arrangements and locations of farm buildings. Besides distance, the locations of farmsteads are affected by physical features such as groves of trees, drainage, soil characteristics, and so forth. Farm buildings are often located on the

PRINCIPLES OF SETTLEMENT AND LAND USE

FIGURE 12–1 Alternative farmstead locations on square farms.

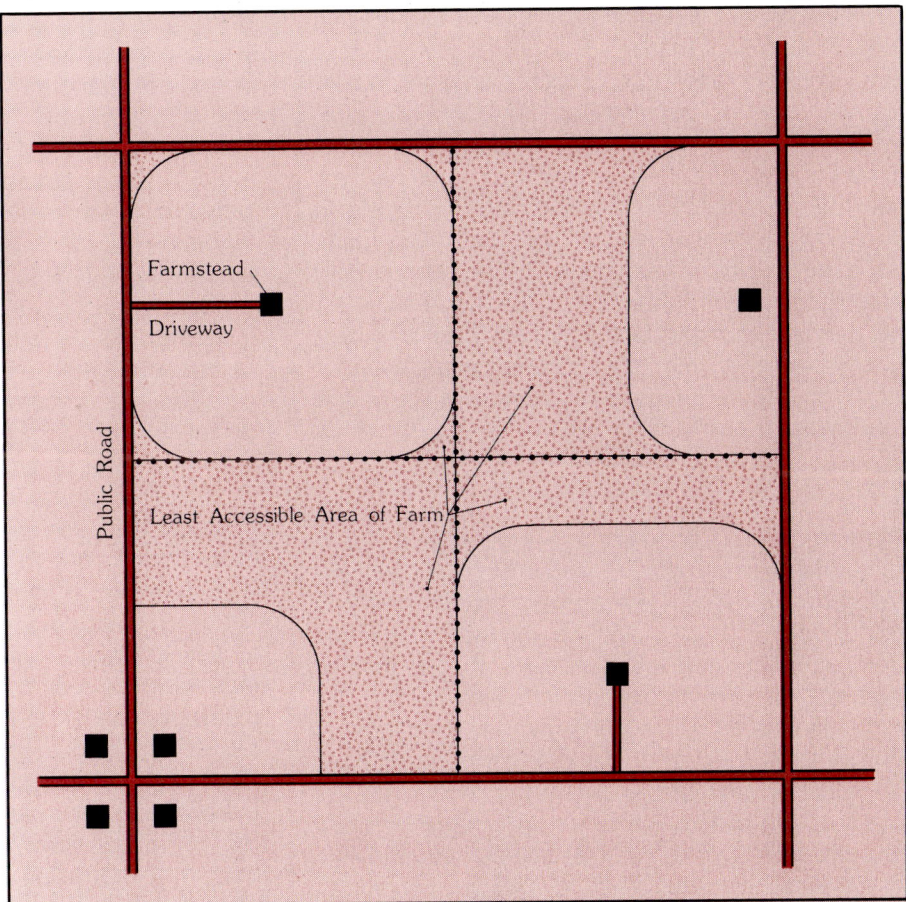

farm's worst land so the best land can be used for farming. Each farmer makes a "location analysis" to determine the best place for the farm house and other buildings.

Location of farm buildings and attention to distances on a farm may appear to be trivial problems; however, movement is costly, on a farm or elsewhere, in terms of both time and fuel. Time and fuel costs increase as distance increases. Farmers also have to pay to transport their products to market. That cost, added to driveway maintenance costs, increases as the length of the driveway increases. Thus, farmers with building locations such as those in examples A and D (Figure 12–1) often build grain storage facilities and livestock loading pens close to the public road, even if their main buildings are some distance from the road.

Another factor to consider with the principles of settlement and land use is the *law of diminishing returns.* In agriculture, each successive hour of work yields a smaller return. A practical farmer stops work at a point on the curve of diminishing returns (Figure 12–2) where work begins to increase more rapidly than yields, resulting in less intense farming at greater distances from the farm house. Because the time consumed in traveling must be added to the cost of producing at the more distant fields, each field of equal size on a farm does not have equal

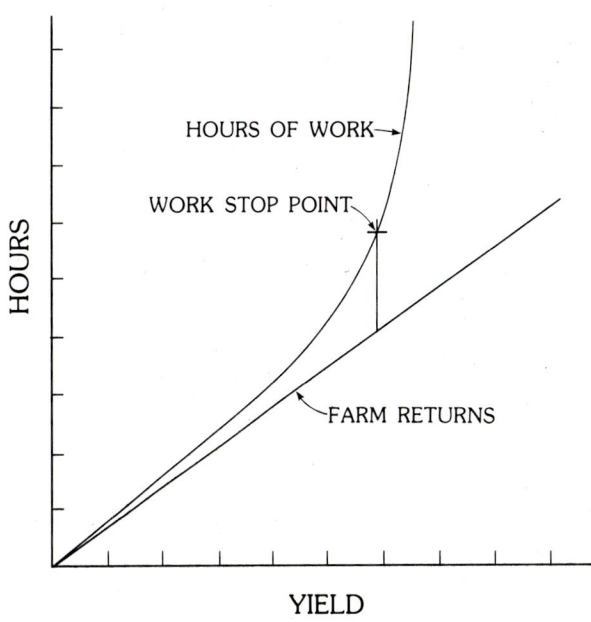

FIGURE 12–2 Curve for law of diminishing returns.

261

production costs. Each farm is in a sense an "isolated state," as in von Thünen's theory that we discussed in Chapter 10, and crop production changes in concentric zones as distance from the farm house increases. Vegetable gardens, feedlots, and other places that require intensive care are located near the farm house. Crops are usually rotated from field to field, but those that require more cultivation (corn, soybeans, cotton) are grown more economically closer to the farm house than those that require less care (wheat and hay). Settlement and land use, then, are influenced by a number of distance factors, each of which affects the resulting patterns we see on the landscape.

Patterns of Settlement

Patterns of rural settlement on a larger scale than the individual farm are also influenced by several factors. We generally describe a settlement pattern merely as *dispersed* or *clustered*, and we will use those terms here, although there are other types of patterns. The problem with the dispersed and clustered designations lies in determining the degree to which a distribution is dispersed or clustered. In other words, how dispersed or how clustered are the phenomena that make up the pattern? One measure geographers use to determine this degree is the *nearest-neighbor* statistic, which indicates whether a pattern is *regular* (Figure 12–3, Example A), *clustered* (Figure 12–3, Example B), or *random* (Figure 12–3, Example C). The magnitude of the nearest-neighbor result indicates to what degree the distribution is clustered or dispersed. A random pattern is neither clustered nor dispersed, but an identifiable pattern where "chance" probably determined locations.

All regular patterns are not identical. The most perfectly regular pattern appears as regular hexagons when the locations are connected by straight lines, as in Example A, Figure 12–3. Clustered patterns also produce variations. In Example D, Figure 12–3, for instance, the pattern is more clustered than dispersed, but because it is stretched into a line, it is called a *linear* pattern. Each type of pattern appears on the rural landscape, and each distribution is influenced by historical and environmental factors.

We find regular, clustered, and random patterns in places that have been occupied for centuries and in those that have been settled recently. The general rule, however, is that more recent settlements adhere to regular patterns, and older settlements tend to be clustered and random. The size of land holdings does not seem to affect the patterns of settlement, because clustered and dispersed arrangements can be found in areas with large farms as well as those areas where holdings are small. Thus, neither the historical dimension nor the size of land holdings tells the entire story behind a particular settlement pattern. Patterns do vary, however, according to what part of the world we are talking about, so we can conclude that customs and traditions play a part in place to place differences in settlement patterns.

Physical Factors and Settlement Patterns

On a global scale, human habitation is limited to places that are not too high, too hot, too cold, too wet, or too dry. Many hardy folks do live under extremely difficult environmental conditions, but most people live where circumstances are less extreme. Agricultural production areas are even more limited than those where people can live. Rural settlement is generally associated with agriculture, so the environmental limits on agriculture also limit settlement.

Two climatic factors that control agricultural production are *temperature* and *precipitation*. They determine where a particular crop can be grown, as to both optimum growth area and limits to growth. Figure 12–4 illustrates these two constraints. The optimum growth area is the place where the greatest yields are achieved under normal conditions. Moving outward from that area, yields decrease and costs of production increase until the physical limits are reached. Beyond those limits, no production occurs.

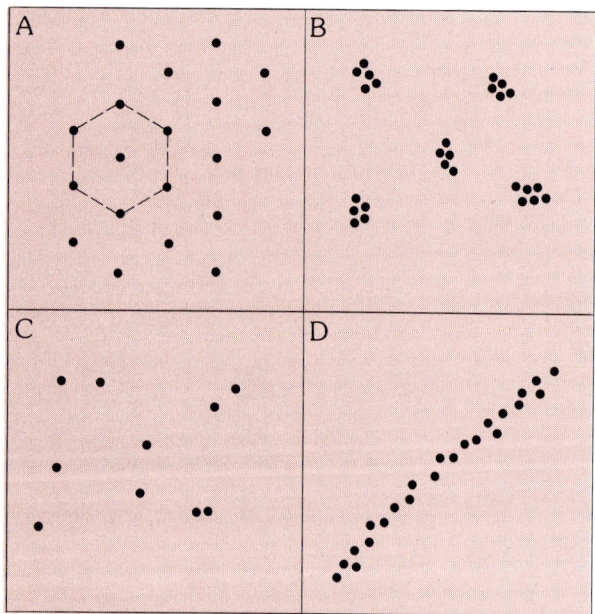

FIGURE 12–3 Rural settlement patterns: (a) regular (hexagonal); (b) clustered; (c) random; (d) linear.

Values for temperature and precipitation both increase upward and to the right of the origin (O) of the graph.

The physical limits to crop production (Figure 12–4) can be changed by human intervention. Irrigation, for example, has moved the "too dry" limit towards the origin of the graph for some crops in some areas. Greenhouses and other shelters are also used to grow crops outside their normal environmental limits. Research has created the development of hybrid strains of wheat, corn, and other crops that has increased their optimum growth areas. Farmers find the optimum region of production through trial and error. They experiment with new hybrids and try new methods of farming to increase production. Obviously, unusual or unpredicted weather conditions account for most crop failures, but they often occur because farmers try to grow certain crops outside their normal environmental limits. The Oklahoma dust bowl of the 1930s, for example, was created largely because farmers were using the wrong crops for the region.

Rural settlement patterns, especially population density, correlate with optimum growth regions. In northern Oklahoma, the early settlers tried to grow corn, as they had in the upper midwest from where they came. Oklahoma is on the fringe of the optimum growth region for corn, and the crops failed for many years. The rural population density was at its greatest in the 1920s. Later, wheat growing replaced corn. Wheat is a less intensive crop that requires fewer people, so the population decreased accordingly. Other regions of the world have experienced the ebb and flow of rural population as certain crops have been tried and found to be unsuitable. In some places, the normal weather conditions have changed over time, causing a change in optimum growth of crops. This in turn affected population density. Rural settlement in many areas, then, is in a state of flux, and the change is partly in response to changes in the physical limits of crop production.

ANCIENT SETTLEMENT PATTERNS

The first farmers probably practiced some form of migratory agriculture. They probably cleared small areas of grass and weeds, grew grain for two or

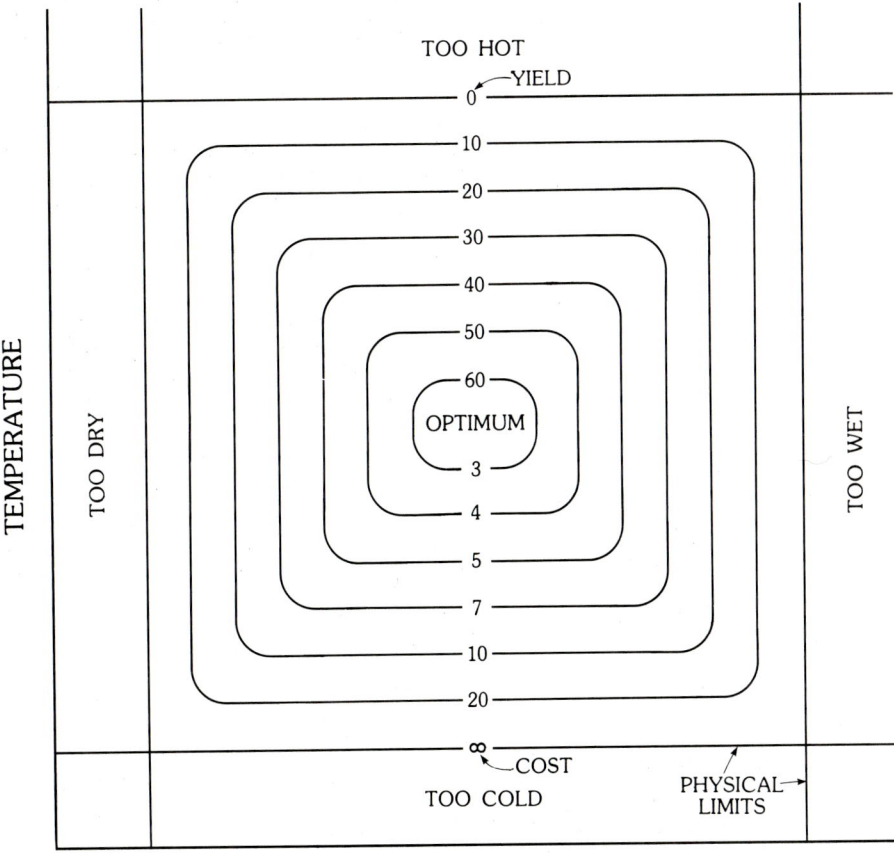

FIGURE 12–4 Climatic limits on agriculture. (From Harold H. McCarty/James B. Lindberg, A PREFACE TO ECONOMIC GEOGRAPHY, © 1966, P. 61. Adapted by permission of Prentice-Hall, Inc., Englewood Cliffs, N.J.)

CHAPTER 12 RURAL SETTLEMENT PATTERNS

three seasons, then moved on to other areas. They certainly knew nothing about soil depletion, except through experience. Shifting agriculture remains as an occupation today (Chapter 10). The first enduring rural settlements came about when folks found that periodic river flooding not only irrigated the crops, but also replenished the soil. Rural settlement began, then, on the floodplains of rivers. The first known settlements were in the Middle East, in what is now Iraq.

In shifting agriculture, land is considered to belong to everyone. The clan or tribe that clears the brush and trees from an area has temporary ownership, but relinquishes their right to it when they leave. As settlements became permanent, however, a system of *land tenure* became necessary. Land tenure refers to ownership of the land, and different ownership systems evolved. *Freehold* tenure refers to individual ownership of particular plots of land. It is common in many areas of the world, and became traditional in the United States. With all nonfreehold types of land tenure, the land is owned by a group rather than by individuals. These include *tribal* tenure, *corporate* tenure, *institutional* tenure, and *government* ownership. The complex laws and customs connected with land tenure have evolved from ancient times.

Freehold land tenure depends on the establishment, acknowledgement, and continued use of boundary lines. Boundaries are necessary to separate the holdings and to define the extent of each plot of ground (Chapter 16). Boundaries often determine the pattern of settlement, as well. Settlement along rivers, for example, often led to linear land holdings. Boundaries of individual farms were put at right angles to the rivers (Figure 12–5). With this arrangement, each farm received the annual replenishment of soils through river-borne sediment. Each farmer could use the river for irrigation, yet all dwellings could be located on the bluffs above the periodically-flooded lowlands. The farmers' dwellings formed lines parallel to the river. The first rural settlement patterns undoubtedly were of this type.

As irrigation techniques improved, farmers began to live away from the rivers. They learned to build canals extending outward from the rivers, and to control the water so they could apply it when needed. These changes in techniques led to changes in settlement. Farmers began to congregate into farm villages for mutual protection. The farm villages

FIGURE 12–5 Linear settlement along a river.

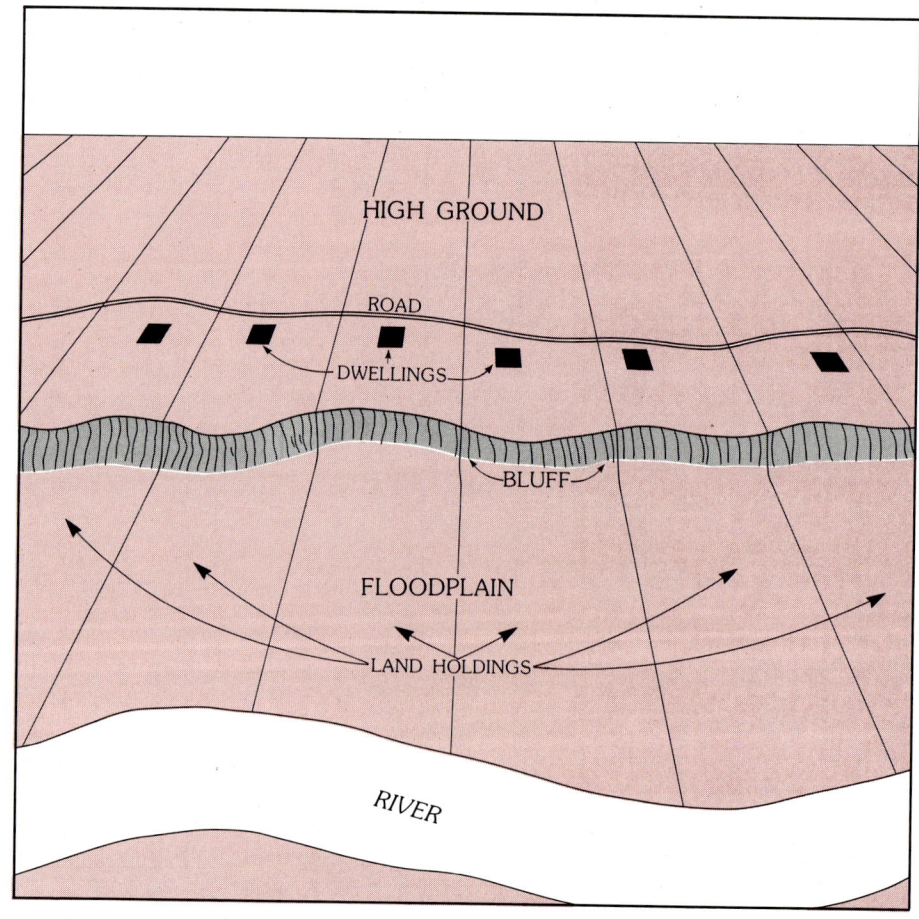

ANCIENT SETTLEMENT PATTERNS

soon became walled towns, and some eventually grew into cities. Living in farm villages, the farmers could not occupy their land holdings. They had to walk to the fields to care for their crops. The protection afforded by the walled villages was worth the extra work of walking to their fields. Settlement patterns were clustered, but over time, individual land holdings became fragmented and dispersed (Figure 12–6). The land became divided politically, through marriage and inheritance, and it was also divided because the farmers wanted a variety of slope and soil types for growing various types of crops. Thus, parcels were traded back and forth. The original land holdings nearest to the village were small, but as the population grew and more land was brought into cultivation, the newer plots became larger. Land allotments were almost always linear, much like the riverfront arrangement, but in this case, the purpose of linear lots was for access to roads rather than for irrigation.

Land Reform

Farm villages and the fragmented land holdings surrounding them became common throughout the world. Much of the land, however, came under the ownership of people who did not farm it. This political situation led to a need for *land reform.* Many bloody revolts have occurred in the cause of land reform, usually forcing the owners of the large tracts of land to sell or otherwise relinquish their holdings to the tenant farmers who live on the land. Land reform usually causes two events: (1) fragmented parcels are eliminated, and (2) the farmers move from farm villages to live on their newly acquired holdings. Thus, farm villages are abandoned, and rural settlement changes from clustered to dispersed. Historically, then, rural settlement began as linear patterns along rivers, then clustered in farm villages, and then became dispersed through land reform.

Land reform began in Europe shortly after the Middle Ages and continues today in other parts of the world. It has been a constant political theme for revolutionaries. Major land reforms began shortly after World War II when new nations came into being, and many local uprisings occurred because of the need for reform. Before 1948, over half the land in Japan and Korea was owned by landlords; today, the figure is less than ten percent. A 1959 program in Pakistan transferred more than six million acres from

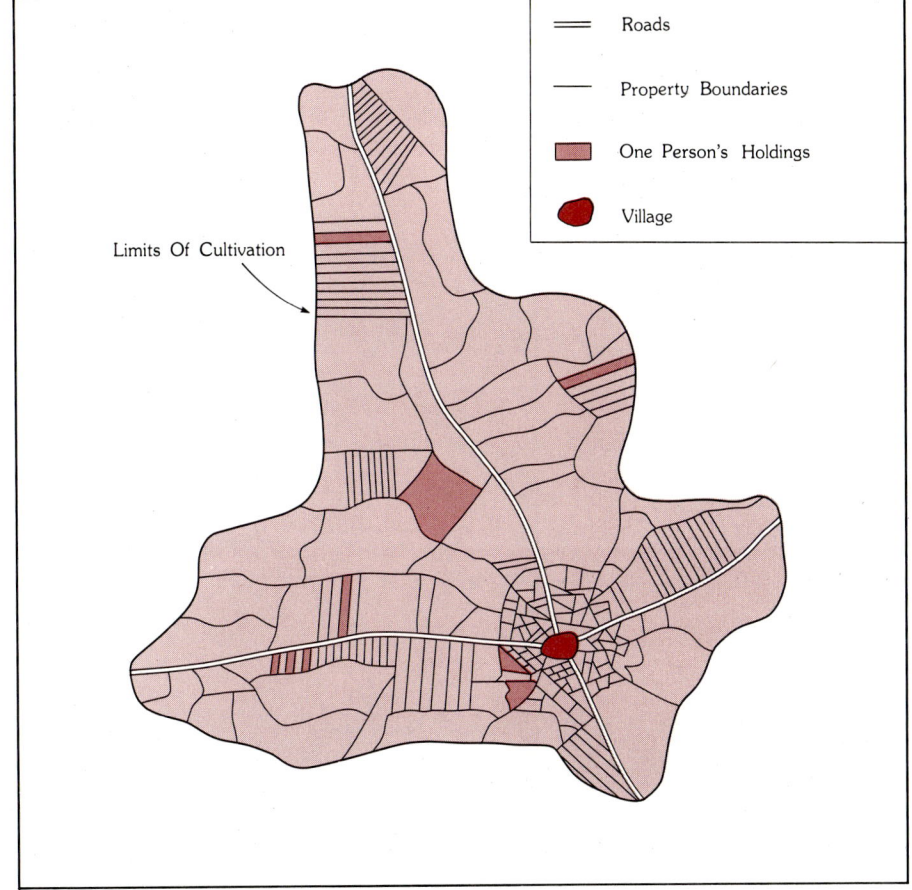

FIGURE 12–6 A Middle Eastern farm village and land holdings. (From Samuel N. Dickens and Forrest R. Pitts, *Introduction to Cultural Geography* [Ginn, 1970], p. 241. By Permission of John Wiley & Sons, Inc.)

6,000 landlords to two million tenant farmers. Land reform in the Middle East has been called a turning point comparable to the abolition of feudalism, and dramatic changes have occurred in Africa and Latin America with regard to land ownership. Political action thus creates changes in land tenure, which in turn affects rural settlement patterns.

Roman Influence on Rural Settlement

The fragmented and dispersed land holdings of the Middle Eastern farmers evolved over long periods of time. In contrast, the Romans quickly imposed compact, geometrical farm holdings upon the people of the lands they conquered. The Romans laid out farming areas into square tracts; every square was exactly 776 yards long on each side (Figure 12-7). Their land survey system is known as the *centuriation* method.

Nearly all the flat and rolling hill farming areas of the Roman Empire were divided according to the centuriation principle. Individual farms included square or rectangular plots within the larger centuriated blocks of land, and farmers usually lived on their own land holdings. Thus, rural settlement patterns tended to be regular and uniform. The roads were straight, because they followed the straight boundaries between farms. In the countries of Europe and north Africa that were part of the Roman Empire, modern roads still follow the routes of the ancient Roman roads. Subsequent cultures, however, have obliterated most of the original square land holdings. Some towns in England that have meandering and complex street patterns, for example, lie on top of the ruins of Roman towns that were laid out in square blocks and straight streets. Similar destruction of the orderly patterns happened in the farm fields.

The Roman method of dividing land into square holdings was copied years later by the federal government of the United States. Instead of square blocks of 776 yards on a side, however, the land survey system in the United States is based on one mile (1760 yards). Although the Roman system fell into disuse in countries that were once in the empire, the idea survives in the American system.

RURAL SETTLEMENT IN THE MIDDLE AGES

During the Middle Ages, rural settlement in northern Europe became much less precise than the earlier Ro-

FIGURE 12-7 Roman centuriation system of land survey.

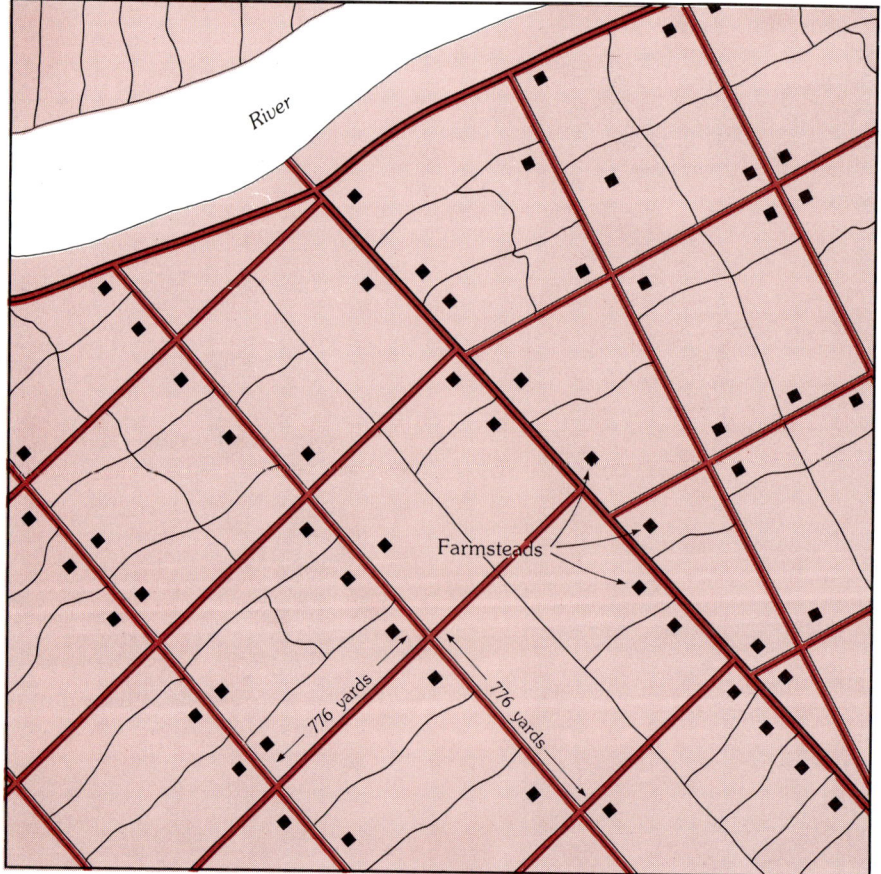

FIGURE 12–8 Settlement and field patterns of the medieval walled circle village.

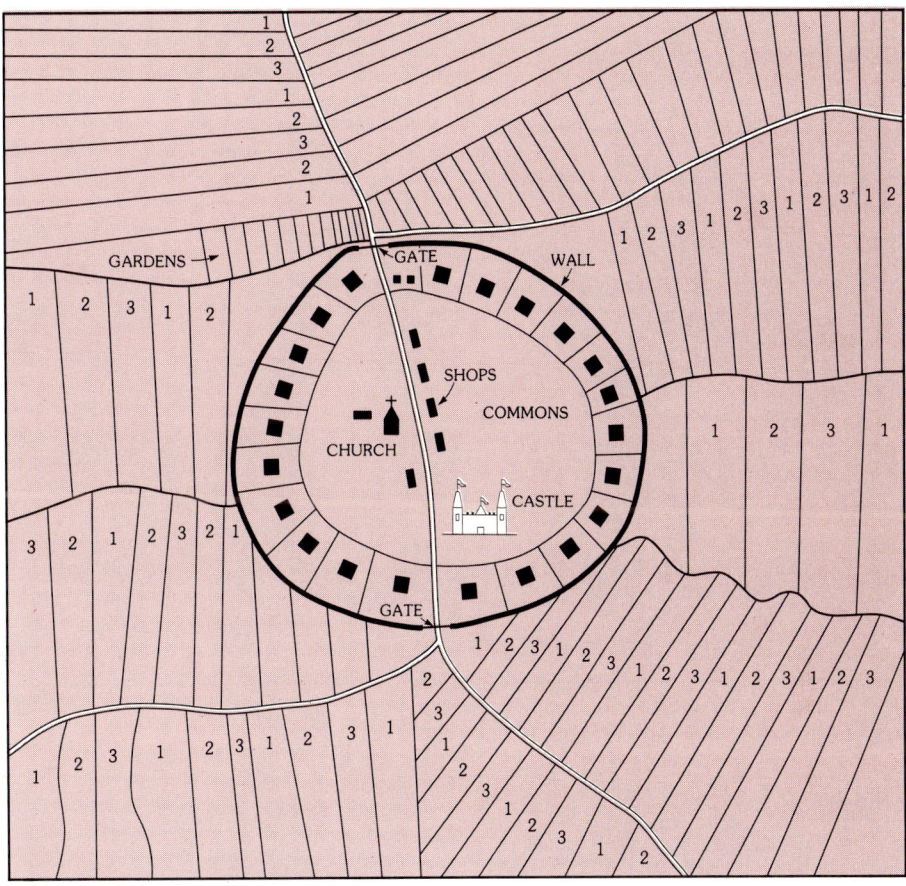

1, 2 and 3 INDICATE CROP TYPE.

man settlement techniques. Farmers were forced to relinquish their land tenure in exchange for protection from marauding tribes. Land holdings changed from the fragmented farm village into large estates ruled by local lords, military campaign winners, or church leaders, a system known as *feudal* land tenure that encompassed the economic, political, and social organizations of the time. The land was worked by *vassals* who were so low in the organization that they were considered part of the land holding. The estates were called *feuds*, worked by *serfs* under an overlord. The serfs worked in exchange for protection and very little else. They paid heavy taxes for the privilege of working the land and overseeing the vassals. Land use and settlement, therefore, were closely tied to the entire way of life.

A feudal farm was usually divided into three parcels in a *three-field* system. The three fields were laid out in strips, or *long lots,* and each strip was farmed on a rotating basis. The people usually lived within walled towns or near castles where they could seek safety in times of danger. The settlements were often *circle villages,* and the central parts of the circular areas, held for common use, became known simply as the *commons* (Figure 12–8). When the feudal lords were overthrown and land reform began, the farmers were left with fragmented and dispersed strips of land. The three-field system remained in use for centuries after the medieval period ended, because the farmers could not agree on land exchanges that would create contiguous holdings. One can still see the results of the three-field system in some of the land holdings of northern Europe and England.

The marauding tribes were eventually subdued, and central governments took control of the countryside. These events, along with increasing population, caused rural settlement to expand beyond the confines of village walls. Dwellings first began to appear along the roads that led to the villages, creating linear settlement patterns known as *line villages* (Figure 12–9a). Line villages were similar in structure to the riverside settlements in the Middle East (Figure 12–5), except their purpose was to allow farmers to live close to access roads rather than to rivers. Sometimes the farmers congregated at major road crossings, which became *irregular cluster villages* (Figure 12–9b.) A cluster of farmers soon needed a church and shops; thus, the village grew, but the irregular pattern of streets and land holdings remained. Villages of this type are common in Europe today. Irreg-

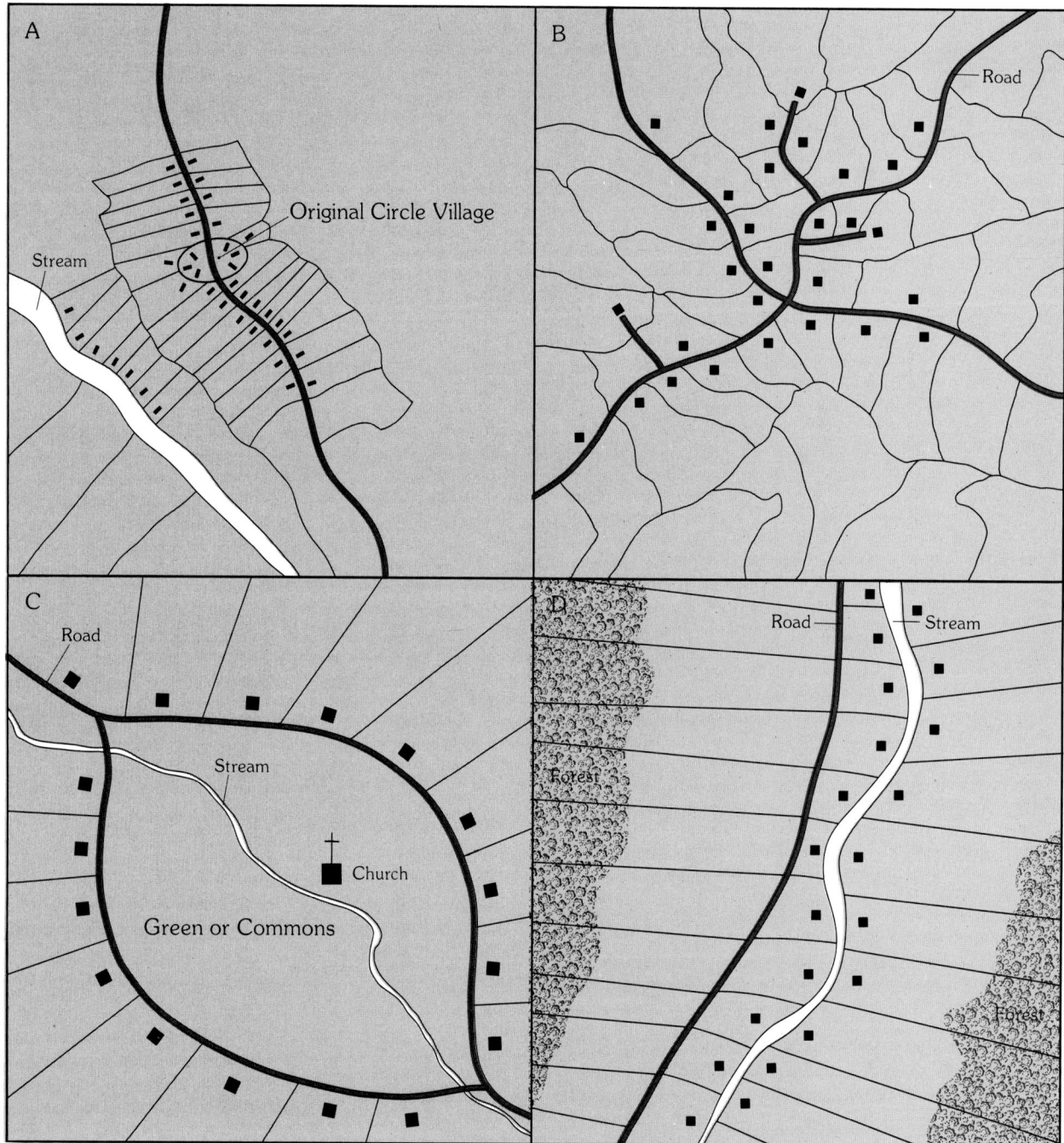

FIGURE 12–9 Rural European settlement patterns: (a) line village; (b) irregular cluster village; (c) ångerdorf; (d) waldhubendorf.

ular field patterns, a hold-over from the medieval period, also remain in many parts of modern Europe.

Another type of line village, the *strassendorf* or "street village," appears in Germany. The small towns consist of groups of farmsteads clustered on both sides of roads, but have no commons or other remnants of circular villages. Another type of German settlement is the *angerdorf* or "meadow village," a combination of the circular village and line village. Most angerdorfs are almond-shaped, with the farmsteads in a line along a split in the road (Figure 12–9c). The commons, sometimes called "the green," is held for public use similar to the circle villages. The angerdorfs are not walled, however, and the farmsteads are on the farmers' land holdings. Another linear type of settlement in Germany is the *waldhubendorf*, or the "village by the forest" (Figure 12–9d). The farmsteads in the waldhubendorf are aligned along a stream, usually within a steep valley. The individual plots of land are long-lots that run up the valley wall, usually terminating in a wooded area that is too steep to farm.

MODERN RURAL SETTLEMENT

Europe

Although farm villages remain common in all parts of Europe, a dispersed rural settlement pattern also exists. The modern trend is to locate farm buildings on the farmers' land holdings. Land reform, consolidation of holdings, and modern farm equipment have all influenced the dispersal of settlement. It is much more common, however, to see farm equipment being transported along country roads in Europe than it is in the United States and Canada, which tells us that farmers in Europe travel by road to their holdings much more than do their Anglo-American counterparts. Land holdings in Europe remain much more fragmented than those in North America.

Asia

Rural settlement in Eastern Europe and the Soviet Union developed in a manner similar to that in Western Europe. The first patterns were linear, followed by circular and almond-shaped, and many of the farm villages were walled. The general pattern, however, was uniform and clustered. A different kind of pattern in the Soviet Union is the communal farm village or *mir*. Large tracts of land were farmed collectively, but the peasant farmers of the Middle Ages clustered into villages. Although the large tracts of land were farmed collectively, each farmer grew garden staples on his own small plot of land. The mirs were semi-autonomous political units, and the Czarist governments of the time taxed the entire mir rather than its individual members. Collectivism was used to control discipline, disputes, work assignments, and other social and economic obligations. The pattern of settlement in a mir was somewhat more orderly than that in Western European farm villages (Figure 12–10). The mir was a planned village rather than one that grew spontaneously.

The ancient mirs were the forerunners of the Soviet Union's large *state farms*. These huge collective farms are run similarly to the mirs in that the farmers are still allowed to care for their small individual plots of land. The peasants' huts of the mirs have been replaced, however, by rows of modern, single-family farm houses, each with its own garden. Dispersal of farmsteads onto the landscape has not occurred. The farmers use modern farm equipment owned by the state. Some farm villages have grown into *farm cities* with populations exceeding 100,000, but the general settlement pattern remains similar to what was established centuries ago.

Farm villages rather than dispersed farmsteads are the rule in all parts of Asia besides the Soviet Union. Oriental farmers have lived for centuries in thousands of small farm villages scattered over miles and miles of countryside. A maze of farm roads and paths lead to the myriad tiny plots of land. The farmers commute daily between their homes in the villages and their fields. They carry hand tools, some lead draft animals, and occasionally a small tractor is seen. In the hilly parts of Southeast Asia, terraced rice paddies occupy the slopes while the dwellings are located on the valley floors. The linear settlement pattern in these valleys is similar to European farm villages, except that the fields do not run back from each farmstead. Also, the general pattern of land use does not appear to be as orderly as in Europe.

Besides the linear patterns of rural settlement in the steep-sloped valleys of Asia, the general settlement pattern there is irregular clustering, much like example B in Figure 12–9. Circle villages appear in India, however, complete with medieval walls or remnants of them. In areas with sufficient rainfall for full farm production, the rural population density is very high. Agriculture is intensive, using small plots of land exclusively, so the farm villages are close together. Most people rarely travel beyond the daily commuting distance to their fields. Pigs, water buffalo, chickens, and cattle are all housed in pens next to the houses; all animals are usually penned and housed together. In drier regions, population density is lower; consequently, farm villages are more dispersed than in the wetter areas. Individual plots of land are also larger in the dry areas than in the wet areas.

Until the Communist land reforms of the 1950s, the Chinese landscape was similar to the rest of East Asia, with a pattern of irregular clustering and farmers, living in scattered villages, who walked to their tiny parcels of land to do their farm work. The only variation from this theme was along the rivers, where long-lots created a linear settlement pattern. Under communism, however, rural settlement became even more clustered than before. Chinese farmers were required to live, like farmers in the Soviet Union, in *commune villages*. The small plots of land were converted to large fields, and the farming was to be done collectively. The communal structure was in-

CHAPTER 12 RURAL SETTLEMENT PATTERNS

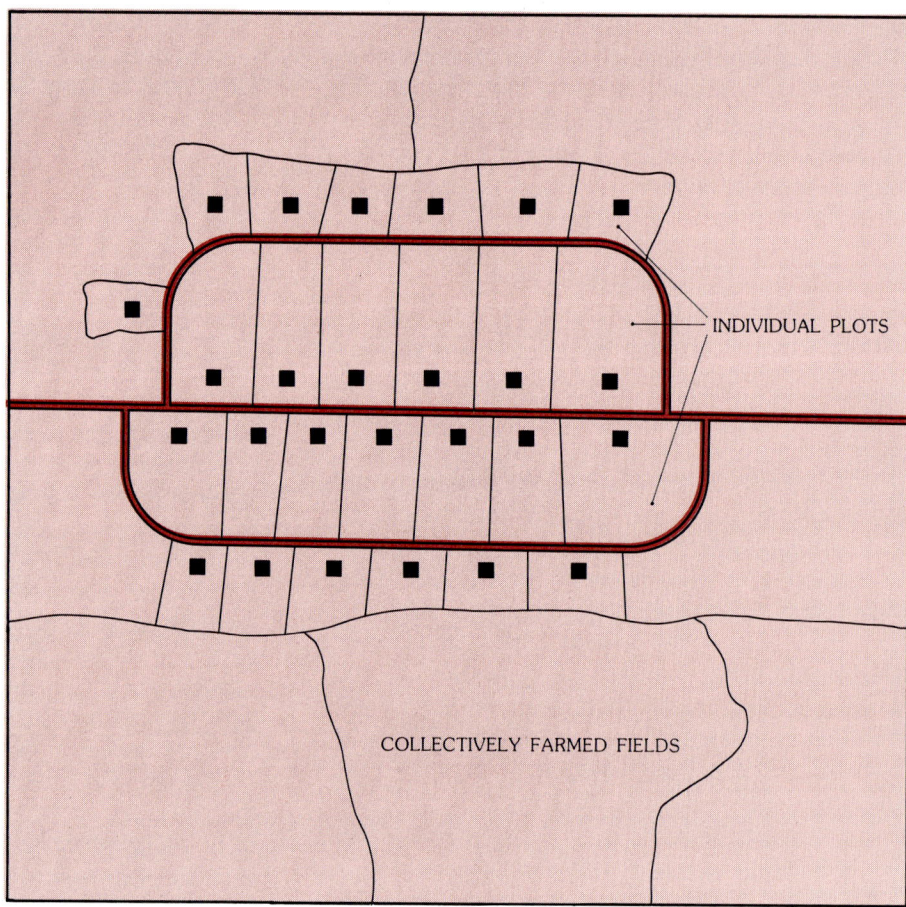

FIGURE 12–10 The settlement pattern of the *mir*, a Russian communal farm village.

tended to provide for even more needs of the people than did the Soviet state farms. Public services included babysitting, schooling, and medical care; on some communes, even eating and sleeping quarters were shared. Nearly everything is owned by the state. During the last few years, however, the strict communal structure has deteriorated somewhat, and farmers are beginning to move back to the traditional farm villages. Despite the government's intervention to try to change the rural settlement pattern to one that is more agglomerated, the farmers are resisting and moving back to the scattered farm villages.

Africa

The theme of rural settlement in Africa is a regular dispersed pattern in the north and south, with irregular clustering in the equatorial region. In some areas along the Mediterranean Sea in the north, the Roman influence of square blocks of land has persisted through the centuries. Citrus, olive, and date groves and small grain fields tend to be orderly and uniform, laid out in square tracts. The European colonial powers carried on the Roman tradition. In South Africa, British and Dutch colonists also tended to place their fields and farm buildings on the landscape in an orderly manner. In tropical Africa, however, slash and burn agriculture (defined in Chapter 10) has been carried on for centuries. This form of survival leads to a hodge-podge of scattered, irregular settlement clusters.

Only about one percent of the land in tropical Africa is devoted to plantation agriculture, and any plantation usually grows only a single cash crop. Most plantations in tropical Africa were established and are financed by foreign corporations, which usually have headquarters in the country that held colonial power over the African nation where the plantation is located. Plantations were designed to: (1) produce crops that will not grow in the higher latitudes of the foreign countries, or (2) to grow certain crops that can be produced more cheaply in the tropics. Cacao is one of the major plantation crops of central Africa. It was introduced to West Africa by the Dutch, but the formerly British colony of Ghana is now the world's leading producer. The British also developed large cotton plantations in East Africa, especially the Sudan, and plantations in Nigeria that produce citrus, cotton, and cacao. Rural settlement in central Africa is largely unaffected by plantations, however, because there are so few.

Latin America

In pre-Columbian Latin America, the Indians lived in small, irregularly clustered farm villages, similar to those in east Asia and central Africa. The people conducted subsistence agriculture by commuting from the villages to nearby farm fields. Spanish and Portuguese colonization resulted in a seizure of tribal lands, however, and the small subsistent farms were turned into giant estates called *haciendas,* although the rural settlement pattern was not disturbed a great deal by the dramatic change in ownership. The Indian farm villages merely became *hacienda villages;* that is, the laborers for the haciendas lived in small clusters that formed villages similar to farm villages of an earlier time. Haciendas are similar to plantations in that they are large estates for growing one commercial crop.

The hacienda village contains a collection of homes for the people who work in the fields of the hacienda. The village is a sort of company town where the buildings, stores, and even the homes are owned by the hacienda owners. The people who work the fields must pay rent for their homes and purchase goods from the hacienda-owned stores. They usually farm a small plot of land on a *sharecropping* basis; about half of what they grow must be given to the hacienda. They receive meager wages, and the hacienda owners retain their services by keeping them in debt most of the time. These peons are little more than indentured servants.

Land reform has been a major issue in many Latin American countries since the colonial period. Governments sometimes take control with "land reform" as a slogan, and are toppled if reform does not come quickly enough. Many problems in Latin America relate to the need for land reform. Where land reform has occurred, the governments tend to plan the local settlements in great detail. Farm villages are operated similarly to a commune, and planning touches almost everything: churches, schools, utilities, and even street patterns. Most of the rural people still live in farm villages, however, so the general scheme of rural settlement does not change when the village structure changes from an unplanned to a planned development.

North America

Settlers in both Canada and the United States began their new lives in America by doing things much the way they had in the old countries. They modeled their settlements after those from where they came. The eastern seaboard regions, then, contain farm villages rather than dispersed rural settlements. The New England *town* consists of both the farm village and the nearby farmland. The early farmers lived in the villages and walked to their land holdings just as millions of subsistent farmers throughout the world.

Many American settlements were established by groups of people who wanted to remain as a unit for protection or for religious, social, or economic reasons. The threat of Indian attack created the need for some walled towns, and many farm villages had stockade walls. Some early German settlements were similar to communes, and these cluster villages still exist in Pennsylvania, Iowa, and Texas. Dutch settlers in the Hudson Valley used a feudal approach complete with the three-field system of strip farming. Plantations were established in the Old South, and the French areas of Canada and Louisiana used long-lots along rivers. All these types of rural settlement were brought to America from the Old World, creating landscapes of settlements clustered into farm villages. These landscapes persist today in the eastern parts of the United States and Canada.

RANGE AND TOWNSHIP

Rural dispersal of the population in Canada and the United States began with westward expansion. It was a planned dispersal. After Americans achieved independence, the original thirteen states relinquished their claims to all the territory west of their boundaries, but east of the Mississippi River and north of the Ohio River—the "Northwest Territory." The area was to be divided in an orderly manner before settlement. During colonial times, land in New England and the Middle Atlantic states had been divided by a system called "metes and bounds." This system was not accurate, because it was based on natural features such as trees, rocks, rivers, or other things that are subject to change over time. The uncertainty of the metes and bounds system led to squabbles and frequent litigation over boundary lines. The new federal government saw a need for a fixed and consistent policy of land allocation and registry (Figure 12–11).

Thomas Jefferson chaired the congressional committee that devised the land division scheme for the Northwest Territory. The committee followed the Roman centuriation example of using square blocks of land, but they decided that the blocks of land should be laid out according to compass directions and adapted the New England system of using six-by six-mile blocks. These large tracts were called

CHAPTER 12 RURAL SETTLEMENT PATTERNS

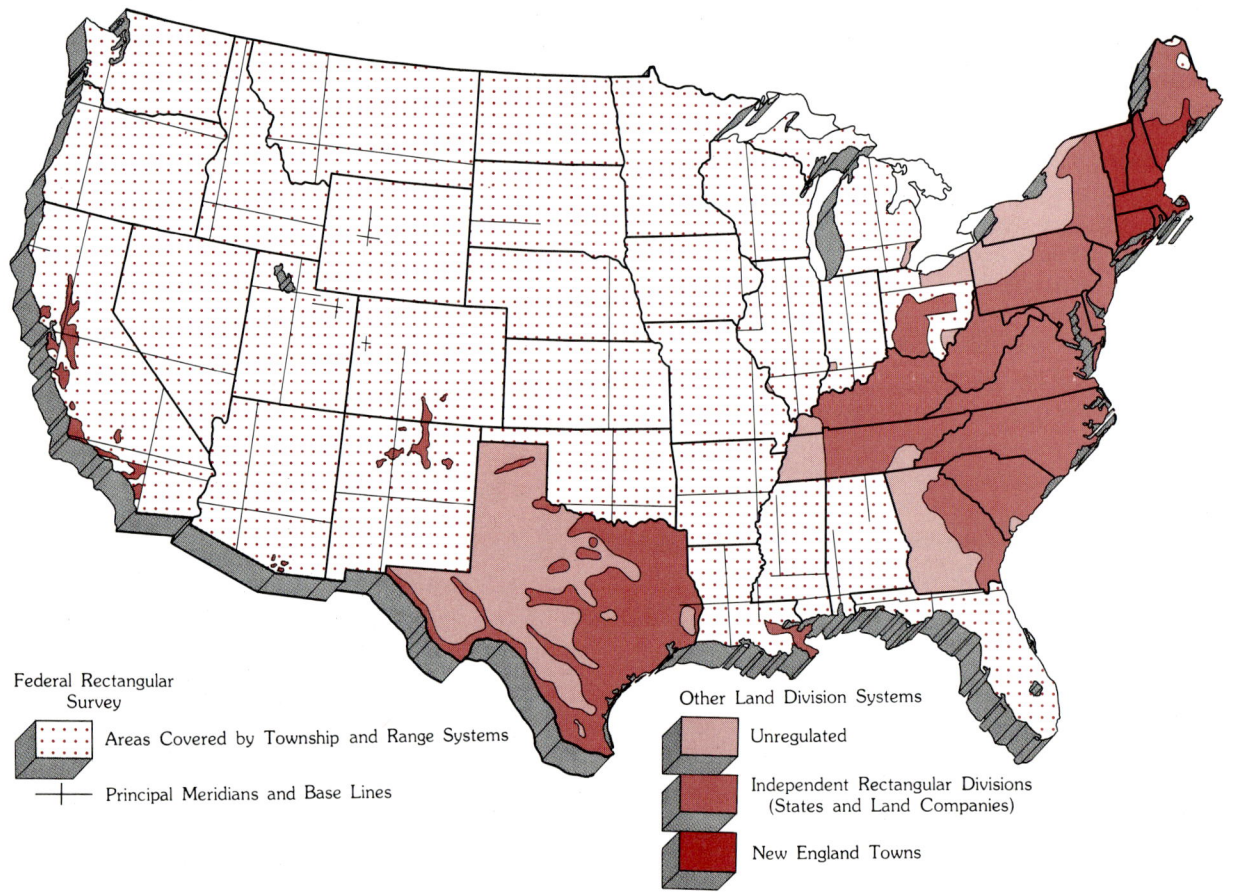

FIGURE 12–11 The U.S. land survey system. (Adapted from F. J. Marschner, *Land Use and Its Patterns in the United States,* 1959.)

townships. Each township was to be divided into 36 square-mile parcels called *sections.* The system was an adaption, then, of previously existing systems, but resulted in a unique land division. The U.S. Congress accepted the committee's proposal, and the *Land Ordinance Act* was passed in 1785. The first survey of the Northwest Territory began that year.

Thomas Hutchins, Geographer to the United States, began the survey of the Northwest Territory by establishing a baseline from which all measurement would be taken. Called the *Geographer's Line,* the line ran directly west from the point where the Ohio River intersects the boundary of western Pennsylvania (Figure 12–12). Every six miles along the Geographer's Line, a survey line was established that ran south toward the Ohio River. The six-mile steps to the west were called *ranges.* The original survey included seven ranges, and "seven ranges west" became a popular catch phrase. The remaining east-west lines were surveyed next, until the area between the Geographer's Line and the Ohio River was blocked off into an accurately measured grid. Townships were established using ranges. The terms "range" and "township" are still used to designate land surveyed in this way.

The Geographer's Line was eventually extended across Ohio to the Indiana border. As the base for most of the range and township surveys made in Ohio, it became known as the *baseline.* The first operation in a new survey was to establish a baseline, then a north-south line. The first north-south line was the western boundary of Pennsylvania. All north-south lines lie on lines of longitude, or *meridians.* The new north-south survey lines became known as *principal meridians.* The intersections of baselines and principal meridians are the beginning points for numbering townships. As the population expanded westward, new baselines and principal meridians were needed, and were eventually used in surveying most of the land west of the Pennsylvania border (Figure 12–11), except for Texas and parts of California and New Mexico.

FIGURE 12–12 The first land survey in the U.S. under the Land Ordinance Act of 1785. (Adapted from C. O. Paullin and J. K. Wright, eds., *Atlas of the Historical Geography of the United States*, 1932.)

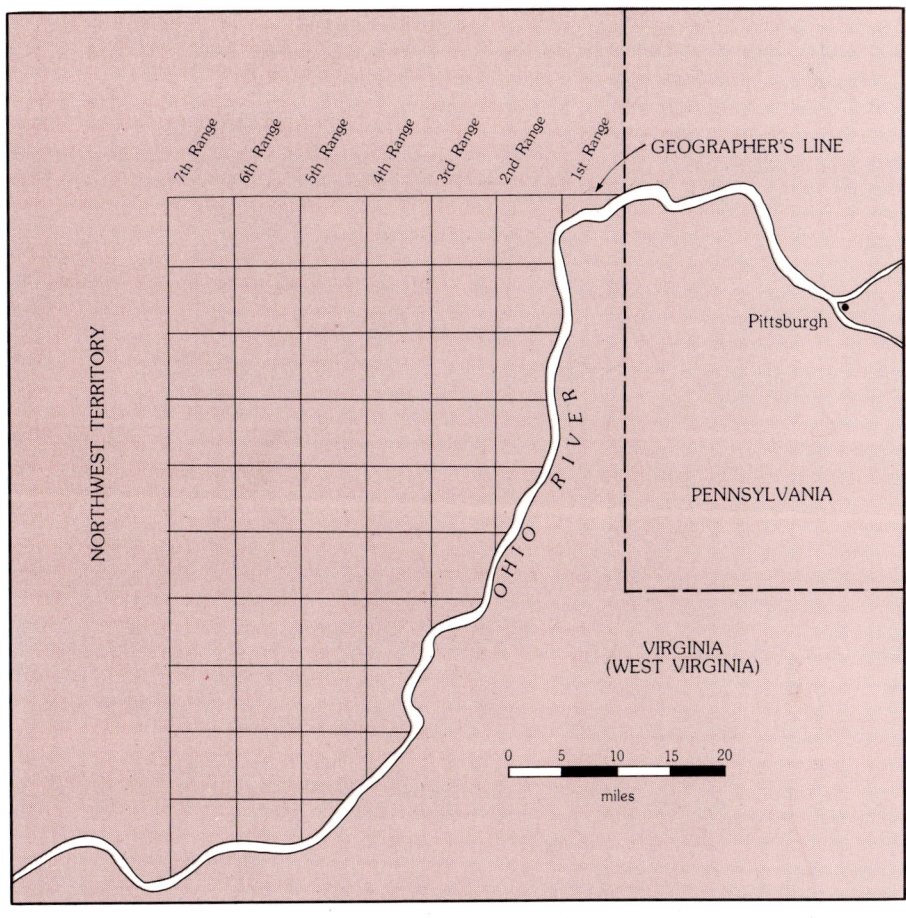

RURAL SETTLEMENT IN THE UNITED STATES

The range and township method of surveying land produced a uniform pattern for the U.S. landscape. It established the grid that led to the uniform pattern of roads, and was a precedent for laying out American cities in grid patterns, permitting an ease of movement not found in most foreign countries. The Land Ordinance Act has had a lasting and positive effect on the American landscape.

The Homestead Act of 1862 assured a uniform pattern of rural settlement in the United States. This law allowed any American citizen to purchase 160 acres of land cheaply. That amount of land, one-fourth of a section, was appropriate for one family to maintain. The square-mile section contains 640 acres; the congressional townships created in 1785 were six miles on a side, so each contained 36 sections, or 23,040 acres (Figure 12–13). The pattern of rural settlement became regular and uniform, because the pioneer farmers lived on their own 160-acre plots. Farmsteads appeared at predictable intervals; the only variations are those shown in Figure 12–1. The Land Ordinance Act created the grid pattern, and the Homestead Act allowed the grid to be filled in with settlement.

The uniform pattern of rural settlement continued throughout the midwestern part of the United States. Going westward, annual precipitation decreases dramatically at about the 100th meridian. To compensate for the lack of moisture, larger farms were needed. Thus, the distances between farmsteads increased. This did not change the uniform pattern of settlement, however; it merely made it more dispersed. Thus, population density decreases dramatically west of the 100th meridian, but the uniform pattern of settlement does not change. Both the mountainous terrain and Spanish influence caused some clustering in rural settlement of the southwest, but in general, the American West is uniformly settled.

Rural settlement in the United States has probably changed more than anywhere else in the world. First, the land was entirely devoid of farmsteads only 200 years ago. Then, in only a few years, farm homes became uniformly dispersed over huge regions. Once the usable land was taken, other

CHAPTER 12 RURAL SETTLEMENT PATTERNS

FIGURE 12–13 Divisions and subdivisions of sections. (From John F. Lounsbury and Frank T. Aldrich, *Introduction to Geographic Field Methods and Techniques* [Charles E. Merrill, 1979], p. 37.)

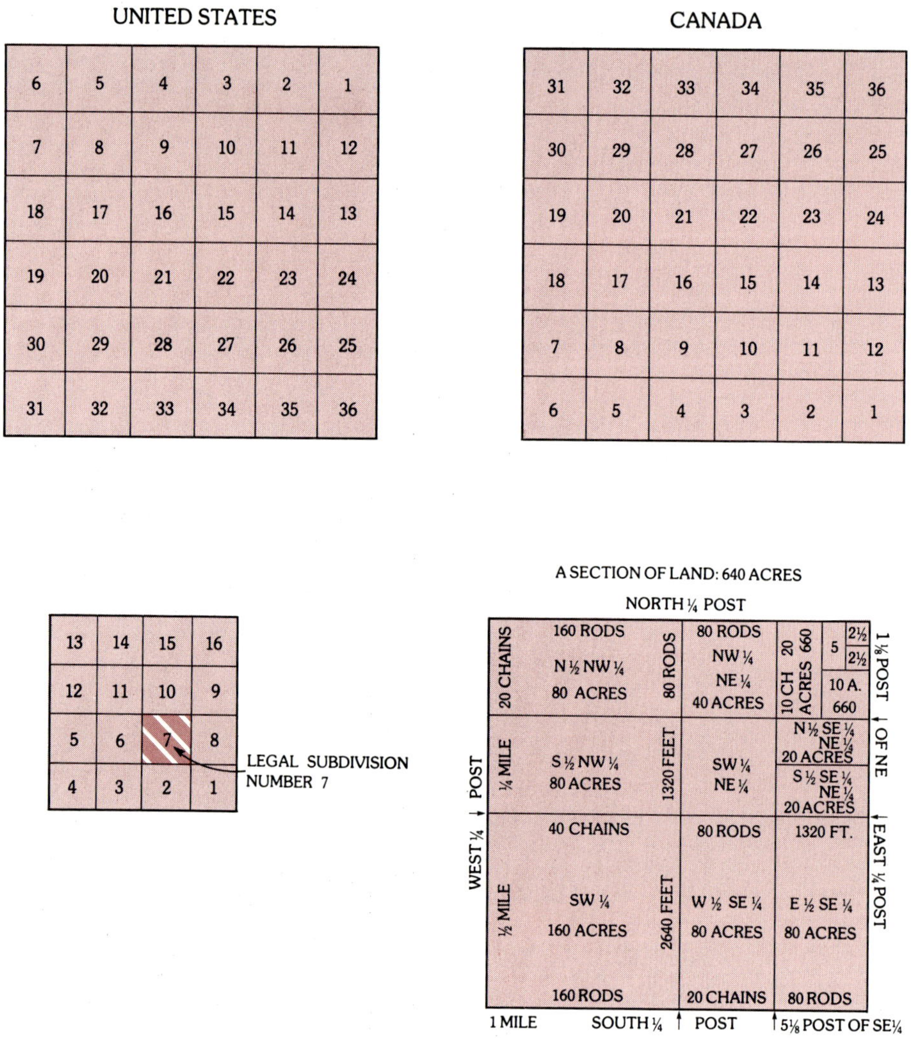

changes began. During the 1930s, the Dust Bowl conditions forced farmers in many midwestern states to abandon their homesteads and move west, usually to California. In the 1950s, cotton production moved out of the traditional growing areas of the South and into the irrigated West. Many farm people began migrating to the cities in search of jobs, leaving the landscape emptier each year. Physical and economic conditions have created changes in settlement patterns, and, unlike other areas of the world, patterns of settlement in the United States change quickly and dramatically.

Changes in rural settlement are occurring now. Mixed farming in the American Midwest is becoming more specialized, and larger machines are being invented. The 160-acre homestead no longer supports a farm family. These factors along with others create a need for fewer farms and farmers. As older farmers retire and move into local towns, their land holdings are purchased by large corporations. The farm buildings are usually abandoned and left to deteriorate. Small farms are consolidated into large farms and eventually into giant holdings. The reverse of land reform is happening. All this leads to lower density and greater dispersal of the rural population, which will affect the pattern of rural settlement.

Another pattern that has begun to appear on the North American landscape is the circle. In the arid west, where irrigation is necessary, one can see large, circular patches of land created by the rotation of overhead irrigation pipes around a center pivot. The pivotal devices have been found to be the best method for carrying irrigation water to crops. Although not strictly related to settlement, these large circles of green on an otherwise brown landscape present a unique and interesting pattern. These and other land use patterns, such as those created by contour and strip farming, are best seen through air travel over the United States.

CONCLUSION

The location and arrangement of human settlement on the world's rural landscapes help us to understand how people use the land and adapt to their environments. The various ways people use land lead to varied and distinctive patterns, distinguishable from each other as well as from naturally occurring patterns. The human imprint on the landscape changes quickly in some areas, but remains the same for centuries in other areas.

Rural settlement patterns are described as *clustered, random, linear,* and *dispersed.* Other terms describe distinctive types of settlements: *angerdorf, mir, strassendorf,* and *waldhubendorf.*

The way humans organize space is of great interest to geographers. The next chapter concerns organization of space and the resulting landscape patterns in urban areas. Use of the land and adaptation to the environment are much different issues in urban areas than in rural areas. In contrast to rural areas, the urban landscape is dominated by human structures, and natural landscapes are preserved only in parks and greenbelts.

KEY WORDS

angerdorf
baseline
centuriation
circle village
cluster village
clustered pattern
commons
commune village
dispersed
farmsteads
feud
freehold tenure
hacienda village
land reform
land tenure
law of diminishing returns
line village

mir
nearest-neighbor analysis
principal meridian
random pattern
range
regular pattern
section
serfs
sharecropper
state farm
strassendorf
three-field system
township
vassals
waldhubendorf
walled village

REFERENCES

AHLMANN, H. W. "The Geographical Study of Settlements." *Geographical Review,* 18 (1928): 93–128.

ALEXANDER, JOHN W., and LAY JAMES GIBSON. *Economic Geography,* 2nd ed. Englewood Cliffs, N.J.: Prentice-Hall, 1979.

BROEK, JAN O. M., and JOHN W. WEBB. *A Geography of Mankind.* New York: McGraw-Hill, 1968.

DEMANGEON, A. "La Géographie de l'habitat rurale." *Annals de Géographie,* 36 (1927): 1–23; 97–114.

DICKEN, SAMUEL N., and FORREST R. PITTS. *Introduction to Cultural Geography.* Waltham, MA: Ginn and Co., 1970.

FOUST, J. BRADY, and ANTHONY R. DE SOUZA. *The Economic Landscape: A Theoretical Introduction.* Columbus, Ohio: Charles E. Merrill Publishing Co., 1978.

JORDAN, TERRY G., and LESTER ROWNTREE. *The Human Mosaic: A Thematic Introduction to Cultural Geography.* New York: Harper and Row, 1982.

JUMPER, SIDNEY R., THOMAS L. BELL, and BRUCE A. RALSTON. *Economic Growth and Disparities.* Englewood Cliffs, NJ: Prentice-Hall, 1980.

LOSCH, AUGUST. *The Economics of Location.* Translated by W. H. Woglom and W. F. Stolper. New Haven, Conn.: Yale University Press, 1954.

MCCARTY, HAROLD H., and JAMES B. LINDBERG. *A Preface to Economic Geography.* Englewood Cliffs, NJ: Prentice-Hall, 1966.

PAULLIN, C. O., and J. K. WRIGHT, eds. *Atlas of the Historical Geography of the United States,* Washington, D.C.: 1932.

TREWARTHA, GLEN T. "Types of Rural Settlement in Colonial America." *Geographical Review,* 36 (1946): 568–596.

ZIMOLZAK, CHESTER E., and CHARLES A. STANSFIELD, JR. *The Human Landscape: Geography and Culture,* 2nd ed. Columbus, Ohio: Charles E. Merrill Publishing Co., 1983.

search of food. Such movement was tiring, time-consuming, and often hazardous, particularly for the young and the old. For you, a trip to the supermarket for a loaf of bread may be inconvenient. But to move yourself back along the time line, imagine you have to walk to the supermarket, that is is located in the next county, that there are hostile street gangs between here and there, and that you have a bad stomachache (from some overripe fruit you ate yesterday) but no medicine.

Sedentary (permanent) settlements evolved gradually as experiments with domesticating plants and animals proved increasingly successful. Domestication (from the Latin word *domus,* for "house") may bring to mind common domesticated animals such as the cat and the dog, but in fact, any plant or animal that has been adapted to the special purpose of humans can be regarded as domesticated. This process was advanced by the selection of plants and animals with desirable traits—a grain with a head more easily separated from its stem, a cow that would yield more milk, and so on. Again, we must remember the slowness of the changes, and that even this domestication process was itself initially nomadic, with the use of forest clearings for patches of cultivation to supplement hunting and gathering. Gradually, then, beginning some 12,000 years ago, domestication advanced, cultivation and animal husbandry complemented each other, and tools such as the plow came into use. Intermittently in time and space, relatively permanent villages appeared. Food surpluses, meaning production beyond that necessary to feed the farmers, enabled people to remain in one place. Surpluses also led to the development of specialized jobs, or what economists refer to as *division of labor.* Masons, priests, or bakers might be fed by the cultivators' surplus.

If a village had some trade advantage—for example, access to a prized material such as gold or obsidian, or a location at the confluence of trade routes—it might grow and begin to appear increasingly urban. Places of worship and defense also often became permanent settlement sites. Restormel Castle (Figure 13–2) was apparently constructed to command a crossing of the River Fowey.

Urban generally refers to places that are predominantly nonagricultural. Early villages, then, were a transitional stage between nomadism and urbanism. Only those favored with advantageous physical and economic environments were likely to persist and develop to the point that they could be regarded as genuinely urban.

HISTORICAL GEOGRAPHY OF URBANIZATION

The time chart in Figure 13–3 and the map in Figure 13–4 show both the temporal and spatial arrangements of the early urban areas of the world. The first region of urban development is considered to have been in the Fertile Crescent, including the Tigris and Euphrates valleys, located principally in what is today the nation of Iraq. Sjoberg (1973) emphasizes the importance of the physical environment—soils and water supply, as well as a moderate climatic region, and the "crossroads" nature of the area, which had the effect of bringing together diverse ideas and skills, and thus stimulating innovation.

Egyptian urbanization came soon after the Fertile Crescent, and the Indus Valley (part of today's Paki-

FIGURE 13–2 Restormel Castle, Cornwell County, England was probably built by Baldwin Fitz Turstin about 1100.

CHAPTER 13 URBANIZATION AND URBAN PLACES

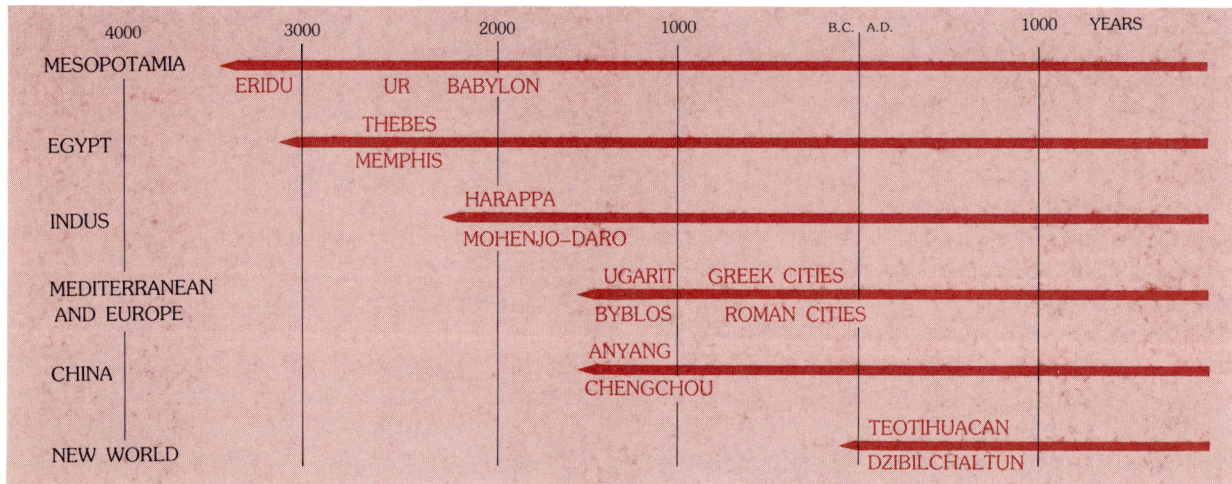

FIGURE 13–3 Sequence of urban evolution. (Adapted from "The Origin and Evolution of Cities," by Gideon Sjoberg. Copyright © 1965 by Scientific American, Inc. All rights reserved.)

stan), the eastern Mediterranean, and China followed. In the Old World, the *diffusion* process was probably important in spreading the idea of the city. In contrast, according to Sjoberg (1973), New World urbanization did not depend on diffusion—Mesoamerican (Central American) cities developed independently. Sjoberg does not regard the Inca culture of the Andes as truly urban, since it had no written language.

The imperialism of various cultures effectively promoted urbanization processes. For example, in the first few centuries A.D., the Romans aggressively colonized most of Europe, taking with them advanced ideas of city planning and engineering. In-

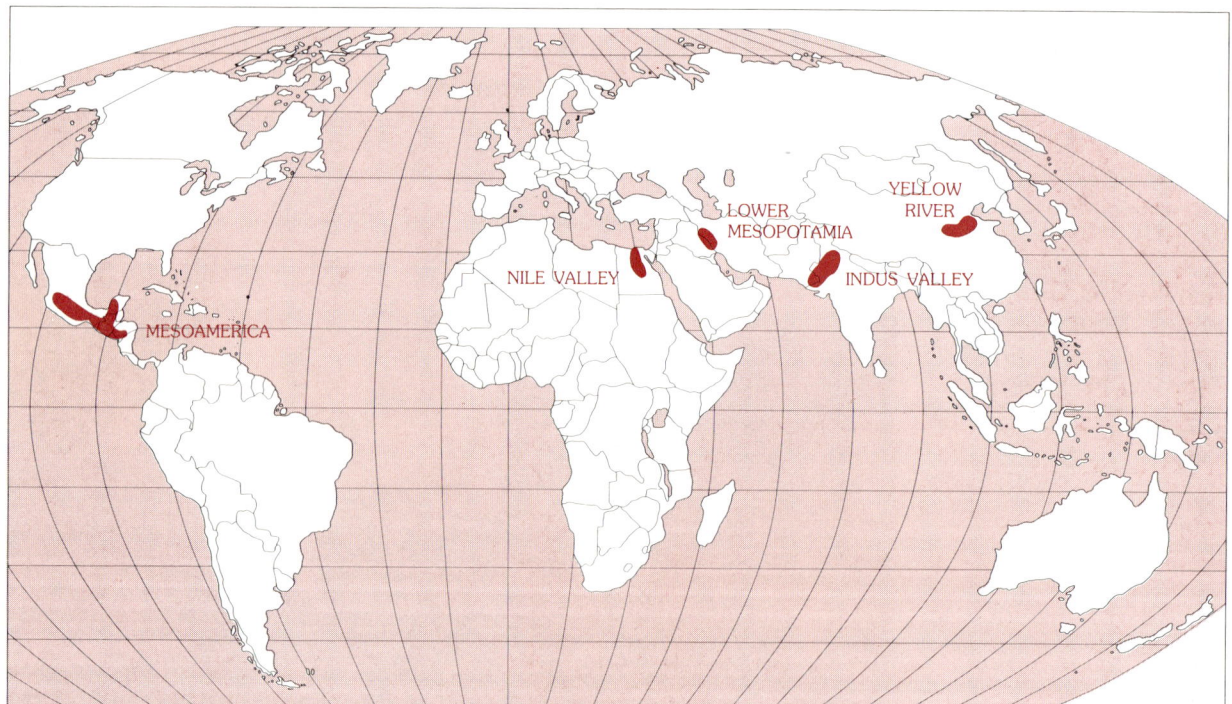

FIGURE 13–4 Areas of earliest urbanization. (Adapted from "The Origin and Evolution of Cities," by Gideon Sjoberg. Copyright © 1965 Scientific American, Inc. All rights reserved.)

deed, the Romans had an excellent grasp of the concepts of urban geography, understanding as they did the importance of the accessibility of public facilities and the significance of comprehensive highway networks. The decline of the Roman Empire was followed by the Middle Ages, a period of urban transformation. One interpretation suggests that the rise of Islam resulted in cutting Mediterranean trade, which in turn led to contraction of urban trade areas and a general shrinkage of markets (Vance, 1977, p. 80). Reestablishment of trade brought new life to cities, but dramatic (in many respects, traumatic) changes were not seen until the *Industrial Revolution* in the 1700s and 1800s. European colonialism had made Europe richer and had enabled more intensive division of labor, including more scientists. Wood, wind, and water came to be replaced by coal, iron, and steam, in Britain at first, but soon after in Europe and North America.

A new form emerged—the industrial city—as a focus for assembling raw materials, processing them, and distributing products. Massive rural-to-urban migration fed needed labor to the industrial city, which was unprecedented in its productivity, and in its capacity to degrade environments and to affect adversely the health and welfare of many who crowded in to operate the machines, dig the railroad cuts, or mine the coal. Social costs, at least initially, were borne entirely by the workers and their families, so production remained highly exploitive. Two responses to this "unbridled capitalism" were the writing of such political philosophers as Karl Marx and, ultimately, the rise of communism.

Parallel with the ascendance of the industrial city and the accompanying urbanization was an increase in the importance of *metropolitan* places, that is, major cities. People have not only tended to move toward cities, but have also tended to be attracted disproportionately to bigger cities. Borchert (1967) shows the ability of U.S. cities to attract development and people to be related to their ability to take advantage of shifts in the technologies of energy and transportation. Borchert identifies four epochs of growth of U.S. metropolitan areas: (1) the Wagon-Sail (1790–1830), (2) the Iron Horse (1830–1870), (3) the Steel Rail (1870–1920), and (4) the Auto–Air–Amenity epoch (since 1920). Figure 13–5 shows how the rise and fall of different energy sources and transportation technologies relate to each of the epochs. In this context, cities can be regarded as experiencing constantly changing conditions, both advantageous and disadvantageous. Thus, a northeastern city located on rivers that provide water power had a great advantage before steam or gasoline engines were invented. Today, by contrast, cities with access to abundant coal or oil have a relative advantage. The skyrocketing cost of energy in the 1980s is leading to a new "advantage pattern"; some observers suggest that Denver, with its proximity to abundant Rocky Mountain coal, is destined for phenomenal

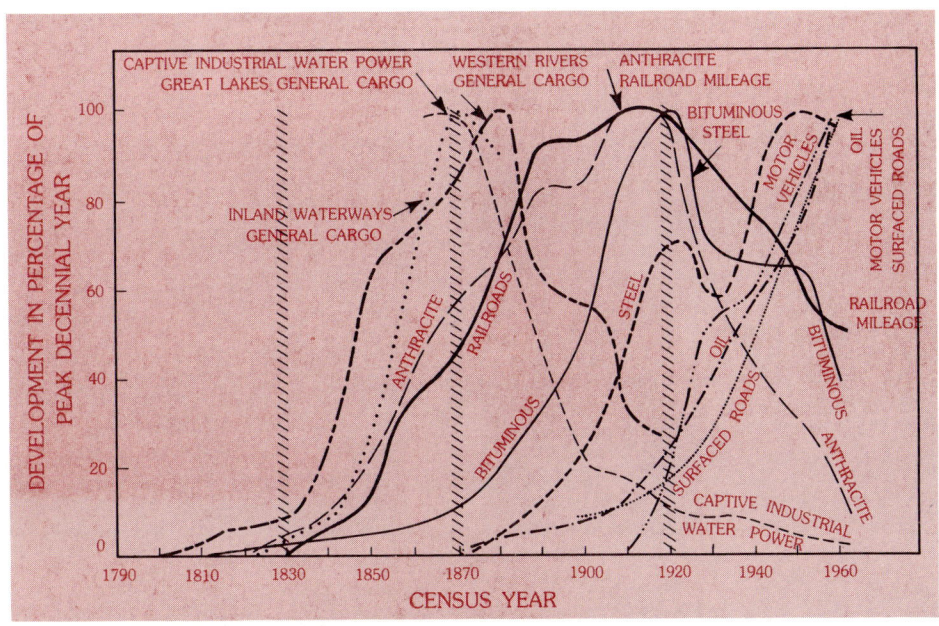

FIGURE 13–5 Rise and decline of 10 indicators of the technology of transportation and industrial energy. (Adapted from *Geographical Review* 57 [1967] with permission of the American Geographical Society.)

CHAPTER 13 URBANIZATION AND URBAN PLACES

growth. On the other hand, a metropolitan area such as Los Angeles, with its ultradependence on gasoline, may at some future time become less competitive as labor costs rise to meet workers' demands for wages adequate to pay soaring gasoline bills.

Recent Urban Population Trends

We have mentioned that urban population has increased dramatically in the last couple of hundred years. Over 40 percent of the world's 4.8 billion people live in cities (Figure 13–1). In the United States, more than 70 percent of the population is classified as "urban," which in numerical terms means about 160 million people. This compares to about 62 percent urban in the Soviet Union, 19 percent in China, 64 percent in Mexico, and 76 percent in Canada. Table 13–1 shows the most highly urbanized nations of the world. Most of these nations are small in area, and the table illustrates that larger countries rarely exceed an urbanized population of 80 percent, because of the greater likelihood of substantial dispersed rural populations. Australia is an exception,

TABLE 13–1 Most highly urbanized nations

Nation	Percent urban*
Malta	94.3
Belgium	87.1
Iceland	86.8
Australia	85.6
Sweden	82.7
Israel	81.9
New Zealand	81.4
Uruguay	80.8

*Excludes Singapore (100%)
Source: United Nations, 1978

partly because so much of its interior consists of sparsely populated desert.

Figure 13–6 shows the urbanization trend in the United States since the first census in 1790. The *early* stage of urbanization can be seen in the period from 1790 to about 1820. At this stage, the processes of industrialization were getting underway. Then the curve steepens to what might be called the *rapid*

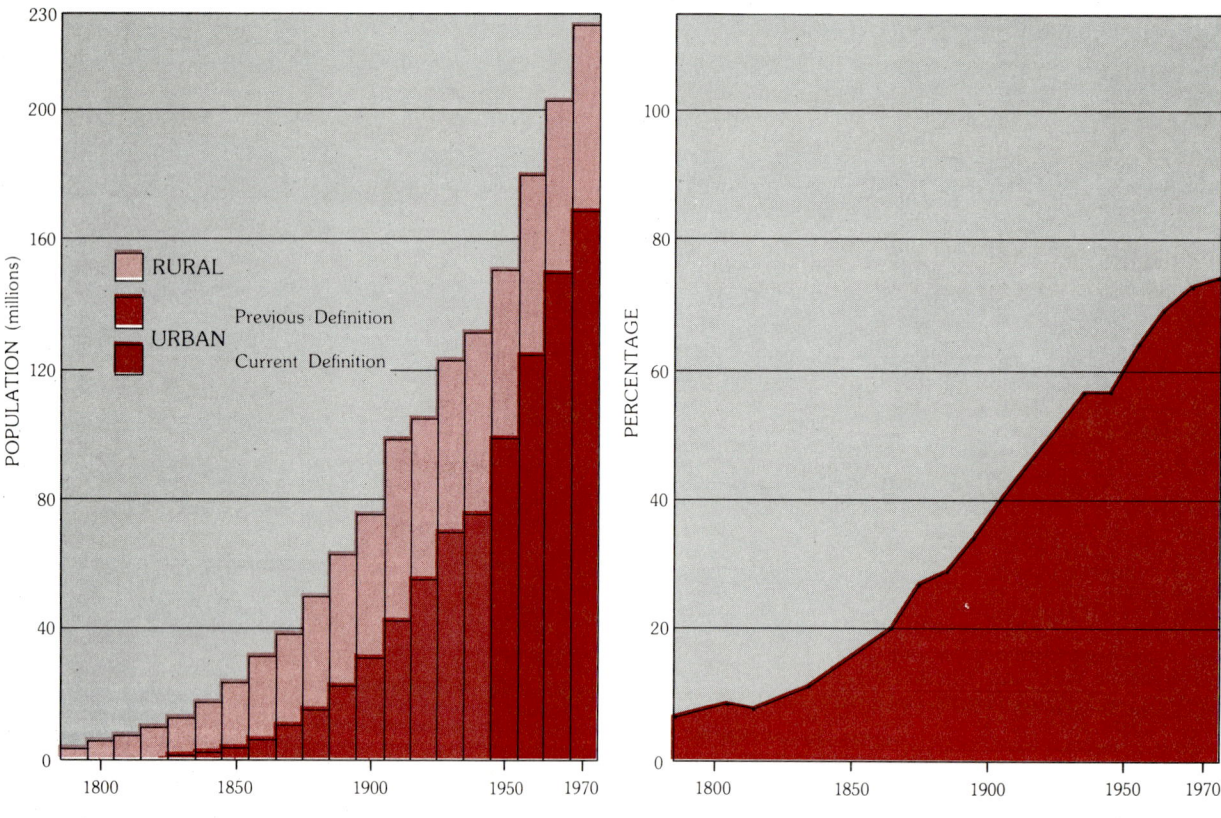

FIGURE 13–6 Numbers of U.S. urban and rural population (left) and percentage of urban population (right), 1790–1980. (From U.S. Department of Commerce [1971], p. 32, and U.S. Bureau of the Census [1981], p. 12.)

stage, during which industrial and agricultural developments simultaneously attracted people to cities and released them from food production. In the decade 1960–1970, there is some sign of a leveling off into a condition of *mature* urbanization. Assuming that there will always be a significant dispersed rural population, it seems unlikely that the level of urbanization in the United States will ever exceed 80–85 percent, though this is admittedly speculative. Note that an urbanization curve such as that in Figure 13–6 is a close relative of the S curve illustrating the cumulative rate of adoption of innovations, discussed in Chapter 8. Conceptually, urbanization can be regarded as an innovation that is adopted slowly at first by a minority, then rapidly by the majority, then slowly again by a "late" minority. This is obviously an oversimplification, because, in reality, people have little choice but to live in cities. Jobs are urban. (As shown in Chapter 8, this S curve is really a normal [bell-shaped] curve redrawn to show a cumulative pattern.)

Figure 13–7 shows the regional pattern of urbanization. The most heavily urbanized states are on the east and west coasts. In general, the West, Southwest, Northeast, and Florida are "peaks" on the "surface" of urbanization; a "valley" trend is visible from the Dakotas southward, and southeastward to Mississippi and the Carolinas. The more heavily urbanized states are those that either developed a strong urban structure early (the Northeast) or that have attracted many migrants more recently (the West, the Southwest, and Florida). This migration pattern is illustrated in part by the shifting center of population in the United States, which has moved in a generally westward direction at every census since 1790 (Figure 13–8).

This trend continued in the 1970s and 1980s. Between 1970 and 1980, the permanent population of the United States grew by over 23 million. Forty-four percent of this growth occurred in the South and West. California added 3.7 million in the decade, followed by Texas and Florida (3.0 million each). The

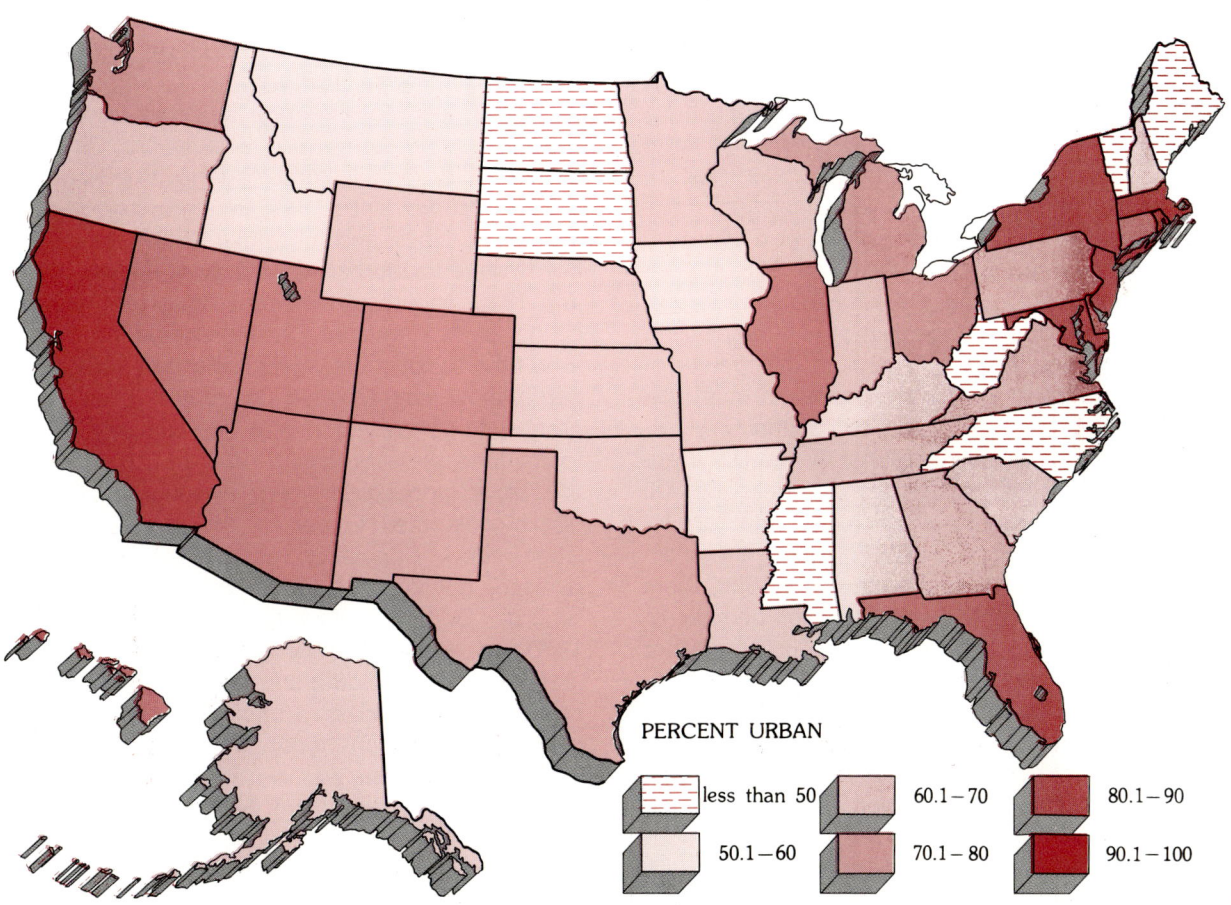

FIGURE 13–7 Percentage of urban population by state, 1980. (From U.S. Bureau of the Census [1981], p. 12.)

CHAPTER 13 URBANIZATION AND URBAN PLACES

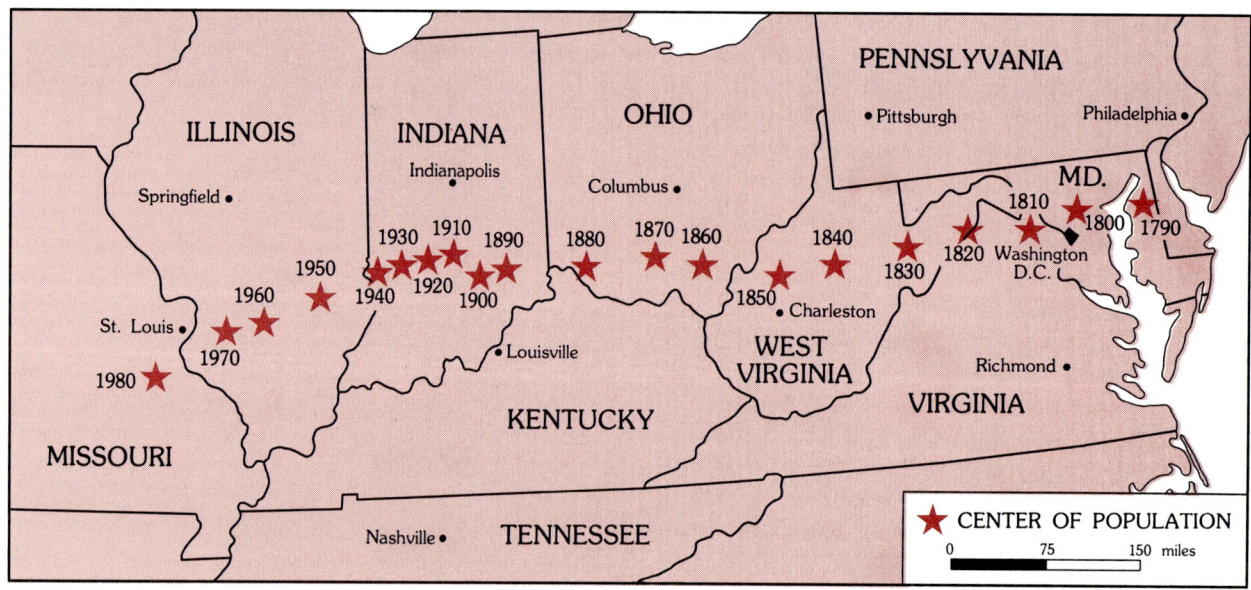

FIGURE 13-8 Movement of centers of population, 1790-1980. (From U.S. Bureau of the Census [1981], p. 7.)

South has become a region of strong population growth, with an increase of 12 million in 16 southern states between 1970 and 1980 (U.S. Department of Commerce, 1982). The pattern of percentage changes is shown in Figure 13-9. Remember, however, that high percentage increases for some states are calculated on a small base population. For instance, the population of Nevada increased from 494,000 in 1970 to 807,000 in 1980, or 61 percent. The population of Georgia increased 878,000, almost three times as much as that of Nevada, but Georgia's was a percentage gain of only 19 percent. Most of this population change is in the growth of cities, but not necessarily in the growth of metropolitan areas. Metropolitan places, called *Standard Metropolitan Statistical Areas* (SMSAs) by the U.S. Census Bureau, are defined as cities of at least 50,000 inhabitants, the counties in which such cities are located, and adjacent counties linked to the main county through commuting patterns. In 1980, there were 318 SMSAs, containing 169 million persons, or 75 percent of the nation's population, on 16 percent of the land area.

Historically, the trend has been for metropolitan areas to grow faster than nonmetropolitan areas, but this trend began to reverse about 1970. Between 1970 and 1980, SMSA population increased by some 16 million persons, whereas nonmetropolitan population increased less numerically but at a faster rate. The biggest SMSAs actually declined slightly in population from 1970 to 1980. New York, Detroit, Philadelphia, and Boston all lost population. Even the Los Angeles and San Francisco SMSAs, which had grown substantially since 1970, did so at less than the 10 percent national growth rate of SMSAs (U.S. Department of Commerce, 1982).

There has been a strong tendency toward suburbanization of the urban population. Continued population growth, in combination with generally rising real incomes since 1945, the deterioration of aging central cities, and (until the 1970s) cheap gasoline, fostered suburban development. Between 1970 and 1980, suburbs grew some 18 percent, whereas central cities stagnated, despite annexation of territory. Ethnic groups, however, tend to remain disproportionately concentrated in central cities. These groups are generally poor and thus relatively less able to buy into the suburbs. In 1980, only 6 percent of the black population lived in suburbs, although blacks constituted 12 percent of the nation's population. Black population growth in central cities stopped, however, at least temporarily, and black suburban population increased 23 percent between 1970 and 1980. This trend reflects the decline in migration out of the South and the gradual emergence of a black middle class, economically capable of entering the suburban housing market. The Spanish surname population was almost evenly divided between cities and suburbs in the 1980s (U.S. Department of Commerce, 1982). (See Appendix C for more details on U.S. population characteristics.)

Rising fuel costs may have an impact on urban population patterns and urban systems in the 1980s and 1990s. Initially, people will adapt to increased

THEORETICAL CONCEPTS

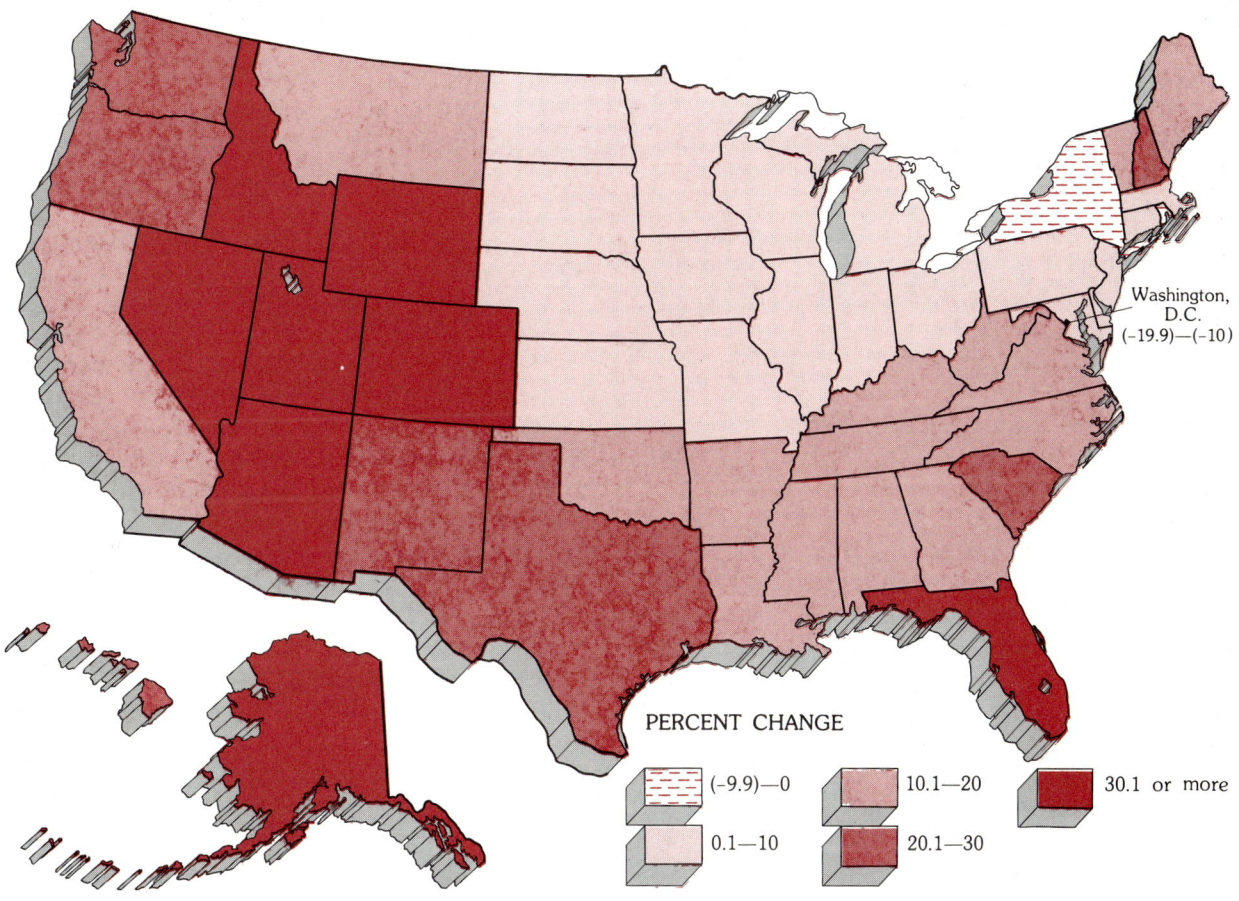

FIGURE 13–9 Percentage of population change by state, 1970–1980. (From U.S. Bureau of the Census [1981], pp. 10–11.)

costs by driving smaller, more fuel-efficient cars. People who are entering the housing market for the first time will place more emphasis on locations closer to workplaces or with good access to mass transit, and people who are relocating will also be more concerned about reducing commuting distances. But the pattern of existing homes, whether apartments or single-family dwellings, is already set, and the scope for adaptation is limited. There is likely to be more emphasis on *infilling* vacant urban land, and very low density suburban and exurban ("beyond the urbanized area") sprawl may be dampened. There will be a lot of discussion about public transportation systems, but few U.S. cities will develop such networks, since low-density sprawl has made public transportation more or less impractical, at least in terms of comprehensive citywide systems.

THEORETICAL CONCEPTS

Urban systems across the world have many common characteristics, and it is easiest to visualize them by discussing a few key theoretical concepts that we can apply to cities we are familiar with. *Theory* may bring to mind dull, sterile charts or formulas, but as we have noted elsewhere, the usefulness of theoretical concepts is that they are efficient—they enable us to learn an idea (a theory or principle) and apply it to many situations. This is much easier than learning a lot of facts and then trying to come up with a theory to fit them! The story of cities reveals some "efficient" ideas with general application.

Locational Competition

Strictly speaking, locational competition is best regarded as a concept, a way of organizing thoughts about why cities are where they are, rather than as a formal theory. Most, but by no means all, cities are located where they are because they offer (or historically offered) certain goods and services needed by people in the city itself and in the surrounding region, sometimes called the *hinterland*, which in the original German meant "behind land."

But this tells us only that we might expect cities to be spaced with some regularity in, say, an agricultural area of fairly uniform productivity. What determines whether a city becomes dominant in its area, or whether it grows to metropolitan status, or to regional dominance—to become a Philadelphia, a St. Louis, a Dallas, or a San Francisco? It is here that the concept of locational competition becomes relevant.

Most big cities rise to dominance because of a combination of advantages. Some are relatively obvious, such as location on a trade route, or a resource, or with easy access to raw materials. Other factors are more subtle—for instance, historical accident, personal location of a key industrialist (e.g., Henry Ford in Detroit), political considerations relating to defense or space contracts, or the location of highly specialized scientific skills or innovations (e.g., "Silicon Valley" south of San Francisco, where microprocessor chip research and production are concentrated). Physical environmental factors such as climate or accessibility to mountains or seacoasts may also constitute significant attractions. Another way to look at this is to say that a city cannot be considered in isolation from its setting. Take two identical cities and put one on a subtropical beach with a high mountain behind it, and the other on a featureless plain with a long, frigid winter. Although the physical forms of these imaginary cities are identical, the cities have become different places.

In effect, cities have advantages or disadvantages that accrue partly from their regional location and partly from special local conditions (the "more subtle" factors). The way this composite of conditions can affect a city is exemplified by New Orleans, Louisiana.

Lewis (1976) points out that the basis of the New Orleans economy is the port, making the city particularly vulnerable to technological changes relating to ocean freight (Figure 13–10). In the last few decades, several events affected New Orleans's strong position as a port. The interstate highway system greatly increased accessibility to many cities. Railroad mergers caused some cities that had been "preferred" by particular railroads (including New Orleans) to be passed over in favor of other ports. The new status of Chicago as a deep-water port, with the completion of the St. Lawrence Seaway, cut into the Midwestern dominance of New Orleans. Technological changes in cargo-carrying techniques led to the rapid emergence of container ships and barge-carrying ships. The location of New Orleans at the junction of the Gulf Intracoastal Waterway and the Mississippi River may offer relative advantage to the barge carriers, which can operate only on waterways, in contrast to the container ships, which can unload to any transportation mode. The competitive position of New Orleans clearly will be affected by new cargo technologies and changes in the national transportation network. If it does not adapt, it will be bypassed in favor of ports that do (Lewis, 1976, pp. 67–70).

This example shows how one specialized type of technological development can mean the difference between life and death for a great city. However, the emphasis must be on the *complexity* of processes of locational competition. Urban and regional systems

FIGURE 13–10 Unloading a ship at the Port of New Orleans using the "ro–ro" (roll on–roll off) technique. (Photo courtesy of the Board of Commissions of the Port of New Orleans.)

THEORETICAL CONCEPTS

are like natural systems in some respects—a change in one part of the system can have repercussions throughout. Thus, the American South in the 1970s and early 1980s has been attracting substantial industrial development, in no small part because trade unions have traditionally been weak in the South and corporations therefore see the South as a low labor cost region. Furthermore, the rural individualism of southerners has meant an attitude opposed to governmental control, which in turn has made it easier for corporations to violate environmental regulations and avoid costs associated with emission controls and other limitations on contamination. A change in attitudes, such as the rise of unions in the South, would have an impact on the entire national urban system and lead to a new round of reassessment of locational advantages and disadvantages.

Accessibility, Interaction, and Land Value

Accessibility, interaction, and land value must be discussed together because they are closely related phenomena. Interaction, or contact among people, cannot occur without some kind of accessibility, whether direct face-to-face contact, or telephone, mail, or media. For a city to thrive, accessibility and interaction must be facilitated. The principal enhancement of accessibility in cities is the connectivity of streets and highways in a network that makes many locations accessible to many others. Usually, the single most accessible district of a city is the downtown business area, commonly called the *central business district* (CBD). Various suburban nodes are usually quite accessible, too, often because of intersecting freeways or other major thoroughfares. These accessible suburban nodes are often the sites of large shopping centers, or are close to such centers. (Figure 13–11).

The concepts of accessibility and interaction are closely linked to land value. For land to be useful for commercial purposes, accessibility is vital. Multipurpose shopping trips and comparison shopping are done most efficiently when driving and walking are minimized. Minimization of effort occurs best in shopping centers, and the best location for centers is at points of convergence of connectivity in the street and highway network. These complementary conditions put a definite premium on more accessible locations that are essential for profitability in certain businesses.

In a competitive situation, potential land users bid against one another, and those who are willing to pay the most for a particular parcel, whether through rent or purchase, will win that parcel. Businesses that bid highest do so on the basis of anticipated profitability. The difference between the amount bid for a more accessible place as compared to a less accessible one is a premium attributable directly to location. Competitive allocation of land uses, based on distance from a "most accessible" point, can be represented by a simple diagram and its associated hypothetical map (Figure 13–12).

In Figure 13–12, distance from the "most accessible" point is represented on the horizontal axis, and the amount bid (per front foot or square foot) by

FIGURE 13–11 A major climate-controlled shopping center.

289

CHAPTER 13 URBANIZATION AND URBAN PLACES

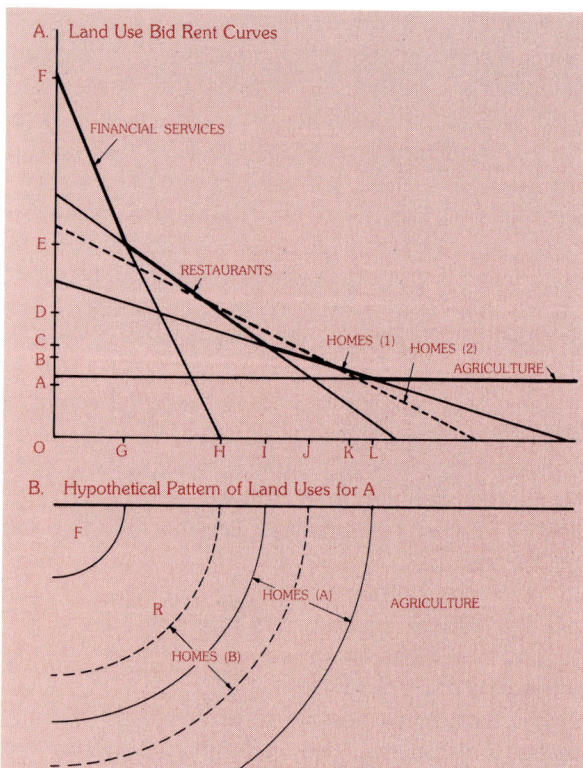

FIGURE 13–12 Competition among land users helps determine use patterns.

various competing uses is on the vertical axis. Assume that financial services (banks, stockbrokers, accountants, computerized money managers, etc.) are willing to outbid all other uses for a central location. At any distance between O and OG, we see that financial services are willing to pay more than any other potential user, at a given distance (Figure 13–12a). Between OG and OI, restaurants outbid any other use. Homes, or residential use, are represented by two curves. Curve 1 represents the residential bid structure under "normal" conditions. Curve 2 shows what may actually be happening today as energy costs, including commuting costs, increase. Home buyers may be willing to pay more to live closer to the center of the city, in effect gambling that the higher cost of land closer in will be more than offset in the long term by increases in gasoline prices. Geographically, this means that the residential zone (Figure 13–12b) shifts toward the center of the city as residential land use outbids other uses in the closer distance range. Agriculture adopts peripheral locations, because *land* is the critical input to the farmer, not location. Theoretically, it makes little difference to farmers or ranchers whether their fields or pastures are in the shadow of downtown skyscrapers or in the boondocks. That is why the agriculture curve in Figure 13–12a is more or less flat.

This is a generalized and simplified representation, or *model,* of the competitive process that sorts land uses and creates a pattern (Figure 13–12b). In reality, many factors upset this neat concentric arrangement. Accessibility is not as uniform as the model assumes—there are hundreds of competing land uses, not three or four; and the physical environment deviates from the model by creating barriers that modify the accessibility network, making land at a particular distance from the center more or less valuable than the simple model suggests. Yet, crude as it is, this model gives a general idea of processes that determine land value, and its validity is confirmed by the urban landscape, where buildings are high in the central city to make maximum use of accessible, extremely valuable land. Commercial uses are common on major streets, whereas residences are generally located on less accessible blocks, even in the suburbs.

Hierarchy

The concept of *hierarchy* is another basically simple idea that helps us understand the geography of cities. Hierarchy may be considered from two perspectives—*interurban* ("between cities") and *intraurban* ("within cities"). A hierarchy is any system in which things are ranked above one another (Figure 13–13). For example, an interurban hierarchy of the United States might be based on city size. New York would stand alone at the top—no other metropolitan area is close to it in size. What comes next in this hierarchy? After New York, Borchert (1972) groups together 7 major metropolitan areas as "second-order" metropolises—Boston, Chicago, Detroit, Los Angeles, Philadelphia, San Francisco, and Washington. Twenty others, ranging in size from Pittsburgh, Pennsylvania, to Portland, Oregon, are "third-order" centers. Figure 13–14 shows these metropolitan areas, along with their associated populations and volumes of retail trade and savings and loan deposits (Borchert, 1972, p. 353).* In this hierarchy, other smaller places, such as Tucson, Arizona; Butte, Montana; and Little Rock, Arkansas, would be regarded as "fourth-order" or lower. This arrangement is a *nested* hierarchy, meaning that at each successively higher level, the cities have all the functions (offerings of goods or services) of the level below, but offer some new or higher-order functions in addition. For example, you can rarely find a big, fancy restau-

---
*Since Borchert's study in 1972, the rank order of SMSAs has changed; in 1980, the top ten were: New York, Los Angeles, Chicago, Philadelphia, Detroit, San Francisco, Washington, D.C., Dallas, Houston, and Boston. The New York SMSA was still preeminent, with 3.5 million more inhabitants than second-ranked Los Angeles.

290

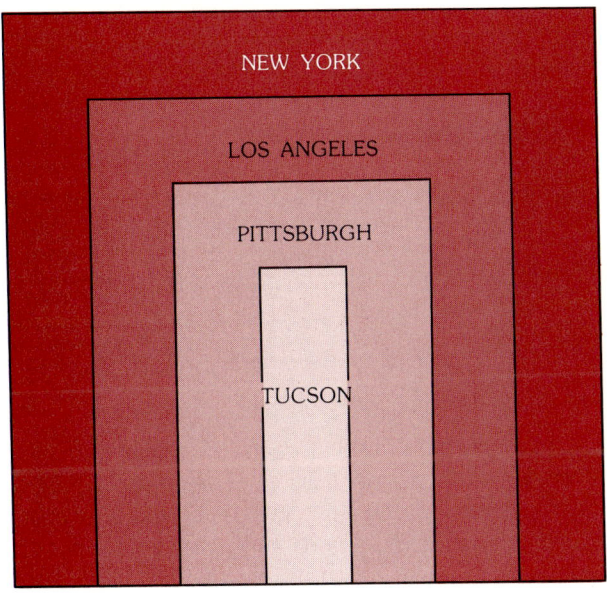
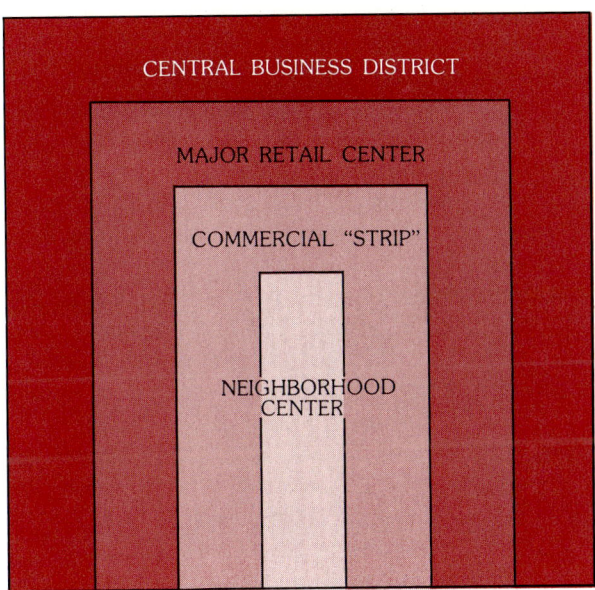

FIGURE 13–13 Interurban and intraurban nested hierarchies, showing the addition of new functions at each higher level.

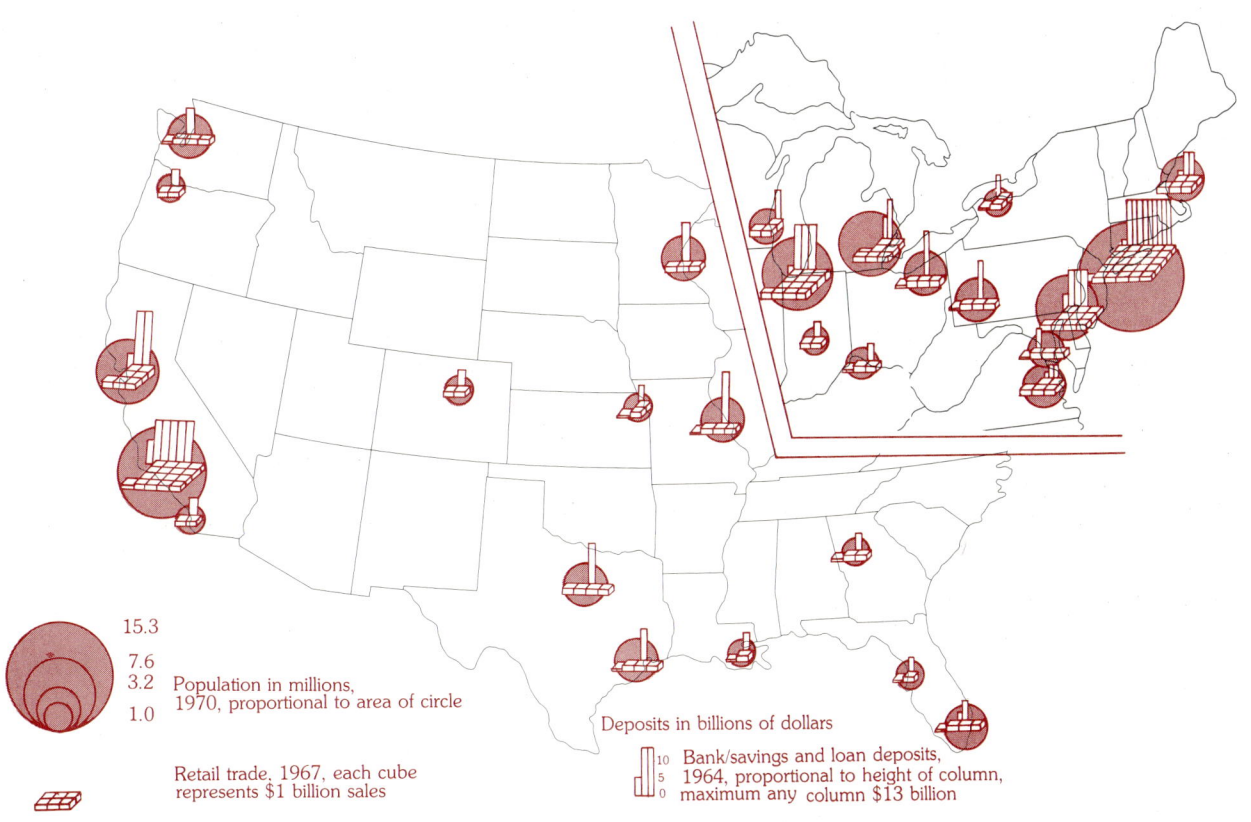

FIGURE 13–14 Borchert's high-order metropolitan areas, showing population, retail trade, and bank/savings and loan deposits. (Adapted by permission from *Annals of the Association of American Geographies* 62 [June 1972]: 353.)

rant in a small town, but as you move up the urban hierarchy, you find bigger and more specialized (e.g., Tahitian food) establishments. Similarly, medical facilities in smaller communities are designed for general treatment. Bigger cities have progressively more specialized facilities, even to the point of having hospitals for particular classes of illness or injury (e.g., orthopedic). Increasingly, small communities are linked to major medical centers in big cities via ambulance helicopters.

Within cities (intraurban), the same principles apply. At the neighborhood level, for example, there are only low-order goods and services—grocery stores, gas stations, and businesses that need relatively few customers for survival. At the other extreme, the central business district and large shopping centers may be regional, drawing customers from surrounding rural areas as well as from the city itself.

We need to touch on the supporting subconcepts of *threshold* and *range* here, and relate them to the concept of hierarchical *order*. A threshold population is the minimum population (or dollar volume) needed to sustain a particular urban function or center. Range refers to the distance a consumer is willing to travel to obtain a particular good or service (Figure 13–15). Presumably, the distance you would go to buy a tank of gas would be the shortest distance consistent with what you consider to be a reasonable price. You wouldn't (or shouldn't) drive 100 km to get gas a penny a gallon cheaper. But a 100-km drive might well be worthwhile to get a good deal on a new car or a major appliance. Higher-order cities or shopping centers have larger threshold populations and ranges compared to those of lower-order (discussed further in Chapter 11).

These few selected theoretical concepts relating to cities provide a preface for considering some of the regularities evident in the structure of North American cities.

REGULARITIES IN URBAN STRUCTURE

We can consider two aspects of urban structure. First, we shall consider why cities seem to develop in certain directions and not in others, and why these directions of development vary over time. Second, we will explain *structure* in more detail. Cities really have several substructures: the *physical city, land uses,* and *social areas*.

Sargent (1972) describes a model that offers a concise and comprehensive basis for understanding the fundamentals of development patterns in cities (pp. 358–61). He suggests that there is a hierarchical arrangement of areas and processes, represented by the *transportation frame,* the *speculative realm,* and the *settlement sphere* (Figure 13–16). The transportation frame represents the transportation system of

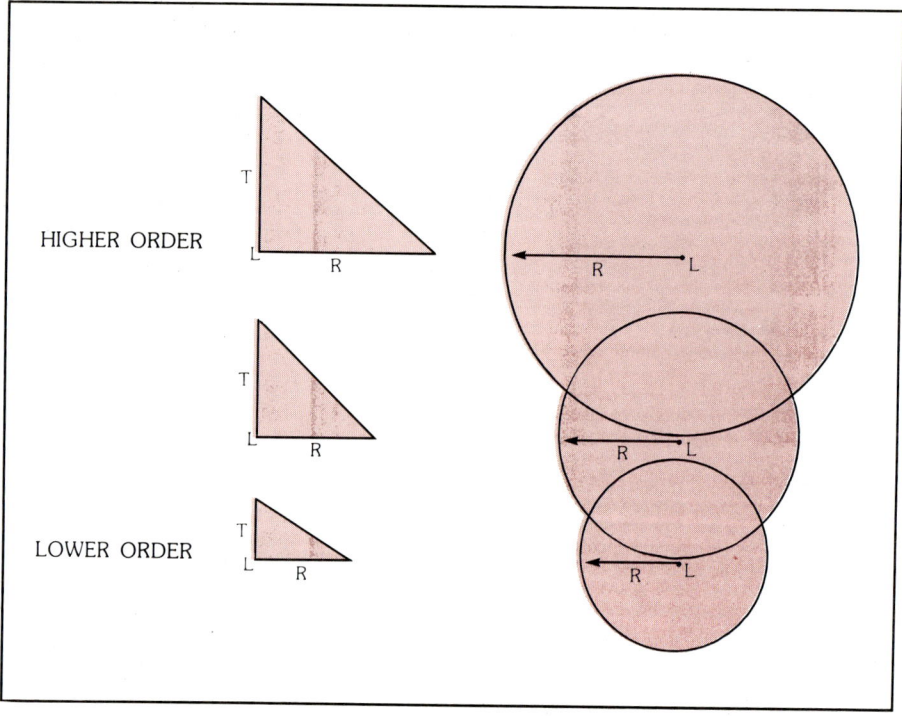

FIGURE 13–15 Concepts of threshold and range, where L represents the location of a store, service establishment, or center; T is threshold measured in population or dollar sales; and R is range. A circle with radius R defines theoretical market area; threshold and range become larger going up the hierarchy from low to high order.

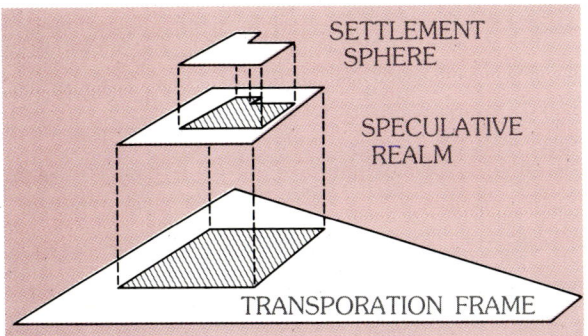

FIGURE 13–16 Nesting of dynamic growth factors. The area that is actually built up is much smaller than the total accessible area ("transportation frame") or the area that provokes the most interest for its development potential ("speculative realm"). (Adapted from Charles S. Sargent, Jr., *Economic Geography* 48 [October 1972]: 357–74.)

a city and its region. Inaccessible areas will not be developed, and those areas that can be reached most easily by public or private transportation will be built up first. The areas accessible within the transportation frame, then, will be subject to speculative interest by developers. The most accessible parts will tend to attract attention earliest. Likewise, not all the speculative realm will be developed at once, even though it may have been *platted* (surveyed, with lot lines drawn to scale) and made ready for subdivision. Within the speculative realm, development will most likely occur in areas that are easily served by utilities, that lack environmental conflicts (e.g., floodable zones), that are physically attractive, and that offer locational advantages with respect to available employment, stores, schools, and other amenities. On the other hand, subdivision also frequently occurs in areas that are subject to mudslides, earthquakes, fires, and floods. Figure 13–17 shows how the contours of the Santa Monica Mountains in Los Angeles have been altered by advancing urbanization.

Just as transportation technology helps to determine patterns of growth and decline *among* cities, so is transportation a critical factor affecting directions of growth *within* urban areas. The alignments of a new interstate highway or of new subway lines may pull development along with them, particularly if other urban services, such as water and sewer, can also be provided. *Physical planning* is therefore extremely important in encouraging development in directions that, insofar as possible, will minimize costs and environmental impacts.

The *physical city* is the product of a complex of processes. Can it be generalized with a model that is reasonably representative of an expectable pattern of development in a typical American city? Mayer (1969) suggests a map that might be described as a *spiderweb model* (Figure 13–18). A highway network radiates from the central business district. The built-up or urbanized area is web-shaped, because people can travel farther in a given amount of time if they are closer to transportation routes than if they are farther away—so the city tends to spread more in areas closer to such routes. Suburban centers, or *nuclei* (often older communities physically separated from the city), are engulfed by the city as it spreads out. Between transportation routes, the less accessible areas gradually fill in at low density (Mayer, 1969, p. 40).

FIGURE 13–17 Urbanization has modified the contours of the Santa Monica Mountains.

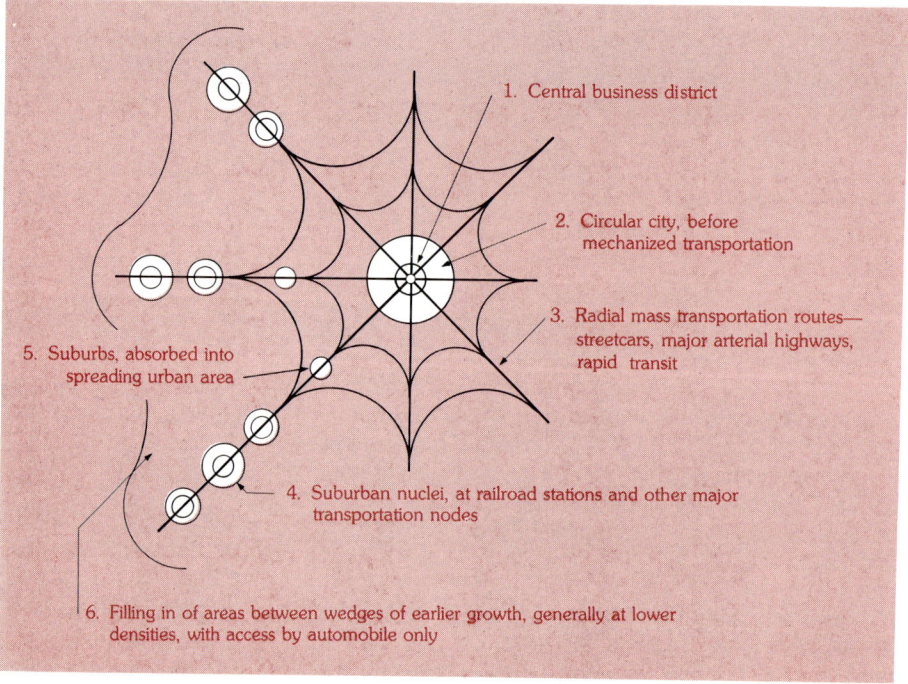

FIGURE 13–18 Spiderweb model of urban expansion. (Adapted by permission from H. M. Mayer, *The Spatial Expression of Urban Growth*, Association of American Geographers, Resource Papers for College Geography no. 7 [1969], p. 40.)

Interpretations of urban *land use* usually emphasize three map models, developed respectively by a sociologist, a land economist, and two geographers. Ernest Burgess, the sociologist, suggested a *concentric zone model* (Figure 13–19a), with the central business district at the center, followed outward by a *transition zone*, a *zone of workingmen's homes*, a *zone of better residences*, and a *commuter zone* (Burgess, 1925). The central business district was, as the name implies, the focus of commercial activity. The transition zone was an area into which commercial activities expanded as the affluent, now able to commute by private car, retreated to the suburbs. In the zone of workingmen's homes, blue-collar workers lived in a residential district close to workplaces. This was succeeded by the zone of better residences and the commuter zone, both encompassing newer dwellings at low density, accessible by train or private car. The land economist, Homer Hoyt, developed the *sector model* (Figure 13–19b). The emphasis was on

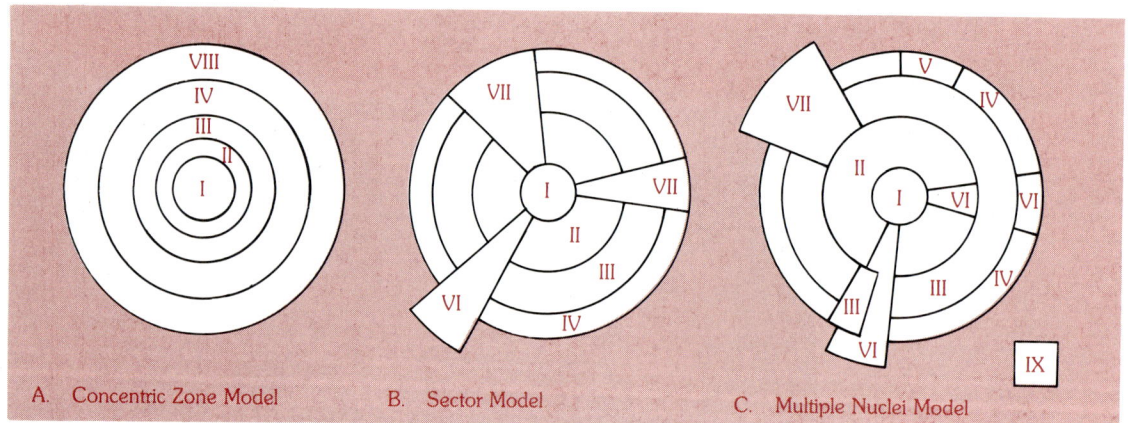

FIGURE 13–19 Urban land use models, in which I = Central Business District; II = wholesale/light manufacturing; III = low-rent residential (multiple family); IV = medium-rent residential; V = high-rent residential; VI = commercial; VII = industrial; VIII = commuter zone; IX = suburb. (From *Urban Geography* by R. M. Northam. Copyright © 1979. Reprinted by permission of John Wiley & Sons, Inc.)

explanation of the pattern of high-rent residential areas, which have such a significant role in guiding overall land use in cities. These areas were found to develop in a sectorial or "pie slice" manner, affected particularly by the alignment of transportation routes (Hoyt, 1939). The *multiple nuclei model,* described by geographers Harris and Ullman, suggested that many nuclei, or activity centers, shape land uses in the city (Figure 13–19c). If we look at American cities in the 1980s, we can see that land uses are indeed a complex of nucleated, sectorial, and concentric patterns.

Social areas display similar complexity. Numerous social area analyses in cities in the United States and elsewhere suggest the existence of three regularities. *Socioeconomic status* (SES) tends to be sectoral (note the similarity to Hoyt's sector model). *Family structure,* meaning stage in the life cycle (for example, are people single, or married with children?), tends to be concentric, with older people toward the center and younger people toward the suburbs. Ethnic or racial groups may be separated from other populations, giving a third pattern—*segregation.* When the three underlying regularities are overlaid, the result appears as in Figure 13–20.

As you may see by now, it is not easy to relate the physical, land use, and social patterns of cities. One way to sort out the complexity is to realize that the similarities among the various map models are not coincidental—in reality, the physical city, the land use city, and the social city are merged together, and the product of this merging is the city itself.

PLANNING THE URBAN ENVIRONMENT

Why plan? The answer is relatively simple. Planning, at its best, allows the orderly development of an urbanized area. In other words, planning provides protection. Home buyers will know that necessary utilities will be available, that street patterns have been designed with some heed to questions of safety and congestion, and that certain minimum standards in terms of lot size, setback (distance of dwelling unit from the street or from neighboring dwellings), and construction have been met. Furthermore, the arrangement of land uses will ideally be controlled in such a way as to limit major conflicts. Noxious industrial uses, such as the manufacture of dynamite, acid, or nuclear warheads, should not be adjacent to residential districts. Medical and educational facilities should be located away from sources of noise or pollution. The zones in the approaches to airport runways should be kept free of residential development,

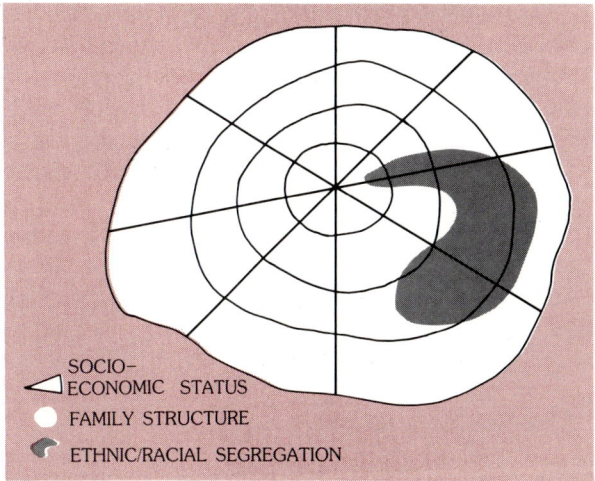

FIGURE 13–20 Social areas in cities.

and areas subject to natural hazards such as flooding, mudslides, or brush fires should be withheld from urban development.

The planning process can do much more than prohibit what is undesirable. Sophisticated planning facilitates *prediction* of the likely impacts of development. Paving an area, for example, will increase runoff and may create a flood hazard where none existed. Studies of population characteristics in new residential areas may allow predictions about the amount of classroom space needed to accommodate additional students in public schools. Efficient provision of public services such as fire prevention, policing, and trash collection needs to take into account changing patterns of population and the characteristics of that population. A neighborhood of elderly people, for example, presents a much different law enforcement problem compared to a neighborhood with many teen-agers. The former is likely to be a *target* of crime—a crime-*importing* area—whereas the latter is more likely to generate crime internally, and also to *export* crime to other neighborhoods.

Urban planning, then, is extraordinarily comprehensive, involving the challenge of understanding the way in which many elements interact in a set of complex processes. Planning is strongly geographical in nature, demanding expertise in the interpretation of the human and physical environments in specific areas. The principles, methods, and data of urban geography can be applied effectively in the planning process. The well-trained urban planner will have expertise not only in urban geography but also in economics, municipal law, architecture, and civil engineering. Quite apart from this demanding academic preparation, an effective planner must possess communication skills and political savvy.

To a considerable extent, the planner's role may be seen as that of a mediator who reconciles the public need for a safe, aesthetic environment with the developer's need for profit. Responsible developers are usually not at odds with the public interest, but the pressure of the profit motive does lead to some irresponsible and dangerous actions, such as placing dwellings in flood zones or in areas with inadequate water pressure or sewer capacity. The involvement of third parties, such as mortgage bankers, often serves as a check on such developments, but third parties may have a conflict of interest in the sense that their profit is linked to the volume of mortgage loans written.

Planning, then, is an extremely challenging profession, and one that can be most rewarding. Urban planning is not a cure-all for the problems of the city, but it can minimize inequities in the provision of neighborhood services that characterize many cities. Some neighborhoods have good schools, good police and fire protection, adequate parks, and high air and water quality, while some do not. Some neighborhoods flood. Some do not. Some have broken streets, leaky water mains and gas lines, clogged sewers, and unreliable electrical supplies. Some do not. Neighborhoods will never be the same in all these respects, but the planning process, incorporating geographical analyses, can help to minimize glaring inequalities.

CONCLUSION

Cities will soon accommodate more than half the world's population. People come together in cities for many reasons, including the availability of employment, housing, services, and amenities. Cities are a relatively new invention, and great increases in the numbers of people living in them have come quite recently. In the United States, the great productivity of agriculture has meant that few people are needed to work the land, so the number of farms steadily declines. A major contributor to the growth of our cities has been rural-to-urban migration. The historical geography of American cities indicates that change has been constant. The great cities of today will probably be relatively less important tomorrow, as their attractiveness fades. Other cities, because of energy riches or mild climate, may see temporary rapid growth.

Understanding of the geography of the city is enhanced through consideration of several theoretical concepts—locational competition, accessibility, interaction, and hierarchy. Just as we can generalize urban processes into theoretical concepts, so can the *form* of cities be represented by general graphic models. In the next chapter, the discussion focuses on the quality of life in cities from a geographer's perspective—which cities rank highest as places to live, and why.

KEY WORDS

city
diffusion
division of labor
domestication
environmental determinism
hierarchy
hinterland
Industrial Revolution
interurban
intraurban

metropolis/metropolitan
model
order
plat
range
SMSA
theory
threshold
urban/urbanization

REFERENCES

BORCHERT, J. R. "American Metropolitan Evolution." *Geographical Review* 57 (1967): 301–32.

_____. "America's Changing Metropolitan Regions." *Annals of the Association of American Geographers* 62 (1972): 352–73.

BURGESS, ERNEST W. "The Growth of the City." In Robert E. Park, Ernest W. Burgess, and Roderick D. McKenzie, eds. *The City.* Chicago: University of Chicago Press, 1925, pp. 47–62.

REFERENCES

HARRIS, CHAUNCY D., and ULLMAN, EDWARD L. "The Nature of Cities." *Annals of the American Academy of Political and Social Science* 242 (1945).

HOYT, HOMER. *The Structure and Growth of Residential Neighborhoods in American Cities.* Washington, D.C.: Federal Housing Administration, 1939.

LEWIS, PEIRCE F. *New Orleans: The Making of an Urban Landscape.* Cambridge, Mass.: Ballinger Publishing Co., 1976.

MAYER, HAROLD M. *The Spatial Expression of Urban Growth.* Association of American Geographers Resource Paper No. 7. 1969. p. 40.

"NEW SPECIES OF MAN: ANCESTORS FROM 'AFAR.' " *Science News* 115 (1979): 36.

NORTHAM, RAY M. *Urban Geography.* 2nd ed. New York: John Wiley & Sons, 1979.

SARGENT, CHARLES S. Jr. "Toward a Dynamic Model of Urban Morphology." *Economic Geography* 48 (1972): 357–74.

SJOBERG, GIDEON. "The Origin and Evolution of Cities." In *Cities: Readings from Scientific American.* San Francisco: W. H. Freeman & Co., 1973, pp. 19–26.

U.S. DEPARTMENT OF COMMERCE, Bureau of the Census. *Number of Inhabitants: U.S. Summary,* PC(1)–A1. Washington, D.C.: U.S. Government Printing Office, 1971.

———. Bureau of the Census, *Statistical Abstract of the United States: 1983* (103d edition.) Washington D.C.: U.S. Government Printing Office, 1982.

———. *Social and Economic Characteristics of the Metropolitan and Non-Metropolitan Population: 1977 and 1970.* Current Population Reports, Special Studies P-23, No. 75. Washington, D.C.: U.S. Government Printing Office, 1978.

———. *Population Profile of the United States: 1978.* Current Population Reports, Series P-20, No. 336. Washington, D.C.: U.S. Government Printing Office, 1979.

VANCE, JAMES E., Jr. *This Scene of Man.* New York: Harper & Row Publishers, 1977.

14
The Quality of Urban Life

THE SOCIOECONOMIC ENVIRONMENT
THE PHYSICAL ENVIRONMENT
A QUALITY OF LIFE STUDY OF U.S. METROPOLITAN AREAS

Oil-coated rocks along the beach of the exclusive Santa Barbara suburb of Montecito, California, after a major spill from offshore oil drilling.

What is the practical value of a geographic perspective on cities? In the last chapter, we touched on some of the historical background, trends, and concepts relating to the geography of cities. Now it is time to illustrate how geographical information can be put to work to help people and institutions make decisions. There are many such applications in the private and public sectors, but we will deal with only one—an application that usually generates a good deal of interest because it relates to emotions as well as to pocketbooks. The label usually given to the kind of studies we will talk about is *quality of life*, abbreviated *QOL*.

QOL can be considered at several geographic levels, or scales. We might compare nations, states, cities, or neighborhoods. Since we are discussing urban geography, it is appropriate to focus mainly on the city and neighborhood levels.

Just what is included in the concept of QOL? Why does it generate so much interest? The work that has been done on QOL has attempted to compare areas or places to find out, quite simply, how they stack up against each other. Such comparisons are difficult for several reasons. People often have strong emotional ties to the places where they live (Chapter 8). In practice, what this amounts to is that people who live in places with low QOL—objectively measured—can feel just as attached to these places as those who live in cities or neighborhoods that are identified as having high QOL. The emotional element in QOL is difficult to measure properly, and in most QOL studies it is ignored. There are no data for any comprehensive set of places, and, furthermore, it is reasonable to assume that most people in any case would say that they like it where they are.

Another difficulty with the assessment of QOL is the difficulty in deciding exactly what to measure, and how to deal with measurements in a QOL index. For example, one person may be concerned with the quality of education in public schools, whereas the next person may see health care as the first priority. Quite apart from the question of *which* elements should be regarded as valid QOL measures, there is the problem of measuring the elements properly. Levels of wages and salaries tell us nothing useful unless we also have information on the cost of living. Measures of health care, such as the incidence of cancer, heart disease, and stroke, may not be informative unless we know something about the age structure of the population. A high level of degenerative diseases in a young population provides us with quite a different set of clues about QOL compared to a high level of such diseases in an older population.

What about the physical environment? In Chapter 8, climate was shown to be one of the principal reasons for interstate migration. How should climate be measured? By the number of frost-free days? Average number of sunny days? Mean temperature or precipitation? Some places that appear favorable in terms of these statistics are desert environments where water shortages and problems with blowing sand or dust may outweigh the advantages of a seemingly pleasant climate. Microclimatic features related to an area's physical geography may mean substantial climatic differences within short distances, as in the case of the coastal and interior zones of California. What about the interface between people and nature in the city? Has urbanization confronted the natural environment in an exploitive way, or has it adapted to natural conditions, minimizing impacts on the preurban ecosystem? QOL studies, in spite of the difficulties in representing the complexity of reality with a simple index of some sort, can provide a basis for comparisons between neighborhoods and cities. (See Helburn, 1982.)

More importantly, perhaps, an understanding of a QOL approach can provide a conceptual framework to help us make our personal or familial locational decisions. If we look at the environment critically and ask perceptive, tough questions about it, we will not only make better locational decisions but will also communicate concerns to employers, realtors, developers, planners, bankers, and others who have the power to shape the cities in which we live.

This chapter is divided into four parts. In the first two, we consider various aspects of the socioeconomic and physical environments that should be included in a QOL index. This discussion is organized on the basis of checklists that could be used in a practical way to assist in personal locational decisions. In the third section, we will discuss some data from a major QOL study of U.S. cities done in the 1970s. In the final part, attention turns to personal locational decision making, an aspect of *applied geography*. This chapter provides a basis for developing a strategy that could help you make the best possible personal locational decisions, which in turn could help you maximize enjoyment of your limited life span and at the same time help you become a potentially more effective citizen.

THE SOCIOECONOMIC ENVIRONMENT

We must emphasize that this discussion of specific indicators of socioeconomic and physical QOL is being painted with a broad brush. We are excluding many aspects of life that could be included in QOL, partly for lack of space, and also in part because general locational data are not available for them. These indicators are psychological factors such as status, dominance, boredom, and friendship. Instead, we will concentrate on major factors for which data can be obtained, either directly or indirectly.

An Environmental Protection Agency study in the 1970s attempted to compile a set of factors that could be regarded as a consensus set of *social indicators,* representing major QOL elements (Table 14–1). The factors are listed in the order of the importance assigned to them by the group that did the selecting. As it happened, this was a fairly affluent group; a group of poor people might have come up with a different list, ranked differently. Housing and economic opportunity, for example, would likely have been ranked higher by the poor.

How do the factors listed in Table 14–1 enter into QOL, and how can they be measured in practice? (The definitions that follow are from U.S. Environmental Protection Agency, 1973).

TABLE 14–1 Social indicators and quality of life

Rank	Factor
1	Democratic process
2	Public participation
3	Health
4	Choices in life
5	Housing
6	Economic security
7	Education
8	Land use planning
9	Essential living costs
10	Economic opportunity

Source: U.S. Environmental Protection Agency, 1973, p. 1–81.

Democratic process The system by which the public [nominally] governs itself in accordance with the principles of equality of rights, opportunity, and treatment.

For purposes of this discussion, focusing on the urban environment, democratic process will be assumed, since the process is not substantially different among U.S. cities, at least in theory—local representatives are elected to city and state governing bodies. Admittedly, the manner in which power is exercised in the democratic process may vary greatly. The outcome of an election is often influenced by economic clout—those interests that can spend enough money to advertise and otherwise promote their candidates often win. At its worst, the democratic process becomes a power struggle among the rich to determine who can buy the most influence. Putting this into a QOL context, there is no meaningful information to help us go about making personal locational decisions. Chicago has probably had the most notoriety for election corruption, but, realistically, few people would decline to move to Chicago purely on the basis of that fact. Some people might actually be attracted to Chicago by the realization that they could benefit from corruption—"get a piece of the action," so to speak.

Public participation The ability of citizens to be heard and to interrogate the decision makers.

To this definition, we might add the concept of an *informed* citizenry, since it is highly unlikely that people will be interested in being heard, or in questioning decision makers, unless they are informed and interested in issues that affect them. Participation, then, can be represented by measures such as access to the media. For example, daily newspaper circulation in 1978 varied from a high of 0.491 per capita in New York State to a low of 0.211 in Maryland. There are similar contrasts in voter participation. In 1978, the percentage of the voting age population that actually cast votes for U.S. representatives was 54.0 in Minnesota, but a mere 16.6 in Georgia. Again, it is unlikely that this factor alone would be crucial in personal locational decision making; however, among people who have a choice, some will prefer to locate in places where there is evidence that the electorate is involved in, and informed about, the issues that affect them.

Health Physical and mental well-being. Ability to detect, treat, and control specific causes and characteristic symptoms of illness and ailments. Quality and quantity of services provided in order to maintain mental and physical growth and development.

Clearly, health is a major concern for many people, especially those who are young or old. There are large and readily measured inequalities in health care at virtually all levels of geographic scale—whether nations, regions, cities, or neighborhoods. Figure 14–1 shows that even pet ownership can pose health and sanitation problems in a densely populated area. Common measures include infant mortality rates, death rates, and the availability of physicians and hospital beds. The United States, rich as it is, does not have one of the highest-ranked medical care systems in the world. Generally, richer nations are "healthier," but the United States stands out as an exception, suggesting that doctors tend to choose highly paid specialties in affluent communities, where their impact on general health care is least (Smith, 1979, p. 255).

Within the United States, there are sharp differences among places and population groups. In 1979, the lowest infant death rate (8.6 per 1,000 live births) was recorded among whites in Vermont. The highest rate (35.1) occurred among blacks in Rhode Island. For the United States as a whole, the black

FIGURE 14–1 High-density human population brings high-density dog population and accompanying problems of sanitation.

infant death rate was almost double that for whites (21.8 compared to 11.4). One difference among cities that has been receiving increasing attention recently relates to the provision of trauma centers that specialize in acute emergency care. The geography of these centers can mean the difference between life and death for significant numbers of people. The typical general hospital emergency room is simply not capable of dealing properly with serious burns, gunshot wounds, or complex traffic accident injuries. Travel time to the nearest trauma center may determine whether the patient lives or dies, and the locations of such centers, quite apart from these other factors, are a real QOL factor. For college students who are either in or approaching the family formation stage of their life cycles, the availability of pre- and postnatal care and of adequate pediatric services should be a relevant concern.

Choices in life The chance, right, or power to make fundamental choices in life usually by the free exercise of one's judgment and the use of one's resources.

This important QOL element is probably best measured indirectly through such factors as education and economic opportunity. Racial and sexual discrimination are good examples of denial of the right to freely use one's resources, and a reasonably effective way to gauge such discrimination is to look at differences in income or occupational status based on race or sex. Discrimination based on race, sex, and other factors is so widespread that it is unlikely that many locational decisions will be based on this factor alone, with the possible exception of those who might decline to move to some southern communities or to smaller cities, fearing that discrimination would be more blatant there than in larger metropolitan areas. The reverse could be true, too. People who enjoy a discriminatory advantage may be reluctant to leave a social environment in which discrimination is aggressively practiced.

Housing The availability of adequate housing facilities.

Like health care, housing is fundamental for most people. Information on housing is critically important in the locational decision-making process. The quality and quantity of available housing not only affect comfort and convenience, but may have a direct bearing on physical health, particularly if heating is inadequate or if conditions are unsanitary. There are substantial place-to-place differences in housing, which can be readily evaluated through the study of information from the Census of Population and Housing (Figure 14–2). Owner-occupied housing is most prevalent in Michigan (74.4 percent of the housing stock) and least so in Hawaii (46.9 percent). Crowded housing is most likely to be found in Hawaii, Alaska, Louisiana, and New Mexico.

In 1981, the median selling price of new single-family houses was lowest in the South ($64,000) and highest in the West ($78,000). This kind of data can be useful for those considering a move between states or regions. The problems of balancing economic advantages (cheaper housing) against human rights disadvantages (more discrimination) are diffi-

FIGURE 14–2 Few people can afford expensive waterfront property like this.

THE SOCIOECONOMIC ENVIRONMENT

cult, but are best dealt with on the basis of the fullest possible information.

Economic security The degree to which one can maintain his economic state in relation to his needs.

Economic security can be measured in terms of levels of income, unemployment, productivity, and the "mix" of economic activities, all of which can be viewed geographically. In 1981, for example, Alaska had the highest per capita income among the states ($14,190), followed by Connecticut, New Jersey, and California. At the other end of the spectrum were Alabama, South Carolina, Arkansas, and (in last place with $7,256) Mississippi. Income levels alone by no means tell us enough about "economic security." High pay may go along with high prices and with temporary activities such as the construction of the Alaska pipeline. Also, per capita income may be high, but most of the wealth may be in few hands. Cities or regions that are heavily dependent on one economic activity (e.g., automobiles, construction) may rate poorly on economic security because they are hit hard when demand for that product falls off, with ripple effects that may be far-reaching. This problem is worth taking into account in locational decision making.

Education The knowledge, skills, character, and so forth of the population and the process of obtaining and developing them by schooling, training, and other means.

To tell college students that education is important is at the same time a conflict of interest (the authors are educators) and redundant. (Why would you be a college student if you didn't think college was likely to prove useful in some way?) Studies by noneducators show that, in general, more education is associated with higher income levels, and a generally higher level of economic security and overall QOL. Education is in many respects the key to QOL. Those who are unable to gain access to education are likely to find themselves in lower-paying, less secure jobs, with lower-quality housing and inferior standards of health care (Figure 14–3).

Like other QOL factors, education varies geographically. In general, places with lower income levels are also places with less educated populations. For the purpose of locational decision making, information on geographical variations in education may be most practical as a guide to the quality of public school systems and institutions of higher education. The presence of major educational institutions enhances the quality of life in cities through direct education, cultural events, and advanced medical facilities.

Land use planning The well-organized, planned, and presumably beneficial use of the land.

Land use planning should be considered as both a *socioeconomic* and a *physical* environmental factor. Land use in populated areas is affected by human decision making, but there is interaction between

FIGURE 14–3 U.C.L.A. is one of many colleges and universities in Los Angeles.

human and physical factors. We will discuss land use as a physical environmental factor at the city or neighborhood level beginning on p. 304.

Essential living costs The portion of total income required to satisfy basic human needs such as food, clothing, shelter, and so on.

The earlier brief discussion of income levels has no meaning unless income levels are related to costs. If cities with the highest wages also have the highest prices and taxes, the cities may offer no distinct advantage (or disadvantage) compared to cities with lower wages and prices.

Data on the cost of a selected group of goods and services, including food, housing, and transportation, for a four-person family in 1981 showed substantial geographical differences. The cost was almost $2,000 more in metropolitan areas compared to nonmetropolitan. Among metropolitan areas, Honolulu, Boston, and New York were high, Dallas and Austin low. Locational decision making should take into account prices as well as wages.

Economic opportunity Circumstances favorable to improvement of an individual's material welfare in relation to his ability.

Conceptually, this is similar to "choices in life," and can be thought of in terms of factors such as income differentials between races or sexes, educational opportunities (including vocational and on-the-job training), and other measures that tell us to what extent individual potential can be maximized in the marketplace. Areas noted for discriminatory practices or for weak educational systems are less likely to provide "economic opportunity" in this broader sense, as compared to simply providing a job.

These 10 socioeconomic factors provide a partial basis for developing a framework for thinking about the QOL concept. To these 10, we must add another set to reflect the quality of the physical environment (Table 14–2).

THE PHYSICAL ENVIRONMENT

As we mentioned, land use should be regarded as both a social and physical environmental indicator. In urban areas, land use changes often have dramatic impacts on the physical environment, directly or indirectly. Direct impacts are particularly noticeable in relation to drainage patterns. Natural surfaces such as grass and trees have the effect of slowing down storm runoff—some water penetrates the soil, some

TABLE 14–2 Physical environment indicators and quality of life

Rank	Factor
1	Land use
2	Air pollution
3	Water pollution
4	Recreational resources
5	Noise pollution
6	Solid waste
7	Climate-weather
8	Utilities
Unranked	Visual pollution

Source: U.S. Environmental Protection Agency, 1973, p. 1–81.

is absorbed by the plants directly, and some is prevented from running off by the obstructing action of stems and plant debris. When an area is substantially paved and roofed with impermeable (nonporous) surfaces, runoff is essentially instantaneous. This in turn means that creeks and streams reach their peak sooner, and that the peak is higher than before development.

The problem is compounded by the fact that residential subdivisions are usually *imposed* on the landscape, disrupting the natural drainage pattern. When a *drainage basin* is developed piecemeal, and each developer fails to interrelate drainage patterns, drainage problems can become progressively worse downward through the basin, until, at the lowest levels, street flooding is commonplace, creating an obstacle to neighborhood accessibility. Ironically, such shallow-water flood areas are not necessarily on floodplains, yet flooding is a much more frequent (though less serious) problem than on true floodplains. From a locational decision-making perspective, this problem is elusive, because even the most careful study of topographic maps would fail to show any hazards. Inadequate drainage regulations in cities mean more downstream impacts—more *costs*. Tighter, or less permissive, rules mean more attention to impacts and higher initial costs (more money spent on design and construction of drainage improvements). But in the long term, costs are less than without proper design, and inconvenience and risk to life are minimized. Another benefit may be a more *aesthetic* environment.

Indirectly, land use may create new environmental conditions or modify old ones. Urbanization creates new kinds of air pollution. Water is polluted by running off contaminated surfaces and through various industrial emissions into streams. Climate is modified. In short, land use causes various levels of environmental impact depending on the specific use.

Shopping centers or industrial plants may be focal points of air and noise pollution, for example. A park, on the other hand, should make antipollution contributions by absorbing carbon dioxide, generating oxygen, and slowing storm runoff, quite apart from its powers of spiritual restoration and physical recreation. Figure 14–4a shows the approach to Meadowlark Airport in Orange County, California, through an entirely residential neighborhood. Figure 14–4b shows the influence of zoning ordinances at

FIGURE 14–4 Land use in California. The lighter area at the top of the picture in (b) marks the top of the smog layer; the arrow marks the border of Beverly Hills.

(a)

(b)

the border between Beverly Hills, zoned for single-family residential (left), and unincorporated Los Angeles County with its famous Sunset Strip entertainment district (right).

Air pollution The amount of foreign and harmful substances in the air from all possible sources.

Health, particularly for the young or for those already weakened by lung diseases such as emphysema, can be seriously affected by air pollution. Anyone who has suffered the runny eyes and nasal congestion associated with smog, or who has been compelled to curtail physical activity on account of air pollution, knows that air quality is a very real QOL factor.

Air pollution is not solely an urban problem. In a survey of rural residents of Oklahoma in the 1970s, air pollution was identified as the first-ranked environmental problem—due not to auto or industrial emissions, but to dust. This dust is not necessarily the red dust of the dry fields of the plains, either—it may come from billowing clouds of tree pollen (and other plant pollens) that boost the sales curves of sinus medicines.

Pollutants are of two types—primary and secondary. *Primary* pollutants come directly from specific sources—natural (volcanoes, fires, dust, pollen), man-made, or "man-accentuated," as in the case of fires caused by humans. *Secondary* pollutants develop through interaction with the atmosphere itself (Bryson and Kutzbach, 1968, p. 9). Air pollution is strongly affected by the interrelation of natural conditions such as climate and man-made conditions, and there are major place-to-place differences. For example, Buffalo, Chicago, and Cleveland are high in suspended particulates, and Phoenix, Birmingham, and Baltimore stand out with high levels of sulfur oxides.

Generally, air pollution is associated with higher-density areas in cities, so the poor and minorities who are concentrated in central areas are most heavily affected. This problem is particularly acute in Gary, Chicago, Cleveland, and Newark. It has been suggested that "the race-related disparities in exposure to air pollution are even more glaring than those associated with income" (Lakshmanan and Chatterjee, 1977, p. 8).

Water pollution The amount of foreign and harmful substances in the water from all possible sources.

The most directly relevant QOL question about water is whether the supply of domestic drinking water is pure. Water drawn from major rivers that are also used as sewers for residential, industrial, and agricultural wastes may need expensive filtration and other treatments to reduce health risks.

Recreational resources The availability of nonpersonal resources for use in leisure activities.

The place-to-place availability of recreational resources varies substantially, partly because of variations in the opportunities presented by the natural environment. For example, in the extreme case of Alaska, the federal government owns 1.5 million km^2 (570,000 mi^2), or an area more than twice the size of Texas. Such a large publicly-owned area offers possibilities for recreational development. At the urban scale, one should consider the availability of neighborhood and city parks, including their levels of use and maintenance (for suggested standards, see Claire, 1973, p. 185).

Noise pollution The production of sounds at a level that can be considered annoying and possibly harmful.

Noise can interfere with sleep, speech communication, leisure activities, and students in schools (Stevenson, 1972, p. 223). Noise is therefore an important factor, particularly in locational decisions for homes and schools, as well as for the sources of the noise. Airport noise is particularly critical, affecting as it does large swaths of metropolitan areas. Many homes have been removed from runway approach zones, as at Los Angeles International Airport, and vast soundproofing schemes for homes have been undertaken, as in London. It is important to realize that those who benefit from airport use (passengers, employees, and airline stockholders) do not pay the costs of the noise produced. These costs are passed on to metropolitan residents who must absorb them as a kind of tax or penalty on location.

Solid waste The problems engendered by the requirements to effectively and permanently dispose of the residual matter remaining after the initial use or consumption of society's products.

While a main concern of households is regular removal of solid waste, the disposal of wastes is a major problem for many cities. New York City uses a vast landfill, and Los Angeles has used it to fill canyons in the Santa Monica Mountains, which were then converted into parks. From a QOL perspective, it is important that cities have effective strategies for dealing with solid waste (and other utilities) and that they give proper attention to recycling.

Climate/weather   The impact of long-term (climate) and short-term (weather) atmospheric and solar conditions.

It has already been shown (Chapter 8) that climate is a major factor in determining interstate migration in the United States. People are attracted by what they perceive as favorable climatic conditions, represented most typically by mild temperature. The winter migration of "snowbirds" (people from northern states) to Arizona and Florida illustrates this. Climatic preference, like many other aspects of QOL, is a personal matter, but it may be worth considering that air pollution problems are linked to climatic conditions, and that severe winter locations represent cost disadvantages in terms of space heating. Construction costs are also higher because of the need for heavier insulation. At the extremes in this respect are such cities as Honolulu and Duluth, Minnesota. In Honolulu, the mean daily temperature in the coldest month (22.4°C or 72.3°F) is only 4.7°C (8.4°F) cooler than the temperature in the warmest month (27.1°C or 80.7°F), compared to a difference of 14.0°C (57.1°F) between the coolest and warmest months in Duluth.

Precipitation patterns and the likelihood of hazards such as tornadoes and hurricanes may also be worth considering. People in New York City may not have too much trouble with an annual average of 73.7 cm (29 in.) of snow. Upstate in Buffalo, however, where the average expectation is 236 cm (92.9 in.), enthusiasm for the white stuff is no doubt less. Rainfall, and other aspects of climate, differ qualitatively from place to place. In Florida, the Midwest, and other areas where thunderstorm activity is common, storm rainfall may be rated according to whether it is a "gulley washer" or a "toad strangler"! Similarly, most people appreciate that 32°C (90°F) is *felt* much differently in low humidity compared to high.

One additional point in connection with climate and weather is that urban conditions are quite different from rural conditions. Cities are warmer, cloudier, less humid, less windy, and have more precipitation than surrounding rural environments (Bryson and Ross, 1972, p. 52).

Hazardous substances   Materials located in the environment in such a way as to constitute a threat to human health.

This catchall category overlaps to some extent with air and water pollution. The problem has been dramatized by Morganthau and Hager (1980):

> In Woburn, Mass., health authorities shut down two city water wells found to be contaminated with trichloroethylene, an industrial solvent known to cause cancer. Deaths from cancer have risen 17 percent in five years among Woburn residents, and state officials are now preparing a block-by-block survey to find out how widespread the town's health problems really are.
> In Elizabeth, N.J. . . . an abandoned chemical dump crammed with 34,000 barrels of toxic waste caught fire and blew up. Dozens of firemen were overcome by the smoke, and hundreds of nearby residents reported symptoms of chemical poisoning. In the end, one official said, "No one got a dangerous dose—but it was just dumb luck" [p. 34].*

To these examples, we could add the radiation problems of the Three Mile Island nuclear power plant in Pennsylvania, and the horrors of Love Canal, New York, a chemical dump that awakened the United States to the toxic waste issue. Hazardous substances, many with a yet undetermined impact on health, are found universally, on farms (fertilizers, herbicides, pesticides, DES), in factories, in homes, and in various dumps, as well as in the air and in watercourses. Unfortunately, there is no comprehensive set of data that can be included in a QOL index. In making residential locational decisions, one should investigate potential locations carefully and ask a lot of questions. What was this land used for previously? Where do local industries dispose of their wastes? How is this site located with respect to the prevailing wind direction and the location of industrial plants?

Visual blight   Ugly landscape.

Everyone agrees that some things are ugly, but no two people necessarily agree that the same things are ugly. In other words, visual blight is subjective—like beauty, it is in the eye of the beholder. Visual blight is an element in QOL, but again we face the problem of measuring it in some comparative way. From the viewpoint of the locational decision maker, the solution is easy—don't locate in ugly places!

In fact, many people have become increasingly angry in recent decades about what they see as the rape of the American landscape, with indiscriminate dumping, jumbles of signs, neighborhood decay, and

---

*Copyright 1980, by Newsweek, Inc. All rights reserved. Reprinted by permission.

CHAPTER 14 THE QUALITY OF URBAN LIFE

FIGURE 14–5 This abandoned house symbolizes residential decay.

what amounts to exploitation of the environment in a time when resource depletion tells us plainly that our emphasis should be on conservation, restoration, and adaptation. The burned out and abandoned house in Figure 14–5 makes the adjacent houses less desirable, which can reinforce neighborhood decline. (A short, interesting discussion of visual blight is found in Lewis, Lowenthal, and Tuan, 1973. See also Lowenthal, 1968.)

A QUALITY OF LIFE STUDY OF U.S. METROPOLITAN AREAS

The socioeconomic and physical environmental checklists provide a possible basis for developing a QOL index. This raises the question of how places actually score when a QOL index is calculated. One such index, which included a broad array of socioeconomic and physical environmental indicators, was developed for 243 U.S. metropolitan areas (Liu, 1975). It incorporated data for 123 QOL factors divided among five components: (1) *economic,* (2) *political,* (3) *environmental,* (4) *health and education,* and (5) *social.* These are considered in turn, and maps illustrate the ratings of the 65 metropolitan areas containing more than 500,000 people in 1970. For each component, factors are divided into two types—*individual* level and *community* level.

1 **Economic Component** Examples of some of the factors included under each economic component heading are shown in Table 14–3. On the rating scale, ranging from *outstanding to substandard* (Figure 14–6), the weakest large metropolitan areas were concentrated in the South and along the northeastern seaboard, plus Honolulu.

2 **Political Component** Individual factors reflected considerations such as media information and voter participation. Local factors described conditions such as professionalism among police and fire personnel, performance of local government, and levels of welfare assistance (Table 14–4). On this component, the South was conspicuously weak, while western and northeastern metropolises fared better (Figure 14–7).

3 **Environmental Component** As we have noted, some conditions cannot be compared easily across cities because they are totally subjective or because no national data base has been developed. Environmental comparisons, then, depend

TABLE 14–3 Selected factors from the economic component

Individual Level	Community Level
Personal income per capita	Percentage of families with income above poverty level
Savings per capita	
Median value, owner-occupied, single-family housing units	Productivity
	Unemployment rate

Source: Liu, 1975, p. 6.

308

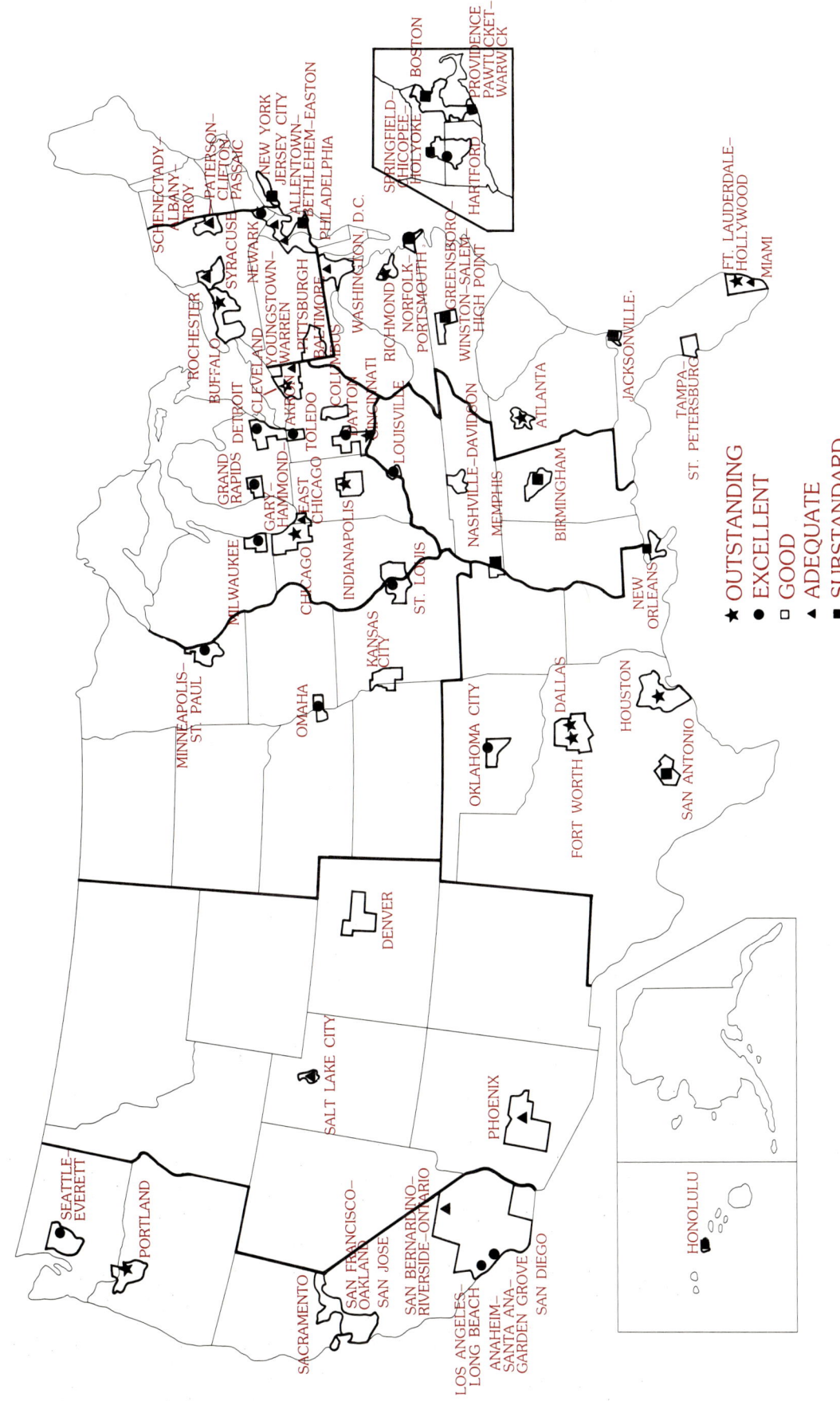

FIGURE 14-6 Geographic distribution of ratings, economic component. (Adapted from Ben-Chieh Liu, *Quality of Life Indicators in the U.S. Metropolitan Areas, 1970: Summary* [1975], p. 12.

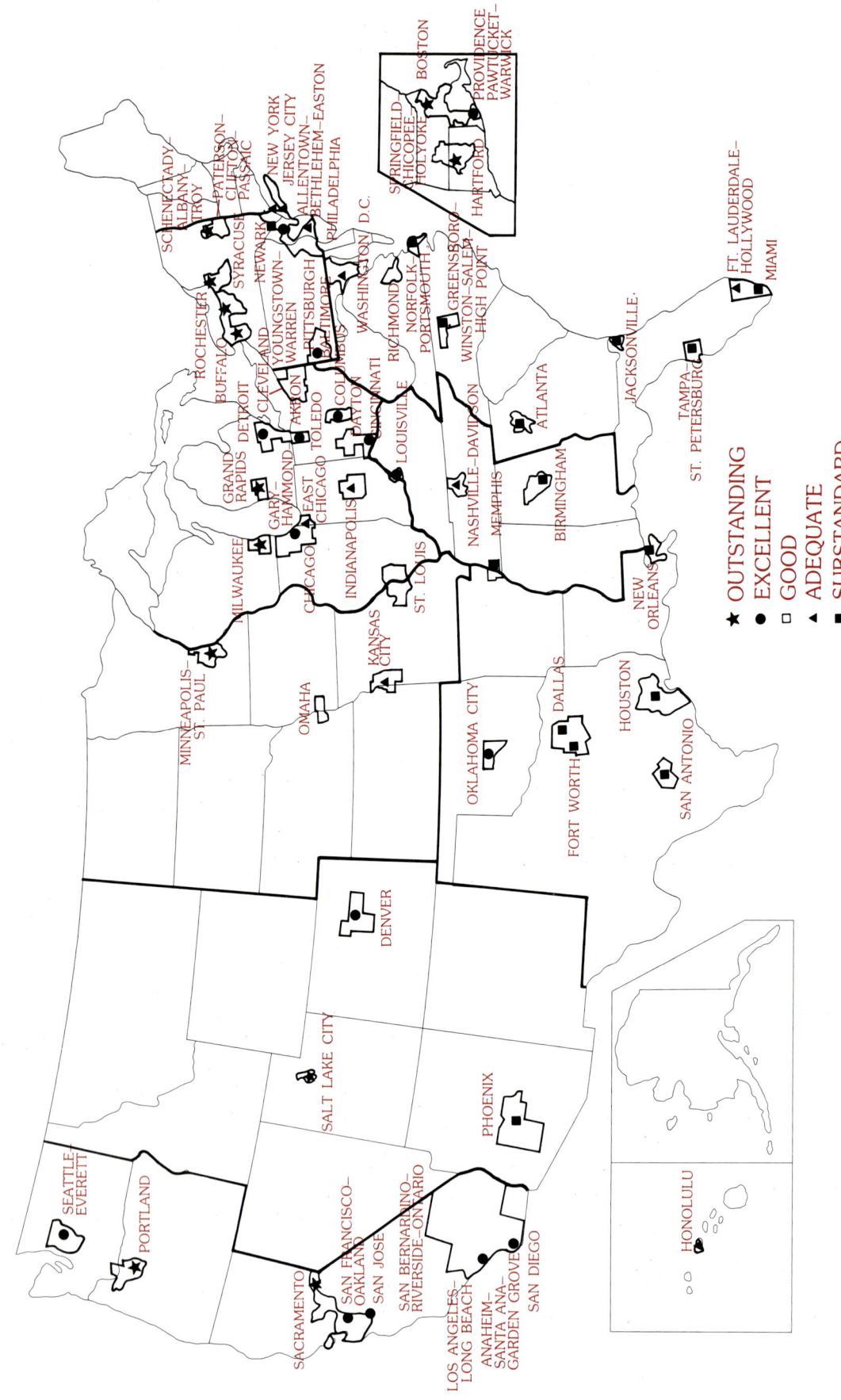

FIGURE 14-7 Geographic distribution of ratings, political component. (Adapted from Ben-Chieh Liu, *Quality of Life Indicators in the U.S. Metropolitan Areas, 1970: Summary* [1975], p. 14.)

CONCLUSION

TABLE 14–4 Selected factors from the political component

Individual Level	Community Level
Sunday newspaper circulation per 1,000 population	Average monthly earnings of full-time teachers
Radio stations per 1,000 population	Violent crime rate per 100,000 population
Ratio of presidential vote cast to voting-age population	Average monthly payments to families with dependent children

Source: Liu, 1975, p. 6.

on what is really partial information. In the Liu study, a division was made between the individual and institutional environment and the natural environment. Selected data types in each category appear in Table 14–5. The geographical distribution of environmental ratings for the large metropolitan areas shows a sharp difference between East (lower ratings) and West (higher ratings) (Figure 14–8). This regional pattern has to do with the eastern cities having been established longer, often with older, dirtier kinds of industrial activity as compared to the West.

4 **Health and Education Component** Chances for a fulfilling life for individuals and families are enhanced by the availability of good health care and high-quality educational facilities and personnel (Table 14–6). Southern metropolitan areas were conspicuously weak on this component (Figure 14–9); those in the West were mostly "outstanding" or "excellent."

5 **Social Component** The largest number of factors—54—was included in this component,

TABLE 14–5 Selected factors from the environmental component

Individual and Institutional Environment	Natural Environment
Air pollution (particulates and sulfur dioxide)	Possible annual days of sunshine
Noise (includes motorcycle registrations per 1,000 population)	Number of days with temperature freezing or below
Water pollution index	Acres of parks and recreational areas per 1,000 population

Source: Liu, 1975, p.6.

TABLE 14–6 Selected factors from the health and education component

Individual Conditions	Community Conditions
Infant mortality rate per 1,000 live births	Number of hospital beds per 100,000 population
Death rate per 1,000 population	Number of physicians per 100,000 population
Median school years completed by persons 25 years old and over	Per capita local government expenditures on education

Source: Liu, 1975, p. 6.

under headings of "Individual development," "Individual equality," and "Community living conditions" (Table 14–7). Again, the regional split between East (low) and West (high) is apparent (Figure 14–10). The variation between highest and lowest metropolitan areas was greatest for the health and education and social components, suggesting that the areas rated lowest have further to go to catch up compared to ratings on the economic, political, and environmental components (Liu, 1975, p. 9).

The relative inferiority of southern and many northeastern metropolitan areas is also apparent in the data for those classified as medium and small. And whether metropolitan areas, cities, or states are considered, the relative deprivation of the South is apparent. In a related QOL study at the state level, Liu identified nine states as having "substandard" living conditions (1973, p. 7). Of these nine, only Alaska and Arizona were outside the South (see also Liu, 1976).

CONCLUSION

Increased wealth and mobility in advanced nations means that locational choices are wider than ever before, and that they can be changed relatively easily. Within certain political, economic, and cultural limitations, people may choose what nation they prefer to live in, and again within certain limitations, a region, a city, and a neighborhood. These choices are nearly worldwide for the very rich, and nonexistent for the very poor and for certain ethnic and racial minorities.

Most of you are upwardly mobile, socially and economically. You are also mobile in the sense that

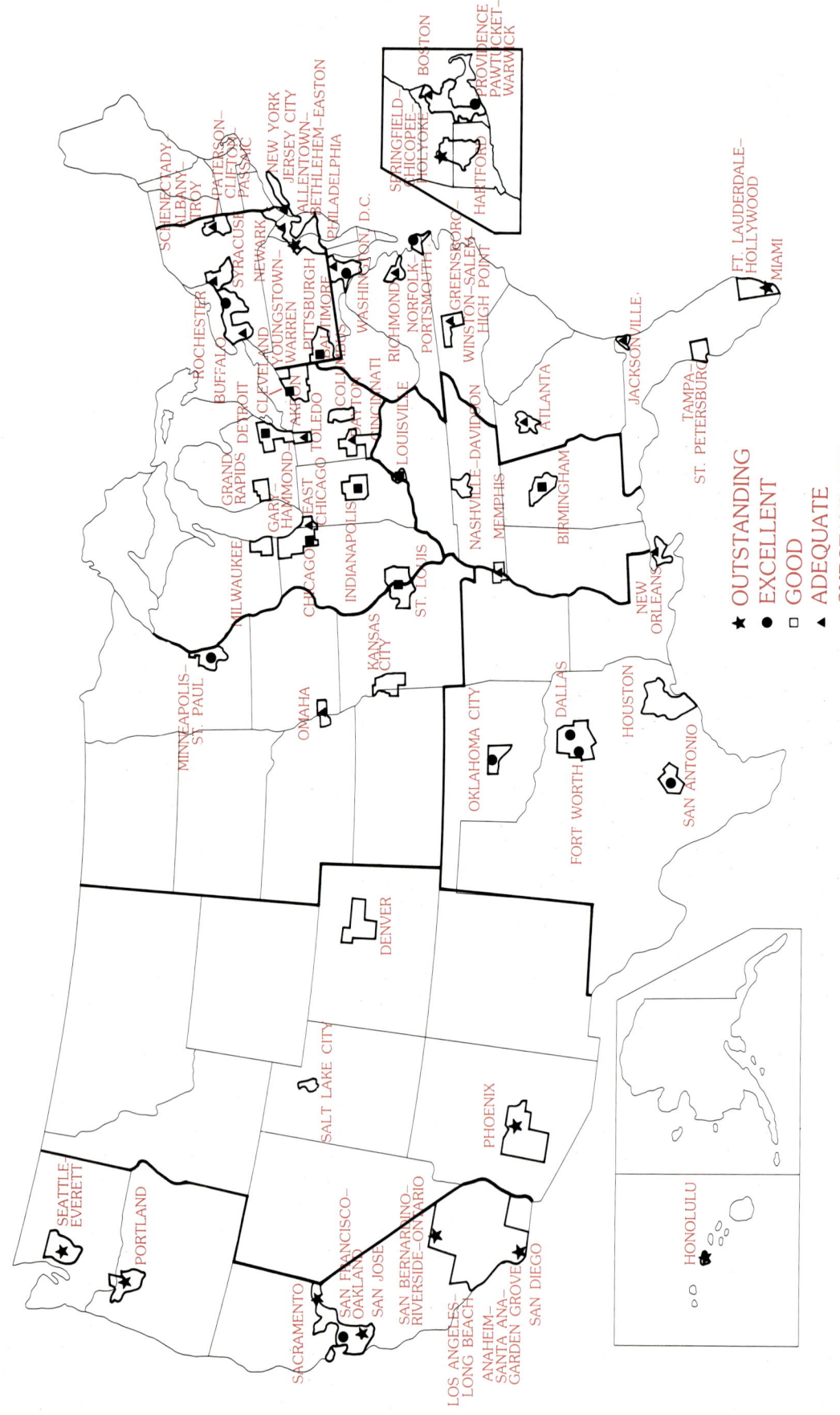

FIGURE 14–8 Geographic distribution of ratings, environmental component. (Adapted from Ben-Chieh Liu, *Quality of Life Indicators in the U.S. Metropolitan Areas, 1970: Summary* [1975], p. 16.)

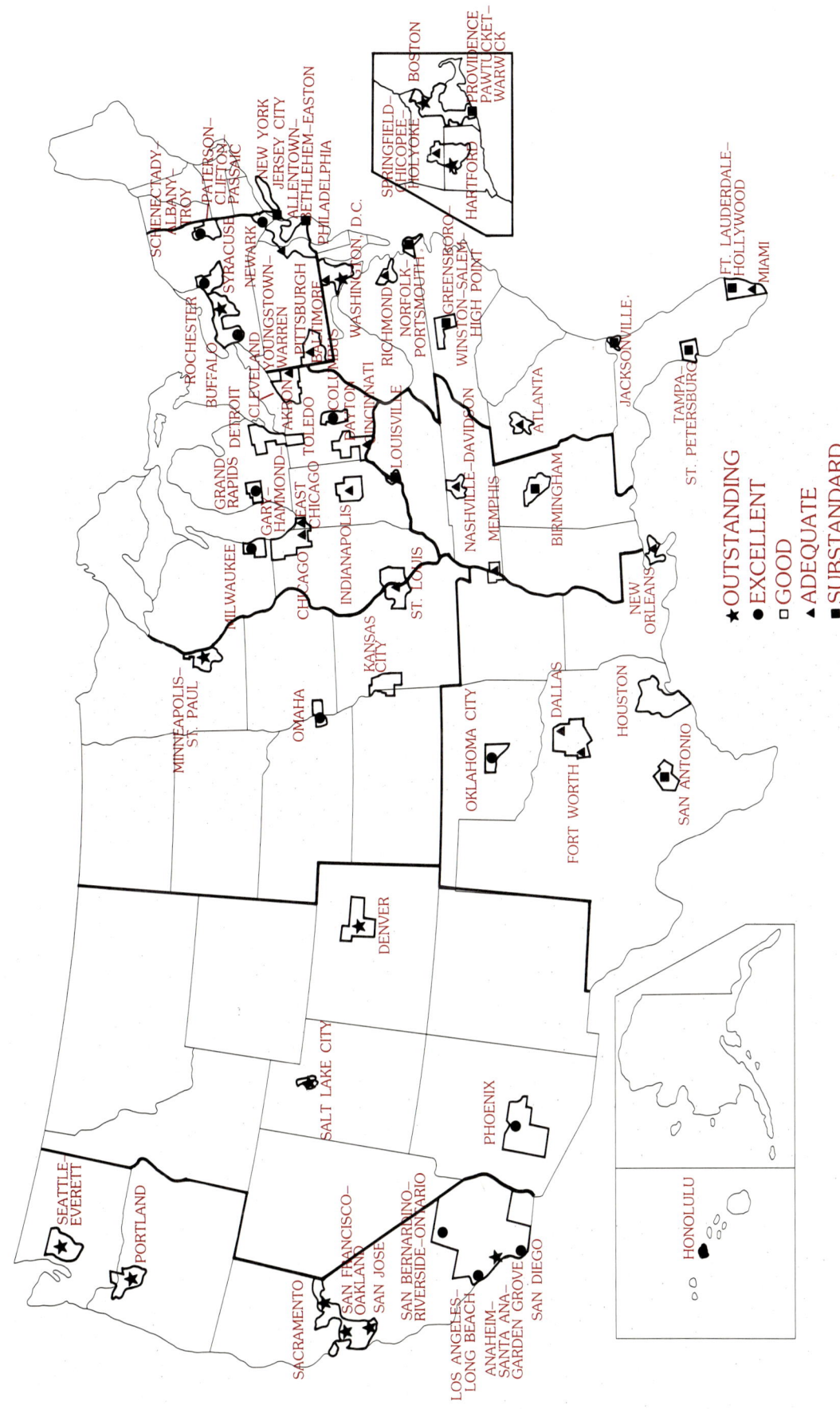

FIGURE 14—9 Geographic distribution of ratings, health and education component. (Adapted from Ben-Chieh Liu, *Quality of Life Indicators in the U.S. Metropolitan Areas, 1970: Summary* [1975], p. 18.)

313

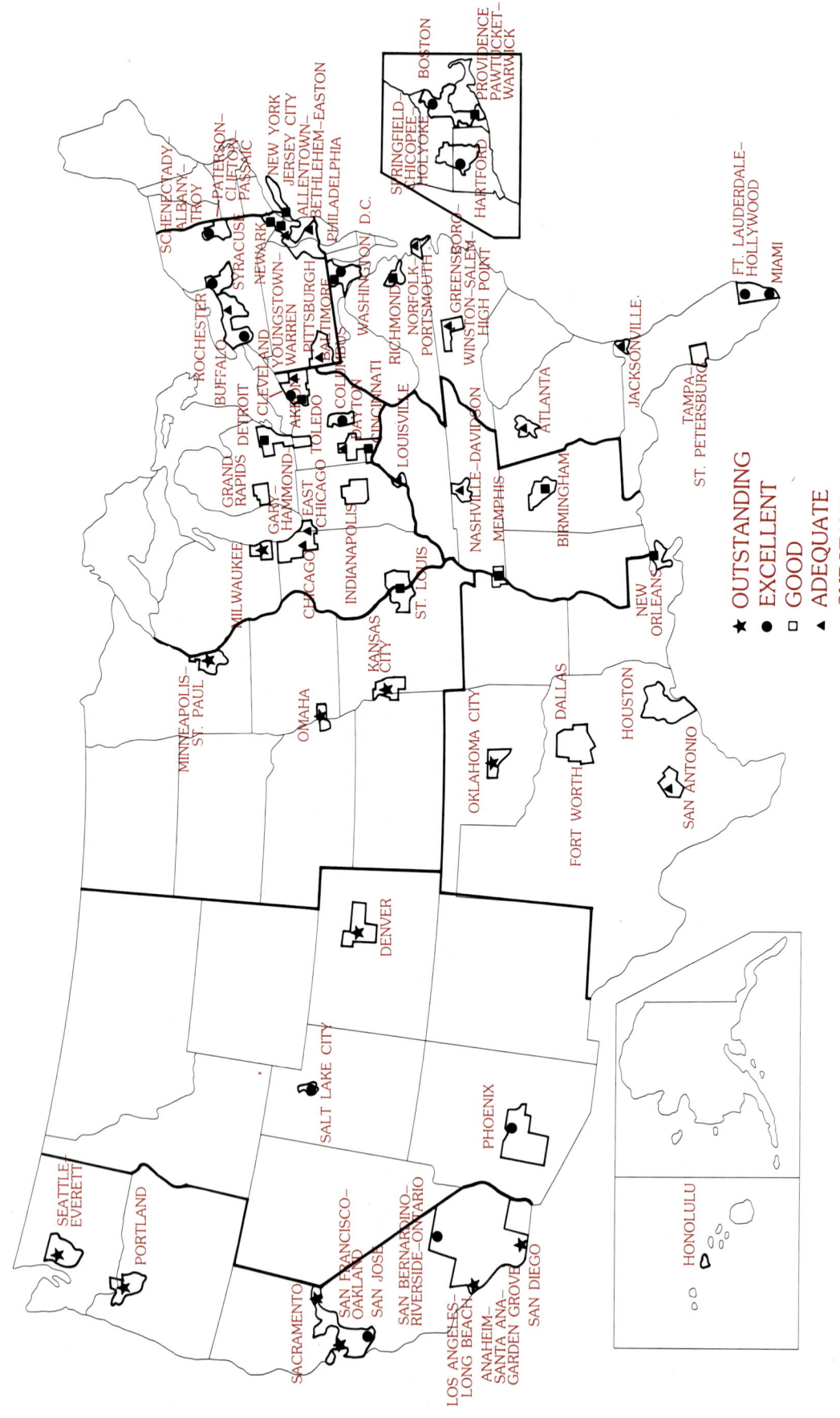

FIGURE 14-10 Geographic distribution of ratings, social component. (Adapted from Ben-Chieh Liu, *Quality of Life Indicators in the U.S. Metropolitan Areas, 1970: Summary* [1975], p. 20.)

TABLE 14–7 Selected factors from the social component

	Individual Development	Individual Equality	Community Living Conditions
	Labor force participation rate	Ratio of black to total persons' median family income, adjusted for education	Percentage of families with income above poverty level
	Individual health index	Ratio of male to female unemployment rate, adjusted for education	Volumes of books in main public library per 1,000 population
	Individual and institutional environment index	Housing segregation index	Cultural events in metropolitan area

Source: Liu, 1975, p. 7.

you will have a wide range of locational possibilities from which to choose. In Chapter 8, we saw that the most mobile population group, in terms of interstate migration, are those who are at about the age of college graduates (early twenties). We have seen in this discussion of Quality of Life that migration decisions, whether interurban or intraurban, can have a profound impact on lifestyle and, in extreme cases, on life itself. Locational decision making is both a science and an art. In a scientific sense, we can compare statistics of various QOL indicators. But this factual approach ignores emotional considerations and the important point that there are trade-offs—to gain an advantage from locating in a particular place, it may be necessary to accept a disadvantage. Much of the art of locational decision making consists of evaluating these tradeoffs. This chapter provides a framework for locational decision making in the hope that better informed decision makers will, in fact, make better decisions.

In the next chapter, the focus shifts to consideration of the interrelationships between politics and geography. The pattern of political boundaries on the earth's surface has a profound effect on patterns of economic development, resource bases, individual freedoms, and other considerations.

KEY WORDS

aesthetic environment
applied geography
floodplain
metropolitan area
physical environment
place identity
QOL
smog
social indicator
socioeconomic environment
topographic map

REFERENCES

BRYSON, REID A., and KUTZBACH, JOHN E. *Air Pollution.* Association of American Geographers Resource Paper No. 2. 1968.

BRYSON, REID A., and ROSS, JOHN E. "The Climate of the City." In Thomas R. Detwyler and Melvin G. Marcus, eds. *Urbanization and Environment.* Belmont, Calif.: Duxbury Press, 1972, pp. 51–68.

CLAIRE, WILLIAM H., ed. *Handbook on Urban Planning.* New York: Van Nostrand Reinhold Co., 1973.

HELBURN, NICHOLAS. "Geography and the Quality of Life", *Annals of the Association of American Geographers* 72 (1982): 445–456.

LAKSHMANAN, T. R., and CHATTERJEE, L. R. *Urbanization and Environmental Quality.* Association of American Geographers Resource Paper No. 77–1. Washington, D.C., 1977.

LEWIS, PEIRCE F., LOWENTHAL, DAVID, and TUAN, YI-FU. *Visual Blight in America*. Association of American Geographers Resource Paper No. 23. Washington, D.C., 1973.

LIU, BEN-CHIEH. *Quality of Life in the United States, 1970: Index, Rating, and Statistics*. Kansas City: Midwest Research Institute, 1973.

———. *Quality of Life Indicators in the U.S. Metropolitan Areas, 1970: Summary*. Kansas City: Midwest Research Institute, 1975.

———. *Quality of Life Indicators in U.S. Metropolitan Areas: A Statistical Analysis*. New York: Praeger Publishing, 1976.

LOWENTHAL, DAVID. "The American Scene." *Geographical Review* 58 (1968): 61–88.

MORGANTHAU, TOM, and HAGER, MARY. "Coping with Toxic Wastes." *Newsweek*, 19 May 1980, pp. 34–35.

SMITH, DAVID M. *Geographical Perspectives on Inequality*. New York: Barnes & Noble, 1979.

STEVENSON, GORDON M., JR. "Noise and the Urban Environment." In Thomas R. Detwyler and Melvin G. Marcus, eds. *Urbanization and Environment*. Belmont, Calif.: Duxbury Press, 1972, pp. 195–228.

U.S. DEPARTMENT OF COMMERCE, Bureau of the Census. *Statistical Abstract of the United States: 1979*. Washington, D.C.: U.S. Government Printing Office, 1979.

U.S. ENVIRONMENTAL PROTECTION AGENCY. *The Quality of Life Concept*. Washington, D.C.: U.S. Government Printing Office, 1973.

15
The Bounded Earth

PERSONAL SPACE
PERSONAL PROPERTY
LOCAL GOVERNMENTS
CITY BOUNDARIES
STATE BOUNDARIES
INTERNATIONAL BOUNDARIES
OCEAN BOUNDARIES
MULTINATIONAL BOUNDARIES

The town of Texarkana straddles the state line between Texas and Arkansas.

Political geography is the study of the relationship between politics and terrestrial space. *Politics* includes all human tactics used in seeking personal gain and in conducting public affairs. *Terrestrial space* refers to the earth's surface and that part of the earth above and below the surface that humans use. Thus, political geographic studies range from the personal level (microscale) to the world level (macroscale).

One important aspect of political geography is the way humans *partition* terrestrial space into territories that they protect and utilize. Partitioning occurs at all levels from the microscale through the macroscale. The earth's entire land surface and most of its water bodies have been partitioned into well-defined areal units. The units are delimited by boundaries; thus, boundaries are the major threads in the fabric of any discussion about this part of political geography.

Although the major purpose of a boundary is to define the limits of territorial control, a boundary also exists to govern the interaction between the two areas separated by the boundary. To "govern" the interaction usually means to retard or restrict it rather than to promote or enhance it. For instance, the flow of commodities and migrators is often restricted by international boundaries, some of which are marked by walls, fences, and armed guards. The white picket fence across someone's lawn is put there to restrict foot traffic, and barbed wire stops the free movement of livestock. In fact, fences are so common that we tend to ignore their significance. We forget that all territory is partitioned into units, and that each unit is carefully outlined with a boundary.

We will talk about a seven-tiered hierarchy of partitioned territories: (1) personal space, (2) land holdings, (3) local governments, (4) city governments, (5) state and regional structures, (6) nation-states, and (7) multinational organizations. The sequence goes from the micro level to the macro and includes most of the types of territories humans use.

PERSONAL SPACE

The concept of *personal space* relates to political geography in that individual territories are similar to political territories. Both personal spaces and political spaces are delimited by boundaries and defended from encroachment, and occupants of each space interact with others of their kind. Personal space refers to both the *portable territory* people carry with them and the *fixed territory* they may stake out for their personal use. Boundaries of both portable and fixed territories are well defined, but those for portable territories are invisible whereas those for fixed territories are observable.

The size of personal (or political) space is a function of the location of the boundary that encloses it. A general rule is that humans each need at least 2 square feet of space, the minimum requirement for a person standing in a crowd. (Of course, the minimum varies according to a person's size.) Outward from that minimum and enclosing it on all sides lies the boundary of the portable territory. The distance the boundary lies from the person is called *individual distance*, and varies from culture to culture, from person to person, and for the same person under varying conditions. Personal space, then, sets the limits for the spacing that individuals maintain between themselves and others. Some people need more self-space than other people. The English and the Americans, for instance, generally keep farther apart than Arabs and Latins. And, in any culture, personal space disappears almost entirely under crowded conditions (Figure 15–1).

Portable territory is not circular, because individuals will allow strangers to come closer to their sides than directly in front of them (note the placement of furniture in a bus terminal). The boundaries of these areas, although invisible and not spherical, generally correspond to the areas enclosed when one stands in one place, extends both arms, and rotates 360°. The boundaries are flexible, however, changing shape under pressure.

Nonportable or fixed personal space refers to those areas individuals retain as their own personal preserve. The region may be a favorite chair or room where someone retreats for privacy. On the other hand, it could be a temporary place in a public setting, such as space at a library table or in a cafeteria. The boundaries of this kind of space are usually marked by personal items. For example, in a college library, students place books and coats around themselves on a table; the items outline the boundaries of their personal space and act as barriers to stop others from intruding into their private realm. *Space retainers* are the items left in a public place to reserve a particular area while the user is temporarily absent.

FIGURE 15–1 The bathers on this beach in Cornwall, England, may find it difficult to maintain personal space under these crowded conditions.

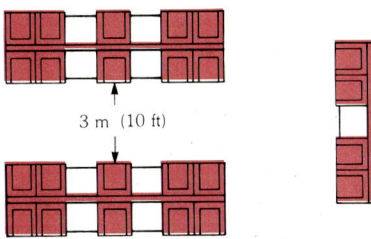

A. WAITING ROOM—
PUBLIC TRANSPORTATION

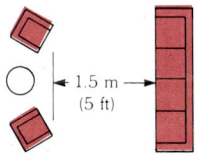

B. LIVING ROOM—
PRIVATE HOME

FIGURE 15–2 (a) Sociofugal or formal arrangement, designed to keep people separated; (b) sociopetal or informal arrangement, designed to bring people together.

A coat hung on a chair at a library, a towel draped over a lounge chair at a pool, and a glass turned upside down on the handle of a slot machine are examples of space retainers. They are just as effective as "Occupied" signs on airline seats.

The study of the distances that define personal space is called *proxemics.* Modern rooms are designed on the basis of proxemics. For example, in public waiting rooms where people want to be apart, such as airline terminals, the seating arrangement is fixed so that no one faces anyone else in close proximity. This is an example of a *sociofugal* arrangement (Figure 15–2a); that is, the design intention is to allow people to be separated. In areas where the purpose is to bring persons together, the arrangement is *sociopetal* (Figure 15–2b). In a living room, the chairs are situated so that people can face each other and talk. Large, formal rooms can be made into small, informal areas by arranging the furniture in a sociopetal manner.

People often become edgy, even outright angry, when their personal space is violated. Try sitting down in a public place where someone has staked a claim but is temporarily absent. When the "owner" returns, the immediate hostility is obvious. This experiment should indicate on a small scale the frustration and anger generated when a country's territory is invaded. The leap from the micro to macro scale is but a short one as the relationship between personal space and political space becomes obvious.

PERSONAL PROPERTY

Personal property in the form of real estate is the most basic resource in the world. Land is not only a financial asset as a commodity; it also provides the space in which humans live, work, and play. Most of the world, and certainly all of the United States, is divided into units of public and private land. Every unit is delimited by precise boundaries, and many of the boundaries are demarcated by various types of fences, walls, and other barriers. Private property often resembles a country, because the owners "rule" their estates from their domicile (capitol), guard the borders, and make agreements (treaties) with their neighbors as to the maintenance of fences. And, as in international affairs, squabbles between neighbors are common.

A unit of land can be considered a three-dimensional part of space, because property rights extend both above and below the land surface (Figure 15–3). Property rights are the legal defenses for property owners to use in protecting their property from outside encroachment. Property rights give owners legal control of: (1) the *airspace* over a piece of property; (2) the *land surface* itself; and (3) the *subsurface,* or subterranean part of the land. Three

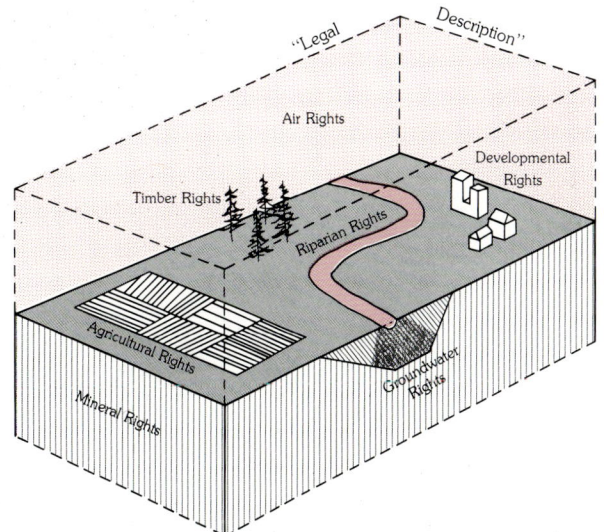

FIGURE 15–3 Property rights included in private land ownership. (From Rutherford H. Platt, *Land Use Control: Interface of Law and Geography* [Washington, D.C.: Association of American Geographers, Resource Papers for College Geography No. 75–1, 1976], p. 4. Reprinted by permission.)

different levels of legal control are necessary for a piece of property—one for the airspace, another for the surface, and still another for the subsurface.

The airspace over a parcel of land includes the volume of *usable space* immediately above the land, although there is no clear definition of usable air space. But since the tallest building in the world today is the 443.2-m (1,454-ft) Sears Tower in Chicago, reasonable definition of usable air space might be about 450 meters (1,500 ft) above the land surface. That height also corresponds with most laws on the lowest allowable altitude for the operation of aircraft.

Airspaces are protected by laws because they have economic importance. In fact, airspace can be purchased or leased from the surface owner. The Merchandise Mart in Chicago, for example, bought the airspace over the Northwestern and Illinois Central Railroad tracks for construction of its building. And many overhead railroads and highways are constructed in leased airspaces (Figure 15–4). Airspace can be sold and leased, and it can be polluted. Air pollution, whether in the form of noise or chemical irritants, can lower property values. Surface owners can take legal action against polluters on the basis of their airspace rights.

The rights granted to the surface owners of property are similar in intent to airspace rights, but they are much more numerous. There are more things of value on the land than in the air; consequently, there are more reasons to trespass. Land surface rights are of two general types: (1) rights to use the property as the owner wants, and (2) rights to exclude other persons from using the property. Uses of property, however, cannot infringe on the rights of others, or go against established laws. The general rule in the United States is that federal, state, and local governments can suppress certain uses of private property that are offensive or detrimental to public health, safety, morals, or welfare.

Generally, the exclusive-use laws are designed to control trespassing, encroachment, and occupancy by illegal means. *Trespassing* refers to a person's entering onto another person's land without permission, whereas *encroachment* is the use of another person's land without permission. For example, a burglar or poacher trespasses, but a misaligned fence constitutes encroachment. *Illegal occupancy* of land occurs when squatters take over unoccupied land parcels and live on them without acquiring ownership.

Subsurface rights granted to landowners are usually called mineral rights. These rights, however, include exploitation privileges for all subterranean commodities, not just minerals. The rights to the subsurface space can be sold or leased while the surface rights are retained, or owners can sell the land on the surface and keep the mineral rights. Thus, it is possible to have three strata of ownership for a single parcel of land—one of the airspace, another of the surface, and a third for the subsurface. Boundary lines around private land extend downward into the earth as far as what is "reasonably usable" space. The deepest oil well rarely exceeds 7,500 m (25,000 ft) in depth; thus, 9,000 m (30,000 ft) might be a reasonable limit.

The general rule is that boundaries are to be respected, even at the subterranean level of landownership. However, some interesting exceptions occur for this level. For example, a mine shaft can penetrate neighboring property as long as it extends downward, and as long as it follows a proven mineral-laden vein of rock. This exception is called an *extralateral* mining right. Also, a pool of oil can be pumped legally from under adjacent property, because oil must be "captured" before it can be owned. A curving or slanted drill hole that penetrates subterranean boundaries is illegal, however (Figure

FIGURE 15–4 Overhead railways must purchase or lease airspace over the land on which they are constructed.

 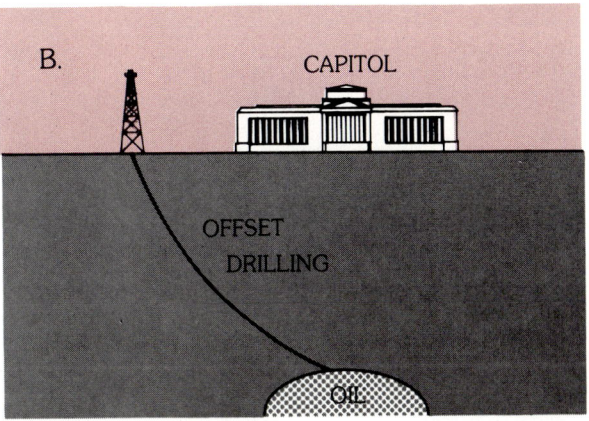

FIGURE 15–5 To extract oil from beneath the Oklahoma capitol, the drilling rig was placed as close to the building as possible (a), and the drill hole was curved as drilling progressed (b), an illegal method if the drill hole crosses a property line.

15–5). Another ownership exception arose in 1980, when the Texas Supreme Court ruled that a surface owner could mine coal on a parcel of land without paying royalty to the owner of the mineral rights. Only strip mining techniques were permissible, but this case may create the need to redefine *surface* and *subsurface*.

Thousands of regulations, statutes, ordinances, and laws pertain directly to landowner rights, land transactions, and land boundary problems. Everyone is a user of some real estate. The purchase of a home is the largest financial transaction in most people's lives. In fact, nearly 10 percent of all employed persons in the United States work in real estate and construction. Furthermore, construction expenditures alone account for about 12 percent of the annual gross national product of the United States. The laws governing landownership vary from state to state, making the political geography of private land incredibly complex.

LOCAL GOVERNMENTS

The next-higher increments of land designation in the United States are *special districts, townships,* and *counties*. These areas differ from private land and personal space in that they are politically formed territories; that is, the territories are designated areas used for the common good of the people who live in them. Thus, the intended use of the delimited area is for political rather than personal gain.

Special Districts

Special districts are designed to provide basic services to the people of a local area and could therefore be called *service areas* (see Figure 15–6). Funds for services are acquired through taxes or special assessments. The most common method of raising money is a property tax. When a district is created, boundaries are drawn around a small territory according to the purpose of the district and the number of people to be served. A library district, for example, can serve more people and a larger area than a fire protection district.

The most common type of special district in the United States is the *independent school district*. Nearly the entire land surface area is divided into these small single-function territories. During the 1930s, when the one-room rural schoolhouse was typical of elementary education in this country, there were more than 100,000 school districts. Consolidation decreased that number to about 10,000. The children who would have once filled 30 or 40 rural schools can now be accommodated in one *consolidated school*.

Special districts have governing bodies whose members are usually elected by citizens of the district. The governing body of a school district, for example, is the school board. Board members are elected by their neighbors in the district, and are charged with duties related to the single function of providing education for the children in the district. The most important responsibility of the board is to hire personnel to operate the schools—superintendents, principals, and teachers. The board members have other responsibilities as well, but all relate to the proper functioning of the local schools. Other special districts have similar governing bodies charged with the responsibility of maintaining the function for which the district was designed. Special districts, then, are not only the smallest units of local

FIGURE 15–6 Road signs marking special district boundary lines.

government in the United States, they are also the most basic governmental organization

The number of school districts in the United States continues to decline because of consolidation, but the number of nonschool special districts is increasing rapidly. There are over 25,000 nonschool special districts, located in both urban and rural areas of America. Special districts are popular because they can be tailored as to size and function, but they are difficult to manage, and create planning problems when there are too many of them. District boundaries can overlap with districts of another type, and the districts themselves are small or large, depending on the service need. They can cover a few blocks in a city, or parts of several counties.

After school districts, fire protection districts are the next most numerous type of special district. The districts whose numbers are growing most rapidly, however, are those related to environmental protection. There are air and water pollution control districts, solid waste management districts, and conservation districts. Both urban and rural residents are concerned with drainage control, flood protection, and soil conservation, and create special districts to have an outlet to express that concern. Out of the 15 most common types of districts, 5 are related to environmental problems (Table 15–1).

Townships

Townships are small unit areas that serve as political subdivisions of counties. Originally, they were created with local self-governments that provided the basic needs of rural Americans. The smallness of the townships allowed representatives to meet without having to travel long distances. Townships were modeled after *towns,* which are the local governments of many New England states. A typical midwestern township was a 36-square-mile area that formed a square 6 miles along each side. The 36 sections of land within a township were each 640 acres (one square mile). Usually, each section of land had four farms of 160 acres each. The national government authorized the organization of townships; thus, they have been called *congressional townships.* And the Homestead Act of 1862 allotted 160 acres of land to each settler. The political organization of the land therefore corresponds with the land survey system (Figure 15–7).

Only 23 states have had township governments, mostly in the Northeast and Upper Midwest (Figure 15–8). Many counties have abolished the township form of government, and two states have eliminated their township structure entirely. Some states (Connecticut, for example) have disbanded their county governments as well. The need for small governmental units decreases as transportation systems improve.

The most common services that township governments provided related to schools, roads, and environmental cleanliness. The elected board of supervisors was given the power to levy taxes to pay for the services rendered. Besides these services, some township governments provided their citizens with parks, libraries, cemeteries, trash collection, fire protection, dog control, water hydrants, judges, vocational education, police protection (via justices of the peace), repair and cleaning of drains and ditches along roads, census taking, and zoning regulations. Some of the more bizarre services that township governments perform include prairie dog eradication in Kansas, hedgefence trimming in Indiana, noxious weed control in Illinois and Iowa, administration of

TABLE 15–1 Ranking of special districts in the United States

	Rural		Urban
Rank	Function	Rank	Function
1	Education	1	Fire protection
2*	Soil conservation	2	Utilities
3*	Irrigation and water conservation	3*	Sewage disposal
4	Highway	4	Housing and urban renewal
5	Fire protection	5	Education
6	Utilities	6*	Drainage
7	Cemetery	7*	Soil conservation
8*	Flood protection	8	Parks and recreation
9	Housing and urban renewal	9*	Irrigation and water conservation
10*	Sewage disposal	10	Cemetery
11*	Drainage	11	Hospital
12	Parks and receation	12	Highway
13	Hospital	13	Library
14	Health	14	Flood protection
15	Library	15	Health

*Related to environmental problems.
Source: U.S. Department of Commerce, Bureau of the Census, *Census of Governments* (Washington, D.C.: U.S. Goverment Printing Office 1972).

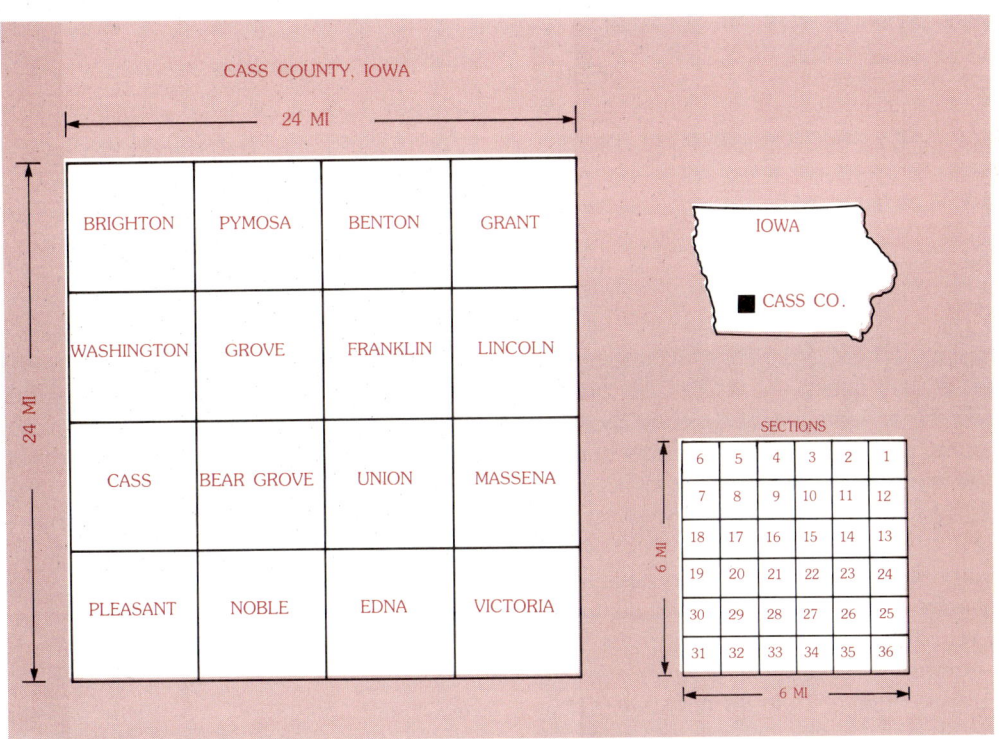

FIGURE 15–7 The 16 congressional townships of Cass County, Iowa, each of which has a name. Each contains 36 sections (one square mile or 640 acres), with each section designated by a number and identifiable by the *range and township* system or by township name. (Adapted from Norris and Haring, *Political Geography* [Charles E. Merrill, 1980], p. 201.)

325

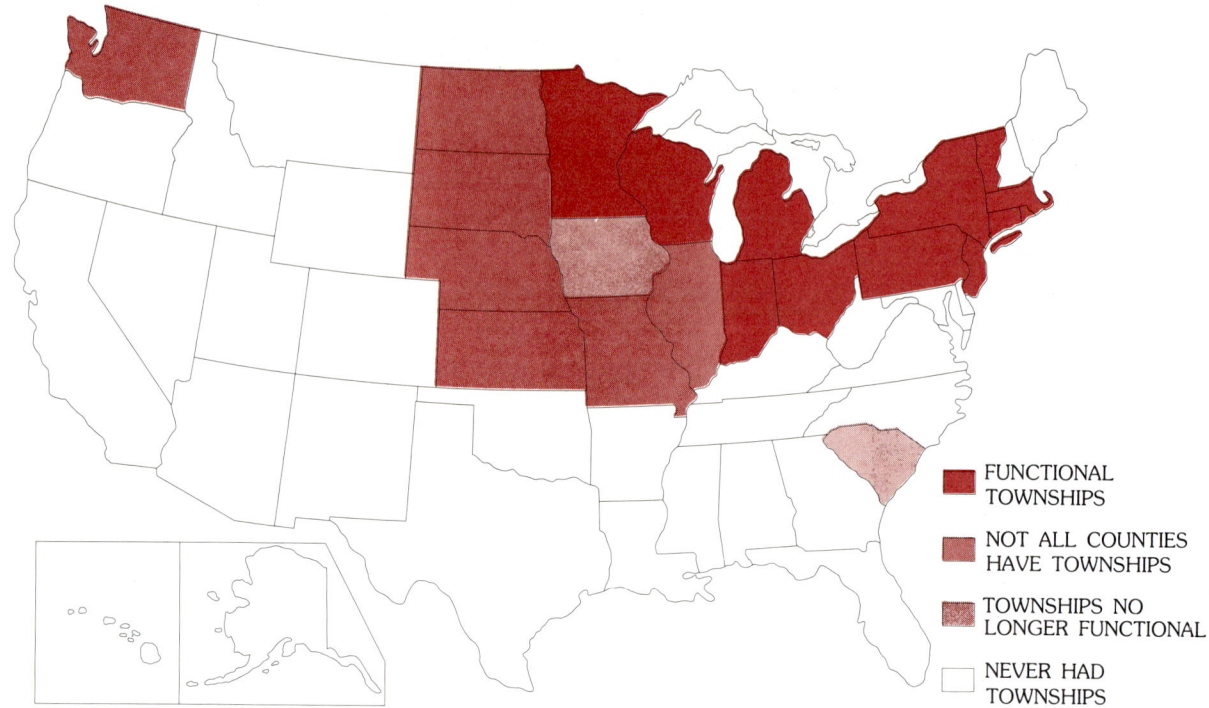

FIGURE 15–8 States that have townships. Half of these no longer use townships for government purposes. (Adapted from Norris and Haring, *Political Geography* [Charles E. Merrill, 1980], p. 200.)

"outdoor poor relief" in Ohio, and "cemetery control" in Iowa. Many township services have been taken over by single-function special districts.

Counties

Counties, the political subdivisions of states, number slightly over 3,100 in the United States. This figure includes 29 *census divisions* in Alaska and 64 *parishes* in Louisiana. There are also 41 counties that contain independent cities, in which the original county governments have been replaced by combined city/county governments. The average number of counties per state is 62, ranging from 254 in Texas to 3 in Delaware. The states in the Midwest and Southeast have the most counties; the small New England states and the large western states have fewer than the average. The states in New England are smaller and require fewer counties, but in the West the smaller number is related to the fewer numbers of people. The number of counties per state is thus related to the historical settlement patterns of the region (Figure 15–9).

San Bernardino County, California, is the largest county in the United States, with 20,117 square miles of territory. Eight census divisions in Alaska, however, are larger than San Bernardino County. The average size of the subdivisions in Alaska is 19,532 square miles, with the Upper Yukon alone measuring 84,142 square miles (similar in size to Minnesota, the twelfth-largest state). The smallest county is New York County in New York, which is only 23 square miles. The average county size increases from east to west across the United States, as exemplified by the New York and San Bernardino examples, and, as we said, relates to the regions' original settlement patterns. Before a county could be formed, it had to have a minimum population; thus, in the sparsely populated West, the counties were made larger in area to meet the population requirement.

The word *county* is from the French word *conté* and originally described the small administrative district of a country rather than the subdivision of a state. The word came to the United States from England, where it described the region governed by a count. English counties generally coincide with what were called *shires;* in fact, many of the present English county names end with "-shire." The town or city containing the county government is the *county seat.* A *county farm* is a plot of publicly-owned land used by the county as a home for persons incapable of supporting themselves. It is often called the county *poor farm.*

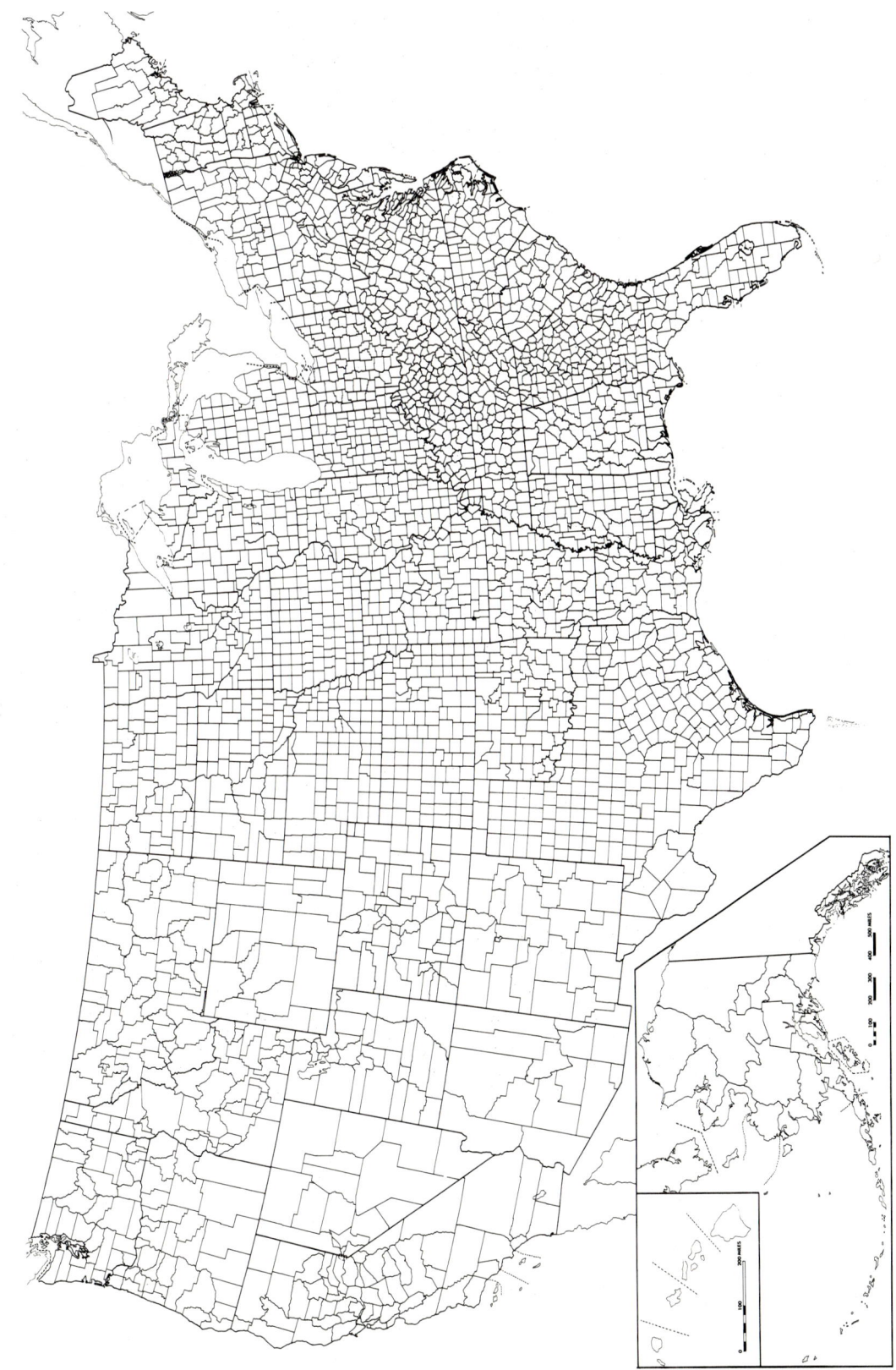

FIGURE 15–9 County boundaries in the U.S. Counties tend to become larger as one moves westward.

CHAPTER 15 THE BOUNDED EARTH

Counties are administered by elected officials usually called the *board of supervisors* or simply the *county board*. The board contains representatives from the various districts of the county as well as the officials of such offices as the auditor, treasurer, recorder, sheriff, county attorney, assessor, highway engineer, social services, veterans affairs, and clerk of the district court. County sheriffs are usually considered the most important county officials because they are the chief law enforcement officers, and perhaps because they have been made familiar (if not famous) by American western movies.

With today's rapid communication and transportation, the number of counties could be reduced without a loss in function by combining a number of smaller counties into a few large ones. For example, many states in the Midwest have about 100 counties, each with its own facilities and paid officials. Most states could operate efficiently with half as many counties. County governments are difficult to eliminate, however, because they are backed by tradition as well as by a sense of local control by the citizenry.

CITY BOUNDARIES

City boundaries are unique because they are more subject to change than any other boundary type. As a city grows, it annexes new territory and the city "limits" expand. When we consider the sprawl of an urban place over time, the growth process appears as a diffusion. That is, the areal spread can be mapped at time intervals and the boundary changes can be observed and studied.

City growth can be blocked by physical or man-made barriers. Physical barriers include difficult terrain such as mountains, and bodies of water such as swamps, rivers, lakes, and oceans. Man-made barriers are economic or political. An economic barrier exists, for instance, when property value is set too high for normal urban use, and development bypasses the expensive area in favor of less expensive property. Political barriers include other cities, counties, and states that halt growth by their own boundaries. Urban boundaries, therefore, are rarely straight lines—a city commonly has growth appendages, *exclaves*, and gaps reflected in its boundaries.

In the United States all city governments are chartered by state legislatures. Legally, cities are corporations, hence the phrase "to become incorporated." The city charter lists the powers of the city, and in order to pass through the state legislature, no power of the city can supersede state laws. In 28 states, cities are controlled completely by the state governments. The remaining states allow their cities some degree of *home rule* (Figure 15–10). Cities under home rule have broader powers of self-government. Some states have also passed laws favoring territorial growth of cities. These laws are called *anti-incorporation* because they make it illegal for a new

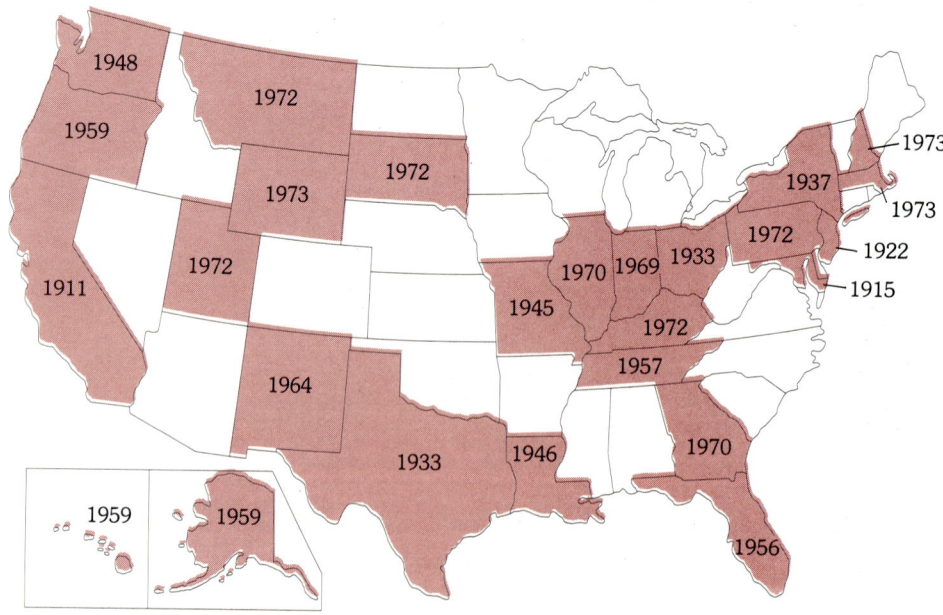

FIGURE 15–10 Years in which state legislatures or voters authorized home rule. State legislatures control the incorporated areas in states not shaded. (Adapted from Norris and Haring, *Political Geography* [Charles E. Merrill, 1980], p. 229.)

town to become incorporated within an established city's potential growth area. Potential growth areas have been defined as belts of land of varying widths around the city limits.

Many problems arise when a city grows in area. A simple boundary change can cause reverberations throughout the urban area. The new city boundaries begin to overlap other boundaries. Take as an example the situation of a small town engulfed by a sprawling city. Street names and addresses are subject to change. Local school districts, police, and fire protection may be affected, as may libraries, parks, and street maintenance. In some cases, even public utilities such as electricity, gas, telephone, and sewage disposal are altered. Generally, people do not want to give up local autonomy, believing that big city governments are not as responsive to the local needs of the community. On the other hand, consolidation may have financial merit. Many public services can be provided more cheaply through centralization, thus saving tax money.

When a city is created or when it takes over new territory, many new boundaries appear. The urban land is subdivided (platted) into small unit areas, with each parcel having specific boundary designations. Thus, the potential for boundary disputes increases dramatically. All the boundary rules we mentioned that pertain to private property hold for urban areas (Figure 15–11). Each owner has air, surface, and subterranean property rights. *Zoning ordinances* regulate the use of the land to a certain extent, however. Land use restrictions in urban areas are geared toward public safety, welfare, health, morals, convenience, and prosperity over the private misuse, abuse, or disuse of the land. Restrictions include such things as the size of yards, courts, and other open spaces as well as population density (see Figure 15–12). Zoning laws were first established to prevent objectionable land use in residential neighborhoods (e.g., factories, stockyards).

Zoning in itself creates new boundaries in the urban area. Zoning ordinances regulate the use of land within zones or districts. They maintain uniformity of land use and building type within each zone, and the area of each zone is specified by a boundary. In addition, special districts are created in each urban area, all designated with boundaries. Many of these boundaries overlap. Thus, the urban landscape is literally crisscrossed with boundary lines, although many of the lines are boundaries for a multitude of functions. For example, a major street might be a boundary between school districts, zones for land use, police precincts, voting precincts, fire protection districts, conservation districts, mosquito abatement districts, flood control districts, and welfare districts, as well as numerous other political units, zones, and private land. There are thus a myriad of problems relating to a city's external and internal boundaries.

FIGURE 15–11 These city property lines are marked by signs embedded in sidewalks (a) in San Antonio, Texas, and (b) in New York City. (Lower photo courtesy of Victoria Lord Kikuchi.)

STATE BOUNDARIES

The government of the United States is classified as a *federation* because of the formal geographical division of political power. Each of the states in the federation has certain political powers. The founding fathers *delegated* specific powers to the national government and *reserved* certain others for the states. Each state is a geographical entity with specifically defined boundaries. As each new state was added to the federation, boundaries were set; few changes have occurred in those original boundary lines, so the outline of each state is quite familiar. The states serve not only as more or less independent political entities but also as administrative subdivisions for the federal government.

CHAPTER 15 THE BOUNDED EARTH

FIGURE 15–12 New York City, where buildings extend as close to property lines as possible and where we see a regular pattern of land use. (Photo courtesy of U.S. Geological Survey.)

Most countries of the world have some system of areal subdivision. These smaller areas facilitate administration, but perhaps more importantly, they give the citizens a "local turf" with which to identify. The names of the lower-order administrative entities vary from country to country (see Table 15–2). Many countries have a pyramid structure of administration as each first-order governmental unit is divided into a number of smaller, second-order units. The second-order units are subdivided further, and so on. With each lower order, the units become smaller in area and larger in number. For example, France has 100 departments, 300 arrondisements, 3,000 cantons, and 38,000 communes.

The same term may represent different orders of subdivisions in different countries. As an example, the common designation for first-order subdivisions in South America is *departamento;* Bolivia, Colombia, Paraguay, Peru, and Uruguay all use that name. In Argentina, however, the *provincia* is the first-order unit, while the *departamento* is second-order. And *communes* in France are fourth-order, while in West Germany they are third-order.

The shape of a political unit is a function of its boundary, and both are related to the history of the unit. The early settlers in the United States used a system of *metes and bounds* to identify land parcels. This system was based on relative locations and physical features of the landscape. The phrase "the largest oak tree located 40 paces due north of the fork in the stream" is an example of this system. Many of the state boundaries in the eastern half of the United States are irregular because they were based on the metes and bounds concept. Rivers were frequently

TABLE 15–2 Political subdivision names

Country	Subdivision		
	First-Order	Second-Order	Third-Order
United States	State	County	Township
France	Department	Arrondisement	Canton
West Germany	Land	County	Commune
England	County	District	Parish
Mexico	Estado	Municipios	
Canada	Province	County	
Soviet Union	Republic		
Switzerland	Canton		

used as boundary lines (Figure 15–13). The states west of the Mississippi River have more regular shapes primarily as a result of federal legislation.

The *Land Ordinance Act* of 1785 required that land be designated on a square-mile basis. Then, the *Homestead Act* of 1862 divided land into 160-acre farms for settlement. In this way, a regular geometrical pattern of land use developed, with geometrical (straight-line) boundaries used for state boundaries. These lines were drawn before settlement, so there was no concern that they might bisect an existing town or an individual's property. The Homestead Act gave the western states their regular shapes, epitomized by Wyoming and Colorado, which are both precise rectangles.

Many states have *panhandles,* a descriptive term for an extension of the main body (like the handle of a pan). Oklahoma and Idaho have classic panhandles,

FIGURE 15–13 The Current River forms part of the boundary of a southern Missouri town (a), and in Europe, German, French, and Swiss borders meet in the middle of the Bodensee (b).

(a)

(b)

CHAPTER 15 THE BOUNDED EARTH

while other states such as Alaska, Texas, Missouri, Louisiana, Mississippi, Alabama, Florida, West Virginia, Maryland, and Pennsylvania have extensions of territory often called panhandles. These odd shapes, whether termed panhandles, boots, or appendages, can be attributed to historical and political circumstances. Each formed in an unusual way; the Oklahoma and Idaho panhandles, for example, were parcels of land left over after the formation of the boundaries of bordering states. Problems sometimes arise because of the physical isolation of these areas from the main bodies of their states.

Throughout the history of the United States, there have been numerous disputes over the precise location of state boundaries. Some of these arguments have brought bordering states to the brink of war. Today, problems are handled in the courts. River boundaries cause more disputes than any other kind of boundary. Large rivers would seem to make ideal boundaries, but they do not, because they meander. A boundary that originally followed the deepest part of a river *(thalweg)* must remain fixed, even when the river changes course. This means that territory belonging to a state on one side of the river could end up on the other side (Figure 15–14), causing many jurisdictional questions. It is natural for rivers to meander, so the problem is common wherever rivers are used as boundaries.

The significance of state boundaries lies in the changes that occur at the lines. The fact that a person lives on one side or the other of an invisible, finite line determines many aspects of his or her social, economic, and political life. For example, marriage laws vary from state to state, dictating different requirements for lawful age, blood tests, and waiting period. Other varying laws restrict when, where, and at what age liquor can be purchased. Differences in tax laws affect gasoline purchases, incomes, inheritances, retail sales, and other economic transactions. Amounts paid in property tax also vary. There are variations among the states in what is considered a crime, and even in what penalties are prescribed for the same crime. Salaries of state employees such as governors, legislators, teachers, and highway patrol officers vary considerably from state to state. The list of changes that occur at a state boundary is indeed very long (see Chapter 9).

Most states have divided their territories into regional administrative districts, creating even more boundaries to consider (Figure 15–15). No standard regions have been established, however. Each administrative function has its own region. The criteria for establishing regions are usually population, economics, or area. For example, judicial districts and congressional voting districts are based on population, and the voting district boundaries change after

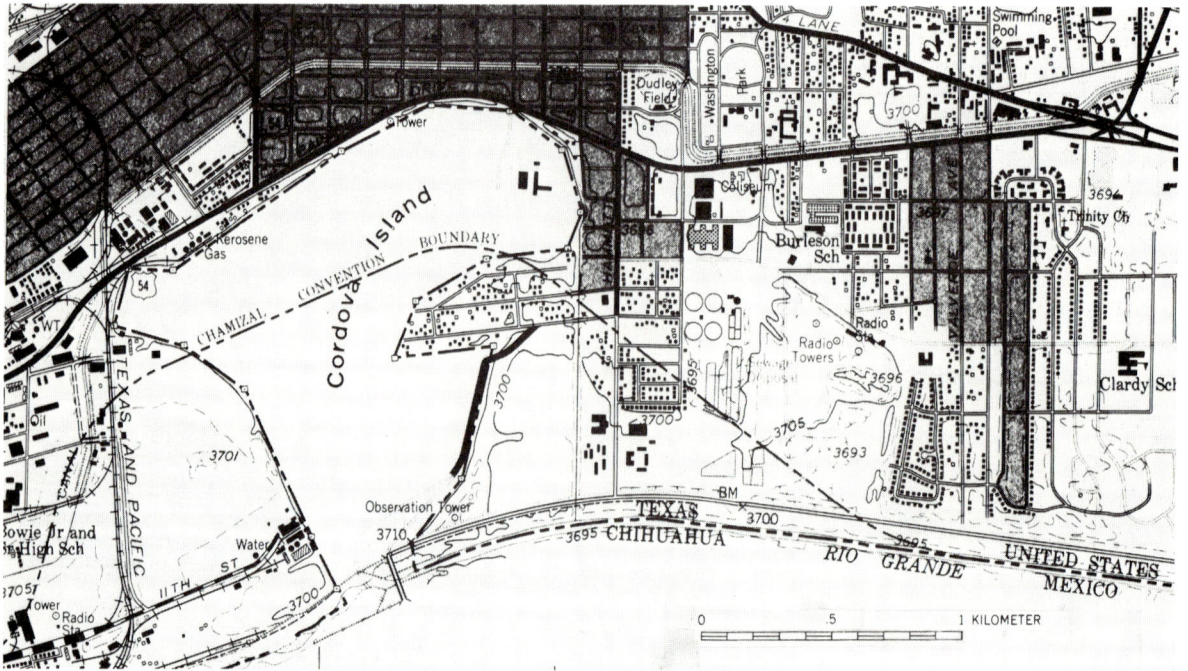

FIGURE 15–14 As rivers change course, boundary lines remain in place, causing jurisdictional problems. Cordova Island between El Paso, Texas, and Juarez, Mexico, was created this way.

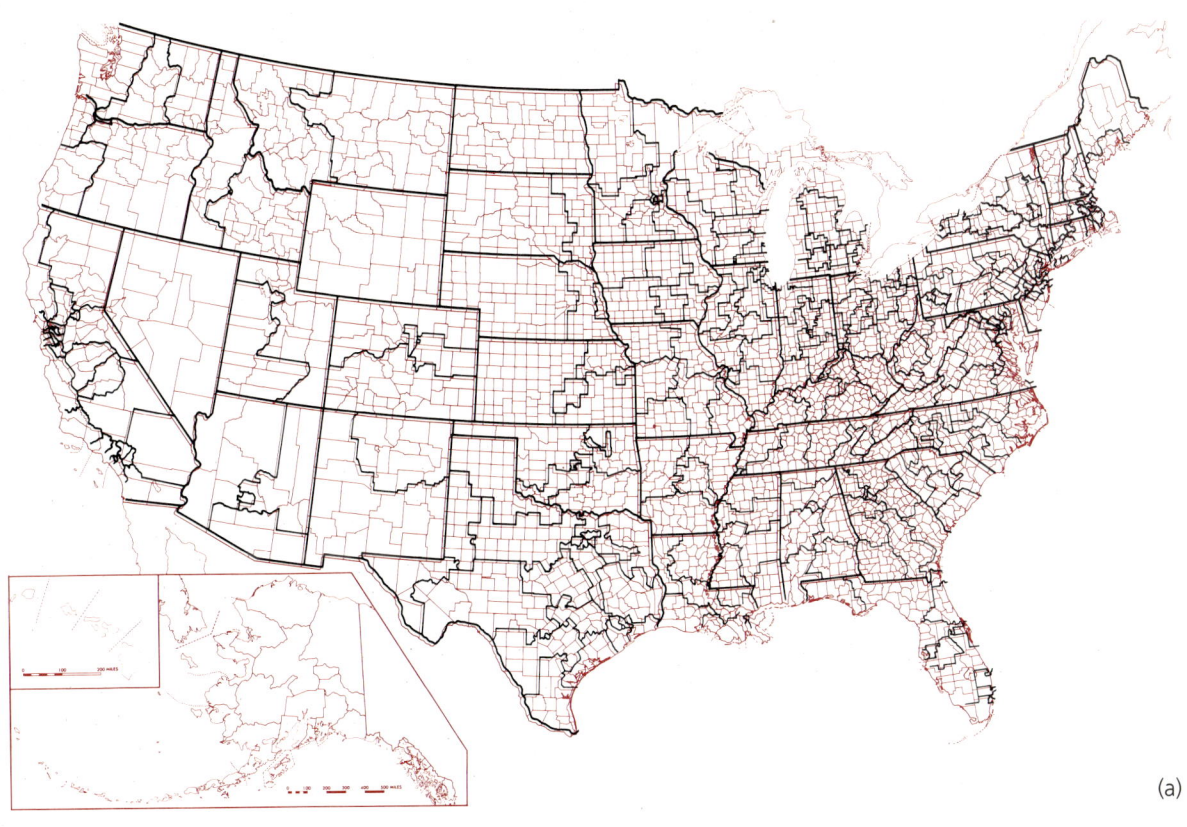

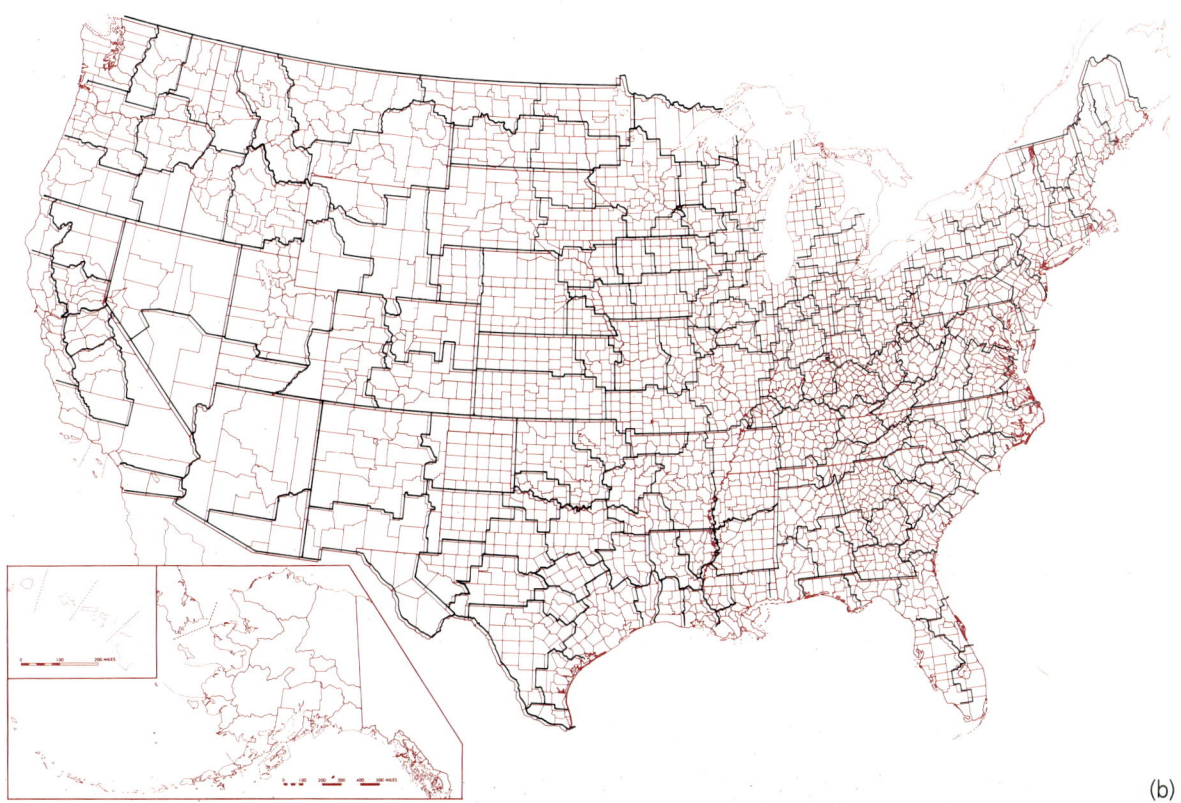

FIGURE 15–15 State functional regions: (a) congressional districts based on population; (b) state economic areas, formed by combining counties with similar economies.

CANADIAN SEPARATISM

The separation of any national state into two or more territories weakens the state and causes numerous disruptions in the lives of the people. Living under hostile conditions, however, also can wear heavily on daily living conditions. Hostility between people tends to increase when they do not speak the language of the adopted country. In many places of the world, however, linguistic enclaves exist. The people in these places often seek independence from the larger state. One example occurs in Canada.

Canadian settlement was pioneered by the French. The French established the cities of Quebec (1608) and Montreal (1642) and claimed the territory as their colony (New France). Meanwhile, Great Britain acquired Nova Scotia as part of its American expansion. The two countries extended their eighteenth century European conflicts into the New World, where Britain emerged the victor. Although New France was taken over by the British, the French retained the rights to their own language, religion, and civil law. This was guaranteed by the Quebec Act of 1774. About 100 years later (1867), the British North American (BNA) Act established the Dominion of Canada. This document became the country's written constitution. Canada now is an independent member of the British Commonwealth. This brief history lesson was designed to point out that the French language has been an integral part of the country's makeup, especially in Quebec.

French-speaking people in Quebec province today make up about 85 percent of the population. Quebec is the largest province in size, and the second largest in population. Feelings of separatism have run strong in the province for many years. In fact, the premier of the province won election on the basis of his separatist leanings. Since that 1976 election, national unity has been a major political issue in Canada. A referendum vote in 1980, however, clearly defeated a proposal to begin separatist negotiations with the national government. Some people in Quebec realize that separation could have a staggering effect on the politics and economics of both units.

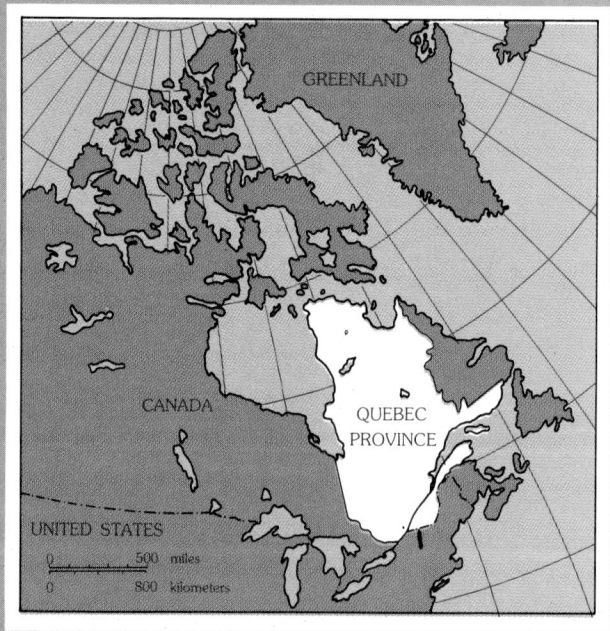

each federal census *(reapportionment)*. Substate economic areas are created by both the federal and state governments for federal and state planning purposes. Other substate regions based on area include highway commissioner and patrol districts, wildlife conservation districts, and special state areas such as tourist districts.

Substate regional boundaries are usually drawn along existing county boundary lines; thus, regions consist of groups of contiguous counties. There are many exceptions to this rule, however. The purpose in grouping counties is to attempt to use small areas that have some internal similarities in terms of both physical and human geographies. Economic development and planning can be accomplished easier within regions than by individual counties.

INTERNATIONAL BOUNDARIES

Primitive societies separated their core areas by zones. As the *heartlands* expanded, the intervening space was reduced. Sharply defined boundaries between historically emerging states did not come into existence until some time after states appeared. For many centuries, boundaries remained vague transition zones known as *frontiers,* and were generally based on physical features. Today, the earth's entire land surface (except Antarctica) is claimed by some national state; the lines that surround the claimed territory are carefully defined and located. A nation's boundary is the thin skin that touches the outside world; it has been called the "zone of friction" because it contacts and "rubs against" neighbors. This contact frequently results in inflamed emotions, border trouble, and outright conflict, and has probably caused more wars than any other factor.

The national boundary is of major concern to political geographers because it is a part of the national state. It defines the size and shape of the state, and separates a multitude of economic, political, and cultural factors that vary among states. The location, surveillance, and maintenance of a boundary is a national state function of prime importance. A major purpose of any government is to protect the territory of the state, and it's at the boundary that the protection is most evident. The Berlin Wall, for example, has vehicle traps, wire fences, and spotlights, and no nearby vegetation (Figure 15–16). Walls, fences, guardhouses, police, and other obstacles to free passage have been used to restrict movement across boundaries. Most national states are willing to risk war to protect their territory from invasions across their borders. The importance of international boundaries cannot be overemphasized.

Boundaries are *delimited* by drawing lines on a map, and *demarcated* by survey crews who establish actual markers in the field. Delimitation is easy, whereas demarcation can be quite difficult. *Antecedent boundaries* are boundaries drawn before human settlement. Many of these are geometrical, that is, they follow meridians, parallels, *rhumb lines,* or other geometrical determinants. The northwestern boundary between the United States and Canada is an antecedent boundary that follows the 49th parallel (Figure 15–17). *Subsequent* boundaries take into consideration both the cultural and physical landscapes. They are established after human settlement.

FIGURE 15–16 The most closely guarded boundary in the world is the Berlin Wall. (Photo courtesy of Paul Dumas.)

FIGURE 15–17 The boundary between Canada and the United States is visible from space because of the differences in land use. The light-colored area south of the line is Montana's wheat fields; the darker area north of the line is rangeland in Alberta. (Photo courtesy of NASA.)

Subsequent boundaries drawn as a consequence of cultural variation are called *consequent boundaries*. Such lines turn and twist like meandering rivers. The India–Pakistan border, for example, was drawn on the basis of religion, and language was the basis for redrawing the post–World War I boundaries of Europe. Both are examples of consequent boundaries. *Superimposed boundaries* are subsequent lines drawn *without* regard to existing cultural factors. That is, they are *superimposed* upon the indigenous people of a region. These kinds of lines were drawn by the Spanish colonial power, and now separate the Indian people living in the Andean basins between Peru and Ecuador and between Chile and Argentina.

National boundaries are classified in many other ways. They can be categorized according to the *function* they perform, or according to the *physical feature* they follow. There are also *historical* boundaries, which are relics of past division lines, as well as *complex* and *compound* boundaries, which adhere to more than one classification scheme. Many boundaries are based on a variety of physical and cultural features, making categorization difficult.

The number of national land boundaries has increased steadily over the years, and continues to do so. Every time a new sovereign nation emerges, new boundaries are created. Since 1815, a total of 22 European national states have disappeared, and 27 have been created. The international boundary map of Europe has been adjusted numerous times to accommodate these changes. In Africa, changes have been even more recent and more rapid (Figure 15–18). Thirty-three new African nations have joined the United Nations since 1960. These new boundaries are the results of countless armed conflicts, both internal revolutions and wars between nations.

OCEAN BOUNDARIES

A national boundary along an ocean would seem to be ideal, because it would not "rub against" a neighbor. It would also be clearly visible on a map, and relatively permanent. International debate continues, however, on determining how far offshore a coastal country's jurisdiction should extend. The Law of the Sea treaty, designed to conclude the debate, was finalized in August of 1980, but the United States government has refused to sign the treaty because of a "share the wealth" provision backed by Third World countries.

Ocean boundary rights include rights concerning sanitation regulation, customs inspection, illegal or undesirable behavior, exploitation of mineral and animal resources, and national protection.

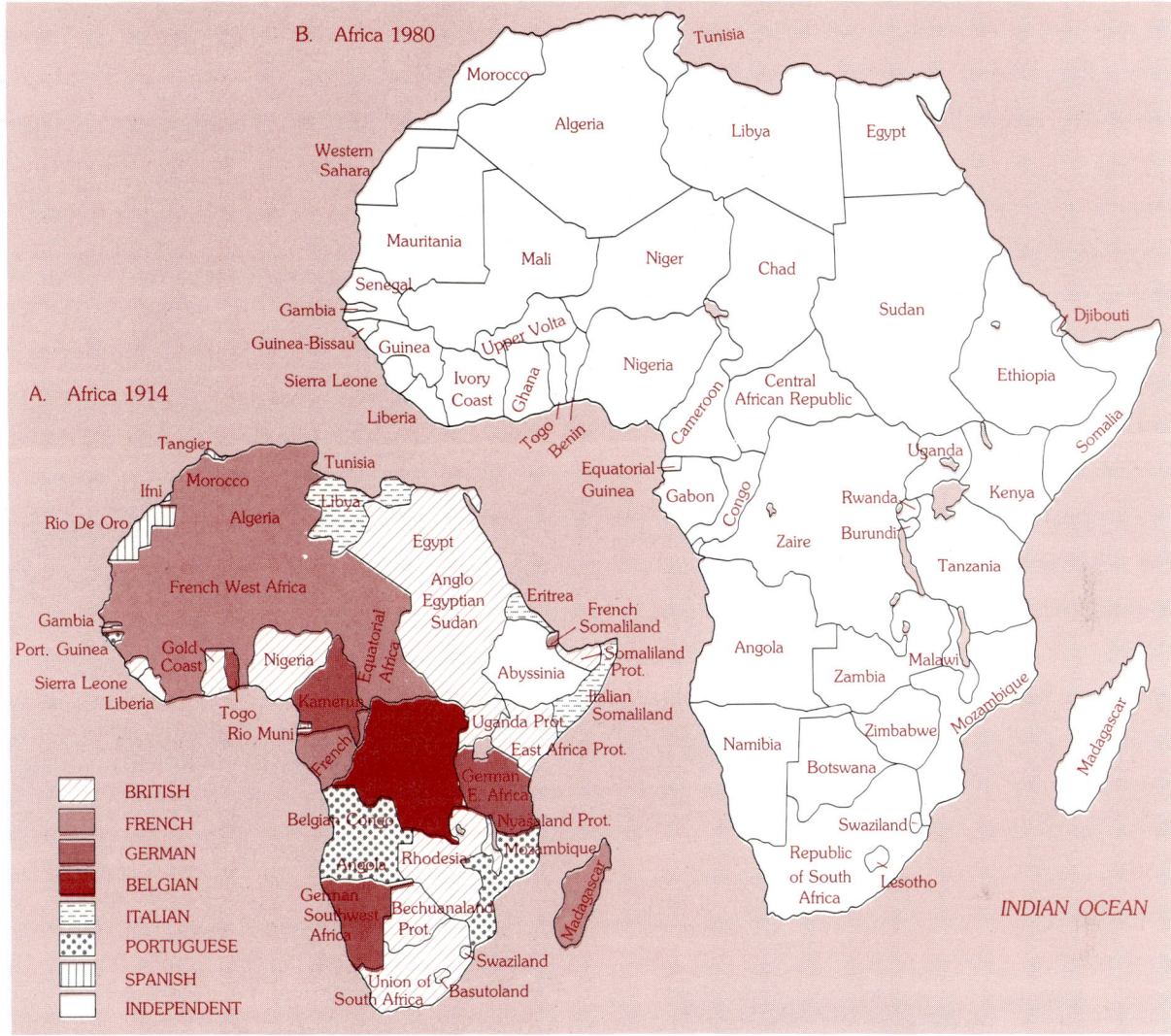

FIGURE 15–18 Boundary changes in Africa have resulted as countries gain independence from colonialism.

Until recently, a 3-mile limit was traditionally recognized as the seaward extent of territorial waters. This distance was established in the age of land-based cannons, whose shot would carry about 3 miles (see Figure 15–19). The boundary limit was therefore the logical distance over which a nation could enforce its laws against sea vessels. Beyond this limit were the open seas, a vast waterway upon which all nations could legally travel freely ("freedom of passage," established by Dutch jurist Hugo Grotius in 1609). When negotiations began at the Law of the Sea conferences, however, 50 countries had extended the 3-mile limit to 5, 6, or 12 miles, with claims ranging as far as 200 miles off shore. The freedom of passage rule was jeopardized in many areas, and seabed mining operations ignored even the 200-mile limit. The Law of the Sea treaty of 1980 covers these problems, and nearly every other conceivable issue dealing with the oceans.

According to the agreements among the 156 participating countries at the Law of the Sea conferences, a coastal nation's sovereignty extends for 12 miles off its shore, but each nation also has exclusive access to a 200-mile "economic zone." The economic zone includes any portion of the continental shelf that may extend beyond 200 miles. This means that coastal states have exclusive jurisdiction over marine resources—both fishing and seabed mining rights—within their economic zones. Two world agencies have been established to arbitrate disputes and oversee the use of resources—the Law of the Sea Tribunal and the International Seabed Authority,

ASEAN

The Association of Southeast Asian Nations (ASEAN) was formed in 1967 to promote political cooperation and mutual protection among the non-Communist states of Southeast Asia. The member nations are Indonesia, Malaysia, the Philippines, Singapore, and Thailand. Economic cooperation through agriculture, trade, finance, and transportation is advanced at the annual meetings in Jakarta.

The most immediate threat to any ASEAN country comes from Vietnam. As shown in the following table, the combined efforts of the five ASEAN countries do not match up well against the one Communist country:

	ASEAN	Vietnam
Population	249,600,000	49,300,000
Army		
Personnel	466,500	600,000
Tanks	480	900
Combat aircraft	431	300

The population of ASEAN is approximately five times that for Vietnam, but Vietnam has the larger army and tank force. This is not the largest problem, however. The major concern is that ASEAN is fragmented into thousands of islands and odd-shaped countries. Should Vietnam attack Thailand, for example, aid from the other ASEAN countries would be difficult to muster. The small overall combat forces and the huge fragmented area leaves doubts about ASEAN's mutual protection capabilities.

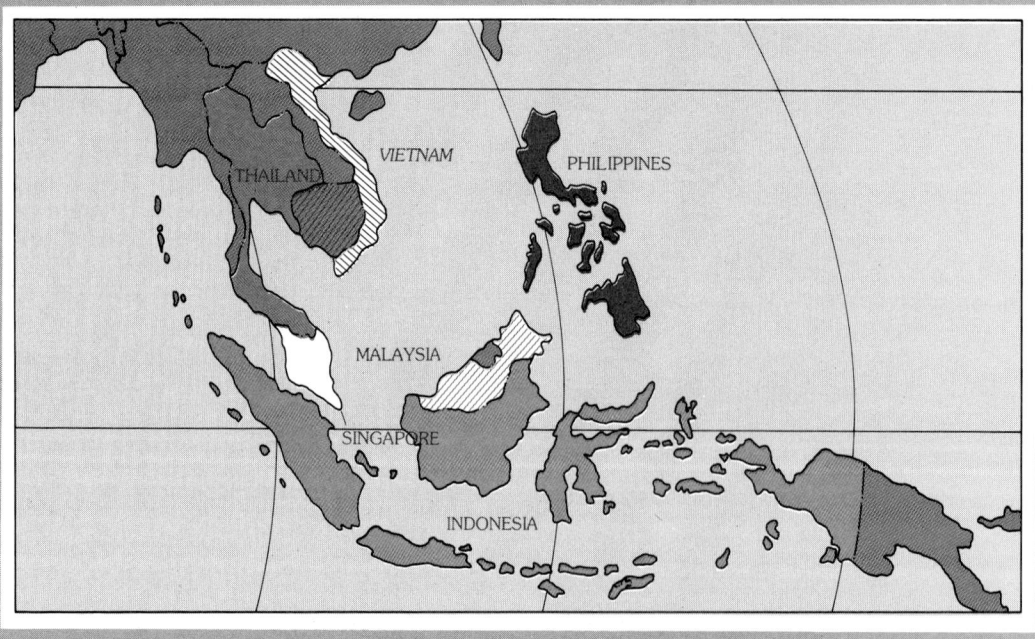

MULTINATIONAL BOUNDARIES

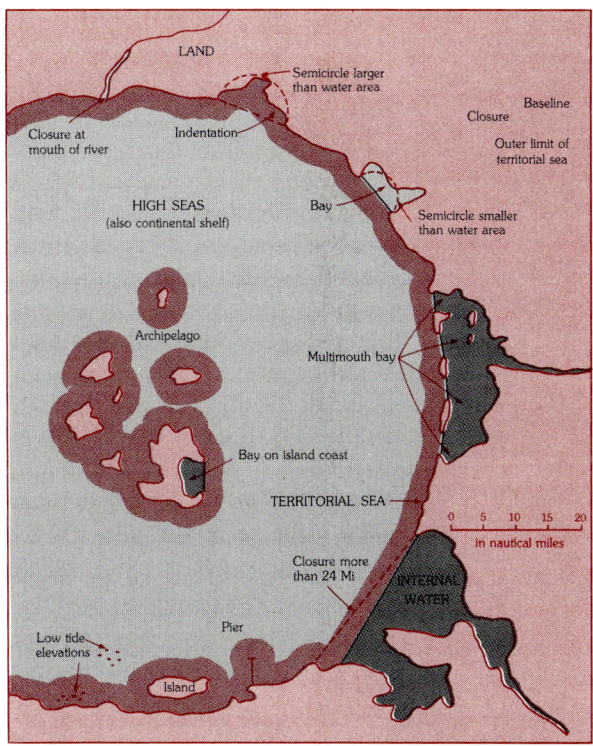

FIGURE 15–19 Baseline from which territorial waters are measured. (From the U.S. Department of State.)

respectively. Many new world boundaries, both political and economic, are created each year.

MULTINATIONAL BOUNDARIES

The last level of man-made boundaries on the earth's surface is made up of those boundaries formed by groups or countries for ideological, military, or economic purposes. These international alliances have been as simple as bilateral statements of mutual intent and as complex as unions attempting to unite all nations of the world. Some have been based on detailed treaties explicit in their directions to members, whereas others have been general in tone and vague in language. Although it is impossible to neatly categorize these organizations, three general types are evident. One exists in the hope of installing a world order, another is the regional association of nations, and the last is the grouping of states that find one ideology or economic interest strong enough to override all other concerns.

The two major organizations that have attempted to bring law and order to the anarchy of the autonomous national state system are the League of Nations (1920–1946) and the United Nations (1946–present). The stated purpose of the League of Nations was to solve international problems and reduce armaments, but it was hampered by the absence of many world powers* and because it had no effective means of policing its decisions. The 50 founding states of the United Nations patterned their organization after the League of Nations, but hoped to avert weakness by having a police force. The major problem with the United Nations today is its unbalanced representation. The proliferation of small states since 1960 allows representatives of less than one-fourth of the earth's people to control the vote in the General Assembly. Regardless of problems and failures of the United Nations, some of its agencies (UNESCO and UNICEF, for instance) have served humankind by alleviating suffering and ignorance throughout the world.

There are numerous regional associations of nations that reflect common economic, cultural, or military interests. These alliances represent a regional bias; that is, the primary binding element is the spatial proximity of members. The most prominent regional boundary in Europe—possibly in the world—is the Iron Curtain, which runs from the Arctic to the Mediterranean and divides eastern and western Europe. The countries east of the line belong to the Warsaw Treaty Organization (Warsaw Pact, a military alliance) and the Council of Mutual Economic Assistance (COMECON, an economic and social alliance). Countries west of the Iron Curtain are organized into one military alliance—the North Atlantic Treaty Organization (NATO)—and numerous economic groups (Figure 15–20). The European Communities (EC) combine three subsidiary organizations—the European Economic Community (EEC), the European Coal and Steel Community (ECSC), and the European Atomic Energy Community (EAEC). The European Economic Community, known as the Common Market, has 10 permanent member nations, 5 associate members, and 49 affiliated states.**

Regional alliances exist on every continent, some extending over two or three continents. For example, the League of Arab States extends over most of North Africa and the Middle East, a distance of 8,000 km (5,000 mi) from Oman to Morocco. The Organization of African Unity includes about 50 countries with similar political, cultural, and economic aspirations, and represents almost all of Africa. The Orga-

---

*The United States never joined the League of Nations; the Soviet Union was a member for only a few years; Germany, Japan, and Italy withdrew in the 1930s.

**The original EEC member nations were France, Germany, Italy, Belgium, the Netherlands, and Luxembourg; the United Kingdom, Ireland, and Denmark joined in 1972, and Greece became a permanent member in 1981.

339

CHAPTER 15 THE BOUNDED EARTH

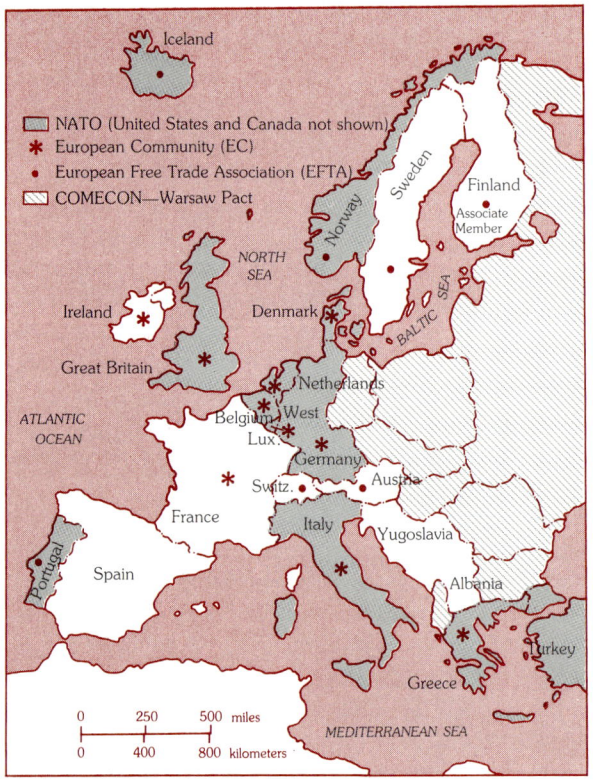

FIGURE 15-20 European economic and political associations. (Adapted from Norris and Haring, *Political Geography* [Charles E. Merrill, 1980], p. 167.)

nization of American States (OAS) is made up of most of the countries of the Western Hemisphere south of the United States–Canadian border. The Organization of Petroleum Exporting Countries (OPEC) consists of a diverse group of countries with the similar special interest of promoting economic and political returns from oil production. OPEC countries are found in Latin America, central Africa, North Africa, the Middle East, and Southeast Asia (Figure 15–21).

In the third type of multinational organization, countries are grouped together because of some outside influence or economic condition. For example, the British Commonwealth of Nations, the French Community, and the Communist world are groups of countries tied not especially from their alliance with each other but rather because of past or present political factors over which most members have little control. Often, the only thing many Communist countries have in common is their basic form of government, yet they are often considered an influential world force. The only similarities of many Commonwealth and Communist nations are their colonial ties to their mother countries.

Another common way of categorizing countries into multinational groupings is to use a scheme of "worlds." These include the First, Second, Third, and Fourth Worlds, and will be discussed in greater detail in Chapter 16.

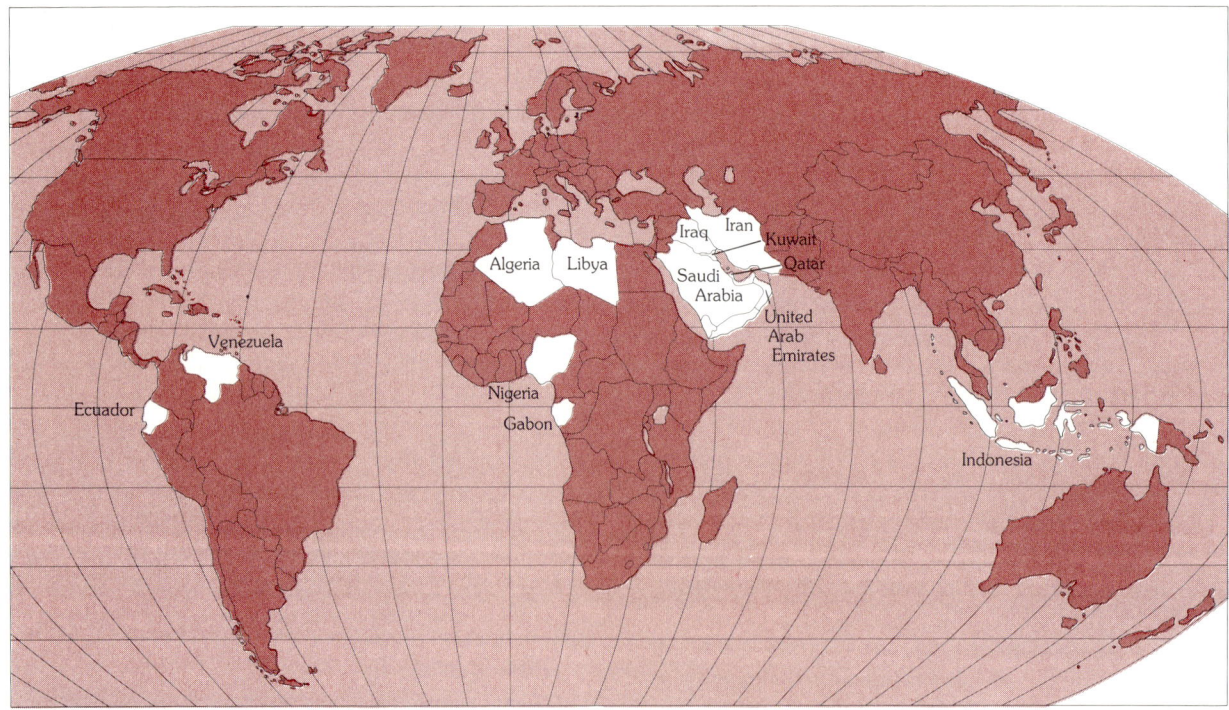

FIGURE 15-21 Locations of the national states belonging to OPEC. (Adapted from Norris and Haring, *Political Geography* [Charles E. Merrill, 1980], p. 169.)

CONCLUSION

We find boundaries at all levels of human organization. An individual's personal space is defined as critically as the frontier between multinational organizations. All boundaries are similar in that they define areas of jurisdiction and form protective covers over the inhabitants of the areas. Although some boundaries overlap and some have gaps between them, most boundaries of a similar type separate contiguous areas. Boundary problems and disputes are common at all scales from the micro to the macro.

Boundaries indicate how humans have divided the earth's surface into unit areas for various reasons. The most common purpose for boundaries is to separate the individual units that comprise the complex patchwork of personal properties. A world without boundaries is difficult to imagine, although it is safe to say it would be extremely chaotic.

KEY WORDS

air space
antecedent boundary
anti-incorporation law
complex boundary
compound boundary
consequent boundary
consolidated school
county
delimit (a boundary)
demarcate (a boundary)
federation
frontier
heartland
historical boundary
home rule
Homestead Act
independent school district
individual distance
Land Ordinance Act
Law of the Sea conferences

League of Nations
metes and bounds
mineral rights
panhandle
personal space
politics
proxemics
reapportionment
rhumb line
sociofugal
sociopetal
subsequent boundary
subsurface
superimposed boundary
terrestrial space
thalweg
United Nations
usable space
zoning ordinance

REFERENCES

ALLEN, EDWARD W. "Territorial Waters and Extraterritorial Rights." *American Journal of International Law* (1953): 478–480.

ARDREY, ROBERT. *The Territorial Imperative.* New York: Dell Publishing Co., 1966.

BOGGS, WHITTEMORE. *International Boundaries.* New York: Columbia University Press, 1940.

————. "National Claims in Adjacent Seas." *Geographical Review* 41 (1951): 185–209.

BRIGHAM, ALBERT PERRY. "Principles in the Determination of Boundaries." *Geographical Review* 7 (1919): 201–19.

HARTSHORNE, RICHARD. "Suggestions on the Terminology of Political Boundaries." *Annals of the Association of American Geographers* 26 (1936): 56–57.

HOLDICH, SIR THOMAS H. *Political Frontiers and Boundary Makings.* London: Macmillan & Co., 1916.

JOHNSON, DOUGLAS W. "The Role of Political Boundaries." *Geographical Review* 4 (1917): 208–13.

JONES, STEPHEN B. *Boundary Making.* Washington, D.C.: Carnegie Endowment for International Peace, 1945.

JOOS, LOUIS C. D. "Bored with Borders." *European Community* 164 (1973): 15.

KRISTOFF, LADIS K. D. "The Nature of Frontiers and Boundaries." *Annals of the Association of American Geographers* 49 (1959): 269–82.

KUHN, DELIA, and KUHN, FERDINAND. *Borderlands.* New York: Alfred A. Knopf, 1962.

McFEE, WILLIAM. *The Law of the Sea.* Philadelphia: J. B. Lippincott Co., 1950.

MINGHI, JULIAN V. "Boundary Studies in Political Geography." *Annals of the Association of American Geographers* 53 (1963): 37–46.

NORRIS, ROBERT E., and HARING, L. LLOYD. *Political Geography.* Columbus, Ohio: Charles E. Merrill Publishing Co., 1980.

PEARCY, G. ETZEL. "Geographical Aspects of the Law of the Sea." *Annals of the Association of American Geographers* 49 (1959): 1–23.

PRESCOTT, J. R. V. *Geography of Frontiers and Boundaries.* Chicago: Aldine Publishing Co., 1965.

SOMMERS, ROBERT. *Personal Space: The Behavioral Basis of Design.* Englewood Cliffs, N.J.: Prentice-Hall, 1969.

SPYKMAN, NICHOLAS J. "Frontiers, Security, and International Organization." *Geographical Review* 38 (1948): 5–29.

16
Politics and Location

Boundaries, as we discussed in the preceding chapter, are basic to political geography because they are the implements used to divide the earth's territory into thousands of unit areas. Boundaries have an impact on human activity and give size and shape to the areas they designate. Another critical factor in political geography that occurs because of boundaries is the *location* of the individual unit areas. A country's latitudinal and continental locations both influence its climatic conditions, and its location determines a country's resource base—Kuwait is a good example. Most importantly, however, location determines a country's neighbors. Thus, location has an impact on daily living conditions (climate), economic activities (resources), and governmental actions (relationships with neighbors).

NATIONALISM AND NATION-STATES

Historical Development of the State Idea

The world is not divided equally into a checkerboard of countries. Most people live under administrations that have evolved from a tribal stage through a fuedal organization, eventually resulting in the system of administration common today. But because there is a special bond between humans and territory, the evolution of governments is closely tied to the evolution of the use of space. Tribes were mobile groups that depended on hunting and gathering (see Chapter 10). Although they had no fixed administrative center, within the territory of each tribe was a special place, such as a burial site or home of the tribal gods. And the territory had a peripheral boundary

NATIONALISM AND NATION-STATES
IMPACT OF LOCATION
INTERACTION AND ECONOMICS
ECONOMICS AND POLITICS

State capitols are usually solid and impressive-looking, to give citizens confidence in their government.

beyond which members traveled at their own risk. Separating tribal territories was a zone of "no-man's-land," which served to reduce conflicts. These tribal territories with special centers and nebulous boundaries were the forerunners of the modern states with administrative centers and strictly defined boundaries.

The human tie with the land existed in all parts of the world, but it was in northwestern Europe that the state idea evolved most rapidly. The tribal system there was followed by the feudal organization of territory. The central location of the feudal governments was a castle fortress, occupied by a warrior lord and his retinue (Figure 16–1). The warriors defended their territory and upheld what little social stability there was. They did so by making their own laws, such as those pertaining to heavy taxation. The common people worked the land but did not own it. In fact, they were considered part of the land. When control of the land changed from one noble to another, the people who worked the land also changed ownership. Hundreds of these serfdoms existed, some until the middle of the nineteenth century. The Holy Roman Empire alone was composed of over 300 tiny states, which helps to explain the hundreds of castles that dot the European landscape today. And in the British Isles, the British Ministry of Public Works lists 138 habitable castles and hundreds of historic halls, houses, gardens, and privately owned palaces.

The first national states of Europe formed when the numerous territories of the serfdoms coalesced. The common people continued their close association with the land. This human-land relationship remained strong even when governments changed from absolute monarchies to republics. The relationship is the basis of *nationalism,* which is a territorial behavior in humans. Such allegiance to a country makes it possible for a government to administer law and order. Because absolute monarchs and dictators demand loyalty to themselves rather than to the state, they are rarely successful for long periods. Thus, the kings of Europe were eventually replaced by democratic republics, and the concept of the nation became the basis for governing all the earth's territory. The boundaries between nations became an integral part of the world order, and changes in boundaries brought population movement, mingling, and displacement as empires, kingdoms, and states have expanded, contracted, and disappeared (Figure 16–2).

Colonialism

Colonialism is a policy whereby a national state seeks to extend its political control over territory that lies beyond the national boundaries. Most of the ancient empires, such as the Inca in the Western Hemisphere and the Roman in Europe, were built through colonial acquisitions. Because these empires, as well as newer states such as India, the Soviet Union, and the United States, extended their boundaries into contiguous areas, they are usually not thought of as colonial powers. European colonialism, on the other hand, was marked by the acquisition of territory located far beyond the national boundaries (Figure 16–3). The wave of territorial expansion that began in the fif-

FIGURE 16–1 Castles, like this one in Chepstow, Wales, were once the administrative headquarters for small local kingdoms.

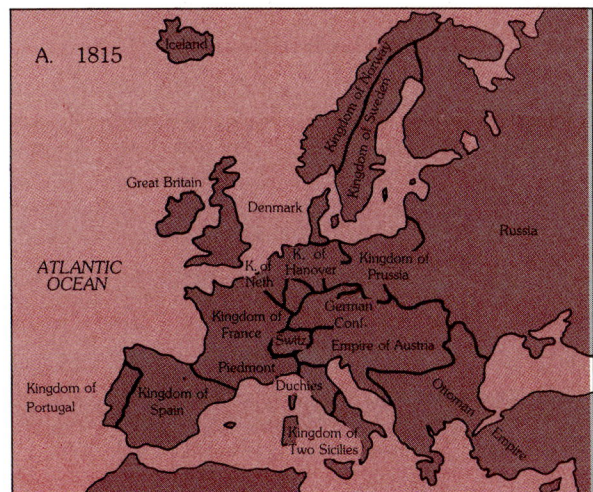 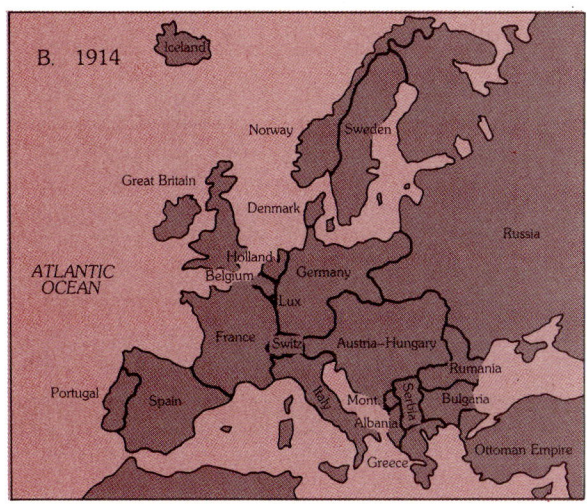
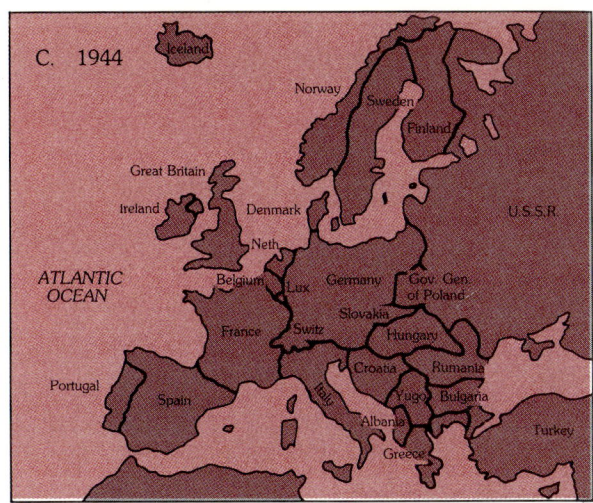 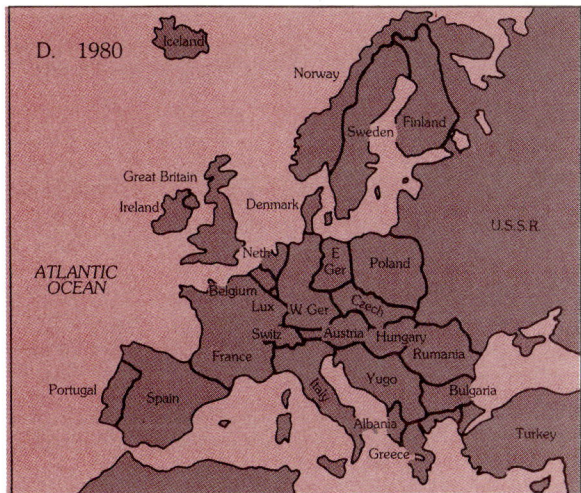

FIGURE 16–2 Sequence of boundary changes in Europe over the nineteenth and twentieth centuries.

FIGURE 16–3 The European influence in Africa can be seen in the architecture of urban centers. (Photo courtesy of John McKinstry.)

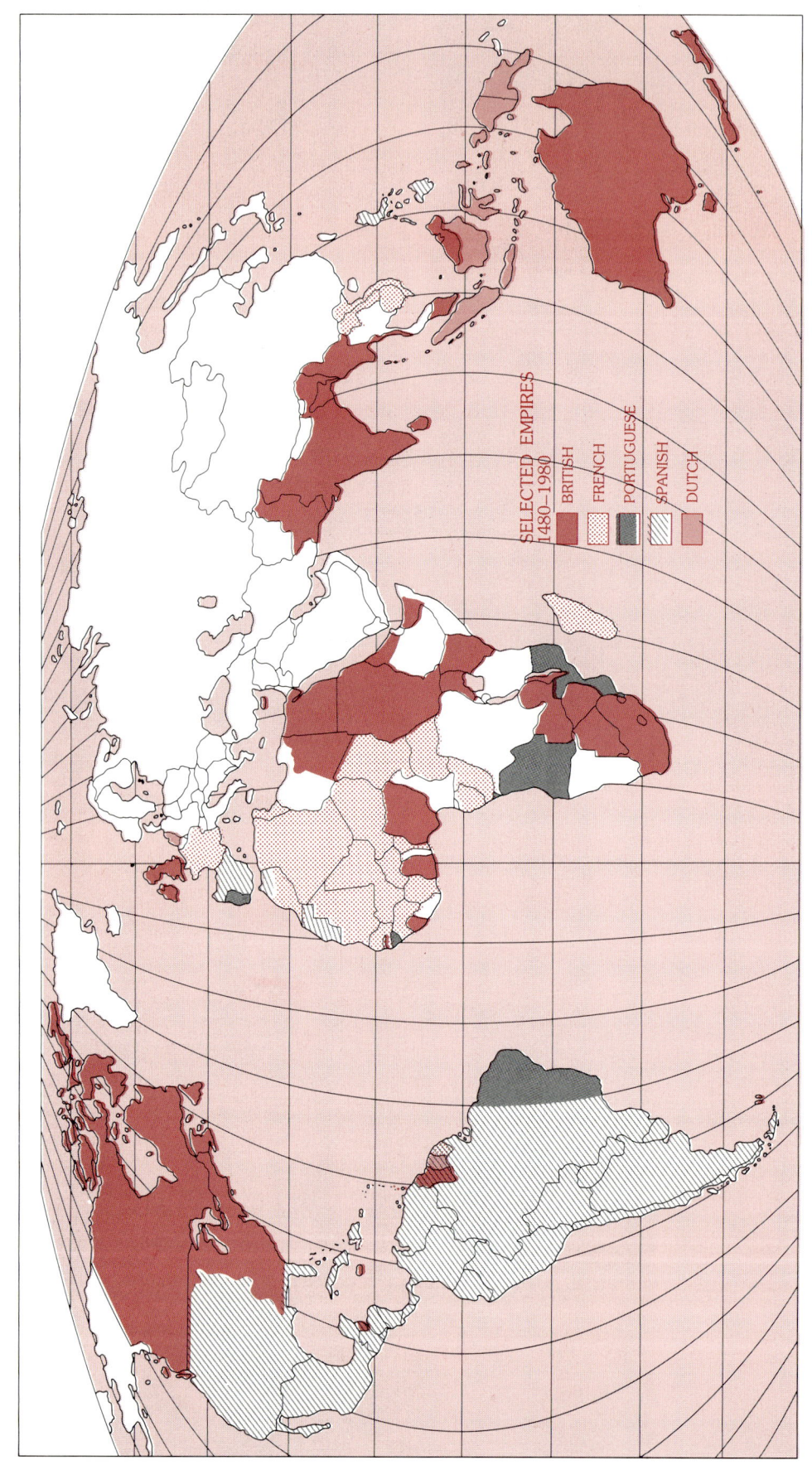

FIGURE 16–4 Colonial empires at their greatest extent.

NATIONALISM AND NATION-STATES

teenth century was of unprecedented scale. It lasted over 500 years and affected every continent (Figure 16–4). Britain once ruled an empire that covered a quarter of the earth's surface, and as recently as 1975, Portugal held territories 23 times its own area.

Colonialism was prompted by economic interests. At first, the explorers were looking for sources of gold, silver, and other riches. Later, the major European states were eager to obtain overseas possessions to serve as exclusive markets. In addition to markets, the industrializing European states wanted places that could supply duty-free raw materials. Economic penetration through trade was followed by political control. Today these holdings are gone, and the number of people who are not members of their own national state is less than 1 percent of the earth's total. Strong ties, however, still exist among member nations of some ex-colonial empires. Probably the most enduring and successful international associations based on ex-colonial ties are the British Commonwealth and French Community.

Decolonization

Independence from colonial rulers began in 1776, when the United States proclaimed its independence from Great Britain. Decolonization came sporadically and slowly to most European colonies until World War II. In 1941, Lebanon declared independence and over half the national states that exist today have come into existence since then. The banner year for the emergence of new nations was 1960, when 17 sovereign, independent African countries appeared on the world political map (see Figure 16–5). Ideas such as democracy, political equality, and nationalism diffused rapidly after World War II, and the spread of these ideas and the declarations of independence continue today.

Countries that gain independence from European colonial rulers usually model their political structures after the European state system. Two major problems arise with this adaptation. First, the boundaries of the new states (especially in Africa) are

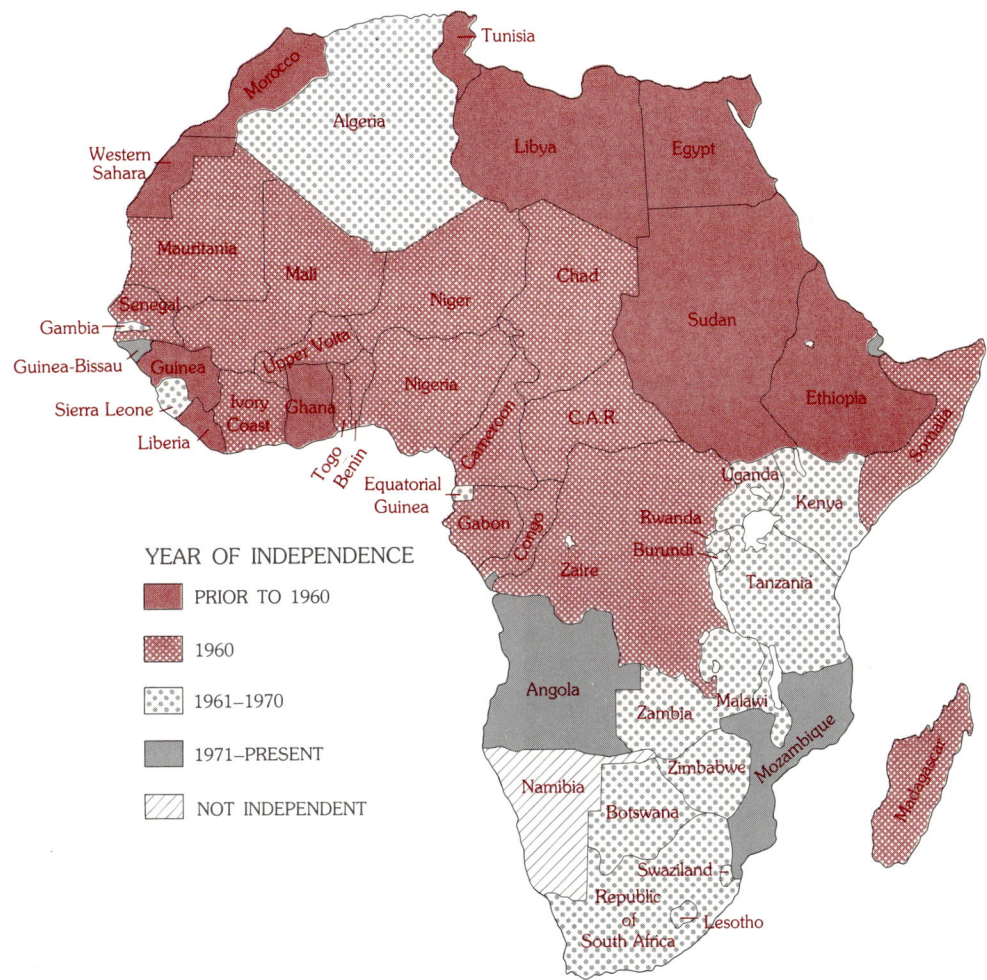

FIGURE 16–5 Years in which African nations achieved independence.

drawn according to the colonial divisions rather than along tribal or cultural lines. Thus, the new international boundaries tend to separate some people with similar cultures and languages and force others who are different to live together. The second problem arises because tribal loyalties are often greater than national loyalties. The feelings of nationalism that help hold the European states together, then, tend to be weaker in the tribe-oriented people of the ex-colonies, resulting in a weaker national state.

Assimilation or Separation

National states are eager to generate in all their citizens a national culture or consciousness. Sometimes this task proves difficult, as most states contain minority groups that must be assimilated into the majority culture for cohesiveness. These minority groups often speak their own languages and follow their own religions. Common examples are the German-speaking people of France, Italy, and Czechoslovakia, and the French-speaking people of Canada. Figure 16–6 shows the Kurdish homeland, which, if it were a national state based on Kurdish culture, would include Kurdistan as well as adjacent parts of Iraq, Syria, and the Soviet Union. There are Moslems in India and Hindus in Pakistan, as well as minority Moslem sects in various Middle East countries. These minority groups can cause problems, especially if they demand independence.

An area of a national state that contains a minority group historically or ethnically related to people of another national state is called an *irredenta*. The policy or desire by the outside state to incorporate an irredenta is called *irredentism*. These terms derive from *Terra Irredenta*, an area claimed by Italy in 1878 that contained a large percentage of Italians *(irredentists)*. In the 1930s, German citizens of Poland, Hungary, and Czechoslovakia created problems for their countries. The Third Reich encouraged the disruptions and used them to justify taking over large territories. Similar problems persist today in many areas of the world. For example, the Shiite Moslems of eastern Saudi Arabia identify with Iran, and many Chinese in eastern Africa and Southeast Asia are loyal to their home state.

Minority group assimilation into the national state is difficult because of the ethnic association within the group. Each ethnic unit has a large number of shared experiences and beliefs—its members may enjoy the same music, eat the same food, and fear or love the same *icons*. Usually, however, the factors that are most important to minority group cohesion are language, religion, and common heritage.

Nearly every national state has an ethnic minority that advocates group identity at the expense of national solidarity. The United Kingdom has experienced separatist tendencies in Scotland, Northern Ireland, and Wales. Spain has its rebellious Basques. In Yugoslavia, the Serbs, Croats, and Slovenes are each moving toward political confrontation with the government. Present demands in Nigeria could eventually lead to nearly 200 states based on ethnic differences. These separatist factors within a state are called *centrifugal forces,* because they tend to tear a state apart.

Nation-States

To become politically powerful, a state must have internal cohesion. When sufficient assimilation has occurred that most of the people maintain a sense of national cohesion, we identify the area with the term *nation-state*. Other terms have been used to describe international political units—for example, *nation*, *country*, and *state*—but political geographers use *nation* to mean a group of individuals who possess a sense of unity based on shared common factors. Therefore, a nation does not necessarily have its own territory. *Country,* on the other hand, refers only to the territory that a nation occupies. The word *state* best describes the international political unit, but is often confused with the subdivisions of the United States. The term *nation-state* should perhaps be used for all international political units regardless of whether or not the place has internal cohesion.

FIGURE 16–6 Kurdistan, the Kurdish homeland, is in the valleys of northwestern Iran's Zagros Mountains and eastern Turkey's Tauras Mountains.

Once a nation-state is established, there are several significant ways to hold the diverse elements together. These *centripetal forces* include schools, military training, communication media, and churches. These forces direct divergent political activity toward the central concept of the nation-state. Schools teach a common language, history, and geography. Military training emphasizes nationalism and response to national icons. Telephones and postal systems are integral parts of a unified state. And religion establishes a common climate of thought that is politically useful. Becoming a true nation-state involves not only having a central government with effective administrative control over a precisely defined area, but also developing a national and relatively uniform culture.

IMPACT OF LOCATION

Although the location of a point on the earth is fixed, continuously changing political and economic conditions alter the implications of location. As Figure 16–7 shows, for example, resources must be extracted where they are found, no matter how

MALTA

Malta is a rocky Mediterranean island country located off Sicily. The main island (Malta) is only 246 km² (95 mi²); Gozo and Comino add another 70 km² (27mi²). During World War II, Malta was called the "unsinkable aircraft carrier" because of its size and strategic location. Its coastlines are indented with many cliffs, and the interior is a series of low hills. The population of Malta, slightly less than 350,000, is mostly of Italian descent, and primarily Roman Catholic (98 percent). Malta's official languages, however, are English and Maltese.

Malta was founded as a British colony in 1814, gained its independence in 1964, and became a Republic in 1974. On 1 April, 1979, the last British sailor left the island, after 179 years of British military presence. At Malta's Grand Harbor, British and Maltese officials unveiled a monument symbolically depicting the departure. Prior to British rule, Malta had been governed by Phoenicians, Romans, Arabs, Normans, the Knights of Malta, and France. Malta had thus been a colony for centuries.

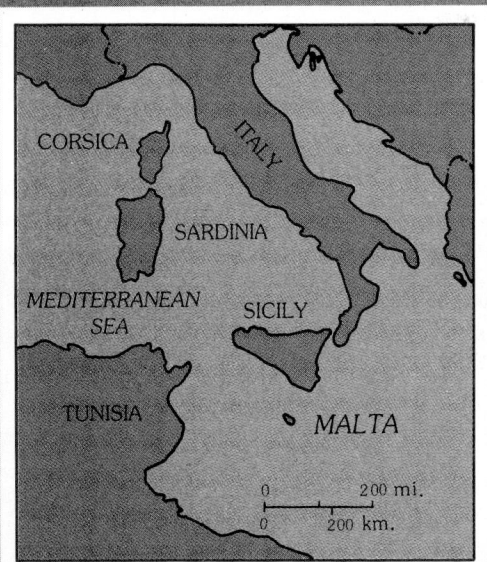

Malta today is neutral politically and tends to play the East against the West. The country's self-proclaimed protector is Libya, and China is helping to build a drydock for supertankers. The U.S. Sixth Fleet is barred from liberty visits to Malta, and Soviet military ships cannot use the facilities. The tiny, rocky island country is working to maintain its national existence in a location loaded with geopolitical significance.

strange or exotic the location. Until about 80 years ago, the United States was on the periphery of the world, but today, of course, its location is more significant. The same might be said about the Middle East, but for a slightly different reason. The United States became prominent in world affairs through agriculture, manufacturing, and technology—that is, by means of many resources. The Middle East, on the other hand, became an area of world concern because of one resource—petroleum. The location of a nation-state affects not only the ordinary citizens but also the thinking of statesmen and military strategists.

Relations with Other States

The location of a nation-state determines the number and location of its neighbors. It is significant, for example, that the United States shares boundaries with only 2 other countries, whereas the Soviet Union has common borders with 11 other nation-states. The larger the number of bordering states, the greater the potential for boundary disputes, and the greater the likelihood of problems in the neighboring states spilling over the border. Having more neighbors increases concern for what is happening in neighboring states. Conversely, with fewer neigh-

BALUCHISTAN

Pakistan is a federation of the four provinces of Sind, Punjab, the North-West Frontier, and Baluchistan. The people of each province have a strong sense of regional identity; Baluchistan's nationalism is the strongest. Baluchistan province is part of a tribal nation that extends into eastern Iran and southern Afghanistan. The tribal nation was split by the British during the time of imperialism and has remained in parts of the three countries ever since. Despite the politics that separate them, the Baluch have remained loyal to their tribal nation.

Baluchistan is a desert region with a landscape corrugated by rugged mountain ranges. The province contains some oil, coal, and natural gas, but little else of value. About 60 percent of the people are nomadic tribesmen who live much the same as the people of the region lived hundreds of years ago. Tribal values are based on honor, and great importance is placed on keeping that honor.

Baluch identity rests in loyalty to a harsh region and to tribalism—an outdated, dying form of social structure. It is difficult for an outsider to understand the Baluch militant persistence in maintaining such strong nationalistic feelings. How do you convince a turbaned, bearded, Muslim guerrilla whose prized possession is an ancient British Lee–Enfield rifle that there is a world beyond his tribe?

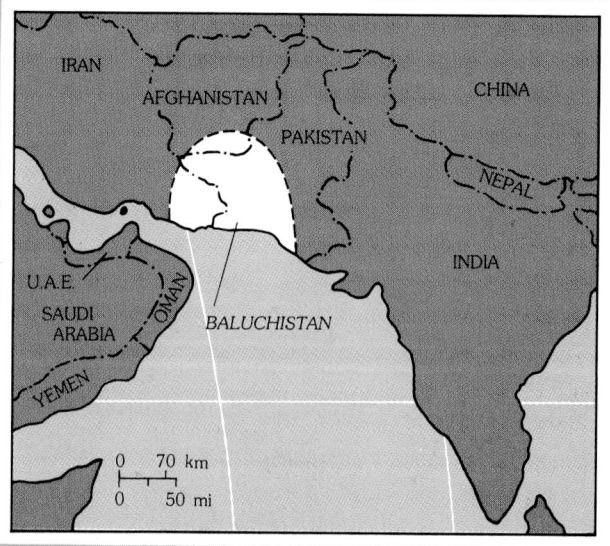

IMPACT OF LOCATION

FIGURE 16–7 Oil drilling rigs (a) in the North Sea off the coast of Scotland and (b) near Dakar, Senegal, on the west coast of Africa. (Photos courtesy of Phillips Petroleum Company.)

bors, it is easier to develop *isolationist* attitudes—attitudes that are often expressed by a lack of interest for neighbors or the world outside the homeland.

Fear of actual or potential attacks by neighbors has been used as a reason for countries to take over adjoining territory. The expansion of Germany and Japan during World War II was based on this excuse. Israel used the same rationale during its expansion years, as have many other nation-states. A small country surrounded by potentially hostile neighbors is especially vulnerable to take-over.

These attitudes and fears are psychological factors and thus susceptible to distortion. This means that spatial relationships, especially those regarding location, can distort the political outlook of international relations. Sometimes, the foreign policies of nation-states are based on these distortions.

Buffer States

In some areas of international conflict, often called *hot spots*, tension-easing devices are used. Hot spots usually occur where two or more powerful states border one another. To reduce the friction caused by the locational factors, a small, independent state may be created as a buffer between the larger, hostile countries. *Buffer* states are usually located in transition zones between the stronger neighbors. In Europe, Belgium, Luxembourg, and Switzerland have served as buffers between France and Germany. Uruguay is a buffer state in South America, and many states in Asia (Afghanistan, Burma, Laos, Mongolia, Nepal, and Thailand) either have been or still are buffers between larger neighbors (see Figure 16–8).

The states of eastern Europe were created after World War I as buffers between the opposing ideologies of the Soviet Union and the countries of western Europe. The buffer aspect as well as the political fragmentation of eastern Europe led to the term *shatter belt*. The region today is neither a buffer nor a shatter belt, however, for it has been completely absorbed into the sphere of influence of the Soviet Union. The opposing ideologies of the East and West now rub against each other at such hot spots as the Berlin Wall.

Landlocked States

When a nation-state has no direct access to an ocean, it is said to be *landlocked*. There are over 30

353

CHAPTER 16 POLITICS AND LOCATION

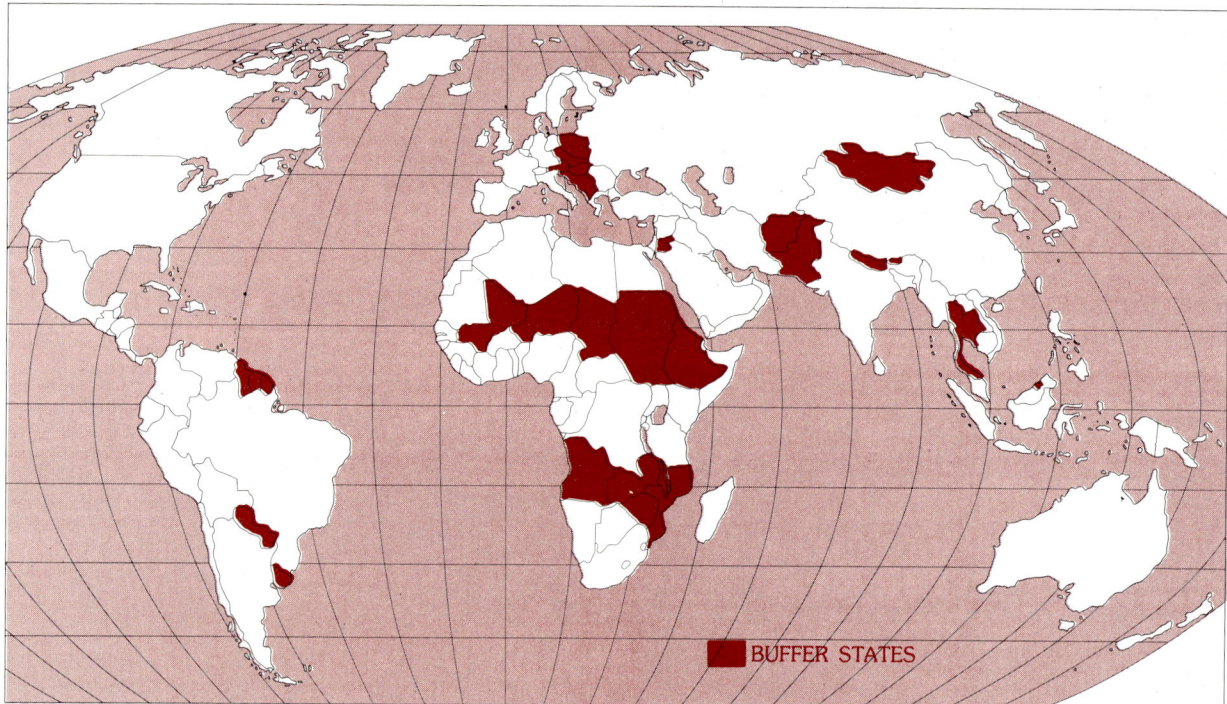

FIGURE 16–8 World states created as buffers between other states or that act as buffers because of their location.

such states in the world today (Figure 16–9). These states are at the mercy of their neighbors as far as foreign trade is concerned. Not only does a landlocked state have to bear the greater expense of overland haulage, it must also maintain good relations with at least one neighboring state through which it can move its goods to a coastal port. The state must thus share some transport route as well as port facilities. Because there is no international law or agreement to protect the landlocked countries, there is always the possibility that the coastal country will decide to stop sharing the facilities.

Another disadvantage confronting landlocked states is their lack of access to the resources of the oceans and the continental shelves along the coast. All coastal states support fishing fleets, some much larger than others. Fish and other edible ocean products, however, are rare and expensive in such landlocked states as Afghanistan, Chad, and Mongolia. The petroleum and other mineral resources found in the continental shelves are extremely important, as evidenced by the years of deliberations over their ownership during the Law of the Sea conferences. None of these resources, however, is available to Paraguay, Botswana, Nepal, or any other landlocked state.

The most extreme example of a landlocked state is that of a state completely surrounded by only one other country. The landlocked state has no alternative but to get along with the state encompassing it; it cannot play one neighboring country against another. Fortunately, these places are rare. Only Basutoland (Lesotho), surrounded by South Africa, is of any size. The tiny European states of San Marino and Vatican City are also landlocked by one country (Italy). It is also rare for a landlocked state to have only two neighbors—the only examples are Andorra (Spain and France), Liechtenstein (Switzerland and Austria), Mongolia (China and the Soviet Union), and Swaziland (South Africa and Mozambique). All of these states are too small to act as buffers between their two neighbors, except possibly Mongolia.

Corridors and Proruptions

Some landlocked states have sought access to oceans through expansion of their territory. Sometimes, states use narrow strips of land, which appear on the map as strange appendages, for access to oceans or navigable rivers. These parcels are called *corridors.* The Finnish extension to the Arctic Ocean (Petsamo) and the Polish territory that reached to the Baltic Sea are important historical examples of corridors. Neither remains today, but between the two world wars they were valuable extensions *(proruptions)* to the two states. Figure 16–10 gives examples of proruptions.

354

INTERACTION AND ECONOMICS

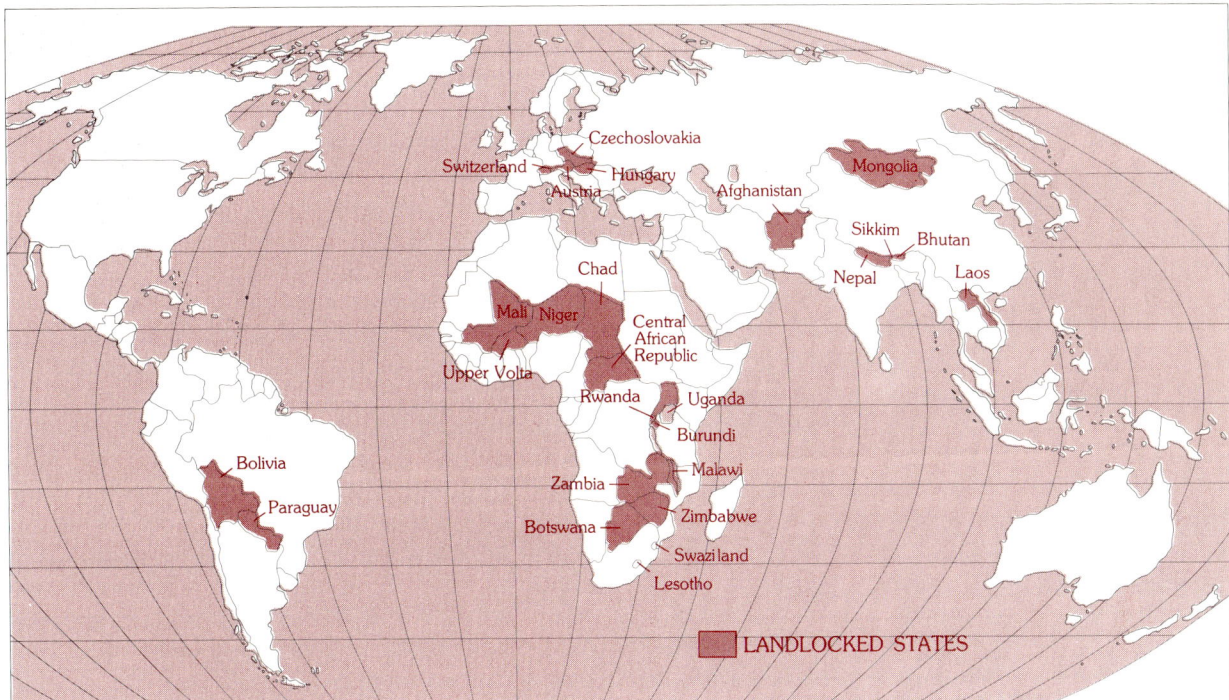

FIGURE 16-9 Landlocked countries.

Currently, examples of proruptions to state territories that serve as corridors for access to desired areas are in Bolivia (to the Paraguay River), Colombia (to the Amazon), Iraq (to the Persian Gulf), Jordan (to the Gulf of Aqaba), and Zaire (to the Atlantic Ocean). Other strange proruptions served as forward points of growth during settlement periods. These, called *wachstumspitzens,* include the Caprivi Strip of Southwest Africa and the Alaskan Panhandle. Other proruptions, such as the eastern extension of Afghanistan, were designed as buffer areas. Interestingly, this part of Afghanistan, once a buffer between India and the Soviet Union, now lies between Pakistan and the Soviet Union.

INTERACTION AND ECONOMICS

The earth's 148.36 million km² (57.28 million mi²) of land area is divided into 167 national states which contain the 4.32 billion people of the earth. If there were an average state, it would contain about 27 million people in an area of about 927,000 km² (358,000 mi²). This imaginary, average national state would be about the size of, and have a population similar to, the combined U.S. states of California, Arizona, and Nevada. And if every one of our average states *(real states)* sent one messenger to every other state, it would take 27,722 persons to carry out the exchange. If you put 167 dots on a piece of paper and connect each dot with every other dot, the resulting 13,861 lines might give you an indication of

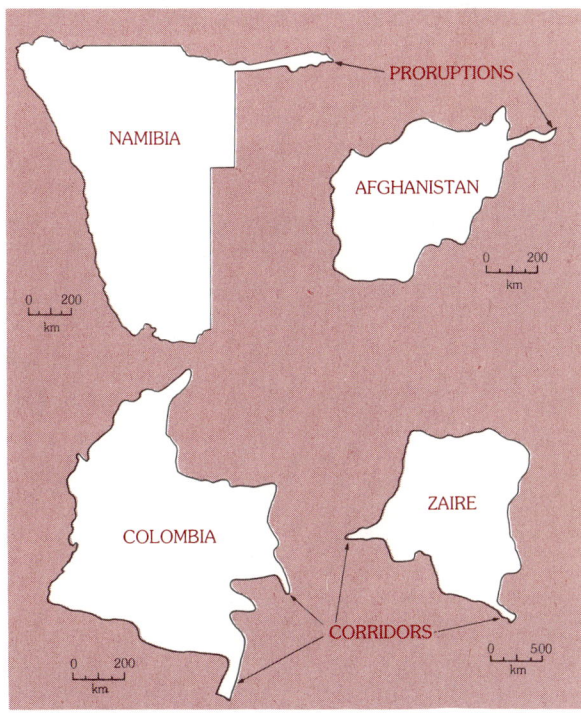

FIGURE 16-10 Examples of proruptions.

the incredibly complex nature of international interaction.

Migrants and Refugees

One aspect of international interaction is the movement of individuals from one nation-state to another. Human history has had many periods of great migrations. Age-old paths of movement follow natural routes provided by the physical features of the earth. More recently, natural barriers have been replaced by political rules that restrict and direct movement. Every nation-state has laws governing *immigration* (moving in), and most states restrict *emigration* (moving out).

Political action restricts movement, but often encourages it as well. Both ancient and modern migration streams have resulted from hostile political environments at the origin. Moses and the Israelites fled from Egypt to escape bondage. A modern-day counterpart is the flight of Indochinese from Cambodia, Laos, and Vietnam. Similar pressures motivate the desperate escape attempts across the Berlin Wall as well as the dangerous voyages of Cubans, Haitians, and South Vietnamese from their homelands. In each of these cases, the people are not politically directed to leave, but escape, with or without permission, from what they believe to be intolerable economic and political conditions. The transfer of large groups of people as a result of political persecution may be called *forced migration,* a term also applied to other situations.

The transfer of large groups of people by government directive contrasts sharply with the situation of refugees eluding a government. Emerging national states in Africa have sometimes sought ethnic purity by expelling minority groups. Kenya, for instance, ejected 192,000 Indians and 39,000 Arabs solely because they were ethnically unacceptable. After both world wars, millions of people in Europe were relocated from their countries of residence to their countries of ethnic origin (Figure 16–11). In 1923, the governments of Greece and Turkey, in recognition of new post–World War I boundaries, supervised the transfer of 2 million Greek and Turkish nationals. After World War II, 12 million ethnic Germans were transferred back to West Germany. Millions of other ethnic groups were directed to move across national boundaries after each war. In fact, most wars create misery and suffering by forcing millions of people from their homes. Forced migration, therefore, can occur from an adverse political environment, by conscious political actions, or as a consequence of political activity.

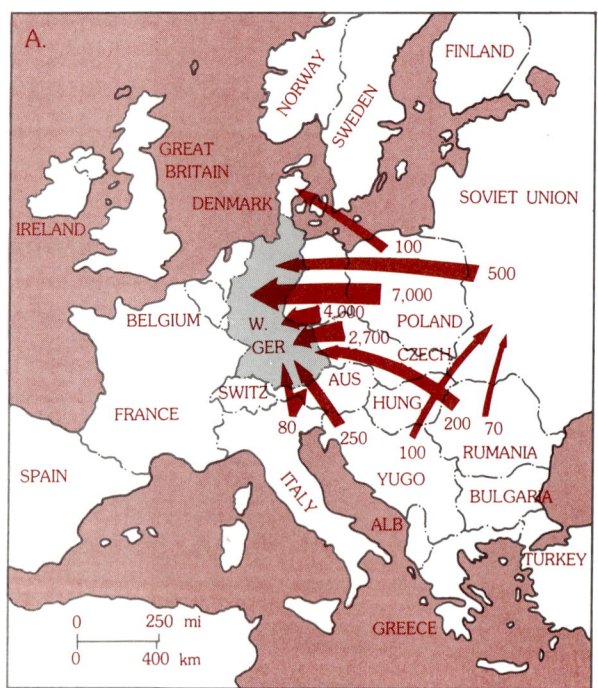 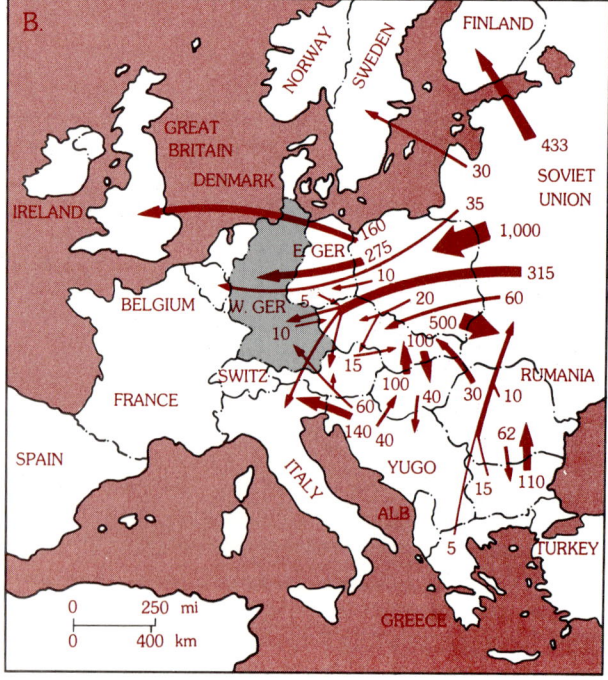

FIGURE 16–11 Redistribution of people following World War II: (a) transfer evacuation, and flight of ethnic Germans; (b) movement into and out of countries by non-Germans. Figures are in thousands and exclude movements within states. (Adapted from Norris and Haring, *Political Geography* [Charles E. Merrill, 1980], p. 145.)

INTERACTION AND ECONOMICS

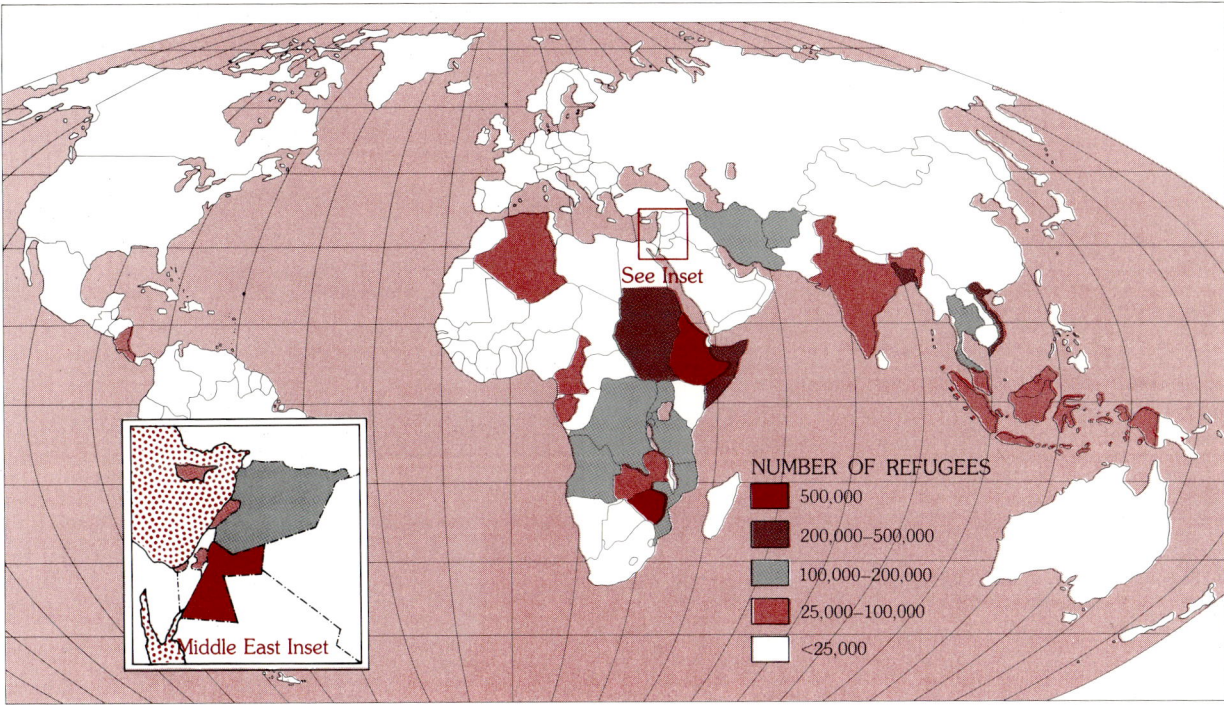

FIGURE 16–12 Number and location of world refugees. (Adapted from UNESCO.)

At one time, *population pressure* was thought to be a major cause of forced migration. Today, however, new arrivals almost always move directly to areas that are already overcrowded. In the United States, over 60 percent of the immigrants settle in cities, where they usually cluster in ethnic enclaves. There are, for example, over 500,000 Cubans in Miami, and twice that many Chicanos in Los Angeles. These groups establish miniature nations of their own, and often cause burdens to their adopted countries. Some countries have attempted to solve this situation with laws that require migrants to remain in specified areas for certain periods of time (see Figure 16–12). The number of potential homes for political refugees is shrinking, unless they begin to settle in underdeveloped areas or in areas of backward economic situations. That is contrary, however, to trends.

Haves and Have-Nots

A major cause for past and present migration is the place-to-place difference in economic factors. A good economy acts like a magnet, attracting persons seeking to improve their condition in life. Just as gold discoveries have attracted fortune hunters, a good economy attracts job seekers. A region's economic development is always limited and conditioned by its natural geographical features. Some national states have overcome the contraints of their natural environments through trade and colonization, while other areas that are rich in natural resources remain underdeveloped. Generally, however, economic development has been associated with physical conditions such as available mineral resources, climate and soil, topography, and waterways.

Countries that are well endowed with a balanced combination of good natural features have become strong economically and, consequently, strong politically. At one time, it was fashionable to point out that all the highly developed countries lie in the Northern Hemisphere between 35° and 70° of latitude. This economic preeminence was attributed to the region's "invigorating climate." This environmental explanation ignored the fact that that area of the world contains major supplies of iron ore and coal, the two commodities most needed in industrial development (Figure 16–13). The region is also blessed with rich soils and reliable rain during the growing season, making it an excellent area for the agriculture needed to supply foodstuffs to industrial workers. These factors, more than the invigorating climate, contributed to the industrial progress of the countries of the region.

The industrial giants and the most politically powerful nations are still in the 35° N–70° N belt. Historical momentum of industrialization, rather than present circumstances, accounts for this pattern, for

357

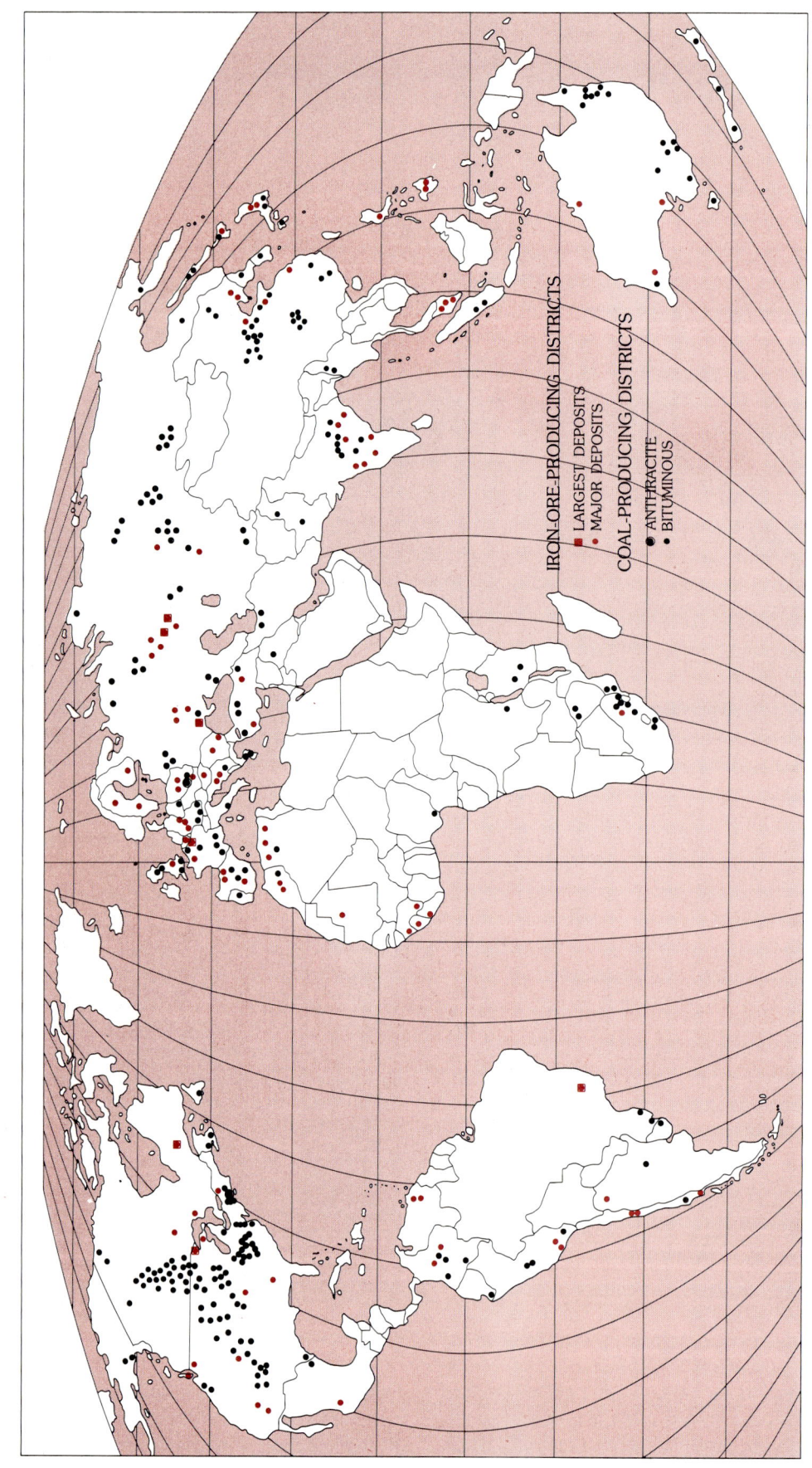

FIGURE 16-13 Location of iron ore mines and coal fields.

no nation today has adequate domestic supplies of all minerals, and few even approach self-sufficiency. Political rivalries can thus be interpreted in terms of the struggle for raw materials—minerals, petroleum, or foodstuffs—and relative location remains an important determinant of political and strategic policy.

The economically and politically powerful civilizations of the past flourished in the tropical and semitropical regions of the world. The three pre-Columbian civilizations of the Americas—the Aztecs, Incas, and Mayas—were in the tropics, and the cradle of civilization, Mesopotamia, was in the subtropics. Similar climatic regions today contain some of the most densely populated areas of the world. In these places, industrial production is low because per capita agricultural production is low. India, Southeast Asia, and southern China must first feed their people before they can establish industries. India, for example, has good supplies of iron ore and coal, but cannot develop significant industrial production because its agriculture barely feeds its people. Southeast Asia and China have coal but no iron ore, plus the foodstuff problem. The tropics, although favorable to life, have not been favorable to diversified economic development, including industrialization.

The cold regions, the deserts and mountains, and the equatorial rainforests may have adequate raw materials for industrialization, but they usually cannot support agriculture. In addition, the climate of these areas is generally not conducive to human habitation. These harsh regions constitute huge portions of each continent, leaving only about 10 percent of the earth's land surface suitable for agricultural production (Figure 16–14). This proportion ranges from less than 3 percent in Oceania to about 37 percent in Europe. Most of the world's economically underdeveloped countries are located where it is too cold, too hot, too dry, or too wet for agriculture.

Industrialization, Modernization, and Development

Countries that have become industrialized have had either the right combination of natural resources or the ability to obtain them through trade. The United States is a classic example of industrialization. The hard-coal beds of Pennsylvania were complemented by the iron ore deposits of northern Minnesota. The two commodities were brought together by cheap water transport over the Great Lakes. Moreover, the Midwest contains thousands of square kilometers of relatively flat land with excellent soils, and cyclonic storms provide moisture during the growing season. The combination of location and physical factors makes the Midwest the greatest agricultural area of the world. Of course, the people of the United States and their form of government were strong factors in development of the resources, but the geography made industrialization possible.

Other places that have become industrialized have not had the tremendous geographical advantages enjoyed by the United States. The Soviet Union, for example, has nearly unlimited supplies of iron ore and coal, but Soviet agriculture is limited. With hot summers and extremely cold winters, most of the country receives less than 50 cm (20 in.) of rainfall annually. Smaller countries, such as West Germany and England, have the appropriate combination of factors, supplemented by imports of iron ore, but their agricultural areas are small. Probably the most amazing industrial giant is Japan. This country is the world's third leading steel producer (after the United States and the Soviet Union), yet it must import nearly all its iron ore. Also, the agriculture that sustains the industries must be carried on in very limited parts of the country (see Figure 16–14) because of the extreme topography.

Modernization usually follows or corresponds with industrialization. Industrial democracies whose economic and political development has given them a favored position in world affairs are called *First World* countries (see Figure 16–15). This group of politically strong nations recognizes no single leader, although the United States has played an important role. The First World is the modern world.

The *Second World* refers to most, but not all, of the Communist states. China and the Soviet Union are the leading Second World countries. Despite its advanced technology and sophistication in aircraft and space industries, the Soviet Union cannot be called modern, for it lacks consumer products, especially automobiles and household appliances. The idea of modernization appeals to leaders of the Communist world, but implementation is retarded by a commitment to military strength. Some of these countries have made themselves politically strong by channeling their resources to their military—resources that could otherwise be used to modernize.

A large group of emerging but underdeveloped nations in Asia, Africa, and Latin America comprises the *Third World*. These countries form a group because of their common lack of industrial development and low standards of living. Most have not established any deeply committed ties with the First or Second World. Some of the Third World states, such as Kuwait, are among the world's wealthiest on a per capita basis.

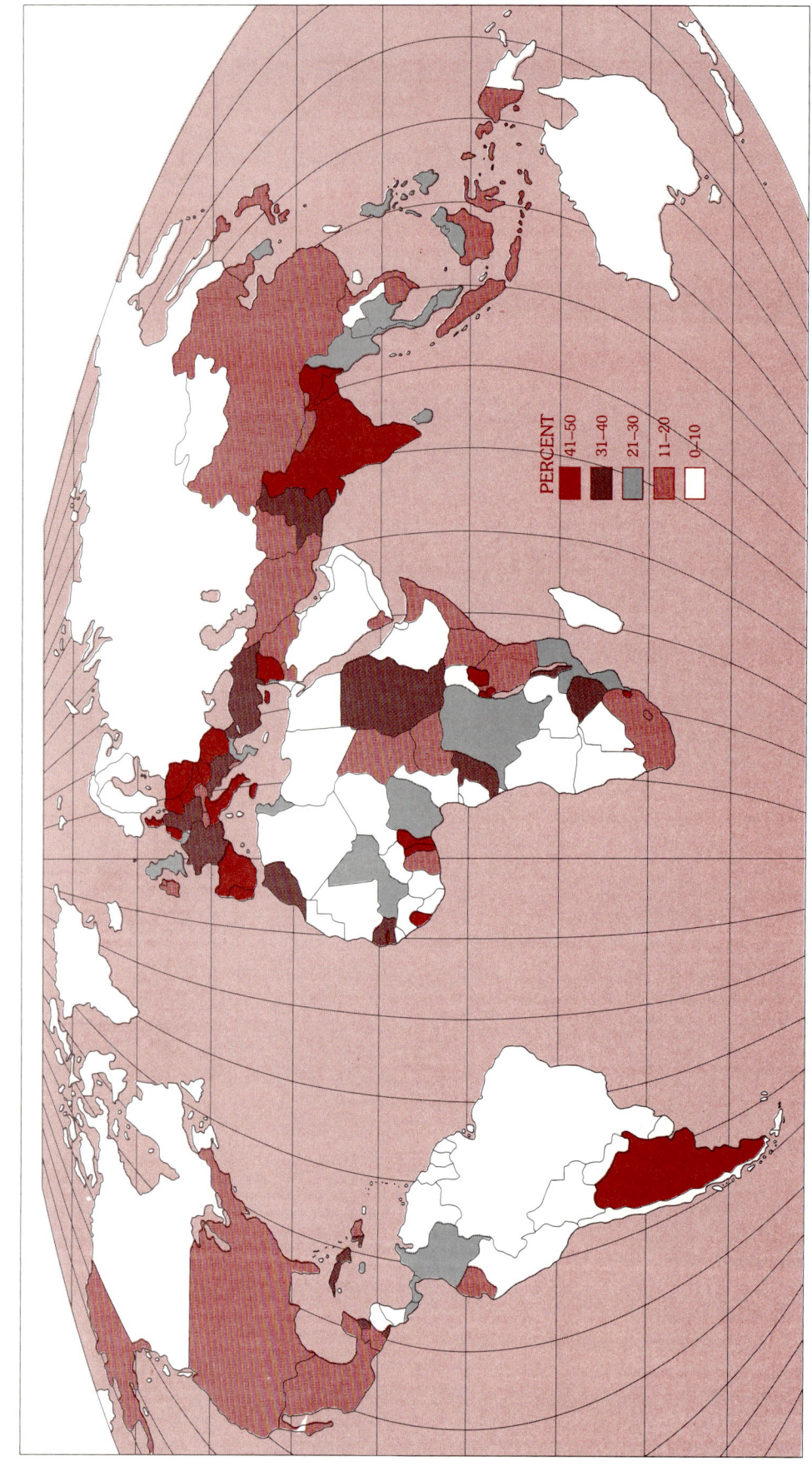

FIGURE 16–14 The world's arable land in percentages of land under cultivation in each country (see also Fig. 10–9, pp. 212 and 213). (From CIA, 1980.)

ECONOMICS AND POLITICS

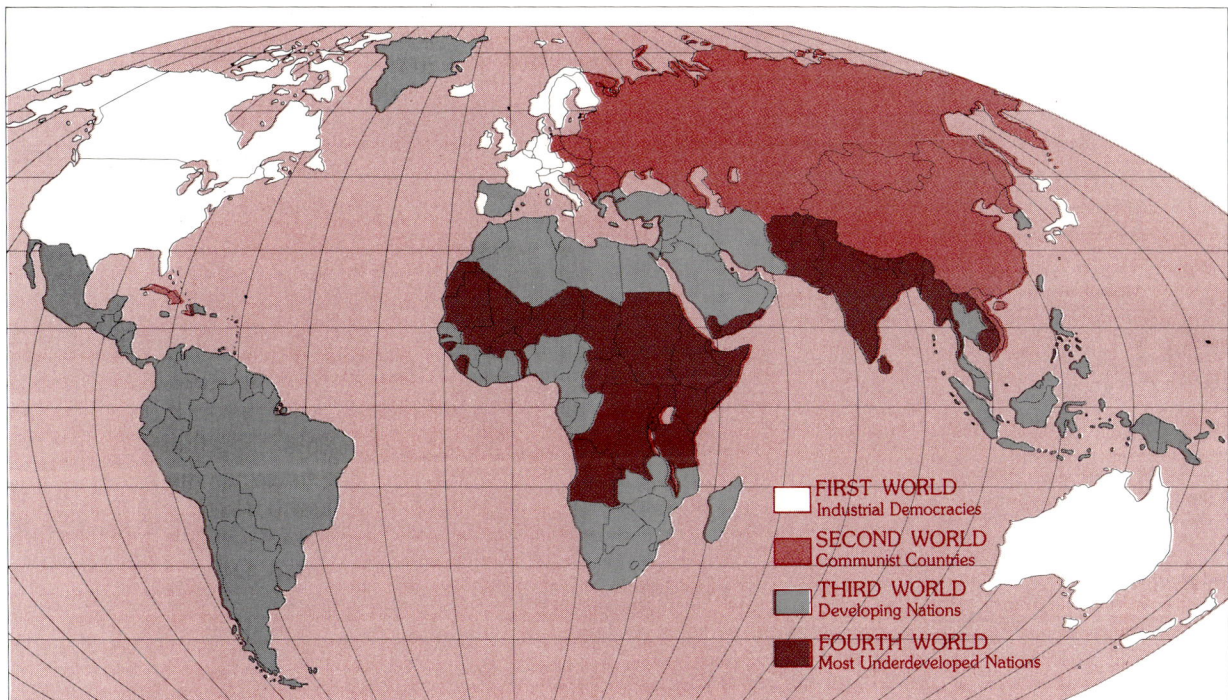

FIGURE 16–15 The four "worlds" classified by levels of economic development. (Adapted from Norris and Haring, *Political Geography* [Charles E. Merrill, 1980], p. 172.)

The least modern and poorest countries in the world are designated *Fourth World* states. These states are so poor (less than $150 annual per capita income) and underdeveloped that they appear to have little hope of becoming competitive economic units, let alone modernized. Grinding poverty is not conducive to stable world conditions, because it accentuates imbalance among nations. A major obstacle to progress in these countries is their resistance to altering existing cultural practices, such as religion, to make economic productivity and modernization possible. The 1979 political upheaval in Iran demonstrated how economic modernization conflicted dramatically with the religious tenets of the Shiite Moslems. About one billion of the world's people reside in the Fourth World, a world that may never see modernization.

ECONOMICS AND POLITICS

Over one-half of the world's four billion people live in the Third and Fourth worlds. And, finding common political cause in their economic backwardness, they are beginning to demand an increased share of the world's material wealth. A world revolution may or may not be coming, but one thing is certain from a historical view—the present political map of the world is a temporary picture.

States are born, evolve through stages, and sometimes die and disappear. This cycle has led to a biological analogy for the political development of states. The analogy is useful for comparing economic and political development with regard to aggression and world political upheaval.

Life Cycles of States

The system of life cycles of states as described by Samuel Van Valkenburg includes four distinct stages of national development. In the earliest stage after the birth of a state—called the *young state*—there is an attempt to consolidate the internal structure. The state devotes energy to putting its national house in order. All new nations commonly go through a period in which they attempt to strengthen their economic forces. They wish to be left alone, and in essence are extremely isolationist. Since they must get organized before they can aggress against anyone, their neighbors need not fear them. Most of the Third and Fourth World countries can be considered young states.

Eventually the new state enters a growth period known as the *adolescent stage*. The necessity for peace and tranquility disappears as the state becomes economically sound. That, coupled with the state's strong desire for territorial expansion, makes this a dangerous period for neighbors. Dynamic political concepts like Manifest Destiny in the United States encourage aggression. During America's adolescence (1800–1900), for example, wars over territory were fought with the Indians, Great Britain, Mexico, and Spain, not to mention the "in-house" squabble between North and South. Current adolescent states might include Israel and the nations of eastern Africa, as well as some of the Second World powers, such as the Soviet Union and China.

When a state enters the *mature stage*, it becomes stable; it does not want to upset its status quo. It becomes a stabilizing force in world politics, seeking peace and international harmony. The mature state will fight for its internal integrity and safety but will relinquish outlying parts not integral to the nation. This is the reason decolonization occurred only after the colonial powers matured. Currently, most First World industrial democracies can be classified as mature countries.

Finally, as with plants and animals, the state deteriorates. The biological process continues through the *old-age stage*, where withering and weakening occurs. Internal decay may lessen the state's resolve to resist internal and external forces, which can destroy it. The history of state government tends to indicate that old age is inevitable. The Roman and Ottoman empires declined from large, strong states to small, weak ones; then they died. Some suggest that the United States is entering its old age, citing internal corruption and decadence combined with the retreat from Vietnam and the release of the Panama Canal as examples of old-age activities.

The number of years varies for each stage in the aging process. In addition, the development stages may be disrupted at any time and begun again. In fact, not many young nation-states live to be old ones. While these cycles are not definitive, they do demonstrate that political and economic changes occur simultaneously.

The Cost of Arms

Political power at the international level has been described as a state's economic ability to wage war. According to Thomas Paine, "war has but one thing certain, and that is to increase taxes." There is no doubt that the preparation for war is costly. Even peacetime preparedness (defense budgets) is extremely large.

Some national states place a higher priority on defense spending than do others (Figure 16–16). This can be judged by comparing a state's annual defense budget with the annual government receipts from taxes, duties, and other fees. For example, the gross national product of the United States for fiscal year 1983 was $3.311 trillion; the defense budget for the same year was $275 billion. This means that 8.31 percent of the GNP went to national defense. Because it is difficult to obtain figures for other countries, especially Communist countries, we have to make estimates.

General Dwight Eisenhower, one of the most widely known military leaders of the twentieth century, proposed a simple model for estimating *military power*. The model is

$$MP = A \times ES \times PW$$

where A equals the arms available, ES is a measure of economic strength, and PW is an estimate of the political will of the people. The United States and Germany at the time of World War II could be compared (on a scale of one to ten) as follows:

United States: $7 \times 8 \times 10 = 560$
Germany: $8 \times 7 \times 7 = 392$

Whereas, in the Vietnam conflict, the military power factor might have been

United States: $10 \times 10 \times 1 = 100$
North Vietnam: $5 \times 10 \times 3 = 150$

The Eisenhower model is practical in that a state must compare its strengths with those of its adversaries. Problems may arise, however, in estimating the political will of the people—both the enemy's will and that of the people of the home state. Table 16–1 displays information about the United States and the Soviet Union that can be used to compare the military power and industrial strength of the two. Notice how Soviet military power outweighs that of the United States, while the economic strength of the United States is much greater. Thus, the potential for military power is much larger in the United States than in the Soviet Union. As in the Eisenhower model, the most important factor may be the will of the people.

CONCLUSION

The concept of the nation-state began in northwestern Europe and spread from there throughout the world. Colonialism later helped to spread the concept, and in the process established many of the economic ties between the First and Third worlds that exist today. Assimilation of language and cultural groups into national states is an important aspect of the state's internal cohesion.

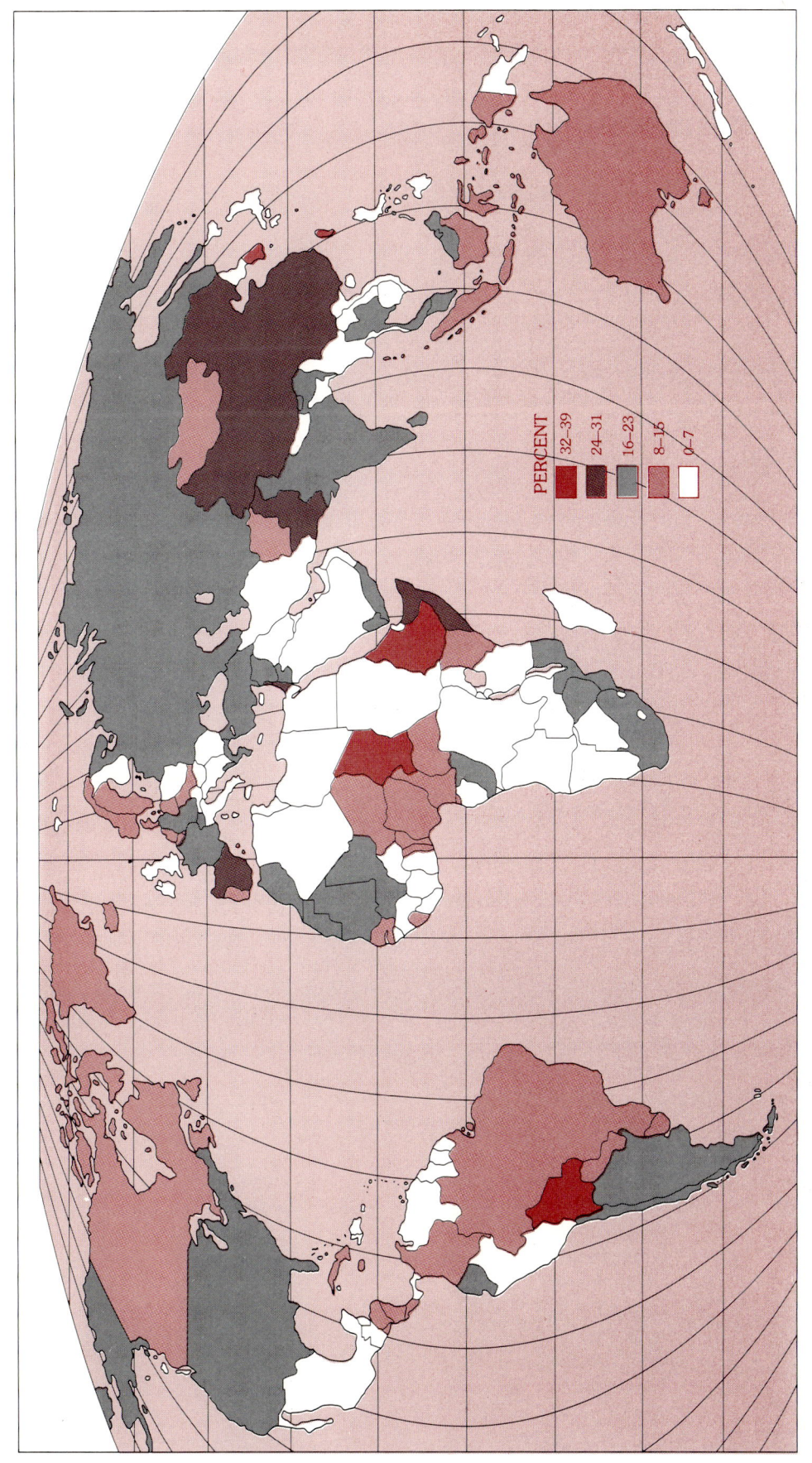

FIGURE 16–16 Arms expenditures as percentages of governments' total budgets. (From CIA, 1980.)

CHAPTER 16 POLITICS AND LOCATION

TABLE 16–1 Comparisons between the United States and the Soviet Union

	United States	Soviet Union
Population		
Total (1980) (*millions*)	227	261
Annual increase (%)	0.58	0.89
Life expectancy (*years*)		
Males	68.7	64.0
Females	76.5	74.0
Area		
Total (10^6 mi^2)	3.6	8.7
Population per square mile	63.1	29.8
Per capita arable land (*acres*)	2.1	2.2
Production		
GNP (1979) (*$ billions*)	2,088	700
Steel prouced (1978) (10^6 *tons*)	126.5	151.4
Per capita income (1977) (*$*)	7,686	2,600
Trade		
Imports (1978) (*$ billions*)	183.1	50.6
Exports (1978) (*$ billions*)	143.6	52.2
Armed forces personnel (1979)		
Persons in uniform	2,026,345	4,400,000
Reserves	819,700	6,800,000
Total	2,846,045	11,200,000
Army equipment		
Tanks	12,100	50,000
Field artillery	5,500	20,000
Air force equipment		
Strategic missiles	4,702	4,998
Tactical aircraft	5,364	8,000
Navy equipment		
Aircraft carriers	13	2
Cruisers, destroyers	161	284
Submarines	81	195

The world's migrants and refugees are made homeless by political pressure, and the gap between the 'haves' and 'have-nots' is widening. The modern world spends money on arms that could go to help feed starving people in underdeveloped countries. Political geography, or any study that lends understanding, can help alleviate these problems.

KEY WORDS

adolescent state
buffer state
centrifugal force
centripetal force
colonialism
corridor
country
emigration
First World
forced migration
Fourth World

hot spot
icon
immigration
irredenta
isolationists
landlocked state
Law of the Sea conferences
mature state
modernization
nation
nationalism

nation-state
old-age state
proruption
Second World
shatter belt

state
Third World
wachstumspitzen
young state

REFERENCES

CIA. *National Basic Intelligence Fact Book.* Washington, D.C.: 1980.

CRESSEY, GEORGE B. *The Basics of Soviet Strength.* New York: Whittlesey House, McGraw-Hill Book Co., 1945.

HAYES, CARLETON J. H. *The Historical Evolution of Modern Nationalism.* New York: Macmillan Co., 1948.

HERZ, JOHN H. "The Rise and Demise of the Territorial State." *World Politics* 9 (1957): 138–46.

HAUSER, PHILIP M. *Population and World Politics.* New York: Free Press, 1958.

NORRIS, ROBERT E., and HARING, L. LLOYD. *Political Geography.* Columbus, Ohio: Charles E. Merrill Publishing Co., 1980.

PEARCY, G. ETZEL. *World Sovereignty.* Fullerton, Calif.: Plycon Press, 1977.

PIGON, A. C. *The Political Economy of War.* London: Macmillan & Co., 1939.

STOESSINGER, J. G. *The Might of Nations.* New York: Random House, 1963.

STRAUZ-HUPE, ROBERT, and HAZARO, HARRY W., eds. *The Idea of Colonialism.* New York: Praeger Publishing, 1958.

VAN VALKENBURG, SAMUEL. *Elements of Political Geography.* New York: Prentice-Hall, 1939.

WEIGERT, HANS W., et al. *Principles of Political Geography.* New York: Appleton-Century-Crofts, 1957.

WHITTLESEY, DERWENT S. "The Impress of Effective Central Authority upon the Landscape." *Annals of the Association of American Geographers* 25 (1935):85–97.

17
Geography at Work

We have thus far presented an overview of the processes and patterns associated with human occupancy of the earth. Before summarizing and drawing to a conclusion, we will explore some approaches geographers take to real-world problems. Like other social scientists, geographers in recent decades have become more aware that their intellectual and technical skills are applicable to various questions of public and private policy.

APPLIED GEOGRAPHY

Applied geography is the application of geographic concepts, methods, and perspectives to the solution of problems. Although a number of geographers were involved in applied work in the early decades of the twentieth century (Frazier, 1982, pp. 9–13), the father of applied geography was the British geographer L. Dudley Stamp, Professor of Social Geography at the London School of Economics until his retirement in 1958 (Figure 17–1). Stamp was noted for a massive land-use mapping project in Britain, conducted in the 1930s (Stamp, 1948). In his first book on applied geography, published in 1960, Stamp outlined the field. He regarded the unique contribution of the geographer as "the holistic approach in which he sees the relationship between man and his environment, with its attendant problems, as a whole" (Stamp, 1960, p. 9). Population geography, land use, land planning, and urban planning were prominent in Stamp's view of applied geography. He also saw the significance of what we call *remote sensing*—the use of aerial photography and satellite imagery to gather data about patterns on the earth's surface. Stamp called it *photogeography* (Figure 17–2). Aerial photography has greatly

APPLIED GEOGRAPHY
SUBJECT MATTER OF APPLIED GEOGRAPHY

Aerial view of Boston showing how extensive landfills have created new land along the shoreline. (Photo courtesy of NASA.)

CHAPTER 17 GEOGRAPHY AT WORK

FIGURE 17–1 L. Dudley Stamp, pioneer in the field of applied geography. (Photo courtesy of Prof. M. J. Wise, The London School of Economics and Political Science.)

SUBJECT MATTER OF APPLIED GEOGRAPHY

The field of applied geography has retained Stamp's concerns for land-use planning and conservation, but its scope today is probably even broader than its early practitioners anticipated. A partial list of topics that actively involve applied geographers today includes natural resource development and conservation, social issues, land use, population geography, transportation, electoral geography, and urban and regional development (Briggs, 1981, p. 3).

Approaches and Methods

In any vital discipline or organization, there is constant tension between conflicting viewpoints. Geography is no exception, and one of the more powerful debates has been between individuals who represent different positions on the political spectrum. Inevitably, applied geography has been drawn into the discussion. Those on the political right, the conservatives, defend the status quo. In the U.S., this means defense of capitalism, a system that conservatives view as ideally suited to maximizing productivity through the incentives provided by opportunities for individual wealth.

On the left, radical geographers take the position that capitalism perpetuates and magnifies social and economic inequities, thus deepening the rift between the haves and the have-nots. The left also sees the exercise of unrestrained capitalism as a recipe for disaster at the international level, as rich countries become richer and the poor poorer.

Applied geography becomes embroiled in the crossfire between these conflicting viewpoints. When the geographer adopts the stance of problem solver, he or she must decide whether to do so within the context of the existing sociopolitical framework (an essentially conservative position), or as a radical who is unwilling to accept existing institutions. In the latter scenario, the approach to the problem becomes the solution. Proponents of this position argue that society is restructured, and capitalism is replaced by a more equitable alternative.

What have emerged, then, are essentially two kinds of applied geography. One, *radical geography*, operates outside "the system." Radical geographers are not hired by government agencies or corporations because they question the very existence of those agencies and firms. Whether or not one is sympathetic to the radical perspective, there is no question that radical analyses have raised important questions and caused us to rethink not only *what* problems we will consider but also *how* we consider

improved the rate at which land-use mapping can be accomplished. Fundamentally, Stamp's posture toward applied geography was rooted in recognition of the importance of *planning* and *conservation*. His emphasis on "the need to understand . . . what this earth holds for us, and how we should develop its resources by their careful conservation" sounds as relevant today as it did when it was written (Stamp, 1960, p. 196).

The early promise of applied geography, however, was not fulfilled. Its focus remained on land-use mapping, while the field of geography as a whole was passing through a period of dramatic methodological change known as the *quantitative revolution*, involving the application of statistical methods to geographic questions. Though work that was recognizable as applied geography continued in the interim, a specialty in the field did not reemerge for nearly twenty years after publication of Stamp's pioneering book. At this time, 1978, an ongoing series of annual applied geography conferences began in the United States. The first volume of the journal *Applied Geography* appeared in 1981, and evidence suggests the reemergence of applied geography as a promising and exciting branch of the discipline.

FIGURE 17–2 A LANDSAT image of part of Oklahoma. (Photo courtesy of Center for the Applications of Remote Sensing, Oklahoma State University, Dr. Stephen J. Walsh, Director.)

them. The other kind of applied geography is "establishment" oriented. Geographers of this school typically work for governmental agencies and private firms. Their main preoccupation is the analysis of conditions in the context of society's prevailing organization. This is not to say that these applied geographers necessarily approve of conditions as they find them, but presumably they regard working within the system as a more effective way to implement constructive change compared to the radical approach. (For related discussion, see Peet, 1975, and Harries, 1975.)

The methods of applied geography are adaptations of methods used throughout geography in general. Briggs (1981, p. 3) suggests five main interdependent stages to applied research:

- *Problem definition* The nature of the problem to be investigated is outlined, often in the form of an hypothesis, or hunch, to be tested on the basis of available evidence.
- *Inventory and mapping* The necessary data are gathered, in the field or from sources such as government agencies or corporations. The various U.S. censuses are often valuable data sources in applied geography, but the researcher may also design her or his own survey instrument to assess people's values and attitudes.

- *Problem analysis* At this stage, computers are often used as tools to process substantial amounts of information. The researcher may use the computer for statistical analysis, preparation of maps and other graphics, and word processing.
- *Formulation of solutions and strategies* Results of the analysis may allow one to draw conclusions about the problem that was formulated at the first step. Quite often, however, no clear answer emerges, and the most sensible course is to suggest several alternative approaches to solving the problem, perhaps based on different sets of conditions, or "scenarios."
- *Strategy selection* In consultation with the client, the applied geographer suggests the most appropriate course of action given current or anticipated conditions.

At any stage, moral and political issues and value judgments may pose problems for the applied geographer. Quite apart from the philosophical split between radical and conventional applied geographies, there is the problem that recommendations based on careful analysis and responsible balancing of relevant viewpoints may be scratched in favor of purely political decisions. These may be based on favoritism, nepotism, croneyism, or a lobbyist's well-placed campaign contribution. Applied geographers who work with environmental problems may have to make value judgments about trade-offs between agricultural productivity and soil erosion or runoff contamination from fertilizers, insecticides, or herbicides. Those who work on urban planning may be compelled to consider the effects of a new highway on neighboring residents, and balance the advantages of accessibility against the disadvantages of noise and air pollution (and neighborhood disruption, if highway cuts or embankments are involved).

Clearly, becoming an applied geographer involves achieving a high level of training in conventional scientific geographic methodology. Beyond that, one also needs skills best described, perhaps, as intellectual and personal maturity. Ultimately, the applied geographer must be able to weigh options, evaluate methods, interpret analyses, and predict what will happen as a result of decisions. If we are to control the systems we live with, we must improve our ability to predict (Briggs, 1981, p. 5).

Case Studies

Brief summaries of some recent studies in applied geography will illustrate contemporary work in the field. These studies relate to medical geography, Third World energy resources, crime, natural hazards, management of water resources, and urban planning.

Medical Geography Hunger continues to be a world problem of overwhelming proportions (Figure 17–3). So far, it has defied the best efforts of individuals and organizations, both public and private. Efforts must continue, however, and two geographers, Aggarwal and Bhardwaj (1982), developed strategies to deal with malnutrition in ten villages in the state of Haryana in northwestern India. Initially, they con-

FIGURE 17–3 Hunger is a persistent problem in India and other countries of the world. (Photo by Michael Putnam, © Peter Arnold, Inc.)

ducted fieldwork to assess the study areas and collect data. Then they appraised children's nutritional status and identified nutritional determinants in the region. Finally, planning directives outlined intervention strategies for solving the problem. The strategies stressed the importance of targeting nutritional improvement efforts toward specific groups, in contrast to a blanket coverage approach. Administrators of nutrition programs must understand local cultural factors because some groups' dietary preferences and practices actually preclude the need for nutrition programs. Local physicians need basic education in nutrition so that they can spread information about proper nutritional practices in their local communities. Finally, each primary health center should have a nutritionist on its staff. This study showed how an understanding of medical, cultural, and social geographic processes could be used to more efficiently utilize nutritional resources.

In a survey of the health-care-seeking behavior of the elderly in Johnson City, New York, Henry (1981) found that females were much more interested than males in home health care delivery. Females were more dependent on modes of transportation other than the private automobile and thus had less personal mobility compared to males. As a result of this survey, Henry recommended that pilot efforts in home health care should be aimed at elderly women. The population geography of Johnson City was studied to locate concentrations of elderly women. A primary target zone was identified on the south side of the city, allowing the most effective dissemination of home health care information, thus reducing costs for local health planners.

Third World Energy Resources Using the West Indies as an example of a less-developed region heavily dependent on imported petroleum as its energy source, Schaeper (1981) explored alternative energy resources in the context of the region's physical and cultural geographies. Two study areas were selected: the Windward Islands (Dominica, St. Lucia, St. Vincent, and Grenada) in the Eastern Caribbean, and Jamaica. Physically, the West Indies are characterized by exposure to the constant northeast trade winds. The windward sides of the islands are typically shrouded in cloud as condensation occurs in the warm moist air rising over the mountainous topography. Precipitation on the windward side is heavy. The lee or "rain shadow" sides of the mountains are sunny. The islands are culturally diverse and densely populated. Agriculture is the principal economic activity. Three different projects were introduced to meet specific local needs: solar horticultural dryers, using polyethylene plastic to create a "greenhouse effect" in a sunny leeward location; a wind-driven electric turbine, utilizing the trade winds, to supply electricity for a rural school; and a small hydroelectric turbine, made partly of gravy ladles, to electrify a plantation home and its offices in a location that had abundant precipitation. These projects showed how knowledge of physical, cultural, and social geography is vital for adapting modern technologies to Third World environments. In this example, principles of applied geography and engineering technology were combined to allow appropriate siting of energy sources independent of petroleum. Technology alone is inadequate; human and physical environmental factors must be taken into account. It is particularly important to gauge people's attitudes—the slickest technology is worthless junk if people refuse to accept it.

Crime Crime is usually measured by ratios of crime events to population. Thus we can say that the homicide *rate* in Nevada in 1980 was 20.0 per 100,000 people; in South Dakota the rate was 0.7 per 100,000. For some crimes, however, population may not be an appropriate rate base, since the entire population may not be "at risk." In a burglary, for example, property is stolen, not people, and a property measure such as assessed valuation should be the base for measurement. An appropriate base for rape rates would be young females, since 80 percent of rape victims are under 26 years of age. For vehicle theft, number of vehicles as a base is preferable to total population. The population-based vehicle theft rate in Los Angeles is often about twice that of New York City, but when number of vehicles is used as the base, the New York rate is much higher than that of Los Angeles. The point is that per capita automobile ownership is much lower in New York than in Los Angeles. Cities or neighborhoods within cities may rank quite differently for various crime rates when those rates are calculated on different bases. This knowledge is important in several respects. When appropriate bases are used to map crime rates, a more fitting allocation of law enforcement resources can be made. Crime patterns can be understood more readily when crimes are related to risk conditions, and public information about crime can be more helpful when environmental opportunities are linked to crime occurrences. Availability of appropriate crime rate data enhances both law enforcement education and policy decisions by public officials. Police departments conduct geographical analyses of crime on a routine—often daily—basis. Applied geographers have brought their expertise to bear by offering new approaches to the interpretation and manipulation of crime data (Harries, 1981).

Natural Hazards Many unanswered questions remain in relation to people's locational decision making in areas subject to natural hazards such as floods, earthquakes, and tornadoes (Figure 17–4). Montz (1981) examined the relationship between housing prices and floodplain location in Binghamton, New York. She found that floodplain homes were cheaper than those out of the floodplain; however, floodplain residences were older than those elsewhere, and older dwellings generally command lower prices. Floodplain homes did not remain on the market any longer than those outside the hazard area. What seemed to be happening in Binghamton was that floodplain housing was *filtering down* to lower income people, partly because of lack of alternatives combined with high demand for housing. This finding has implications for policymakers and planners, for it suggests that floods will have their greatest economic impact on those in the community who are less able to deal with the hardship. The role of the applied geographer in this context is to relate social and physical environmental processes to provide an accurate picture of hazard effects. (For further discussion of applied geographical analysis of floods and floodplains, see Douglas, 1973, pp. 74–82.)

Water Resource Management At a time when competing claims of industrial, agricultural, and domestic water users make water an extremely valuable resource, proper management of water resources is a vital skill. Problems of water resource management are inherently geographical, since the resource and its users are unevenly distributed. Furthermore, demands and supplies also vary over time and space. The spatial components of water resources are extremely complex owing to the maze of water districts and laws governing water rights that overlay the locational arrangement of water and users. Fernald (1981) developed a matrix, or table, that set geographic elements against stages in the management process so that management gaps for any particular geographic units could be readily seen.

Urban Planning The expansion of cities into their surrounding rural areas is a continuing source of concern, as agricultural land is taken out of production and formerly isolated rural settlements are swallowed up by advancing suburbs. Figure 17–5 shows the change in an intersection in Orange County, California, where the population increased by 101.8 percent in a ten-year period, and bean fields became sites for service stations, banks, and stores. The problem of urban expansion is particularly acute in densely populated regions such as parts of northwestern Europe. Newcomb (1977) reports on a project in Denmark in which a large group of geographers, technicians, and geography students gathered data on 105 villages in the vicinity of the city of Århus, to provide the city with a data base for appropriate planning of urban expansion. The research group reported on the physical milieu, population

FIGURE 17–4 The Salt River flooding in Phoenix, Arizona, in 1980.

FIGURE 17–5 The intersection of Springdale and Warner Streets in Orange County, California, (a) in 1967 and (b) in 1977.

characteristics, services, and economic profiles of all the villages. The group classified and mapped the villages according to quality of life and identified those with possible historical preservation value. Quite apart from the reports provided to local policymakers, planners received a computerized data base capable of answering most planning-related questions and providing a baseline for historical comparisons in subsequent years.

These six case studies illustrate the types of work that applied geographers become involved in. They show how a distinctively geographical perspective offers insights to problems that cannot be obtained from other disciplines. Underlying this perspective is a sensitivity to the coexistence and interaction of both the human and physical worlds, and a strong awareness of the power of regional and local cultures in shaping peoples' attitudes. The satellite view in Figure 17–6 reminds us of the interrelationship between humans and their physical environment. Additional studies are cited in the References to encourage further reading on applications of geography.

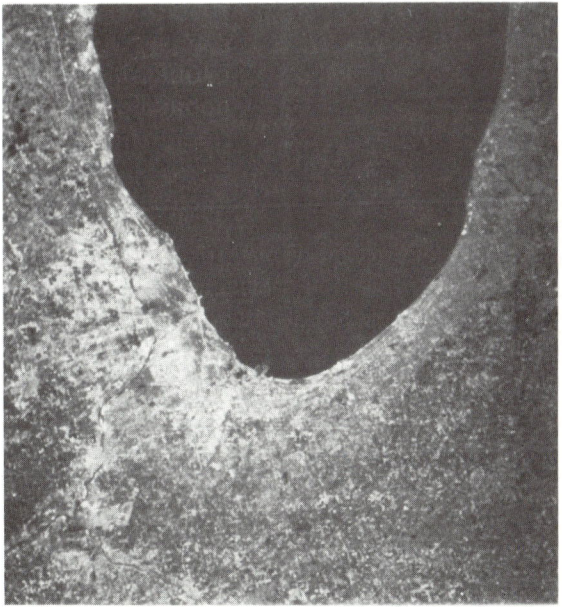

FIGURE 17–6 Satellite view of the Chicago area and Lake Michigan. (Photo courtesy of NASA.)

CHAPTER 17 GEOGRAPHY AT WORK

CONCLUSION

Elements of the Geographic Perspective

Maps For most geographers, maps are both stores of data and tools for problem solving. Many geography students become so interested in maps and mapmaking that they become *cartographers,* or mapmakers. Developing map skills is a significant element in a liberal education. A society whose citizens can read and construct useful maps will be more productive than societies that lack these skills. Map skills are applied in a vast range of situations, civil and military: from the newspaper delivery route map to the digital map in the computer of a nuclear missile. Maps often suggest interrelationships that do not appear when data are presented in words or statistical tables. Concerns with *location* and *distance* are linked to the geographer's interest in maps (see Chapter 1).

Culture Geographers understand that current cultural patterns are the product of long and complicated processes of change and diffusion. Historical geography studies the interface between geography and history in which lies much exploration of today's cultural patterns. An understanding of cultural geography involves an appreciation of how people formulate attitudes and what motivates their actions. This appreciation requires careful study of many phenomena: population dynamics, patterns of language and religious beliefs, and social, economic, and political systems. Other social sciences, including anthropology and sociology, share the geographer's interest in cultural phenomena.

Geometry of Space We can best solve some geographic questions by applying mathematical concepts in such techniques as *network analysis* and *nearest neighbor analysis.* Problems involving optimal location of facilities, spatial allocation of resources, or redistricting political boundaries, for example, call for a sound understanding of economic, social, or political processes, as well as familiarity with mathematical methodologies. The student who is familiar with the geographic perspective knows that geographers must call on quantitative methods when appropriate.

Regionalism As we noted in Chapter 1, geographers have traditionally been concerned with delimiting and analyzing regions. We defined various types of regions in Chapter 1; it is sufficient here to note that awareness of what regions are and of approaches to their definition are parts of the geographical perspective. The geographer's interest in *distributions* also relates to regionalism. Historically, *regional geography* was the strongest aspect of the discipline, but in recent decades *topical,* or *systematic geography,* has gained favor. (This book is organized topically rather than regionally.) The regional view incorporated the tradition of *descriptive* geography. Whereas accurate description is still considered important, it has been balanced by the growth of *prescriptive* or problem-oriented geography. There have recently been signs of reemergence of a newly vigorous regional geography, as new methods and approaches are applied to regional problems (see House, 1978).

The Physical World Human and physical systems are interdependent and cannot be separated except arbitrarily, for convenience of discussion. Ultimately, human life depends on the availability of natural energy sources. Geographers have traditionally been trained to develop an understanding of the interface between the human and physical worlds. Our failure as a society to acknowledge this interdependency has led to tragic environmental abuses, including the existence of numerous toxic waste dumps that will cost billions of dollars to clean up in the 1980s (Figure 17–7).

Change Built into the geographer's thought processes is the realization that we can depend on the constancy of change in the physical and human environments. Much change is imperceptible, while other events—volcanic eruptions or wars, for example—produce immediate and dramatic effects. In the 1980s we see the restructuring of the American economy as the smokestack industries decline and high technology activities expand (Figure 17–8). This restructuring creates profound regional change as areas that depend on the traditional heavy industries lose employment and their tax base, while other regions experience booming prosperity. In the late 1970s the expert consensus was that gasoline prices were destined to move only upward. Few anticipated weakening world demand for petroleum in the early 1980s, disabling the OPEC cartel and resulting in a period of sharply lower prices. Such changes have profound effects on the geographies of economic and social phenomena. Astute planning anticipates such scenarios and at least speculates about the consequences so that they come as less of a shock if and when they materialize. Concern for the role of

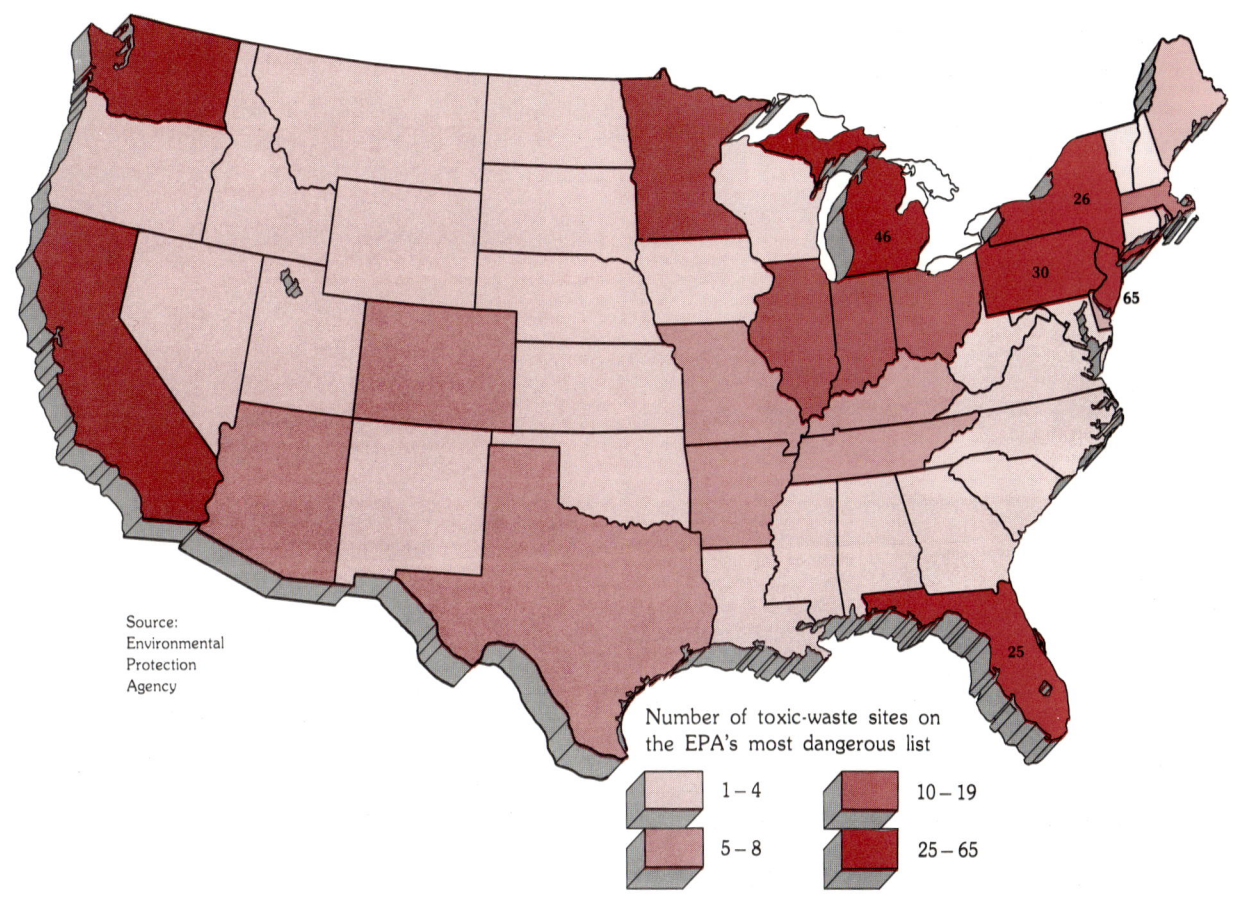

FIGURE 17–7 Locations of the 418 most hazardous waste sites in the U.S. in 1982, excluding federal sites and those currently active. (Adapted by permission from *Newsweek*, January 3, 1983.)

FIGURE 17–8 Smokestack industries such as this steelworks on the Cuyahoga River in Cleveland, Ohio, are on the decline.

change in our life systems is shared among the social sciences and is not unique to geography.

Application Modern geography has moved from a posture based solely on explanation to one that also seeks solutions to problems. The long tradition of fieldwork in geography has allowed geographers to become familiar with problems at firsthand. This willingness to relate to the real world, combined with greater social and political awareness, fostered the emergence of applied geography.

KEY WORDS

applied geography
cartographer
capitalism
change
conservation
crime rate
culture
descriptive geography
filtering
floodplain
geographic perspective
geometry of space
medical geography

natural hazards
physical environment
planning
prescriptive geography
quantitative revolution
radical geography
regionalism
remote sensing
systematic geography
Third World
topical geography
water resource management

REFERENCES

AGGARWAL, SURINDER K., and SURINDER M. BHARDWAJ. "Applied Medical Geography in the Developing World." In John W. Frazier, ed., *Applied Geography: Selected Perspectives.* Englewood Cliffs, N.J.: Prentice-Hall, 1982, pp. 84–106.

BRIGGS, DAVID J. "The Principles and Practice of Applied Geography." *Applied Geography* 1 (1981):1–8.

DEVORSEY, LOUIS, JR. "Florida's Seaward Boundary: A Problem in Applied Historical Geography." *Professional Geographer* 25 (1973): 214–220.

DOUGLAS, IAN. "Water Resources." In John A. Dawson and John C. Doornkamp, eds., *Evaluating the Human Environment: Essays in Applied Geography.* New York: St. Martin's Press, 1973, pp. 57–87.

EDMUNSON, WADE. "Applied Nutritional Geography: Priorities and Praxis." *Social Science and Medicine* 14D(1980): 133–137.

FERNALD, EDWARD A. "Managing Water Resources." *Proceedings of Applied Geography Conferences* 4(1981): 353–363.

FRAZIER, JOHN W. "Applied Geography: A Perspective." In John W. Frazier, ed., *Applied Geography: Selected Perspectives.* Englewood Cliffs, N.J.: Prentice-Hall, 1982, pp. 3–22.

FRAZIER, JOHN W. "On the Emergence of an Applied Geography." *Professional Geographer* 30(1978): 233–237.

HARRIES, KEITH D. "Applications of Alternative Crime Rate Denominators in Crime Monitoring." *Proceedings of Applied Geography Conferences* 4(1981): 310–317.

HARRIES, KEITH D. "Rejoinder to Richard Peet: The Geography of Crime: A Political Critique." *Professional Geographer* 27(1975): 280–282.

HARRISON, JAMES D., and ROBERT D. LARSEN. "Geography and Planning: The Need for an Applied Interface." *Professional Geographer* 29(1977): 139–147.

HENRY, NORAH F. "Socio-Spatial Dimensions of Health-Seeking Behavior in an Urban Elderly Population." *Proceedings of Applied Geography Conferences* 4(1981): 34–38.

HOUSE, J. W. *France: An Applied Geography.* London: Methuen, 1978.

ISACHENKO, A. G. "On the Method of Applied Landscape Research." *Soviet Geography* 14(1973): 229–243.

Journal of Geography 78(1979). Several articles in this issue were devoted to applied geography.

MONTZ, BURRELL E. "The Floodplain as a Housing Submarket: A Preliminary Analysis." *Proceedings of Applied Geography Conferences* 4(1981): 321–326.

NEWCOMB, ROBERT M. "The Århus, Denmark, Village Project: Applied Geography in the Service of the Municipality." *Geographical Review* 67(1977): 86–92.

PEET, RICHARD. "The Geography of Crime: A Political Critique." *Professional Geographer* 27(1975): 277–280.

PHLIPPONNEAU, MICHEL. "The Rise of Applied Geography." *International Social Science Journal* 33(1981): 133–160.

PRYDE, PHILIP R. "The Residential Landscape Conservation Zone as an Example of Applied Geography." *Geographical Review* 66(1976): 200–208.

SCHAEPER, HERBERT R. A. "Alternate Energy Resource Development in the West Indies." *Proceedings of Applied Geography Conferences* 4(1981): 364–372.

SOCHARA, V. B. "Problems in Applied Geography in Connection With the Baykal-Amur Mainline Rail Project." *Soviet Geography* 17(1976): 159–171.

STAMP, LAWRENCE DUDLEY. *Applied Geography.* Harmondsworth, England: Penguin Books, 1960.

STAMP, LAWRENCE DUDLEY. *The Land of Britain, Its Use and Misuse.* London: Longmans, Green, 1948.

Glossary

Absolute distance. Distance measured with a standard unit such as a mile or kilometer.

Acculturation. Process by which people become accustomed to a new environment.

Adobe. Sun-dried brick made of clay and straw.

Adolescent stage. Second stage of development of a national political unit, when expansion and aggression are common.

Aesthetic environment. That part of the environment which evokes feelings or evaluations concerning beauty.

Agglomerated distribution. Type of spatial distribution where objects are located close together; opposite of *dispersed distribution*.

Airspace. Usable space above the surface of the earth that is considered the property of the surface owner; usually 460 meters (1500 ft) above private land; on the international level, to the height reached by manned aircraft.

Alloy. Less valuable metal mixed with a more valuable one, usually to give hardness.

Ångerdorf. Almond-shaped farm village created by splitting a roadway.

Animism. Derived from the Latin *anima* (soul), the belief that material objects and animals, as well as people, have souls.

Antecedent boundary. Border between two political units that was delimited before human occupation of the region.

Anthracite. Hard coal that gives off extreme heat and little smoke.

Anti-incorporation law. Provision in some U.S. states that favors territorial expansion of cities by making it illegal for a new town to incorporate within the city's potential growth area.

Applied geography. Application of geographic information and theories to decision making or problem solving.

Arctic Circle. Imaginary circle located at 66½° north latitude, usually used to designate the north polar region.

GLOSSARY

Asceticism. Extremely austere or self-denying life style; an ascetic refrains from indulging in pleasures generally regarded as normal.

Awareness space. Area of which an individual is aware; usually more extensive than *action space (contact space)*, which refers to the area individuals cover in the course of regular activities.

Babylonian exile. Deportation of the inhabitants of Jerusalem in the sixth century B.C.

Bailey. Outer wall or court of a medieval castle.

Barbed wire. Wire with evenly-spaced barbs used as fencing, primarily for cattle.

Barbican. Defensive tower at the gate of a medieval castle.

Base metal. Primary metal in an alloy.

Baseline. East-west line used as the beginning of land measurement in the range-and-township survey method.

Bastion. Projection from a fortification used to give a wider range of fire.

Bilingualism. Situation in which two languages are dominant; e.g., English and French in Canada.

Bituminous. Hard, dark coal that burns with a yellow, smoky flame, used in coking.

Black-and-white houses. Timber-frame houses built in England in the Middle Ages, with timbers painted black and areas between the timbers painted white. (Same as half-timber houses.)

Brahmans. Class of hereditary priests in early Hinduism.

Broadleaf tree. Trees, such as oak, maple, and cottonwood, that have broad, fanlike leaves.

Buffer state. Small, independent state created between larger, more powerful states.

Cartographer. One who practices cartography (mapmaking).

Capitalism. Economic system in which people take the risk of investing personal funds (capital) in business enterprises.

Caste. Class system involving thousands of occupations and racial and ethnic groups in India.

Caucasoid Racial label used to indicate peoples who are generally pale-skinned and long-headed.

Central place. City or town that provides goods and services for its own population as well as for the people in the surrounding agricultural region.

Central place model. Theoretical structure that aims to predict the location of central places and to explain the spatial arrangement of towns.

Centrifugal forces. Negative influences on a state's internal cohesiveness, such as ethnic differences, irredentism, and language or religious differences.

Centripetal forces. Positive influences on a state's internal cohesiveness, such as a common language or religion and universal military training.

Centuriation. Land survey system developed by the ancient Romans, based on squares of land 776 yards long on each side.

Chain-link fence. Metal fence made from flexible series of joined links rather than woven.

Choropleth map. Map that portrays various quantities, aggregated by unit areas, through shades of one color or through various colors.

Circle village. Small farm village where houses form a circle and face a common or a public use area.

City. Collection of relatively large concentration of people, permanently settled, and working principally in nonagricultural employment.

Climate. Summary statement of weather conditions averaged over a long period of time for a particular place.

Cluster village. Farm village where houses are clustered together but with no distinct pattern of settlement.

Clustered pattern. Agglomerated pattern created by clustering the phenomenon under study.

Coarse pattern. Anything distributed so that the elements are spread out rather than agglomerated.

Coking coal. Industrial fuel created by heating coal to remove most gases; burns with intense heat and little smoke.

Colonialism. System in which a country maintains political control over foreign territories to exploit them economically.

Commercial dairy farming. Occupation that specializes in milk production.

Commercial producers. People who produce a surplus of a commodity and then exchange it for profit.

Commodity flow. Movement of goods among places that is created through trade.

Commune village. Village where most services are run on a communal basis.

Complementarity. Concept that explains trade between two areas when one has a need for a surplus produced in the other.

Complex boundary. Border between two political units delimited on the basis of two or more factors, such as geometric lines drawn along physical features.

Compound boundary. Border between two political units delimited for part of its length on the basis of one factor (e.g., a physical feature), and for the remainder by another factor (e.g., cultural variations).

Conifers. Needleleaf evergreen trees that produce woody fruit or cones; 450 species of conifers exist.

Consequent boundary. Border between two political units that is delimited on the basis of existing cultural features.

Conservation. Practice of protecting or keeping intact various resources, including soil, oceans, forests, and natural ecosystems.

Consolidated school. Large school district created by uniting many small school districts.

Consumption. Economic activity in which produced items are used (consumed).

GLOSSARY

Contour map. Type of isoline map, usually one that portrays landforms with elevations above sea level.

Core. Central part of a cultural region.

Corinthian. Culture of Corinth, an area of ancient Greece; now designates the most elaborate of the three forms of Greek architecture. (See also *Ionic, Doric.*)

Corridor. Strip of land extending out from the main body of a country, used for access to oceans, navigable rivers, or other valuable areas.

Cost-benefit analysis. Formal or informal process of relating costs of an action to its likely benefits. In reality, this is an imperfect process at the personal level—people generally "make do" rather than make ideal decisions (optimize).

Country. Political unit on the international level that may or may not be independent.

County. Primary political and areal subdivision of most states in the United States.

Covered bridges. Early American wooden bridges covered with a barnlike structure to preserve the wood.

Craft guild. Group of people in the same craft or trade, bound together to uphold standards, promote business, and protect members.

Creationist. One whose interpretation of the Bible is literal; creationists believe the universe, life, and humans are not part of an evolutionary process.

Creole house. Small, square cottage with a front porch, adapted by Louisiana blacks from an old French design.

Crime rate. Number of crimes expressed in relation to some environmental indicator, typically population; e.g., we say that the homicide rate is 15 per 100,000 people.

Crowding. Shortage of personal space.

Cultural-technological adjustments. Nonbiological human response to modify or eliminate environmental stress, such as development of clothing and energy sources to combat cold environments.

Culture. Way of life of a group of people.

Culture region. Area within which one or more culture elements, such as language, or religion, are similar.

Deciduous tree. Tree that discards its leaves (needles) in the fall and replaces them in the spring (or during periods of drought in tropical areas).

Demarcate (a boundary). Designating a boundary on the landscape with a series of monuments, a fence, or other markings.

Demographic transition. Four-stage process describing how a nation moves over time from high birth and death rates to low birth and death rates.

Demography. Science of the study of population.

Density. Element of spatial distribution that refers to the number of objects per unit area.

Dependent variable. Variable a researcher wishes to explain (e.g., crop yield). (See *independent variable.*)

Descriptive geography. Type of geography devoted to description of conditions, with little or no emphasis on analysis or prediction. (See also *prescriptive geography.*)

Desert. Region that receives less than ten inches of annual precipitation and has high temperatures, especially in the summer.

Desertification. Spread of the world's deserts, caused primarily by poor land use practices.

Dialect. Variation within a language of pronunciation and word usage. Dialects are usually identified with specific regions.

Diaspora. Greek word meaning *dispersion*, applied to the forced migration of Jews out of Palestine. Also used to describe Jews who lived outside Palestine, or the countries in which they lived.

Diffusion. Spread of some phenomenon (e.g., a language, a religion, or a disease) over the surface of the earth.

Diocese. Church district under the jurisdiction of a bishop, made up of several parishes.

Dispersed distribution. Type of spatial distribution where objects are spread out; opposite of *agglomerated distribution.*

Distance decay. Theory of human behavior stating that interactions will diminish with distance away from a source point.

Division of labor. Specialization of people in particular tasks or jobs.

Doctrine of first effective settlement. Notion that the first group to have viable or lasting settlement in an area makes a major impression on the area's culture.

Dogtrot house. Lowland, southern cottage built with two parts under one roof and a breezeway (dogtrot) between the parts.

Domain. Area in which a culture is dominant, but with less intensity than in the core area.

Domestication. Adaptation of plants and animals to human use.

Doric. People, language, or culture of Doris, an area of ancient Greece; designates the oldest and plainest style of Greek architecture. (See also *Ionic* and *Corinthian.*)

Dot map. Map that portrays spatial distribution by using a dot to represent a number of objects. Also, various sizes of dots can be used to represent varying quantities of objects.

Double-pen house. Log house that doubled in size by adding a second "pen" to the side of the original cabin away from the chimney. (See *saddle bag house.*)

Drystone fence. Stone fence made without mortar by careful placement of various sized stones.

Dust bowl. Area centered in Oklahoma and Kansas created by the droughts and poor land use practices of the 1930s.

Economic distance. Distance measured in terms of cost rather than miles or kilometers.

Economic surface. Imaginary surface created over the map of an area that indicates one or a combination of economic factors in the area.

Ecosystem. Group of organisms and the environment with which they interact.

Embargo. Government order prohibiting entry or departure of commercial ships at its ports.

Emigration. Leaving one country or region to settle in another.

Endemic. Locally prevalent.

Environmental determinism. Theory in geography proposing that human behavior is determined by physical environment.

Epidemic. Local outbreak of disease.

Eschatology. Doctrines relating to death and afterlife.

Ethnic group. People of the same race or national origin who also share a common cultural heritage.

Ethnocentrism. Belief that one's own culture is superior to others.

Etiology. Study of causes.

Evergreen tree. Tree that discards and replaces its leaves (needles) continually rather than seasonally.

Evolution. Change over time; biological organisms are subject to evolution, as are cultural elements such as language and religion.

Exchange. Economic activity that increases the value of something by moving it, trading it, or both.

Farm cities. Communal farm villages that have grown into small, modern cities, still primarily oriented to agriculture.

Farmsteads. Individual farm settlements including house, barn, and other buildings.

Federation. Union of a group of territories in which each member agrees to subordination to a central authority.

Fertile Crescent. Agricultural region located between the Nile and Tigris Rivers and the Persian Gulf.

Fetish. Based on the Portugese *feitico*, meaning "made" or "created," refers to the belief that spirits can be controlled. Purpose of a fetish was to ward off evil.

Feudal. Social, economic, and political system of the Middle Ages in which estates were worked by serfs.

Filtering. Process by which housing as it ages and deteriorates is occupied by groups of progressively lower economic status.

Fine pattern. Distribution of elements so they are close together rather than spread out.

First World. Group of modern industrial democracies whose economic and political development puts them in the world's most favorable position.

Floodplain. Margins of a watercourse that customarily flood following heavy runoff. The edge of a floodplain is often identified by a significant change of slope.

Food chain. Sequence of transfers of energy in the form of food from organisms in different levels of the system.

Forced migration. Transfer of large groups of people from one country to another because of political turmoil or persecution.

Fossil fuel. Remains of dead plants and animals from previous geologic ages that can be burned to release energy.

Fourth World. Least modern, poorest countries of the world.

Freehold tenure. Individual ownership of land.

Friction of movement. Factors involved in overcoming distance, including cost, time, congestion, road conditions, safety factors, or a combination of these.

Frontiers. Zone along the edges of a settled area or country that faces an unexplored region or another country.

Functional region. Region established to perform a function; usually an administrative device, such as counties within a state.

Generic. General, referring to all members of a class or group.

Genetic. Inborn trait or characteristic independent of learned behavior, such as eye and skin color. Also used to mean "specific," as in the study of toponyms.

Genetic drift. Accidental change in a population's genetic structure.

Geographical perspective. Viewpoint emphasizing the spatial interrelationships and interactions of phenomena. May be compared to historical perspective; the geographical perspective is to space as the historical perspective is to time.

Geography. Explanation of the spatial distribution of phenomena.

Geojurisprudence. Geography of systems of laws.

Geometrical increase (progression). Sequence with the same ratio between successive terms (e.g., 2, 4, 8, 16, or 3, 9, 27, 81).

Geometry of space. Application of geometrical concepts to the solution of geographic problems.

Ghetto. Urban area to which a minority population is confined, either by law or by social and economic forces such as discrimination and poverty.

Golden Age. Describes the tenth to thirteenth centuries, a period of flourishing Judaic culture. (The term also has more general application.)

Graffiti. Writing on walls or other surfaces in public places.

Grammar. Set of rules governing construction of a language.

Habitat. Place where any organism lives and grows.

Hacienda village. Farm villages in Latin America where hacienda employees live; the hacienda is a large plantation devoted to commercial agriculture.

Half-timber house (See *black-and-white house*.)

Hard wheat. Wheat grown in dry regions; low in moisture content, resists spoilage, and its flour rises well with leavening agents. (See *soft wheat*.)

Hardwood tree. Tree with heavy, compact, and hard wood, such as oak and cherry.

Hearth. Source area of particular cultural characteristics.

Heartland. Geopolitical term referring to the core area of a nation-state that dominates the surrounding agricultural or industrial area.

GLOSSARY

Heavy industry. Industry, such as steelmaking, in which heavy equipment or heavy raw materials are used.

Hedgerow. Hedge grown as a fence or barrier along farm fields.

Hierarchy. Progressively stepped pattern or organization such that there are fewer large entities (e.g., cities) and many smaller ones.

High technology. Chemical, electronic, and other industries that require high levels of research.

Hinterland. [literally, "behind land" (German)]. Area that contributes to, and depends on, a city.

Historical boundary. Border between two political units delimited on the basis of a division line from earlier (historical) times.

Home rule. Law in 28 states of the United States that provides cities with broad powers of self-government (as opposed to complete state government control of cities).

Homestead Act. U.S. law (1862) granting each settler a 160-acre tract of public land for development into a farm.

Homo sapiens sapiens. Biological label denoting the human species.

Homo sapiens. Modern human; the only surviving species of the *Homo* genus.

Hot spot. Small area where friction between states creates international tension.

Hypoxia. Form of high-altitude stress caused by insufficient oxygen to maintain normal body functions.

Independent variable. Variable used to explain a condition; e.g., precipitation may be regarded as an independent variable explaining crop yield. (See *dependent variable*.)

Indo-European. A language family originating somewhere in the region from India to Europe.

Information field. Subset of a mental map or maps indicating an area about which people have information.

Intensity theory. Notion that crowding intensifies human reactions to situations, whether positive or negative.

Interaction. Response in one or more environmental variables to change in another variable.

Interaction field. Area within which interactions occur.

Intermediate-scale map. Map that portrays an intermediate-sized area of the earth's surface. (See *large-scale map; small-scale map*.)

Interurban. Literally, "between cities"; refers to studies of sets of cities, or comparisons among cities. (see *intraurban*.)

Intervening opportunity. Intervening source of supply located closer to the area of need than the original source.

Intraurban. Literally, "within cities"; refers to studies of the structure and relationships of cities. (see *interurban*.)

Ionic. People, language, or culture of Ionia, an area of ancient Greece; designates the middle of the three types of Greek architecture. (See *Doric; Corinthian*.)

Irredenta. From Italian, meaning "unredeemed"; territory of a country inhabited by people who formerly held it and wish to recover it.

Irredentism. Policy of irredentists to recover territory for their homeland.

Isogloss. Boundary separating language areas; from the Greek words meaning equal *(iso)* and language *(gloss)*.

Isolated state. Theoretical area created to isolate economic factors so as to analyze them.

Isolationists. People who want their country to be free of any international alliances.

Isoline. Line on a map that connects points of equal value.

Kaaba. Sacred Moslem shrine at Mecca containing a black stone given to Abraham by the angel Gabriel.

Keep. Yard inside medieval castle walls used for gardens, cattle pens, and out buildings.

Landlocked state. International political unit that has no outlet to the world oceans.

Land Ordinance Act. U.S. law (1785) requiring land to be designated with precise measurements, such as square-mile units (as opposed to *metes and bounds*).

Land reform. Governmental intervention that forces owners of large land holdings to subdivide and sell their land to peasants and tenant farmers.

Land tenure. Ownership of the land, such as "corporate tenure" vs. "freehold tenure."

Language. System of spoken and written communication.

Large-scale map. Map that portrays a small area of the earth in great detail; *large-scale* refers to a large ratio (fraction) between the map and the earth.

Latitude. System of parallel lines on a globe representing angular measurement from the center; used to measure distances north and south of the equator.

Law of diminishing returns. Theory that increasing amounts of work do not create proportionately larger yields.

Law of the Sea. Results of a treaty by United Nations members designating offshore limits of coastal nations as well as other factors related to the world's oceans. [Note: the treaty had not been signed by the United States as of early 1983.]

Law of the Sea conferences. Series of international meetings to establish laws on ocean problems such as offshore boundary limits.

LDC. See *Less Developed Countries*.

League of Nations. Obsolete international organization founded to maintain world peace by solving international problems and reducing armaments; dissolved in the 1920s.

Less Developed Countries (LDCs). Countries of the Third and Fourth Worlds that are less developed economically, socially, and politically than those of the First and Second Worlds.

Light industry. Industry such as cloth making that requires lightweight raw materials and usually simple machines.

Lignite. Low-grade, brown coal with woody texture.

Line village. Settlement wherein houses form a linear pattern, usually along a road or river.

Lingua franca. Language used for trade or general communication among several countries.

Linguists. Scientists who study languages.

Livestock ranching. Commercial farming in which large parcels of land are used to graze cattle, sheep, or goats.

Location quotient. Degree of concentration of particular types of manufacturing.

Longitude. System of lines on a globe running from pole to pole representing angular measurement from the center; measure distances east and west of the prime meridian.

Machine space. Area of a city set aside for motor vehicles.

Machine tools. All the precision devices used to make parts for machinery.

Maginot Line. System of heavily fortified pillboxes located along France's northeast border with Germany; named after Andre Maginot, the French minister of war who supervised their construction.

Manufacturing. Process in which raw materials are changed into finished products.

Map scale. Ratio between the distance or area on a map and the distance or area of the earth's surface portrayed by the map.

Marginal producer. Someone who produces a product or commodity at the break-even margin; neither makes nor loses money in the operation.

Market city. City within von Thünen's hypothetical isolated state that receives the goods produced by the region's farmers.

Mathematical location. Location based on coordinates, such as a grid or polar coordinate system.

Mature stage. Third stage of development of a national political unit, when stability in economic and political matters is achieved.

MDCs. See *More Developed Countries*.

Medical geography. Study of the geographic aspects of disease and health care.

Mental map. Mental image of the spatial relationships of a place or area.

Mentifacts. Psychological or other phenomena such as religion, superstition, astrology, and language.

Mesopotamia. Ancient country located between the Tigris and Euphrates Rivers in what is now Iraq; generally accepted as the "cradle" of civilization.

Metes and bounds. System of land measurement based on location of landmarks.

Metropolis; metropolitan. A large city; pertaining to a large city or cities. (See *urban; SMSA.*)

Metropolitan area. In the United States, a city of at least 50,000 persons and the surrounding county or counties that are economically and socially integrated with the central city. (See *SMSA.*)

Migration. Relocation of individuals, families, or peoples.

Mineral rights. Privileges granted to the subsurface owner of terrestial space that grant exploitation rights for subterranean commodities such as minerals.

Minor metal. One of the least expensive and most common industrial metals, such as mercury or cobalt.

Mir. Ancient Russian village occupied by farm peasants.

Mixed farming. Agricultural specialization that utilizes crop rotation and mixed land use patterns for conservation and market advantages.

Moat. Ditch, usually filled with water, surrounding a medieval castle, used as part of the castle's defense system.

Model. Simplified representation of a condition or process, such as a map, chart, diagram, formula, verbal statement, or some other forms.

Modernization. Conforming to present-day practices; applied to countries, means use of modern transportation, communication, and medical equipment to ease citizen work and hardship.

Monetary metal. Metal that has been or is used to make coins.

Mongoloid. Racial label to describe peoples of Asiatic origin who are light-skinned and often flat-faced, with double eyelids giving the characteristic "almond" eyes.

Monotheism. Belief in a single god.

Moral code. Guide for a people's behavior.

More Developed Countries (MDCs). Countries of the First and Second Worlds that are more developed economically, socially, and politically than countries of the Third and Fourth Worlds.

Motte. Artificially raised mounds of earth used by the Normans in old England to construct castles at a higher elevation than the surrounding land.

Multifactor region. Region based on more than one factor, such as a combination of landforms, climate, culture, and economic activities.

Multilingualism. Presence within a nation of several significant language groups.

Nation. Group of people related through tribal heritage (e.g., the Sioux nation), but who do not necessarily have their own territory.

Nationalism. Emotional allegiance to a particular country.

Nation-state. State on the international level where there is a sense of national cohesion.

Natural hazard. Natural event that interacts with humans and inflicts death, injury, or property loss.

GLOSSARY

Nearest-neighbor analysis. Method for measuring the clustering vs. the dispersal of a distribution.

Needleleaf tree. Tree such as fir, pine, or spruce that has long, narrow, needle-shaped leaves and usually produces its fruit in woody cones.

Negroid. Racial label describing peoples who are generally dark-skinned.

Nodal region. Region based on movement patterns to or from one central point (node) and peripheral points.

Nominal location. Location identified only by the name of the place.

Offa's Dyke. Ditch and low mound of earth running the length of the Welsh-English border, used as a barrier and constructed during King Offa's reign (757–796).

Old-age stage. Final stage of development of a national political unit, when weakness and internal decay are common.

Order. Term synonymous with *level*, as in *higher-order cities, lower-order cities,* referring to the degree of sophistication of goods and services offered.

Palisade. Row of large pointed stakes set in the ground to form a fence used for fortification.

Pandemic. Worldwide outbreak, usually of disease.

Panhandle. Extension or proruption to the main body of a political unit that resembles the handle of a pan.

Parapet. Bank of earth formed to protect troops; sometimes placed on top of a rampart or motte. (See *motte.*)

Parish. British church district with one church under the charge of one clergyman; a group of parishes make up a diocese. (See *diocese.*)

Pattern. Arrangement of phenomena in space.

Peat. Partially decayed vegetable matter found in marshes; often cut, dried, and used for fuel.

Pentagon. Five-sided office building in Arlington, Virginia, that houses the U.S. military establishment.

Percentile. Division into 100 groups with equal frequencies.

Perception. Understanding about the way something is; may or may not resemble reality.

Periodic market. Marketplace or central place that provides goods or services on a periodic basis rather than continuously.

Permeability. Rate at which water can move through soil.

Personal space. Space close to people; space that people see as their own "space bubble."

Petrochemical. Petroleum-based chemical such as gasoline, ethylene gycol, or ethylene oxide.

Physical environment. That part of the environment associated primarily with geologic, climatic, and biologic processes.

Physical geography. Science of the pattern and processes of the physical environment (atmosphere, lithosphere, hydrosphere, and biosphere).

Physical model. Small version of a real thing, such as a globe or model airplane.

Physiological adjustment. Unconscious responses in the human body to environmental stress; generally reversible, such as responses to reduced levels of oxygen at high altitudes.

Place identity. Notion that people have an emotional attachment to places.

Plat. "Plot" or map, as for a residential subdivision; an area divided into surveyed lots is said to have been *platted.*

Polar coordinate system. Mathematical system for locating points, based on distance and direction from a known point.

Polarized. Refers to a situation in which a given condition exists mainly at the extremes (e.g., a society in which people are either rich or poor).

Political culture. Way in which affairs of government are conducted.

Politics. Science of government; principled conduct of public affairs with a definite governmental organization.

Polytheism. Belief in many gods.

Population pressure. Condition in a country or region where population begins to outstrip resources.

Population pyramid. Graphic device portraying a population's age and sex composition.

Prescriptive geography. Geographic work that attempts to recommend action to solve problems. (See also *descriptive geography.*)

Primary production. Activities such as farming, fishing, mining, and forestry in which products are taken directly from the earth.

Prime meridian. Longitude line passing through Greenwich, England, serving as the origin (beginning point) for the measurement of longitude. It is half of a great circle that continues beyond the poles as the International Date Line.

Principal Meridian. Longitude line used as the baseline for land measurement in the range-and-township survey method.

Probability theory. Mathematical principle used as the basis for statistical analyses.

Process. Actions or interactions among components of systems producing changes.

Proruption. Any appendage or extension of territory protruding from the main body of a state.

Proxemics. Study of individual distances that define limits and dimensions of personal space.

Psychological distance. Distance measured as it is perceived rather than in absolute terms.

QOL. Abbreviation for Quality of Life.

Quantitative revolution. Methodological upheaval in geography that occurred in the 1960s and resulted in adoption of quantitative methods in geographic research.

Quarternary production. Work, such as research, that produces wealth but is not a service or manufacturing activity.

Race. Population group distinguished by certain physical characteristics.

Radical geography. View of geography that seeks radical change as solutions to contemporary problems.

Random pattern. Distribution between dispersed and clustered wherein the phenomenon under study is situated in "chance" locations.

Range. East-west measurement of land, six miles long, used to designate congressional townships; component of the rectangular land survey system *(township and range)*; distance people are prepared to travel to shop at a particular store or center.

Rate. Expression of a phenomenon as a ratio to some base; e.g., number of hospital beds per 100,000 population.

Reapportionment. Realignment of voting district boundaries based on a new census to assure equalization of population for each new district.

Reformation. Sixteenth-century reform movement led by the "protestants" who objected to prevailing conditions in the church; Martin Luther and John Calvin were central figures.

Regional social philosophy. Sectional, or state-to-state, variations in people's reactions to social issues.

Regionalism. Interpretation of phenomena based on division of states or nations into homogeneous areas called *regions*.

Relative distance. Distance measured with respect to the cost or time it takes to move from one point to another.

Relative location. Location of an unknown place given by relating it to something known; location of an area with respect to other areas.

Remote sensing. Science of studying the earth's surface from a distance using various forms of photography and electromagnetic radiation to detect land-cover differences.

Round village. Similar to a circle village, but without the commons.

Russification. Process of domination of Soviet ethnic peoples by the Russian majority; cultural values of ethnic minorities gradually disappear.

Saddlebag house. Log houses that were doubled in size by adding a second "pen" to the chimney-side of the original cabin. (See *double-pen house*.)

Scale. Proportion of the distance on a map to the corresponding distance on the ground.

Secondary production. Economic activities, such as manufacturing, in which value of something is increased through change (i.e., raw material is changed to a finished product).

Second World. Group of Communist countries with aspects of advanced technology, but whose development is retarded because of lack of sufficient agriculture or consumer products.

Section. Square parcel of land, one mile on each side; consists of 640 acres.

Sedentary subsistence farming. Type of farming in which farmers live on the land and till crops for their own use; world's largest single occupation.

Serfs. In the feudal system, people who were bound to the land and transferred with it to new owners when the land was sold.

Service industry. Industry that caters to human needs or desires, such as hotels, grocery stores, and eating places.

Sentence disparity. Difference in punishment for similar criminal offenses.

Sharecropper. Tenant farmer who works the land for a share of the crop produced.

Shatter belt. Region, such as eastern Europe, that has been "shattered" by political fragmentation.

Shifting cultivation. Type of agriculture in hot, rainy areas where farmers move their homes and fields every 3 to 4 years. (See *slash-and-burn agriculture*.)

Shotgun house. Long, narrow cottage of African design popular with Louisiana slaves of early America.

Silicon. Nonmetallic chemical element that combines with oxygen to form silica, the hard, glossy mineral in quartz, sand, and opals.

Single-factor region. Region identified by one factor, such as corn production or newspaper circulation.

Slash-and-burn agriculture. Type of shifting cultivation in which farmers cut down (slash) and burn the tropical trees to make room for their fields; known as *milpa* in Latin America, *chena* in Asia, *fong* in Africa, and many other local names.

Small-scale map. Map that portrays a large area of the earth with few details; *small-scale* refers to a small ratio (fraction) between the map and the earth.

SMSA. Standard Metropolitan Statistical Area; city of at least 50,000, the county in which the city is located, and other counties linked by significant commuting patterns.

Snake fence. Split-rail fence built in a zig-zag fashion so that stakes would hold the rail-ends together. (See *split-rail fence*.)

Social indicator. Factor or variable that measures a specific social condition (e.g., median years of education in a city or neighborhood).

Social space. Space defined in terms of social relationships, such as *familial space*.

Socioeconomic environment. That part of the environment represented by various social and economic conditions.

Sociofacts. Elements of human social organization, including family, educational institutions, legal systems, and forms of government.

Sociofugal. Refers to arrangement of furniture designed to keep people separated; used in public places such as airline terminals.

GLOSSARY

Sociopetal. Refers to arrangement of furniture designed to bring people together; used in informal settings such as living rooms.

Sod house. Early American house built on the treeless prairie and constructed with layers of sod.

Soft wheat. Wheat grown in wet areas that is high in moisture content and spoils easily; its flour does not respond well to leavening agents. (See *hard wheat.*)

Softwood tree. Tree with wood that is cut easily, such as most conifers.

Space model. Device used by geographers to illustrate factors and relationships among factors that act upon the location of activities. (See *model.*)

Spatial distribution. Arrangement in space of anything that can be mapped; in geography, spatial distribution usually refers to things that appear on the surface of the earth, or things that can be measured and that vary from place to place, such as prices, temperatures, rainfall amounts, and so forth.

Spatial interaction. Interaction between people or groups occurring across geographic space.

Spatial rights. Notion that peoples' rights vary from place to place; e.g., behavior that is legal in one location may not so be in another.

Special district. Small territory established for a single purpose or function, such as fire protection or education, where funds are raised for the function through taxation of property owners or by some other means.

Specific value. Value of a commodity per a unit of its weight; diamonds have high specific value, rocks low.

Sphere. Area where the influence of a particular culture is apparent, but weaker than in the core and domain areas.

Split-rail fence. Early American wooden fences constructed by laying consecutive rows of rails (split from logs) on top of each other.

Spring wheat. Wheat that is sown in the spring and harvested in late summer. (See *winter wheat.*)

State. Political unit on the international level; also, the subdivision of many international political units.

State farm. Large farm owned by a government and worked by groups of farmers.

Steppe. Large, treeless plains that receive between ten and twenty inches of annual precipitation.

Stochastic. Chance or random; a stochastic process involves randomly occurring events.

Stockade. Barrier created by driving stakes in the ground side by side.

Strassendorf. Linear farm village created along a road.

Subsequent boundary. Border between two political units that is delimited after human occupation of the region.

Subsistence producer. One who produces and consumes for his own needs, with virtually nothing left over for trading.

Subsurface. Subterranean part of terrestrial space.

Superimposed boundary. Border between two political units that is delimited without regard to existing cultural factors.

Survey research. Information gathering directly from the individuals about whom information is sought.

Systematic geography. Study of geography by means of phenomena rather than regions.

Technology. Application of knowledge for practical purposes.

Terrestrial space. Air, surface, and subterranean levels of the earth used by humans.

Territoriality. People's or animals' defensive or possessive feelings about areas or places.

Tertiary production. Economic activity that produces wealth through service to others.

Thalweg. Deepest and most rapidly flowing part of a river.

Thematic map. Map that usually portrays the distribution of one category of information, on which shades, lines, or other symbols are assigned values.

Theory. Statement used for general explanation of a phenomenon.

Third World. Group of countries with a common lack of industrial development and low standards of living.

Three-field system. Farming system developed in the Middle Ages wherein land parcels were divided into three strips and the strips were farmed on a yearly rotating basis.

Threshold. Minimum number of people or dollars needed to sustain a commercial activity; level above or below which conditions change significantly in some way, e.g., the threshold percentage of infection in a population—beyond the threshold level, the disease spreads much more rapidly.

Thünen rings. Concentric zones, observed in the 1820s by Johann von Thünen, that existed around a town and were created by the products produced at particular distances from the town.

Tidewater cottage. Type of early American house built on a six- to eight-foot superstructure to protect it from periodic flooding.

Ton-mile. Index of transportation cost calculated by multiplying the weight of a commodity in tons by the distance traveled in miles.

Topical geography. Synonymous with *systematic geography.*

Topographic map. From the Greek *topo,* meaning "place," map that shows topography, referring to the detailed shape of the land.

Topography. Description of the earth's surface features, including landforms and other objects.

Toponym. Place name.

Town. Rural or urban unit of local government in some New England states; analogous to *township* in most other states.

Township. North-south measurement of land, six miles long, designating congressional townships.

Trade surplus. Imbalance of foreign trade in which exports exceed imports.

Trap-rock. Steplike formations of dark-colored igneous rock found in other rock.

GLOSSARY

Transferability. Cost of moving goods, individuals, or messages from one place to another; usually measured in terms of distance.

Transportation cost. Cost associated with moving any commodity a specified distance.

Transportation mode. Type of conveyance (vehicle) used to move commodities.

Transport gradient. Line on the von Thünen model created by connecting the price paid for a product at the market with the location of the marginal producer, or distance from the market where profit can be made after paying transportation costs.

Tree line. Line beyond which tree growth stops, either from increased elevation (on a mountain) or increased latitude (proximity to the poles).

Truck farming. From the French *troc*, meaning "barter," to raise vegetables near urban markets.

Tudor. Style of architecture characterized by much paneling, flat arches, and shallow moldings, used extensively during the Tudor reign (1485–1603) in England.

Unbounded plain. Theoretical area that is flat and has no restrictions on movement, such as mountains or rivers.

Uniform plain. Plain hypothesized by von Thünen as devoid of variation in physical features.

Urban, urbanization. Related to cities; the process through which the proportion of people living in cities increases.

Usable space. Part of terrestrial space utilized by humans.

Variable. Anything that can assume a succession of values.

Vassal. Feudal tenant of the Middle Ages who held land and serfs, but pledged fealty to an overlord.

Vedas. The four parts of a massive and complex literature brought to India by the Aryans; means "knowledge."

Vernacular region. "Popular" region; region based on people's perceptions rather than on statistical criteria.

Wachstumspitzen. From the German *wachsen*, "to grow," and *spitz*, "point"; extension of a state's territory that is a remnant of earlier settlement patterns and was considered a forward point of growth.

Waldhubendorf. Village aligned along a stream in a forest.

Walled village. Village of the Middle Ages encircled by a protective wall, usually of stone.

Water resource management. Management of water resources to ensure continuing supplies of pure water at least cost.

Weight-loss ratio. Percentage of weight of a raw material lost in the manufacturing process.

Winter wheat. Wheat that is sown in the fall and harvested in early summer. (See *spring wheat*.)

Young stage. Earliest stage of development of a national political unit, when consolidation of internal structures is sought.

Zebu. Type of humped cattle found in tropical areas.

Zoning ordinance. Land use regulation established by U.S. cities to provide for public safety, welfare, and health.

APPENDIX A
Climatic Classification

The purpose of a climatic classification is to illustrate how climate varies from place to place. The global map with Köppen classification system in Figure A–1 reveals a pattern of climates described by a simple lettering scheme, where the letters correspond to climatic characteristics. Early in the twentieth century, Köppen constructed this classification using annual average values of temperature and precipitation. The lack of weather data forced him to use vegetation as an indicator of the climate in an area. Five basic climate groups, designated by capital letters A, B, C, D, and E, were further subdivided to recognize distinctive characteristics within each major group. Table A–1 is designed to indicate the criteria for the major categories shown on the global map.

TABLE A–1

Major Group	Subgroups	Discriminating Characteristics
A—Tropical rainy Coldest month's temperatue >18°C (64.4°F)	Af—Tropical wet	No dry season; driest month >6 cm (2.4 in.)
	Aw—Tropical wet and dry	Winter dry season; driest month <6 cm (2.4 in.)
	Am—Monsoon	Short dry season but sufficiently wet year-round from high total rainfall

B—Dry
Evaporation exceeds precipitation
	BS—Semiarid (steppe)
	BSh–Tropical and subtropical
	BSk—Middle-latitude
	BW—Arid (desert)
	BWh—Tropical and subtropical
	BWk—Middle-latitude
	where
	  h = average annual temperature >18°C (64.4°F)
	  k = average annual temperature <18°C (64.4°F)
		Short moist season
		Meager rainfall, mostly in summer
		
		Constantly dry
		Constantly dry

C—Humid mesothermal
Coldest month's temperature between 18°C (64.4°F) and −3°C (26.6°F)
	Cs—Dry summer subtropical
	Cf—Humid subtropical
	Cw—Marine climate
	and where a third letter is added:
	  a = hot summer, warmest month >22°C (71.6°F)
	  b = cool summer, warmest month <22°C (71.6°)
	  c = short, cool summer, less than 4 months, >10°C (50°F)
		Summer drought, winter rain
		Rain in all seasons
		Winter dry

D—Humid microthermal
Coldest month's temperature < −3°C (26.6°F);
Warmest month's temperature >10°C (50°F)
	Df—Humid continental
	Dw—Humid continental
	and where a third letter is added:
	  a = hot summer, warmest month >22°C (71.6°F)
	  b = cool summer, warmest month <22°C (71.6°)
	  c = short, cool summer, less than 4 months >10°C (50°F)
	  d = average temperature of coldest month < −38°C (−36.4°F)
		Rain in all seasons; humid winters
		Dry winters

E—Polar Warmest month's temperature 40°C (50°F)	ET—Tundra EF—Ice cap Average annual temperature <0°C (32°F)	Meager precipitation year-round Meager precipitation year-round
H—Undifferentiated highlands	At the scale of most maps, it is impossible to display that climate changes with an increase in elevation.	

APPENDIX A

In summary, four of the major groups have been defined with temperature values, whereas the B group (dry climates) was identified with precipitation values. Within the B group, classifying an area as BS (steppe) or BW (desert) requires manipulation of several formulas, which use annual rainfall (r) and average temperature (t) as shown in Table A–2.

TABLE A–2

	Boundary between BS and Humid Climates	Boundary between BS and BW
Rainfall evenly distributed	$r = 0.44t - 8.5$	$r = \dfrac{0.44t - 8.5}{2}$
Rainfall maximum in summer, 10 times more in wettest summer month than in driest winter month	$r = 0.44t - 3$	$r = \dfrac{0.44t - 3}{2}$
Rainfall maximum in winter, 3 times as much in wettest winter month as in driest summer month	$r = 0.44t - 14$	$r = \dfrac{0.44t - 14}{2}$

Source: Formulas from Glenn T. Trewartha, *An Introduction to Climate,* 4th ed. (New York: McGraw-Hill Book Co., 1968).

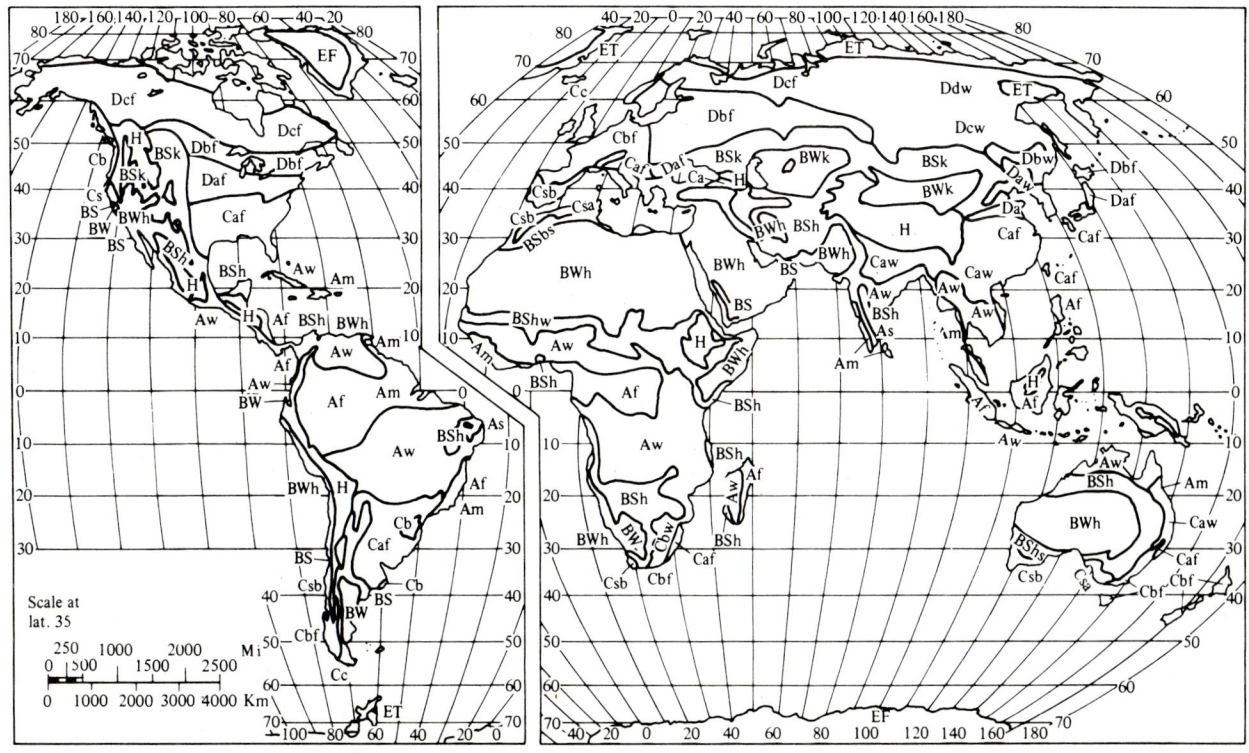

Legend. Af, Am: Tropical wet. Aw: Tropical wet, dry winters. BSh: Tropical and subtropical steppe. BSk: Middle latitude steppe. BWh: Tropical and subtropical desert. BWk: Middle latitude desert. Cs: Dry summer subtropical. Ca: Humid subtropical. Cb, Cc: Marine. Da: Humid continental, warm summer. Db: Humid continental, cold summer. Dc, Dd: Subarctic. ET: Tundra. EF: Ice cap. H: Undifferentiated highlands.

FIGURE A-1 Climatic Classification System

APPENDIX B
The United States Population Data Sheet of the Population Reference Bureau, Inc.

APPENDIX B

Regions, Divisions, and States	Resident Population, July 1, 1983 (in 1000s)	Resident Population, April 1, 1980 (in 1000s)	Population Change, April 1, 1980 to July 1, 1983 (in 1000s)	Resident Population Change, April 1, 1980 to July 1, 1983 (percent)	Rank Order of Population, April 1, 1980	Rank Order of Population Size, 1983/1980	Resident Population Projected to July 1, 1990	Total Area, 1000s of Sq. Miles	Persons per Sq. Mile of Land Area, 1983/Rank Order	Estimated Net Migration, April 1, 1980 to July 1, 1983 (in 1000s)	Crude Birth Rate, 1981	Crude Death Rate, 1981	Infant Mortality Rate, 1981	Total Fertility Rate, 1980	Births per 100 Deaths, 1980-1983	Population Born in State Where Now Residing, 1980 (percent)	Population Below Age 18, 1983 (percent)	Population Age 65 and Over, 1983 (percent)	Black Population, 1980 (percent)	Hispanic Population, 1980 (percent)	Per Capita Personal Income, 1983	Unemployment Rate, April 1984	Projections of Population of Voting Age, 1984 (in 1000s)	Electoral Votes
UNITED STATES	233,981	226,546	7,435	3.3	203,302	—	249,203	3618.8	66	2,048	15.8	8.6	11.9	1.8	183	64	26.7	11.7	11.7	6.4	$11,675	7.6	173,936	538	U.S.
NORTHEAST	49,519	49,135	383	0.8	49,061	—	48,423	168.9	304	−255	13.4	9.5	11.6	1.8	142	70	24.9	12.9	9.9	5.3	12,814	6.8	37,495	113	N.E.
NEW ENGLAND	12,489	12,348	141	1.1	11,847	—	12,733	66.7	198	−29	13.2	8.9	10.5	1.5	146	66	24.5	13.0	3.8	2.4	12,845	5.2	9,520	36	N.ENG.
Maine	1,146	1,125	21	1.9	994	38/36	1,229	33.3/39	37/36	1	14.6	9.2	10.9	1.7	159	73	26.8	13.0	0.3	0.4	9,619	7.5	848	4	ME
New Hampshire	959	921	38	4.1	738	41/45	1,139	9.344	107/20	18	14.4	8.2	9.7	1.7	180	49	26.2	11.6	0.4	0.6	11,620	4.5	722	4	NH
Vermont	525	511	14	2.7	445	48/47	575	9.643	56/30	3	15.4	8.4	7.7	1.7	173	62	26.6	11.7	0.2	0.6	10,036	7.4	391	3	VT
Massachusetts	5,767	5,737	29	0.5	5,689	11/9	5,704	8.3/45	739/3	−38	12.8	9.2	9.7	1.5	138	72	23.9	13.2	3.9	2.5	13,089	5.0	4,422	13	MA
Rhode Island	955	947	8	0.9	950	42/39	951	1.2/50	910/2	−2	13.0	9.6	11.8	1.5	133	68	23.8	14.1	2.9	2.1	11,504	6.6	733	4	RI
Connecticut	3,138	3,108	30	1.0	3,032	27/25	3,136	5.0/48	640/4	−11	12.7	8.5	12.1	1.5	148	58	24.2	12.7	7.0	4.0	14,826	4.3	2,404	8	CT
MIDDLE ATLANTIC	37,029	36,787	243	0.7	37,213	—	35,690	102.2	371	−226	13.5	9.6	11.9	1.6	140	71	24.9	12.9	11.9	6.3	12,804	7.4	27,974	77	M.A.
New York	17,667	17,558	109	0.6	18,241	2/1	16,457	49.1/30	373/3	−136	13.8	9.6	12.4	1.6	145	69	25.0	12.6	13.7	9.5	13,146	6.5	13,326	36	NY
New Jersey	7,468	7,365	103	1.4	7,171	9/8	7,513	7.846	996/1	8	13.0	9.1	10.7	1.6	142	57	25.0	12.3	12.6	6.7	14,057	6.6	5,659	16	NJ
Pennsylvania	11,895	11,864	31	0.3	11,801	4/3	11,720	45.3/33	265/8	−98	13.5	10.1	11.9	1.6	133	82	24.7	13.8	8.8	1.3	11,510	9.2	8,989	25	PA
NORTH CENTRAL	58,953	58,866	88	0.1	56,590	—	60,265	766.4	78	−1,265	15.9	8.8	12.2	1.8	180	72	27.2	12.0	9.1	2.2	11,494	8.8	43,035	137	N.C.
EAST NORTH CENTRAL	41,531	41,682	−151	−0.4	40,263	—	42,372	248.5	170	−1,091	15.6	8.7	12.6	1.8	180	72	27.3	11.5	10.9	2.6	11,599	9.7	30,244	90	E.N.C.
Ohio	10,746	10,798	−52	−0.5	10,657	6/5	10,763	41.3/35	262/9	−278	15.5	8.9	12.3	1.8	172	73	27.1	11.6	10.0	1.1	10,567	9.8	7,846	23	OH
Indiana	5,479	5,490	−11	−0.2	5,195	14/11	5,679	36.2/38	153/15	−134	15.4	8.6	11.7	1.8	180	71	27.8	11.4	7.6	1.6	10,567	9.4	3,969	12	IN
Illinois	11,486	11,427	60	0.5	11,110	5/4	11,503	56.3/24	207/10	−212	16.2	8.9	13.9	1.9	182	69	27.1	11.6	14.7	5.6	12,626	9.5	8,410	24	IL
Michigan	9,069	9,262	−193	−2.1	8,882	8/7	9,394	58.5/23	159/14	−403	15.3	8.2	13.1	1.8	184	72	27.7	10.8	12.9	1.8	11,574	11.0	6,530	20	MI
Wisconsin	4,751	4,706	45	1.0	4,418	16/15	5,033	56.2/26	87/24	−64	15.7	8.6	10.4	1.9	182	77	27.1	12.6	3.9	1.3	11,132	7.6	3,490	11	WI
WEST NORTH CENTRAL	17,422	17,183	239	1.4	16,328	—	17,894	517.8	34	−174	16.5	9.1	11.1	2.0	180	72	27.0	13.2	4.6	1.2	11,243	6.7	12,792	47	W.N.C.
Minnesota	4,144	4,076	68	1.7	3,806	21/18	4,353	84.4/12	52/32	−46	16.7	8.0	10.3	1.9	205	75	27.2	12.3	1.3	0.8	11,666	6.5	3,044	10	MN
Iowa	2,905	2,914	−9	−0.3	2,825	29/24	2,983	56.3/25	52/33	−70	15.8	9.2	10.0	2.0	168	78	27.1	13.9	1.4	0.9	11,048	7.9	2,119	8	IA
Missouri	4,970	4,917	54	1.1	4,678	15/13	5,077	69.7/19	72/27	−38	15.6	9.9	12.6	1.9	158	70	26.4	13.6	10.5	1.1	10,790	8.0	3,682	11	MO
North Dakota	680	653	28	4.3	618	46/44	678	70.7/17	10/45	5	18.8	8.3	11.2	2.1	222	73	28.8	12.5	0.4	0.6	11,350	5.3	491	3	ND
South Dakota	700	691	9	1.3	666	45/40	699	77.1/16	9/46	−12	18.5	9.3	11.5	2.4	200	71	29.1	13.6	0.3	0.6	9,704	4.5	498	3	SD
Nebraska	1,597	1,570	27	1.7	1,485	36/34	1,640	77.4/15	21/41	−13	17.2	9.3	9.9	2.0	183	70	27.6	13.3	3.1	1.8	10,940	4.1	1,163	5	NE
Kansas	2,425	2,364	62	2.6	2,249	32/28	2,463	82.3/14	30/37	(z)	17.3	9.1	11.4	2.0	187	63	26.7	13.2	5.3	2.7	12,285	5.4	1,794	7	KS
SOUTH	79,539	75,372	4,167	5.5	62,813	—	87,594	898.6	91	2,272	16.1	8.7	13.0	—	187	65	27.3	11.5	18.6	5.9	10,701	7.1	59,153	177	S.
SOUTH ATLANTIC	38,805	36,959	1,846	5.0	30,679	—	43,144	278.9	145	1,131	14.6	8.9	13.6	1.7	166	57	25.6	12.4	20.7	3.2	11,020	6.1	29,512	88	S.A.
Delaware	606	594	12	1.9	548	47/46	630	2.0/49	319/7	−2	15.4	8.5	13.4	1.8	187	52	25.6	10.8	16.1	1.6	12,442	5.6	457	3	DE
Maryland	4,304	4,217	87	2.1	3,924	19/21	4,491	10.5/42	439/5	−3	14.4	8.0	12.6	1.6	180	54	25.4	10.1	22.7	1.5	12,994	5.1	3,259	10	MD
District of Columbia	623	638	−15	−2.4	757	—	502	0.1	10,383	−24	14.5	11.0	25.1	1.5	136	39	21.6	11.8	70.3	2.8	16,409	10.7	482	3	DC
Virginia	5,550	5,347	203	3.8	4,651	13/14	5,961	40.8/36	140/16	81	14.6	7.8	12.5	1.6	188	60	25.7	10.0	18.9	1.5	11,835	4.3	4,203	12	VA
West Virginia	1,965	1,950	15	0.8	1,744	34/30	2,037	24.2/41	82/25	−13	14.3	9.8	13.0	1.8	147	79	27.5	12.8	3.3	0.7	8,937	14.9	1,433	6	WV
North Carolina	6,082	5,882	200	3.4	5,084	10/12	6,473	52.7/28	125/17	−13	14.1	8.3	13.1	1.6	173	76	26.3	11.0	22.4	1.0	9,656	6.3	4,559	13	NC
South Carolina	3,264	3,122	142	4.5	2,591	25/26	3,560	31.1/40	108/19	58	16.4	8.0	16.1	1.8	201	73	28.4	9.8	30.4	1.1	8,954	7.3	2,386	8	SC

APPENDIX B

	Population, 1983	Population, 1980	Change, 1980-1983	% Change, 1980-1983	Population, 1970	Population Rank, 1980	Population, 1990	Area/Rank	Pop. Density/Rank	Net Migration	Birth Rate	Death Rate	Infant Mortality	T.F.R.	Birth/Death Ratio	Born in State	<18	65+	% Black	% Hispanic	Per cap. income	Unemployment	Voting Ages	Elec. Votes	
Georgia	5,732	5,463	269	4.9	4,588	12/16	6,175	58.9/21	99/23	120	16.2	8.1	13.8	1.9	203	71	28.3	9.8	26.8	1.1	10,283	5.8	4,204	12	GA
Florida	10,680	9,746	933	9.6	6,791	7/10	13,316	58.7/22	197/11	831	13.6	10.8	13.3	1.7	129	31	23.0	17.5	13.8	8.8	11,592	5.7	8,529	21	FL
EAST SOUTH CENTRAL	**14,946**	**14,666**	**280**	**1.9**	**12,808**	**—**	**16,121**	**181.9**	**84**	**—43**	**15.7**	**9.0**	**13.2**	**1.9**	**175**	**77**	**28.1**	**11.8**	**19.6**	**0.8**	**9,056**	**9.5**	**10,861**	**36**	**E.S.C.**
Kentucky	3,714	3,661	54	1.5	3,221	23/22	4,074	40.4/37	94/23	—24	15.6	9.1	12.2	1.9	172	79	28.0	11.6	7.1	0.7	9,162	9.4	2,700	9	KY
Tennessee	4,685	4,591	94	2.1	3,926	17/17	5,073	42.1/34	114/18	8	14.5	8.8	12.6	1.7	166	72	26.6	11.8	15.8	0.7	9,362	8.5	3,476	11	TN
Alabama	3,959	3,894	65	1.7	3,444	22/19	4,214	51.7/29	78/26	—19	15.7	9.0	13.0	1.9	174	79	28.1	11.9	25.6	0.9	9,235	11.0	2,875	9	AL
Mississippi	2,587	2,521	67	2.6	2,217	31/29	2,761	47.7/32	55/31	—8	18.2	9.3	15.4	2.2	199	79	31.0	11.7	35.2	1.0	8,072	9.4	1,810	7	MS
WEST SOUTH CENTRAL	**25,788**	**23,747**	**2,041**	**8.6**	**19,326**	**—**	**28,329**	**437.7**	**60**	**1,184**	**18.6**	**8.1**	**12.1**	**2.1**	**232**	**69**	**29.4**	**10.2**	**14.9**	**13.3**	**11,173**	**7.1**	**18,779**	**53**	**W.S.C.**
Arkansas	2,328	2,286	42	1.8	1,923	33/31	2,580	53.2/27	45/35	—2	15.6	9.8	11.9	2.0	158	69	27.9	14.1	16.3	0.8	9,040	8.6	1,694	6	AR
Louisiana	4,438	4,206	232	5.5	3,645	18/20	4,747	47.8/31	100/22	78	19.1	8.4	13.7	2.2	232	78	30.6	9.6	29.4	2.4	10,406	8.9	3,147	10	LA
Oklahoma	3,298	3,025	273	9.0	2,559	24/27	3,503	70.0/18	48/34	186	17.3	9.2	11.9	2.0	191	63	27.8	11.9	6.8	1.9	11,187	7.0	2,452	8	OK
Texas	15,724	14,229	1,494	10.5	11,199	3/6	17,498	266.82	60/29	922	19.1	7.5	11.6	2.1	259	68	29.5	9.4	12.0	21.0	11,702	6.4	11,487	29	TX
WEST	**45,970**	**43,172**	**2,797**	**6.5**	**34,838**	**—**	**52,920**	**1,785.0**	**26**	**1,297**	**17.9**	**7.4**	**10.4**	**—**	**240**	**45**	**27.2**	**10.3**	**5.2**	**14.5**	**12,368**	**7.7**	**34,253**	**111**	**W**
MOUNTAIN	**12,331**	**11,373**	**958**	**8.4**	**8,290**	**—**	**15,404**	**863.6**	**14**	**470**	**19.7**	**6.9**	**10.4**	**2.2**	**285**	**44**	**29.7**	**9.7**	**2.4**	**12.7**	**10,864**	**6.2**	**8,928**	**40**	**MTN.**
Montana	817	787	30	3.8	694	44/41	888	147.04	5	18.0	8.5	10.7	2.1	214	57	28.7	11.4	0.2	1.3	9,999	8.7	591	4	MT
Idaho	989	944	45	4.8	713	40/42	1,214	83.6/13	12/43	4	20.5	7.2	9.2	2.5	278	49	32.2	10.6	0.3	3.9	9,342	7.7	681	4	ID
Wyoming	514	470	45	9.5	332	49/48	701	97.89	5/49	20	22.1	6.5	10.6	2.4	370	39	31.1	7.9	0.7	5.2	11,969	6.5	365	3	WY
Colorado	3,139	2,890	249	8.6	2,210	26/33	3,755	104.18	30/38	141	17.5	6.5	10.0	1.8	269	42	27.0	8.6	3.5	11.8	12,580	5.1	2,365	8	CO
New Mexico	1,399	1,303	96	7.4	1,017	37/37	1,536	121.65	12/44	38	20.0	6.5	9.8	2.2	303	52	30.8	9.3	1.8	36.6	9,560	7.4	997	5	NM
Arizona	2,963	2,718	245	9.0	1,775	28/35	3,994	114.06	26/40	147	18.4	7.7	11.8	2.1	237	33	28.2	12.0	2.8	16.2	10,719	5.1	2,200	7	AZ
Utah	1,619	1,461	158	10.8	1,059	35/38	2,040	84.9/11	20/42	50	27.3	5.5	9.8	3.2	500	66	37.6	7.6	0.6	4.1	9,031	6.7	1,040	5	UT
Nevada	891	800	91	11.3	489	43/49	1,275	110.67	8/47	65	16.7	7.0	11.2	1.8	230	21	25.7	9.1	6.4	6.7	12,516	7.2	689	4	NV
PACIFIC	**33,639**	**31,800**	**1,839**	**5.8**	**26,548**	**—**	**37,516**	**921.4**	**38**	**827**	**17.3**	**7.6**	**10.3**	**1.9**	**225**	**46**	**26.3**	**10.5**	**6.3**	**15.1**	**12,920**	**8.2**	**25,326**	**71**	**PAC**
Washington	4,300	4,132	168	4.1	3,413	20/23	5,012	68.120	65/28	49	16.5	7.6	10.5	1.8	214	48	26.7	11.0	2.6	2.9	12,051	10.3	3,202	10	WA
Oregon	2,662	2,633	29	1.1	2,092	30/32	3,319	97.1/10	28/39	—37	16.2	8.2	10.9	1.8	193	44	26.7	12.5	1.4	2.5	10,920	10.0	1,961	7	OR
California	25,174	23,668	1,506	6.4	19,971	1/2	27,526	158.73	161/12	750	17.4	7.6	10.2	1.9	224	45	26.0	10.4	7.7	19.2	13,239	7.7	19,063	47	CA
Alaska	479	402	77	19.2	303	50/50	522	591.01	1/50	50	24.3	4.1	12.7	2.3	517	32	32.1	3.0	3.4	2.4	16,820	11.8	345	3	AK
Hawaii	1,023	965	59	6.1	770	39/43	1,138	6.5/47	160/13	15	18.6	5.1	9.8	2.1	375	58	27.8	8.7	1.8	7.4	12,101	5.4	755	4	HI

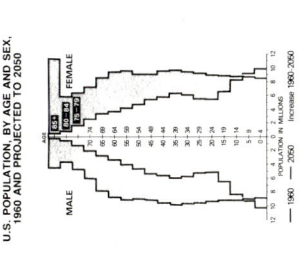

U.S. POPULATION, BY AGE AND SEX, 1960 AND PROJECTED TO 2050

Source: U.S. Bureau of the Census

General Notes

Modeled on PRB's other well-known *Data Sheets*, such as the *World Population Data Sheet* and the *World's Children Data Sheet*, this fourth edition of *The United States Population Data Sheet* presents a unique collection of statistics in a level and form useful for teachers, students, businesspeople, planners and all who are concerned with people and population in the United States. Data are presented for the United States, the 50 states and the District of Columbia, the four Census Regions (Northeast, North Central, South, and West), and the nine Census Divisions (New England, Middle Atlantic, East North Central, West North Central, South Atlantic, East South Central, West South Central, Mountain, and Pacific). Dashes (—) indicate that a category is not applicable, z indicates that a statistic rounds to zero. Totals may not add nor be precisely identical to totals published elsewhere due to rounding or the use of preliminary data.

Related PRB Publications

Users of *The United States Population Data Sheet* interested in a further look at population change may order the PRB's *Population Handbook*, a quick guide to population terms (also available in Spanish), and the *Population Bulletins*, "The 1980 Census: The Counting of America" (Vol. 34, No. 4), "U.S. Population: Where We Are, Where We're Going" (Vol. 37, No. 2); "Black America in the 1980s" (Vol. 37, No. 4); and "U.S. Hispanics: Changing the Face of America" (Vol. 38, No. 3). Price list available upon request.

Footnotes

[1] Resident population totals (which exclude armed forces overseas) are from U.S. Bureau of the Census, *Current Population Reports*, Series P-25, No. 944, September 1984.

[2] Estimates of the Population of States: July 1, 1981, to 1983 (Advance Report)." The 1960, 1970, and the 1960 Census counts used for rankings are from the *1980 Census of Population*, PCB0-1-A1, *Number of Inhabitants, United States Summary*.

[3] Projections from U.S. Bureau of the Census, *Current Population Reports*, Series P-25, No. 937, "Provisional Projections of the Population of States, by Age and Sex: 1980 to 2000." These projections assume that American women will average 1.9 children each in the long run, that projected national survival rates apply to each state, and (most importantly for future geographic distribution) that the internal migration patterns of the 1970s will continue unchanged.

[4] Total area includes 3,539,289 sq. miles of land and 79,481 sq. miles of water. (Note: 1 sq. mile = 2.59 sq. kilometers.) Area data are from U.S. Bureau of the Census, *Statistical Abstract of the United States, 1984*, Table 338, and were revised for the 1980 Census.

[5] Components of change data (births, deaths, and migration) from advance tables provided by the U.S. Bureau of the Census, to be published in a forthcoming issue of *Current Population Reports*. The number of births per 100 deaths, or "birth-death ratio," is determined by both actual fertility levels within a state and its age structure. Thus, states with low birth rates and "old" populations may even so experience natural decrease as the number of deaths outnumbers births.

[6] The crude birth rate is the annual number of births per 1,000 population as given in the National Center for Health Statistics' *Monthly Vital Statistics Report* (MVSR), *Advance Report of Final Natality Statistics, 1981*, Vol. 32, No. 9, Supp. The crude death rate is the annual number of deaths per 1,000 population and the infant mortality rate is the annual number of deaths to infants less than one year of age per 1,000 live births in the year. These data are from MVSR, *Advance Report of Final Mortality Statistics, 1981*, Vol. 33, No. 4, Supp.

[7] The total fertility rate (TFR) is the average number of children born to a woman during her childbearing years at the rates of a given year. TFRs given above are from unpublished tables provided by the Division of Vital Statistics, the National Center for Health Statistics.

[8] 1980 Census data as given in U.S. Bureau of the Census, *County and City Data Book, 1983*.

[9] Estimates from U.S. Bureau of the Census, *Current Population Reports*, Series P-25, No. 951, "Estimates of the Population of States, by Age: July 1, 1981 to 1983."

[10] Data from the 1980 Census of Population, Vol. 1, PC80-1-B1, *General Population Characteristics, United States Summary*.

[11] Estimates from U.S. Dept. of Commerce, Bureau of Economic Analysis, *1983 State Per Capita Personal Income*, News Release BEA 84-22, April 29, 1984.

[12] Estimates from U.S. Dept. of Labor News, USDL 84-260, *State and Metropolitan Area Employment and Unemployment: April 1984*.

[13] Projections from U.S. Bureau of the Census, *Current Population Reports*, Series P-25, No. 948, "Projections of the Population of Voting Age for States: November 1984."

Copyright © 1984 *The Population Reference Bureau, Inc.*

APPENDIX C
1985 World Population Data Sheet

APPENDIX C

Region or Country[1]	Population Estimate mid-1985 (millions)[2]	Crude Birth Rate[3]	Crude Death Rate[3]	Natural Increase (annual, %)[4]	Population "Doubling Time" in Years (at current rate)[5]	Population Projected to 2000 (millions)[6]	Population Projected to 2020 (millions)[6]	Infant Mortality Rate[7]	Total Fertility Rate[8]	%Population Under Age 15/Over Age 64[9]	Life Expectancy at Birth (years)[10]	Urban Population (%)[11]	Per Capita GNP, 1983 (US$)[12]	Total Area (1000's of sq. miles)/Percent Cultivated[13]
WORLD	4,845	27	11	1.7	41	6,135	7,760	81	3.7	35/6	62	41	$2,760	51,720/11
MORE DEVELOPED	1,174	15	9	0.6	118	1,271	1,351	18	2.0	23/12	73	72	9,380	21,344/12
LESS DEVELOPED	3,671	31	11	2.0	34	4,863	6,409	90	4.2	39/4	58	31	700	30,375/10
LESS DEVELOPED (Excl. China)	2,629	36	12	2.4	29	3,666	5,121	101	5.0	41/4	56	34	880	26,670/10
AFRICA	551	45	16	2.9	24	869	1,433	110	6.3	45/3	50	31	750	11,711/6
NORTHERN AFRICA	128	41	12	2.9	24	190	282	97	6.0	43/4	56	42	1,190	3,291/4
Algeria	22.2	45	12	3.3	21	35.5	53.5	109	7.0	46/4	60	52	2,400	919.6/3
Egypt	48.3	37	10	2.7	26	67.3	94.2	80	5.3	40/4	57	44	700	386.7/2
Libya	4.0	46	11	3.5	20	6.7	11.5	92	7.2	46/2	58	64	7,500	679.4/1
Morocco	24.3	41	12	2.9	24	37.5	58.8	99	5.9	46/3	58	42	750	172.4/19
Sudan	21.8	46	17	2.9	24	33.2	51.3	118	6.6	45/3	48	21	400	967.5/5
Tunisia	7.2	33	10	2.3	30	9.7	12.9	85	4.9	40/4	61	52	1,290	63.2/31
WESTERN AFRICA	166	48	18	3.0	23	272	454	118	6.4	47/3	48	29	580	2,372/10
Benin	4.0	51	23	2.8	25	6.3	10.9	149	7.0	49/5	43	39	290	43.5/16
Burkina Faso (Upper Volta)	6.9	48	22	2.6	27	10.5	17.7	149	6.5	44/3	44	8	180	105.9/10
Cape Verde	0.3	36	9	2.7	26	0.4	0.5	77	4.5	31/4	57	20	360	1.6/10
Gambia	0.8	49	29	2.0	35	1.0	1.6	193	6.4	43/3	35	21	290	4.4/14
Ghana	14.3	47	15	3.2	22	22.9	36.5	107	6.5	46/3	5[illegible]	40	320	92.1/12
Guinea	6.1	47	23	2.4	29	8.9	14.3	147	6.2	43/3	[illegible]	22	300	94.9/6
Guinea-Bissau	0.9	41	22	1.9	36	1.2	1.8	143	5.4	44/5	43	27	180	13.9/8
Ivory Coast	10.1	46	18	2.8	25	16.0	29.0	122	6.7	45/3	47	42	720	124.5/12
Liberia	2.2	46	15	3.1	22	3.7	6.9	112	6.7	47/3	49	39	470	43.0/3
Mali	7.7	49	21	2.8	25	11.4	19.2	137	6.7	46/3	42	18	150	478.8/2
Mauritania	1.9	50	21	2.9	24	3.0	5.3	137	6.9	46/3	44	35	440	398.0/z
Niger	6.5	51	23	2.8	25	10.5	18.4	140	7.1	47/3	43	16	240	489.2/3
Nigeria	91.2	48	17	3.1	22	156.5	258.0	105	6.3	48/2	50	28	760	356.7/33
Senegal	6.7	50	19	3.1	22	10.5	17.9	141	7.1	45/3	43	42	440	75.7/27
Sierra Leone	3.6	47	30	1.7	41	4.9	7.3	200	6.1	41/3	34	28	380	27.7/25
Togo	3.0	45	17	2.8	25	4.7	8.3	113	6.1	44/3	49	20	280	21.9/25
EASTERN AFRICA	159	48	17	3.1	23	258	452	109	6.8	47/3	49	17	300	2,454/7
Burundi	4.6	48	21	2.7	26	7.0	10.4	137	6.4	44/3	44	7	240	10.7/47
Comoros	0.5	46	16	3.0	23	0.7	1.0	88	6.3	46/3	50	19	–	0.8/42
Djibouti	0.3	46	20	2.6	27	0.4	0.7	122	6.8	45/3	47	74	–	8.5/0
Ethiopia	36.0	43	22	2.1	33	54.8	88.5	142	6.7	45/3	43	15	140	471.8/11
Kenya	20.2	54	13	4.1	17	37.3	68.0	82	8.0	52/2	53	16	340	225.0/4
Madagascar	10.0	45	17	2.8	25	15.6	26.8	67	6.4	44/3	50	22	290	226.7/5
Malawi	7.1	52	20	3.2	22	11.4	20.5	165	6.9	48/2	45	12	210	45.7/20
Mauritius	1.0	21	7	1.5	47	1.3	1.6	26.9	2.7	33/4	67	43	1,150	0.7/58
Mozambique	13.9	45	17	2.8	25	21.4	36.0	110	6.1	46/5	49	13	–	309.5/4
Reunion	0.5	23	6	1.7	42	0.7	0.8	14	2.6	33/5	66	41	3,710	1.0/22
Rwanda	6.3	53	17	3.6	19	10.7	20.3	110	7.3	46/3	49	5	270	10.2/39
Seychelles	0.1	26	7	1.9	37	0.1	0.1	14.4	4.1	37/7	70	37	2,400	0.1/21
Somalia	6.5	47	21	2.6	27	9.1	14.1	143	6.5	44/4	43	34	250	246.2/2
Tanzania	21.7	50	15	3.5	20	37.3	70.7	98	7.1	46/4	50	14	240	364.9/6
Uganda	14.7	50	15	3.5	20	24.5	43.7	94	6.9	48/2	52	14	220	91.1/25
Zambia	6.8	48	15	3.3	21	10.9	20.7	101	6.8	47/3	51	43	580	290.6/7
Zimbabwe	8.6	47	12	3.5	20	14.5	28.1	70	6.6	48/3	56	24	740	150.8/7
MIDDLE AFRICA	62	45	18	2.7	26	95	163	119	6.1	44/3	48	34	420	2,553/4
Angola	7.9	47	22	2.5	28	12.0	20.2	149	6.4	45/3	42	24	–	481.4/3
Cameroon	9.7	44	18	2.6	27	14.4	23.1	117	6.5	43/4	48	42	800	183.6/15
Central African Republic	2.7	46	22	2.4	29	3.9	6.3	143	5.9	43/4	43	41	280	240.5/3
Chad	5.2	44	23	2.1	33	7.6	12.4	143	5.9	42/4	43	22	–	495.8/2
Congo	1.7	44	19	2.5	28	2.6	4.5	124	6.0	44/3	47	48	1,230	132.0/2

Region or Country[1]	Population Estimate mid-1985 (millions)[2]	Crude Birth Rate[3]	Crude Death Rate[3]	Natural Increase (annual, %)[4]	Population "Doubling Time" in Years (at current rate)[5]	Population Projected to 2000 (millions)[6]	Population Projected to 2020 (millions)[6]	Infant Mortality Rate[7]	Total Fertility Rate[8]	%Population Under Age 15/Over Age 64[9]	Life Expectancy at Birth (years)[10]	Urban Population (%)[11]	Per Capita GNP, 1983 (US$)[12]	Total Area (1000's of sq. miles)/Percent Cultivated[13]
LATIN AMERICA	406	31	8	2.3	30	554	752	62	4.2	38/5	65	66	$1,890	7,935/9
MIDDLE AMERICA	105	33	6	2.7	26	151	211	55	4.9	43/4	65	63	1,940	963/12
Belize	0.2	32	7	2.5	28	0.2	0.3	27	4.5	44/4	70	50	1,140	8.9/2
Costa Rica	2.6	31	4	2.7	26	3.6	4.8	19.3	3.5	37/4	73	48	1,020	19.6/13
El Salvador	5.1	28	6	2.1	33	7.8	12.4	42.2	5.6	45/3	65	39	710	8.1/34
Guatemala	8.0	43	8	3.5	20	12.2	19.7	62.4	6.1	46/3	59	39	1,120	42.0/16
Honduras	4.4	44	10	3.4	20	7.1	12.2	82	6.5	47/3	60	37	670	43.3/16
Mexico	79.7	32	6	2.6	27	112.8	150.7	53	4.7	42/4	66	70	2,240	761.6/12
Nicaragua	3.0	44	10	3.4	20	4.9	7.8	76	5.9	47/3	60	53	900	50.2/10
Panama	2.0	25	5	2.0	34	2.7	3.5	26	3.5	38/4	71	49	2,070	29.8/8
CARIBBEAN	31	25	8	1.8	39	39	51	55	3.3	35/6	67	54	–	92/26
Antigua and Barbuda	0.1	15	5	1.0	67	0.1	0.1	11.1	2.4	28/6	66	34	1,730	0.2/18
Bahamas	0.2	24	5	1.9	37	0.3	0.3	24.7	2.5	38/4	69	65	4,060	5.4/1
Barbados	0.3	18	8	1.0	72	0.3	0.3	14.2	2.0	28/10	71	42	3,930	0.2/77
Cuba	10.1	17	6	1.1	64	11.6	13.1	16.8	1.8	29/8	73	70	–	44.2/28
Dominica	0.1	22	5	1.7	40	0.1	0.1	12.6	3.4	41/6	65	–	970	0.3/23
Dominican Republic	6.2	33	8	2.5	28	8.4	11.5	64	4.1	41/3	63	52	1,380	18.8/30
Grenada	0.1	25	7	1.8	39	0.1	0.2	15.4	2.9	36/6	71	–	990	0.1/41
Guadeloupe	0.3	20	7	1.4	51	0.4	0.4	23	2.6	31/7	70	46	–	0.7/22
Haiti	5.8	36	13	2.3	30	8.4	14.1	108	5.5	44/3	53	28	320	10.7/32
Jamaica	2.3	28	6	2.2	32	2.8	3.5	28	3.4	37/6	70	54	1,300	4.2/24
Martinique	0.3	18	7	1.1	62	0.3	0.4	20	2.4	28/8	71	71	4,270	0.4/17
Netherlands Antilles	0.3	19	6	1.3	53	0.3	0.4	26	2.9	33/5	71	66	–	0.4/8
Puerto Rico	3.3	20	6	1.3	52	3.8	4.7	16.0	2.7	32/8	73	67	2,890	3.4/15
St. Kitts-Nevis	0.04	29	11	1.8	39	0.05	0.05	42.8	3.6	37/10	64	45	820	0.1/0
Saint Lucia	0.1	31	6	2.5	28	0.1	0.2	26.1	4.2	50/5	69	40	1,060	0.2/27
St. Vincent and the Grenadines	0.1	26	6	2.0	35	0.1	0.2	46.8	4.0	44/5	65	–	860	0.1/50
Trinidad and Tobago	1.2	25	7	1.9	37	1.5	1.7	28	2.9	34/6	70	23	6,900	2.0/31
TROPICAL SOUTH AMERICA	225	32	8	2.4	29	308	422	70	4.2	38/4	63	66	1,860	5,446/7
Bolivia	6.2	42	16	2.7	26	9.5	17.0	124	6.3	44/3	51	46	510	424.2/3
Brazil	138.4	31	8	2.3	30	187.1	251.3	71	4.0	37/4	63	68	1,890	3,286.5/9
Colombia	29.4	28	7	2.1	33	39.0	50.6	53	3.6	37/4	64	67	1,410	439.7/5
Ecuador	8.9	35	8	2.7	26	13.2	20.0	70	5.0	42/4	64	45	1,430	109.5/9
Guyana	0.8	28	6	2.2	31	0.9	1.2	35	3.3	37/4	68	32	520	83.0/2
Paraguay	3.6	35	7	2.8	25	5.3	7.8	45	4.9	42/4	65	39	1,410	157.0/5
Peru	19.5	35	10	2.5	28	27.7	38.3	99	5.2	41/4	59	65	1,040	496.2/3
Suriname	0.4	28	8	2.0	34	0.5	0.6	31	4.1	43/5	69	66	3,520	63.0/z
Venezuela	17.3	33	6	2.7	25	24.7	35.4	39	4.1	41/3	69	76	4,100	352.1/4
TEMPERATE SOUTH AMERICA	46	24	8	1.6	44	56	67	32	3.1	30/8	70	83	2,020	1,433/12
Argentina	30.6	24	8	1.6	44	37.2	45.6	35.3	3.4	30/8	70	83	2,030	1,068.3/13
Chile	12.0	24	6	1.8	39	14.9	18.1	23.6	2.6	32/6	70	83	1,870	292.3/7
Uruguay	3.0	18	9	0.9	77	3.4	3.8	33.2	2.8	27/11	69	84	2,490	68.0/8
EUROPE	492	13	10	0.3	240	509	507	15	1.8	22/13	73	73	8,200	1,881/29
NORTHERN EUROPE	83	13	11	0.1	465	84	83	9	1.8	21/15	74	75	9,680	608/11
Denmark	5.1	10	11	-0.1	–	5.0	4.6	8.2	1.4	20/15	74	83	11,490	16.6/62
Finland	4.9	14	9	0.5	154	5.0	4.9	6.0	1.7	20/12	74	60	10,440	130.1/7
Iceland	0.2	19	7	1.2	60	0.3	0.3	7.1	2.2	27/10	77	89	10,270	39.8/z
Ireland	3.6	19	9	1.0	71	4.3	5.8	10.5	3.0	31/11	73	56	4,810	27.1/14
Norway	4.2	12	10	0.2	365	4.2	4.1	7.8	1.7	21/15	76	71	13,820	125.2/3
Sweden	8.3	11	11	0.0	6,930	7.9	7.4	7.0	1.6	19/16	76	83	12,400	173.7/7
United Kingdom	56.4	13	12	0.1	630	57.0	55.9	10.1	1.8	20/15	73	76	9,050	94.5/29
WESTERN EUROPE	155	12	11	0.1	729	154	144	10	1.6	20/14	74	83	10,870	383/30
Austria	7.5	12	12	0.0	–	7.5	7.3	12.0	1.6	20/15	73	55	9,210	32.4/19
Belgium	9.9	12	11	0.1	1,155	9.8	9.2	11.3	1.6	20/14	73	95	9,160	11.7/25
France	55.0	14	10	0.4	198	56.8	57.5	9.0	1.8	22/13	75	73	10,390	211.2/34

APPENDIX C

399

INDEX

A

Abraham, 89, 126
Absolute distance, 16, 156
Absolute space, 155
Acid soil, 227
Adaptability, of religion, 93
Adobe, 114
Adolescent state, 361
Aenglisc, 25
Aerospace industry, 249
Afghanistan, 58, 352–55
Age cohort, 35
Age of Exploration, 7, 8, 238
Aggarwal, Surinder K., 370
Agglomerated distribution, 18
Agglomeration oriented factories, 238
Aggregate data, 156, 157
Airplane industry, 249, 250
Airspace, 321
Alabama, 195, 303, 332
Alabama, University of, 161
Alaska, 133, 169, 218, 222, 302, 303, 306, 311, 326, 332
Alaskan panhandle, 355
Alaskan pipeline, 303
Aleutian Islands, 25
Alexander the Great, 4, 89
Algeria, 225
Alkaline soil, 227
Allen, Harold B., 65
Allied Stores, 254
Alps, 70
Alsace, 108
Aluminum, 237
Amarillo, Texas, 50
Amazon River, 227, 355
American Revolution, 111
Anatolia, Turkey, 241
Andes, 282
Andorra, 354

Angerdorf, 268
Angles, 25, 70
Angola, 225
Angora, goats, 215
Animism, 86, 95
Annual Housing Survey, 170
Antarctica, 7
Anthropogeography, 8
Anti-incorporation law, 328
Apes, 23
Appalachian coal fields, 244
Apple Computer, 248
Apples, 219
Applied geography, 20, 300, 367
Apricots, 219
Arabia, 6, 13
Arabian Peninsula, 95
Arab oil embargo, 250
Arabs, 95, 320, 356
Arc de Triomphe, 125
Archaeology, 64
Architecture, 105–10
  Colonial, 110
  Corinthian, 106
  Doric, 106
  Gothic, 107, 108
  Ionic, 106
  Medieval, 107
  Romanesque, 106
  Tudor, 110
Arctic Ocean, 339
Argentina, 205, 215, 254, 330, 336
Arhus, Denmark, 372
Aristotle, 4
Arizona, 40, 133, 218, 219, 307, 311, 355
Arkansas, 40, 169, 303
Arles, France, 107
Arlington, Virginia, 126
Armstrong, Neil, 251

Artifacts, 50–52
Aryan, 74, 97
Asia Minor, 25
Asoka, 98
Association of American Geographers, 2
Association of Southeast Asian Nations (ASEAN), 338
Atlantic Ocean, 165, 229, 355
Attica prison, 196
Austin, Texas, 304
Australia, 7, 26, 57, 171, 194, 205, 211, 214, 215, 225, 245, 254, 284
Australopithecus, 23, 24
Austria, 243, 354
Automobiles, 250
Automotive industry, 249
Awareness space, 173
Aztec Empire, 106, 359

B

Babylonia, 90
Bailey castle, 108
Bakersfield, California, 136
Balboa, 7
Baldassare, Mark, 164
Baltimore, Lord, 79
Baltimore, Maryland, 14, 79, 306
Baluchistan, 352
Bamiyan, Afghanistan, 126
Bananas, 210, 216, 219
Bangladesh, 44, 239
Baptists, 58
Barbed wire, 211
Barley, 204, 216
Baseball, 132, 147
Baseline, 272
Basketball, 132, 147
Basques, 350
Basutoland (Lesotho), 354

INDEX

Battle of Tours, 95
Beach Boys, 147
Beans, 210
Beatles, 147
Bedouins, 208
Beef, 205
Begin, Menachem, 100
Belgium, 75, 121, 242–44, 254, 353
Bell-shaped curve, 285
Bench mark, 16
Berlin Wall, 118, 335, 353, 356
Bethlehem, Israel, 126
Beverly Hills, California, 156, 306
Bhardwaj, Surinder M., 370
Bigotry, 85
Bilingualism, 75
Binghamton, New York, 372
Bioclimatology, 2
Birmingham, Alabama, 306
Birmingham, England, 242
Birth rate, 31
Black and Decker Company, 255
Black and white houses, 110
Black Belt of South, 132
Black Country of England, 242
Black Death (Bubonic Plague), 185
Black Sea, 241, 245
Blue Bell Company, 254
Bluegrass music, 147
Body language, 78
Bolivia, 31, 218, 222, 330, 355
Bolshevik Revolution, 245
Bombay, India, 89
Bon Marché department store, 253, 254
Borchert, J. R., 283
Borneo, 209
Bos indicus cattle, 214
Boston, Massachusetts, 136, 159, 286, 290, 304
Bos turus cattle, 214
Botswana, 354
Boundaries, 319, 328, 335, 336
    antecedent, 335
    city, 328
    complex, 336
    compound, 336
    consequent, 336
    delimited, 335
    demarcated, 335
    functional, 336
    historical, 336
    international, 335
    subsequent, 335
    superimposed, 336
Bourbon Street, 159
Bowness-on-Solway, England, 117
Brahmans, 97
Brazil, 26, 65, 207, 209, 218, 219, 225, 245, 248, 251, 254, 260

Brewing, 241
Briggs, David J., 368
Britain (*See also* Great Britain; England), 71, 185, 189, 194, 283, 349, 367
British Commonwealth, 340, 349
British Isles, 346
Brothels, 56
Brunn, Stanley, 53
Brussels, Belgium, 76
Buddha, 126
    Gautama, 98
Buddhism, 97, 98, 128, 133
Buddhist temples, 106
Buffalo, dairy, 215
Buffalo, New York, 244, 306, 307
Buffer states, 353
Bug Tussle, Oklahoma, 80
Bulgaria, 219
Burgess, Ernest, 294
Burkett's lymphoma, 189
Burma, 239, 353
Bushmen, 28
Butte, Montana, 290
Butter, 215
Byzantine Empire, 93

C

Cabot, John, 7
Cacao, 216, 219, 220, 270
Calcutta, India, 280
California, 26, 38, 41, 55, 80, 114, 133, 135, 136, 143, 145, 147, 163, 171, 182, 194, 195, 218, 219, 222, 253, 272, 274, 285, 300, 303, 305, 355
California encephalitis, 190
California, University of, 161
Calvin, John, 95
Cambodia (Kampuchea), 356
Cambridge, England, 126, 136
Camels, 215
Canaan (Palestine), 90
Canada, 1, 36, 57, 75, 76, 136, 171, 194, 219, 225, 226, 253, 254, 269, 271, 284, 334, 335, 350
Canadian Riviera, 36
Canadian Rockies, 36
Cancer, 182, 184, 185, 300, 307
Cantaloupe, 219
Canterbury, England, 78
Cape Saint Vincent, 7
Capitalism, 181
Caprivi Strip, 355
Carboniferous era, 221
Carolina piedmont, 147
Cartographer, 10, 374
Cashmere, 215
Caspian Sea, 222, 241

Cassava, 210, 211, 219
Caste system, 97
Castles, 108, 346
Catalan forge, 241
Catalan, Spain, 241
Cathedral, 107
Catholic Church, 14, 40, 58, 93, 95, 100, 140, 142, 143, 194
Cattle, 205, 211, 214–16, 252, 269
Caucasoid, 28
Caucasus Mountains, 241
Celtics, 241
Cemeteries, 126–27
Central Business District (CBD), 289
Central Park, 159
Central place theory, 167, 252
Centrifugal force, 350
Centripetal force, 351
Centuriation, 267
Chad, 354
Chang Jiang (Yangtze Kiang), 41
Charcoal, 242
Chaucer, 71
Cheese, 215–16
Chelmsford, England, 78
Chelyabinsk, USSR, 245
Chepstow, England, 118
Cherries, 219
Chicago, Illinois, 128, 240, 253, 288, 290, 301, 306
Chicago, University of, 8
Chicanos, 356
Chickens, 269
Chile, 229, 336
China, 40, 41, 95, 99, 115, 209, 218, 222, 225, 245, 253, 282, 284, 354, 359, 362
Chinatown, 133, 136
Chinese, 132, 133, 135, 350
    pagodas, 106
Cholera, 185
Christaller, Walter, 251, 252
Christian religion, 5, 19, 88
Chronic diseases, 182
Cigarettes, 219
Circle village, 267
Citrus, 269–70
City planning, 167
Clark County, Nevada, 56
Cleveland, Ohio, 244, 251, 306
Climatologist, 8
Clothing, retailing, 253
Cluett Company, New York City, 254
Cluett, Sanford, 254
Coal, 49, 221, 222, 225, 242–44, 283, 359
Coalbrookdale, England, 242
Coca-Cola, 253
Codes, local, 52

INDEX

Coffee, 216, 219, 220
Cologne, West Germany, 244
Colonialism, 346, 349, 362
Colorado, 147, 163, 331
Collectivism, 269
Colombia, 210, 219, 222, 330, 355
Columbia, Maryland, 14
Columbus, Christopher, 7, 214
Commercial farming, 207, 216
Commercial fishing, 229
Commercial herding, 207, 211
Commune village, 269
Communicable diseases, 182
Computer, 247–48
Concentric zone model, 294
Connecticut, 303, 324
Conservation, 367
Consolidated schools, 323
Constantine, 92
Constantinople, Turkey, 93
Consumption, economic, 204
Continental shelves, 229
Copper, 221, 237
Corinth, Greece, 106
Corn, 19, 51, 205, 210, 211, 216, 218, 262–63
Coronado, Francisco, 7
Corridors, 354, 355
Cortes, Hernando, 7
Cost/benefit analysis, 168
Cotton, 26, 218, 239, 252, 262, 270, 274
Council of Mutual Economic Assistance (COMECON), 339
Country and western music, 147
County, 323, 326
Craft Guilds, 238
Crematorium, 165
Creole house type, 114
Crime, 197–99
Croats, 350
Cro-Magnon, 24
Crowding, 163
Crusades, 6, 95, 238
Cuba, 38, 132, 169, 171, 218
Cubans, 26, 135, 196, 359
  refugees, 184
Cultural geography, 155
Cuyuna Range, Minnesota, 225
Cybriwsky, R., 146
Cyprus, 89, 92
Cyrillic alphabet, 73
Czechoslovakia, 350

D

Dallas, Texas, 1, 288, 304
Danube River, 70, 117, 218
Darby, Abraham, 242
Darius, 89

Darwin, Charles, 8
Dates, 270
Decolonization, 349
De Kalb, Illinois, 123
Delaware, 326
Demographic transition, 31
Denmark, 225, 372
Density, 18–19, 163
  distribution, 18
  population, 163
Denver, Colorado, 183
Dependency ratio, 35
Descartes, Rene, 15
Deseret, 142
Desertification, 19, 44
De Soto, Hernando, 7
Des Plaines, Illinois, 253
Detroit, Michigan, 147, 163, 244, 250, 286, 288, 290
DeVise, Pierre, 191
Dialect 57, 63
Diaspora, 90
Diffusion
  expansion, 176
  hierarchical, 176
  relocation, 176
  spatial, 19, 50–51, 92, 174–76, 185, 189, 282, 328
Dioceses, 107
Disease ecology, 189
Dispersion, 18
Distance-decay, 167
Distilling, 241
Division of labor, 51, 235, 238, 250, 281
Dogon people, 100
Dogtrot house type, 111, 114
Dominican Republic, 239
Dominica, West Indies, 371
Donetsk, USSR, 245
Doris, Greece, 106
Double doors, 112
Double-pen house type, 111
Doughnut, 65
Drainage basin, 304
Dravidians, 97
Dublin, Ireland, 173
Duluth, Minnesota, 307
Dusseldorf, West Germany, 244
Dutch doors, 112
Dust Bowl, 136, 274

E

Eastern Orthodox Church, 58, 93
East Indies, 95
Economic distance, 16
Economic geography, 176, 203, 235
Economic space, 156
Ecuador, 222, 336

Egypt, 88, 90, 95, 239, 281, 356
Egyptians, 3, 106, 124
Eisenhower, Dwight D., 362
El Al, 100
Elazar, Daniel, 55
El Djem, Tunisia, 107
Elizabeth, New Jersey, 307
El Paso, Texas, 118
El Segundo, California, 99
El-Shaddai, 89
Emphysema, 306
Encroachment, 322
England (*See also* Britain; Great Britain), 1, 57, 109, 117, 124, 193, 215, 238–44, 266, 326, 359
English, 19, 132, 320
Environment, 158
Environmental determinism, 8, 280
Epidemics, 185
Episcopalian Church, 58
Erotosthenes, 4
Eschatology, 89
Essen, West Germany, 244
Essential living cost, 304
Ethiopia, 44, 204, 239
Ethnocentric, 88
Etiology, 185, 190
Eudoxus, 4
Euphrates River, 89, 117
  valley, 281
Eureka, California, 80
European Atomic Energy Commission (EAEC), 339
European Coal and Steel Commission (ECSC), 339
European Economic Commission (EEC), 339
European Community (EC), 339
Everett, Washington, 128
Evolution, 50–51
Exclaves, 328
Exclusive Economic Zones (EEZ), 230, 337
Extractive industries, 221
Extralateral mining rights, 322
Exurban, 287

F

Factories, 235
Familial space, 156
Family structure, 295
Fault lines, 259
Federal Aeronautics Administration (FAA), 52
Federal Trade Commission (FTC), 52
Fences, 121–23
Fertile Crescent, 89, 281
Fertilizer minerals, 226, 370
Fetish, 86

403

INDEX

Feuds, 267
Fiji, 26
Filipino, 26, 132–35
Financial occupations, 204
First World, 359, 362
Fish, 229, 354
Flanders, Belgium, 76–77
Flint, 3
Floodplain, 304, 372
Florida, 38, 40, 86, 147, 218–19, 285, 307, 332
FM radio, 51
Folk houses, 115
Football, 132, 136, 147, 163
Ford, Henry, 250, 288
Ford, Larry, 147
Forestry, 226, 227
Fossil fuels, 221
Four Noble Truths, 98
Fourth World, 361
Fowey River, Cornwall, England, 281
France, 31, 36, 53, 70–71, 107–8, 118, 121, 194, 218–19, 225, 330, 241–44, 249, 251, 254, 330, 350, 353–54
Franks, 58
Freedman, Jonathan L., 165
French Community, 340, 349
Frontiers, 335
Furman vs. Georgia, 195

G

Gabon, 225
Gandhi, Mahatma, 75
Ganges River, 126
Garment district, New York City, 159
Garreau, Joel, 150
Garrison, William, 8
Gary, Indiana, 306
Gasoline, 49, 283–84, 286, 290
Gastil, Raymond, D., 149
Gateway Arch, 125
Gaul, 25, 91, 120
Gems, 226
General Electric Company, 255
General Motors Company, 250
Genetic drift, 26
Geographer's Line, 272
Geographic fact, 18
Geojurisprudence, 52
Geomorphology, 2, 8
Georgia, 194, 286, 301
Georgia, USSR, 241
Germans, 55, 57, 132, 135, 287, 356
Germany, West, 8, 24, 41, 90, 95, 108, 118, 242–46, 248, 250, 268, 353, 362
Ghana, 31, 219, 270

Ghetto, 90, 136–37, 164, 168, 199
    Black, 132
Gibbs, Lois, 183
Glaciation, 24
    Riss, 24
    Wurm, 24
Glidden, Joseph F., 123
Goats, 214–16
Gogebic, Wisconsin, 225
Goiter, 189–90
Gorillas, 23
Goths, 25, 107
Gould, Peter, 161, 163, 176
Graffitti, 146
Grand Banks, Newfoundland, Canada, 229
Granite, 14
Grapefruit, 219
Grapes, 219
Gravity model, 169
Great Britain (*See also* Britain; England), 110, 214, 219, 225, 349, 362
Great Divide Basin, Wyoming, 79
Great Lakes, 219, 244, 359
Great Plains, 36
Great Sandy Desert, Oregon, 79
Great Wall of China, 115, 117, 121
Great Wall of the Missing, Cambridge, England, 126
Greece, 4, 23, 88, 92, 219, 356
Greeks, 4, 106, 241
Greenbelt, Maryland, 79
Greenhouse effect, 371
Greenland, 6, 25
Greensboro, North Carolina, 254
Grenada, West Indies, 371
Grotius, Hugo, 337
Gold, 281, 349
Guadalquivir, 70
Gulf Intracoastal Waterway, 288
Gulf of Aqaba, 355
Gulf of Mexico, 229, 237
Gulf stream, 229
Gypsum, 226

H

Haciendas, 271
Hadrian's Wall, 117–18
Hager, Mary, 307
Haiti, 38, 160, 239
Haitians, 26, 196, 356
Half-timber house, 110
Harries, Keith D., 53
Harris, Chauncy D., 295
Haryana, India, 370
Hawaii, 26, 40, 133, 135, 218, 302

Hay, 262
Hazardous substances, 307
Hazard perception, 160
Heart disease, 184–85, 300
Heartland, 335
Heavy industry, 236, 241–44
Hecataeus, 4
Heikkala Lake, Minnesota, 79
Herbicides, 19, 370
Henry, Norah F., 371
Hierarchy, 167, 290
    interurban, 290
    intraurban, 290
    nested, 290
High specific value, 238
High technology, 236, 245–46
Hinayana (Lesser way), 98
Hindu, 95, 128, 220
Hinterland, 287
Hispanic, 14, 40, 140
Hittite Kingdom, 89
Holistic approach, 367
Holy Ghost, 86
Holy Spirit, 86
Homer, 4
Home Rule, 328
Homestead Act, 273, 324, 331
Hominid, 23, 64
Homo erectus, 23–24
Homo sapiens, 23, 25, 40, 85
Hong Kong, 254
Honolulu, Hawaii, 304, 307–8
Honyocker, 65
Hooker Chemical Company, 183
Hopedale, Massachusetts, 79
Horvath, Ronald J., 143
Hot spots, 353
Hot Springs, Arkansas, 79
Houston, Texas, 124, 251
Hoyt, Homer, 294–95
Huang He (Huang Ho), 41
Hudson River valley, 271
Humanities, 1, 2
Hungarian Plain, 218
Hungary, 31, 169, 350
Huns, 25
Hunting and gathering, 207
Huntington, Ellsworth, 8
Hutchins, Thomas, 272

I

Ice cream, 215
Ice hockey, 132
Iceland, 6
Icons, 350
Idaho, 143, 191, 218, 331–32
Illegal occupancy, 322

INDEX

Illinois, 56, 133, 142, 182, 218, 324
Incas, 359
India, 7, 71–75, 89, 95, 97, 99, 205, 218–19, 225, 239, 245, 251, 336, 346, 355, 359, 370
Indiana, 272, 324
Indians, 25–26, 86, 131–33
   Aleut, 25
   American, 131
   Asian, 26
   Cherokee, 133
   Comanche, 86
   Eskimo, 25
   Huron-Iroquois, 80
   Pawnee, 86
   Seminole, 86
   Yanonana, 65
Individual distance, 320
Individualistic political culture, 55
Indochinese, 356
Indonesia, 24–26, 222, 225, 338
Indus River, 95, 281
Industrial Revolution, 238, 241, 244, 283
Infant death rate, 301–2
Infilling, 167, 287
Influenza, 184, 189
Information field, 173
Innovations, 51
Insecticides, 370
Intensity theory, 165
International Business Machines (IBM), 248
International Seabed Authority, 337
Ionia, Greece, 106
Iowa, 174, 218, 271, 324, 326
   University of, 8
Iran, 53, 58, 88–89, 140, 214, 350, 361
Iraq, 95, 217, 222, 350, 355
Ireland, 57, 70–71
Irish, 132, 136
Iron, 221, 225, 243, 245–46
   Age, 225, 241
   Curtain, 58, 339
   industry, 242
   ore, 49, 283, 359
Irredenta, 350
Islam, 58
Isobars, 12
Isobaths, 12
Isochrones, 12
Isoglosses, 65
Isohyets, 12
Isolated state, 206, 262
Isolationist, 353, 361
Isolines, 163
Isotherms, 12
Israel, 100, 194, 353, 362
Italians, 135
Italy, 92, 218, 240, 244, 350

J

Jacob, 89
Jainism, 100
Jamaica, West Indies, 371
Jamestown, Virginia, 214
Japan, 81, 99–100, 124, 194, 222, 229, 230, 245–51, 253, 265, 353, 359
Japanese, 132
Japanese-Americans, 133, 137
Java, 209
Jefferson, Thomas, 121, 261, 271
Jericho Tower, 124
Jersey City, New Jersey, 159
Jerusalem, Israel, 90, 126
Jesus, 90, 92
Jews, 135
John Hancock Building, Chicago, Illinois, 159
Johnson City, New York, 371
John the Baptist, 92
Jordan, 355
Jordan River, 126
Journey
   to shop, 167
   to work, 166
Juarez, Mexico, 118
Judaism, 88–89
Jute, 216
Jutes, 25, 70

K

Kangaroo, 23
Kansas, 136, 217, 324
Kaufman-Broad Company, Los Angeles, 255
Kaunonen Lake, Minnesota, 79
Kaups, Matti, 81
Keltoi (Celts), 70
Kentucky, 147, 219
Kenya, 239, 356
Kindergarten, 19, 57
King Ranch, Texas, 214
Koran, 53, 95
Korea, 99, 251, 265
Krishna, 97
Kroc, Ray, 253
Kshatriya, 97
Kurath, Hans, 65
Kurdistan, 350
Kuwait, 204, 222, 345, 359
Kuznetsk Basin, USSR, 245

L

Labor intensive, 220
Labor-oriented factories, 237
Labrador, Canada, 6, 244
Labrador Current, 229
Lake Superior, 225, 244
Lake Titicaca, 218
Landlocked states, 353–54
Landmarks, 159
Land Ordinance Act, 272, 278, 331
Land planning, 367
Land reform, 265, 271
Landscape influences, 99
Land tenure, 264, 267
   corporate, 264
   feudal, 267
   freehold, 264
   institutional, 264
   tribal, 264
Land use, 294, 303, 367
   planning, 303
   urban, 294
Language, 57, 63, 65–66, 70–76, 79–80, 90, 100
   Altaic, 72
   Arabic, 70
   Assamese, 73
   Baltic, 70
   Bengalese, 70, 73
   Breton, 70
   Cantonese, 70
   Castilian, 70
   Caucasian, 72
   Celtic, 70–71
   Chinese, 6, 70
   Cornish, 70
   Danish, 71
   Dravidian, 70
   Dutch, 65, 70–71
   English, 63, 66, 71, 74–76, 80–81, 100
   Finnish, 71, 79, 81
   French, 65, 71, 75–76, 80
   Gaelic, 70
   Gallic, 70
   German, 65–66, 71, 90
   Greek, 66
   Gujarati, 73
   Hebrew, 90, 100
   Hellenic, 70
   Hindi, 70, 73–75
   Hittite, 66
   Indo-Aryan, 66
   Indo-European, 66
   Italic, 66
   Japanese, 70
   Kannada, 73
   Korean, 70

INDEX

Language (continued)
   Latin, 23, 70–73
   Malayalam, 73
   Marathi, 73
   Melanesian, 86
   Old English, 71
   Oriya, 73
   Paleoasiatic, 72
   Persian, 75
   Polynesian, 86
   Portuguese, 86
   Punjabi, 73
   Rajasthani, 73
   Russian, 70, 73, 75
   Sioux, 80
   Sino-Tibetan, 70
   Slavonic, 70
   Spanish, 63, 65–66, 70, 80–81, 100
   Swahili, 58
   Tamil, 73
   Telegu, 73
   Teutonic, 71
   Thai, 70
   Ukranian, 73
   Uralian, 72
   Urdu, 75
   Vietnamese, 70
   Welsh, 70
   Wu, 70
   Yiddish, 90
Laos, 353, 356
Las Vegas, Nevada, 56
Latins, 320
Laws, 52–53, 230, 336–37, 354
   Anglo-American common, 52–53
   Chinese, 53
   Nordic (Scandanavian), 53
   of diminishing returns, 261
   of the sea, 230, 336–37, 354
   Romano-Germanic civil, 52–53
Lead, 225
League of Arab States, 339
League of Nations, 339
Lebanon, 89, 100, 227, 349
Lemons, 219
Less Developed Countries (LDC), 29, 31, 34, 41, 45, 219
Levi Strauss Company, 254
Lewis, Peirce F., 288
Lexicon, 63
Ley, David, 146
Liberia, 225
Liberty, Statue of, 125
Libya, 225, 239
Liechtenstein, 354
Life cycle of states, 361
Light industry, 236, 239
Limestone, 14, 226

Lincoln, Abraham, 126
Lindbergh, Charles, 251
Lingua franca, 58, 71, 74–75
Linguistic geography, 65
Line villages, 267
Little Big Horn, Montana, 126
Little England, 136
Little Italy, 136
Little Rock, Arkansas, 290
Little Scotland, 136
Liu, Ben-Chieh, 308, 311
Livery companies, 238
Llamas, 215
Location analysis, 261
Location factors, 236
Locational competition, 287
Log cabin, 111
London, England, 41, 78, 173, 242, 280
London School of Economics, 367
Long lots, 267
Lorraine Region, France, 108
Los Angeles, California, 40, 133, 147, 159–60, 168, 173, 251, 284, 286, 290, 293, 306, 356, 371
   east, 145
   County, 306
Los Angeles Times, 139
Louisiana, 13, 114–15, 218, 222, 225, 302, 332, 336
   Purchase, 126
Louisville, Kentucky, 115
Love Canal, New York, 182–84, 307
Love, William T., 183
Lumbering industry, 204
Luther, Martin, 95
Luxembourg, 244, 353
Lynch, Kevin, 159, 160

M

Macedonia, 92
Machinery, 236
Machine space, 143
Machine tools, 246
Macroscale, 319
Magellan, Ferdinand, 7
Maginot Line, 118
Magnitogorsk, USSR, 245
Mahayana (Greater Way), 98
Mail-order sales, 253
Maine, 111, 218
Mainyu, Angra, 89
Malaria, 190
Malaysia, 26, 338
Mali, 100
Malta, 351
Malthus, John, 34
Mana, 86
Manchester, England, 136

Manifest Destiny, 362
Manilatown, 135
Manor house, 109–10
Manufacturing, 204, 235
Map, 10–12
   choropleth, 10–12
   contour, 11–12
   dot, 10
   isoline, 10–12
   projection, 10
   statistical, 10
   thematic, 10
Map scale, 10
   global, 10
   large, 10
   local, 10
   small, 10
Marco Polo, 6
Market, 13, 236
Market oriented factories, 237
Mar Vista District, Los Angeles, California, 168–69
Marx, Karl, 283
Maryland, 14, 191, 301, 332
Massachusetts, 111-12, 191
Material culture, 56
Mathematical location, 15
Mature state, 361
Mauritius, 26
Mayan Empire, 106, 359
Mayer, Harold M., 293
Mazda, Ahura, 89
McCarty, Harold H., 8
McDonald's restaurants, 253
McDuffie, Arthur, 196
Meadowlark Airport, Orange County, California, 305
Mecca, Saudi Arabia, 95
Median family income, 156
Medical geography, 370
Medicine Hat, Canada, 81
Medicine man, 88
Medina, Saudi Arabia, 95
Mediterranean, 4, 89, 122, 218–19, 229, 270
   climate, 218–19
   Sea, 229, 270
Meinig, Don W., 142
Melanin, 26
Menominee, Michigan, 225
Mental maps, 158
Mentifacts, 50, 52
Mercedes, 208
Merchandise Mart, Chicago, 322
Mesabi Range, Minnesota, 225
Mesopotamia, 89, 216, 359
Messiah, 90
Metals, 225

INDEX

Meteorologist, 8
Metes and bounds, 271, 330
Methodist Church, 142
Mexican-Americans, 135, 139, 146
Mexicans, 26
Mexico, 35, 40, 132, 143, 171, 210, 218, 222, 237, 251–54, 284, 362
Mexico City, Mexico, 124
Miami, Florida, 24, 135, 196, 254, 356
Michigan, 133, 183, 250, 302
Microchips, 247
Microcomputers, 19, 51
Microscale, 319
Middle Ages, 5–6, 90, 110, 118, 121, 238, 265–66, 269
Middle East, 58, 81, 222, 238, 264, 266–67, 283, 339, 350, 352
Middle Path, 98
Migration, 24–26, 169–71, 173, 255, 283, 285, 307, 356
  emigration, 356
  forced, 356
  immigration, 40, 356
  illegal, 40
  legal, 40
  refugees, 40
  modern, 26
  prehistoric, 24
  pull factors, 169
  push factors, 169
  rural-to-urban, 283
Millet, 210
Minneapolis, Minnesota, 173, 204
Minnesota, 79, 81, 163, 301, 326, 359
  University of, 161
Minorca, Spain, 78
Mir, 269
Mississippi, 147, 191, 218, 285, 303, 332
  River, 271, 288, 331
  Valley, 115, 218
Missouri, 142, 174, 182, 332
Mixed farming, 216
Model, 20
  land use, 290
  mathematical, 20
  of military power, 362
  multiple nuclei, 295
  physical, 206
  sector, 294
  statistical, 20
Mohair, 215
Mohammed, 58, 95
Mongolia, 209, 239, 353–54
Mongoloid, 28
Mongols, 25
Monotheism, 89

Monroe, Bill, 147
Montana, 163
Montreal, Canada, 334
Montz, Burrell E., 371
Monuments, 124
Moors, 90
Moral code, 85
Moralistic political culture, 55
Moral Majority, 58, 140, 143
More Developed Countries (MDC), 28, 31, 41, 43
Morganthau, Tom, 307
Mormons, 55, 142, 151
Morocco, 226, 339
Moscow, USSR, 93
Moses, 90, 356
Moslems, 6, 13, 90, 126, 220
Mosquitoes, 190
Motherland statue, 124
Mount Everest, 165
Mount Rushmore, 126
Mozambique, 354
Multilingualism, 58, 71, 75
Multinational boundaries, 338
Multiple Listing Service (MLS), 173

N

Napoleon, 125
National Geographic, 2
Nationalism, 346, 350
National Religious Party (Israel), 100
Nation-state, 350
Natural gas, 221, 225
Natural hazards, 372
Natural selection, 26
Nazis, 8
Neanderthal, 24, 88
Nearest-neighbor statistic, 262, 374
Nebuchadnezzar, 90
Negroid, 28
Neighborhood, 156
  effect, 175
  homogeneous, 156
  social acquaintance, 156
  space, 156
  unit, 156
Nelson, Lord, 125
Nepal, 98, 353–54
Nepotism, 370
Netherlands, 53, 118, 219, 225
Network analysis, 374
Nevada, 40, 56, 286, 355, 371
Newark, New Jersey, 306
Newcastle-upon-Tyne, England, 56
Newfoundland, Canada, 6, 229
New Guinea, 209, 218
New Hampshire, 111
New Jersey, 147, 185, 303

New Mexico, 40, 133, 147, 163, 272, 302
New Orleans, Louisiana, 79, 128, 288
New York, 112, 136, 142, 147, 171, 182, 191, 195, 301, 326, 371
New York City, 40, 50, 78–79, 126, 146, 158, 173, 280, 286, 290, 304, 306–7, 371
New York County, 326
New Zealand, 26, 171, 215–16
Niagara Falls, 183, 237
Niagara River, 183
Nigeria, 41, 118, 225, 239, 270, 350
Nile River, 88–89
Nile River Valley, 41
Nirvana, 98
Noble Eightfold Path, 98
Nodes, 159
Nogales, Arizona, 118
Nogales, Mexico, 118
Nonmetallic minerals, 226
Normandy, France, 145
Norris, Robert E., 340
Norsemen, 6
North Atlantic Treaty Organization (NATO), 339
North Carolina, 133, 147, 219, 254
North Dakota, 182, 204, 218
Northhampton, England, 136
Northern Ireland, 53, 100–102, 194, 350
North Pole, 16
North Sea, 222
Northwestern and Illinois Central Railroad, 322
Northwest Territory, 271–72
Norway, 225
Nova Scotia, Canada, 7
Novosibirsk, USSR, 245

O

Oats, 204, 216, 218
Obsidian, 281
Occidental legal system, 52
Ocean boundaries, 336
Ocean currents, 229
Odyssey (Homer), 4
Offa, King of England, 118
Offa's Dyke, 118
Official Language Act (Canada), 76
Ogden, Utah, 142
Ohio, 142, 326
Ohio River, 271–72
Ohio River Valley, 115
Oil, 49, 95, 221, 283
Oklahoma, 133, 182, 191, 222, 263, 306, 331–32
Old-age state, 361

407

INDEX

Olds, Ransom E., 250
Old Testament, 89
Olives, 219, 270
Oman, 339
Orange County, California, 372
Oranges, 205, 219
Order of goods, 251
Ordinances, 52
Oregon, 143
Organization of African Unity, 339
Organization of American States (OAS), 340
Organization of Petroleum Exporting Countries (OPEC), 205, 222, 340, 374
Osaka, Japan, 245
Ottoman Empire, 95, 362
Overcrowding, 165

P

Paavola Creek, Minnesota, 79
Pacific Ocean, 204, 229
Paine, Thomas, 362
Pakistan, 58, 95, 189, 239, 265, 281, 336, 352, 355
Paleoenvironments, 2
Palestine, 89, 92, 95, 100
Palestine Liberation Organization (PLO), 100
Palm, Risa, 173
Palo Alto, California, 247
Panama Canal, 362
Pandemic, 185, 189
Panhandles, 331–32
Paradise, California, 79
Paraguay, 239, 330, 354
Paraguay River, 355
Parimutuel betting, 56
Paris, France, 41, 108, 253–54
Pasta, 219
Patagonia, Argentina, 86
Paths, 159
Patterns of distribution, 18
Peaches, 219
Peanuts, 210
Pearl Harbor, 137
Pedologist, 8
Pennsylvania, 79, 112, 144, 147, 169, 182, 272, 332, 359
Pennsylvania State University, 163
Penn, William, 79
Pepsi Cola, 253
Perception, 158
Persia (See also Iran), 89, 95
Persian Gulf, 222, 355
Personal property, 321
Personal space, 156, 319–20
Peru, 210, 218–19, 230, 336

Peru Current, 229
Pesticides, 19
Petrochemical industry, 246
Petroleum, 222
Pharynx, 24
Philadelphia, Pennsylvania, 147, 286, 288, 290
Philippines, 208–9, 254, 338
Philistines, 89
Phoenicians, 3, 241
Phoenix, Arizona, 251, 306
Phonology, 63
Photography, 367
Photosynthesis, 229
Physical geography, 2, 204
Pidgin English, 58
Pieris papae (butterfly), 174
Pig iron, 245
Pigs, 269
Pillsbury, Richard, 144, 147
Pineapple, 216, 219
Pittsburgh, Pennsylvania, 244, 290
Pizarro, Francisco, 7
Plankton, 229
Plato, 4
Platted land, 293, 328
Pleistocene epoch, 190
Ploesti, Rumania, 222
Plums, 219
Poland, 53, 90, 222, 350
Polar coordinate system, 15
Polders, 260
Political geography, 319
Political power, 329
  delegated, 329
  reserved, 329
Pollutant, 306
  primary, 306
  secondary, 306
Pollution, 304-6
  air, 305–6
  noise, 305–6
  water, 304–6
Polybrominated biphenyl (PBB), 183
Polytheism, 88
Population, 34–35, 356
  pressure, 356
  pyramids, 34–35
Portland, Oregon, 40, 136, 290
Ports-of-entry, 36
Portugal, 7, 70, 95, 349
Portuguese, 7, 58
Potatoes, 218
Power-oriented factories, 237
Prague, Czechoslovakia, 128
Presbyterian Church, 58
Prestatyn, England, 118
Primary production, 203, 235
Prince Henry, 7

Principal meridians, 272
Printing press, 6
Private property, 53
Probability theory, 8
Professional occupations, 204
Property rights, 53
Property tax, 323
Proruptions, 354–55
Prostitution, 56
Protestants, 58, 95, 194
Protestant work ethic, 59
Proxemics, 321
Prudhoe Bay, Alaska, 222
Psychological distance, 17
Psychological space, 158
Psychology, 155
Puerto Rico, 132
Puritans, 55
Pyle, Gerald, 189
Pyramids, 124
  Djoser step, 124
  Egyptian, 124
  Cheops, 124
  Quetzalcoatl, Mexico, 124

Q

Quality of life (QOL), 299–308, 315
Quantitative revolution, 8, 367
Quaternary production, 204
Quartzite, Arizona, 79
Quebec, Canada, 75, 174, 334

R

Rabies, 190
Radical geography, 367
Ramses II, 90
Ranges, 272
Rangoon, Burma, 128
Rapid growth model, 35
Ratzel, Friedrich, 8
Raw materials, 236, 247
Reapportionment, 335
Recreational resources, 306
Reformation, 5, 95, 107
Regina, Canada, 80
Regionalism, 374
Regions, 12–14
  functional, 13–14
  multifactor, 13
  nodal, 13
  single factor, 13
Relative distance, 16, 155
Relative location, 14, 359
Relative space, 156
Religion, 85–90
Remote sensing, 367
Renaissance, 5, 95, 110
Resource-oriented factories, 236

INDEX

Restaurants, 253
Restormal Castle, Cornwall, England, 281
Retailing, 252
Rhine River, 25, 117
Rhode Island, 301
Rhumb lines, 335
Rhythm and blues, 147
Rice, 51, 205, 210–11, 216–19, 252
Rickets, 24
Rig Veda, 97
Ritter, Karl, 8
Rituals, 85
Robot welders, 246
Rocky Mountains, 13, 283
Rocky Mountain Spotted Fever, 190
Rome, 70, 78, 88, 92, 117, 266
   ancient, 4–5, 25, 106, 107, 241, 282–83
   Empire of, 5, 25, 92, 107, 266, 283, 346, 362
Rooney, John F., Jr., 147
Roosevelt, Theodore, 126
Rostock, Germany, 205
Rubber, 216
Rubin, 145–46
Rugby football, 136
Ruhr District, West Germany, 41, 244–45
Rural settlement patterns, 259–62
Rushmore, Mount, 126
Russification, 73
Rye, 218

S

Saar District, West Germany, 244
Saddlebag house type, 111
Sahara Desert, 13, 19, 102, 225, 227
Sahel, 43
St. Albans, England, 78
St. Lawrence River, 190
St. Lawrence Seaway, 244, 288
St. Louis, Missouri, 125, 288
St. Lucia, West Indies, 371
St. Vincent, West Indies, 371
Salem County, New Jersey, 185
Salisbury plain, England, 124
Salt, 3
Salt Lake City, Utah, 142
San Bernardino, California, 253
San Bernardino County, California, 326
San Diego, California, 79, 168, 251
San Francisco, California, 40, 79, 133, 247, 286, 288, 290
San Jacinto, battle of, 125
San Jose, California, 247
San Marino, 354
Sanskrit, 74, 97
Santa Barbara, California, 79, 160

Santa Monica Mountains, California, 293, 306
Sargent, Charles S., Jr., 292
Saskatchewan, Canada, 80
Saudi Arabia, 31, 204, 208, 222, 350
Sauer, Carl O., 50
Sawtelle District, Los Angeles, California, 133
Saxons, 25, 70
Scandinavia, 185
Scandinavians, 55, 135
Schaeper, Herbert R. A., 371
Schistosomiasis, 190
School of fish, 229
Scotland, 57, 70–71, 194, 350
Scovill Company, 255
S-curve, 175, 285
Sears, Roebuck Company, 253
Sears Tower, Chicago, 128, 159, 322
Seattle, Washington, 15, 40, 251
Secondary production, 203, 204, 235
Second World, 359, 362
Section, 272
Segregation, 295
Seine River, France, 41
Semishifting agriculture, 209
Semiskilled occupations, 204
Semitic tribes, 89
Semple, Ellen C., 8
Serbs, 350
Serfs, 267
Serra dos Dourados Mountains, 207
Serra, Father Junipero, 114
Service industries, 235
Service occupations, 204
Settlement sphere, 292
Severn River, England, 242
Shaman, 88
Share-cropping, 271
Shatterbelt, 353
Sheep, 211, 214–15
Shifting agriculture, 264
Shifting cultivation, 209
Shih Huong Ti (Chinese emperor), 115
Shiite Moslems, 95, 350, 361
Shotgun house types, 114
Shrines, 124–26
Shudras, 97
Shwe Dagon Pagoda, Rangoon, Burma, 128
Siberia, USSR, 222
Sicily, 351
Siegfried Line, 118
Silicon, 247
Silicon Valley, California, 247–48, 288
Silver, 349
Sinai Desert, 89
Singapore, 335
Singer Co.,

Sjoberg, Gideon, 281–82
Slash and burn agriculture, 209, 270
Slavs, 135
Slaves, 26
Slovenes, 350
Smallpox, 182
Smith, Joseph, 142
Smog, 306
Soccer, 132
Social geography, 155
Social indicators, 300
Social interaction field, 168
Social space, 155–56
Social trips, 155
Socialism, 181
Socialist/communist legal system, 52
Socioeconomic status, 295
Sociofacts, 50–52
Sociology, 1, 155
Sociopetal, 321
Sociopolitical influences, 99
Sociofugal, 321
Sod house type, 114
Soft drinks, 241
Solid waste, 306–7
Somalia, 239
Soogan, 65
Sopher, David, 99
Sorghum, 216, 218
South Africa, 57, 171, 215, 354
South Carolina, 195, 303
South Dakota, 133, 182, 191, 371
South Korea, 239
Southern Baptist, 140
Southern Baptist convention, 142
Southern homicide region, 193
Southern violence syndrome, 194
Soviet Union (*See also* Union of Soviet Socialist Republics) 1, 53, 57, 71–75, 90, 169, 209, 211, 214, 216, 219, 225, 245, 246, 253, 269, 284, 346, 350, 352–55, 359, 362
Soybeans, 216, 218, 252, 262
Space models, 205
Space retainer, 320
Spaghetti, 57
Spain, 14, 53, 58, 70, 90, 92, 95, 107, 215, 241, 253, 350, 354, 362
   Castile district, 70
   Catalan district, 70
Spatial distributions, 10, 18
Spatial interaction, 156
Spatial rights, 56
Special districts, 323–24
   conservation, 324
   fire protection, 324
   pollution control, 324

INDEX

Special districts (continued)
  school, 323
  solid waste management, 324
Specialization, 238
Specific value, 221
Speculative realm, 292
Spencer, Joseph, 50
Spinning wheels, 238
Sri Lanka, 26, 100, 219
Stalingrad, USSR, 124
Stamp, L. Dudley, 367
Standard Metropolitan Statistical Areas (SMSA), 286
Standard Oil Company, 80
State boundaries, 329
State farms, USSR, 269
Statue of Liberty, New York City, 126
Steel, 225, 243, 245–46
Steinbeck, John, 136
Stonehenge, 124
Strabo, 4
Straits of Gibraltar, 125
Strassendorf, 268
Stroke, 184–85, 300
Structural approach, space perception, 159
Stochastic approach, 99
Subsistence farming, 207, 209–10
Subsistence herding, 207–8
Subsurface property rights, 321–22
Suburbanization, 171
Sudan, 239, 270
Sugar, 26
  beets, 218
  cane, 13, 210, 216, 218
Sulfur, 242
Sulfur oxides, 306
Sunbeam Company, 255
Sun City, Arizona, 79
Sunni Moslems, 95
Sunset Strip, Los Angeles, California, 159, 306
Superdome, New Orleans, Louisiana, 128
Swaziland, 354
Sweden, 1, 31, 35
Switzerland, 95, 353–54
Syria, 89–90, 95, 214, 350

T

Tabu, 86
Taif, Saudi Arabia, 95
Taj Mahal, Agra, India, 126
Tampa, Florida, 196
Tasaday tribe, 208
Taunton, 136
Tea, 219–20
Telecommunication, 173
Television, 51
Ten Commandments, 90
Tennessee, 111, 147
Territoriality, 165
Tertiary economic activity, 251
Tertiary production, 204, 235
Texas, 38, 114, 133, 135, 163, 171, 195, 214–15, 218–19, 222, 254–55, 271–72, 285, 306, 326, 332
Texas Supreme Court, 323
Terrestrial space, 319
Textile industry, 238–39
Thailand, 204, 210, 338, 353
Thalweg, 332
Thames River, England, 41
Thatched roof house type, 109
Third World, 239, 336, 359, 370–71
Thomas, William, 50
Three-field system, 267
Three Mile Island, Pennsylvania, 307
Threshold, 189
Threshold and range, 251–52, 292
Third Reich, 350
Thünen rings, 207
Tibet, 99, 215
Ticks, 190
Tidewater cottage house type, 114
Tigris River, 89
  Valley, 281
Timber-frame house type, 109
Times Square, New York City, 159
Tin, 221
Tobacco, 26, 219
Tokyo, Japan, 173, 245, 280
Tomatoes, 210
Tombstone, Arizona, 126
Topical geography, 20
Tortillerias, 139
Township, 272, 323–24
  congressional, 324
Toxic waste, 307
Trade surplus, 245
Traditional political culture, 55
Trafalgar Square, Longon, England, 125
Transportation frame, 292
Transport gradient, 207
Trees, 227
Trespassing, 322
Truck farming, 219
Tucson, Arizon, 290
Tunisia, 249
Turkey, 89–90, 214–15, 219, 239, 241, 356

U

Uganda, 210
Ukraine, USSR, 218, 245
Ullman, Edward L., 295
UNESCO, 28, 339
UNICEF, 339
Uniform plain, 206
Uniform products, 236
Union of Soviet Socialist Republics (USSR) (*See also* Soviet Union), 222, 226, 227, 230, 241, 249–51
United Kingdom (*See also* Britain; Great Britain; England), 31, 222, 227, 350
United Nations, 100, 336, 339
  General Assembly, 339
United States, 1, 79, 85, 131–32, 136, 140, 143, 145, 147, 166, 171, 173, 181, 183–85, 190–95, 204–5, 210, 214–19, 222, 226, 237, 242, 244–53, 255, 260, 264, 266, 269, 271, 273–74, 283–85, 295, 300–301, 307, 321–26, 330, 335, 340, 346, 349, 352, 355–56, 362
United States Armed Forces, 170
United States Census Bureau, 286
United States Census of Population and Housing, 302
United States Constitution, 182, 195
United States Department of Commerce, 133
United States Environmental Protection Agency, 300
Universality of religion, 93
Upper Yukon, Alaska, 326
Ural Mountains, USSR, 222, 245
Urban geography, 283
Urbanization, 171, 279, 283
  early stage, 284
  mature stage, 285
  rapid stage, 284
Urban planning, 367, 372
Urban-regional space, 156
Urban structure, 292
Uruguay, 204, 215, 330, 353
Usable space, 322
Utah, 143

V

Vaisyas, 97
Valdez, Alaska, 222
Valencia, Spain, 78
Vancouver, Canada, 36
Vandals, 25
Van Valkenburg, Samuel, 361
Varenius (Bernhard Varen), 8
Varnas, 97
Vasco da Gama, 7
Vassals, 267
Vatican City, 354
Vectors, 189

INDEX

Vedas, 97
Venezuela, 65, 222, 225
Venice, Italy, 6
Vermillion Range, Minnesota, 225
Vermont, 112, 142, 301
Vernacular regions, 149
Vicksburg, Mississippi, 126
Victoria, Queen, 80
Videotape recorders, 51
Vietnam, 26, 169, 171, 239, 338, 356, 362
Vietnamese, 356
Vietnam War Memorial, 126
Vikings, 6, 25
Vinyl chloride, 184
Virginia, 26, 112, 147
   University of, 122
Vishtaspa, 89
Visual blight, 307
Volga River, USSR, 222
Volgograd, USSR, 124
Volcanic soil, 219
Von Humboldt, Alexander, 8
Von Thünen, Johann Heinrich, 205–7, 262
Voyager space project, 158

W

Wachstumspitzen, 355
Waldhubendorf, 269
Wales, 57, 71, 193, 350
Wallonia, Belgium, 76–77
Walls, 121–22
Wallsend-on-Tyne, England, 117
Warsaw Pact, 339

Warsaw Treaty Organization, 339
Warwick, England, 136
Wasatch Mountains, 142
Washington, 15, 133, 290
   University of, 8
Washington, D.C., 14, 78, 126
Washington, George, 79, 126
Water buffalo, 269
Watts District, Los Angeles, California, 139, 156
   riot, 196
Weald District, England, 242
Weight-loss ratio, 227
West Germany, 194, 219, 222, 225, 260, 330, 359
West Indies, 371
West Wall, 118
West Virginia, 332
Weymouth, England, 136
Wheat, 51, 205, 216–18, 252, 263
Whirlpool Company, 255
White, R. R., 176
Whizbang, Oklahoma, 80
Wholesaling, 252
Wichita, Kansas, 251
William and Mary College, 66
Windmills, 211
Windward Islands, 371
Wine, 216
Woburn, Massachusetts, 307
Wood-frame house type, 111
Wood products, 227
Worcester, Massachusetts, 136
World Trade Center, New York City, 128

World War I, 95, 125, 133, 254, 353, 356
World War II, 121, 124, 254, 265, 349, 351, 353, 356, 362
Wrangler jeans, 254
Wyoming, 147, 331

X

Xerxes, 89
Xeta tribe, 207

Y

Yaks, 215
Yale University, 8
Yams, 210–11
Yogurt, 215
Yokohama, Japan, 245
Young, Brigham, 142
Young state, 361
Yugoslavia, 350

Z

Zaire, 239, 355
Zaporozhe, USSR, 245
Zebu, 214
Zelinsky, Wilbur, 80, 135–36, 140, 149
Zero Population Growth (ZPG), 31, 171
Zinc, 225
Zionism, 90, 110
Zoning ordinances, 328
Zoroaster, 88
Zoroastrianism, 88